Multilingualism in Spain

MULTILINGUAL MATTERS SERIES

Series Editor: Professor John Edwards, *St. Francis Xavier University, Antigonish, Nova Scotia, Canada*

Other Books in the Series
Beyond Bilingualism: Multilingualism and Multilingual Education
  Jasone Cenoz and Fred Genesee (eds)
Can Threatened Languages be Saved?
  Joshua Fishman (ed.)
Community and Communication
  Sue Wright
Identity, Insecurity and Image: France and Language
  Dennis Ager
Language and Society in a Changing Italy
  Arturo Tosi
Language Attitudes in Sub-Saharan Africa
  Efurosibina Adegbija
Language, Ethnicity and Education
  Peter Broeder and Guus Extra
Language Planning in Malawi, Mozambique and the Philippines
  Robert B. Kaplan and Richard B. Baldauf, Jr. (eds)
Language Planning in Nepal, Taiwan and Sweden
  Richard, B. Baldauf, Jr and Robert B. Kaplan (eds)
Language Planning: From Practice to Theory
  Robert B. Kaplan and Richard B. Baldauf, Jr. (eds)
Language Reclamation
  Hubisi Nwenmely
Linguistic Minorities in Central and Eastern Europe
  Christina Bratt Paulston and Donald Peckham (eds)
Quebec's Aboriginal Languages
  Jacques Maurais (ed.)
The Step-Tongue: Children's English in Singapore
  Anthea Fraser Gupta
A Three Generations – Two Languages – One Family
  Li Wei

Other Books of Interest
Encyclopedia of Bilingual Education and Bilingualism
  Colin Baker and Sylvia Prys Jones
Language, Culture and Communication in Contemporary Europe
  Charlotte Hoffman (ed.)
Studies in Japanese Bilingualism
  Mary Goebel Noguci and Sandra Fotos (eds)

Please contact us for the latest book information:
Multilingual Matters, Frankfurt Lodge, Clevedon Hall
Victoria Road, Clevedon, BS21 7HH, England
http://www.multilingual-matters.com

MULTILINGUAL MATTERS 120
Series Editor: John Edwards

Multilingualism in Spain

Sociolinguistic and Psycholinguistic Aspects of Linguistic Minority Groups

Edited by
M. Teresa Turell

MULTILINGUAL MATTERS LTD
Clevedon • Buffalo • Toronto • Sydney

Library of Congress Cataloging in Publication Data
A catalog record for this book is available from the Library of Congress.

British Library Cataloguing in Publication Data
A catalogue entry for this book is available from the British Library.

ISBN 1-85359-491-1 (hbk)

Multilingual Matters Ltd
UK: Frankfurt Lodge, Clevedon Hall, Victoria Road, Clevedon BS21 7HH.
USA: UTP, 2250 Military Road, Tonawanda, NY 14150, USA.
Canada: UTP, 5201 Dufferin Street, North York, Ontario M3H 5T8, Canada.
Australia: P.O. Box 586, Artarmon, NSW, Australia.

Typeset by Aarontype, Bristol.
Printed and bound in Great Britain by the Cromwell Press Ltd.

Contents

Foreword
Viv Edwards vii

Acknowledgements
M. Teresa Turell ix

The Contributors xi

1   Spain's Multilingual Make-up: Beyond, Within and Across
    Babel
    M. Teresa Turell   1

Part 1: The Larger Established Minorities

2   The Catalan-speaking Communities
    Miquel Àngel Pradilla 58
3   The Basque-speaking Communities
    Jasone Cenoz and Josu Perales 91
4   The Galician Speech Community
    Carme Hermida 110

Part 2: The Smaller Established Minorities

5   The Occitan Speech Community of the Aran Valley
    Jordi Suils and Àngel Huguet 141
6   The Asturian Speech Community
    Roberto González-Quevedo 165
7   The Sign Language Communities
    Rosa Vallverdú 183

Part 3: The Other Established Minorities

8   The Gitano Communities
    Ángel Marzo and M. Teresa Turell 215
9   The Jewish Communities
    Bárbara Vigil 235

Part 4: The New Migrant Minorities

10   The Brazilian Community
     M. Teresa Turell and Neiva Lavratti 254
11   The Cape Verdean Community
     Lorenzo López Trigal. 271
12   The Chinese Community
     Joaquín Beltrán and Cresen García 282
13   The Italian Community
     Rosa M. Torrens 301
14   The Maghrebi Communities
     Belén Garí. 329
15   The Portuguese Community
     Lorenzo López Trigal. 344
16   The UK Community
     M. Teresa Turell and Cristina Corcoll 355
17   The US American Speech Community
     M. Teresa Turell and Cristina Corcoll 373

Foreword

This book will be an important landmark in our understanding of multilingualism in society. One of its many achievements will be to extend the debate on linguistic diversity beyond the English-speaking world where it has been focused in recent decades.

Challenges to myths of monolingualism are now commonplace in Australia, Canada, New Zealand the UK and the USA. Here they include attempts to chart the nature and extent of different varieties of English, as well as discussions of the so-called 'lesser used' indigenous languages which have been increasingly displaced in recent centuries. In relatively recent times, the languages of migrant groups have also emerged from centuries of marginalisation and 'inaudibility'.

Such is the linguicism of the English-speaking world that administrators, policy makers – and even linguists – have seldom sought to look beyond the situation on their doorsteps to consider similar situations elsewhere. Yet the evidence presented in this volume reminds us that the same assumptions and behaviours associated with multilingualism in the English-speaking world are also influential well beyond. These findings are important for the purposes of description; but they have implications, too, for attempts to understand issues which, it may be argued, have been undertheorised to date.

Multilingualism in Spain reminds us very powerfully that Castilian is only one of the languages spoken in Spain: while no one would wish to underplay the central unifying role which it plays, we ignore the other languages – indigenous and migrant, spoken and signed – at our peril. We are also reminded of the social and political dimensions involved in charting and exploring multilingualism. And while the issues raised have global significance, another important achievement of *Multilingualism in Spain* is to place developments concerning linguistic diversity in Spain very firmly and clearly within a European legislative framework.

Some of the papers report information which is widely available in the Spanish-language literature but rarely discussed in English; some represent the very first attempts to describe a particular community in either Spanish or English. *Multilingualism in Spain* will thus be an invaluable resource for many several groups of readers: those with an interest in Spanish sociolinguistics, those wishing to find out more about a particular community, and those interested in multilingualism *per se*. Well argued, well documented and clearly presented, *Multilingualism in Spain* adds force to arguments that linguistic diversity is a human resource to be nurtured and cherished, not a problem to be overcome.

Viv Edwards

Acknowledgements

This book is the final product of a long, intense and exciting process which started back in 1993 when the research project, *Sociolinguistic and psycholinguistic aspects of linguistic minority groups in Spain*, was first conceived. It has been possible in the first place thanks to the disinterested contribution from all our consultants from the different communities into which we have entered. On behalf of all the researchers and on my own behalf I want to express my warmest thanks to all these anonymous consultants who are the real protagonists of this book, designed as it is to become a brick in the building of the desperately needed bridge between cultures, communities and people, particularly now at the turn of the 21st century.

My very special thanks are also due to all the researchers who were originally involved in the project when it was launched as I was co-directing, between 1988 and 1993, a Master's course in Teacher Education in Spanish as a Foreign Language offered by the University of Barcelona, who were part of the research group for several years, but who could not finally finish their research for a number of personal and professional reasons. I want to specially mention the following people: Aliou, Lina Anguera, Alexia Delgado, M. Felicitas Diolazo, Beverley Holliday, Antonio Molina, Francho Nagore, Mercè Pujol and Rocío Vilaró. And naturally, I also want to thank all those researchers who finally contributed to the project and to this book. More specifically, I want to thank Catia Tavares for doing a very good job when transcribing the recordings from the members of the Brazilian community that participated in the pilot study. The highly complex task of bringing together 18 researchers to describe 16 communities has involved on everybody's part compromise and patience, but above all it has resulted in a lot of sharing of knowledge and intercultural attitudes, something which has enriched all of us both personally and professionally. Without them the project and the book would not have materialised.

Some people who offered their help at different stages of the project have contributed with their information, their knowledge and their comments on the general aims and methodology. I am particularly grateful to Viv Edwards, John Edwards and David Sutcliffe for their support for my ideas, helping me develop my own thinking and commenting on some methodological decisions. Many thanks are due to Chris Nicol and David Sutcliffe, who translated a number of chapters which were originally written in Spanish or Catalan, because their work not only involved the sometimes mechanical task of translating but also some adaptation work and the contribution of some very relevant translator's notes which were incorporated to the text; to our research assistant Cristina Corcoll for helping me to put the final manuscript together and performing a marvellous editing job, and to Susi Bolos and Judith Champion, from the administrative office of the Department of Translation and Interpreting at the Universitat Pompeu Fabra (Barcelona), who helped us in the administrative work involved in research networking.

Finally, I would like to acknowledge the following people and institutions: Manuel Gracia from the Social Services Department at the *Diputació de Barcelona* for allowing me to use their documentation archives and several reports and documents on migration in Catalonia, and the Spanish *Comisión Interministerial de Ciencia y Tecnología* (CICYT) for their support in granting three successive research projects on linguistic minority groups: PBS90-0580, SEC93-0725 and SEC96-0627.

M. Teresa Turell

The Contributors

Joaquín Beltrán (PhD in Sociology and Political Science, Universidad Complutense de Madrid) is a social anthropologist and a specialist in Chinese studies. He has spent a number of years in the People's Chinese Republic where he conducted research into Chinese international migration. His publications include several articles on topics related to China, Chinese international migration and intercultural exchange. At present he is a lecturer at the Centre for International Studies (Universitat Autònoma de Barcelona) and he is also the Director of the series 'Biblioteca de China Contemporánea' (Edicions Bellaterra, Barcelona). He is currently conducting a research project on the Chinese community in Catalonia which focuses on integration, family and education.

Jasone Cenoz is Associate Professor of English Applied Linguistics at the University of the Basque Country (Spain) and has conducted research on bilingualism, multilingualism, second and third language acquisition. Her publications include *Beyond Bilingualism: Multilingualism and Multilingual Education* (co-edited with Fred Genesee, Multilingual Matters) and *English in Europe: The Acquisition of a Third Language* (co-edited with Ulrike Jessner). She is currently conducting research on the influence of Basque and Spanish on L3 production and is co-editing a book on early bilingual acquisition.

Cristina Corcoll obtained her degree in Translation and Interpreting (English and French) at the Universitat Pompeu Fabra (Barcelona) in 1996. Since then, she has been working as a research and teaching assistant at the same university. She has been involved in several research projects, one of which aimed at describing, both linguistically and socially, linguistic minorities in Spain. Her research has resulted in a number of papers that have been read at international conferences, and also provided the basis for her PhD research paper, where she proposes a reassessment of the notion of syntactic calque based on data obtained from two linguistic minorities residing in Catalonia, namely, the British-English and the American-English communities.

Belén Garí received her degree in Spanish Philology from the Universitat de Barcelona in 1986, within the speciality of Literature. She subsequently entered the field of teaching Spanish as a foreign language, focusing on the specific problems of the Maghrebi Community in Spain. In this context she has taught Spanish to Maghrebi immigrants at the Bait

Al-Thaqafa Centre in Barcelona, as well as developing a teacher's training seminar for volunteers at the centre. In addition she has created a series of didactic units tailor-made for the Maghrebi Community. She gained her Master's Degree in Teacher Education in Spanish as a Foreign Language, from the Universitat de Barcelona in 1991, and presented her research report on Learning Strategies in the Maghrebi Community in 1994. At present she is teaching Spanish at the Modern Languages Centre (SIM – Servie d'Idiomes Moderns) at the Universitat Autònoma de Barcelona. She is currently giving a seminar on the integration of illiterate students into Spanish classes, at the Postgraduate Course for Teaching Spanish as a Foreign Language at that university.

Cresencia García has a BA Honours degree in Anthropology (Université de Genéve) and a Master's degree in Teacher Education in Spanish as a Foreign Language (Universitat de Barcelona). Since 1981 she has devoted herself to the teaching of adults. She specialises in literacy and teaching of Spanish as a foreign language to non-EU migrants in Spain. She has been a teacher and a researcher in several adult education centres in Barcelona. At present, she combines teaching with being Director of the *Escola d'Adults del Barri Gòtic de Barcelona*, which is sponsored by the Catalan autonomous government (Generalitat de Catalunya). She has published extensively in the fields of literacy, adult education and teaching of Spanish as a foreign language.

Roberto González-Quevedo (PhD in Anthropology, Universidad Autónoma de Madrid) has conducted extensive research on anthropology and anthropological linguistics. The results of his research have appeared in a number of specialised journals both national and international. His recent publications include *Roles Sociales y Cambio Social* (Barcelona: Ed. Anthropos, 1991) and *Antroploxia Lingüística* (Oviedo: Academia de la Llingua Asturiana, 1994). He is a member of the Academia de la Llengua Asturiana and the Director of its journal *Cultures, Revista Asturiana de Cultura* since 1980. His present research interests include topics related to language and ethnic identity, and also language contact.

Carme Hermida is Associate Professor at the Universidade de Santiago, where she teaches Galician in its Faculty of Communication Studies, and member of the scientific committee of the Instituto da Lingua Galega (Galician Language Institute). Her research interests include language in the mass media, lexicography and social history of language. Results of her research on language in the mass media have appeared in *Cadernos de Lingua, A Trabe de Ouro*, and others. She has participated in the compiling of several dictionaries such as the *Diccionario Galego-Castelán* (Galaxia) and the *Diccionario Castelán-Galego* (Xerais). In the field of the social history of language she is the author of *O Rexurdir da Conciencia Idiomàtica.*

Reivindicación e Uso do Galego durante o Rexurdimiento (1840–1891) (Xerais) and *A Reivindicación do Galego durante o Rexurdimiento* (Consello da Cultura Galega).

Àngel Huguet (PhD in Psychology and Pedagogy, Universitat de Lleida) is a lecturer at the Universitat de Lleida (Catalonia, Spain) where he lectures on bilingualism and education. He specialises in bilingual education in unbalanced language contact situations and the results of his research appear in a number of specialised journals. Together with Jordi Suïls, he is currently involved in several research projects which aim at evaluating the effect of multilingualism in the domain of the school both from the point of view of educational achievement and linguistic attitudes, and the role of language in individual and social identity formation.

Neiva Lavratti was trained in languages and linguistics, first in Brazil where she was born and then in Spain where she lives. She has two Master's degrees: one in Spanish literature and language from the Instituto de Cooperación Iberoamericana (1981) and another in Teacher Education in Spanish as a Foreign Language from the Universitat de Barcelona (1992). She has been involved in a number of research projects on foreign language instruction and learning strategies in foreign language acquisition. Since 1992 she has been teaching Brazilian Portuguese as a foreign language in the Centro de Estudos Brasileiros in Barcelona. Her current research interests include topics on language acquisition and language contact of Brazilian migrants in Spain.

Lorenzo López Trigal is Professor of Human Geography at the Universidad de León (Spain). He specialises in theory of geographical thought, urban geography, regional geography, political geography and geography of migration. He has evaluated the Hispano-Portuguese Programme on Educational and Cultural Action, jointly sponsored by the Portuguese and Spanish governments, and has also supervised the project on Portuguese migration in Spain. He is the author of *La Migración de Portugueses en España* (León: Universidad de León, 1994) and has also published extensively in the fields of geography and migratory movements.

Ángel Marzo is a psychologist and a teacher in primary education, and since 1978 he has devoted himself to the teaching of adults. He specialises in literacy and education within the Gitano community in Spain, more specifically in Barcelona and Girona. As a literacy expert, he has also been a teacher and a researcher in some of the major prisons in Catalonia. At present, he combines teaching with being Director of the journal *Diálogos. Educación y Formación de Adultos.* He has published extensively in the fields of literacy, in-training service and adult education. His publications include several books *Educación de Adultos. Situación Actual y*

Perspectivas (1990); *Alfabetización en el Medio Penitenciario* (1990) and articles in various specialised journals.

Josu Perales works for the Basque Government HABE Institute (Institute for the Teaching of Basque and Basque language Literacy to adults) and is the editor of *HIZPIDE*, the journal for teachers of Basque to adult learners. His main research areas are minority languages, languages in contact, new technologies and testing. He has publications on second language pedagogy, testing, motivation and oral communication strategies. He is currently conducting a research study on individual and social psychological factors affecting the acquisition of Basque by adult learners.

Miquel Àngel Pradilla is an Associate Professor of Catalan Philology at the Universitat Rovira i Virgili (Tarragona, Spain). He has conducted research in the fields of Catalan sociolinguistics and phonological variation. Results of his research have appeared in several specialised journals (*Estudios de Fonética Experimental; Diálogos Hispánicos*). He has been involved in joint co-ordinated research projects (*Atles Toponímic Valencià; Atles Lingüístic de la Comunitat Valenciana; Variació i Models Lingüístics a les Terres de l'Ebre*). He is the author of *El Baix Maestrat: una Cruïlla Fonètica* (1996), co-author of *Comentari Lingüístic de Textos. Teoria i Pràctica* (1990), and editor and author of *El Món dels Sons* (1998), *Ecosistema Comunicatiu. Llengua i Variació* (1998) and *La Llengua Catalana al Tombant del Mil.lenni. Aproximació Sociolingüística* (1999).

Jordi Suïls (PhD in Catalan Philology, Universitat de Lleida) is a lecturer at the Universitat de Lleida (Catalonia, Spain) where he specialises in grammar and sociolinguistics. His present research is into language minority groups in the area of the Pyrenées, in particular the Occitan community. Together with Àngel Huguet, he is currently involved in several research projects which aim at evaluating the effect of multilingualism in the school domain, both from the point of view of educational achievement and linguistic attitudes, and the role of language in individual and social identity formation.

Rosa Maria Torrens is an Associate Professor of Italian at the Universitat de Barcelona where she teaches Business Italian at the School of Business Studies and Italian as a Foreign Language in the Faculty of Philology. Her research is concerned with interactive discourse analysis, and in particular the study of code-switching phenomena, both in natural language situations (native vs. non-native) and teaching–learning contexts. She is currently conducting a research project on the experimental use within the classroom of Hypertext as an instrument that can be used to produce expression and comprehension written tasks in a foreign language. She is also involved with the diffusion of pedagogical material addressing the learning of Italian by means of the electronic journal, *On-Line Specialised Italian*, of which she has been the Director since 1998. In addition to her individual research activity, she is supervising work on a course of Business Italian with the participation of Spanish and Italian scholars specialised in Italian Linguistics, Didactics and Applied Computer Science.

M. Teresa Turell (PhD in Catalan Philology, Universitat de Barcelona) is Professor of English Linguistics at the Universitat Pompeu Fabra (Barcelona) and Head of the English Section of the Departament de Traducció i Filologia at this same university. She has conducted extensive research on Catalan and English sociolinguistic variation, and more recently on qualitative and quantitative studies of language contact. Results of this research have appeared in *Language Variation and Change*, *Language in Society* and *Treballs de Sociolingüística Catalana*. She is the author of *No One-to-One in Grammar* (1983), *Elements per a la Recerca Sociolingüística a Catalunya* (1984), *Nuevas Corrientes Lingüísticas* (1990), *La Sociolingüística de la Variació* (1995). She has carried out and supervised extensive research on the interplay between internal and external factors in the bilingual speech modes of linguistic minority groups in Spain. Her recent research interests include the analysis of the interface between lexicon and syntax, and between syntax and pragmatics in language contact studies, and global approaches to code-switching practices.

Rosa Vallverdú has a BA Honours degree in Catalan Philology and a Master's degree in Teacher Education in Catalan as a Foreign Language, both from the Universitat de Barcelona. She has extensive experience as a researcher within the Sign Language community and has learnt Sign Language at the School of Catalan Sign Language. She has been involved in research within other language minority groups in Spain, and has developed educational materials for the teaching of Catalan specifically for these minorities. She is currently developing her expertise in Sign Language and subtitling at TV3, the autonomous Catalan television channel.

Bárbara Vigil has a BA Honours degree in Semitic Philology (Hebrew and Aramaic) and a Master's degree in Cultural Administration, both from the Universitat de Barcelona. She has been awarded several scholarships to study and conduct research in several Israeli universities. Her research interests include cultural administration and cultural exchange. At present she combines the teaching of Hebrew in several institutions with being a cultural administrator at the Associació de Relacions Culturals Catalunya-Israel (Catalonia-Israel Association for Cultural Relations).

Chapter 1

Spain's Multilingual Make-up: Beyond, Within and Across Babel*

M. TERESA TURELL

The Genesis of the Book

Multilingualism in Spain deals with the sociolinguistic and psycholinguistic aspects of both *established* and *new migrant* minority groups in Spain. The philosophy behind the topic of this book involves the idea of a multilingual Europe where all official languages of the historical European nations are respected on an equal footing, and where all the so-called 'lesser used' languages of the regions of Europe are backed and reinforced. However, the philosophy of this book goes beyond that. It promotes respect for all those mainly non-European linguistic minority groups and speech communities, which have had to migrate and leave their country of origin for whatever reason, so that they are respected and given equal social, educational and linguistic opportunities.

Article No. 3 of the Spanish Constitution (1978) recognises Spain's national and linguistic plurality to the extent of granting an official status not only to the Spanish language in the whole territory, but also to the other 'Spanish' (that is, pertaining to Spain as a state) languages spoken in the Autonomous Communities commonly known as 'historical', that is, Basque, in the Basque country, Catalan, in Catalonia and the other Catalan-speaking countries (the Valencian country, including València, Castelló and Alacant and the Balearic and Pitiuses Islands, comprising Majorca, Minorca, Eivissa and Formentera) and Galician, in Galicia. This legal recognition has brought with it twin consequences, as Siguán (1992: 9) points out. In the first place, the fact that nowadays, slightly over 40% of Spanish citizens live in these Autonomous Communities in which Spanish shares its official status with Basque, Catalan and Galician; in the second place, the issuing and implementation of linguistic policies by these 'historical' communities' statutes designed to defend and promote these languages. In my view, this legal recognition takes a stand which has had and will have further, more subtle consequences: the recognition that there are migrant communities and many other languages spoken in Spain.

However, this new deal will have to fight its way through because in origin it is actually a response to not very positive reactions to already

1

existing bilingualism in the above-mentioned *established* 'historical' communities involving, as mentioned, Catalan, Basque and Galician, and to ignorance of the other *in situ* languages of Spain: Aragonese, Astur-Leonese or Bable and Aranese. The achievement of these new goals will have to confront (1) the monolingual speakers' linguistic intolerance towards speakers of the main minority languages, and of these other *in situ* languages of Spain, and (2) society's linguistic intolerance towards speakers of regional dialects, not only of Spanish (Andalusian, etc.) but also of Catalan, of Basque and of Galician, with preference for the Standard variety and clear attempts to make linguistic diversity non-existent. Furthermore, the achievement of this new deal will have to overcome widespread ignorance of the 'lesser known' but also *established* communities, by which I mean the deaf communities, on the one hand, and the Gitano[1] and the Jewish communities, which migrated in the past but have long been established in Spain, on the other, and the languages they use. The latter include the different Sign Languages, the Caló spoken by some members of the Gitano communities in Spain, and Yiddish, Jaketía, and Judeo Español or Ladino. In the case of the *new migrant* communities, there is a marked hierarchy of host community preferences or attitudes towards them and the languages they speak, so that some languages (and speakers) are granted higher prestige (French, English, Italian, German) than others (Arabic, Chinese, Portuguese, Tagalog, Igbo, Walof, Yoruba, Hausa).

Linguistically speaking, therefore, beyond the implementation of European programmes such as *Erasmus, Lingua* and *Socrates*[2] and the 'official' European policy in relation to education,[3] a correct, complete and consistent proposal of multilingualism would have to be predicated on the following: (1) respect for the existing linguistic diversity, and for all the languages of all the countries and nations that constitute Europe, (2) respect for the right of each individual to use her or his own language, not only within that person's territory, but also outside it, and not only by all the citizens from all the states already recognised as forming the future Europe, but also by all those who have abandoned their country and homeland, and (3) respect for the enriching right of each individual to learn and use, two, three or more languages, intent on better communication between humans, based upon understanding and not misunderstanding. The implementation of these premises necessarily involves having information on these minority groups' languages and the extent of linguistic plurality.

Apart from Siguán's *España Plurilingüe* (1992), which only analyses the situation of official and co-official languages as established by the 1978 Constitution, there is no other extensive account of language diversity in Spain. From what has been said above, it should be clear that apart from Spanish, which is the only official language in the whole of the Spanish territory and which has been thoroughly analysed and described, both formally and from the point of view of its variation, and Catalan, Basque and Galician, which are co-official with Spanish in Catalonia, the Valencian

Country, the Balearic and Pitius Islands, the Basque Country, Nafarroa (Navarre) and Galicia, respectively, there are many more languages, and many more speech communities. These have either been present *in situ* for many centuries and contributed to the grounding of what is now known as contemporary Spain, have settled in Spain as a result of past migration, or are relatively recent having migrated into Spain during the last 20 years.

The genesis of this book has to be traced back to the period of 1988–93 when I was co-directing a Master's course in Teacher Education in Spanish as a Foreign Language whose participants originated from many of the communities that have been migrating and settling in Spain for the last two decades. Their motivation for taking such course was basically educational – to be able to teach Spanish to the members of their own minority group and do it with more awareness of their pedagogical and methodological needs. Yearly, the Ministry of Social Affairs provides information on migration, which is published in the *Anuario de Migraciones*. However, available information includes only demographic information on the *new migrant* communities, and although there exist isolated, basically anthropological, studies, there is no integrated account of the historical, social, and especially linguistic patterning of their settlement in Spain. Preliminary observation of these communities also confirmed that there was no detailed study on a number of variables that would give us a more global idea of such aspects. Accordingly, in 1993 a project[4] on linguistic minority groups in Spain was set up to investigate the sociolinguistic and psycholinguistic aspects of these communities in order to achieve better understanding of Spain's multiethnic and multilingual make-up.

In this respect, the main aim of this book, which derives directly from the need to have available comprehensive accounts of language plurality, is to contribute to the description of all these languages and communities, considering in particular those which have never been described and updating the available data on the officially recognised languages of Spain with the exception of Spanish. A secondary aim is to learn more about the different languages and communities that constitute this multilingual organism in order to contribute to the ever necessary understanding between people and peoples, migrant and host, in a changing world whose future can only be conceived in terms of intercultural exchange.

Minorities in Spain

In the last two decades minority groups have emerged as a major concern for educational and language planning policies. Definitions and taxonomies are always difficult to make in a time of change, and in particular the concept of 'minority' is very difficult to define but, following

Churchill (1986), three types of minority groups can be established: *indigenous*, *established* and *new migrant* minorities. They are generally distinguished by their specific linguistic and cultural traits, although language is not always a decisive factor since a minority group may not have a distinctive language of their own and still be a minority. According to this author, *'Indigenous' peoples* are 'groups long-established in their native countries whose life style follows a traditional mode considered archaic by contemporary industrial societies' (p. 6). *'Established' minorities* are 'groups long-established in their native countries whose life style has generally tended to evolve along the same lines as that of the remainder of their national society, though sometimes falling behind in the rate of evolution (p. 6).[5] *'New migrant' minorities* are 'groups perceived to have migrated recently to their current place of residence' (p. 6).

For analytical and taxonomic purposes, the terms adopted in this book to refer to minority groups in Spain are *established* and *new migrant* minorities, since they are particularly relevant to set up the context of study of *Multilingualism in Spain*. Large *established* communities include the Basques, the Catalans, and the Galicians, that is, the 'historical communities' (so described by law) which have been granted certain linguistic rights in the 1978 Constitution and some social, historical and economic rights through the different Statutes of Autonomy, as well as some economic advantages through the Central Government policy known as the 'Estado de las Autonomías' (the State of the Autonomies).[6] Smaller *established* minorities also include the Astur-Leonese speakers, in Asturias, the speakers of Aragonese, in Aragón, and the Aranese people, the Occitan speech community of the Aran Valley. The Gitano and the Jewish communities, on the other hand, do not fit any of these definitions. In the case of the Gitanos because, even if their life-style is considered traditional and archaic by Spanish contemporary industrial society, they are part of the grounding of present-day Spain; in the case of the Jewish communities because, even if they have adopted the language(s) of the host community and their life-style has generally evolved as that of the rest of the their national society, they keep their traditions and religious practices. And in both cases, while being originally migrant communities, they migrated to Spain many centuries ago, and particularly in the case of the Gitano community, they have been prosecuted for over five centuries; therefore, for our purposes they will both be considered *established* minorities. Finally, the Deaf communities in Spain will also be considered *established* minorities because they have always been present in Spain although they have seldom been granted any recognition and respect.

The *new migrant* minorities are easier to define. They include those communities that have migrated recently or not so recently for several reasons. These include minorities from Western Europe such as, the Austrian, Belgian Danish, Dutch, Finnish, French, German, Greek, Southern Irish, Italian, Luxembourgian, Norwegian, Portuguese, Swiss, Swedish, and

British; from South America, such as, the Brazilian;[7] from North America, that is, the US American and Canadian, and other English-speaking countries, including New Zealand and Australia; others from Black Africa (the Gambian and Senegalese), from the Maghreb (the Moroccan and Algerian), from Cabo Verde, and Egypt; still others from Asia, including the North Korean, Japanese, Indian, Pakistani, the Middle East (the Lebanese and Jordanian) and Philippino; and finally, from Eastern Europe, including Russia and the former URSS.

Many taxonomies have been proposed (Churchill, 1986; Fishman, 1989; Fase *et al.* (eds), 1992) to characterise minorities. In the case of minority groups in Spain, their study has allowed to establish the most important factors that define them. These factors can be grouped under three typologies: *sociodemographic, sociolinguistic* and *sociocultural* patterns. *Sociodemographic* patterns have to do with absolute numbers (large minorities, such as the Catalan, the Basque and the Galician vs. smaller minorities, such as the Aranese in the Aran Valley, the Astur-Leonese in Asturias, or the Aragonese in Aragón; large migrant minorities continuing to increase, such as the Maghrebi vs. large stable migrant minorities, such as the British); length of settlement (long-standing minorities, such as the three 'historical' minorities, and also the Gitano and the Jewish minorities vs. more recent migrant minorities, such as the *new migrant* minorities; type of settlement (rural (i.e. the Black Africans and some sections of the Maghrebi communities in Catalonia; the Cape Verdeans in León and other areas of Castile) vs. urban (some other sections of the Maghrebi communities, the Gitano communities in their present-day settlement), and other factors such as motivation, family structure and social conditions. *Sociolinguistic* patterns are related to issues such as language maintenance (among the *established* minorities, the Catalans; among the *new migrant*, the Chinese community), language shift (the Jewish communities from Central and Eastern Europe which settled in Spain in the 1880s and adopted the language(s) of the host communities), and different degrees and types of bilingualism (Lambert, 1975): *additive* (in the case of the children of the so-called 'historical' communities vs. *subtractive* (in the case of the *new migrant* minorities from the Third World, such as the Maghrebians, the Black Africans, the Cape Verdean). Finally, *sociocultural* patterns have to do with their culture and traditions, the degree of culture proximity/distance, their degree of contact with the members of the host communities, and their degree of social organisation and political awareness ranging from (1) minorities which migrate and integrate, and have been described as *more open* (i.e. the Brazilians, the Italians, the US Americans), (2) minorities which integrate without giving up their own traditions and customs (the UK community, the Maghrebi communities), although some may give up their language(s) (some of the Jewish communities), have been described as *less open*, and some attain structured social organisation patterns, and finally, (3) those minorities characterised by different degrees of cultural isolation (the Gitano communities) and even ghettoisation (the Chinese community).

In this book, the terms 'minority' and 'community' have been used indistinctively, although it may be useful to point out that the term 'minority' seems to be more adequate to refer to its situation *vis-à-vis* the state, in this case, the Spanish state. Conversely, the term 'community' seems to be more relevant to refer to its internal idiosyncratic characteristics.

The Context of Study and the Methodology Used

This categorisation of minority groups is hardly precise since the social phenomena that frame these groups are very complex and undergoing fundamental changes. In the case of the minorities present in Spain it was observed that there are three guiding analytical research approaches that cut across them: *language, migration* and *discrimination.* Alladina and Edwards's (1991) framework of analysis to describe language plurality in the British Isles was considered a good starting point to situate these three guiding analytical research approaches proposed in this book. The first area of analysis is the *sociolinguistic situation* in the country of origin and in the host country, that is, the languages spoken and their status, the standard language question, and also the degree of literacy of the minority group. The second area of analysis refers to *migration* and *settlement patterns*, in terms of (1) the nature and distribution of each speech community and linguistic minority group, (2) the history of arrival and settlement, (3) the migratory conditions, whether the migration is political or economical, (4) the particular characteristics of the community, in their place of origin and their place of arrival, that is, whether they are of rural/urban origin, whether they are traders or industrialists, professionals or artisans, and (5) also the settlement patterns, i.e. if the settlement is concentrated in small geographical areas, the migrants are going to be able if they wish to maintain very strong community ties, something which is not possible if the settlement takes place over a wide and dispersed area. The third area of analysis has to do with *institutional support*, in terms of the links and the support that the minority group receives from their community or country of origin through any kind of institution or organisation, either religious, cultural or secular, and also from the host country, through employment or the social and public services. The fourth are of analysis the *role of education*, and what Alladina and Edwards (1991: 20) refer to as 'language reproduction', distinguishing three main strands: the family, the community and the school. The fifth area of analysis deals with the changing *patterns of language use*, that is, language choice and codeswitching. Finally, a sixth area of analysis, which proved useful to account for the psycholinguistic aspects of the communities under analysis, refers to the *learning and communicative strategies* used by migrants in the process of learning the host community's language(s).[8]

Thus, it was considered that the first issue which is relevant to the topic under analysis in this book, that is, *language*, would be addressed by considering information related to area 1 (the sociolinguistic situation), area 4 (the role of education), area 5 (the patterns of language use) and area 6 (learning and communicative strategies), although it was felt that in order to understand language maintenance and code change processes it would also be useful to analyse the specific schooling situation and the domains of language use. Secondly, it was considered that the second research approach proposed, that is, *migration*, would be described by considering data collected in area 2 (migration and settlement patterns), particularly in relation to the *new migrant* communities; however, it was felt that some general information should be added on the scope of the migratory processes in Spain and their demographic, social and attitudinal aspects in order to be able to understand their real nature and extent. Finally, it was considered that the third research focus suggested, that is, *discrimination*, would be accounted for by the information collected in area 3 (institutional support) with additional consideration of international and European migratory policy, Spanish legislation on migration and its discriminatory consequences, the policy of 'quotas', and the specific forms that racism takes in Spain.

It was soon noticed, however, that not all three aspects would equally apply to all minorities in the same way: some are characterised by language, migration and discrimination (the Maghrebians, the Cape Verdeans and other African communities, the Brazilian, the Portuguese); other communities are only defined by language and migration, but their members are not discriminated against, socially and culturally speaking (the US Americans, the British, the Italians, the French, the German, the Jewish in contemporary Spain); another group of communities are not characterised by recent migration, but they are discriminated against and/or their languages not even officially recognised (the Gitano, the Aranese, the Astur-Leonese, the Sign Language communities). Lastly, there are some other communities – the ones which have been referred to as the so-called 'historical' Autonomous Communities (primarily, Catalonia, the Basque Country and Galicia) – that do not find enough legal and institutional support and their languages may suffer discrimination in certain situations or find themselves in an asymmetrical situation *vis-à-vis* Spanish.

When the project on linguistic minority groups in Spain (SPALIMG) started in 1993, a common methodology was proposed with which to enter the communities and investigate them from the point of view of the three research approaches mentioned above (*language, migration* and *discrimination*) and the proposed six areas of study (*sociolinguistic situation, migration and settlement patterns, institutional support, role of education, patterns of language use,* and *learning and communicative strategies*).

In order to investigate the sociolinguistic situation, researchers were asked to consult official educational documents and any documentation on language normalisation and standardisation, illiteracy and language planning. A similar procedure was used to find out more about the communities' migration and settlement patterns, the role of the host country's education in the maintenance of their mother tongue and culture, the institutional support that they receive both from their country of origin and the host country, and the communities' organisational network in the host country.[9]

Two basic instruments were proposed to investigate these several areas of study: an adapted form of *sociolinguistic interview*, which incorporates elements taken both from the *life story*, an instrument used in anthropological analysis, and from the *sociolinguistic interview* itself, as used in sociolinguistic analysis. The modules forming this version of the sociolinguistic interview ranged from personal domains (family and friendship, both in the country of origin and the host country) to social and professional domains (education, languages used at school, employment, neighbourhood), and included two or three questions which would allow the researcher to elicit narratives and indirectly determine the effect of style (i.e. more or less informal) in the specific forms of the informants' linguistic behaviour and use, and patterns of language contact. This particular instrument was thus devised to investigate the above-mentioned patterns of language use and language contact, and to achieve this end the researchers were asked to use two different versions of this same method. Modality A involved the researchers being members of the minority group under investigation. They were asked to conduct the sociolinguistic interview in the informant's mother tongue, in order to describe the modalities of discourse and language contact patterns that the speakers would produce in the $L1 \rightarrow L2$ direction (i.e. interference from L2). Modality B involved the researchers being from the host country and using the same instrument conducted in Spanish or any of the other officially recognised languages in order to collect data on the $L2 \rightarrow L1$ direction and thus indirectly investigate what learning and communicative strategies they were using.

A second method was used to investigate the patterns of language use and language contact. This is referred to as the *family recording* and it consisted in the recording of a family gathering (a meal, a meeting) or a community meeting, depending on the social structuring of each specific community. In order to comply with the ethical requirements of ethnographic research, one of the family members or a community representative would have authorised the recording and supervised the technological questions related to the carrying out of the recording.

In order to investigate the most psycholinguistic aspects of the present study, that is, the learning and communicative strategies involved in the process of learning and acquiring Spanish or any of the other officially recognised languages of Spain, two instruments were used. One instrument, used with members of the Maghrebi, Brazilian and Chinese communities, had to do with *class observation* for which the researchers developed an observation template. The other instrument was a sophisticated *questionnaire* on the strategies used by learners when trying to learn the sounds, the vocabulary and the grammar of the Spanish language, in the context of traditional learning skills (speaking, writing, listening and reading).

General information on the total distribution of each community was available from Spanish statistical institutions, such as, the Instituto Nacional de Estadística (INE), research institutions and public institutes, such as the Centro de Investigaciones Sociológicas (CIS) and the Spanish Ministry of Social Affairs, which publishes the *Anuario de Migraciones.*[10] The specific sample selection for each community was done on the basis of several criteria: (1) community representation (community leaders), (2) overall representative social factors (age, sex, profession), and (3) the researchers themselves, so that being a community member could help in entering the group.

The Final Scope of the Study

Multilingualism in Spain was conceived to give an account of language plurality in Spain via an in-depth study of all non-Spanish speaking minority groups and their languages or varieties of language. In the final version of the book, small *new migrant* minorities, such as the Brazilian or the Cape Verdean and small *established* communities, such as the Aranese or the Astur-Leonese receive as much attention as the 'historical' *established* communities, such as the Catalan, the Basque and the Galician. This apparent imbalance requires an explanation, and so does the fact that very significant *new migrant* minorities, such as the Black African (Gambian and Senegalese), the Indian, the German and the French are not included.

The initial project did not include information on the three 'historical' communities, Catalonia, the Basque Country and Galicia, and the three major officially recognised languages apart from Spanish, that is, Catalan, Basque and Galician, basically because they have been vastly considered, both at structural and sociolinguistic levels. As the project advanced, the editor of the book, the series editor and the publishers envisaged the possibility of including information on these 'historical' minority groups and languages and the other established minorities in order to update and complete available information on them.[11] The latter involved the consideration of the Occitan community of the Aran Valley, the Astur-Leonese community and the Aragonese community and, therefore, the other indigenous languages of Spain, that is, Aranese, Astur-Leonese (or Bable) and Aragonese.[12] The Sign Language communities in Spain were also considered as *established* communities sharing two of the guiding research lines with other *established* minorities, that is, the issues of language and discrimination. And finally, the Gitano and the Jewish communities were also considered as long-established, even if they were also constrained by migration in the past.

As to the *new migrant* minorities, the final selection was done via the application of two basic criteria: (1) the overall number of members (above 5000), which seems a reasonable figure to guarantee community perspective, and (2) a minimum of five-year settlement at the moment when the project started (1993) to guarantee community stability. According to the data published in the latest available edition of the *Anuario de Migraciones* (1997), there would be 47 migrant minority groups, excluding the Spanish-speaking South American migrants. If criteria (1) and (2) are applied, the number of *new migrant* minorities which should have been considered is 16,[13] including 10 European minorities (the UK (68,359); the German (45,898); the Portuguese (38,316); the French (33,134); the Italian (21,362); the Dutch (13,925), the Belgian (9,847); the Swiss (7,138), the Swedish (6,545); the Danish (5,107)), two communities from the American continent, one from the North (the US (15,661)) and one from the South (Brazil (5,694)), one in Africa (the Moroccan (77,189)), three from Asia (the Philippino (11,770); the Chinese (10,816) and the Indian (6,882)).

Out of those 16 communities which should have been considered in the first place, the non-inclusion of minorities, such as the Belgian, the Danish, the Dutch, the Swedish and the Swiss was due simply to problems in finding any researchers to analyse them. A similar problem was faced with some of the communities which were originally included in the first proposal but have not been incorporated to the book because the researchers dropped out of the project and failed to finish their work for a number of reasons. This applies to the Indian, the Philippino, the French, and the German minorities. Other communities from Eastern Europe, like Ex-Yugoslavia migrants, were not included at all because they involve a much more recent migration.[14]

The final version of *Multilingualism in Spain* includes the analysis of eight *established* and eight *new migrant* minorities. The *established* minorities include large 'historical' *established* communities such as, the Catalan-speaking, the Basque-speaking, and the Galician, 'smaller' *established* minorities such as the Aranese, the Astur-Leonese and the Sign Language communities, and 'other' *established* minorities, such as the Gitano and the Jewish communities. The *new migrant* minorities include the Cape Verdean,[15] the Brazilian, the Chinese, the Italian, the Maghrebi, the Portuguese, the UK and the US American communities. It is hoped that in the near future another project will be able to investigate the remaining minorities of Spain and offer a more complete picture of Spain's multilingual make-up.

Language

Essential to the nature of the situation and future prospects of both *established* and *new migrant* minorities in Spain is the status of the community language at different levels: (1) as symbol of personal identity and community belonging, (2) as an exponent of language maintenance, language loss and bilingualism, and (3) as an instrument in education to contribute to the cognitive development and socialisation of minority language children. Hence, the importance of establishing the status of community languages.

An approach which has proved useful in the conceptualisation of minority languages in Spain is that of John Edwards (1992). He considers different elements in an attempt to build a useful and generalising taxonomy of minority languages. The first criterion proposed by Edwards is that of the status of the minority language *vis-à-vis* the state: *unique* minority languages are 'unique to one state', *non-unique* minority languages are those which are non-unique but 'are still minorities in all contexts in which they occur', and *local-only* minority languages are those which 'are minority varieties in one setting but majority varieties elsewhere'. The second criterion proposed by Edwards has to do with 'the type of geographical connection between speakers of the same minority language in different states'. In order to conceptualise this situation, Edwards suggests the terms *adjoining* and *non-adjoining*. The third criterion refers to the amount of 'internal spatial cohesion' that there exists among minority language speakers and this criterion gives rise to the terms *cohesive* and *non-cohesive*, which are self-explanatory (Edwards, 1992: 38–9).

Drawing from this approach, in Spain it would be possible to classify minority languages in several groups, depending on whether we refer to *established* communities or *new migrant* minorities. As far as *established* minorities are concerned, group 1 (*non-unique, adjoining, cohesive*) would include Catalan in the Principality of Catalonia and in some of the Balearic Islands (especially, Menorca), Basque, Galician and Astur-Leonese (Bable), spoken in Asturias and parts of León; group 2 (*non-unique, adjoining, non-cohesive*) would include Catalan in the Valencian Country, that is Valencià,[16] group 3 (*non-unique, non-adjoining, cohesive*) would include Catalan spoken in l'Alguer (Sardinia) and Occitan spoken in the Aran Valley, and group 4 (*non-unique, non-adjoining, non-cohesive*) would include Caló and the different varieties of Judeo-Español (Ladino throughout Spain and Jaketía in Ceuta and Melilla). As to *new migrant* minorities, further distinctions can be established. Group 5 (*local-only, non-adjoining, cohesive*) would include all the well-established languages, such as English, French, Italian, Arabic and Portuguese, and finally, group 6 (*local-only, non-adjoining, non-cohesive*) would include primarily the Kriolu, spoken by Caboverdeans, and Chinese Mandarin and other Chinese languages.

In the context of language diversity and multilingual settings several aspects are relevant to understand the specific linguistic exponents of minority groups. On the one hand, at the macrolinguistic level the complementarity of issues such as language maintenance, language shift and bilingualism, and on the other, at the microlinguistic level, the whole question of language contact.

Language maintenance, language shift and bilingualism: the role of education

In the context of large *established* community languages in Spain, that is, Catalan, Basque and Galician, the question of language maintenance and language loss has been framed around the principles of individuality and territoriality. The latter issue can be, and frequently is, politicised, arguing that a specific community, speaking a specific language, lives in a specific territory and therefore has certain national rights, which among other things involves their demand for a state. The path to nationalism is served and language is used as a political flag to serve political ends, a pheno- menon described as linguistic nationalism. Naturally, while it is true that in all three communities language is used by nationalisitc politicians as a political weapon, it is also true that not all three languages are in as vigorous use as they might be. While the situation of Catalan is more or less optimistic, particularly in Catalonia, Basque and Galician are not advancing as healthily as Catalan.

The results presented in this book illustrate that the language plan- ning policies implemented by the autonomous governments exclusively respond to their own need to defend their own minority language, offi- cially recognised in the Constitution, that is, Catalan, Basque and Galician. The basic linguistic laws issued by the autonomous governments of those communities regulate the teaching of Catalan (in Catalonia, the *Llei de Normalització Lingüística* (1983), in the Valencian Country, the *Llei d'Ús i Ensenyament del Valencià* (1983) and in the Balearic Islands, the *Llei de Normalització Lingüística* (1986); Pradilla, Ch. 2); of Basque (in the Basque Country, the *Euskararen Erabilpena Aranzkotzeko Oinarrizko Legea* (1982) and in Nafarroa (Navarre), the *Euskari Buruzko Foru Legea* (1986); Cenoz and Perales, Ch. 3) and of Galician (*Lei de Normalização Lingüística* (1983); Hermida, Ch. 4). However, in both the case of the central government and that of the autonomous governments, the administrations are too busy defending 'their own patch' for there to be space to defend the smaller *established* minority languages of Spain. The two exceptions would be Catalonia, where the Generalitat de Catalunya (Catalan autonomous government) cautiously recognises Aranese although leaves it to the local authorities and private initiatives to promote and strengthen the Aranese language and culture (Suils and Huguet, Ch. 5), and the Principality of Asturias, where community and private initiatives (*Conceyu Bable* (1974) and *Academia de la Llingua Asturiana* (1980)) forced the Asturian auto- nomous government to take the first steps in bringing Asturian into the school system (González-Quevedo, Ch. 6).

What seems to characterise the situation for these large *established* community languages is their necessary living together with Spanish, which involves considering the whole question of bilingualim. The fact is that almost 34% of the Spanish population (13 million people) live in Autonomous Communities with two official languages (Catalonia, the Valencian country, the Balearic and Pitius Islands, the Basque Country, Nafarroa (Navarre) and Galicia). However, the co-existence between the four official languages of Spain (Spanish, Catalan, Basque and Galician) has not been particularly peaceful over the course of the middle decades of the 20th century,[17] particularly during Franco's regime when all languages other than Spanish were repressed and banned from public life and relegated to private settings, and their teaching was forbidden. As mentioned, the new Spanish Constitution recognised this bilingual situation and has protected it since its approval in 1978. So with the dawning of the new democratic era, from 1977 onwards, Catalan, Basque and Galician were granted official status. However, this multilingual richness has not been recognised in state institutions (Parliament, Senate, etc.), or only very recently under pressure from nationalist parties in the Autonomous Communities mentioned above; moreover, people's attitudes, particularly in monolingual Spain (that is, outside the Basque-speaking countries, the Catalan-speaking countries and Galicia) and above all in centralist-oriented regions (Castilla La Nueva and Castilla La Vieja)), have always lagged far behind what was being legislated.

However, it is still the case in contemporary Spanish politics, particularly in monolingual areas, that any linguistic and cultural differentiation would endanger the view of Spain as an indivisible unit. Obviously, Spain's 'historical' *established* minorities view this imposition as an attempt to maintain the *status quo*, only recognising the co-official status of these minority languages on paper and relegating them to an incomplete paradigm, not used in all domains or for all functions.[18] In this context, there is another aspect of bilingualism that should be mentioned. Usually, not only is a monolingual norm all too easily imposed on a community and on an individual, but also it seems that this monolingualism has to be monolithic as well, in the sense that only the standard variety is accepted, ignoring the fact that dialectal varieties,[19] and other varieties linked to register, context and style, can contribute through an imaginative and creative use of language to develop sensitivity for different linguistic forms and for suitable use in a specific context.

In parallel to all that there are other languages, those spoken in the host territory by the members of the *new migrant* minorities, often forgotten and neglected. There are speakers of those languages to whom the principle of individuality must be applied, at the same time that their right to learn the host community language or languages must be ensured. And just as it is not possible simply to consider language as a symbol of personal identity from the point of view of the individual, because one's individuality is collective at the same time, it is impossible to defend the territory just in community and territory terms because communities and territories are constructs which would not have been perceived and created unless there had been individuals constituting those communities and living in those territories. Furthermore, the individual right to use one's language is only one of the many rights that a human being has to demand. Apart from this linguistic right, people have the right to a job, to a dignified lodging, to public services, to developing their own culture, and cultivating their own art. And ideally, these rights would have to be enjoyed, not only in the country where one is born, but also in the country where one ends up and lives, whatever reason there is for a migration to another country. It is also known that in order to be able to reach a balanced personal identity and benefit from a successful educational and professional upbringing it is important to have a high level of self-esteem. And this self-esteem is developed through the socio-cultural norms and values that one acquires through early socialisation within one's ethnic and social group. And what is more, language is the most important means of human communication and of the transmission of such norms and values. If the role of language is so clear in socialisation and education, it is obvious that socialisation and education should take place primarily in the first language of the people involved, because children acquire their cognitive, socialising and linguistic skills in an integrated way, not in isolation.

Moreover, in the context of migration and minority groups the approach towards bilingualism can and should also be positive. Naturally, anyone that takes that approach will have to overcome a lot of linguistic and educational prejudices. It was during the 1970s that scholars began to consider as beneficial the cognitive and intellectual effects of bilingualism (Cummins & Swain, 1986), and nowadays teachers are beginning to think more in terms of transfer of abilities and less in terms of linguistic interference (Cenoz & Genesee, 1998). Unfortunately, bilingualism has different connotations for minority group and majority group individuals, since most minority group speakers tend to learn the host community language and become bilingual, whereas majority group speakers seldom learn the migrants' language(s). Moreover, bilingualism in minority group children is all too often *subtractive* (Lambert, 1975) where the learning of the host community's language(s) – their L2 – is at the expense of the maintenance and development of their L1, as is the case for most children from those *new migrant* communities in Spain whose L1 is not prestigious (i.e. Arabic, Portuguese, Tagalog, Yoruba, Igbo, Chinese). On the other hand, many majority group children develop an *additive* (Lambert, 1975) type of bilingualism, by being schooled extensively via their L2 but not at the expense of their L1. This would be the case of children in at least two of the historical communities, Catalonia and the Basque country, which can be considered minority groups *vis-à-vis* Spain as a whole, but are majority groups in their own territory, or at least their language (Basque and Catalan) is as prestigious, locally, as the state language (Spanish). Conversely, for the children from a Spanish-speaking background, usually third generation children from those families which migrated to Catalonia and the Basque country from areas of Spain during the 1960s and 1970s, different models may be adopted, ranging from immersion programmes in their L2 to schooling in their L1 with the gradual introduction of the L2, as Pradilla (Ch. 2), and Cenoz and Perales (Ch. 3) illustrate.

So, even admitting that the newcomers to a state have to try to integrate[20] − rather than *assimilate* − and learn the language of the host community, it is important for the immigrants and their children, above all, to be able to have access to equal opportunities in education. In fact, recent research has shown that *additive* bilingualism in minority group children, particularly from *new migrant* communities, is better attained when their schooling occurs via their L1 (Cummins, 1986; Skutnabb-Kangas, 1983). Also, educationalists and teachers have to learn, respect and in some cases know the language spoken at home by the migratory group, so that the migratory group's linguistic rights are ensured. Every citizen of every country − indigenous or immigrant − has the right to continue using his/her language and the immigrant minorities should be given the equal opportunity of learning the language of the host country and communities.

Accordingly, information is needed on the cultural and linguistic patterning of these minorities. Most of the contributions to this volume include a reference to the sociolinguistic context in the communities' country of origin, in terms of the languages spoken and their status, and its patterning once the communities settle in Spain. In some societies the questions of bilingualism and multilingualism are central issues. In Cabo Verde two languages co-exist, Portuguese and a creole (*Kriolu*), as a result of the country's history in which West African and European Portuguese mingled (López Trigal, Ch. 11) and the linguistic situation becomes more complex as the Cape Verdean community settles in Spain. Maghrebi people (Algerians and Moroccans) live in a complex trilingual situation, where French (the High status language), Arabic (with two status levels, High and Low) and some of the Berber languages of the area from where these migrants come (in this case, the Low languages) are present in a triglossic system (Garí, Ch. 14).

The question of literacy constitutes a point of contrast between communities, the result of different traditions. The majority of Southern and Northern European countries have attained extended literacy,[21] whereas some parts of Africa (Black Africa, the Maghreb, Cabo Verde) are still pre-literate in the case of the majority of their populations. Obviously, different reading and writing systems, such as we find in the Chinese community (Beltrán and García, Ch. 12), are decisive as to the difficulties the migrants encounter when in some instances not having even achieved a satisfactory degree of literacy in their own language, they are in the process of becoming literate in the host community's language (García, 1993).

The standard language issue is also relevant when considering the sociolinguistic context in the different communities' country of origin. Interestingly, in both China and Italy the path followed in the prioritisation of the standard language variety over other dialects is very similar, although this happened at different periods of their history. Chinese has eight linguistic varieties officially considered in China as dialects (Beltrán and García, Ch. 12), even though these are as different phonetically and lexically as French or Spanish, and beyond that, local variants and dialects can be mutually unintelligible. In Italy, the dialect of Florence (the Tuscan variety) is the basis of a national literary language, largely as a result of the prestige of Dante, Bocaccio and Petrach. This influence was consolidated and codified in the 16th century in a series of grammars. The leap from literary to everyday language – which became the standard spoken variety – has only really been achieved since political unification in 1861. Highly divergent varieties, derived from the original fragmentation of Italy in small states and the substratum effects of ancient languages were used for very long after the unification, and are still used nowadays. From a purely linguistic point of view these varieties, officially considered in Italy as dialects in all cases, could be considered as linguistically independent systems and, therefore, different languages (Torrens, Ch. 13).

When settling in Spain, an inevitable decision that migrants usually face is language choice, since in many areas of the so-called 'historical' Autonomous Communities, the other officially recognised languages (Catalan, Basque and Galician) are in extensive use. In other words, the migrants will have to decide whether they take Spanish, or any of the other languages, as a means of communication and take any formal instruction in one or other of these. Later on, the question of language shift from their mother tongue to the local or national language becomes relevant, although usually the situation involves 'a gradual development (shifting)' rather than total shift (Clyne, 1992: 18). The extent of this shift will vary according to the intersection of several types of factors, beginning with the nature of migration and duration of the settlement: long-standing communities may need to maintain or recover their mother tongue whereas for more recently arrived groups, the acquisition of Spanish and/or one of the other 'official' languages of Spain (Catalan, Basque and Galician) may be a priority and the shift will occur more rapidly. Equally important are socio-individual factors such as the degree of contact with the receptive community or degree of identification with own mother tongue and culture, the community's social structure, social trajectory, culture distance or proximity, duration of contact, and positive attitudes towards the host community.

For example, it is interesting to note that communities which, in principle, are very distant in culture and language, such as the Black Africans and the Maghrebis, show very positive attitudes towards the host communities, soon learn their languages and integrate well,[22] while keeping their own customs and traditions. It is possible to refer to their second generations as having language shifted, although this shift has been accompanied by attempts to achieve language stability. That is, that there has been a reaction towards the learning of their mother tongue and fostering of the culture by the communities' adults and children. At the other end of the scale, it is possible to find communities (Beltrán and García (Ch. 12) on the Chinese), whose adult members can spend 10 or 12 years in the host country without understanding or speaking any Spanish or any of the other official languages. Their children are encouraged to learn Spanish or the other languages because they value progress and social mobility, without excluding the learning of the Chinese language and culture that they use in the family and among friends. Other communities, although they show very positive attitudes and are in fact culturally close (Torrens, Ch. 13) on the Italian community), tend to learn and use Spanish or any of the other languages but rarely to the point of being involved in a process of language shift.

The Jewish and the Gitano communities in Spain, very different in nature from each other in many respects, but traditionally characterised as long-established communities also framed by migration in the past, seem to follow broadly the same pattern as to their attitudes towards the language(s) of the host community. In different periods of their long-established settlements, both communities seem to have adopted the language(s) where they settle (Spanish and/or Catalan, Galician or Basque) and restricted the use of their own language or variety of language to private domains (family, religion, peer group) and to specific functions, depending on the community's cultural and identity patterns. In the case of the Gitano community, the language used is *Caló*, a Spanish based variety of Romani, which is used as an instrument of self-defence *vis-à-vis* the non-Gitano population (Marzo and Turell, Ch. 8).[23] In the case of the Jewish community, a distinction must be made between the long-established Jewish communities which settled many generations ago and seem to have integrated and have adopted the languages spoken where they settled (the Catalan Jewish community, the Sefardies, in Melilla), and the most recent groups of Israeli citizens. For the former, the use of Hebrew, for example, responds to religious needs and traditional individual pride related to 'a glorious past'; for the latter, that use responds to political and national reasons (Vigil, Ch. 9).

Most communities which have migrated to Spain express a will to maintain their own language and culture. This will towards the maintenance of mother tongue and minority culture finds its way through the family at first, as is the case within the Chinese community (Beltrán and

García, Ch. 12) in which Chinese families ensure that their second generation members, who attend schools in the Spanish educational system, are not excluded from the learning of the Chinese language and culture, either paying for private teachers or having them study Chinese as a second language in language schools. This may then spread to the wider community, as is the case of the Portuguese community (López Trigal, Ch. 15) which settled in León and whose members participate in the Portuguese Language and Culture Programmes, sponsored by the Portuguese government.

A further important factor in the discussion of the migrants' language behaviour and use has to do with domains of language use, in Fishman's (1972) sense. Some patterns are constrained by the age factor. For example, in the Gitano community (Marzo and Turell, Ch. 8), *Caló* is used by the older people, among friends, and as a code of self-defence or distinguishing feature of their group. The Maghrebi communities in Spain, particularly the Moroccan, show a very rich network of domains, using five languages (Garí, Ch. 14): Berber in the family and friendship domains, national varieties of Arabic within the family, with friends and in the cultural centre, Classic Arabic in the Mosque, Spanish at work, in the cultural centre and among friends, and French also at work, in the cultural centre and among friends. Other patterns are basically functional, as for example in the Portuguese community (López Trigal, Ch. 15), whose members try to use Spanish as much as they can outside the home, for employment reasons, whereas they show a high use of Portuguese in their communication among adults, parents and children at home. At the same time they mix Portuguese and Spanish and make use of mixed codes such as *Portunhol*, mentioned by López Trigal (Ch. 15), the same as the Brazilian community makes use of both *Portunhol* and *Españogués* (Turell and Lavratti, Ch. 10).

The school can play a decisive role in the direction of language maintenance of a minority language and language shift towards a host community language, and can also affect other domains of language use, particularly in the context of migration. Unfortunately, institutional involvement in the ensuring of the respect for the legitimate right and needs of large numbers of bilingual children is almost non-existent in Spain as far as migrated linguistic minority groups are concerned. The educational policy implemented by the Spanish central government reflects the need that the central administration feels that it has to defend the Spanish language in the monolingual areas and bilingual areas of Spain where it coexists with other languages other than Spanish. In the 'historical' Autnonomous Communities the basic linguistic laws issued by the autonomous governments of those communities regulate the teaching of Catalan, Basque and Galician and the situation of these three languages in the field of education.[24] This means in practice that Spanish primary education involves either the use of Spanish for monolingual children, or the application of policies that involve different degrees of bilingualism, while the languages of immigrant minority groups are ignored, in general. And yet, there is strong evidence that suggests the effectiveness of bilingual education, of using the mother tongue as both a medium and a subject for children from minority communities (Skutnabb-Kangas & Cummins, 1988; Artigal, 1993). Obviously, this would bring extra issues to worry about when training teachers (experienced bilingual support teachers) and when providing resources (books, posters, music), pedagogical tools, language awareness, and other matters. This explains, but does not justify, why there has not been any institutional involvement in Spain's linguistic diversity beyond the seven *in situ* languages (Spanish, Catalan, Basque, Galician, Aranese, Aragonese and Astur-Leonese).

There are some exceptions, apart from individual initiatives on the part of some teachers, but nothing planned from the administration, in spite of the fact that the LOGSE (the latest Spanish Educational Act) calls for a compensation of pupils' differences and an adaptation of the teaching methods to their individual characteristics. This point has been taken over by private institutions, such as the Servei Gironí de Pedagogia Social (SERGI)[25] where a pilot experience was designed and is being organised around three axes by means of which the implications of linguistic and cultural diversity are really acknowledged: (1) the understanding of the school, family and social background of the migrant pupil, (2) the development of the pupil's mother tongue, particularly for the metalinguistic advantages that this will involve, and (3) the mastery of the host community's majority language.

However, the Spanish educational system in general reinforces a sort of pathology model whereby a lack of knowledge of any of the recognised languages involves a situation in which something is to be cured. Moreover, it is a model basically centred on the teacher and frequently involves a use of language which is still too artificial, although huge efforts are made to implement more communicative approaches and methods (Pérez Vidal, forthcoming). The model is, consciously or unconsciously, based upon racist, sexist,[26] monocultural, monolingual/bilingual, assimilative parameters. In fact, bringing in new parameters along the lines of pluralism, multilingualism and intercultural integration would involve a new educational context (Churchill, 1986; Spolsky, 1972, 1986) in which the practice of the classroom would imply that (1) minority languages are considered as a *resource*, and not as a problem, and that the family language is worked upon and used, rather than being abruptly substituted by the new language(s) of the host community(ies); (2) there is a mainstream teacher and a support teacher; (3) all courses are taught in the mainstream language, and by the same teacher, and the support teacher organises specific tasks for the minority language speakers, both to be able to continue using their own language and to learn the new school language, which is also socially dominant outside their own ethnic group;

(4) curriculum subjects are used as a vehicle to learn the new language;
(5) the teaching is based upon information, discussion and participation.

Language contact

Language contact (LC from now on) constitutes one of the most important linguistic exponents of social contact between the members of *new migrant* and *established* minorities, and also between those from larger and smaller *established* minorities. In the Spanish context, three areas of study can be identified in order to account for LC patterns in which members of linguistic minority groups engage. One area would consider the bilingual speech modes of minority groups speakers that result from the insertion of (Muysken, 1994) or alternation of (Muysken, 1994, Myers-Scotton, 1993a, 1993b) linguistic units from an embedded language (in this case Spanish, or Catalan, Basque and Galician) in the utterances of a matrix language (in this case, their mother tongue), or result from different manifestations of language interference, such as borrowing and calque. Another comparable area to be investigated involves the reverse situation, that is, when such speakers use the language of the host community, which then becomes their matrix language, and then insert or alternate linguistic units from their original mother tongue, the embedded language, either in the course of their same turn, or in different turns. Another related area which will not be considered in this volume is that of mother tongue convergence on or divergence from the standard language or any dialect of the *in situ* communities, and the longer-term processes of language change observed in the varieties of language spoken by immigrant communities away from their countries of origin.

The analysis of the LC patterns observed in the *established* communities and the *new migrant* minorities under consideration in this book is based upon two complementary concepts, that of LC phenomena produced as *reflection*, and LC used as pragmatic *resource*. LC as *reflection* involves the use of *unmarked* (1) codeswitching or situational codeswitching which occur almost unconsciously within the linguistic mode of a speaker who is not trying to achieve a specific goal, or produce an effect on the interlocutor, (2) borrowing, (3) syntactic and semantic calque, and any contact unit produced as a result of language interference at the system level. LC produced as *resource* refers to *marked* use of any manifestation of LC which occurs as a communicative strategy of the speaker who designs his/her linguistic mode in accordance with the different components of the linguistic situation (participants, topic, purpose, tone), and is shaped by the goals to be achieved and the effects to be produced on the other participants in the interaction. Observations within the communities and minorities under study also confirmed the viewpoint taken elsewhere by other scholars (Muysken, 1991; Clyne, 1992; Turell, 1997) that LC

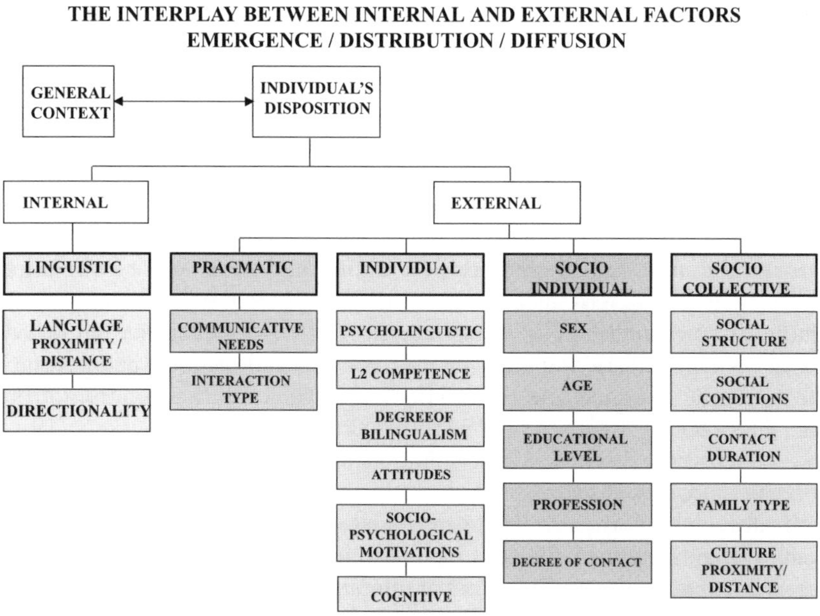

**THE INTERPLAY BETWEEN INTERNAL AND EXTERNAL FACTORS
EMERGENCE / DISTRIBUTION / DIFFUSION**

Figure 1.1 Language interaction integrated model (own source)

patterns vary in accordance with several internal and external factors, including degree of proximity or distance between languages, degree of identification with the first language and culture, along with the size of the community, its degree of organisation, and the amount of time that the group has been established in the host country. This being so, LC needs to be accounted for within an integrated, multifactorial model.

The idea behind one such model, namely the *Language Interaction Integrated Model* (Turell, 1997) which is represented in Figure 1.1, is that both internal and external factors constrain LC phenomena. By *internal* factors what is meant are factors of a linguistic nature, basically language proximity/distance which determines the LC type. More specifically, these factors are: (1) the order of constituents, (2) morphological typology, (3) marking typology in the predicate/arguments relationship, and (4) contrastivity of phonological typology and the degree of lexical/ morphosyntactic distance/proximity; *external* factors require several subclassifications: (1) *pragmatic* factors, such as communicative needs (in turn affected by socio-collective factors, as will be seen) and interaction type, and others; (2) *individual* factors related to the individual speaker: (a) psycholinguistic, that is, the individual's degree of competence in L2 and degree of bilingualism (with implications for FLA and SLA), (b) cognitive and (c) attitudinal, with positive or negative attitudes towards the host community, its culture and language, which however very much depend on what the group's attitudes as a whole are, and as such these factors interact with the socio-collective and socio-psychological ones; (3) *socio-individual*, that is, factors such as sex, age (first generation, second generation), educational level, which are individual indices of the speaker's belonging to a specific group; family type (mixed or not mixed); the degree of contact, which, in turn, will interact with the previous psycholinguistic and attitudinal factors, (4) *socio-collective*, that is, factors relating to the community's social structure (that is, whether it is *more* or *less open*), the community's social history (social type of migration and settlement pattern: stability or non-stability of the settlement, social status of community before and after migrating, reasons for migration, social prestige before and after); and finally, cultural distance or proximity (between the migrated and the host communities) and the duration of the contact situation.[27]

The use of codeswitching

Codeswitching is one of the most extensive forms of LC, both as a *marked* or an *unmarked* choice, which has become a major and outstanding research topic, as the proliferation of references testifies.[28] Historically, the beginning of this development can be traced back to a crucial study done by Blom and Gumperz (1972) through which codeswitching acquired a new positive status: that of a *skilled performance*, as Myers-Scotton (1993a) puts it, and a new taxonomy was proposed: that of *situational* and *metaphorical switching*. All the work done during the 1970s and 1980s, which refers to the social motivations of codeswitching, derives from Gumperz' contribution in terms of seeing speakers as exploiting linguistic choices (in this case codeswitching) as part of an interaction and as a social strategy within an interaction.

In the last decades or so, codeswitching has been investigated from very different perspectives. Evidence of these different perspectives was presented at the different Symposia organised by the ESF Network on Codeswitching and Language Contact between 1989 and 1991. These perspectives range from accounting merely for internal linguistic factors, what Muysken (1994) describes as the grammatical dimension of codeswitching (which would include models suggested by Poplack (1980) on universalist grounds; Muysken (1994), Myers-Scotton (1993a)), to cognitive factors (Fontana and Vallduví, 1990), socio-psychological and socio-pragmatic factors (Myer-Scotton 1993b), pragmatic factors (Gumperz, 1982; Auer, 1992), sociolinguistic and contact situation-bound factors (Pujadas and Turell, 1993; Turell, 1994b, 1995b, 1997).

The observations that derive from the analysis of the bilingual speech modes produced by the members of the linguistic minority groups considered in this book show that when codeswitching occurs as a *resource/ marked* phenomenon, and particularly when the speakers' degree of bilingualism is very high, speakers codeswitch in any of the grammatical slots or within any of the sites that have been proposed (Poplack, 1990; Myers-Scotton, 1993a; Muysken, 1994), that is, (1) *intersententially* (where use of two languages corresponds to two sentences in the same turn, and as such, *alternation*s between sentences or clauses, (2) *intrasententially* (switching which occurs when both languages are used in the same sentence, including *one-word codeswitches*,[29] or *constituent switches*, and (3) *extrasententially* (involving peripheral elements of the sentence such as discourse cues, that is, *tags, confirmation checks* and *clarification checks*[30] ('oi' (right?) in Catalan, '¿vale?' (okay?) in Spanish, and so forth). However, even if it is also true that speakers seem to be using any and all types of switches, there are certain patterns in terms of type and frequency that appear to predominate and this distribution can only be explained through another group of factors that most models and explanations tend to ignore, that is, the cognitive ones.

Following the general model proposed, a set of predictions can be formulated in relation to the emergence of codeswitching and its diffusion in the context of the migration (into the Basque Country and Catalonia) that took place during the 1960s, but particularly within the linguistic minority groups that migrated to and settled in Spain.

Prediction 1. It is predicted that intrasentential codeswitching (where language directionality is L1 → L2) will appear in individuals and later on be extended to the community if the following factors coincide: relatively high competence, language proximity, cultural proximity, high contact, positive attitudes, communicative needs, need for upward mobility, open-community or open-settlement type, youth, female.

Some of the extracts that follow are from several of the speakers from different *new migrant* minorities considered in this book who conform to the socio-cultural patterns mentioned and make use of codeswitching.[31] In (1), Cintia is a 22-year-old Brazilian who migrated to Spain with her family and who now works as a secretary in Barcelona. She took classes in Catalan before formally taking classes in Spanish, as she mentions:

(1) **Cintia:** Bom, a escola era super difícil, porque eu não sabia nada, nem sabia o **castellano**, e tive que aprender o **català**. Entao, me confundi mais do que eu primeiro tivesse só aprendido o **castellano**, ou depois o **català**. Mas como a sociedade pede que você saiba um poco mais, então ... Por isso que eu fui fazer o curso, mas ... eu não estava preparada para ... para **começar a estudiar** o **català**.

Well, it was very difficult at school, because I couldn't speak anything, I couldn't speak **Spanish**, and I had to learn **Catalan**. Then, I got more confused than if I had

> learnt **Spanish** before, and then **Catalan**. But, because
> society demands your knowing more, then ... That's why I
> began a course, even if I wasn't ready to ... to **start**
> **studying Catalan.**
>
> (Lavratti, 1992)[32]

Qualitative observation shows that there is a tendency for more young
women than men within the Brazilian community to make more extensive
use of intrasentential codeswitching in general. This observation can be
explained in terms of socio-psychological motivations within the Brazilian
community: the fact of viewing themselves as non-prestige migrants or
members of a non-prestigious ethnic group, and thus of indexing status
mobility through the use of codeswitching. First-generation migrants
show a less extensive use of codeswitching, as predicted.

Within the Italian community, quite a prestigious one in Spain and
Catalonia, also viewed as prestigious by its own members, competence in
Spanish and positive attitudes towards the receptive community, in this
case Catalonia, favoured the appearance of codeswitching.[33] In (2), Tina is
a 26-year-old Italian, who has been in Catalonia (Spain) for six years and
first came as an Erasmus student, but is now working as a translator and
teacher of Italian, and has attended formal classes of Spanish:

(2)   **Tina:**   (... fanno un mischio terribile no, e questo l'ho notato invece
              se vai nei paesi già il catalano è più stretto, questo si nota
              propio assai cioè il **el tornillu** o parole che **amarillu** o cose
              strane che propio, questo si, il catalano qua credo che **en**
              Cataluña el catal bueno Cataluña, a Barcellona il catalano
              non si parla propio bene non so se è una mia impressione o
              so ... parlano un catalano schifosissimo.

              ... they mix terribly, I noticed this in the villages where
              Catalan is purer, you can tell by words such as **screw** [Spanish
              loan with phonological integration into Catalan) and words
              such as **yellow** (same as above). I really think that **in**
              Catalonia, Catal, well in Catalonia, rather in Barcelona, it
              is not real Catalan that is spoken, I don't know, it's my own
              view, really ... they speak a broken Catalan.

              (Torrens, 1996)

Prediction 2. It is predicted that codeswitching will be less extensive, if
present at all, or will primarily take the form of lexical codeswitching (involving less cognitive effort) with the following speaker profile:
a speaker of a typologically distant language (from Spanish and Catalan),
from a culturally distant community, of a very 'endogamic' type, and
therefore, with low degree of contact, negative or neutral attitudes, no

socio-psychological motivations for mobility, and few communicative needs in the language of the host community.

Along these lines, it wouldn't be surprising then to find that there is no codeswitching within the Chinese community. The members of the latter community have been migrating to Spain over the last 30 years (Beltrán and García, Ch. 12), and constitute a *less open*, culturally distant community type. This pattern, which applies to first-generation and second-generation migrants, is no longer followed by third-generation Chinese migrants, who attend Spanish-speaking and Catalan-speaking schools and make use of a bilingual mode with codeswitching patterns ; however, there is no recorded evidence of this in the linguistic minority groups' corpus. Another group of communities which would fit this pattern would be the Arabic-speaking and Berber-speaking Maghreb communities, the Algerian, and above all, the Moroccan community.

The interplay between internal and external factors

That internal factors, such as language proximity, are not the sole factors explaining the emergence of codeswitching, is shown by the fact that speakers from communities whose languages are very distant from Spanish also adopt codeswitching as a usual modality of discourse. The socio-psychological motivation behind this has to do with positive attitudes towards the receptive community and a wish to integrate in it.[34] Such is the case of the Israeli community, whose members migrated to Spain, more specifically to Catalonia, in 1992, after the Gulf War. Their language is Modern Hebrew, although their speech will also reflect the use of some loans from Yiddish and Jewish-Spanish (Judeo-Español). In (3), Tania, a 40-year-old Israeli woman, who migrated with her husband and small children in 1992 and usually speaks Hebrew to them, codeswitches into Spanish in the middle of her conversation with them:

(3)   **Tania:**   ... yesh li **queja** be inyan ha ze.
              (I have a **complaint** in this matter)

              ... im ein leja **enchufe** lo tujal lehicanes le sham.
              (You won't be able to get that job, if you don't have **influence,** (i.e. someone on the inside to help you))
                                                                (Vigil, 1997)

The differences observed between the codeswitching practices of the members of the US and the UK communities illustrate the intersection between internal and external factors involved in the model proposed in Turell (1997). Given that internal factors, such as language typology, cannot apply in this case because there are virtually the same structural differences between Spanish or Catalan and American English as between Spanish or Catalan and British English, there would have to be other factors, having to do with community-type and degree of contact and social integration, responsible for any differences in this case. Indeed, the qualitative analysis of the two communities' settlement pattern, degree of contact and overall social integration showed that in its settlement in Spain, the American English US community emerges as a *more open* community, while the British English UK community tends towards a *less open* community type (Turell & Corcoll, 1998; Turell & Corcoll, Chs. 16 and 17).

Qualitative observation showed that the *more open* type of community, such as the US, typically produce LC phenomena which involve more interference than others: for example, borrowings with various degrees of interference, calques and both lexical and grammatical codeswitches (Fontana & Vallduví, 1990) which involve a free option for the speakers, in the sense that they may be using another language segment when they could have used their own language. In this way, these phenomena become a sort of indicator of their positive attitudes towards the host community's language and culture. Speakers from *less open* types of communities tend to use LC units, particularly one-word codeswitches or lexical codeswitches[35] which are constrained by the sentence linguistic context in which they are produced, filling in the slots with words in the host community's language that could not have been English, because either the term or the concept, object, entity, participant or particular cultural overtone did not exist in their culture or in everyday life back in their country.

Extracts (4) and (5) illustrate the point which has just been made in relation to community type. (5) involves the modality of discourse of one member of the US American-English-speaking community in Spain. J.B. is a 37-year-old truck driver who has been in Spain for more than five years, with no formal instruction in Spanish or Catalan.

(4)   **J.B.:**   'Like today, I had, at work, I had a piece of, a tool, what do you call it? **un cepillo** [plane], you know, a carpenter's ... thing, well, somebody put on there ***averiado*, no tocar, *averiado*** [do not touch, out of order] and, of course, they spelled ***averiado* con b en vez de v** [with a b instead of a v]. I knew that right off, you know, that it was wrong, but ... I mean, there are some things that are difficult in Spanish [spelling], but, very few' ...

(Turell, 1992)

(6) reflects the modality of discourse of one member of the UK British-English-speaking community and informs us of what on first analysis seems to be the most usual codeswitching parameter among members of this community, that is, insertions. James, a 50-year-old plumber, with no formal instruction in Spanish, migrated to Spain more than five years ago.

(5) **James:**   ... we go to Tarragona and I find, the services are OK, in the middle of the afternoon they seem to sort of stop, possibly the drivers have a **siesta** [nap], I don't know, but, but then, I can understand that because in the old days Tarragona had a **siesta**[36] but now it doesn't, it's open all day ...

(Corcoll, 1996)

Language typology is another internal factor that constrains codeswitching patterns. The data drawn from the communities under study shows that (1) codeswitching between typologically close languages, such as, Brazilian → Spanish/Catalan (Turell & Lavratti (Ch. 10) on the Brazilian community), Italian → Spanish/Catalan (Torrens (Ch. 13) on the Italian community), English → Spanish/Catalan (Turell and Corcoll (Chs. 16 and 17) on the US American and UK communities) takes the form of both lexical and grammatical intrasentential codeswitching, although the former would be more extended than the latter, whereas (2) data sets involving codeswitching between typologically distant languages, such as, Hebrew → Spanish (Vigil (Ch. 17) on the Jewish community, or Basque → Spanish (Cenoz & Perales (Ch. 3) on the Basque community) would primarily present lexical insertion codeswitching or the use of other resources to avoid the use of complex grammatical relations or categories. In an example of intrasentential codeswitching from Basque → Spanish, as shown in (6), the speaker avoids the conjugation of the Spanish verb and uses the infinitive form after the conjunction:[37]

(6) Bai, nik makina elektrikoa erabiltzen dut sartu folioa eta gero **poner a ciento cincuenta y seis** eta bete folioa.

Yes, I use a typewriter and put the sheets in; then you **to fix it at a hundred and fifty six** and you fill in the sheets.

(Cenoz, 1994)

Language contact unmarked choices

The most typical pragmatically *unmarked* choices are borrowing and calque, but *unmarked* codeswitching also occurs.[38] Borrowing, as the most extended form of *unmarked* LC phenomenon, is defined as the incorporation of lexical elements from one language into another, adapting this material to the phonological and morphological patterns of the receptor language (Grosjean, 1990; Muysken, 1991; Poplack, 1990; Pujadas & Turell, 1993). Borrowing usually occurs as an unmarked choice in relatively long-standing situations of LC. Catalan-Spanish contact offers the best examples of unmarked borrowing occurring between typologically close languages.[39]

Another contact situation which is relevant to illustrate the use of *unmarked* choices is the very long-standing contact situation of the

Sephardim Jewish community living in Ceuta and Melilla (North Africa), whose ancestors came from the Jewish community expelled by Isabel and Ferdinand, the Spanish Catholic Monarchs, back in 1492. After Expulsion some Jewish communities migrated to several places in North Africa and in their settlements they started using another variety of language called *Jaketía*, extensively studied by Bendalac (1995). This variety constitutes a mixed code containing elements of Old Spanish, Hebrew and local Arabic, with some borrowings from Berber, Portuguese, French and English. The most frequently noted mixed formation in the above-mentioned variety consisted in taking an Arabic or Hebrew verb root morpheme and conjugating it according to Spanish verb inflectional morphology. Examples are shown in (7), (8) and (9):

(7)   lais**near** (from *lasan* [to speak badly of people, gossip])
(8)   **en**ka'as**arse** (from *ka'as* [to get angry])
(9)   **des**jame**zar** (from *jamets;* jars where baking powder has been used [to clean the *jamets*])

The last type of LC phenomena to mention is calque which, together with borrowing, constitutes a pragmatically *unmarked* pattern of language mixing, at all events less overt than codeswitching. It has been traditionally defined as the literal translation from one language to another of certain idiomatic phrases (semantic calque) or syntactic constructions (syntactic calque), with no external indication of its other-language provenance (Poplack, 1990). More recent accounts of syntactic calque define it as 'the calque by a L2 of the particular syntactic structure underlying an utterance conveyed in terms of L2 words, but L1 syntax'[40] (Corcoll, 1999: 14–15), as is illustrated in (10), uttered by a member of the US community in Spain:

(10) Possibly, because I think it's something that **the people** have invented to keep themselves occupied, possibly.

                                                                                    (Turell, 1992)

where all the lexical items are produced in English but the internal structure of the NP (in bold) is either Catalan or Spanish, since it involves the use of the definite article which is obligatory in these two languages but not canonical in English, at least in this specific communicative context.

In sum, the research conducted within the minorities and speech communities object of study in this book has shown that different LC phenomena can be taken as indicators of inter-ethnic contact and that several factors can constrain the emergence, diffusion, type and frequency of these phenomena. These phenomena include *marked/unmarked* codeswitching, as in Pradilla (Ch. 2) on the Catalan-speaking community in Catalonia; codemixing, associated with low competence in the two languages in contact and sometimes involving the use of a mixed variety,

Portunhol, as in López Trigal (Ch. 15), and *Portunhol* and *Españogués*, as in Turell and Lavratti (Ch. 10) on the Portuguese and the Brazilian community, respectively; loan and calque, as *unmarked* forms of LC, and language shift, as a consequence of the substitution of one language in contact by the other.

The first generations of almost all communities adopt a wide range of borrowings from the host community's language and culture that they adapt to the phonological and morphological structure of their own language. With time they will not only borrow individual words but they will also calque a whole syntactic structure (syntactic calque) or they will borrow from the host community's language the meaning of a particular expression even if the words are in their mother tongue (semantic calque). If they achieve a good competence in the new language, they then adopt more sophisticated forms of LC, such as codeswitching where the two systems are kept separate. Obviously, this behaviour will also be constrained by other factors, such as the duration of the contact situation. Second and subsequent generations adopt LC patterns that show much more adaptation where words and phrases from Spanish (or any other officially recognised languages) are inserted into the mother tongue's grammatical structure.

For some communities of the *less open* type it may be difficult if not impossible to find LC phenomena. At one extreme of the scale, the older generations within the Chinese community would be classified within this group. The correlation of *more open* type community, positive attitudes and high competence in the host community language would favour the occurrence of codeswitching modalities, where the codeswitch is a context-free option (Torrens (Ch. 13) on the Italian community, and Turell and Corcoll (Ch. 17) on the US American community), as well as LC types which reflect more interference with the other language, such as loan and calque. In the case of *less open* communities, the data confirm that their members seem to maintain the two languages more separate and that when codeswitching they use a codeswitch which is context-bound, that is, less of an option, as tends to happen within the UK community (Turell and Corcoll, Ch. 16).

Learning and communicative strategies

It is widely accepted nowadays that in the context of both second and foreign language acquisition the role of learning strategies (LS from now on),[41] which involve learning how to learn, is unquestionable. The origins of this interest in strategies have to be traced back to the 1970s but fuller development occurred during the 1980s and 1990s and continues to this day.

This early interest was framed by several issues which are fundamental to the nature and occurrence of strategies in learning processes: (1) the question of 'successful learners' (Naiman *et al.*, 1978), (2) the relation between the development of interlanguages and 'process-oriented under-lying mechanisms', which would later on be called, simply, 'strategies' (Faerch & Kasper, 1983), (3) the effect of bilingualism and multilingualism on the process of learning a new language, (4) the incorporation of the notion of 'communicative competence' (linguistic, sociolinguistic, dis-course and strategic), first proposed by Hymes (1974), to acquisition and learning contexts (Canale & Swain, 1980), and finally, (5) the development of the study of the notion of interlanguage as being constrained by both free and systematic variability (Tarone, 1988; Adamson, 1990). This approach and framework of analysis led scholars to highlight the instru-mental character of language.

Several definitions of learning strategies have been proposed. In fact, the first scholars to actually name them as such were O'Malley and Uhl (1990). Others have attempted a hierarchic classification, but the most complete taxonomy, which is taken in this book as a reference model and is illustrated in Figure 1.2, was proposed by Oxford (1990).

Learning strategies have been considered from several points of view, but maybe the most relevant in the context of second and foreign language learning and acquisition are: the learner's autonomy, the learning strategies' teachability, and finally the relation between learning strategies and social identity. The issue of autonomy arises from attempts to distinguish between the factors that together comprise the learning context (the learners, the teacher, the educational institution, the country's educational system, the parents, in the case of young learners, and the company or firm, in the case of adult learners) and those factors which have an effect on the learner's learning process. The latter would form the answer to a question formulated to the learners themselves: How do you prefer to learn? Accordingly, a useful definition of LS would be that proposed by Garí (1995: 15) according to whom LS involve 'the set of actions that the learners take in a voluntary and conscious way to optimise learning not only at the cognitive but also at the affective and social levels in such a way that their autonomy in learning is increased.' The question of the possible teachability of LS involves the viewing of LS as means to

LEARNING STRATEGIES	DIRECT STRATEGIES	MEMORY STRATEGIES COGNITIVE STRATEGIES COMPENSATION STRATEGIES
	INDIRECT STRATEGIES	METACOGNITIVE STRATEGIES AFFECTIVE STRATEGIES SOCIAL STRATEGIES

Figure 1.2 Learning strategies system
Source: Oxford (1990)

realising possible learning tasks, and in the process of performing these tasks learners combine and practise different skills (reading, writing, speaking and listening) applied to different linguistic levels (usually, vocabulary and grammar) in the context of which the teaching of second and foreign languages is framed.[42]

Maybe the most relevant issue to the context of language learning among migrant communities is the relationship between LS and social identity, where the learners of the host community's language(s) face this challenge immersed in an apparent contradictory situation. They have to learn a new language, and thus be exposed to a new culture in order to integrate into the social dynamics of the host country and be respected as new citizens on an equal footing with the indigenous people, and at the same time, they stick to their own culture and their own view of the world. This in turn means maintaining their own language, and claiming respect for their culture and language. It should not be forgotten either that language is an exponent of individual and social identity and that through language one can express solidarity or disrespect, and also that one of the main aims behind the learning of languages other than one's own is to promote intercultural understanding between peoples.

Unfortunately, only six communities (the Brazilian, the Chinese, the Gitano, the Italian, the Maghrebi, and the Sign Language communities) have been investigated from the point of view of their learning strategies when they learn Spanish or any of the other co-official languages of Spain. The correlation between the learning strategies used by learners of Spanish (or the other languages) and the typological nature of the migrant's mother tongue and the host community's language showed interesting patterns that suggest new directions for research to be taken in the future. When the two languages in question are typologically distant, as is documented in Beltrán and García (Ch. 12) in the case of Chinese and Spanish, and in Garí (Ch. 14) in the case of Arabic and Spanish, the learners do not modify their own language as a possible interlanguage because of the typological distance; they rather use direct and metacognitive strategies (Oxford, 1990), visual memory, analogy, contrasts and opposites, as well as social strategies, learner autonomy and self-direction; in other words, strategies directly related to their own culture, language and values, although there may be other factors affecting their learning process (i.e. other languages learnt before, degree of expertise and competence in their own language, age, gender). In contrast, when the two languages involved are typologically close, as documented in Turell and Lavratti (Ch. 10) on the Brazilian community, and in Torrens (Ch. 13) on the Italian community, particularly in the early stages of learning, communicative interaction in the new language is reinforced by using particular language items of the mother tongue which is used as a sort of interlanguage bridge.

Finally, the analysis of the language acquisition and learning aspects of migrant communities in Spain also sheds some light on the intrinsic relation between the ultimate goals of education, its pedagogical aspects and teaching content. What could be viewed as school underachievement may be in fact related to the different nature of the discourse used at school (conceptually based) and the community's everyday language (analogy based), as in Marzo and Turell (Ch. 8) on the Gitano community. The Sign Language communities (Vallverdú, Ch. 7) provide evidence of the debate concerning the advantages of the oral method or the sign method for the education of the deaf people.

Migration

The context and the scope of migration

J.K. Galbraith (1994) describes migration as 'a historical need in our era' in the sense that the migrants do the jobs that the indigenous people do not want to do. But not all opinions are so optimistic. Migratory flows in modern times are governed by economical laws: the need for cheap and/or dirty labour (i.e. doing dirty jobs no one else wants) in the Western world and the dramatic situation in the Third World. However crude and drastic this last statement about migration may seem, what it suggests is that in order to predict future migratory patterns, on a general scale as well as within particular situations, it will be fundamental to have information at a world level on economy and population growth. The world's population increased at an average rate of 97 million inhabitants every year over the last decade of the 20th century and 83% of that increase took place in the big cities.[43] The population of the world, estimated at present at five thousand seven-hundred (5700) million people approximately, will double by the middle of the 21st century, and this will mean 10 thousand million people unequally distributed and with unequal resources.

At the same time, the 1992 UNDP (United Nations Development Programme) report revealed that inequality had doubled in the previous 30 years and that one-fourth of humanity lived in worse conditions (financially and in other ways) than even 15 years ago. Some of the items considered in this report need to be highlighted, particularly in relation to health. Life expectation was 75 in developed countries, while it only reached 63 in underdeveloped countries, and in these countries 1500 million people did not have health services and 2500 million were living in unsanitary conditions. And there were 80 countries where 40% of the population suffered from poor or insufficient water supplies; 800 million people from several countries were hungry (of these one-fourth of the children below 5),[44] and 180 million suffered from malnutrition (*Source: La Vanguardia*, Revista, p. 2 (23 April 1992).

With such perspectives it is not surprising that people from these poor countries feel compelled to migrate to be able to survive. According to 1993 UN sources, over the two previous decades 100 million people –

2% of the world's population – were compelled to migrate to other countries in order to be able to survive due to the precarious economic or political situation in their countries of origin. Of these, 17 millions were refugees and 20 millions escaped from violence, drought and environmental destruction. Over the preceding 30 years or so, around 35 million people had migrated from South to North, and this figure was increasing by one million every year. Every year, according to the same source, between one and two million people from the Third World applied to legalise their position in developed countries. The report went on to say that in the future environmental change and decay would bring about massive migration, because many islands, coasts and deltas would become flooded and uninhabitable, and environment refugees would become a fact. These same sources concluded that the growth of migration could become the greatest crisis of our times.

Present-day migration as an international issue can be characterised as: (1) urban, either internal migration in which people are drawn from the country to the big cities, or external migration where foreign migrants settle in big cities as well; (2) one-way type of migration, either as a 'brain-drain', where privileged migrants develop their abilities and careers and join well-equipped research groups, or as a job-seeking migration, where the migrants occupy the vacuum left by the indigenous workers who no longer want to take certain types of jobs; and (3) illegal migration, since 90% of the residence-permit applications handed in by migrants are refused and, therefore, they are condemned to become illegal residents, at least temporarily.[45]

International migration patterns differ from one region to another. Between 1980 and 1992, Europe welcomed 15 million migrants, the majority of whom sought a permanent and stable settlement in the country and community to which they moved. Since 1960 oil-producing countries have attracted migrant workers from the Middle East and Asia in different migratory flows. Internal and external migration patterns in Africa and Asia are changing very rapidly and are difficult to summarise here. People from Central America and the Caribbean are migrating to the US, Brazil and Venezuela.

In Europe, the 1960s and 1970s were decades of both within-Europe migration (Spanish, Portuguese, Italian and Greek people migrating to Germany and France) and extra-European migration (Maghrebi and Turkish people migrating to these same countries, and Caribbean and Asian people migrating to the United Kingdom). However, in the 1980s migration decreased and this was due to the 1982–85 crisis which obliged many European governments to facilitate the migrants' return to their countries of origin. But in fact the return was only feasible for those migrants who could really survive in their own countries; the majority stayed, either as nationalised citizens or in precarious conditions. According to EU sources, in 1995 the distribution of biggest immigrant groups to continental Europe included 2,000,000 Turks, the majority of them settling in Germany, 1,500,000 Maghreb migrants, most of them living in France, and 600,000 migrants from the ex-Yugoslavian countries, who concentrated in Germany as well.

In contrast with this development, at present within-Europe migration has been reduced to the minimum, to the point that only 2% of Europeans live in a member state and come from another, although this average percentage is distributed unevenly depending on the member states: Luxembourg and Belgium are above 5%, France, Germany and Ireland are above 2%, whereas Spain and Portugal don't reach 1%. According to a EU questionnaire on workforce, between 1987 and 1991 only 1,500,000 people moved from one state to another, which involves an average of 300,000 people per year and represents less than 0.1% of the total EU population.

During the decade 1990–2000 Europe experienced high rates of external migration from outside the EU. In 1990, West Germany and France showed that the figure for foreign-born population was 8.4% and 6.4%, respectively, while the EU countries as a whole registered 13 million of foreign people. Even Eastern and Central European countries, such as, Hungary, Poland, Slovakia and the Czech Republic have been receiving immigration flows over recent years. In 1991 and 1992 half of the population growth there was due to migration, and in the case of Germany this accounted for about three-quarters of the growth. Between 1990 and 1993 one million people acquired the nationality of a country forming part of the EU. The majority of these people being from Turkey (43,000), Morocco (31,000) and ex-Yugoslavia (26,000). However, only 26,000 Europeans (including 6500 Portuguese and 4000 Italians) adopted another communitarian nationality over the same period. By countries, France is the leading destination, having nationalised 223,000 people, followed by Great Britain (218,000) and the Benelux countries (204,000).

In the future, a very interesting development to consider is birth-rate and population aging since these are going to be crucial factors when predicting the future of Europe's demographic make-up and further migration processes. According to the UN Population Foundation (1992), Europe's low birth-rate and its increasingly aging population are reaching such levels that in year 2025, it is calculated, Western and Southern Europe will see their workforce reduced by 14 million workers (11%), while it will be increased by 56.6 million people in North Africa. This loss of workforce is already being caused by falling birth-rate which reduces the young sections of a country's population, and the disproportion is further increased by the extension of life expectancy which increases the number of elderly people. In spite of the growing rejection of migration by EU countries, developed countries demand for working populations will actually increase the South → North migration, which will concentrate in urban areas as recent developments have already shown. Over the decade of the 1990s, (1) 83% of population growth was in cities, (2) already in 1990, 45% were living in urban areas, and (3) at present there are 20 megacities in Europe which have 8 million or more inhabitants. In these urban areas, migrants will live together with the poorest sections of the indigenous populations and they will suffer the worst part.[46]

The context of migration in Spain

The context in which the process of migration to Spain takes place includes demographic, social and attitudinal aspects with which migrants are faced and which help define the social and cultural make-up of Spain as a destination for many people. Demographically speaking, in a century Spain has doubled its population, which at the turn of the millennium stands at 40,000,000 people approximately. Estimates from unofficial censuses put the Spanish population in 1897 at 18,108,600 people, while the 1996 municipal census (approved by the Spanish government, 11 July 1997) assessed Spain's population to be 39,652,700 people, which means that the Spanish population has increased 108% over the course of the 20th century and in fact over the last 135 years from the time of writing the increase has been 151%. However, contrary to the growth tendency of the world's population, which was increasing by 97 million people per year over the last decade of the 20th century, in Spain the population will start decreasing after the turn of the new century and millennium. This decrease will be caused by a low birth-rate (1.3, occupying position 174, second lowest in the world), in spite of the fact that life expectancy is one of the highest in the world (80.5 years for women and 73.4 for men) and that mortality at birth is one of the lowest (5 children for every 100,000 live births) (*Source*: 1995 UN Report on Human Development). The last available Spanish census (1991) indicated that there were in Spain 798,805 more women than men, and this was also due to greater life expectancy among the female population.

Socially speaking, according to the 1994 UN report on Human Development, Spain occupied the twenty-third position in terms of quality of life. The results of the same report in 1995 show that Spain leapt to the ninth position and this was due to spending on education in particular. On the other hand, Spain, with one of the highest European rates of unemployment (2 million compared with the 17 million in the whole of Europe), occupies a mid-way position in the UN ranking (1995) as to hypothetical workforce (active population). Only 39% of its total population are actually working. However, the most important aspect to take into account in this case is the spectacular influx of women in the employment domain, something which changed Spanish society quite remarkably between 1982 and 1994. Over the course of the 1990s, 9 out of 10 new work places created were taken by women. Of the 16,255,600 women comprising Spain's active female population, 5,726,600 women (35.2%) are actually in employment. The most important sectors occupied by working women are trade, health, education, executive work, hotels, public administration, domestic service, textiles, food, finances. One important consequence of this overwhelming incorporation of the women into the world of work is that the family's structure will change because there will be fewer housewives to look after the youngest and the elderly living in the household. Notwithstanding, the 1995 UN report on Human Development also showed that there are other aspects, particularly development related to women's issues, which lowered the ranking. And this is basically due to the fact that in spite of the overwhelming proportion of young women who are employed, women are still not present in all areas of employment and their salaries can in some cases be 30% lower than men for the same work.

As to attitudes, according to a survey carried out by the Centro de Investigaciones Sociológicas (CIS (Spanish Centre for Sociological Research) for the 1995 International Social Survey programme (ISSP) in 22 countries, Spanish society emerges as a population that demands equality and has, in fact, reduced inequality. Moreover, it is perceived by its members as very egalitarian, while at the same time identifying many differences within itself. In spite of this, this same survey shows that Spain is undergoing a long period of dissatisfaction, pessimism, defeatism and hypercritical attitudes, being in first place in what has been defined as 'the culture of complaint'. More specifically, the population making up the different indigenous communities complain because they feel badly done by in relation to the others, with the persistence of regional stereotypes whereby which Andalusians are happy-go-lucky people, always celebrating, Aragonese people are conceited big heads, Basque people are rough and/or separatists, Catalans are tight-fisted or money-minded, Galician people are untrusting, closed and mystical, people from Madrid are conceited big mouths, and Valencian people are skilful. These stereotypes undergo fundamental differences depending on whether the community is being perceived by its own members or by other indigenous communities in Spain (*Source: Datos de Opinión*, No. 1, Bulletin of the Centro de Investigaciones Científicas ((CIS) Centre for Sociological Research))).

But in spite of this carping attitude the fact is that Spain is at present a relatively peaceful country, with frequent industrial unrest, but no social conflict. The welfare state that was initiated during the 1980s has had negative effects in promoting insolidary attitudes, with unfortunate consequences: Spanish citizens have been spending more than they actually have, working less and trusting in a providential state. With the economic crisis at the end of the 1980s and beginning of the 1990s, they have had to tighten their belts. From 1994 onward, Spanish people emerge as more optimistic about their future, particularly as to the economic situation, and even further, a 1995 survey conducted by the Centro de Investigación de

Mercados Españoles e Internacionales ((CIMEI) Research Centre for Spanish and International Markets) shows that in general the Spanish citizen's happiness rate is surprisingly high, although this rate translates in very materialistic terms, since 40% of the interviewees respond that to be able to be happier they would need more money, only 16% associate happiness with having a stable job, 13% with health, and 10% with love and a good family atmosphere.

Characterisation of immigration to Spain

The Spain of the 1960s and 1970s could be characterised as a country of both *external* migration (migrants from several provinces in Spain migrating primarily to Germany, Switzerland and France) and *internal* migration (migrants particularly from Andalusia and Extremadura migrating to other regions of Spain such as the Basque Country and Catalonia in particular). During the 1980s, and in some cases long before that, Spain started welcoming a number of communities whose members had to abandon their country of origin for political, and above all, economic reasons. Since then, from a situation of external migration, Spain has become primarily a country of destination for immigration, becoming the host country for a range of communities which have come to join the long-standing ones.

The analysis of *internal* migration, that is, Spanish citizens moving to different areas and regions in Spain, is not the object of study in this book and would, therefore, require a separate volume. In its turn, *external* migration can be legal or illegal, depending on whether or not this migratory process runs up against legal restrictions, and the speed at which it is accomplished will depend on the prestigious or non-prestigious status of the group of migrants in question, or of course, the professional group to which each individual migrant may belong.[47] Another interesting item of information from the Ministry of Social Affairs, in which the nature of migration to Spain is characterised, refers to the degree of stability of this migration once the migrants have settled. Spain has stopped being a country primarily receiving 'through-traffic' going to another destination to become a stable destination. In fact, only 20% of migrants are planning to go back to their country of origin.

Initially migration to Spain could be characterised in terms of four big groups of foreigners whose distribution is now beginning to change and also varies by Autonomous Community. One group includes the Northern European retired immigrants who benefit from the tax differences between their countries of origin and Spain, who have seldom added their names to the census and whose illegality remains unnoticed. Another group comprises qualified technicians whose standard of living is above the average in Spain. A third group is composed of relatively qualified workers who migrate to better their position, in general either Europeans or South-

Table 1.1 Distribution of foreign residents in Spain
by country of origin (non-Spanish speaking)

Morocco	77,189
United Kingdom	68,359
Germany	45,898
Portugal	38,316
France	33,134
Italy	21,362
EE.UU	15,661
Holland	13,925
Philippines	11,770
China	10,816
Belgium	9,847
Switzerland	7,138
India	6,882
Sweden	6,545
Brazil	5,694
Denmark	5,107

Source: Anuario de Migraciones 1997: 236–45

Americans who want to get away from the deterioration of the middle
classes in their countries of origin. Finally, those migrants who want to
escape from hunger and redundancy and come to Spain to work on farms, in
the building industry and in low-qualified services. There is a fifth group of
quite often short-term migrants, who are in fact political refugees. According
to the 1993 INSERSO[48] report at present there are 3850 political refugees in
Spain, but in fact, between 1985 and 1992, 4000 applications for political
asylum were made to Spain, of which only 10% were granted. During 1993,
by far the highest number of applications was from Bosnian citizens (68%).

Although it is difficult to document the exact number of migrants living
in Spain because some half of them are illegal residents, it is estimated that
there are 800,000 in all. According to the last published census (1991),[49]
the foreign population in Spain accounted for by the census represents
around 1% (360,655 people) of the total 1991 population (39,433,930)
people).[50] According to more recent data, recorded in 1996 by the Spanish
Ministry of Interior,[51] the total number of foreign residents amounts to
538,984 (around 0.73% of the total 1996 population). Table 1.1 includes
the major groups of foreign residents distributed by countries of origin.

As to the migrants' profile in terms of the migration patterns that have been observed, the members of the *new migrant* minorities that have been considered in this volume either have economic motivations (the Chinese, the Brazilian, the Maghrebi, the Portuguese, the Cape Verdean), or can be described as an elitist migration where migrants come in search of individual socio-cultural growth or jobs in technology (the Italian, the British, the US American). This is so even though it is usually claimed that in many migration contexts it is very difficult to discern between political and economic reasons (Alladina & Edwards, 1991: 16), It is also interesting to look at the variety of origins of the minorities considered in this study, in terms of their social and organisational structure. Some communities come from rural areas (the Gitanos, the Portuguese and the Cape Verdeans), others come from both rural and urban areas (the Chinese, the Maghrebi) and still others come from urban areas almost exclusively (the Italians,[52] the British, the US Americans).

The settlement patterns also offer a variety of situations. Some communities concentrate in relatively small areas, and therefore they are able to develop and maintain strong social networks, either in rural settings: the Black African communities (Gambia, Senegal) in rural Lleida, a province of Catalonia; the Portuguese, in mining, fishing, or agriculture, or more urban structures: the Maghrebi in the small villages or neighbourhoods in the Maresme.[53] Others concentrate in big connurbations, seeking jobs in the services sector (the Chinese, the Portuguese). The majority of the communities from Western European countries follow a double settlement pattern: if their motivation for migration is primarily to seek employment, they usually settle in big cities where professionalism develops and where big companies are most usually located, although they often live in the outskirts of these big cities or have a second house in the countryside; if they come for retirement reasons, then they will prefer to settle in small seaside areas. One special settlement pattern is associated with the Gitanos, long-established communities which back in the 15th century settled in different parts of Spain, conserving their own identity and keeping links with their lineage; and the Jewish, also long-established communities with very unhappy episodes in their history: above all their expulsion by the Spanish Kingdom, a historical event which was painful for the community and shameful for 'la España de los Reyes Católicos' and for its descendants.

The duration of the migrants' settlement, therefore, is also of particular relevance, with there being a clear distinction between, (1) those minorities which have been in Spain for centuries, such as the different Jewish communities,[54] and the Gitano communities, with their characteristic nomad pattern, (2) well-established minority groups of recent times, such as the Chinese, Italian, German, Russian, French, US American, and British communities, which have maintained a presence for several decades, and (3) the still more recently arrived communities, such as the Black Africans, the Maghrebi, the Indians, the Pakistanis, and the Middle Eastern communities, whose migration was constrained by economic factors.

A further distinction can also be made by considering the communities' stability and the communities' expectations to return to their country of origin. In this sense, it is possible to distinguish, (1) communities which cherish the so-called *myth-of-return*, whereby their members organise their life around their return to their country of origin (the Maghrebi, the Black Africans, the Philipinos), (2) 'annual migrants' (Alladina & Edwards, 1991: 16), such as the Japanese community, and (3) the retired or wealthy people who settle in various seaside towns and villages along the Spanish Mediterranean coast and the Canaries for six or eight months a year, spending the rest of the year in their country of origin (the British, the French, the Dutch, the German).

Another relevant dimension is the minorities' degree of contact with the home country. Some communities, such as the Chinese, even if they have little or no contact with their country of origin, are decided in their resolve to keep their ethnic identity, live in relative isolation and try to build similar patterns to those they would find if they were involved with their own country's culture and habits back home. Other communities, such as the Maghrebi, although also keeping to themselves and standing by their religious obligations and cultural patterns, live for their 'annual summer return', travelling freely to their country of origin. Some other communities, such as the British, although predominantly of the *less open* type in many respects, also like to mix with the people from the host country. Finally, there is another group of communities of what can be described as the *more open* type, whose members are very proud of being so, for example, US American and Italians, who mix much more frequently, marry members of other communities, and enjoy adopting some of the host country's cultural patterns.

Discrimination

The discriminatory aspects that affect minorities in Spain, in particular, *new migrant* communities, involve state legislation (both European and Spanish), planning policies and intentions, on the one hand, and the attitudes of the Spanish society, on the other. However, discriminatory paths affect the members of these minorities differently depending on their different nature and origin. At the same time, the existence of discrimination has generated reactions of institutional and social support on the state and the society's side.

Migratory policy and legislation and their discriminatory consequences

In present-day Europe, the increase in the number of expulsions of foreign migrants from each member state can be attributed to the Schengen agreement, subscribed by the Benelux countries, France, Germany, Greece, Italy, Portugal and Spain and implemented in 1995, which involved the elimination of national borders and the free circulation of people in those nine countries. In the run-up to the actual implementation of the Schengen agreement, the subscribing countries were interested in reducing the number of illegal migrants in view of the more than probable increase of new illegal fluxes of migration after implementation. This increase in expulsions was preceded by a toughening of the EU members' migratory policy and bilateral agreements between several EU state members, which took place during the last decade of the 20th century. In terms of bilateral relations between EU members, it must be mentioned as well that in 1992, France and Spain called upon Morocco to tighten control on their migration to Europe and in exchange they committed themselves to ensuring dignified conditions and increase in co-operation on development. Also at the end of 1992, Portugal and Spain agreed to control illegal migration and to sign in 1993 an agreement to readmit illegal migrants from third countries. In Germany, there was an attempt to reduce the generous German right of asylum to 70% of applications.

In democratic Spain, the Spanish Parliament can legislate and implement any law in relation to migration, establishing the conditions of entry, exit and settlement for foreigners, determining immigration and emigration policy, and institutionalising asylum and nationality rights. Migratory legislation was framed in general terms in the 1978 Spanish Constitution. Later, the 1985 Immigration Act on foreigners' rights and liberties in Spain, commonly known as the 'Ley de Extranjería', explicitly developed the fundamental rights of foreigners and legislated on the migrants' entry, residence and exit. A year later (1986), the executive regulation of the 'Ley de Extranjería' [Immigration Act] was approved. This regulation developed the law restrictively in such a way that it almost only emphasised the aspects of control, and it has, therefore, been criticised by the migrants' groups and associations, and non-governmental organisations (NGOs). The law established that a foreigner will only be considered a legal resident when he or she obtains a residence permit. If this person wants to engage in a professional activity, he or she will have to apply for a work permit, which will only be granted when it is confirmed that there are no redundant Spanish workers in the work sector/branch where the migrant would like to work. Notwithstanding, lack of Spanish workers in any activity or sector will always be a reason for granting work permits to migrants. It is worth mentioning that the fact of being a legal resident does not mean one has the same rights as a Spanish citizen.

Once the Immigration Act was approved (1985), the government offered the migrants the possibility of legalising their situation during 1987. Several years later, on 7 June 1991, the government approved a bill giving immigrants a second chance to legalise their position in Spain. In spite of these measures, which legalised the situation for many people, the temporary nature of the permits, which grant the right to legal residence, and the restrictive application of the law have had many discriminatory consequences for many others who do not have their papers in order. Besides, these regularisations, the last of which was brought into effect in 1992, ushered in what ever since has been known as the 'política de cupos' [legalisation quota].

The first annual residence and work permits which had been granted to foreign workers expired in June 1992 and, therefore, new regulations were thought necessary to stabilise the foreign population in such a way that any immigrant who had been a holder of an annual residence and work permit would be able to have permits renewed automatically for another five-year-period. In parallel to this, starting in 1993, the Spanish Ministry of Labour drew up a plan whereby it was proposed that a fixed number of legal migrants, known as a 'cupo' [quota], would be established every year. Through this 'cupo' [quota], negotiated with the trade unions and the employers associations, only 20,600 migrants would be accepted, the majority to work in domestic service and as farm workers. Half of these (10,500) would come to Spain to work on a temporary basis and the other half (10,100) would stay and live in Spain on a permanent basis. But in March 1993, in view of the high rate of total unemployment, the Spanish government relented this plan and suggested a reduction of the overall fixed number. In the end, however, the reduction was slight and the same figure was proposed for 1994.

In 1995, the Spanish government relaxed the requirements needed to obtain and renew the visa and considered the possibility of extending the residence permit for periods greater than a year. The culmination of this came in 1996 with the reform of the so-called 'Ley de Extranjería' [Immigration Act] obliging all countries signatory to Maastricht and the Schengen Agreement (mentioned later) to do away with internal borders. Under this new regulation, (1) non-EU illegal foreigners can regularise their situation and have a four-month period to apply for the work or residence permit, (2) a permanent permit is created for those foreigners who have been living in Spain on a legal basis for more than six years, (3) a new residence permit, similar to the Spanish ID card, comes into existence, and (4) the immigrants' children's rights are protected and family grouping is contemplated. This new reform, although positive in terms of smoothing the way to migrant integration, has been questioned by migrants' organisations and NGOs because it condemns the most precarious migrants in the most precarious position to restriction of their free access to employment and health attention, except in the case of children, and arbitrariness in the issuing of visas and entry permits.

The prospects as far as present-day nationalisation procedures follow similar discriminatory paths, showing what has been called the 'two track system', that is, the fast first-class route and the slow second-class route, depending on whether the applicant is a famous or an anonymous candidate for nationalisation. The requirements are the same for everybody: a visa or residence permit obtained through marriage, which should have taken place a year before applying. However, the fast track for famous people (such as football players or other sports personalities, actors, influential people) usually takes between two or three months and one year, whereas the slow track involves between two or two and a half years of patient effort plus a further six-month period to apply for the Spanish ID card.

Corruption and abuse

Migrants from Third World countries (Maghreb, Black Africa) themselves suffer from the effects of corruption and abuse (i.e. fraudulent dealing with work permit application, especially in the case of Maghrebi migrants) and others suffer from extortion, sometimes committed by members of their own communities (foreign Chinese mafias), but the majority of times by professionals such as lawyers and agents that organise paperwork for people and take deliberate advantage of the migrants' precarious status. These people have been prosecuted and condemned as criminals. However, the Spanish Ombudsman has condemned several times the indiscriminatory imprisonment of illegal migrants who are also treated as delinquents.

With the 'Ley de Extranjería' [Immigration Act] and the hardening of the procedures leading to legalisation, for some years (1992–94) some members of these migrant minorities reacted by bending the rules of society and committing minor crimes, such as petty theft or by turning to major crimes, thus avoiding expulsion. They took advantage of Spanish laws which do not permit repatriation of those people who are charged with an offence. They avoided repatriation and expulsion, but then claimed that they suffered from ill treatment at the hands of the police. In 1994 a new regulation was brought in whereby expulsion was allowed not only of illegal immigrants but also of persistent delinquents who commit minor crimes (with prison sentences of less than six years), threaten citizens, or pose a threat to society in general.

In the last 10 years the most pathetic situation, caused by the migrants' need to migrate, can be seen in the *pateras* [smallish open boats powered by an outboard motor] which attempt to disembark on the Spanish coasts. These *pateras*, into which a large number (greater than the boat can really take) of North African migrants (the majority from Morocco and Algeria, but some also from Black African countries) are crammed, and are frequently stopped by the police before their passengers can even disembark. These passengers, who spend their last penny on the journey and suffer abuse from the intermediaries involved in the process, are in the majority of cases repatriated. In fact, these intermediaries ask for enormous amounts of money for a journey which will either end in death by drowning or successive attempts until they succeed in cheating the coastguards.

Another form of abuse that migrants suffer has to do with permits which are either not issued or not renewed because the authorities are taking into account the migrants' 'criminal record' involving crimes related to the 'Ley de Extranjería' [Immigration Act]. This fact is in real breach of the original agreements and regulations. In the case of political migrants, while in the majority of Western countries legal action can be taken to suspend any governmental decision to expel an applicant for political asylum, in Spain the judge only intervenes when the Alto Comisionado de las Naciones Unidas para los Refugiados (ACNUR)[55] manifests its disagreement with the decision to deny asylum, and is therefore in the administration hands.

Racism in Spain: the form it takes

Looking back in Spanish history, it would not be an exaggeration to assert that Spanish society has often been one of the most racist and xenophobic in Europe. Our past history confirms it: the Jews were expelled in the 15th century, and so were the Moors with the 'Reconquista', and families of the Spanish and Catalan oligarchy amassed huge fortunes from slave trading until the middle of the 19th century. In recent times under the Franco regime, it was the Church and the state which favoured racism with their brutal repression of anybody or anything which had to do with different races, cultures and religions. Nowadays the fact is that Spain continues to show the gloomy face of racism: many are the complaints from parents who do not want migrant children as course-mates of their own children because they are African, Maghrebi, Gitano, or from locals who would want to see migrants from these communities somewhere other than their own village, neighbour-hood or small town. And as in any other country, discriminatory and derogative language is present in the public language of politicians and in private circles, as something readily acquired and difficult to get rid of. This is reinforced by the proliferation of implicitly racist educational texts and videos, which have been disseminated throughout Europe, and Spain has not been exempt from this.[56] However, according to the 1995 Centro de Investigaciones Sociológicas (CIS) report, Spain nowadays is the least racist country in Europe and is becoming more and more tolerant. In general, Spanish people are becoming more conscious of the discrimination that migrants suffer, since they have worse living and have greater difficulties in finding a job. Spaniards want to see their families reunited, with better housing, health care, equal job opportunities, public education. And although it is also true that a high percentage of Spanish people are still in agreement with the government establishing annual entry quotas per year, on the whole Spanish society seems much more tolerant than even 10 years ago.

At a more general level, notwithstanding, in most European countries profound changes have been taking place within society, in the state, and also in the context of the relationship between culture and nation, which create favourable conditions for the emergence of racism. Also, the situation of economical crisis is fertile ground for the emergence of racism. And the racist message appeals, at the migrants' expense, to the importance of maintaining and defending the threatened national societies. Hence its proximity to certain types of nationalism. The politicians in these national societies with nationalistic tendencies use the fact of being different to claim that one is better, leading to cultural absolutism.[57] With the construction of Europe, the danger would be to shift from such national cultural identities, which may feel under threat from massive migration from the Third World, to a European culture, which would attempt to dissolve these migratory groups and their distinctive traits, particularly in the case of the Muslims. Among these distinctive traits there is one which must be considered as fundamental and paradoxical: this European identity is forged through the extension of the very means of production that directly cause the migration that is then rejected.

This view of national cultures and a more recent superposed European culture is fundamented in the idea that they derive from a single root. Nothing is further from the truth, since history teaches us that culture is forged and fortifies itself through contact and mixing, that is, cross-fertilisation between different human groups. And this applies to our present times. Nowadays, culture cannot be exclusively Spanish (or just French or German; not even European, in any 'pure' sense), but is rather hybrid, 'bastard' (Juan Goytosolo, 1994), fertilised by the very civilisations which have been the victims of ethnocentrism. And the narcissist Eurocentrism of which some people are so proud actually impedes understanding that Europe and its North American extension are the result of the interplay of many external influences. The same is true of the Spanish situation where Spanish centralist nationalism[58] remains blind to the existence of many other cultures, Basque, Catalan, Galician, Andalusian, Gitano, Jewish, Islamic, etc. Moreover, it seems that not only Spanish nationalism, but also Catalan, Basque and Galician nationalism do not seem by choice to leave space for the many other cultures and languages that are present in Spain for migratory reasons. Cultures and languages which, if a positive atmosphere is achieved — obviously without necessitating their dissolving themselves in any of the majority cultures — will fertilise them and bring about mutual benefit. In other words, it is hoped that the idea of cultural interchange[59] will substitute terms such as integration, assimilation, or even multiculturalism, the latter referring to a plurality of cultures without making reference to the relations among them, and that the issue of *interculturality* will make people more tolerant and respectful with other peoples and their culture.

Institutional and social support

From the beginning of the 1990s, migration became a public issue in Spanish society, and the administration, particularly Gonzalez's socialist government with their policy of greater sensitivity to social affairs, had to respond to a demand from society to smooth the migrants' path towards integration, maintaining respect for their idiosyncrasies and for their historical and cultural identity. However, they continued to show very little sensitivity to their linguistic rights and their consequences in the education of the migrants' children, young and adolescent. A more political reaction came from Europe: since 1995 the EU has brought the struggle against racism and xenophobia into schools.[60] Also regional and local initiatives have been taking place in Spain. In Catalonia, for example, one million school-children participated in a programme organised by the regional government and several NGOs (*Intermón, Fundació per la Pau*).[61]

Institutional support has brought about a number of amendments to the 'Ley de Extranjería' [Immigration Act] and the nationality legislation. For instance, in 1993 the extension of the right to Spanish nationality to the migrants' children was approved in the Plan General para la Inmigración (General Plan for Immigration). In 1994, the Spanish Ministry of Interior proposed a modification of this Act so that the migrants could have their most immediate relatives join them in the nuclear family, in such a way that the issuing of residence permits would be considerably faster and easier.[62]

In 1992 the Spanish government made religious freedom official by signing a series of agreements with the religious authorities of the other main faiths present in Spain, apart from the Catholic Church, that is, the Moslems, the Jews and the Protestants. These agreements cover attendance of religious services in the army and in the public health and prison, religious teaching in public education and more beneficial taxation. In 1994, the army subscribed to and implemented these agreements by granting and recognising these religious rights for soldiers. The celebration of the 'Forum Civil Euromed' [the Euromed Civil Conference] in 1995 laid the foundation for the promotion of a new attitude towards immigration, a more solidary, enriching, respectful attitude, where the removal of the legal obstacles will have to go hand in hand with education, in schools and via the mass media, to reinforce a more positive view of immigrants, as people with a culture which can enrich the host country one rather than create problems or provide a breeding ground for crime. At the educational level, this forum recommends backing affirmative action education for the children of migrants, respecting their own cultural resources and taking into account the migrants' language and culture of origin. At the same time, the migrants are expected to learn the language(s) of the host country on equal footing with the nationals, rather than form ghettos, and be able to obtain their diplomas and degrees regardless of their legal situation in the host country. Apart from this forum which is now permanent, there is also an 'Observatorio de la

Inmigración' [Immigration Watchdog Committee],[63] which will work towards the real social integration of migrants and foreign workers.

Socially, alongside this apparent increase of racist and xenophobic attitudes around the world which particularly affect migrants and refugees away from their countries of origin, there has been an opposite current of positive reactions – for respect and tolerance and the condemnation of racism coming from very different sections and groups within Spanish society – which has been gathering strength over the last decade. Since 1992 demonstrations against racism and backing migrants have been taking place regularly every year in which many people from different sectors and ages of Spanish society participate; it is worth mentioning the 1992 Madrid and Barcelona demonstrations with more than 50,000 people in each. Social support has involved the emergence of societies, networks and celebrations, such as the 'Diada Multicultural de Catalunya' [Catalonia Multicultural Day] which has been taking place since 1993 and has now been extended to the rest of Spain. Moreover, there is an antiracist European network in which Spain is also represented.

In Spain, the experts in law have undertaken legal action on several fronts. In 1993, *Judges against Racism* asked the government to make racist societies illegal and spoke out against hidden racism inherent in the accusations that migrants take advantage of the social services system and that they restrict the job market for the nationals. In 1995 some of the most celebrated prosecutors proposed heavy sentences for violent racist acts. The Committee for the Defence of the Individual's Rights of the Barcelona Lawyers Association also raised the question of reforming the present law because it discriminates, marginalises and criminalises foreign people living in Spain. Even the notaries have spoken up to ensure respect for sexual, ethnic, religious and cultural differences as human rights to be included in the New Spanish Civil Code and to oppose any aggression against people on these grounds in entrepreneurial, employment, political or associational areas.

The less political initiatives come from the artistic and intellectual world: the Catalan Palestinian Association has since its founding in the 1980s been organising a celebration in which Jewish, Catholic, Protestants, Arabs and the non-confessional sit together to see out Ramadan. In 1991, the private Baruch Spinoza Foundation was created first of all to show, particularly in Catalonia and Spain, the universal values that Jewish people have contributed to the Western world. But perhaps more importantly, it was created to defuse racism by pointing out differences and combat the use of genetic explanations to justify consideration of one social group or another as inferior.[64] The letter of presentation of this Foundation was the The City of the Difference exhibition which was set up in 1996 in the Women's Patio of the Centre de Cultura Contemporània de Barcelona (CCCB) [the Barcelona Centre of Contemporary Culture]. At about the same time the Writers Against Racism initiative, in the context of the 1995

International Literature Seminars, as well as the *Associació d'Escriptors en Llengua Catalana*, organised the 1996 International Seminar against Racism, Intolerance and Xenophobia in Barcelona. Many other groups of professional people, including journalists, have participated in a number of actions against racism. In Barcelona an agreement to protect minorities was signed by the Dean of the Journalists' Association and the counsellor of Social Affairs at the Barcelona Town Council

Turning to the social support generated within the most discriminated *new migrant* minorities, it would not be possible to mention here all the numerous self-help associations of very widely differing nature that there exist in almost all the Autonomous Communities in Spain. These back, defend and protect the migrants' rights and take the form of political,[65] educational,[66] secular[67] and religious[68] associations. Typically, such support comes from the migrant communities themselves or from the host communities, or from intercultural experience. Other instances of support are provided directly by the local and national administrations, including the municipalities. Maybe the most important of the initiatives coming from the immigrants themselves to mention is the Federació de Col.lectius d'Immigrats a Catalunya (FCIC) which brings together between 20 and 25 different associations from different migrant groups and whose main objectives are: (1) to defend the migrants' rights and dignity, (2) to promote migrants' integration defending at the same time the development of their own culture and language maintenance, (3) to combat racism and xenophobia. These component associations give support to the migrant communities at the cultural, sports and economical levels.

Focusing more specifically on the *new migrant* minorities considered in this book, analysis shows that some minorities which have been established for a long period of time may keep strong links with the country of origin, through the postal service, phone, TV and the investment of property, as reported in Beltrán and García (Ch. 12) on the Chinese community, while others contribute to a very impressive range of social, political, religious and cultural activities in the host country, often implemented through a complex network of organisational involvement, as illustrated in Turell and Lavratti (Ch. 10) on the Brazilian community). These organisations provide a natural arena for language and culture maintenance and also a setting for language reproduction. Recent arrivals, particularly if the motivation for migration is purely economic, generally have little time or energy to spend on community life, but may become involved in community gatherings as they attend Spanish classes, as reported in Garí (Ch. 14) on the Maghrebi communities in Barcelona.[69]

The Structure of the Book

The book could have been structured according to several criteria: by the nature of minority group, by its size, by the communities' patterns of settlement, by geolinguistic areas, by language, by country of origin, by communities as such. The fact that very clear types of minorities emerged from the analysis was a good reason for deciding on a combination of two basic criteria. Thus, the final structure of the book is based first of all on a community criterion, defined by the nature of the minority, that is, whether it was an *established* or a *new migrant* community, and its size, distinguishing between 'larger', 'smaller' and 'other' *established* minorities. In the specific description of each minority, linguistic criteria were used, distinguishing between 'speech communities', where the linguistic and political-administrative borders coincide, 'speaking communities', where the same language may involve two political administrations, and 'communities' in those situations in which it was not possible to find a single adjective that would capture the total linguistic and cultural complexity, since the community could include speakers of different languages with very different cultural patterns, or it was not possible to say to which linguistic area a language should belong and where the boundaries should be drawn.

This book has four parts. Part 1, on the larger *established* minority groups, comprising three articles: The Catalan-speaking Communities (Ch. 2), written by Miquel Àngel Pradilla; The Basque-speaking Communities (Ch. 3), by Jasone Cenoz and Josu Perales, and The Galician Speech Community (Ch. 4), by Carme Hermida. Part 2, on the smaller *established* minorities, contains three articles, The Occitan Speech Community of the Aran Valley (Ch. 5), written by Jordi Suïls and Àngel Huguet; The Astur-Leonese (Bable) Speech Community (Ch. 6), by Roberto González-Quevedo, and The Sign Language Communities (Ch. 7), by Rosa Vallverdú.

Part 3, on the other *established* minorities, incorporates two more articles, The Gitano Communities (Ch. 8), written by Ángel Marzo and M. Teresa Turell, and The Jewish Communities (Ch. 9), by Bárbara Vigil. Finally, Part 4, on the *new migrant* minorities, contains eight articles included in alphabetical order: The Brazilian Community (Ch. 10), written by M. Teresa Turell and Neiva Lavratti; The Cape Verdean Community (Ch. 11), by Lorenzo López Trigal; The Chinese Community (Ch. 12), by Joaquín Beltrán and Cresen García; The Italian Community (Ch. 13), by Rosa M. Torrens; The Maghrebi Communities (Ch. 14), by Belén Garí; The Portuguese Community (Ch. 15), by Lorenzo López Trigal; The UK Community (Ch. 16), by M. Teresa Turell and Cristina Corcoll, and finally, The US American Community (Ch. 17), also written by M. Teresa Turell and Cristina Corcoll.

Notes

* I would like to thank the Spanish *Comisión Interministerial de Ciencia y Tecnología* for their support in granting three consecutive projects (PBS90-0580, SEC93–0725 and SEC96–0627) on minorities in Spain.

1. I owe this term to Yaron Matras (U. of Manchester).
2. With one of their more clearly linguistic implications being that in time every member of the European Union should know two more member state languages besides their own.
3. Since Maastricht (1992, Article 126/2), this policy aims at 'developing the European dimension in education, especially, through the learning and the spreading of the member state languages'.
4. Namely, the *Sociolinguistic and Psycholinguistic Aspects of Linguistic Minority Groups in Spain* (SPALIMG).
5. In my view, Churchill s statement 'falling behind in the rate of evolution' sounds quite reductionist in favour of mainstream, westernised, official societies. The question would be, the rate of evolution towards what?
6. In this 'Estado de las Autonomías', which devolves Spain into 18 Autonomous Communities, the other communities whose linguistic rights are to be recognised are the Valencian Country and the Balearic Islands, in the case of Catalan, and Nafarroa (Navarre), in the case of Basque.
7. The reason why other migrant South American minorities are not mentioned is because only non-Spanish speaking communities are considered in this study.
8. It was also thought that methodological proposals, in the direction of the production of didactic and pedagogical materials, derived from the information gathered in point 6 (learning and communicative strategies) could be directed towards the development of a communicative competence in the new language (including the linguistic, sociolinguistic, discourse and strategic competences in Hymes's terms (1974), although these would have to be the object of another volume. Ultimately, this development could help in the integration, but not assimilation, of the members of linguistic minority groups, and the non-frustrating maintenance of linguistic, and therefore, social interaction with the host communities, without the denial of their language and culture.
9. It should be mentioned that in the case of some of the communities under investigation, the amount of documentation and sources is very sparse since they have been investigated for the first time.
10. Sometimes, the reader will find that there is a mismatch between the figures presented in this introduction and those referring to specific minorities. This is due to the fact that the general figures regarding the communities under study which are presented in this introduction have been up-dated with the latest available version of the *Anuario de Migraciones*, something which has not always been done in the case of each separate article where the figures presented by the authors have been respected.
11. Consequently, the methodology used to do research in these six established speech communities was not the same as the one used for those linguistic minority groups that migrated, considering above all that there is a considerable amount of academic and scientific information on the former.
12. Unfortunately, the Aragonese speech community could not be included in the final version of the book due, as in other cases, to the researcher's inability to accomplish the investigation.
13. These communities are mentioned by decreasing number of members in each group.
14. Except in the case of the minority comprising citizens of the former USSR, at present people from Russia and other republics, which was initially considered in spite of its small size (958 people) because it is a quite long-established community presenting idiosyncratic aspects, but finally could not be included for both the same reasons exposed above.
15. Which was included in spite of its small size (2166 people) because it is not as well known as other Black African communities, such as the Gambian and Senegalese, and features some very idiosyncratic aspects.
16. Which is a variety of Western Catalan with Aragonese and Arabic influence. In the Valencian Country, sections of the community, namely, the 'españolistas' (Hispanist nationalists) refer to it as *Valenciano* and claim that it derives from Spanish.

17. See Nadal (1992) for the history of the Catalan language.
18. In any case, in particular with regard to Catalonia, the people's irrevocable will to use their own language is a good reminder of the symbolic potential of language within the framework of ethnic identity.
19. In 1995, 200 Catalan philologists demanded a Standard Catalan which would reflect dialectal varieties (*La Vanguardia*, 18 November 1995).
20. In the context of this book the term integration is understood as a bi-directional process, that is, the migrants integrate into the host community s world and the host community people integrate into the migrants' world. The new term coined for such a process is that of *interculturality* (see Carbonell *et al.*, 1995).
21. There are still pockets of illiteracy in countries such as Italy, Spain, Portugal and Greece. Also, between 8% and 10% of the population of Britain could be partially illiterate (David Sutcliffe, personal communication).
22. It would be desirable to speak about more or less close intercultural relations rather than integration, because the latter is ostensibly unidirectional and always refers to the migrant's integrating into the host community and not vice versa.
23. More recent trends include the Gitano community of Portuguese origin (López Trigal, Ch. 15), whose members speak Portuguese and Caló, and learn Spanish.
24. At the pedagogical and teaching-methodology level there are the very interesting experiences of the immersion programmes in the Basque Country (Cenoz and Perales, Ch. 3; Cenoz (1998); Cenoz and Valencia (1994) and in Catalonia (Artigal, 1993; Pérez Vidal (forthcoming), where children are immersed in Basque or Catalan, and at the same time, but only in some of the immersion proposals, take advantage of their second language, in these cases Spanish. These programmes co-exist with two other models which are based on the recognition of two types of situation: one which involves the use of either Catalan or Basque as a medium of instruction, with Spanish being introduced as a school subject; the other which involves the opposite situation, Spanish being used as a medium of instruction and Catalan or Basque introduced as school subjects.
25. A centre of Social Pedagogy in Girona (one of the provinces in Catalonia) where teachers have worked upon the basis of intercultural relations within the educational setting. They have recently gained a UNESCO award for their work.
26. In November 1992, the Generalitat de Catalunya (Autonomous Government in Catalonia) banned two linguistic games intended to be educational materials: *Quinto d'Accions*, for sexist contents, and *Aventura en la Selva*, for racist contents, both included in the set of games called, *Olivia, jocs de llengua*, games that were already being used in some schools.
27. The model presented needs further testing with the linguistic minority groups data and with many other data sets. The basis for this will be provided by the project that the European Language Interaction in Plurilingual and Plurilectal Speakers (LIPPS) group is setting up to constitute an international database which will include many bilingual pairs of typologically close and typologically distant languages. There is also a need for revision and further analysis of the data, in terms of dissecting the typological nature of languages, instead of just discriminating according to morphological criteria, and this will provide the basis of such a revision, looking for the interface between syntax and pragmatics in bilingual discourse. Finally, it is believed that this model opens a new path in codeswitching studies which can be useful in other areas of study, such as, language acquisition and the understanding of the genesis of pidgins and creoles.
28. We refer readers to the exhaustive review done by Myers-Scotton (1993a).
29. One-word codeswitching, which is referred to as insertion in Muysken's (1994), is termed *lexical codeswitching* in Fontana and Vallduví (1990). In fact, this lexical codeswitching could also include two or more word constructions such as idioms, toponyms, etc., as reported in Turell and Corcoll (1998).
30. See Doughty and Pica (1986).
31. When considering the effects of codeswitching on language learning by bilinguals, it is not enough to take account of linguistic juxtaposition and mixing in the bilinguals

discourse. Sometimes even if there is almost no interference nor switching between the two languages used, what takes place is a much more subtle form of switch, but not of linguistic structures – that is, there is no observation of borrowing, interferences and lexical calque – but rather of discourse practices and communicative styles (Tosi, 1991). These practices and styles are characteristic of each speech community, and therefore, they have to do with their cultural patterns.

32. The surnames and dates which appear in parentheses after every extract indicate the interviewer's name and the year that the recording was made.

33. Incidentally, this reason for codeswitching is the opposite of the one observed among Brazilians.

34. Such use might become the *unmarked* modality as in Myers-Scotton (1993a) or the *reflection* type as in Turell (1994b).

35. Less marked cognitively and therefore more frequent, according to Fontana and Vallduví (1990).

36. Notice that siesta is an established loan in English.

37. This and similar processes should be taken in consideration when comparing LC phenomena and the emergence of Pidgins and Creoles.

38. In Catalonia, a context of migration which resulted from the massive internal migration during the 1960s and 1970s of migrants from the South of Spain, this *unmarked* choice is known as the *accommodation* norm (*sequential unmarked codeswitching*, in Myers-Scotton (1993b)), that is, unconscious switching into Spanish used by Catalan speakers in their exchanges with immigrants. It also ocurred in exchange with administration people who represented the state under Franco's regime from Central Spain. There are other *unmarked* choices described in the same situation where Catalan speakers quote Spanish speakers in their original Spanish, etc., and this behaviour becomes a sort of *reflection* of their usual discourse practices (Pujadas & Turell, 1993; Turell, 1994b, 1995b).

39. LC between typologically close languages has allowed researchers to look at the range of variation in borrowings in a different and arguably more insightful way, by distinguishing between loans that are not only cognates but superficially **close** to the corresponding word in the receptive language (i.e. Sp **casi** – Cat. **quasi** [nearly]; Sp. **mitad** – Cat. **meitat** [half])) and those loans that do not have a close correlate in the receptive language, and are superficially **distant** (i.e. Sp. **hasta** – Cat. **fins** [until]; Sp. **pues** – Cat. **doncs** [then]) (Turell, 1995a, 1995b).

40. Where the distinction between L1 and L2 helps to distinguish between any two languages at play and is therefore not related to first and second language acquisition.

41. In fact, the interest for strategies in general involved consideration of two more types of strategies, namely, *production* strategies which do not involve solving any communicative problem, and *communicative* strategies, by which the learner reformulates, simplifies, reduces, or even abandons the message.

42. For a complete list of the possible combinations of types of LS (Figure 1.2) and the four skills and the levels of vocabulary and grammar, see Garí (1995: 25).

43. Paradoxically, side by side to this demographic explosion, according to the Worldwatch Institute, the disappearance of aboriginal tribes, and their cultures with them, is taking place at an unprecedented speed in the history of the world, menaced by national and multinational cultures. Half the languages of the world – which store and express the people's intellectual heritage – will be extinct in less than a century. According to the Cultural Survival Association (Massachusetts), one-third of the languages of the American continent and two-thirds of Australia's languages have disappeared since 1800, the majority of them since 1900.

44. This is particularly shocking since a fifth of the world *over*eats.

45. This last category may overlap with some of the others.

46. But without any doubt, within these poor sections those who get the worse deal are the women. According to the Migration International Organisation (MIO), between 200,000 and 500,000 women are victims of sexual traffic organised by European mafias. These are

increasingly women from Eastern Europe who are replacing the traditional victims of this kind of traffic, that is, South American, Caribbean and Asian women. This traffic, which takes place in the context of migratory processes, is only one aspect of the many faceted nature of general traffic involving people, in the context of which migrants are exploited at the work level. In the case of women who are the object of illegal traffic, they are obliged to become prostitutes or are used for 'marriages of convenience' where they may be sexually exploited.

47. This question will be further developed in the section on Spanish legislation and its discriminatory consequences.

48. The INSERSO (Instituto Nacional de Servicios Sociales) is a Spanish government's agency which pays attention to elderly people, among other social groups.

49. Data published in the Anuario de Migracions, 1997. Madrid: Ministerio de Asuntos Sociales, p. 225. *Source*: National Census, Instituto Nacional de Estadística.

50. As to their origin, the 1991 regularisation of foreign nationals carried out in Catalonia showed that the number of migrants from the South was higher than that of the North: 62% came from the Third World whereas 38% came from a developed country.

51. Data published in the *Anuario de Migraciones*, 1997. Madrid: Ministerio de Asuntos Sociales, pp. 236–45. *Source*: Dirección General de la Policía, Ministerio del Interior.

52. Differently from what happened with Italian migration into Great Britain where migrants who settled in industrial areas (Bedford) were originally from rural Calabria and Sicilly (David Sutcliffe, personal communication).

53. The latter is a county in east central Catalonia, where Maghrebis work in the services sector or in agriculture, and live in villages or small towns.

54. Since the *Seferad* (Sephardic) community from before the expulsion in 1492 does not have much to do with the Jewish community of present day Spain, and the Jewish community of the *diaspora* is not the same as the Israelian Jewish community (Vigil, Ch. 9).

55. Spanish acronym for the United Nations High Commission for Refugees (UNHCR).

56. This information was provided by the Simon Wiesenthal Center (1993).

57. At the individual level, Panikkar (1993) proposes the term 'culturismo' [culturism] which involves the 'absolutisation' of the individual's own culture.

58. The view that Madrid and the Spanish language are the hub.

59. This term was first proposed at the 1994 conference on Interculturality sponsored by the SERGI Foundation (Servei Gironí de Pedagogia Social).

60. Also, in the European campaign against racism ('Somos iguales, somos diferentes'[we are equal, we are different]), European youth participated in many ways; the most important one perhaps being the creation of the First Youth Forum Against Racism, Xenophobia, anti-Semitism and Intolerance, which coincided with the celebration by the UN of the International Day Against Racism.

61. This programme included the distribution of a folder with school cards or worksheets, documents on racism, intolerance and the organisations that combat racism, a video, Josep Espinas' book, *Aprendre a Conviure* (1984) [Learning how to live together] and a competition on 'Public Spiritedness'.

62. Another initiative of this sort, although with very little political impact because it was to be effected at the municipal level, was the motion to defend foreign immigrants' right to vote for those with more than five years of residence in Spain and which was approved by the town council of El Prat de Llobregat, a locality close to Barcelona with a very high percentage of immigrants.

63. Sponsored by the Dirección General de Migración, which comes under the Ministerio de Asuntos Sociales.

64. According to Cavalli-Sforza (1994), the concept of race is quite useless; genetic differences do not justify the concept of race, nor that of racism; all population groups are carriers of practically all the existing genes and therefore, the differences are minimal. One of his most important findings is that culture and language are more important than the genes when it comes to differentiate populations, and that the map of genetic differences coincides with that of linguistic differences.

65. In Catalonia, for example, the Centre d'Informació per a Treballadors Estrangers (CITE) which depends on Comissions Obreres (CC.OO) [the Worker's Commissions Union].
66. In Girona (one of the provinces in Catalonia with a high proportion of immigrants, from Black African countries, in particular), the Servei Gironí de Pedagogia Social (SERGI) or the Grup de Recerca i Actuació sobre Minories Culturals i Treballadors Estrangers (GRAMC).
67. Also in Girona, the Comissió d'Associacions i Organitzacions No Governamentals de les Comarques de Girona), which published a manifesto.
68. Such as *Justicia i Pau, Caritas* and others.
69. Whose members attend Spanish courses in the *Bayt Al-Thaqafa* centre. The latter was created in 1974, and legally registered as the *Asociación Española de Amistad con los Pueblos Árabes.*

References

Adamson, H.D. (1990) *Variation Theory and Second Language Acquisition.* Washington, DC: Georgetown University Press.
Alladina, S. and Edwards, V. (eds) (1991) *Multilingualism in the British Isles.* London and New York: Longman.
Anuari (1997) Barcelona: Centre d'Informació per a Treballadors Estrangers (CITE).
Artigal, J.M. (1993) Catalan and Basque immersion programmes. In H. Beatens Beadsmore (ed.) *European Models of Bilingual Education.* Clevedon: Multilingual Matters.
Auer, P. (1992) Introduction: John Gumperz' approach to contextualization. In P. Auer and A. Di Luzio (eds) *The Contextualization of Language* (pp. 1–37). Amsterdam/Philadelphia: John Benjamins.
Bendalac, D.Y. (1995) *Diccionario Sefardí.*
Blom, J.P. and Gumperz, J.J. (1972) Social meaning in structure: codeswitching in Norway. In J.J. Gumperz and D. Hymes (eds) *Directions in Sociolinguistics* (pp. 407–34). New York: Holt, Rinehart and Winston.
Canale, M. and Swain, M. (1980) Theoretical basis of communicative approaches to second language teaching and testing. *Applied Linguistics* 1, 1–47.
Carbonell, F. *et al.* (eds) (1995) *El Sistema Educatiu i l'Educació.* Barcelona: Diputació de Barcelona.
Cáritas Española (1993) *Report.*
Cáritas Catalana (1995) *Report: Aproximació als Immigrats Estrangers des de les Diòcesis Catalanes.* Barcelona.
Cavalli-Sforza, L.L. (1994) *The History and Geography of Human Genes.* Princeton: Princeton University Press.
Cenoz, J. (1998) Multilingual education in the Basque Country. In J. Cenoz and F. Genesee (eds) *Beyond Bilingualism. Multilingualism and Multilingual Education* (pp. 175–91). Clevedon: Multilingual Matters.
Cenoz, J. and Valencia, J.F. (1994) Additive trilingualism: Evidence from the Basque Country. *Applied Psycholingusitics* 15, 195–207.
Cenoz, J. and Genesee, F. (eds) (1998) *Beyond Bilingualism. Multilingualism and Multilingual Education.* Clevedon: Multilingual Matters.
Centro de Investigaciones Sociológicas (CIS), 1995 *Report.*
Centro de Investigación de Mercados Españoles e Internacionales (CIMEI), 1995 *Report.*
Churchill, S. (1986) *The Education of Linguistic and Cultural Minorities in the OECD Countries.* Clevedon: Multilingual Matters.
Clyne, M. (1992) Linguistic and sociolinguistic aspects of language contact, maintenance and loss: towards a multifacet theory. In W. Fase *et al.* (eds) *Maintenance and Loss of Minority Languages* (pp.17–36). Amsterdam/Philadelphia: John Benjamins.
Comissió d'Associacions i Organitzacions No Governamentals de les Comarques de Girona (1993) *Report.*

Corcoll, C. (1999) *A Reassessment of the Notion of Syntactic Calque: Grammatical and Sociolinguistic Evidence.* Unpublished Masters Thesis, Barcelona: Universitat Pompeu Fabra.

Cummins, J. (1986) Empowering minority students: A framework for intervention. *Harvard Educational Review* 56, 18–36.

Cummins, J. (1988) Educational implications of mother tongue maintenance in Minority-Language groups. In T. Skutnabb-Kangas and J. Cummins (eds) *Minority Education: from Shame to Struggle* (pp. 395–416). Clevedon: Multilingual Matters.

Cummins, J. and Swain, M. (1986) *Bilingualism in Education.* London: Longman.

Doughty, C. and Pica, T. (1986) Information gap tasks. Do they facilitate second language acquisition? *Tesol Quarterly* 2 (20), 305–25.

Edwards, J. (1992) Sociopolitical aspects of language maintenance and loss: Towards a typology of minority language situations. In W. Fase *et al.* (eds) *Maintenance and Loss of Minority Languages* (pp. 37–54). Amsterdam/Philadelphia: John Benjamins.

Espinás, J.M. (1984) *Aprendre a Conviure.* Sabadell: Caixa d'Estalvis de Sabadell.

Euzkararen Eralbipena Aranzkotzeko Oinarrizko Legea (1982) (Linguistic Normalization Law of the Basque Language in the Basque Country).

Euskari Buruzko Foru Legea (1986) (Linguistic Normalization Law of the Basque Language in Nafarroa).

Faerch, C. and Kasper, G. (1983) *Strategies in Interlanguage Communication.* London: Longman.

Fase, W. *et al.* (eds) (1992) *Maintenance and Loss of Minority Languages.* Amsterdam/Philadelphia: John Benjamins.

Federació de Col.lectius d'Immigrats de Catalunya (FCIC) (1995) *Report* (Catalan Federation of Migrants). Barcelona.

Fishman, J.A. (1972) *Language and Nationalism.* Rowley, MA: Newbury House Publishers.

Fishman, J.A. (1989) *Language and Ethnicity in Minority Sociolinguistic Perspective.* Clevedon: Multilingual Matters.

Fontana, J.M. and Vallduví, E. (1990) Mecanismos léxicos y gramaticales en la alternancia de lenguas. In M.T. Turell (ed.) *Nuevas Corrientes Lingüísticas. Aplicación a la Descripción del Inglés* (pp. 171–92). Granada: *RESLA*, Anejo I.

Galbraith, J.K. (1994) *La Cultura de la Satisfacción.* Barcelona: Ariel.

García, C. (1993) *La Adquisición del Español como Segunda Lengua por Personas Analfabetas: una Propuesta Didáctica.* Unpublished Masters Thesis. Barcelona: Universitat de Barcelona.

Garí, B. (1995) *Estrategias de Aprendizaje en el Seno de una Comunidad Magrebí.* Unpublished Masters Thesis. Barcelona: Universitat de Barcelona.

Goytisolo, J. (1994) El bosque de las letras. *El País – Babelia* (8 January 1994).

Grosjean, F. (1990) The psycholinguistics of language contact and codeswitching: Concepts, methodology and data. *Papers for the Workshop on Concepts, Methodology and Data* (pp. 105–16). ESF Network on Codeswitching and Language Contact. Basel, 12–13 January 1990.

Grup de Recerca i Actuació sobre Minories Culturals i Treballadors Estrangers (GRAMC), No. 4, January 1996 (Research Group on Cultural Minorities) Barcelona.

Gumperz, J.J. (1982) *Discourse Strategies.* Cambridge: Cambridge University Press.

Hymes, D. (1974) *Foundations in Sociolinguistics.* Philadelphia: University of Pennsylvania Press.

Institute Opina (1993) *Report.*

Instituto Nacional de Estadística (INE) (1993, 1994, 1995) *Reports.* Madrid.

Instituto de Servicios Sociales (INSERSO) (1993) *Report.* Madrid.

International Migration Organisation (IMO) (1992) *Report.*

International Social Survey Programme (ISSP) (1995) *Report.*

International Unesco Conference on Education (1994) *Report.* Paris.

Justicia i Pau (1993) *Report.* Barcelona.

Lambert, W.E. (1975) Culture and language as factors in learning and education. In A. Wolfgang (ed.) *Education of Immigrant Students.* Toronto: Ontario Institute for Studies in Education.

Lei de Normalização Lingüística (1983) (Linguistic Normalization Law of Galician). Santiago de Compostela.

Ley de Extranjería (1985) (Immigration Act). Madrid.

Ley de Ordenación General del Sistema Educativo (L.O.G.S.E) 1990 (Education Act). Madrid.

Llei d'Ús i Ensenyament del Valencià (1983) (Linguistic Normalization Law of Catalan in the Valencian Country). València.

Llei de Normalització Lingüística (1983) (Linguistic Normalization Law of Catalan in Catalonia). Barcelona.

Llei de Normalització Lingüística (1986) (Linguistic Normalization Law of Catalan in the Balearic Islands). Palma de Mallorca.

Maastricht Treaty on European Union (1992) (Article 126/2).

Ministerio de Trabajo y Asuntos Sociales. *Anuario de Migraciones 1997*. Madrid.

Muysken, P. (1991) Needed: A comparative approach. *Papers for the Symposium on Code-switching in Bilingual Studies: Theory, Significance and Perspectives* (pp. 252–72). ESF Network on Codeswitching and Language Contact, Vol. I. Barcelona, 21–23 March 1991.

Muysken, P. (1994) The typology of codeswitching. In F. Sierra Martínez and M. Pujol Berché (eds) *Las Lenguas en la Europa Comunitaria* (pp. 11–21) *Diálogos Hispánicos 15*, Amsterdam: Ed. Rodopi.

Myers-Scotton, C. (1993a) *Duelling Languages: Grammatical Structure in Code-switching*. Oxford: Clarendon Press.

Myers-Scotton, C. (1993b) *Social Motivations for Codeswitching: Evidence from Africa*. Oxford: Clarendon Press.

Nadal, J.M. (1992) *Llengua Escrita i Llengua Nacional*. Barcelona: Quaderns Crema.

Naiman, N. *et al.* (1978) *The Good Language Learner*. Toronto: OISE.

O'Malley, J. and Uhl. Y. (1990) *Learning Learning Strategies in Second Language Acquisition*. Cambridge: Cambridge University Press.

Oxford, R.L. (1990) *Language Learning Strategies*. New York: Newbury House Publishers.

Panikkar, R. (1993) Racismo y culturismo. *La Vanguardia* (4 February 1993).

Pérez Vidal, C. (forthcoming) Language teacher training and bilingual education in Spain. In *Intertalk, Aspects of Implementing Plurilingual Education, ELC Report*. University of Jyväskylä (Finland).

Poplack, S. (1980) Sometimes I'll start a sentence in Spanish y termino en español: Towards a typology of codeswitching. *Linguistics* 18, 581–618.

Poplack, S. (1990) Variation theory and language contact: Concepts, methods and data. *Papers for the Workshop on Concepts, Methods and Data* (pp. 33–66). ESF Network on Code-switching and Language Contact. Basel, 12–13 January 1990.

Pujadas, J.J. and Turell, M.T. (1993) Els indicadors sociolingüístics del contacte inter-ètnic. *Actes del IXè Col.loqui Internacional de l'Associació de Llengua i Literatura Catalanes*. Alacant (1991), 301–18.

Schengen Agreement (1985).

Servei Gironí de Pedagogia Social (SERGI) (1992) *Report* (No. 1, Autumn).

Siguán, M. (1992) *España Plurilingüe*. Madrid: Alianza Editorial.

Skutnabb-Kangas, T. (1983) *Bilingualism or Not: The Education of Minorities*. Clevedon: Multilingual Matters.

Skutnabb-Kangas, T. and Cummins, J. (eds) (1988) *Minority Education: from Shame to Struggle*. Clevedon: Multilingual Matters.

Skutnabb-Kangas, T. and Cummins, J. (eds) (1990) Legitimating or delegitimating new forms of racism: The role of researchers, *Journal of Multilingual and Multicultural Development* 2 (1 & 2), 77–100.

Spanish Census (1991) *Report*. Madrid.

Spolsky, B. (ed.) (1972) *The Language Education of Minority Children*. Rowley, MA: Newbury House.

Spolsky, B. (ed.) (1986) *Language and Education in Multilingual Settings*. Clevedon: Multilingual Matters.

Tarone, E. (1988) *Variation in Interlanguage Communication.* London: E. Arnold

Tosi, U. (1991) First, second or foreign language learning? *Papers for the Symposium on Codeswitching in Bilingual Studies: Theory, Significance and Perspectives* (pp. 353–68). ESF Network on Codeswitching and Language Contact, Vol II. Barcelona, 21–23 March 1991.

Turell, M.T. (1994a) Beyond Babel: Across and within. In F. Sierra Martínez and M. Pujol Berché (eds) *Las Lenguas en la Europa Comunitaria* (pp. 23–40) *Diálogos Hispánicos* 15. Amsterdam: Ed. Rodopi.

Turell, M.T. (1994b) Codeswitching as communicative design, *Actas del XVI Congreso de AEDEAN* (pp. 59–78). Valladolid (1992): Universidad de Valladolid.

Turell, M.T. (1995a) Una primera aproximació a l'anàlisi quantitativa dels préstecs. *Llengua i Literatura* 6, 201–16.

Turell, M.T. (1995b) L'alternança de llengües i el préstec en una comunitat inter-ètnica. In M.T. Turell (ed.) *La Sociolingüística de la Variació* (pp. 259–93). Barcelona: PPU.

Turell, M.T. (1997) Bilingual speech modes in linguistic minority groups: The interplay between internal and external factors. In L. Díaz and C. Pérez Vidal (eds) *Views on the Acquisition and Use of a Second Language, Proceedings* (pp. 237–52) Barcelona: Universitat Pompeu Fabra.

Turell, M.T. and Corcoll, C. (1998) The effect of socio-collective factors on the bilingual speech modes of British and American English-speaking communities. Paper presented at the Sociolinguistics Symposium 12, 26–28 March 1998. Institute of Education. University of London.

United Nations Development Programme (1992) *Report.*

United Nations Population Foundation (1992) *Report.*

United Nations Human Development Programme (1995) *Report.*

Universal Declaration of Linguistic Rights (1995).

Chapter 2

The Catalan-speaking Communities

MIQUEL ÀNGEL PRADILLA

Communities Distribution and Regional Context

The Catalan-speaking communities are distributed across political borders such that the Catalan language is spoken at present in four countries: Spain, where the majority of Catalan speakers live, France, Italy and Andorra. In Spain, it is spoken in five autonomous communities: (1) Catalonia, south of the Pyrenees (31,426 km^2 and approximately 6,000,000 inhabitants), except for the Aran Valley, where Occitan is spoken,[1] (2) the Balearic and Pitius Islands (5014 km^2 and 700,000 inhabitants, (3) the Catalan-speaking part of the Valencian Country (13,612 km^2 and 3,800,000 inhabitants),[2] (4) the Franja de Ponent (4449 km^2 and 50,000 inhabitants), a strip of land about 20 km wide along the eastern edge of the Community of Aragón, and (5) the Carxe (300 km^2 and 2500 inhabitants), a group of settlements in the extreme north-east of the Community of Murcia, resettled in recent times by Valencian immigrants. In France, Catalan is spoken in the northern area of the Pyrenees, also known as North Catalonia (4086 km^2 and 350,000 inhabitants). In the city of Alguer (224 km^2 and 40,000 inhabitants), on the Italian island of Sardinia, Catalan is also still spoken. And lastly, Andorra (468 km^2 and 40,000 inhabitants) constitutes the last of these Catalan-speaking areas.

Like all languages, Catalan has regional varieties, even though it is one of the most uniform of the Romance languages. This fact has been brought about in part by the relatively small size of its territory and by the strongly unifying action exercised by the Royal Chancellery in the mediaeval period. It was in the 15th century that the dialectal differences began to become sharper, because of lack of government support, and still more so as from the 18th century, when it was forbidden to speak Catalan. Despite certain disagreements among philologists, the classification of the geographical varieties of Catalan proposed by Veny (1978), and shown in Figure 2.1 and Map 2.1, is still valid.

In this chapter, the three larger Catalan-speaking regions in Spain are discussed: Catalonia, the Balearic and Pitius Islands, and the Valencian Country. These are Autonomous Communities where Catalan is officially

Eastern Catalan (català oriental)	Rossellonese (rossellonès) **Central** (central) **Balearic** (baleàric) **Alguerese** (alguerès)
Western Catalan (català occidental)	North-Western (nord-occidental or Ileidetà) Valencia (valencià)

Figure 2.1 Geographical varieties of Catalan (Veny, 1978)

recognised (as a community language) alongside Spanish (the official language of Spain). The objectives are to describe the general sociolinguistic situation of each one of the political-administrative regions, to present the data on the linguistic proficiency of the different Catalan-speaking communities that inhabit these regions, and to look more deeply at one area where linguistic planning has achieved quite substantial advances.

A Short History of the Catalan Language

Catalan belongs to the group of western Latin-based languages, together with Spanish, French and Portuguese, to mention only the main languages in this group. Around the 8th century, the language spoken in the French counties of the Spanish March could already be considered a different language from Latin. Once the split had been made between the spoken (Catalan) and written (Latin) languages, the first texts written in Catalan began to appear: the Catalan translation of the *Forum Iudicum*, the set of Visigothic laws dating from the second half of the 12th century; the *Homílies d'Organyà*, a collection of sermons from the end of the 12th and beginning of the 13th centuries, etc. On the other hand, poetry was mainly written in Occitan, or Langue d'Oc, until the 15th century, as a result of the prestige enjoyed in Europe by the troubadours from that area.

Throughout the Middle Ages, Catalan became established as a language in its own right and a true language of culture. Among the different factors which contributed to this phenomenon, two kinds are most important: (1) Historical and political factors: the independence of the counties of the Catalunya Vella (Old Catalonia) and the later territorial expansion Southwards and Eastwards (Lleida, Tortosa, Majorca, Valencia, Sardinia, Naples, Sicily, etc.); (2) Cultural and literary factors: Ramon Llull, who laid the foundations of cultured Catalan prose, produced an enormous number

Map 2.1 Geographical varieties of Catalan
Source: Veny (1978)

of works, and was the first European writer to write on philosophical and
scientific topics in a Romance language. The four great historical *Chronicles*
were written by Jaume I, Ramon Muntaner, Bernat Desclot and Pere El
Cerimoniós. Among other writers from this period, Bernat Metge wrote
Lo Somni, an achievement which made him the most representative humanist writer in Catalan. The Golden Age of Catalan literature
was the 15th century, when great works such as *Tirant Lo Blanch*, by
Joanot Martorell, *Espill*, by Jaume Roig, and *Curial i Güelfa* (anonymous),

appeared. Ausiàs Marc was the most important poet and was the first to write poetry in a Catalan free of Occitan expressions, and his vast work, of great overall unity, made him the most important writer of the old lyric poetry. In the last third of the 15th century, Rois de Corella emerged as an outstanding humanist, poet and prose writer, both religious and non-religious.

One characteristic of Catalan literary prose in the Middle Ages was its uniformity. The *Cancelleria Reial* (Royal Chancellery) was the body which spread it throughout the land, and the linguistic model propagated by its documents became the model for good writing.

The unfavourable political and social situation during the 16th and 17th centuries meant that Catalan literary production suffered a severe setback. The death of King Martí l'Humà in 1410 with no heir led to the *Compromís de Casp* (the Casp Agreement) in 1412. The result was that the Catalan crown passed to a Spanish family, the Trastámaras. The 16th century saw the beginning of a process in which the aristocracy and part of the intellectual class used Spanish, and became more and more influenced by it. The fact that at this time high culture revolved around the court meant that Catalan suffered. At the same time, the poor, the Catalan bourgeoisie, the bureaucracy and part of the nobility, particularly the rural part, continued to speak and write in Catalan. In the meagre literary production of the 16th century, *Los Col.loquis de la Insigne Ciutat de Tortosa*, by Cristòfor Despuig, and the poetic work, *El Rector de Vallfogona*, by Francesc Vicent Garcia, are outstanding. On the other hand, there was plenty of literature produced by the poorer classes, who did not speak Spanish. These sectors produced and consumed a large quantity of poetry and regularly attended theatrical performances derived from Mediaeval dramatic works. And at this time, without any stabilising linguistic authority, the language began a process of creation of dialects.

The War of Succession had disastrous political-economic and cultural-linguistic consequences, since the territory of the *Corona d'Aragó* (Aragó Kingdom) took side against Philip V. When this pretender won the battle for the crown, he proclaimed the decrees of the *Nova Planta* in the various parts of Catalonia (in 1716 in Catalonia). In this way, the community language was officially prohibited and its use repressed in Catalonia, in the Valencian Country and in the Balearic and Pitius Islands.

Despite the setback implied by the imposition of Spanish over Catalan, there was enough resistance to keep the flame of the Catalan language alight during the 18th and 19th centuries. One example is the continual publication of new editions of the *Instruccions per a l'Ensenyança de Minyons*, by Baldiri Reixac (1749).

In the first half of the 19th century, the dominance of Spanish in all kinds of literary publications was reinforced, and there was more and more linguistic interference from Spanish in the Catalan language. This hispanicisation made great strides among the bourgeoisie, while it was the poorer classes which remained faithful to their own language. In the middle of the 19th century, the arrival of the European romantic ideals encouraged the revindication of national cultures and a return to the splendour of the mediaeval era. This cultural awakening, together with the new spirit born of the industrial revolution, was to provide the basis for a new political and cultural movement which would take the name of *Renaixença* (renaissance), in opposition to the three previous centuries of *Decadència* (decadence). This was a bourgeois-based movement, which in Catalonia began around an emblematic year, 1833, when Bonaventura Carles Aribau's ode *La Pàtria* (the homeland) was published. In Valencia it began with the publication of a poem by Tomàs de Villaroya, while in the Balearic Islands it came later. It should be noted that while the *Renaixença* movement began with the intention of dignifying the literary language, in the last third of the century it included the aim of standardising the language in all senses. In Catalonia, the linguistic and cultural revindications went hand in hand with the emergence of what has been called political Catalanism.

At first, the Jocs Florals (poetry contests in Catalan) embraced a large part of the literature in Catalan, and they became the platform for popularising authors such as Jacint Verdaguer, one of the founders of the contemporary Catalan cultural language, Narcís Oller, who took the novel to its definitive consolidation, and Àngel Guimerà and Frederic Soler, the most important representatives of Catalan theatre. The lack of a public used to reading in its own language and the absence of grammatical rules which would tame the orthographical chaos were major factors behind the slow and difficult access gained by Catalan to the printed media. In 1870, the first newspaper appeared in Catalan, *Diari Català*, and the first satirical magazine, *La Campana de Gracia*. From then on, production in Catalan increased and improved at a hefty pace. Modernism was the artistic and cultural movement which continued on the struggle at the end of the 19th century. On the literary side, authors of the class of Raimon Caselles, Joaquim Royra, Joan Maragall, Santiago Rosiñol, Prudenci Bertrana, Caterina Albert 'Víctor Català', Ignasi Iglésias, etc., were all important.

The 20th century brought the political consolidation of Catalanism in Catalonia, when in 1907 Enric Prat de la Riba was elected President of the Diputació de Barcelona. This linguistic effervescence reached a milestone in 1906 with the holding of the First International Conference on the Catalan Language, proposed by the Majorcan canon Antoni M. Alcover. A month later, the *Institut d'Estudis Catalans* (Institute of Catalan Studies) was created, an institution whose mission was to standardise the language and promote research. In the field of Philology, Pompeu Fabra forged the tools which made Catalan an appropriate language for all kinds of uses and for all the areas where it was spoken. His publications include his *Normes Ortogràfiques* (Spelling Rules) (1913), *Gramàtica Catalana* (Catalan Grammar) (1918), and the *Diccionari General de la Llengua Catalana*

(General Dictionary of the Catalan Language) (1932). Francesc de Borja Moll and Manuel Sanchis Garner adapted Fabra's rules to the Balearic and Valencian varieties respectively, with the aim of consolidating the linguistic unity of the three varieties. Historical reasons have meant that the linguistic communities have not always coincided with the administrative communities, so that, with the intervention of other factors such as the political use of the language by certain sectors seeking linguistic secession, the common language has received a variety of names according to the local area and the political purpose intended. Thus, Valencian, Majorcan, Minorcan and Eivissan co-exist with the name Catalan, with which the international community of Romance language scholars designates the language as a whole. At the same time, the language extended its use into new areas (education, press, radio, etc.), and new literary movements appeared (*Noucentisme* and *Avantguardisme*), as well as the works of such worthy writers as Carles Riba, Josep Carner, Salvat-Papasseit, J. V. Foix, Josep Pla and others.

During the period of the Franco Dictatorship (1939–75), the Catalan language was once again prohibited and repressed, thus being confined to use within the family. Spanish was the only language allowed in formal, public usage. The death of the dictator meant that freedoms began to be regained. With the re-establishment of the *Generalitat de Catalunya* (1977), the founding of the *Generalitat Valenciana* (1982), and the *Consell Insular de Mallorca* (1983), each region had its own local government and its own *Estatut d'Autonomia* (Autonomy Statute), through which linguistic policies were instituted, to varying degrees, with the aim of recovering Catalan as the language of the Catalan-speaking communities.

Sociolinguistic Characteristics

Language and institutional support

Catalonia

Catalonia is the area where Catalan is in best (though not perfect) health. This obvious fact leads one to establish a correspondence between linguistic health and the level of national consciousness of the group of people who speak the language. This has to do with a feeling of identity, to the sense of belonging to a group which shares certain historical and cultural references based on its own language. One way of evaluating this desire for self-affirmation is to look at the results of the various elections to the Catalan Parliament since the coming of democracy. The repeated victory of the nationalist coalition *Convergència i Unió*, together with the nationalistic revindications which are a feature of the political programmes of the Catalan political parties, is proof of the central role played by the Catalan language in the political and social dynamic of this region.

It is in Catalonia that the official institutions have addressed the matter of the linguistic normalisation in the most rigorous way. Any outline of the linguistic policy carried out by the *Generalitat de Catalunya* (Catalan autonomous government) since the approval of the *Estatut d'Autonomia* (Regional Autonomy Statute) in 1979, must begin with the creation of the *Direcció General de Política Lingüística* (Department of Linguistic Policy), part of the *Departament de Cultura* (Catalan Department of Culture), in 1980. In 1983, the *Llei de Normalització Lingüística* (Linguistic Normalisation Act) was passed, a law of supreme importance. Approved by the consensus of all parliamentary groupings, its starting point was the precarious situation of the Catalan language, and aimed to eradicate its linguistic inferiority, as is fitting given its status as the community and (with Spanish) official language. Catalan became the language of the *Generalitat de Catalunya*, and of other public institutions which fall under its jurisdiction. The law recognised the right of all citizens to carry out their activities and to address the administration, public and private companies and the judiciary in this language. It reinstated the writing of public documents in Catalan, and the standardisation of the spelling. It regulated the right of children to receive their primary education in Catalan, and proposed the creation of mass media in Catalan which would encourage its use and learning. It can be fairly said that it is in the areas of education and mass media where linguistic policy has given the most satisfactory results. In 1989, the *Consorci per a la Normalització Lingüística* (Linguistic Normalisation Consortium) was set up, with the aim of making the normalisation of Catalan reach all sections of society, via the stimulus of its use, linguistic advice and Catalan courses for adults.

The beginning of the 1990s saw the creation of the *Consell Social de la Llengua Catalana* (Catalan Language Social Council), which reflected the desire of the majority of society to continue along the path of linguistic normalisation. It was in this context, in 1991, that the proposal and planning for the *Pla General de Normalització Lingüística* (General Linguistic Normalisation Plan) was conceived. The Plan was approved in 1995, with the aim of creating the institutional framework which would allow 'the continual adjustment of the indispensable social accord between the public powers and the main social agents in the process of the recuperation of the normal use of Catalan' (*Pla General de Normalització Lingüística*, 1995: 10–11). In this way, the socio-cultural change proposed by the linguistic normalisation programme would respond to the particular situation of the moment.

The final episode in this process occurred during 1997 when, by common agreement of all political parties, a new law was debated. The need to create a new legal framework had become more and more obvious with the passing of the years. However, not all the political parties agreed with this proposal, so that the new *Llei de Política Lingüística* (Linguistic Policy Act) was passed by a majority of 80%, and not by consensus as for the previous Act of 1983. This new legal document has as its fundamental objective the increase in the use of Catalan, to be achieved by action carried out in those areas of most need.

A brief look at these different areas will give us an idea of the socio-linguistic situation in Catalonia. Education will be discussed more thoroughly later (see pp. 77–79), but a brief summary would suggest that while in primary education the results have been quite good, with the implementing of such interesting schemes as linguistic immersion programmes, in secondary and higher education the results are negative in many cases, especially at the level of higher education. In state and local government bodies, the level of normalisation can be described as acceptable. The autonomous state administrative bodies and the judiciary are areas which have yet to be tackled. In the area of socio-economic activities, in the general business world and in the world of professional activity, despite some advances, Spanish is dominant at least in the written medium. In the mass media, the spectacular contribution of Catalan Television or *TV3* (1984) and *Catalunya Ràdio* must be highlighted. Over time, the number of public media has increased, with the introduction of Channel 33 in television (1984), *Ràdio Associació de Catalunya*, *Catalunya Música*, *Catalunya Informació*, *Com Ràdio*, and a large number of municipal radio stations. In contrast, in the large commercial stations Spanish is still clearly dominant. In printed media, the panorama shows a strong imbalance in favour of Spanish. The growing number of newspapers in Catalan, with *Avui* (1976) and *Punt Diari* (1979) as pioneers, only covers about 12% of a market which is basically in Spanish. One ray of hope is the initiative by *El Periódico* (1997), which now produces a dual edition, one in Spanish and another in Catalan. Far and above the most optimistic predictions, the Catalan edition almost equals the Spanish one in number of daily sales. After showing the economic viability of a Catalan newspaper, this fact may overcome the conservative inertia of some other publications. Local provincial newspapers show an enviable linguistic vitality, and the same could be said of the cultural magazines, such as *L'Avenç*, *Serra d'Or*, *Revista de Catalunya*, etc. However, the presence of Catalan in fields such as sports papers, magazines of satire or humour, women's magazines, etc. is practically absent. Finally, in the culture industry, one must highlight the advances in the book publishing world. The number of books published in Catalan has steadily increased to reach some 5000 titles a year. But looking at the size of the editions, we might well conclude this to be the case of 'lots of books but not many readers'. On a positive note, the theatre in Catalan functions quite well, but cinema, video and vocal music are marginal.

Despite the impression of a precarious situation which one might gain from the number of areas where Catalan is not used sufficiently, progressive improvement can be seen. Catalan society sees its own language as an instrument of prestige, which encourages social integration, and as useful for success at work. If the Linguistic Policy Act is successfully implemented, the Catalan language will take an important step forward towards occupying the dominant place in those regions in which it is the community language.

The Balearic and Pitius Islands

In a similar way to the rest of the Catalan-speaking areas, the factors which explain the present relatively more precarious nature of the community language in the Balearic and Pitius Islands are the following: the lack of official recognition and the consequent repression, as from the 18th century, which meant that schooling was overwhelmingly in Spanish; the large wave of non-Catalan-speaking immigrants in the 1960s, and the introduction of the mass media, largely in Spanish, although tourism has brought about substantial presence of English and German.

The Estatut d'Autonomia (Regional Autonomy Statute) was passed in 1983, and established the co-official nature of Catalan, in its Balearic variety, together with Spanish. It also encouraged government bodies to report on the linguistic normalisation process, and granted the University of the Balearic Islands official authority in matters of linguistic standardisation. Between 1983 and 1999 the Balearic government has been in the hands of a conservative, Spain-wide party, the *Partido Popular* which postulated a kind of non-interventionist linguistic liberalism. The parliamentary opposition criticised this lack of interest in, or even opposition to, a more affirmative policy. It is from the non-governmental organisations that serious and committed initiatives have arisen. The *Obra Cultural Balear* (Balearic Cultural Association) is the most outstanding of these groups in the movement for linguistic normalisation. The *Llei de Normalització Lingüística* (Linguistic Normalisation Act) of the Balearic Parliament was the first legislation of this type which was approved in 1986. Its positive aspect is that in some respects it improved upon the previous legislation. Firstly, in stating the co-official nature of Catalan and Spanish, it differentiated between the two. Catalan is official because it is the language of the Autonomous Community, and Spanish is official because it is the language of the whole of the Spanish state. And furthermore, it encouraged collaboration between the various Catalan-speaking areas in the areas of culture and communication.

The lack of governmental interest in the normalisation of its own language in the Balearic Community is shown by the absence of any Department of Linguistic Policy. For this reason, in 1989, the *Obra Cultural Balear* (Balearic Cultural Association) arranged a pact between governmental institutions directed by various political groupings, which resulted in the creation of a Campaign for linguistic normalisation. The main objective was to make the government react, and to put into practice the proposals contained in the Act. It can definitely be said that the improvements in this area have been slight, since the linguistic legislation has not been applied. The lack of jurisdiction in certain areas, especially education and mass media, has also been a negative factor. There has only been a timid Catalanisation seen in official institutions, in the inadequate language training of the civil servants, the writing of signs, etc., only in Spanish. Only in education, as will be seen later (pp. 79–81), can we find a positive trend. Both in the government and in the private sector, lack of funds has been the excuse for not giving higher priority to this area, and the common denominator has been the absence of local media.

From 1988 to 1991, *Ràdio-4 a les Illes* (Spanish National Radio) was a reference point in Catalan-speaking media, and since this station disappeared there have only been a few programmes in Catalan on *Ràdio-5*. Only *Ràdio Jove* and a few local stations offer programmes in Catalan, and on the rest of the stations Catalan has no, or at best only symbolic, presence. In television, there has only been a limited replacement of some national programmes on Spanish TV by local programmes, and some programmes on local television, with a very small audience. In fact, there is television in Catalan but it comes from the mainland, especially from Catalonia. On the initiative of the *Obra Cultural Balear* (Balearic Cultural Association), a company called Voltor was created, which set up a network of repeaters which allowed the reception of *TV3*, *Canal 33*, *Catalunya Ràdio*, etc., and *Canal 9*, the Valencian TV and radio stations.

In the printed media of the Balearic Islands, Catalan can be found in magazines such as *Lluc*, and in a few contributions to the mainland press. A turning point was the 1996 decision of the *Baleares* newspaper, written in Spanish, to become *Diari de Balears*, totally in Catalan. Until then, one could only read the newspaper in Catalan by way of the mainland press, *Avui, El Temps*, etc. Lastly, in industry and commerce, the community language has only a symbolic presence. Clearly, the fact that the island economy revolves around the strong tourist industry means that Spanish, and to some extent English and German, are the languages of international communication.

Despite what has been said above, it should be noted that the legalisation of Catalan has changed the attitude of the local Balearic population towards their own language. Its prestige, and the consciousness of the need to encourage its use, have steadily increased.[3] However, it is necessary that the government share the desire of part of the society to carry out a real linguistic normalisation.

The Valencian Country

The socio-linguistic situation in the Valencian Country has a major factor in common with the Balearic and Pitius Islands, which is the failure of its autonomous government to face its responsibilities regarding the linguistic policy that needs to be put into practice.

The passing of the *Estatut d'Autonomia* (Autonomy Statute) in 1982 allowed the celebration of the first autonomous regional elections the same year. Until 1995, the government was in the hands of the *Partido Socialista Obrero Español*, a national (Spanish) social democrat party. During this period, the two most important milestones in linguistic planning were the passing of the *Llei d'Ús i Ensenyament del Valencià* (Use and Teaching of Valencian Act) in 1983, and *the Pla Triennal per a la Promoció de l'Us del Valencià a la Comunitat Valenciana* (Three Year Plan for the Promotion of the Use of Valencian in the Valencian Country), of 1990. The Act limits the co-official nature of Catalan to education and the autonomous government administration, and merely mentions the mass media.

Since 1995, a conservative political party, the *Partido Popular*, has been in power in the Valencian Generalitat. This party abstained in the vote on the *Llei d'Ús i Ensenyament del Valencià* (Use and Teaching of Valencian Act) and represents those social sectors which are most reticent with regards to regaining the public use of Catalan; so that the timid advances made during the previous government may come to an end because of the lack of interest of the new government. This situation has been worsened by the political pact between the governing party and *Unió Valenciana*, a party which defends a kind of linguistic secession, regarding the so-called 'Valencian language' as a different language from Catalan.

While the official panorama is not heartening, the social pressure to redress the linguistic imbalance is quite considerable. *Acció Cultural del País Valencià* (Valencian Cultural Organization) is the main organisation on this front, and since 1995 the *Bloc de Progrés Jaume I* (The Progressive Front Jaume I) has become the co-ordinator of the civil movement for linguistic revindications. That said, there is a paradoxical situation. Although the democratic, institutional framework is *a priori* favourable, and some historic gains have been made, such as the legalisation of the use of Catalan in public, and its introduction into schools (although not into public institutions), it is difficult at the same time to ignore the feeling that the process of linguistic normalisation which has been carried out has not lived up to expectations, especially for those sectors most sensitive on this matter.

Valencian society, in general, is uninformed, unaware of its own history, manipulated by 'official' information which says that it is not really very different from the other regions of Spain. The vision both within and without Valencia is one which denies it the condition of a 'historical nationality' (similarly to the Basque Country, Catalonia and Galicia), as would correspond to its history and its language. The available data shows that Valencian is used by those with middle to low socio-economic status, a largely rural population (Ros, 1982). The surveys carried out by the *Servei d'Estudis d'Investigació Sociolingüística* (Sociolinguistic Research Studies Service) provide empirical evidence that leading sectors of this society are in favour of the normalisation process, and would even like it to move more quickly. These sectors are the advanced tertiary sector, young people, and in general the urban and better educated (Pitarch, 1994: 53). This fact, if it is definitely confirmed, would constitute a real revolution in the socio-linguistic behaviour of the country.

One positive development is that as a result of the legalisation of Valencian, its dominance has increased among those sectors with a higher academic level, an increase which is slight in the speaking skill, but significant in reading skills. Of those with higher studies, 54.5% read Valencian, whereas of those with primary school studies only 28.1% read it. These are clearly encouraging data and show that Valencian is spoken in the most modern and influential sectors of society.

Spanish is spoken by the upper and upper middle classes, which gives it high prestige, and this means that the Valencian-speaking population has tended to replace Valencian with Spanish as it improves its economic and educational levels, especially in an urban context, although, as mentioned above, this appears to be changing. At the same time, the Spanish-speaking immigrants from other parts of Spain are indifferent towards a language which the Catalan-speaking population abandons.

As to whether the name of the language should be Valencian or Catalan, Ferrando (1991) has studied this question in detail. It is true that since the second half of the 15th century, the Valencian people have generally chosen the former, which emphasises the unique nature of the language, and this has often expressed the desire to differentiate the language from Catalan, in a context of ideological manipulation.

The above-mentioned misinformation and manipulation have encouraged a certain kind of ideology, which evolved under Franco and takes the guise of a linguistic secessionism, in opposition to the 'Catalan peril'. An artificial conflict has been created between Catalan and Valencian to hide the real conflict, which is between Valencian and Spanish. The end result has been the growing linguistic defection and self-hatred. Some recent surveys suggest that the access to Valencian in schools will gradually solve this surprising question. No doubt the calculated ambiguity in the wording of the Autonomy Statute, where the differential term 'Valencian' is not accompanied by any explicit statement as to its ideological connotations, has contributed to this conflict over what to call the language. Thus far, the *Generalitat Valenciana* (Valencian autonomous government) has only introduced Valencian as a subject in primary and secondary school, has reserved a place for it in the Valencian Radio and TV, and occasionally makes a token use of it in public. The creation of *Radiotelevisió Valenciana-Canal 9* (TVV) aroused great hopes for the consolidation of the process begun in the area of education. However, the result has been disappointing. Not only has *TVV* not been the normalising tool that was hoped for (the percentage use of the community language has gone down to approximately 40% at present), but it has helped to consolidate the diglossic patterns of linguistic behaviour. Furthermore, for a language model, it has used a dialect that has been corrupted by linguistic interference from Spanish at all levels. The increase in the audio-visual possibilities for the Catalan language has come as a result of the activities of the association *Amics de TV3* (Friends of TV3), which, despite the many governmental obstacles, at the end of the 1980s managed to ensure that Catalan Television could be received all over the Valencian Country. To top it all off, the oral use of Valencian by governmental institutions is practically nil. The most important offender is the Parliament, when it should be the reflection of, and model for, the citizens' linguistic behaviour. In the cultural sector, too, there is hardly any Catalan. Only in publishing is there any progress, where the more intellectual cultural activities show quite a lot of activity in Catalan. Obviously, the above would seem to suggest a diagnosis of serious illness for Catalan in the Valencian Country. However, there is a part of society which does not give up hope of a better future. Any improvement in the linguistic situation in this region will depend on the pressure which it can bring to bear in order to turn the tide.

Language proficiency

Linguistic censuses and demographic changes

There are several ways of presenting the data on the use of Catalan in the various political and administrative regions of Spain. At the moment, there is a great deal of information about this which has been obtained via censuses and surveys, most carried out by government agencies although there have also been some private initiatives. The method used here is that which best allows the comparable data on the three Catalan-speaking regions discussed in this article.

The most interesting part of the following data is that which comes from the 1991 census, in the statements on language proficiency in Catalan:

1. I do not understand it.   4. I speak it.
2. I understand it.   5. I speak and read it
3. I understand and read it.   6. I speak, read and write it.

Also, an attempt has been made to compare this data with that from earlier censuses.[4] Lastly, for reasons of clarity and simplification, these six answers have been analysed in terms of the four basic linguistic skills: listening, speaking, reading and writing.[5] In 1991, the total population of the Catalan-speaking areas was slightly more than 11 million people. In the area discussed by this chapter, the total is around 10 and a half million. Table 2.1 shows an important increase over the first period from 1975 to 1981 (a total of 603,000 inhabitants, and some 100,000 per year), when immigration from other areas of Spain was still high.

Table 2.1 Population in Catalonia, the Valencian Country and the Balearic Islands, 1975–91 (thousands of inhabitants)

	Km^2	*1975*	*1981*	*1986*	*1991*	hab/km^2 *1991*
Catalonia	31,895	5,660	5,956	5,979	6,059	190
Balearic Islands	4,965	598	655	680	709	143
Valencian Country	23,005	3,397	3,647	3,733	3,831	166
Total	59,865	9,655	10,258	10,392	10,599	178

Source: National and municipal population censuses for the three countries

Language proficiency in Catalan: An overall view

As one can see from Table 2.2,[6] the most encouraging figures refer to the level of oral understanding, as the vast majority do understand Catalan. However, the total of a million people who do not understand it is a faithful reflection of the abnormal situation which exists. The majority also speak it and a smaller majority read it, whereas only a third of the population states that they know how to write in Catalan. The obvious difference between a passive oral understanding and the active skill of speaking is even greater when one looks at reading and writing. As far as this last skill is concerned, the rather dramatic conclusion is that the inhabitants of these areas are mostly illiterate in their own language. Figure 2.2, on the other hand, shows the situation of the four basic skills.

A breakdown of the data by political-administrative region (as in Table 2.3) shows the strong imbalance between the three areas.

The analysis of the data in terms of age clearly suggests some very interesting conclusions. Firstly, the 10–25 age group stands out in each

Table 2.2 Overall Catalan proficiency in Catalonia,[a] the Valencian Country[b] and the Balearic Islands,[c] 1991

	N	*%*
I understand Catalan	9,201,745	89.3
I speak it	6,389,275	61.8
I read it	5,786,834	50.6
I write it	3,108,321	30.1
I do not understand it	1,044,316	10.1
Did not answer	66,035	0.6
Proficiency coefficient	–	0.580

[a] Population aged two years or more. [b] Population aged three years or more. [c] Population aged six years or more

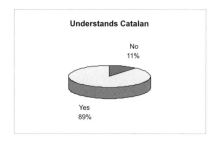

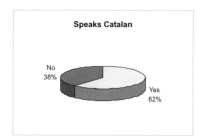

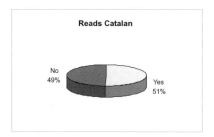

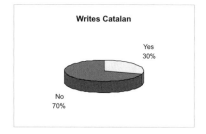

Figure 2.2 Overall Catalan proficiency in Catalonia, the Valencian Country and the Balearic Islands
Source: 1991 population censuses for Catalonia (INESCAT), the Valencian Country (IVE) and the Balearic Islands (IBE)

region, that is, Catalonia, the Valencian Country and the Balearic Islands. The use of Catalan in the school is obviously the most important reason. But it will be necessary to look more closely at each region. Secondly, the number of people who use Catalan decreases with an increase in age, except for the speaking skill, which increases after the age of 50. The level of comprehension is clearly greater than for the other skills, which can be explained by the fact that in the older age groups there are more native speakers, although here we find the highest proportion of those non-native speakers who do not understand Catalan. For those between the

Table 2.3 Catalan proficiency in Catalonia, the Valencian Country and the Balearic Islands, by region

	Catalonia	*Valencian Country*	*Balearic Islands*	*Total*
I understand Catalan	5,557,855	3,056,794	587,096	9,201,745
I speak it	4,065,841	1,882,094	441,340	6,389,275
I read it	4,019,276	1,403,739	363,819	5,786,834
I write it	2,376,201	560,880	171,240	3,108,321
I do not understand it	371,322	607,831	65,163	1,044,316

ages of 20 and 50, the fact that schooling was in Catalan for only a very few of them (as for those over 50 also) has caused a decline in the level of speaking, reading and writing (most accentuated in writing and least in speaking).

Finally, the analysis of the data from the 1986 and 1991 censuses allows one to see the change over time and shows the trends for the lack of proficiency in the various skills. In general, all inhabitants increased their level of proficiency, i.e. their lack of knowledge decreased. Whereas the speaking skill has been most resistant to change, the problems of reading and writing, addressed by literacy campaigns, are those which have undergone a change for the better.

Language proficiency in Catalan: Differences by community

Catalonia

Table 2.4 gives quite a clear idea of the use of Catalan in Catalonia. Almost all the population understands it, two-thirds say they speak and read it, and finally, only one-third say they can write it.

Looking at the change from 1986 to 1991, we can see an improvement in each area. The increase in linguistic competence is most noticeable in the skills where proficiency is lowest, that is, writing (+8.3%) and reading (+6.9%), both skills being aspects of literacy in Catalan. On the other hand, speaking (+4.1%) and oral comprehension (+3.2%) have increased to a lesser extent.[7] However, this clearly positive trend should not blind us to the fact that there is still a large deficit. Over three and a half million people cannot write Catalan, almost two million cannot speak or read it, and approximately four hundred thousand do not understand it.

When analysing the linguistic data, Reixach *et al.* (1997) divide Catalonia into four geographic-demographic areas which are sociologically important: Area 1, the city of Barcelona (27.1% of the population

Table 2.4 Catalan proficiency in Catalonia (population aged two years or more), 1986 and 1991

	1986	*1991*	*Increase in linguistic competence*
I understand Catalan	90.6	93.8	3.2
I speak it	64.2	68.3	4.1
I read it	60.7	67.6	6.9
I write it	31.6	39.9	8.3
Proficiency coefficient	0.62	0.67	0.05
Does not answer	0.3	–	–
Total	100	101.6	1.6

Source: INESCAT, population census (1991) and municipal census (1986)

Table 2.5 Catalan proficiency by areas (population aged two years or more), 1991

	Understand Catalan	Speak it	Read it	Write it	Do not understand it	Proficiency coefficient
1	95.4	70.1	70.7	40.1	4.7	0.69
2	87.8	50.7	53.6	29.3	12.2	0.55
3	93.2	66.2	65.5	40.8	6.8	0.66
4	96.8	80.3	75.7	46.7	3.2	0.75
Total	93.8	68.3	67.6	39.9	6.2	0.67

Source: INESCAT, 1991 population census

of two or more years of age); Area 2, the rest of the metropolitan area of Barcelona (the outlying suburbs) (22.1%); Area 3, the rest of the Barcelona province (18.7%); and Area 4, the rest of Catalonia (32.1%). Table 2.5 shows language proficiency in Catalan in the four areas.

The imbalance is clear. The highest percentages are found in Area 4 (rest of Catalonia) far ahead of the others in all four skills. This area is followed by the city of Barcelona (Area 1) and the rest of the Barcelona province (Area 3), respectively, although for writing the order is reversed. The area where Catalan is least known involves the outlying suburbs of Barcelona (Area 2), where most of the immigrant families from other areas of Spain live.

The skill of speaking is the one which shows the greatest geographical imbalances. Looking at smaller regional areas ('comarques' or counties), the difference between Terra Alta (94.8%) and Baix Llobregat (53.4%) is 41.4%. But in the other skills, the differences between the different geographical areas tend to be less, although there are some variations. Looking at cities of over 25,000 inhabitants, the progress made in all four skills tends to level out the statistics.

In an analysis of the National Census of 1981 and the Municipal Census of 1986, Reixach (1985: 23–3, 1990: 66–7) described certain areas of greatest deficit, called pockets of 'non-Catalanisation'. This referred to a municipality or a district of a municipality where the percentage of non-comprehension of Catalan was 25% or more of the population. At the moment, the spectacular growth of this skill suggests that this criterion should be updated[8] and based on the speaking skill. Attention should now be centred on *Sectors d'Inferior Competència* (SIC; areas of low proficiency according to age and geographical differences; Reixach *et al.*, 1997). In the SICs, 25% or more of the population of a municipality or a municipal district between the ages of 15 and 19 cannot speak Catalan. According to this new classification, 71 SICs have been detected, most of which are concentrated in the Barcelona metropolitan area, but which also appear in other towns such as Balaguer, Girona, Lloret de Mar, Reus and Tarragona. The fact that a considerable number of young people cannot express themselves in Catalan, despite its use and teaching in schools, illustrates the long road ahead before the milestone of linguistic normalisation is reached.

Balearic and Pitius Islands

As Table 2.6 illustrates, the data from the 1991 census shows that in the Balearic Islands the level of understanding of Catalan is quite high (88.7%), slightly less than that of Catalonia, but more than that of the Valencian Country. A majority also speaks it (66.7%) and reads it (55%). The largest shortfall is in writing, since only a quarter of the population considers itself to be proficient in this skill.

An analysis of the data for each island shows that the results are very heterogeneous. Table 2.6 is shows a breakdown of the percentages of the data for each island and the capital of Majorca, Palma.

The most recent data available, from the 1991 census, shows that Minorca is ahead (the percentages for the four skills are higher than in Catalonia, except for writing), while Eivissa (Ibiza) and Formentera are last.

It is especially interesting to see the change in level of Catalan language proficiency in the Balearic Islands, as here there is a unique phenomenon. Surprisingly, there has been a decline in understanding in the island of Majorca, including in Palma, and in speaking in all of the islands. On the other hand, the figures for reading and writing have increased significantly. The explanation for this is clear: reading and writing are skills associated with literacy in Catalan. But the declines are difficult to explain. Several studies (Guitart, 1995: 135–1; Moll, 1995: 23–34) suggest that the reason for the decrease in percentages could be the different ways in which the question has been asked. Whereas in 1986, the census asked whether the person understood, spoke, read and wrote 'the language of

Table 2.6 Catalan proficiency by islands in the Balearic Islands, 1986–91

	Majorca		*Minorca*		*Eivissa and Formentera*		*Total*		*Palma*	
	1986	*1991*	*1986*	*1991*	*1986*	*1991*	*1986*	*1991*	*1986*	*1991*
I do not understand it	9.7	10.1	4.6	4.9	16.2	12.4	9.9	9.9	12.4	12.5
I understand it	89.7	88.6	94.6	94.7	83.4	84.8	89.6	88.7	87.6	86.2
I speak it	70.4	66.1	84.6	81.3	61.8	58.9	70.8	66.7	61.6	56.9
I read it	46.5	54.8	60.4	71.1	29.8	42.9	46.0	55.0	47.2	51.5
I write it	16.0	25.7	26.4	34.8	12.4	19.7	16.6	25.9	16.5	22.8
Proficiency coefficient	0.56	0.59	0.67	0.70	0.47	0.52	0.56	0.59	0.53	0.54
N ('000)	509	531	55	60	63	70	627	661	272	278

Source: IBE: 1991 population census, and 1986 municipal census

the Balearic Islands', in 1991 it was made explicit that this language was 'Catalan'. The correctness of this hypothesis is supported by the special historical importance of this name and the long history of manipulation and misinformation about this question which the Islands have suffered, in a similar way to the Valencian Country.

Finally, it is interesting to consider the generational structure of Catalan language proficiency in the Balearic Islands which shows in contrasted data that cannot be reproduced here a relatively homogeneous behaviour in the different age groups, with the minimum in the 6–9 group. The highest figure for proficiency is generally between the ages of 10 and 19. As regards speaking, the progressive decline shown until the age of 39 gives way to a gradual increase until it reaches the highest point with the elderly. On the other hand, reading and writing continue to decline as from the 10–15 age group.

The Valencian Country

Looking at the Valencian Country as a whole, the data show that there is a high level of understanding of Catalan (82.2%), but that only half the population speaks it (50.6%), about a third reads it (37.7%) and only a minority writes it (15.1%).[9] The data have been broken down into geographical regions or provinces.[10] Table 2.7 shows the Catalan language proficiency from 1986 to 1991.

If one looks at the data for 1991, one can see that the Castelló province is far ahead of the others. At the other extreme, and with the lowest levels seen in this study, is Alacant. Valencia is in the middle, and the largest difference with Castelló can be seen in speaking. Both overall and in each area, the trend from 1986 to 1991 is clearly one of improvement. Progress in each of the four skills is in the following order: reading (+13.4%), writing (+8.1%), oral comprehension (+5.1%) and speaking (+1.2%). This last figure has special sociolinguistic significance.

Table 2.7 Catalan proficiency in the Valencian Country, 1986–91

	Alacant		Castelló		València		Total	
	1986	*1991*	*1986*	*1991*	*1986*	*1991*	*1986*	*1991*
I understand Catalan	60.6	68.2	90.3	93.2	84.0	88.2	77.1	82.2
I speak it	36.5	37.0	67.0	67.9	53.4	55.0	49.4	50.6
I read it	13.1	23.1	28.6	46.1	30.0	44.7	24.3	37.7
I write it	4.4	9.9	8.7	19.8	8.2	17.1	7.0	15.1
Proficiency coefficient	0.29	0.35	0.49	0.57	0.44	0.51	0.40	0.46
N ('000)	1,169	1,243	422	431	2,007	2,046	3,599	3,721

Source: IVE, data from the Municipal Census and the 1991 National Census

The division of the Valencian Country into Spanish-speaking and Catalan-speaking counties makes it especially interesting to know the figures for only the Catalan-speaking counties: oral comprehension (87.7%), speaking (56.1%), reading (42%) and writing (16.8%). One can see an increase of about 5% or 6% although less for writing.

Education

Catalonia

Since 1978, when the Catalan government took power, education has played a special part in the normalisation of the Catalan language. The point of departure was the Royal Decree 2092/1978, by means of which the use of Catalan became obligatory in schools.[11] The Catalan Education Department began with the intention of ensuring students attended a minimum of three hours' Catalan classes per week in every school. Later, it became clear that due to the particular sociolinguistic conditions, which made Catalan a minority language in so many situations, three hours a week are not enough to achieve the same level of proficiency as in Spanish. As from 1981, it was clear that more vigorous action was needed to obtain a minimum number of hours in Catalan, and so three basic acts were introduced (Arnau & Artigal, 1995: 23):

(1) The Act of 11 May 1981, increased the number of hours of Catalan to four, making it equivalent to the number of hours of Spanish, and raised the concepts of 'main learning language' and of 'introduced language', with the aim of allowing each school to design its own educational project, in accordance with its own sociolinguistic environment.

(2) The Act of 16 August 1982 introduced the distinction between Catalan and Spanish curricula, determined by the choices made by each school of the above-mentioned concepts.

(3) The Decree 270/1982, of 5 August 1982, meant that schools which chose to teach mainly in Catalan did not have to ask for permission to do so. Now, for the first time, a minimum number of hours in Catalan was determined, beginning in secondary school.

The *Llei de Normalització Lingüística* (Linguistic Normalisation Act) of April, 1983, initiated a new era of more profound intervention by the Education Department in this area. Now, the objective was to increase the presence of Catalan in schools, both in teaching and in the related administration. To this end, the Act of 8 September 1983, laid down the obligation to teach and learn in Catalan in at least one of the two streams, humanities or sciences, from third to fifth year primary school, and in both streams from sixth to eighth year. It now granted to each School Board the power of deciding which linguistic option was most adequate, according to their understanding of the students and the context in which the school was situated.

This step gave rise to three models of schools (Alsina *et al.*, 1983):

(1) Schools of maximum Catalanisation (normalisation model), where the teaching and communicative language is Catalan from the very beginning, except for the Spanish classes and one other subject.

(2) Schools of medium Catalanisation (immersion model), where schooling begins in Spanish and gradually introduces Catalan as a language of communication until it reaches the same level of use as Spanish.

(3) Schools of minimum Catalanisation, where Spanish is the teaching and communicative language, and Catalan is only used as far as it is legally obligatory.

The data for schools from the period 1984–93 (Arnau and Artigal, 1995: 27–8) shows perfectly clearly the change in percentages for the kind of school chosen. While the maximum Catalanisation model increased spectacularly in numbers (1984: 45.1% of schools and 23.3% of students; 1993: 88.8% of schools and 72.9% of students), the medium Catalanisation model fell to a minority of 10%, and the minimum Catalanisation model has tended to disappear (1993: 0.9% of schools and 3.45% of students).

Curriculums of 'linguistic immersion' in Catalonia are those which work towards the maximum Catalanisation model in a school where at least 70% of students are not Catalan speakers, and which are located in non-Catalan-speaking areas.

Arnau and Artigal (1995: 29) outline the political, psychological and linguistic basis for this 'schooling mainly in Catalan for students whose language at home and in their immediate social environment is Spanish'. From a psycholinguistic point of view, it is justified by the fact that the acquisition of languages is a function of their meaningful use in context, and in this sense the making of Catalan a minority language can be seen in the lack of contexts in which it is used. The school is thus seen as a place of use and learning of primary importance. Politically and linguistically speaking, it is considered that immersion offers the Spanish-speaking child an area of activity where Catalan functions as the main means of communication.

During the 1983–84 course, the linguistic immersion programme was introduced for the first time in 19 schools in Santa Coloma de Gramanet, where there were large numbers of Spanish-speaking students.[12] It began at pre-school age (first at the age of 4, then at 3), and continued until the end of the first period of primary school (EGB), at the age of 7. Later, with the introduction of the Educational Reform in 1992–93, the immersion period was extended to include all of primary school, from 3 until 12 years of age. The data for the school year 1992–93 show some more revealing percentages: 43.6% of the schools in Catalonia (53.3% public and 31.2% private) applied the immersion programme to their 85,317 students from 3 to 7 years old.

We have seen how the Catalan immersion model has been applied to schools where the percentage of Spanish speakers is between 70% and 99%. At the same time, we have data which allows us to compare the situation of immersion in Catalonia to other models, essentially those applied in Finland and Canada (where it is applied when 100% of students do not speak the community language,) and in the Valencian Country, the Basque Country or the USA (where the percentage lies between 50% and 69%). So for the 1992–93 school year, 4.3% of all students in Catalonia attended kindergarten and primary school in conditions of maximum Catalanisation where none of the students spoke Catalan in the family, 21.3% did so in classes where between 70% and 99% of the class did not speak Catalan at home, and 3.8% in classes where between 50% and 69% of the students did not do so.[13]

The 1993–94 school year was a turning point in the consideration of Catalan as the main teaching and communicative language in schools. The reason is the changes brought about by the Educational Reform (Decree 75/1992 of 9 March and Decree 94/1992 of 28 April). In this new stage, the three optional models disappear, but most importantly, this proposal for a programme introduces strict criteria for deciding areas of competence, as the regional government increased its powers of decision to the detriment of those of parents and teachers. Although it was flexible, the new programme had only one model. Also, 'the individual linguistic rights of the student would be respected' (Decree 94/1992, Article 6.3), and the parents could demand that their children from 3 to 7 years of age be taught in Spanish.

This step forward suffered a serious shock when on 15 February 1994, the third Supreme Court allowed an appeal to the Constitutional Court against the Linguistic Normalisation Act of 1983, on the grounds that several of its articles may have been anti-constitutional. However, the ruling of the Constitutional Court, on 23 December 1994, granted the Government of the *Generalitat de Catalunya* the right to decide the correct model to be implemented in order to attain the objective of teaching Catalan and Spanish in the area under its jurisdiction. Without doubt, this ruling legitimises the actions of the autonomous government in the area of education, and avoids it having to take several steps backward in its programmes.

Balearic and Pitius Islands

To understand the situation of Catalan in the context of the Balearic Islands, there are three facts which should be emphasised: (1) the late appearance of the *Llei de Normalització Lingüística* (Linguistic Normalisation Act), in 1986, as compared to the Regional Autonomy Statute of 1983; (2) the fact that no institutional body has been created to take charge of the planning and co-ordination of linguistic policy; and (3) the fact that the regional government of the Balearic Islands at the time of writing does not have legal or administrative jurisdiction over education, a fact which makes the design of local curricula and the development of legislative measures impossible.

In the field of education the Linguistic Normalisation Act seeks to allow students to finish their period of compulsory schooling speaking equally well both Spanish and Catalan. Considering Catalan to be the Balearic Islands' own official language, it promotes a gradual increase in its use that will make it usual in pre-university education.[14]

At the same time, the regional government administration has been slow to ensure an effective presence of Catalan in the education system by means of legal regulations. A clear example of this is the Department of Culture, Education and Sport's regulation of 27/8/94, in which the proposed extension of the use and the teaching of Catalan is left exclusively in the hands of the school itself, which, in the context of the Educational Policy, will have to elaborate their own Linguistic Policy.

With regard to types of models for schools in the Islands, there is teaching completely in Catalan, in the minority of cases, and partially in Catalan. Looking at the data for the 1992–93 school year, the situation was as follows (Sbert & Vives, 1994):

(a) In state primary and pre-schools, 20.72% students received their education totally in Catalan, 16.21% partly in Catalan, while 63.07% received it totally in Spanish.
(b) In private and subsidised schools, the percentage of students who receive their education totally in Spanish increases to 89.03%.
(c) A breakdown of the data by the different islands shows that Eivissa is in the worst situation, with 81.47% in Spanish, followed by Majorca, with 57.28%. Minorca has the highest percentage of students who receive their education totally in Catalan, 61.48%.
(d) In primary education, the differences are maintained, with the following percentages of students receiving their education entirely in Spanish: Eivissa, 69.73%; Majorca, 63.07%; and Minorca, 53.70%.

The introduction of linguistic immersion programmes was initiated spontaneously by teachers and parents who were sensitive to the linguistic question. Despite the growing demand for immersion, the lack of serious institutional commitment has meant that this phenomenon has remained purely anecdotal in quantitative terms (2.3%).

The *Associació Illenca de Renovació Pedagògica* (AIRE) (the Island's Association for Pedagogical Reform) brought together and co-ordinated those teachers who voluntarily put into practice linguistic immersion in several schools in Majorca. In 1992–93, nine public schools which come under the authority of the (national Spanish) Ministry for Education and Science, all on the island of Majorca, have carried out linguistic immersion programmes.

About 20 more pre-schools and primary schools have developed linguistic integration programmes, similar to linguistic immersion.

Notwithstanding, the overall situation could be called precarious, based on voluntary initiatives and lacking institutional support.

The Valencian Country

The approval of the Autonomy Statute in July 1982, was the starting point of an educational policy which took Catalan into the classroom. On 23 November 1983, the *Corts Valencianes* (Regional Parliament) passed the *Llei d'Ús i Ensenyament del Valencià* (LUEV) (Use and Teaching of Valencian Act), and created the *Gabinet d'Ús i Ensenyament del Valencià* (Use and Teaching of Valencian Section) of the *Conselleria de Cultura, Educació i Ciència* (Department of Culture, Education and Science). The sub-heading of this law, 'From Valencian to Education', expresses the guidelines of this process.[15]

The first part of the education policy which was followed (1) ensured that *Valencià*, the Valencian variety of Catalan, was an obligatory subject for 3–4 hours a week, (2) drafted a proposal for a Valencian Curriculum, (3) decreed that the texts should follow the norms of the *Institut Valencià de Filologia* (Valencian Institute of Philology),[16] (4) organised the training and hiring of the teachers who would put the policy into practice, and (5) laid down specific regulations for the incorporation of this variety of Catalan into the education system.

For historical reasons, the Valencian Country is divided into two zones, one Spanish-speaking and one Catalan-speaking. This situation is taken into account in the LUEV by adopting two different models (see Figure 2.3) one of monolingual education in Spanish, with 'Valencian' as a subject, in the corresponding zone, and the other of bilingual education, with both Catalan and Spanish as the teaching languages, in the areas where Catalan is the main language spoken.

The bilingual system takes the following form in primary education (Torró & Brotons, 1995: 53–4):

(1) A programme of gradual incorporation of Valencian Catalan. This was aimed at those students who live in a predominantly Catalan-speaking area. With a certain amount of flexibility, Spanish is used as the teaching language.

(2) A programme of teaching in Valencian Catalan. This was aimed at those students in a mainly Catalan-speaking area. The preferred teaching language is their own native language, without ignoring the need to be proficient in the other official language.

(3) Linguistic Immersion Programme. This was aimed at those mainly Spanish-speaking students who lived in a predominantly Catalan-speaking area (or Spanish-speaking area, if circumstances permitted).[17] It is clear that this model implies a change of language from the home to the school.

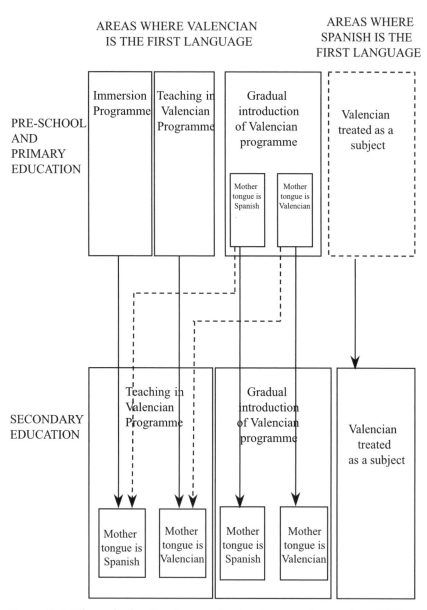

Figure 2.3 Bilingual education in pre-school, primary and secondary (ESO) education
Source: Adapted from Pascual and Sala (1991)

(4) Valencian Catalan as a subject on the school curriculum. This cannot be considered a truly bilingual programme, and is aimed at those students in a traditionally Spanish-speaking area. Its aim of allowing students to learn both languages was rarely achieved, and besides this, it was an optional subject.

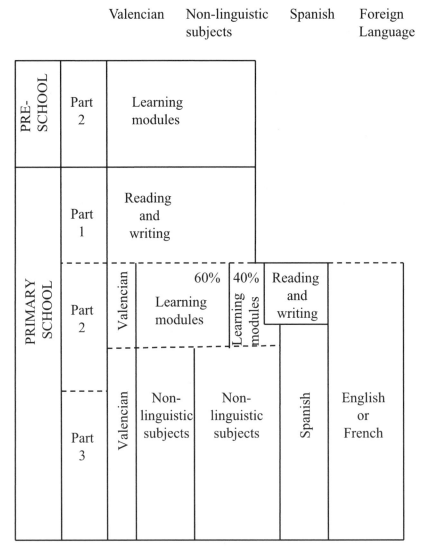

Figure 2.4 The design of the linguistic immersion programme in the Valencian Country
Source: Torró & Brotons (1995: 60)

In 1983–84, the teaching of Valencian Catalan moved strongly ahead, but only in certain areas. It was not a generalised change, as even today there are schools which do not comply with the law, especially in private schools. In this school year, Valencian Catalan began to be taught, at first hesitantly, but gradually the number of schools increased from 10 in 1983 (6 public, 4 private) to 474 in 1993 (457 public, 17 private).

Little by little, the public demand grew for a model which would go further than just teaching Valencian Catalan as another subject, towards a real bilingual programme. This need became especially clear in those towns where everyday use of Catalan had receded in previous decades. It was in this context that the regional government decided on the Linguistic Immersion Programme (Figure 2.4) (the Department of Culture, Education and Science Regulation of 23 November 1990, under the 79/1984 Decree of 30 July which put into practice the *Llei d'Ús i Ensenyament del Valencià* (4/1983) (Use and Teaching of Valencian Act).[18]

According to data from the *Servei d'Ensenyament en Valencià* (Teaching in Valencian Section) (1994), in 1993 47,776 students learnt Valencian Catalan in pre-school, primary school and the first few years of secondary school (EGB) (45,319 in public schools and 2457 in private schools). The same data states that 10,462 studied in the Linguistic Immersion Programme in 1993–94 (10,165 in public schools and 297 in private schools).

Despite the progressive increase in numbers of students studying Catalan since 1983, if we compare the figures for the Immersion Programmes with the total number of students, we can see that it is only a small 22% of the total. So a lot remains to be done, and there are plenty of obstacles. The same government which has laid down a legal framework for more and better teaching of Valencian Catalan has not been so resolute in putting these laws into practice. Finally, one fact on the negative side should be mentioned: this progress, however small it has been, has been under a progressive autonomous government. The coming to power of a conservative government after the local autonomous regional elections of 1995 quite feasibly threatens to move things backwards or, in the best of circumstances, towards an end to further advances.

Language Behaviour and Use Patterns

Language contact phenomena involving the use of Catalan and Spanish made by speakers from the communities considered in this article have been extensively analysed (Pujadas & Turell, 1993; Turell, 1994; Pujol & Turell, 1995; Turell & Forcadell, 1997), in particular, with regards the speech modalities of the different linguistic and cultural groups interacting in Catalonia, indigenous Catalan-speaking and immigrant Spanish-speaking.

Samples (1), (2), (3) and (4) help us characterise the modalities of discourse that can be observed among indigenous Catalan speakers, Catalan-speaking immigrants, Spanish-speaking immigrants from other areas in

Spain with a high degree of contact with the members of the indigenous Catalan-speaking communities, and finally first generation immigrants with maximum contact who make use of rapid codeswitching which results in code-mixing.

(1) is characteristic of speakers of Catalan who use it as their most usual language and make use of loan words, codeswitching, syntactic calques and semantic calques. Typically this modality contains a whole series of switches between Catalan and Spanish, designed by the speakers when they quote the words of Spanish speakers to distance themselves and distinguish themselves from the culture and the attitude of the reported interlocutor.

(1) **I:** Ben ballades (les sevillanes) ... jo, es que ... escolta ... i els hi vaig dir ... i moltes m'ho van vindre a dir, dius, ... diu: 'filla' ... 'quina faceta', diu, **'no lo conociamos esto'**, dic: 'ah, que us penseu'! i vaig i li dic: 'i tú que has après de ballar sardanes?', diu: **'yo no, pero mi hija sí que irá, ... irá'**, ara no ho sé ...

I: Danced well (the sevillanas) ... the thing is ... listen ... and I said to them ... and obviously ... and lots of them came and said, you say ... she says: 'girl' ... 'what hidden talents!' she says, **'we didn't know this [side to you]'**, I say: 'ah, what do you think!' and I went and said: 'and have you learned to dance 'sardanes'?', she says **'I haven't, but my daughter is going to go ... going to go'**, now I don't know ...

(LC/IP:50/88)

(2) shows the **bilingual** modality of the immigrants who now use Catalan as their most usual language. This modality shows that Catalan is the matrix language, since, as illustrated, the speaker switches to Spanish consciously, then uses Catalan again, and thus employs intrasentential switching to 'quote' an idiomatic expression:

(2) **M:** Los castellans se van sentir més ... imposats, també; van dir: **'nosotros** per què *tenim que* (syntatic calque) donar **nuestro brazo a torcer** sempre'?

M: The Spanish felt more ... imposed on, too; they said: why do **we** *have to* **stand there and take it** always?

(LC/MJ:18/88)

There is a second group of immigrants who have a very high index of contact with the other group, and who use a **bilingual mode**, with Spanish as a matrix language, full of codeswitching, as illustrated in (3):

(3) **A:** Y hay que tener una economía para hacer eso. Lo mismo **lo fill** que **lo** padre, estudiar para salir **endavant**, y los padres pa ir dando céntimos pa ir manténiendolos. Y eso muchos no quieren

hacerlo, se creen que **lo fill**. Muchos los tienen, no sé como decirte ... que a los diez años, salen del colegio, y, hala, **(a) treballar**. Y yo, mira, cada uno es como es, pero es lo más bueno que hay; una persona que tenga **(una) mica** de estudios hay mucha diferencia.

A: And you need an income to do that. Both **the son** and **the** father, studying to be able to get **on**, and the parents to be able to keep handing over the cash to maintain them. And a lot don't want to do that, they think that **the son**. A lot have them, how can I put it ... that when they're ten years old, they should leave school and then, come on, get **(to) work**. And look, we're all different, but for me there's nothing finer; someone who has **(a) little** education, there's a lot of difference.

(LC/AF:28/88)

Finally, there is a fourth type of modality that can be characterised as a **mixed code** and which involves a series of rapid switches where sometimes the matrix language is Spanish, and sometimes Catalan. This mode runs counter to the principles (the equivalence constraint, the free morpheme constraint and the constituent morpheme constraint)[19] that have been put forward (Poplack, 1990), the latter having it that switches can occur at certain points in the sentence or noun or verb phrase, and not at others. On the other hand, from the point of view of the psychology of language, this mode also shows that there is a loss of awareness of the two codes as separate languages on the part of the speaker. This modality is illustrated in (4).

(4)   C: **Bueno**, aquí hi ha una cosa. Jo perquè estic dintre d'aquí **(i)** **(a mi) me gusta**. Ara **en cuanto va un baile flamenco** m'agrada. **(Y) si el baile flamenco, pues una sevillana, (o)** ballo (un tango). És clar, ara hi ha més gent forastera. Ara que si aquí **(la) fiesta fuera toda** junta, **tiene que haber un dia** (una) cosa, un dia una altra cosa ...

       C: **Well**, here there is one thing. Because I am in this place, **(and) (I) like it**. Now **when there's a flamenco dance** I like it (base language Catalan). **(And) if there's flamenco, then a sevillana** (dance typical of Seville), **(or)** I dance (a) tango (base language Spanish). Of course, now there are more newcomers. Now, if **there was (one) fiesta** together, **then one day we'd have** (one) thing, and another day another thing ...

(LC/C:12/88)

Concluding Remarks

In summary, it could be stated that Catalan has a different status as a community language in Catalonia, the Balearic and the Pitius Islands, and the Valencian Country. The legislation in these three Autonomous Communities which was passed during the 1980s and which has influenced their members to different degrees, has certainly changed the attitude of the local population towards Catalan in all cases, but the view taken of the language's prestige and the consciousness of the need to encourage its use are also very different in each case. In Catalonia, the prestige of Catalan and the need for encouraging its use have certainly increased; furthermore, the *Generalitat de Catalunya* (the autonomous government) has always been committed to carrying out real linguistic 'normalisation' in all social domains, particularly because the same political nationalist party has been in power continuously since the end of the 1970s. As as a result, Catalan seems to be in best health in this Catalan-speaking area. In the Valencian Country and the Balearic and Pitius Islands the situation seems to be more uncertain and not only for historical reasons. In spite of the fact that the Linguistic Acts which were passed by their respective Parliaments grant the co-official nature of Catalan and Spanish, there are two reasons for viewing the situation as uncertain. One is the fact that historically, and even so today, Catalan was not and is not viewed as prestigious by a majority of the Valencian and the Balearic populations. The other factor is more institutional: the authorities and administration in these two Autonomous Communities, whether progressive or more conservative, have not been so committted to linguistic normalisation policies and, therefore, the legislation which derives from the Statutes and the Linguistic Acts has never been really implemented.

As to language behaviour, some of the patterns mentioned in the section where such behaviour is analysed can be found in the other Catalan-speaking communities considered in this article, particularly in rural areas and other areas where there seems to be interaction and contact between indigenous and immigrant members in the Valencian Country and the Balearic and Pitius Islands. Analysis of urban populations in these two communities remains to be considered.

Notes

1. See Suïls and Huguet (Ch. 5) in this volume.
2. For historical reasons, to do with the resettlement after the *Reconquista* (mediaeval Christian conquest) of the western part of the ancient Kingdom of Valencia, this area was initially Aragonese-speaking, and as from the 5th century this language was absorbed into Castillian. As well as this area, the other Spanish-speaking areas are the Baix Segura and Vinalopó Mitjà counties, because of a process of linguistic substitution caused by Murcian resettlement in the 18th and 19th centuries, and the counties of Pla de Requena-Utiel and Alt Vinalopó, which belonged to Castile until 1851 and 1836 respectively.
3. In fact, in Minorca the vast majority of native Minorcans speak the language and use it as their everyday language.
4. For Catalonia, one can analyse the changes in linguistic use from the 1981, 1986 and 1991 censuses, although they only give information about levels of understanding. For Valencia and the Balearic Islands, the comparison can only be made between the data from 1986 and 1991.

5. I am grateful to Modest Reixach for his generosity in providing me with information on the linguistic data from the 1991 census, even before publication.

6. For the figures in the table, there are methodological differences between each region. The figures for Catalonia refer to a population of two years of age or more, those for the Valencian Country to a population of three years or more, and those for the Balearic Islands to a population of six years or more.

7. One fact that should not be overlooked and which confirms this positive trend is that the increase for these different skills is greater than the population increase (two years or more) which is 1.6%.

8. According to this criterion and the 1991 data, only District 6 of the Municipality of Sant Adrià del Besós could be considered a pocket of non-Catalanisation.

9. Of the three linguistic areas discussed in this chapter, the Valencian Country is the one which shows the lowest levels of linguistic proficiency. The differences are not so great in comprehension, but increase considerably in speaking, reading and writing, in that order.

10. The full complexity of the situation can be appreciated by looking at the data at the level of smaller administrative regions (counties), but it has been simplified here. However, the province should be seen as a group of counties and all together they make up the three large areas in the Valencian Country.

11. In the history of Catalonia, this had only happened once, during the Second Republic (1931–36).

12. From 1955 to 1970, Catalonia received a large number of immigrants, in numbers comparable to that of the host population. These immigrants settled mostly in the metropolitan area of Barcelona, including in Santa Coloma de Gramanet.

13. If the category of immersion were applied to classes of maximum Catalanisation where at least 50% of students were not Catalan speakers, then in 1992–93 in Catalonia some 39.5% of students would have been involved in the immersion programme.

14. Unlike in Catalonia, where the law establishes that the language of use and the contents of the teaching process should be in Catalan, this Balearic legislation does not make explicit this idea of Catalan as the first or local language in the school, and thus as the basis of the educational and cultural proposal.

15. Just how limited, ambiguous and contradictory it is has been is shown by Pitarch (1994).

16. The 'secessionist' trend for the writing, grammar, etc. of the language, which denied the links with the rest of the Catalan-speaking areas, was rejected, thus accepting the norms proposed by Pompeu Fabra, who stressed the unity of the language in all areas where it is spoken. Similarly, in 1997, the *Partido Popular* government, under pressure from its coalition partner *Unió Valenciana*, revoked the linguistic authority granted to this Institute, opening a period of uncertainty until a solution was found to this conflict. Meanwhile, the acceptance of Valencian as a variety of Catalan is still official policy in all areas of the education system.

17. It should be said, however, that in the 1994–95 school year there was still no school in a historically Spanish-speaking area which had got under way a linguistic immersion programme. On the other hand, there were many places near the dividing lines between the two areas where this kind of programme was functioning already.

18. More laws and regulations can be found in Decree 20/1992, by the Valencian government, which laid down the curriculum for primary schools in the Valencian Regional Community, (DOGV 1728, 20/2/92), and in the Department of Education and Science's Regulation of 12/5/94, which regulated the curriculum and timetables of the schools with a linguistic immersion programme.

19. These principles will be considered when a more exhaustive linguistic treatment of Catalan-Spanish contact features is completed, as well as the linguistic state of affairs in the other Catalan-speaking communities (the Valencian Country and the Balearic Islands) giving an objective assessment of degree of bilingualism and the real competence speakers have in the two languages.

References

Alsina, A. *et al.* (1983) *Quatre Anys de Català a l'Escola.* Barcelona: Departament d'Ensenyament.

Arenas, J. (1988) *La Immersió Lingüística. Escrits de Divulgació.* Barcelona: La Llar del Llibre.

Arnau, J. and Artigal, J.M. (1995) El programa d'immersió a Catalunya. In J.M. Artigal (ed.) *Els Programes d'Immersió als Territoris de Llengua Catalana* (pp. 21–47). Barcelona: Fundació Jaume Bofill.

Artigal, J.M. (ed.) (1995) *Els Programes d'Immersió als Territoris de Llengua Catalana.* Barcelona: Fundació Jaume Bofill.

Bastardas, A. (1991) *Fer el Futur. Sociolingüística, Planificació i Normalització del Català.* Barcelona: Empúries.

Bibiloni, G. (1991) La situació del català a les Illes Balears. In J. Martí (ed.) *Processos de Normalització Lingüística: l'Extensió d'Ús Social i la Normativització* (pp. 139–58). Barcelona: Columna.

Ferrando, A. (1991) Les perspectives de normalització lingüística al País Valencià. In J. Martí (ed.) *Processos de Normalització Lingüística: l'Extensió d'Ús Social i la Normativització* (pp. 103–38). Barcelona: Columna.

Generalitat Valenciana (1987) *Patró Municipal d'Habitants / 1986. Coneixement del Valencià.* València: Generalitat Valenciana.

Generalitat Valenciana (1989a) *El Valencià en el Sector Terciari Avançat.* València: Generalitat Valenciana.

Generalitat Valenciana (1989b) *L'Ús del Valencià en l'Administració Autonòmica.* València: Generalitat Valenciana.

Generalitat Valenciana (1990a) *Coneixement del Valencià. Anàlisi dels Resultats del Padró Municipal d'Habitants de 1986.* València: Generalitat Valenciana.

Generalitat Valenciana (1990b) *Dades sobre la Situació Sociolingüística de la Comunitat Valenciana.* València: Generalitat Valenciana.

Ginebra, J. (1992) La política lingüística al Principat de Catalunya (1980–1992). In I. Marí (ed.) *La Llengua als Països Catalans* (pp. 15–28). Barcelona: Fundació Jaume Bofill.

Guitart, J. (1995) Grau de coneixement del català a les Balears. *Actes del Simposi de Demolingüística.* Barcelona: Generalitat de Catalunya, Departament de Cultura, 135–51.

Guitart, J. and Reniu, M. (1990) *Cultura a Catalunya Anys Noranta. Un Nou Impuls a la Política Lingüística.* Barcelona: Departament de Cultura de la Generalitat de Catalunya.

Marí, I. (1991) La política lingüística de la Generalitat de Catalunya. In J. Martí (ed.) *Processos de Normalització Lingüística: l'Extensió d'Ús Social i la Normativització* (pp. 85–102). Barcelona: Columna.

Marí, I. (ed.) (1992) *La Llengua als Països Catalans.* Barcelona: Fundació Jaume Bofill.

Martí, J. (1991a) *Processos de Normalització Lingüística: l'Extensió de l'Ús Social i la Normativització.* Barcelona: Columna.

Martí, J. (1991b) Alguns supòsits per a la normalització lingüística. In J. Martí (ed.) *Processos de Normalització Lingüística: l'Extensió de l'Ús Social i la Normativització* (pp. 25–39). Barcelona: Columna.

Melià, J. (1992) La política lingüística a les Balears. In I. Marí (ed.) *La Llengua als Països Catalans* (pp. 49–85). Barcelona: Fundació Jaume Bofill.

Moll, A. (1995) La situació lingüística a les Illes Balears. *Serra d'Or,* 425, 23–34.

Mollà, A. (1992) La política lingüística al País Valencià. In I. Marí (ed.) *La Llengua als Països Catalans* (pp. 29–48). Barcelona: Fundació Jaume Bofill.

Ninyoles, L. (1982) (ed.) *Estructura Social al País Valencià.* València: Diputació de València.

Pascual, V. and Sala, V. (1991) *Un Model Educatiu per a un Sistema Escolar amb tres Llengües.* Valencia: Consellia de Cultura, Educació i Ciència de la Generalitat Valenciana.

Pitarch, V. (1994) Entre l'immobilisme i la modernitat. In V. Pitarch (ed.) *Parlar i (con)Viure al País Valencià* (pp. 53–8). Barcelona: Publicacions de l'Abadia de Montserrat.

Poplack, S. (1990) Variation theory and language contact: Concepts, methods and data. *Papers for the Workshop on Concepts, Methodology and Data,* ESF Network on Codeswitching and Language Contact. Strasbourg: European Science Foundation, 33–66.

Pradilla, M.À. (1996) Llengua i societat a l'extrem nord del País Valencià. *Mainhardt* 24, 53–9.

Pujadas, J.J. and Turell, M.T. (1993) Els indicadors sociolingüístics del contacte inter-ètnic. *Actes del IXè Colloqui Internacional de l'Associació Internacional de Llengua i Literatura Catalanes.* Alacant, 301–18.

Pujol, M. and Turell, M.T. (1995) El préstamo en una comunidad inter-étnica: una primera elaboración teórica. *Actas del X Congreso Nacional de Lingüística Aplicada.* Valladolid: Universidad de Valladolid, 661–70.

Reixach, M. (1985) *Coneixement i Ús de la Llengua Catalana a la Província de Barcelona.* Barcelona: Departament de Cultura de la Generalitat de Catalunya.

Reixach, M. (1990) *Difusió Social del Coneixement de la Llengua Catalana.* Barcelona: Departament de Cultura de la Generalitat de Catalunya.

Reixach *et al.* (1997) *El Coneixement del Català.* Barcelona: Departament de Cultura de la Generalitat de Catalunya, .

Ros, M. (1982) Percepción y evaluación social de los hablantes de cinco variedades lingüísticas. In L. Ninyoles (ed.) *Estructura Social al País Valencià* (pp. 679–97). València: Diputació de València.

Sbert, M. and Vives, M. (1994) Las lenguas en el sistema educativo de las 'Illes Balears'. In M. Siguán (ed.) *Las Lenguas en la Escuela* (pp. 109–32). Barcelona: ICE/Horsori.

Sbert, M. and Vives, M. (1995) El programa d'immersió a les Illes Balears. In J.M. Artigal (ed.) *Els Programes d'Immersió als Territoris de Llengua Catalana* (pp. 71–83). Barcelona: Fundació Jaume Bofill.

Torró, T. and Brotons, V. (1995) El programa d'immersió al País Valencià. In J.M. Artigal (ed.) *Els Programes d'Immersió als Territoris de Llengua Catalana* (pp. 49–70). Barcelona: Fundació Jaume Bofill.

Turell, M.T. (1994) Codeswitching as communicative device. In *Actas del XVI Congreso de la Asociación Española de Estudios Norteamericanos.* Valladolid, 59–78

Turell, M.T. (1995) L'alternança de llengües en una comunitat inter-ètnica. In M.T. Turell (ed.) *La Sociolingüística de la Variació* (pp. 259–93). Barcelona: PPU.

Turell, M.T. and Forcadell, M. (1997) *Language Interaction Patterns in Catalan-Spanish Discourse.* Paper presented at the International Symposium on Bilingualism, Newcastle.

Universitat de les Illes Balears i Consell Insular de Mallorca (1986) *Enquesta Sociolingüística a la Població de Mallorca.* Mallorca.

Veny, J. (1978) *Els Parlars.* Barcelona: Dopesa.

Vernet, J. (1992) *Normalització del Català i Accés a la Funció Pública.* Barcelona: Fundació Jaume Callís.

Vial, S. (1994) *Barcelona: Enquesta sobre l'Ús del Català a l'Ensenyament Primari. Curs 1989–90.* Unpublished manuscript, Departament d'Ensenyament de la Generalitat de Catalunya.

Chapter 3

The Basque-speaking Communities

JASONE CENOZ and JOSU PERALES

Heuskara, ialgui adi plaçara **(Etxepare, 1545)**
Basque, come out and make yourself heard

The Basque Country has an area of $20,742\,km^2$ and a population of approximately three million. It comprises seven provinces, three North of the Pyrenees (Iparralde) and four in the South (Hegoalde). The Northern provinces are Lapurdi, Nafarroa Beherea and Zuberoa and belong to the Pyrenees Atlantiques community in France. The Southern Basque Country, which belongs to the Spanish state, comprises 92% of the population in the Basque Country. The Southern provinces include the three provinces in the Basque Autonomous Community (Araba, Bizkaia, Gipuzkoa) and Nafarroa (Figure 3.1).

Euskara (Basque) is a unique language in Western Europe for being non Indo-European. Although there have been attempts to relate Basque to Iberian and the Caucasian languages (Bouda, 1960; Lafon, 1933, 1951; Román del Cerro, 1993; Schuchardt, 1907), the hypotheses concerning the origin of the Basque language are still inconclusive (Charlat, 1980; Michelena, 1985, 1988). Basque is a highly inflected language with 16 morphological cases and typologically, it has been defined as ergative and agglutinative (Saltarelli, 1988).

The Basque language has miraculously survived surrounded by powerful Romance languages and these languages are nowadays used in territories where Basque was previously spoken (Echenique, 1984; Tovar, 1981). Latin and Romance languages not only replaced Basque in some areas but exerted some influence on Basque phonology and morphology. The close association between Basque and Romance dialects is also proved by the Basque words used nowadays in Spanish-speaking areas: South of Nafarroa and Rioja.

Even though Basque was used in most areas of the Euskal Herria (Basque Country), Basque has never been widely used at the institutional level and most official documents were written in Romance languages. The disappearance of Basque from important areas of the Basque Country is a relatively recent phenomenon. The Basque language suffered an important retreat in Araba and Nafarroa in the 18th and 19th centuries (Michelena, 1988; Hualde *et al.*, 1995). The use of Basque also decreased during the 20th century and particularly during Franco's dictatorship (1939–75).

Figure 3.1 The Basque Country (own source)

The Basque language not only suffered at the institutional and educational levels but also in the private domain. Several institutions founded at the beginning of the century such as _Eusko Ikaskuntza_ (Society of Basque Studies, 1918), _RIEV_ (International Journal of Basque Studies, 1907) and _Euskaltzaindia_ (Academy of the Basque Language, 1919) disappeared or interrupted their work after the Civil War (1936–39), during the dictatorship. More than 150,000 Basques were exiled and went to France, North America and South America. The political and social changes that have taken place in Spain in the last decades of the 20th century have favoured attempts to maintain and revive the Basque language.

The limited use of Basque at the institutional level, the insufficient number of written texts and the spread of the Basque Country North and South of the Pyrenees can explain the existence of six Basque dialects; three in the Northern Basque Country (Lapurtera, Nafarrera Beherea, Zuberera) and three South of the Pyrenees (Bizkaiera, Gipuzkera, Nafarrera). The Academy of the Basque Language (_Euskaltzaindia_) has played a crucial role in the standardisation of the Basque language at the oral and written levels. Even though dialectal differences are present, Euskara Batua (unified Basque) is the variety based on the central dialects of Basque which is widely accepted in the Basque Country. Nowadays, about 80% of the books published in Basque are published in 'Batua'. 'Batua' is also the variety used for education and official documents. There is an increasing number of grammars and dictionaries in Basque but the standardisation of the Basque language is still an open process.

Basque has a weak written tradition and Basque culture has given a high priority to the oral language. Apart from Basque words in Roman inscriptions and Middle Age documents, the first Basque text, a book of poems by the Northern Basque writer Etxepare, dates from the 16th century (1545). Verbal abilities have always been highly valued at the oral level in '*bertsolaritza*' (extemporaneous oral poetry) and up to the introduction of Basque in education, many Basques were illiterate in Basque but literate in either French or Spanish.

The Basque Language Today

Nowadays, Basque is a minority language within its own territory as a result of its lack of official status in the past and its long-lasting contact with Spanish and French. This contact has increased in the last decades as the result of industrialisation, communications and mass media and the important number of Spanish-speaking immigrants who came to the Basque Country in the 1950s, 1960s and 1970s. The new legislation gives Basque a co-official status with Spanish in the Basque Autonomous Community (BAC) and in the North of Nafarroa. When the census data of the last 10 years are compared it can be observed that the proportion of people who are proficient in Basque has increased in the three BAC provinces but remains the same in Nafarroa (Figure 3.2).

In 1991 there are 95,000 bilinguals more in the BAC than in 1981, mainly because of the educational system (Garmendia, 1994). Nowadays, almost 40% of the children between 5 and 14 living in the BAC are

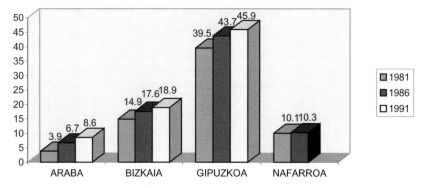

Figure 3.2 Basque speakers in the BAC and Nafarroa
Sources: EUSTAT, 1994, 1995; Government of Nafarroa, 1995

bilingual. Although these data are optimistic for the Basque language, Spanish is the dominant language and Basque-speaking people can only use Basque in their everyday life in sociolinguistically Basque areas.

A recent study carried out by the Basque Government's Secretariat for Language Policy (Aizpurua, 1995) with the collaboration of the Government of Nafarroa and the Regional Council of Aquitaine, included interviews on language proficiency and language use with 5017 subjects who were over 16 and lived in all the Basque provinces. According to this study, 21% of the population is bilingual (Basque-Spanish or Basque-French), and 8% passive bilingual. Monolinguals in Basque are only 1% of the population and monolinguals in either French or Spanish are 70% of the population. Therefore, except for a small proportion of the population, speaking Basque equals being bilingual in Basque and a Romance language.

The Distribution and Use of the Basque Language

Basque-speaking people are not distributed evenly throughout the Basque Country. The data in Table 3.1 indicate that the proportion of Bascophones is much higher in Gipuzkoa than in the other BAC provinces or Nafarroa.

According to recent data, there is also a considerable proportion of Basque-speaking population in the Northern Basque Country (34.16%). Most Basque speakers are found in the provinces of Gipuzkoa, Nafarroa Beherea and Zuberoa, where the number of Bascophones is higher in rural and isolated areas. When towns and cities began to develop in the Southern Basque Country as the result of industrialisation, Spanish-speaking newcomers did not learn Basque and Spanish became the main language of communication. Nowadays, San Sebastian (Gipuzkoa) is the only capital city with more than 25% of Bascophones. The use of Basque in the BAC is more common in villages and towns of less than 10,000 inhabitants. In Spanish-speaking areas (Araba, South of Nafarroa) the number of Bascophones, mainly speakers of Basque as a second language, is higher in bigger towns such as Vitoria-Gasteiz or Pamplona-Iruñea.

Table 3.1 Linguistic competence in the BAC and Nafarroa

	Competent Basque	*Passive bilinguals*	*Spanish only*
BAC	26.3	19.8	53.9
Araba	8.6	20.0	71.4
Bizkaia	18.9	20.5	60.5
Gipuzkoa	45.9	18.6	35.5
NAFARROA	10.3	6.1	83.6

Source: EUSTAT, 1994; Government of Nafarroa, 1994

The BAC census data reveal that the age groups with a higher proportion of Bascophones are the following: 5–9 (40.70%); 10–14 (37.32%); >75 (31.95%) and 70–74 (30.80%). The lowest proportions of Bascophones correspond to subjects aged between 35 and 55 (*Euskara* 81–91, 1994). The census data also indicate that there are no significant differences in the knowledge of Basque in the BAC when male and female subjects are compared (*Euskal Urtekari Estatistikoa*, 1995).

Several factors have been identified as predictors of the use of Basque (Aizpurua, 1995). The most important factor affecting the use of Basque is the number of Bascophones in the subject's social networks. As in most cases speaking Basque equals being bilingual, it is necessary for everybody or almost everybody in the subject's social networks to know and use Basque if this language is going to be used for communication. According to Aizpurua's study, when both parents know Basque, 81% of them use it at home and 8% use Basque and Spanish. When the mother knows Basque and the father is monolingual in Spanish, Basque is the preferred language of the household in 20% of the cases and Basque and Spanish in 18%. When the father speaks Basque and the mother only Spanish, Basque is used in 9% of the households and Basque and Spanish in 11% of them.

The second factor affecting the use of Basque is also related to linguistic proficiency and it is the relative ease that the subject has to use Basque and Spanish: 65% of the bilinguals find it easier or at least not more difficult to speak Basque than Spanish but 35% of the bilinguals find it easier to speak Spanish, which in most cases is their first language.

The third factor affecting the use of Basque is the number of Bascophones in the sociolinguistic area where the subject lives. Other factors which are also influential are the attitudes towards Basque, the use of Basque in the mass media (television and radio) and age.

Bascophones tend to use Basque within the family but they frequently use Spanish in more formal settings (Aizpurua, 1995). The use of Basque in different situations by bilinguals (Basque-Spanish; Basque-French) is shown in Table 3.2.

The percentages in Table 3.2 indicate that Basque is the main language of communication for Bascophones at the market and with the priest. Bascophones also use Basque more often with children than with other members of the family and they tend to use Basque less often when shopping or working. Most bilinguals (77%) listen to the radio in Basque and 82% of them watch television in Basque.

Another recent study on the Basque language (Iñigo, 1994) has measured the use of Basque in the street all over the Basque Country. The study was conducted in towns with more than 5000 inhabitants, that is, towns which concentrate 81.88% of the population. The methodology used was observational and the researchers spent six hours in each town on three different sessions, observed 275,335 people (9.57% of the total population) and recorded the language used in the street, bars and shops.

Table 3.2 Use of Basque by bilinguals

– at the market	76%
– with the priest	71%
– with their children	61%
– with their children's teachers	60%
– with their mother	59%
– with their grandparents	58%
– with their brothers & sisters	58%
– with their father	57%
– at home, at lunch or dinner	53%
– with husband or wife	51%
– in the town hall	48%
– going out with friends	44%
– at the bank	44%
– shopping	43%
– with their colleagues	37%

Source: Aizpurua, 1995.

The general results of this research study conducted in 1993 are given in Table 3.3. According to this study, there has been an important increase in the use of Basque as compared to previous data and all the age groups experienced this change, particularly young people and children.

With the exception of a few months during the Spanish Civil War (1936–39) the Basque language has never had an official or co-official status until 1979. The Statute of Autonomy gives Basque a co-official status in the

Table 3.3 Use of Basque in towns with a population over 5000

	Use 1993 *(%)*	*Increase from 1989* *(%)*
BAC Araba	2.90	+25.51
Bizkaia	9.01	+15.52
Gipuzkoa	25.09	+15.52
Nafarroa	5.73	+44.48
Southern Basque Country (Spain)	11.90	+17.53
Northern Basque Country (France)	4.92	+26.55

Source: Iñigo, 1994

BAC and all citizens in this community have the right to use Basque. The Spanish Constitution (1978) declared Spanish the nation-wide official language and guaranteed the rights of Spanish speakers to use their language. The *Euskararen Erabilpena Arauzkotzeko Oinarrizko Legea* (1982) (Basic Law on the Standardisation of the Basque language) entrusted the public authorities in the BAC to strengthen the use of Basque and the standardisation of its written form as well as the acquisition of new functions normally discharged by Spanish.

Nafarroa is a historically Basque community which was granted its own Statute of Autonomy (1982). The *Euskarari Buruzko Foru Legea* (Foral Law of the Basque language) issued in Nafarroa in 1986 only guarantees the co-official status of Basque in the northern part of Nafarroa. The lack of institutional support for Basque in the Northern Basque Country is affecting its maintenance and revival North of the Pyrenees.

The co-official status of Basque in the BAC makes necessary to incorporate Basque into the public domain in fields in which Basque has not been normally used, such as the administration and education. The Basque Government has made a great effort to teach Basque to civil servants and Basque teachers in order to safeguard the citizens' right to use Basque and to be educated in Basque. According to the Basque Civil Service Law (1989), civil servants need to achieve a specific level of proficiency according to the characteristics of their job and the sociolinguistic area in which they work. Table 3.4 presents a brief description of the four different levels of proficiency 'profiles') (Eusko Jaurlaritza, 1990).

Apart from the four 'profiles' there is profile 5 for specialists in the Basque language and there are also general Certificates of Proficiency (EGA, Official Language School certificate), which are sometimes necessary in order to obtain positions and promotions in those jobs in which the knowledge of Basque is a requirement.

In order to achieve the different profiles, Basque civil servants are given free language classes and leaves of absence for up to a year and a half.

Table 3.4 Linguistic profiles for civil servants

PROFILE 1	Be able to get the general meaning of a written or oral text. Be able to take part in very simple conversations.
PROFILE 2	Be able to get and provide information. Be able to take part in meetings conducted in Basque.
PROFILE 3	Be able to write different types of texts. Be able to use linguistic forms correctly both in oral and written language.
PROFILE 4	Be able to understand and produce technical texts. Oral and written fluency similar to that of those who have completed university studies in Basque.

Almost 26,000 Basque civil servants have been given different deadlines to achieve the linguistic profile necessary for their jobs. Many private companies have also offered Basque courses for their employees although the private sector seems to be more reluctant to invest in linguistic development.

The presence of Basque in the mass media is overshadowed by the dominant role of Spanish. There is only one newspaper in Basque (*Egunkaria*) although several others devote a few pages a week to articles in Basque. There are some magazines and an increasing number of professionally specialised journals written in Basque but with a small circulation.

There are several all-Basque radio stations (one supported by the Government) and others with programmes in Basque. The Basque Government (BAC) finances two television channels, one in Basque and one in Spanish. The Basque television channel is getting an increasing audience including people who are not very proficient in Basque. About 1000 books are published in Basque every year and most of them, approximately 85%, are either literature books or textbooks. In the last years, the number of books in two areas, children's books and translations of books from other languages, has experimented an important increase. Most books (75%) are published by commercial publishing houses and the rest by institutions. The number of books published in Basque in 1993 was 1193. This figure (Torrealdai, 1994) is slightly higher than the one corresponding to books in Galician (1058) but much lower than the one for Catalan (5905) or Spanish in Spain (41,206).

The Use of Basque in Education

Bilingual education is not a recent phenomenon in the Basque Country. Some schools adopted a bilingual and trilingual system by the end of the 19th century and Basque, Spanish and French were used as the languages of instruction. Basque was banned from education during Franco's dictatorship but some Basque schools (*ikastolak*) were re-opened in the 1960s as private schools by groups of enthusiastic parents and teachers. These schools were not officially recognised at first but attracted a large number of students and were finally accepted by the end of the Franco regime.

The new political situation in the Southern Basque Country allowed for a more favourable legislation and by the time the *Euskararen Erabilpena Arauzkotzeko Oinarrizko Legea* (1982) (Basic Law on the Standardisation of the Basque language) was passed, approximately 15% of the students in the BAC attended Basque-medium schools. In 1982, Basque and Spanish became compulsory subjects in all schools in the BAC and three models of language schooling were established: models A, B and D (there is no letter 'C' in Basque).

Model A. This model is aimed at native speakers of Spanish who choose to be instructed in Spanish. Basque is taught as a second language (2 to 4 hours a week).

Model B. This model is aimed at native speakers of Spanish who wish to be bilingual in Basque and Spanish. Both Basque and Spanish are used as languages of instruction for approximately 50% of the school time although there is considerable variation from school to school. This model is similar to Canadian models of partial immersion, in which French and English are the languages of instruction (Genesee, 1987).

Model D. Basque is the language of instruction in this model and Spanish is taught as a subject (2 to 4 hours a week). This model was originally created as a language maintenance model for native speakers of Basque but also includes a large number of children with Spanish as their first language. So, model D can be regarded at the same time as a total immersion programme for majority language students and as a first language maintenance programme for Basque speakers.

Parents can choose the model they want for their children and the different models are available in the public and private sectors. These options are reduced in some areas in which the three models are not present if there are not enough applications for a particular model. The evolution of the models in the BAC since the *Euskararen Erabilpena Arauzkotzeko Oinarrizko Legea* (1982) (Basic Law on the Standardisation of the Basque language) was issued can be seen in Figure 3.3.

The data on Figure 3.3 indicate that instruction in Spanish has experimented a very important decline while the use of Basque as the medium of instruction is attracting an increasing number of students. Model A includes half as many students as in 1982 (75% vs. 34%) and the models which use Basque as the language of instruction show a great increase, from 25% in 1982 to 65% in 1994–95. This trend is the same in all three

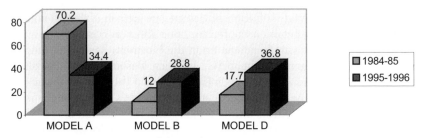

Figure 3.3 Linguistic models in the BAC
Source: Department of Education, Basque Government, 1996

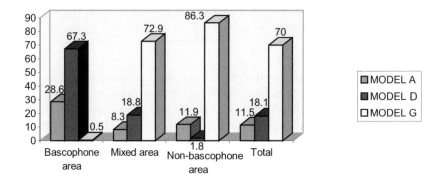

Figure 3.4 Educational models in Nafarroa 1994–95
Source: Government of Nafarroa, 1995

provinces of the BAC but the presence of Basque in Gipuzkoa is more significant and model A has almost disappeared from this territory.

According to the *Euskarari Buruzko Foru Legea* (1986) (Foral Law of the Basque language) three linguistic areas are distinguished in Nafarroa: the Bascophone area in the North, the non-Bascophone area in the South and the mixed area which includes the central area of Nafarroa and its capital city. The Foral Decree 159/1988 (1988) establishes that Basque is only compulsory in the Bascophone area. Therefore, apart from the three models (A, B and D) Nafarroa also has model G with no Basque at all in the mixed and non-Bascophone areas. Model B only exists in the Basco-phone area and it is chosen by less than 4% of the population in that area. The percentages corresponding to the other three models in the three areas are given in Figure 3.4.

The data in Figure 3.4 indicate that there are important differences between the three areas in Nafarroa. In the Bascophone area 67.33% of the students have Basque as the language of instruction (Model D) but only 18.8% of the students in the mixed area and 1.8% of the students in the non-Bascophone area are enrolled in model D. Most students in the mixed area (72.9%) and non-Bascophone area are in Model G with no Basque at all but this model is almost non-existent in the Bascophone area. These data reflect the uneven distribution of Basque speakers in Nafarroa and the important differences between the Bascophone and non-Bascophone areas.

The situation of Basque in education in the Northern Basque Country is weaker than in Nafarroa or the BAC. The first Basque school ('*ikastola*') was open in 1969 and Basque was introduced into the public educational system in 1983. Nowadays, there are four models which are similar (though not identical) to the A, B, D and G models in Nafarroa. However, only a small proportion of the population has access to the models in which Basque is a subject or the medium of instruction (Jauréguiberry, 1993). The use of Basque in education in the Northern Basque Country

Table 3.5 Bilingual education in the Northern Basque Country

	Kindergarten (%)	*Primary (%)*
French only	80.0	85.5
3 hours of Basque	5.1	6.5
50 in Basque	10.2	4.9
Basque in Kindergarten Some French in Primary	4.7	3.1

Source: Jaureguiberry, 1993

has increased in the last years but most students only use French as the medium of instruction (Table 3.5).

Several evaluations of the Basque bilingual programmes have been carried out in the last years and almost 20,000 students have taken part in these evaluations (Gabina *et al.*, 1986; Sierra & Olaziregi, 1989, 1991, and others). The evaluations have focused on several areas: proficiency in Basque and Spanish, academic development and foreign language.

Proficiency in Basque

The results of the evaluations indicate significant differences in Basque proficiency when the three models are compared (Gabina *et al.*, 1986; Sierra & Olaziregi, 1989, 1991). Students in model D are more proficient in Basque than students in model B and these are more proficient than students in model A. Therefore, the time devoted to Basque at school is crucial to develop proficiency in Basque although proficiency is also dependent on the use of Basque in the subjects' social networks.

Proficiency in Spanish (Southern Basque Country)

The evaluation of proficiency in Spanish (Gabina *et al.*, 1986; Sierra & Olaziregi, 1989, 1991) indicates that there are no significant differences among the models. Even model D students, who only study Spanish for 2–4 hours a week and are in many cases native speakers of Basque, achieve a very high level of proficiency in Spanish. Therefore, in the case of the majority language, the exposure to Spanish outside the school seems to compensate for the few hours devoted to this language at school.

Proficiency in French (Northern Basque Country)

The results of the French national tests in the Northern Basque Country indicate that students in bilingual programmes achieve a higher level of proficiency in French than students in regular programmes (Jauréguiberry, 1993).

Academic development

Although there is a need for more evaluations of academic development, the evaluations of mathematics and social sciences conducted so far indicate that there are no significant differences in academic development between students of the different models (Aierbe *et al.*, 1974, 1989). The national tests conducted in the Northern Basque Country also indicate that students in bilingual programmes obtain better results in mathematics than students in regular programmes (Jauréguiberry, 1993).

Foreign language

Evaluations of English language proficiency (Valencia & Cenoz, 1992; Cenoz & Valencia, 1994) show that students who have Basque as the medium of instruction (model D) present significantly higher grades in several English language measures than students instructed in Spanish (model A). These results corroborate other research findings supporting the positive influence of bilingualism on third language acquisition (Ringbom, 1985; Thomas, 1988).

The presence of Basque at the university level is not as important as in primary and secondary education but some advances have been made in the last years. The largest university is the *Euskal Herriko Unibertsitatea* (University of the Basque Country) with campuses in Araba, Bizkaia and Gipuzkoa. In 1994–95 this university had 56,845 students and 86.85% (49,369) studied in Spanish and only 13.15% (7476) in Basque. Although there is still a long way to go, a large number of textbooks and academic nomenclatures have already been published in Basque in order to enable most university courses to be taught both in Basque and Spanish. The presence of Basque in other public and private institutions (*Deustuko Unibertsitatea*, University of Nafarroa, *Nafarroako Unibertsitate Publikoa*) is weaker.

Another educational area that is worth mentioning is the teaching of Basque to adults. Adult schools (*'euskaltegiak'*) are public and private institutions created with the purpose of teaching Basque to adults (*'euskalduntzea'*) and teaching literacy to adults who are literate in Spanish but not in Basque (*'alfabetatzea'*). A Basque Government Agency, HABE (The Adult Institute for developing literacy and proficiency in Basque) was approved by the Basque Parliament in 1983. HABE guides and co-ordinates adult Basque schools in the BAC and offers them pedagogic assistance. HABE also publishes teaching materials, teachers' guides, a journal in Applied Linguistics (*Zutabe/Hizpide*) and a wide variety of audio-visual materials to learn Basque as a second language. In 1994 there were 164 *'euskaltegiak'* (Basque schools) in the BAC and 43,300 adults, including civil servants and teachers, were learning Basque. Most *'euskaltegiak'* receive support from HABE and some of them are public and others private.

There are also public and private 'euskaltegiak' in Nafarroa but only private ones in Iparralde. Private 'euskaltegiak' tend to belong to different associations such as AEK with schools all over the Basque Country.

Bilingual education in the Basque Country involves an enormous effort on the part of the Government, schools and teachers in the fields of teacher development, both methodological and linguistic. Five years before the *Euskararen Erabilpena Arauzkotzeko Oinarrizko Legea* (1982) (Basic Law on the Standardisation of the Basque language) was passed, 95% of all public school teachers could not speak Basque at all and the remaining 5% could speak the language but in most cases did not know its written conventions. The Basque Government offers courses during after-work hours and also gives leaves of absence for those teachers who have reached an inter-mediate level of competence in order to allow them to study Basque on a full-time basis. The teachers who complete these courses are required to take examinations so as to certify that they have attained a sufficient level of proficiency to teach in Basque. Nowadays over 50% of the teachers are qualified to teach in Basque (Zalbide, 1994).

As it has already been described, children study the Basque language at school and adults at 'euskaltegiak'. The teaching methods used at schools include a content based approach in the case of models B and D, and Basque is used as the language of instruction of all or some school sub-jects. The Basque language is also a subject in the curriculum and children in models B and D devote their Basque language classes to the study of Basque grammar and Basque literature. Basque is just a school subject in model A and it is studied as a second language following traditional approaches and structural syllabuses. In 'euskaltegiak', adults take intensive courses which range from 2 to 5 hours a day. The classes are usually smaller (about 12 students) and they follow a structural-functional syllabus which devotes plenty of time to oral communication.

Both adults and children have the opportunity to attend summer courses to improve their Basque. Adult courses are usually 2 or 3 weeks long and the students share a house in a Basque-speaking village. They have 5 or 6 hours of instruction a day and use Basque as the language of com-munication. There is also the possibility for adults to practice their Basque while living with families in Basque speaking villages without taking language courses. Children also have some summer camps and day courses in which they use Basque for leisure activities without formal tuition. Apart from school and summer classes, students also find the Basque television and Basque radio stations very useful to improve their abilities.

Research studies conducted on attitudes and motivation towards learning Basque have proved that there are important differences among the students (Madariaga, 1994; Perales, 1989). Madariaga (1994) con-ducted a study comparing the attitudes of 212 children who had either Basque or Spanish as the language of instruction. He observed that Spanish-speaking children instructed in Spanish presented less positive attitudes towards the Basque language than children instructed in Basque. Perales (1989) conducted a research study on the acquisition of Basque including 434 adult learners from 12 different 'adult schools' (*euskaltegiak*) in the province of Gipuzkoa. His results indicate that adult students of Basque whose parents had been born in the Basque country and/or spoke Basque presented better attitudes towards the Basque community and a more integrative orientation towards learning Basque than adults from non-Basque backgrounds.

The learning of Basque is quite a difficult and long process. One of the main problems is related to linguistic distance due to the fact that Basque, unlike the other languages spoken in Spain, is a non-Indoeropean language. Basque morphology and syntax are complex and it is quite common for non-native speakers of Basque to present grammar mistakes after long years of study or even after having Basque as the language of instruction at school. In a recent study on the oral production of Basque it was found that learners present more pauses when they have to produce verb forms, complex inflections or subordinate clauses (Perales & Cenoz, 1996). Basque is an inflectional language with 15 different inflections including ergative, the ending that is added to the subject of transitive verbs. Verb morphology is particularly complex because the direct and indirect object pronouns are part of the verb forms and also because different auxiliaries are used with transitive and intransitive verbs. Word order is also completely different from Spanish and difficult to be learned.

Another serious problem that Basque learners have to face is the fact that almost all speakers of Basque are bilingual in Basque and either Spanish or French. Therefore, codeswitching into a Romance language is a very common behaviour when communicative problems arise.

Speaking Basque: Some Examples of Codeswitching and Borrowings

A small-scale study was conducted so as to give some examples of the Basque language as used by native and non-native speakers. The specific objectives of this study were the following: (1) to present real data from spontaneous conversations and interviews in Basque; (2) to examine some aspects of the use of Basque as related to context; (3) to analyse the differences between the use of Basque by native and non-native speakers.

A sample of 13 subjects coming from the provinces of Bizkaia and Gipuzkoa was selected for this study. Seven of the subjects were native speakers of Basque while the rest were non-native speakers. Non-native speakers of Basque were included in order to represent the large proportion of non-native speakers among proficient speakers of Basque and also the trend to learn Basque among native speakers of Spanish. The corpus includes oral interviews and spontaneous conversations recorded in several settings: university students at coffee breaks, family conversations at home and oral interviews between teachers and advanced students.

The transcription and analysis of the conversations reveal frequent examples of some phenomena, such as codeswitching and borrowings, which are characteristic of bilingual communities. Although there is some discussion about the definition of these phenomena (Grosjean, 1982; Poplack, 1980; Myers-Scotton, 1990) we consider examples of code-switching those in which the words or expressions uttered in Spanish are not integrated into Basque, that is, when they do not present Basque inflections or Basque pronunciation.

Some examples of codeswitching in our data are illustrated in (1), (2), (3), (4), (5) and (6):

(1) *(NNS) eta orduan e* **relaciones públicas**, *ikasi nuen eta gero ba* (and then I studied **public relations** and later ...)
(2) *(NNS) neretzat ba* **derecho civil**, *da hori hori esaten, du, jendeak* (for me it is **civil law**, that that's what people say)
(3) *(NS) ni esaten ari naiz eta orain zuri gauza berdina esatera nijoa*: **hacer lo menos posible** (I say this and now I tell you the same thing: **do as little as possible**)
(4) *(NNS) arratsaldean ikasten dut e beste kurtso bat deitzen da* **curso de adaptación pedagógica** (I take another course in the afternoon the course is called **pedagogic orientation course**)
(5) *(NS) Gero* **poner a ciento cincuenta y seis** *eta bete folioa* (then **you fix it at a hundred and fifty six** and you fill in the sheets)
(6) *(NS) Bai* **pero** *nahiz eta* ... (yes **but** but ...)

These examples indicate that codeswitching can involve different parts of speech: numerals (5), connectors (6), noun phrases (1), (2), (4) or clauses (3). According to the context, there seem to be different reasons for code-switching. Non-native speakers (1), (2), (4) seem to have problems to find appropriate expressions in Basque and include nominal clauses in Spanish. The different structure of Basque phrases and the dominant presence of Spanish makes some expressions difficult to use in Basque. An interest-ing example was found when the expression 'high jump' was used in Spanish both by a native and a non-native speaker of Basque. The Spanish expression 'salto de altura' is more common than the Basque express-ion 'altuera-jauzia' because of the dominant use of Spanish in the mass media. Basque uses a different structure which is not a word-by-word translation from Spanish and therefore, Basque speakers face more problems when using this type of expression than Catalan speakers who have the same structure in Catalan ('salt d'alçada') and only need a word-by-word translation.

In other cases, when utterances were produced by native speakers (5), codeswitching is the result of common use. Many native speakers who learned mathematics in Spanish and use Spanish when they go to the bank or a tax office use numerals in Spanish when they speak Basque. Native speakers also use Spanish for pragmatic purposes when they feel that an expression in Spanish is more appropriate to convey meaning. For example *'hacer lo menos posible'* (do as little as possible) (3) can be recognised as a fixed expression that would explain its use in Spanish. Nonnative speakers are more aware of codeswitching and try to use it as a communicative strategy when they have linguistic difficulties rather than for pragmatic purposes (Turell, 1994, 1995).

The context in which the conversation takes place and the participants also play and important role in codeswitching. For example, a native speaker of Basque switches into Spanish when explaining some computer instructions and looking at a manual written in Spanish:

zuk disketea sartzen duzu eta idazten duzu **espacio** A bi puntu **espacio** Atik Ara eta orduan galdetzen dizu **inserte disco** (you insert the disc and you write a: **space** a: from a to a and then it asks you to **insert the diskette**).

Borrowings from Romance languages are very common in Basque as Basque has been surrounded by Spanish and French for centuries. Even though it is sometimes difficult to distinguish between borrowings and codeswitching we consider borrowings those words of Spanish origin which are integrated phonologically and morphologically into Basque. Examples of borrowing are illustrated in (7), (8), (9), (10), (11) and (12):

(7)   *(NS)* **Letra**-*tartea ere haunditu behar da eta* **margenak** *ere bai.* (The **spaces** and the **margins** should be bigger)

(8)   *(NNS) etortzen da polizia eta* **mirón bat** *ari zen begiratzen* (the police arrives and there was a **voyeur** watching)

(9)   *(NNS) lehenengo aldiz ikusi nuen* **kuriositateagatik** (the first time I saw it **out of curiosity**)

(10)   *(NS)* **Azidenteak** *eta ikusten dira.* (You can also see **accidents**)

(11)   *(NNS) gerta daiteke ba* **errekurtso** *egiten duenak ba arrazoi edukitzea* (it can happen that the person who makes an **appeal** can be right)

(12)   *(NNS) nik normalean egiten ditut* **kurak** *edo horiek* (I usually give first **aid** or that)

The examples indicate that both native and non-native speakers use borrowings. Some of these borrowings are widespread and accepted by the community while others can be examples of nonce borrowings coinaged by individual speakers (Sankoff *et al.* 1990). Sentences (7) and (11) include borrowings which are accepted in Basque while sentences (8) and (12) include nonce borrowings, that is, borrowings which differ *'from established loanwords only quantitatively -in frequency of use, degree of acceptance, level of phonological integration, etc.'* (Poplack and Sankoff, 1988: 1179). It was observed that borrowings were produced both by native and non-native speakers while nonce borrowings were more common among non-native speakers. Borrowings are a common communication strategy in bilingual communities when the speaker knows that borrowing does not cause communication problems. The fact that non-native speakers use this strategy more often and produce more nonce borrowings could be interpreted as a way to compensate for their lower proficiency in Basque. Sentences (9) and (10) include interesting examples which are difficult to classify either as borrowings or nonce borrowings. The Basque language is still in a process of standardisation and the fact that the use of Basque has been restricted to the private domain for a long time makes it difficult to make a sharp distinction between those borrowings which are accepted by the community and those which are not accepted. It is very common to find words which are accepted in some areas and not in others or words which are included in some dictionaries but not in others. Words such as *'azidenteak'* in (10) and *'kuriositateagatik'* in (9) are frequently used by some Basque speakers but they are not included in most dictionaries and would not be accepted by some Basque academics.

Our findings prove some of the tendencies found in borrowing analysis as most borrowings correspond to nouns although we also found examples of adjectives ('fuerteak' = strong) and verbs ('preparatzen' = prepare). Even though borrowings came from Spanish we also found some borrowings from English such as 'reality show-ri buruz' (about the reality show). Borrowings seem to indicate that the Basque equivalent is not known or that it is not commonly used. The study of codeswitching and borrowings in spontaneous conversations and interviews reflects the situation of the Basque language and the relationship between Basque language use and context. Codeswitching and borrowings are common phenomena found when there is contact between different languages. They are resources that bilingual speakers have at their disposal when they face linguistic problems or when they want to enhance their meanings. Codeswitching and borrowings also reflect the relative status of the languages in contact and their use in different areas. Although this small-scale study presents obvious limitations it can serve to highlight the relationship between everyday use of a language and the historical and sociolinguistic context in which this language is used.

The Future of Basque

Even though there is a revival of the Basque language the future of Basque is still uncertain, particularly in Nafarroa and Iparralde. More speakers of Basque are needed in order to increase its use but the use of Basque among Bascophones also needs encouragement. The achievements of bilingual education in the BAC and North of Nafarroa are important but the revival and maintenance of a language cannot only depend on the school system. As Fishman points out:

The question that remains is whether the Basque competence that the schools of these types achieve can subsequently be maintained in out-of-school and in after-school life, to the point that the general environment too can ultimately be Basquized thereby and this Basquization intergenerationally transmitted rather than artificially engendered from without. (Fishman, 1991: 168–69).

As has been observed (Garmendia, 1994), the future of Basque will depend on the behaviour of the generation who now have Basque as the language of instruction and will be in better conditions for the transmission and use of the language. In sum, the future of the Basque language is not only in the hands of the Basque speech community but it also depends on monolingual speakers of Spanish and French and their wish to become bilingual members of the Basque speech community.

Acknowledgements

The authors wish to express their gratitude to the following institutions: Hizkuntza Politikarako Sailordetza (Basque Government), Euskara Zerbitzua (Goverment of Nafarroa) and Euskal Kultur Erakundea (Iparralde).

References

Aierbe, P., Etxezarreta, J. and Satrustegi, L.M. (1974) Ikastoletako aurren jakite mailaren azterketa konparatiboa. *Zeruko Argia* 603, 1.

Aierbe, P., Arregi, P., Etxeberria Balerdi, F. and Etxeberria Sagastume, F. (1989) Urretxu-Legazpi-Zumarraga Eskoletako Euskararen Egoera. *Kilometroak* 85.

Aizpurua, X. (1995) *Euskararen Jarraipena. La Continuidad del Euskera. La Continuité de la Langue Basque.* Vitoria-Gasteiz: Eusko Jaurlaritza.

Bouda, K. (1960) *Introducción a la Lingüística Caucásica.* Salamanca: Universidad de Salamanca.

Cenoz, J. and Valencia, J. (1994) Additive trilingualism: Evidence from the Basque Country. *Applied Psycholinguistics* 15, 157–209.

Charlat, R. (1980) *Presentación y Análisis de ciertas Correspondencias Vasco-caucásicas.* Bilbao: La Gran Enciclopedia Vasca.

Echenique, M.T. (1984) *Historia Lingüística Vasco-románica.* San Sebastián: Caja de Ahorros Provincial de Guipuzcoa.

Eusko Jaurlaritza (1990) *Euskararen Erabileraren Normalizazioa Herri-administrazioetan.* Gasteiz: Eusko Jaurlaritza.

Etxepare, B. (1545/1980) *Linguae Vasconum Primitiae.* Ed. Crítica de Patxi Altuna. Bilbao: Mensajero.

Euskal Urtekari Estatistikoa 94, (1995) Vitoria-Gasteiz: Eustat.

Euskara 81–91 (1994) Vitoria-Gasteiz: Eustat.

Fishman, J. (1991) *Reversing Language Shift.* Clevedon: Multilingual Matters.

Gabina, J.J., Gorostidi, R. and Iruretagoiena, E. (1986) *Influence of Factors on the Learning of Basque.* Vitoria-Gasteiz: Central Publications of the Basque Government.

Garmendia, M.K. (1994) *Eusko Jaurlaritzako hizkuntza politikarako idazkari nagusiaren agerraldia, berak eskatuta, Eusko legebiltzarreko iraskunde eta herrizaingo batzordearen aurrean.* Vitoria-Gasteiz: Eusko Jaurlaritza.

Genesee, F. (1987) *Learning through Two Languages*. Cambridge: Newbury.

Grosjean, F. (1982) *Life with Two Languages*. Cambridge: Harvard University Press.

Hualde, J.I., Lakarra, J.A. and Trask, R.L. (eds) (1995) *On the History of the Basque Language: Readings in Basque Historical Linguistics*. Amsterdam: John Benjamins.

Iñigo, J.J. (1994) Euskararen kale erabilpena Euskal Herrian: EKBren neurketaren emaitzak. *BAT* 13/14, 51–76.

Jaureguiberry, F. (1993) *Le Basque à l'Ecole Maternelle et Elémentaire*. Pau: Université de Pau et des Pays de l'Adour.

Lafon, R. (1933) Basques et langues kartvèles. *RIEV* 24, 150–7.

Lafon, R. (1951) Correspondences morphologiques entre le basque et les langues caucasiques. *Word* 7, 227–44.

Madariaga, J.M. (1994) Jarreren eragina hezkuntza elebidunean. In I. Idiazabal and A. Kaifer (eds) *Hezkuntzaren Eraginkortasuna eta Irakaskuntza Elebiduna* Euskal Herria (pp. 111–25). Vitoria-Gasteiz: IVAP-Eusko Jaurlaritza.

Michelena, L. (1985) *Lengua e Historia*. Madrid: Paraninfo.

Michelena, L. (1988) *Sobre Historia de la Lengua Vasca*. Donostia-San Sebastián: Seminario de Filología Vasca Julio de Urquijo.

Myers-Scotton, C. (1990) Codeswitching and borrowing: Interpersonal and macrolevel meaning. In R. Jacobson (ed.) *Codeswitching as a Worldwide Phenomenon* (pp. 85–110). New York: Lang.

Perales, J. (1989) Euskara-ikasleen motibazio eta jarrerak. *ZUTABE* 21, 9–50.

Perales, J. and Cenoz, J. (1996) Silence, communicative competence and communication strategies in second language acquisition. In G.M. Grabher and U. Jessner (eds) *Semantics of Silences in Linguistics and Literature* (pp. 67–87). Amsterdam: University of Amsterdam Press.

Poplack, S. (1980) Sometimes I'll start a sentence in English y termino en español: Toward a typology of code switching. *Linguistics* 18, 581–618.

Poplack, S. and Sankoff, D. (1988) Codeswitching. In U. Ammon, N. Dittmar and K.L. Mattheier (eds) *Sociolinguistics. Soziolinguistik. An International Handbook of the Science of Language and Society* (pp. 1174–80). Vol. 2. Berlin: De Gruyter.

Ringbom, H. (1985) *Foreign Language Learning and Bilingualism*. Turku: Abo Akademi.

Roman del Cerro, J.L. (1993) *El Origen Ibérico de la Lengua Vasca*. Alicante: Aguaclara.

Saltarelli, M. (1988) *Basque*. London: Routledge.

Sankoff, D., Poplack, S. and Vanniarajan, S. (1990) The case of the nonce loan in Tamil. *Language Variation and Change* 2, 71–101.

Schuchardt, H. (1907) *Die Iberische Deklination*. Vienna: Akademie der Wissenschaften.

Sierra, J. and Olaziregi, I. (1989) *E.I.F.E. 2: Influence of Factors on the Learning of Basque*. Vitoria-Gasteiz: Central Publications of the Basque Government.

Sierra, J. and Olaziregi, I. (1991) *E.I.F.E. 3: Influence of Factors on the Learning of Basque*. Vitoria-Gasteiz: Central Publications of the Basque Government.

Thomas, J. (1988) The role played by metalinguistic awareness in second and third language learning. *Journal of Multilingual and Multicultural Development* 9, 235–47.

Torrealdai, J.M. (1994) Euskal Liburugintza. *Jakin* 85, 65–77.

Tovar, A. (1981) Orígenes del euskara: parentescos, teorías diversas. In *Euskal Linguistika eta Literatura: Bide Berriak*. Bilbon, Deustuko Unibertsitatea, 7–25.

Turell, M.T. (1994) Codeswitching as communicative design. *Actas del XVI Congreso de AEDEAN* (pp. 59–78). Valladolid: Universidad de Valladolid.

Turell, M.T. (1995) L'alternança de llengües i el préstec en una comunitat inter-ètnica. In M.T. Turell (ed.) *La Sociolingüística de la Variació* (pp. 259–63). Barcelona: PPU.

Valencia, J. and Cenoz, J. (1992) The role of bilingualism in foreign language acquisition: Learning English in the Basque Country. *Journal of Multilingual and Multicultural Development* 13, 433–49.

Zalbide, M. (1994) Bilinguisme scolaire en Pays Basque. *6e Colloque Flarep*. Biarritz: Ikasbi/Flarep, 41–55.

Chapter 4
The Galician Speech Community

CARME HERMIDA

Galicia and the Galicians

In 1981, the writer Álvaro Cunqueiro wrote a text to accompany a book of photographs on Galicia by Raimon Campubrí. This is how the famous Mondoñedo-born author began his description:

> Galicia, Land's End, the westernmost tip of known land. Beyond these craggy rocks lies the Ocean, the Dark Waters, which ends in great chasms at the edge of which swim enormous whales, great hostile beasts. This is where Man's habitat ends, and every evening he can watch the sun die. When the Roman legionaries first set foot here and saw the sun sink into the Ocean they were filled, or so the Latin historian has it, with 'religious awe'. In the east, Galicia is a land of rocky mountains, long flat moorlands and wide valleys. Some small peaks stretch out as far as the sea which in many places on the coastline steals inland, shaping the beautiful estuaries which are so much a part of Galicia and which, for the most part, form deep river valleys. A hundred thousand rivers run through green Galicia and while beech trees grow and wolves run in the mountains to the east, camellias bloom and lemon trees and orange trees bear golden fruits on her western shores (...) The Galician winds blow in from the west, and the damp sea breeze forever caresses this ancient land. The Galician rock is the oldest in all of the Western World, and here where we find broom and gorse, that European *ulex* down with its golden flowers. Galicia has been inhabited since late Palaeolithic times by a people of uncertain origins, but the latter-day Galicians like to think that their protohistorical forefathers were Celts, preferring them to the other races mentioned by the historians, and conferring upon them a special place of honour among their ancestors: a wandering race which lived in the *fisterres* and western isles and which settled in Galicia with its kings, one of whom was the great lord, the Father Breogán, who appears in the national anthem composed by Pondal, and who put up a beacon on the high peninsula of A Coruña, that great lighthouse which lit up the seas all the way to green Eirin (...).

> Finally, this ancient Kingdom stretches from the mountains in the east to the ocean strands like a pregnant, silent woman. And although

there is snow in her mountains, her shoreline is filled with fruit-laden orange and lemon trees and camellia blossom. And in spite of the changing times, a resistant core still remains, feeding the collective and individual life of the nation. The Galician people are quite distinct from by their neighbours in Asturias and León and also from the Portuguese who were once part of the erstwhile Gallaecia. This is a people which lives off the land and the sea and who is still filled with dreams, a curiosity for all things secret and the conviction that things do not end in death. A rather fantastic people, but this very curiosity for the unseen is what makes them a rational people too (...) In his knowledge of the world and in life, a Galician will often switch from reality to fiction. (...)

Friendly winds blow in from the sea and morning mists form in the valleys, and there is always enough rain to slake the thirst of the land and for Galicia to don in its many shades of green. There is a Galician softness of living. Like Ulysses, after a long journey the Galician will always return to his homeland to relieve his strong pangs of '*saudade*' (homesickness). *Saudade* is a strange word which would seem to come from *solitude*, but also from *salutis* (health), and from *suavitatis* (softness). And these words would seem to sum up the perfection of the Galician soul. It is both a rich and a poor people, both wandering and attached to its land, imperialist in the service of other Emperors and a people that sings and loves life and its country much more than it would ever dare tell.[1]

This land situated in the extreme north-west of the Iberian Peninsular, bordered to the north by the Bay of Biscay, to the west by the Atlantic Ocean, to the south by the River Miño and the mountains which mark the diving line with Portugal and to the east with the Provinces of Zamora, León and Asturias, is populated today by some two and a half million inhabitants, to which should be added another million who live outside Galicia, those men and women who had to leave their country and roam the world in search of better living conditions than the ones available to them in Galicia.

The Galician Language: Geographic Spread and Characteristics

Galicia has a language of its own, Galician, which comes from the Latin spoken by the Roman soldiers who first arrived in 137 BC, led by Decimus Junius Brutus Calaicus, returning once again in 61 BC, led this time by Julius Caesar, and finally settling here in 19 BC.

The Galician language is not confined to the administrative limits of Galicia alone, spreading out to the east into the autonomous communities of Castilla-León and Asturias. In the Province of Zamora, Galician is

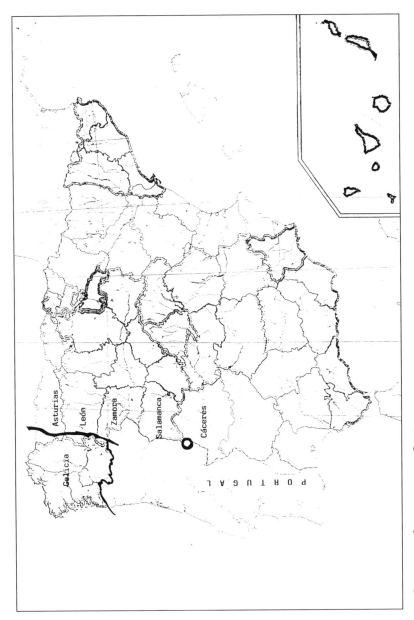

Map 4.1 Galician-speaking areas in Spain
Source: La España Política (Editorial Vicens Vives, 1988)

spoken in the area between Portela da Canda and Portela do Padornelo where we find the towns of Porto, As Pías, Lubián and Hermisende. In León the Galician-speaking area covers the part of the Bierzo situated between the River Cúa and the River Sil, while in Asturias, Galician is spoken in the whole of the area to the west of the River Navía, the western towns of Ibias in the south and in the area located between the River Navía and the River Frexulfe in the north. Its southernmost limits are not quite as clear-cut, however, owing to the fact that modern Galician and modern Portuguese both come from the same branch of languages which linguists refer to as 'Galego-Portuguese', although it should, by rights, only really be referred to as 'Galician' given that Galicia is where the decolonisation of Lusitania, once completely inhabited by Muslims, first began. Thus, the first people to go out to reconquer the Portuguese territory (old Lusitania) were also Galicians who took their language with them.

Linguistically speaking, Galicia has Asturian-Leonese speaking neighbours to the east and Portuguese-speaking neighbours to the south, but Galicia shares no borders with Castillian Spanish.[2] Be that as it may, in light of the fact that Spanish and Galician live side by side in the same territory and bearing in mind the fact that the languages best known to the international world will be Spanish and Portuguese, it was deemed useful to provide a schematic appendix covering some of the major differences between these three languages (see Appendix 1).

Internal Linguistic Variation

Despite the fact that according to Fernández Rei (1991[2]: 36), 'one cannot really talk about Galician dialects as such', this author has himself classified the various diatopical varieties into 3 linguistic blocs, 11 areas, 1 macro-subarea, 20 subareas and 26 micro-subareas. However, in spite of the fact that this variety is based on a combination of distinctive linguistic features which characterise each area, it should be said that, in the words of the same author; 'living Galician is particularly unified'.

The Galician linguistic blocs are determined by the isogloss based on the way the plural of nouns ending in -*n* is formed, i.e. the Western Bloc forms such plurals by adding an -*s* (e.g. *can, cans*), whilst the Central Bloc eliminates the final -*n* before adding an -*s* (e.g. *can, cas*) and the Eastern Bloc eliminates the final -*n* and adds the ending -is (e.g. *can, cais*). There are, however, other distinctive linguistic features which characterise each of these blocs.

As well as forming plurals of the *cans* type, the Western Bloc also has *gheada* (e.g. *amigho, ghato*), postnuclear *seseo*, that is, the use of -s where other varieties have another consonant (e.g. *lus, rapas*), changes in the quality of etymological stressed vowels (e.g. /ɛ/*la*, *h*/ɔ/*ra*, *t*/*e*/*mpo*, /*o*/*llo*), uses the plural ending -*an* (e.g. *irmán, mañán, chan, lan*) and uses the subject pronoun *ti* and the stressed theme vowel *e* when conjugating the preterite of regular second declension verbs in second person (e.g. *vendeches, colleches*). The best defined areas within this bloc are: Fisterra with prenuclear *seseo* (e.g. *sesta, maso*) and where no distinction is made between *te* and *che*, favouring the latter (e.g. *vinche na rúa*); Bergantiños, which uses *i* as the thematic vowel when conjugating the preterite of second declension verbs and third verbs in third person (e.g. *metiu, partiu*); and the macro-subarea of Verdugo-Miño which makes use of a demonstrative system strongly marked by the neutral (e.g. *este, ese, aquel; esta, esa, aquela; isto, iso, aquilo*) and the diphthong -*ui*- (e.g. *muito, cuiro, truita*).

The features which characterise the Central Bloc are the use of the *gheada* in the western part and its absence in the eastern part, the absence of *seseo*, the diphthong -*oi*- (e.g. *moito, noite, coiro*), plurals of the *cas* type, the -*ao* masculine ending (e.g. *irmao, chao*) and the feminine ending -*a* (e.g. *irmá, mañá, la*). The subject pronouns *ti* and *tu* are used in the west and east respectively, the stressed thematic vowel *i*- is used when conjugating the preterite of regular second declension verbs in second person (e.g. *vendiches, colliches*). The *Mindoniense* variety of Galician stands out particularly within this bloc, with the mode and tense marker /ε/ in the present subjunctive regardless of which declension a verb belongs to (e.g. *cant/ε/mos, coll/ε/mos, part/ε/mos*) and with verbal forms such as *seña, teña, sallo*, etc. *in lieu* of their standard equivalents *sexa, estea* and *saio* respectively. *Mindoniense* also uses some vocabulary different to that of other blocs. The *Lucurauriense* area is another particularly striking one with the subject pronoun *il* and a demonstrative system strongly marked by the use of masculine forms (e.g. *iste, ise, aquil; esta, esa, aquela; esto, eso, aquelo*).

The most salient features of the Eastern Bloc are the presence of the diphthong -*ua*- in words such as *cuando, cual, guardar, guardaña*, forms with -*ax*- (e.g. *caxa, baxo, faxa*), the ending -*in* instead of the standard -*iño* (e.g. *camín, padrín/camiño, padriño*), the use of the ending -*is* for nouns ending in -*n* (e.g. *can → cais, corazon → corazois*), the personal number marker -*n* for the first person of the preterite and future of first declension verbs (e.g. *cantein, cantarein*) as well as the person number marker ending -*is* for the fifth person (e.g. *cantais, cantabais*). The best defined areas within this bloc are the 'transfrontier' areas (i.e. areas not within Galicia proper), namely the Asturian area which maintains the Latin intervocalic -*l*- (e.g. *molín, avolo*) with the masculine definite articles *el* or *l'* (e.g. *el día, l'amigo*); and the area of the Ancares with its nasal vocal phonemes, palatalisation of the stressed *a* and with *gheada* and zero-personal number marker for the first person of the preterite of first and second declension verbs (e.g. *collí, partí, fice*). This latter feature is also a characteristic of the Zamora area together with the confusion of the diphthongs -*oi*- and -*ou*- (e.g. *despois-despous, dois-dous, noite-noute, touro-toiro*), a lack of the object pronoun *no* (e.g. *haio, seio, deixouo*) and with plurals of the type *peis, verdais* (sing. *pé, verdá*).

A Social History of the Galician Language

In the north-west of the Iberian Peninsula, Latin split away to form a linguistic variety in its own right which historians believe to have taken shape between the 9th and 11th centuries. The first written document to use this language was produced in the north of Portugal in the year 1214, while the first written document to be found north of the River Miño dates from 1230. From that moment on up until the present day, the social presence of Galician has gone through six different stages.

The Medieval Period

Throughout the Medieval Period (9/11th to 15th centuries), Galician was used in oral communication and as a means of literary expression as well as in the administrative functions of Galicia as testified to by the large production of texts of wide-ranging contents which have survived from that period. Latin and Spanish were both also used alongside Galician in Galicia, albeit to a somewhat lesser degree, and both languages were also used in written documents. But as time went by the use of Latin in written texts, almost all of which date from the very earliest times, dwindled while the number of texts written in Spanish increased (Monteagudo, 1985: 105–7):

Throughout this period, and more especially up until the 13th century, barring some minor dialectal variations, the language spoken in Galicia and Portugal was one and the same. The texts found in the anthologies of verse are a good illustration of the unity which the language spoken either side of the River Miño managed to maintain over such a long period in as much as the writers, regardless of their place of birth, used a language which was geographically unmarked, a sort of *koiné* which makes it impossible to determine their origins to any degree of certainty. In non-poetical texts, however, the differences between the writers from the north and south of the Miño are more striking and can be observed from very early on, as noted by Lorenzo (1985: 81) and Maia (1986: 883 and ff.). As from the 15th century, when the increasingly impermeable political frontier went up between Galician and Portugal, Galicia lost contact with its sister tongue, Portuguese.

Galicia and Portugal have been considered as independent territories as from the year 1096 when King Afonso VI of Castille gave the Portuguese County to one of his daughters, Tereixa, and Galicia to his other daughter, Urraca, thereby effectively splitting up a territory which had until that time always been under the same reign. Portugal won its independence from the Crown of Castilla-León in 1140 during the reign of Afonso Henríquez, and although relations remained very close and fluid even after that date, the independence of Portugal drew a dividing line which, as the years went by, ended up driving ever further apart the two territories, their two peoples, two histories, two cultures and two languages, where there had originally only been one. The political frontiers magnified the original minor differences until they finally became irreconcilable.[3]

Despite the fact that it was under the rule of the King of Castille, Galician managed to maintain its relative independence from the Court until 1350 when a war of succession broke out between Pedro I and Henrique de Trastámara. The Galician nobility backed Pedro I in this battle for the throne but when this cause lost, the Galician nobility suffered a veiled repression which manifested itself in the imposition of a royal envoy, who always came from outside Galicia and in the way in which the Galician nobility were barred from taking up any office within the Galician territory. Following the Civil War between Xoana of Beltranexa and Isabel La Católica, the Galician nobility lost its influence for having backed the former. During the period of the Catholic Kings, Ferdinand and Isabel, Galicia was to suffer a massive influx of civil-servants representing the *Santa Hermandad* (Holy Fraternity) who were appointed as Mayors to the Crown and who served in the Royal *Audiencias*. These people who represented authority spoke Spanish and, as such, constituted the main linguistic inroad into Galicia by this language,[4] because those people who rubbed shoulders with them sought to imitate their linguistic behaviour. Their arrival, together with legal provisions such as those requiring the scribes to sit an exam in Toledo, meant that the Galician language was effectively banished from writing and from public affairs, although it continued to be the language spoken by 99% of the population.

The Dark Ages

The 16th century marked the beginning of a new period characterised by the complete absence of Galician from the linguistic areas typically reserved for cultural matters, i.e. it was barred from administrative, religious and literary affairs. This period is known as the Dark Ages (16th to 17th centuries) because no book from this period is known to exist and because the language was denied any possibility of leaving a permanent mark in time which the written word would have conferred on to the language, thus effectively reducing it to obscurity and the transience of the spoken word. The fact that Galician disappeared from cultural spheres in the 16th century is particularly noteworthy because it was at this very same time, and even earlier, that the Romance languages were beginning to supplant Latin definitively as languages of culture: grammars and dictionaries were being compiled and the discovery of printing brought with it the popularisation of printed texts as compared with the previously much lower level of production provided by the manuscript tradition. By way of contrast, however, no Galician grammars and dictionaries were to appear until as late as the 19th century which was also the century when the first book was printed entirely in Galician.

From the reign of the Catholic Kings, the Castilianisation of Galicia progressed along similar lines to those described by Ninyoles (1978: 101–3) in his analysis of the way Spanish made its way into the Kingdom of Valencia. This analysis gives three ways in which Castilianisation advanced: horizontally, affecting the members of one class only; vertically, involving the Castilianisation of other social classes which came into contact with the agent responsible for the initial spread of Spanish; and multidirectionally, cutting across all sectors of society. The spread of Spanish was horizontal in Galicia during the latter part of the Middle Ages and during the Dark Ages, i.e. the core of the leading classes made up of civil servants from outside Galicia first of all began by Castilianising those Galicians who gravitated to the same circles, later going on to affect other people of the same social rank. The rest of society, i.e. the majority of the population, continued to use Galician as its one and only means of expression.

From the documents available it would seem that the Galicians willingly accepted the disappearance of their language from the spheres of public life, although other data nevertheless indicate that there were also some reactions against Castilianisation. One of these was led by the Countess of Altamira in 1523 when she refused to sign a document on the grounds that it was written in Spanish. In 1597 the Chapter of Santiago de Compostela complained to its Archbishop on the grounds that the best privileges were not only granted to outsiders but, what is more, to people who 'penetibus ignoraban la lengua gallega' (Mariño, 1991: 265). It is also interesting to note that in 1577 F. Xerónimo Bermúdez, the author of two tragedies written in Spanish, *Nise Laureada* and *Nise Lastimosa*, asked the reader to forgive any linguistic errors which were due to him having written in a 'language other than his native tongue', which could be interpreted as a veiled criticism of the Castilianisation of Galicia. Xoan Del Río, one of the poets who took part in the Festas Minervais held by the University of Santiago de Compostela in 1698, took his protests even further.

From the Enlightenment to the pre-Renaissance

The period from the Enlightenment to the pre-Renaissance (1700–1840) involved the continued encroachment of Castilianisation and the process of discrediting and undermining the Galician language which had begun in the Dark Ages. But this period also brought with it the first protests against the state of the language and a call for a change of status. Scientific work was begun on the language and literary production grew to the point where, during the war against the French invaders, it rose to new heights of production on a par with those of the medieval period. This period can be further divided into two subperiods: firstly, the Enlightenment, spanning the whole of the 18th century; and the pre-Renaissance covering the 19th century to 1840.

The Enlightenment (18th century) was marked by the works of four outstanding names: the Priest of Fruíme, Diego Cernadas Castro (1698–1777), Father Sobreira (1745–1805), Xosé Cornide (1734–1803) and, particularly, Father Sarmiento (1695–1772). The works of all four are characterised by their love of Galicia, their desire to rid it of the bad image it had outside Galicia, their esteem for the Galician language and their attempts to win back its dignity by studying it and using it in writing (Pensado, 1989: 74).

However, it was Friar Martín Sarmiento who was to be the foremost champion of Galician in this period. Without a doubt, his ideas and knowledge make him the most interesting figure of his times. This highly learned man of encyclopaedic knowledge produced various works on the Galician language, made several attempts at compiling dictionaries and spoke out against the low esteem that the Galician language was held in. It is a shame that most of his work remained unpublished, for had his ideas on linguistics and pedagogy been made known, they would surely have meant that linguistics and pedagogy could have progressed more quickly than they did. By the 18th century, Sarmiento had already laid down the concept of phonetic law to explain the way Latin evolved into the Romance languages and criticised the pedagogical aberration of teaching children in a language other than their own.[5]

The pre-Renaissance (1800–39) was marked by a historical event which was to be of major importance for the reinstatement of the use of Galician in writing, namely the invasion of the Peninsula by Napoleon Bonaparte's troops in 1808. The means most widely used to call the Galicians to fight off the invaders was pamphlets exalting the bravery of the local population and their courage in the battlefield and the worthiness of the ideal they were fighting for. This jingoistic literature was written in Galician and one of the best examples is the book *Proezas de Galicia*, written by Fernández Neira in 1810, which was also the first book ever to be printed in Galician. The use of Galician carried on after the war in such political writings as *Os rogos dun gallego establecido en Londres* (1813) by Manuel Pardo de Andrade and in the talks, dialogues and colloquies written between 1820 and 1836 such as *a Tertulia na Quintana, a Tertulia de Picaños, a Parola de Cacheiros, o Diálogo na Alameda, o Coloquio na pontella da Chaínsa*, and others.

The writings of Pastor Díaz ('Alborada', and 'Égloga de Belmiro e Benigno') as well as those by Fandiño (especially his play *A casamenteira*), Castro e Neira, Corral and Turnes as well as other anonymous works heralded in the Renaissance for the promotion and use of Galician which was due to set in for good in the latter half of that same century.

The Renaissance Period

In the latter half of the 19th century, (the Renaissance, 1840–1916) the situation of the Galician language underwent radical changes – both for the better and for the worst. The negative change involved the verticalisation of linguistic colonialisation, whereby the linguistic habits of the higher social classes which were already wholly Spanish-speaking began to seep down to the lower social classes which they came into contact with. This meant that Spanish filtered down into the middle classes who sought to imitate the behaviour of their betters, and also affected the less wealthy classes of the nobility and the bourgeoisie who needed to gain social prestige *vis-à-vis* their peers. Another process which came to be of major importance at this time was the way the Galician language came to be discredited and undermined, dogged by such labels as 'un curso' (a sort of course), 'the language of ignorant people', 'unable to express all feelings and all situations', 'responsible for the backwardness of the country', etc.

The positive change began in 1840 when a group of intellectuals started to lay down the foundations of a political ideology which had as its basis the defence of Galicia at all levels. The awareness of the fact that Galicia had become marginalised and discriminated against became widespread and this fact led to a reaction on the part of a sector of society in favour of everything that was typical of the country in an attempt to rid it of the negative image it had. Within this context of its changing image there grew up a defence of Galicia, rejecting the adjectives and attitudes which discredited its language and at the same time singing its praises and the benefits of using it, together with the demand that it be used both orally and in writing and having as its final aim the dignification and complete normalisation of the language. The main effect of this propaganda was to usher in the beginnings of the scientific study of the language with the publication of the first grammars and dictionaries, the publication of newspapers and reviews written entirely in Galician[6] and the final setting up of the *Academia Galega*, after many previous failed attempts, having the promotion of Galician as its main aim.

Without a doubt, the finest achievement of the Renaissance was the beginning of Galician literature, i.e. literature using Galician as its only means of written expression. At the turn of the century, the war had encouraged texts written in Galician and the flow of publications in the language did not stop from that time on. However, the final consolidation of Galician literature did not come about until 1863 with the publication of Rosalía de Castro's *Cantares Gallegos* which was immediately taken up as the symbol of demands in favour of Galician. The same writer, certainly the most outstanding figure in our country's literature of all times, published her work *Follas Novas* in 1880 which took her to the peak of literary expression. Besides Rosalía de Castro, two other writers are considered to be the people who first shaped our national literature; Manuel Curros Enríquez who wrote *Aires da miña terra* in 1880, and Eduardo Pondal, the author of *Queixumes dos pinos* (1886).

The Nós Period

Although the Nós Period (1916–36) was marred by a continued slump in the number of Galician-speakers and by the increased social presence of Spanish, between 1916 and 1936 an important step forward was taken as regards the status of the language. In 1916 the first *Irmandade da fala* (Brotherhood of Speech) was set up in the city of A Coruña, having as its prime objective to work towards the reinstatement of the Galician language, i.e. getting the Galician population which did not use the Galician language to win back the use of the language for its communication needs while ensuring that those people who did speak Galician continued to do so. This initiative first saw the light of day in A Coruña but soon spread to many other places throughout Galicia, finally developing into a great language movement which was also to set the seeds of the *Partido Galeguista* (Pro-Galician Party) This latter organisation which won seats in the Spanish Parliament in Madrid put pressure on the political parties in Galicia to draw up the very first Statutes of Autonomy, which later went on to be approved in a referendum held in 1936. For the first time ever, these Statutes recognised the official nature of Galician (Alonso, 1990; Noia, 1988).

Culturally speaking, this period is looked upon as the Golden Age of Galician culture. It was in this period that a generation, known as the *Nós Generation*, worked to bring Galician literature and all the other scientific and cultural branches up to the highest level they had ever known. Some of this period's most outstanding names include: the historian and novelist, Otero Pedrayo; the painter, artist, humorist, politician, essayist and writer, Castelao; the writer and politician, Vicente Risco; the poet Cabanillas, and many others. The Generation published a journal to spread their ideas, *Nós*, were the main contributors to the paper, *A Nosa Terra*, and also maintained contacts with all of the different currents of thought throughout Europe.

The Second Renaissance

After the Civil War (the Second Renaissance, 1936–present day), the Castilianisation of Galician society became multidirectional, mainly owing to the access people then had to the mass media and to schooling, both of which were provided exclusively in Spanish, being the only approved language.[7] What is more, Galician ceased to be used for public affairs, or whenever it was used in such situations it was only to show up a poor and ignorant society, using the language to scorn and ridicule that society. The Civil War thus effectively cut short the positive evolution geared to the reinstatement of Galician which had got underway hitherto: for 16 years, Galician culture languished as its most outstanding proponents were either forced into exile or had to hold their tongues for fear of reprisals. During the period that Franco was in power, the prestige

Galician had managed to win back for itself since the 19th century was lost at a stroke, becoming a forbidden tongue incurring punishment for anyone who dared use it.

In spite of this hostile context, however, the reinstatement of the Galician cultural tradition and of the Galician literature began with the setting up of the *Galaxia* publishing house in 1950, whose aim it was to encourage the spread of Galician culture. The political forces opposed to Franco's régime and above all, but not exclusively, those groups with a nationalist bent were to play a leading role in the defence and use of Galician. It was thanks to their efforts that Galician society was made aware that its language had a long-forgotten history of its own and that it was just as worthy to be used as any other language (Fernández Rei, 1990).

The legal situation of the minority languages spoken within the confines of the Spanish state was to change considerably when the Spanish Constitution was passed in 1978. Article 3 of its Basic Law states that; 'Spanish is the official language of Spain', but goes on to state; 'the other Spanish languages will also be official in their respective autonomous communities, in accordance with their Statutes'. Article 5 of the Galician Autonomous Statutes approved in 1981, states that Galician is the native language of Galicia, that it will be an official language alongside Spanish and that the Galician public bodies should endeavour to ensure the normal and official use of both languages and will allow for the use of Galician in all domains of public and cultural life and information. Furthermore, these public bodies are charged with setting up mechanisms designed to foster knowledge of the language. In 1983, the *Lei de Normalização Lingüística* (Linguistic Normalisation Act) was issued, a law which led on from Article 5 of the Autonomous Statutes, although it was later challenged in the Constitutional Court by the Spanish Government on the grounds that in one paragraph it stated that all Galicians had the right and the duty to know their language. The Constitutional Court ruled that this paragraph was illegal and so today, Galicians have the right, but not the duty, to know their language.

An Overview of the Current Situation of the Galician Language

Galician in society today

According to the report published in the first volume of the *Mapa Sociolingüístico de Galicia* (Fernández Rei and Rodríguez, 1994, 1995a and 1995b), Galician society is highly proficient in the mastery of the linguistic skills of the Galician language (see Table 4.1), with 97.1% of the population understanding it very well or quite well, 86.4% being able to speak it, 45.1% being able to read it well or quite well and 27.1% being able to write it very well or quite well.

Table 4.1 Comparison of linguistic proficiency, first and usual language for the 16–25 age bracket and for the total population of Galicia

	Total for Galicia	*16–25 age group*
Comprehension of Galician		
Good or quite good	97.1%	97.3%
Poor or not at all	2.9%	2.6%
Proficiency in spoken Galician		
Good or quite good	86.4%	79.3%
Poor or not at all	13.5%	20.6%
Proficiency in reading Galician		
Good or quite good	45.1%	72.6%
Poor or not at all	54.2%	27.4%
Proficiency in writing Galician		
Good or quite good	27.1%	63.9%
Poor or not at all	72.9%	36.1%
First language		
Galician	60.3%	36.7%
Spanish	27.2%	45.3%
Both	11.9%	17.1%
Usual language		
Only or pref. Galician	68.6%	46.5%
Only or pref. Spanish	31.4%	53.4%
Language usually used to write a note		
Only or pref. Galician	22.5%	32.5%
Only or pref. Spanish	77.5%	67.5%

Based on figures from Fernández Rei and Rodríguez (1995a, 1995b)

However, these high levels for language proficiency do not match up with the figures for Galician as first language and as the usual language of the population because only 60.3% have Galician as their first language, and 68.6% use Galician always or most of the time. These overall figures vary substantially when taking into account such factors as age, class, education and location. The highest figures registered for Galician as the first language (80.6%) and as the usual language (84.7%) are to be found in the +65 age group, with the lowest figures being recorded for the 16–25 age group, with 36.7% for first language and 46.5% for usual language.

A class-breakdown of the results yields the following results: the upper-middle class is the class with the lowest level of first language speakers, as well as having the lowest figures for usual language. The lower classes are those which learn to speak Galician more than any other class, as well as being the class which uses it most frequently. As regards the figures for place residence, we find that the figures for Galician as a first language and as the usual language drop progressively as we move from a rural area without public services, to a rural area with public services, to small towns, to the centres near towns and finally to towns and cities. As far as the levels of formal education of the population are concerned, the most interesting figures refer to the use of Galician as their most usual language, it can be observed that the sector of the population which shows the highest figures for the usage of Galician exclusively or preferentially to Spanish is the sector with no formal studies, followed by the sector with incomplete primary education and finally those who had completed their primary education. On the other hand, people who use Spanish more often than Galician have completed higher university studies, basic university studies or have completed their *Bacharelato* (secondary education).

From what has just been said, it can be concluded that in spite of the constant fall in the number of people who have Galician as either their first or usual language of communication, the language spoken by Rosalía de Castro is still the language of the majority of the population in Galicia. However, the varying degrees to which the language is actually used according to social standing, studies, age group and place of residence encourages the continued use of negative labels attached to the language such as the language spoken by old people, used in the countryside and by the lower-middle classes, and by people without basic formal studies. Spanish, on the other hand, is seen as the language of the town-dwellers, spoken by young people and by people with a high level of formal studies and a high income.

The figures in Table 4.2 show the way both of the languages spoken in Galicia are used in a variety of different situations. These figures seem to lead to the following conclusions:

(1) Galician is used more in the home than in any other situation, especially when addressing one's grandparents, parents or one's spouse. Galician is least used when addressing one's own children, which indicates that transmission of the language from one generation to the next is not a generalised phenomenon, as there are Galician-speaking parents who talk to their children in Spanish.
(2) The level of usage for Galician is also relatively high when talking to someone they trust, neighbours and friends, although slightly lower than within the home.
(3) Spanish is most often used in the following settings: the school context, particularly when addressing teaching staff; in the workplace when addressing one's superiors or one's employees; in commercial exchanges when attending to a customer and when the shop is unfamiliar; when dealing with the administration, especially the Xunta de Galicia; and when dealing with other people with a higher level of formal studies and with strangers.

Table 4.2 Average use of Galician and Spanish in different speech contexts (the averages range from one for Spanish only to four for Galician only)

with grandparents	3.36
with parents	3.22
with spouse	3.19
with someone you trust	3.13
with siblings	3.12
with schoolmates	3.12
with neighbours	3.10
with friends	3.06
at work	3.04
in usual shops	3.04
in the townhall	3.00
with offspring	2.97
in the Xunta	2.93
with friends in the playground	2.84
in other shops	2.73
with employees	2.72
with fellow students	2.69
with the G.P.	2.65
with superiors	2.50
with a specialist doctor	2.39
with a stranger	2.36
with customers	2.16
with teachers	1.76

Source: Fernández Rei and Rodríguez (1995a)

From this we can see that the use of Galician is restricted to private settings and to the closest social relations, whereas Spanish is the preferred language for public use and for more distant social *rapports*. Galician is used in situations where the speaker feels s/he can show his/her real self, i.e. informal communication situations, whereas Spanish is reserved for occasions when the speaker wishes to show that s/he is cultured, educated, knowledgeable and has *savoir être*, i.e. in formal communicative settings. In other words, Galicia has a diglossic situation, by which is meant the way two different languages are used according to the communicative situation in which the speaker is involved (Fishman,

Table 4.3 Average use in various settings according to usual language

	Usual shops	Other shops	Townhall	Xunta	G.P.	Specialist
Spanish only	1.03	1.01	1.06	1.09	1.02	1.02
Mostly Spanish	1.73	1.41	1.88	2.04	1.32	1.22
Mostly Galician	3.45	2.85	3.26	3.26	2.70	2.28
Galician only	3.98	3.82	3.91	3.87	3.76	3.51

1971: 74). Diglossia particularly affects people who usually use Galician, as can be observed in the data concerning behaviour in school settings and this is also what happens with speakers who use Galician as their most usual language, 18% of whom use exclusively or mainly Spanish when visiting their GP, rising to 30.8% when consulting a specialist (Fernández Rei and Rodríguez, 1995a: 309, note p. 110). Table 4.3 reveals a similar drop in the use of Galician when visiting an unfamiliar shop. This same table also reveals that those speakers who claim to use Spanish exclusively or most frequently tend to use Galician rather than their usual language when dealing with the townhall or the Xunta (Galician autonomous government).

Galician in schools

The legislation on education issued by the Xunta de Galicia, *Lei de Normalização Lingüística* (Title III of the Linguistic Normalisation Act, 1983) regulates the situation of Galician in the field of education, and can be summarised as follows:

(1) Galician is a compulsory subject at all levels of education up to (but excluding) university, and the number of hours dedicated to the study of Galician must be equal to that given over to the study of Spanish. By the end of their compulsory formal education, all students must be equally proficient in both Galician and Spanish. At university level, both students and lecturers have the right to use either of the official languages.

(2) All pupils have the right to receive their primary education in their mother tongue. At nursery school level and in the first cycle of E.X.B. (primary school), teachers are required to employ the mother tongue of the majority of the pupils in the classroom, although they are entitled to employ whichever of the official languages they prefer for any subject.

(3) The current set up of the educational system is due to be completely phased out with the implementation of the educational reform. Until that time, however, in the second and third cycles of E.X.B. (primary school), it was compulsory for at least the social science subjects to be

taught in Galician, while at *Bacharelato* and *C.O.U.* (pre-university secondary course) levels Galician had to be used as the language of teaching for two subjects to be chosen from any of the following: geography, history, natural sciences, physics and chemistry, maths, computer science and philosophy. At Vocational Training level, the two subjects to be taught in Galician may be chosen from the following: humanities, practical work, technology or maths. The new syllabus due to be brought in when the educational reform takes effect will make it compulsory to use Galician as the language of teaching for subjects from two different fields of knowledge (one of which must be the field of the natural, social and cultural environment) in the second and third cycles (two-year periods) of primary education; in compulsory secondary education, Galician will be the compulsory language of teaching for the social sciences and the natural sciences subjects as well as being optional for the teaching of the environmental sciences and health care studies and for the particular options on offer at the school in question. In the different *Bacharelato* (Secondary School) set-ups, Galician must be used to teach the cross-syllabus core subjects (i.e. philosophy in the first year and history in the second year), one in the first year or two in the second year, specific to each of these *Bacharelato* set-ups and three optional subjects (ethics and the philosophy of law, introduction to the political sciences and sociology and history and geography of Galicia).

(4)   Galician is the language of the administrative bodies dealing with educational matters in Galicia and, as such, most of the activities performed by these bodies are to be carried out in Galician.

The basic thinking underlying the legislation described above is clear: the intention is not to create a special Galician education system having Galician as the language of teaching, but rather to provide legislation designed to guarantee the presence of Galician and which goes some small way beyond the use of the language for teaching Galician language and literature *per se*.

The figures taken from the *Mapa Sociolingüístico de Galicia* (Fernández Rei and Rodríguez, 1995a and 1995b) demonstrate just how little bearing the aforementioned legal provisions have had on Galicianisation and even reveal their failure to maintain the Galician used by schoolgoers. The generation which falls into the 16–25 age group has all received teaching in Galician, and this fact is clearly reflected in their levels of language proficiency when compared with the significantly lower levels for the Galician population as a whole (Table 4.1). However, the fact remains that although Galician is used in teaching, there still remains a considerable percentage of the population who claims to have only a poor or no mastery of the spoken language (20.6%), for reading (27.4%) and of the written language (36.1%).[8]

As far as the education system is concerned, it can be said that it actually tends to degalicianise Galician-speakers, in as much as it encourages those people who have Galician as their first or usual language to use Spanish in this setting, especially when dealing with teaching staff or in writing. This explains why the average use of Galician when dealing with teaching staff (not included in Table 4.2) is 1.96 and 1.1 when writing as compared with the higher levels of usage when communicating with other children in the classroom (3.12) and in the playground (2.84) (see Table 4.2). For people who have Galician as their usual language (Fernández Rei and Rodríguez, 1995a: 269) the averages are 1.21 for writing; 2.20 when dealing with teaching staff; 3.67 with classmates in the classroom; and 3.82 with classmates in the playground (figures not included in Table 4.2). What all of this means is that formal education encourages diglossia in Galician-speakers and does nothing to improve the written proficiency of people who usually use Galician: compared with the figure of 46.5% for people in the 16–25 age group who usually use Galician, only 32.5% choose to use Galician when writing a note (see Table 4.1).

While it is true that including Galician into the syllabus as a compulsory subject for study in itself as well as making it the compulsory language of teaching for certain other subjects in Galicia has not made any significant quantitative improvements to the situation of the language in this domain, it should nevertheless also recognised that this fact is of enormous importance for the normalisation of a language as well as for its social status. Not including a language in the school curriculum is the best way to ensure that it becomes closed in on itself, thus helping towards its disappearance. Not including it as both as a formal subject and as a teaching medium would amount to denying its worth as a means of cultural communication, undervaluing it *vis-à-vis* the other languages and would also mean the speakers of that language remaining ignorant of the way their language works and remaining illiterate in their own language. Presenting the language as both a subject for formal teaching and as a teaching medium for other subjects amounts to putting the language on a par with the other languages and, of course, also means presenting it to the pupils as being perfectly valid for general communication.

The use of Galician in the Church, in the mass media and in advertising

In order to complete the picture of the situation of Galician within society, it is important to analyse the presence of Galician in other areas and institutions. All of the figures which follow are based on small samples and do not, therefore, have the universal value of the *Mapa Sociolingüístico*.

The Church is a deeply rooted institution within Galician society, both in the way it influences social behaviour as well as in the numbers of people who take part in the different religious ceremonies. All in all, the linguistic behaviour of the clergy has little or nothing to do with the language spoken by the majority of their congregation. According to a study carried out by López (1989) who studied the linguistic behaviour of the clergy of the Catholic Church (this being the denomination with the largest following in Galicia), 85% of the clergy use Galician always or most of the time, but not while exercising their profession. When saying Mass, 85.9% never use Galician; 4.2% always say Mass in Galician, 1.8% use Galician in over half of the Masses and 8.2% use it in half or less than half of their Masses. These figures for the linguistic preferences of the clergy yield the following final results: 70% of all Masses performed in Galicia are said in Spanish, with 22.8% in Galician and Spanish and 7.2% in Galician only.

The mass media reflect reality while at the same time the information and opinions they give out condition the reality of the people they reach owing to the fact that they are seen as a prestige role model. For this reason, the language the media use to give out their information is of special relevance because it is a model of prestige. This means that the non-use of a language in the media is immediately perceived by the speakers of that language as an indication that their language is not prestigious enough to be used to convey the model of modern society represented by the media. An overview of the actual use of the Galician language in the various different media yields the following results:

State-owned Television: Four channels (*Antena 3, Canal+, Tele5* and *TVE2*) broadcast in Spanish only. *TVE1* uses Galician in one hour-long slot five days a week with the rest of its broadcasting in Spanish.

Galician Television: Only one channel, *TVG*, which broadcasts in Galician.

Local TV stations: All or almost all in-house productions are in Galician, with such notable exceptions as the local T.V. channels in A Coruña, Vigo and Ponteareas which broadcast in Spanish only.

State-owned radio stations: Practically all state-owned stations broadcast in Spanish only, with the exception of a few stations such as *RadioVoz* which has some Galician-language slots for broadcasts covering either Galicia as a whole or smaller areas, and *Radio Nacional de España, Radio Uno*, which generally broadcasts in Spanish with two and a half hours reserved for Galician-language programmes.

Galician radio stations: There is only the Galician radio station, *Radio Galega*, which broadcasts in Galician.

Local radios stations: Barring a few exceptions, local radio stations run by town councils broadcast in Galician, whereas private radio stations generally opt for Spanish-language broadcasting.

Press (non-daily): There is one Galician-language weekly, *A Nosa Terra* and several local publications which come out at different intervals, such as *A Peneira, O Miñor, O Norte*, etc. as well as a wide range of magazines and journals with only a limited number of copies per edition.

Table 4.4 Evolution of the percentage of Galician used in the daily press

Year	1977	1982	1987	1990	1993
Ideal Galego	2.01	2.27	1.95	3.02	1.04%
Atlántico				4.2	3.01%
Diaro de Pontevedra	0.71	0.44	1.01	2.96	3.93%
Faro de Vigo	1.15	2.25	2.41	2.74	3.94%
La Región	1.28	1.32	1.77	3.60	4.44%
El Progreso	0.77	1.27	3.13	2.63	4.95%
Voz de Galicia	2.76	2.78	1.50	5.39	5.41%
Correo Gallego	2.68	1.62	6.12	9.08	7.23%
Diario 16 de Galicia				3.24	13.54%
Total	1.62	1.71	2.56	4.11	5.29%

The daily press: There is only one Galician-language daily, *O Correo Galego*, which has to compete with the nine other Spanish-language papers published in Galicia as well as the special editions of the papers published in Madrid, i.e. *El Mundo* and *El País*. Table 4.4 shows the varying degrees to which the Galician language was used in the Spanish-language press between 1977 and 1993 (Hermida, 1995: 77). This evolution is characterised by an increase in the amount of information printed in Galician within a range of percentages not exceeding 6% of the total information. *Advertising:* A quantitative study carried out on 3 papers over the week ending 27 August 1992 (Hermida, 1994: 263), revealed a volume of advertising in Galician amounting to 8.15% of the total space devoted to advertising: 63.7% of this advertising came from public bodies with the remaining 31.11% coming from private entities and 5.18% from mixed advertising, i.e. including references to both private and public entities. For the *Televisión de Galicia (TVG)*, which broadcasts exclusively in Galician, the figures for 1994 amounted to 56% of advertising time in Spanish with the remaining 44% in Galician. However, after subtracting in-house advertising for the Galician TV *(TVG)* channel itself, the amount of advertising in Spanish rises to 80% with the amount of Galician dropping to 20%. As far as the advertisers themselves are concerned, 85% of private companies use Spanish for their advertising as compared with only 8% for public bodies. Public bodies opted for Galician in 92% of their advertising whereas only 15% of advertising by private bodies was produced in Galician.[9]

These figures contrast strongly with the conclusions of a study on advertising and the Galician language published by the Department for Culture/Concello da Cultura (Ramallo and Rei, 1995: 77–81) which concludes that over 80% of the population is clearly in favour of the use of Galician in advertising and that the use of Galician could be a strong buying stimulus for between 25% and 40% of the population, with 39.5% of the population feeling attracted to an advertisement simply because it is in Galician and 29.5% would try out a product just because its label was in Galician.

Contact between Galician and Spanish: Language Shift, Codeswitching and Interference

Before going on to deal briefly with language shift, codeswitching and interference, it is worth going back over two facts which, implicitly or explicitly, have already appeared in what has already been said. Firstly, owing to the fact that Galician and Spanish share the same origins – both come from Latin – they are structurally very similar languages[10] which makes for almost complete mutual comprehension. The second fact is that almost the entire population of Galicia is capable of expressing itself in either of the two languages used in Galicia.[11] These two facts might lead one to assume that Galicia offers optimal conditions for the speakers of both languages to remain faithful to their mother tongue, without modifying it in any speech context. And this is precisely what happens with a percentage of the population situated at 38.7% of Galician mother tongue speakers and 10.6% of Spanish mother tongue speakers. However, the basic sociolinguistic situation is one of inequality regarding the conditions which have existed – and still exist – between both languages and it is this imbalance which motivates language shift and codeswitching as well as linguistic interference.

Code change, also known as situational codeswitching (Turell, 1995) or commutation (Nussbaum, 1992) taken to be when someone gives up his/her mother tongue in order to use another language with the aim of resolving a particular speech situation (Silva-Valdivia, 1994: 158). This phenomenon can be observed in both Galician and Spanish-speakers. We believe this phenomenon is caused by four main factors, two of which are common to Galician and Spanish-speakers, namely education and economic or professional interest, one of which is particular to changing from Spanish to Galician, namely respect and courtesy, while the fourth, social prestige, is confined exclusively to Galician-Spanish language shift.

Professional and economic interests can be used to explain language shift in people who forgo their own language in order to use another which they feel will bring them economical or professional gain in certain circumstances and when addressing certain people. This is the case of shopkeepers and professionals who, faced with someone who speaks a language other than their own, will switch over to this other language because they feel that this will bring them greater profit. One clear example of language shift brought about by interest, in this case in the academic setting, can be seen in the linguistic behaviour of the students in the Faculty of Information Sciences of the University of Santiago de Compostela (Castro, 1996: 4–5). The percentages for usual language are as follows: 26% *usually* use only Galician, 62% *usually* use only Spanish and 11% use either language. When asking a question or making a remark during a lesson, 42% of the students use Galician, 25% use Spanish and 31% use either language. These differences between the usual language of the students and the use of both languages in the classroom can be explained by the fact that most of the teaching staff within the aforesaid Faculty use Galician as their teaching medium. Education, which is associated with politeness and courtesy, also causes some people to modify their language in order to express themselves in another language, i.e. people who express themselves in Galician are spoken to in Galician and *vice versa* for people using Spanish, particularly when strangers are involved.

Code change motivated by courtesy and respect is also what occurs when Spanish-speakers address people whom they assume not to know Spanish owing to their age or apparent status. In this case, addressing them in Galician is an act of respect and courtesy towards the people who are assumed to be unable to interpret correctly what is being said. When this occurs, the person who has engaged in this kind of language shift will revert to his/her own initial language as soon as the person being spoken to fails to display the characteristics associated with people who do not know Spanish. To illustrate this, consider the case of a doctor who uses Galician when talking to more elderly patients but ceases to use Galician when dealing with younger patients even if the latter begin the social interaction in Galician.

One of the reasons which motivates language shift in Galician-speakers is the question of social prestige. Those people who address their children's teachers in Spanish, the clergyman who uses Galician when talking to his parishioners but who says Mass in Spanish, the teacher whose usual language of expression is Galician but who gives his/her lessons in Spanish and Galician-speaking shopkeepers who systematically address their customers in Spanish are all behaving in this way in order to avoid giving themselves away as uneducated, rural, backward Galician-speaking country bumpkins, which are the values still associated with Galician in certain circles.

Codeswitching can be described as the conscious or unconscious presence (see Myers-Scotton, 1993) of two languages within the same utterance or speech act and is a phenomenon which affects both Spanish-speakers and Galician-speakers alike. Galician-speakers will occasionally produce utterances such as: 'intentamos convencelos, pero non quixeron vir, así **que les den**' and 'fuimos a la fiesta, pero **érache unha pachangada** y volvimos a la discoteca'. We believe that the conscious insertion of words or expressions into Spanish or use of Galician has one basic aim: to emphasise and to add expressiveness to the concepts or ideas which the speaker wishes to convey.

Linguistic interference, or the persistent use of an incorrect structure in one language conditioned by another language with which it shares the same space (Silva-Valdivia, 1994: 165), affects both the Spanish spoken in Galicia and Galician itself. Very briefly, some Galician features to be found in the Spanish spoken in Galicia can be observed (1) at the phonological and intonational levels, by making use of the Galician seven-way vowel system, the velar nasal phoneme and some Galician intonation patterns; (2) at the syntactic level, by making use of syntactic calques such as, the non-use or misuse of compound tenses, the use of certain typically Galician verbal periphrases, the insertion of the 'solidarity' pronoun (che, lle), in the use of preposition with transitive verbs: *llaman por tí* (you are requested), and (3) at the lexical level, by making use of borrowed vocabulary referring to the household, although today it is possible to observe the use of technical terms which have been made familiar to the public in Galician, but for which the Spanish equivalents are unknown.

The following examples taken from the daily press in Galicia (Goyanes, Núñez, Romero and Túñez, 1996: 29–45) serve to illustrate these and other kinds of linguistic interference: 'la certeza de que **estes** cumplen la normativa' (the certainty that they respect the norms), 'yo no **le** sé (= no sé) nada' (I don't know anything), 'el presidente **ha partici- pado** (= participó) ayer' (yesterday the president took part in), 'me **olvidara** (= había olvidado) de ellos' (I had forgotten about them), '**podería** (= podría) seguir teniendo la misma' (I could go on having the same), 'Nunca lo vimos ni **dimos contactado** (= no pudimos contactar) con ellos' (we never saw or got in touch with them), 'había que **ir esperar** (= ir a esperar) el correo' (we had to wait for the mail), 'señala que ya **se tiene pronunciado** (= se pronunció varias veces)' (it is pointed out that it took decisions on that issue several times), '**de aquella** (= en aquella época) no existía' (it didńt exist at that time), 'la **concelleira** (= concejala)' (the counsellor), 'la red de **sumideros** (= alcantarillas)' (the system of sewers), 'el **pagamiento** (= pago) de los atrasos' (back payments), 'la **subministración** (= suministro) de gas natural' (natural gas supply), 'en un **alpendre** (= cobertizo) próximo' (the next shelter), 'el pan de **mollete** (= hogaza)' (over-baked bread), 'en toda la **bisbarra** (= comarca) de Ortegal' (in the whole county of Ortegal).

Interference from Spanish in Galician mainly affects vocabulary (with words such as **bueno** (well), **siglo** (century), **pueblo** (village), **Dios** (God), **virgen** (virgin), **lentejas** (lentils), **estropajo** (pan scourer), **lejía** (bleach), **escoba** (broom), etc.), but Galician is also influenced by Spanish calque at the morpho-syntactic level, as in the change in gender of words such as 'a sal (salt – sp. la sal), **a leite** (milk – sp. la leche), **o calor** (heat – sp. el calor), **o color** (colour – sp. el color)', etc.; the use of verbal forms such as **anduven** (went), **hubo** (there was), **iba** (was going), etc.; clitic order (e.g. **me dixo**/dixo-me (he said to me)); the use of the preposition **a** in the verbal periphrasis 'ir + inf.' (e.g. **imos a facerllo pagar** (we made him pay)) or with the direct object (e.g. **ver a un neno** (to see a boy)), and others.

Final Conclusions

In order to properly understand the past and the present of the Galician language one must be careful to distinguish between the evolution of the language as used by a community as its means of oral expression, on the one hand, and its evolution in formal domains, on the other. As far as the latter is concerned, the history of Galician can be represented with an upside down M-shape (W), which illustrates how the language went from being present in all formal domains (the Medieval Period), then later becoming completely absent (the Dark Ages) and finally going on to the Renaissance and the Nós Generation when the language won back some of the formal areas of use which it was then barred from between 1936 and 1950. From 1951 onwards, and more especially from 1977, Galician once again became present in all formal areas, although not to the exclusion of other languages as was once the case in the Medieval Period.

On the other hand, the presence of Galician as a language of oral expression and its correct representation can be described graphically as a continual falling line, although the decline does not become very pronounced up until the 19th century, falling away more sharply between the turn of the century and 1936 and with a very noticeable drop starting in the 1940s, with this trend continuing unchanged to the present day. Nonetheless, in spite of this current downward trend, there have never before been as many people able to read and write the language. As things stand, however, prospects for the language look far from bright. If the downward trend for Galician as a first and usual language does not pick up, then Galician, which has always been the language of the majority of the population within its territory although, barring the Medieval Period, it has always been a minorised language, it is bound to end up being ever more a minority language and ever more minorised. The outlook for Galician seems rather bleak, ruling out any great optimism, for the following reasons:

(1) There are still areas that Galician is either wholly absent from or where its presence is very limited.
(2) Some people still harbour prejudices against the language and spurn anything which to them smacks of Galician as well as others who abandon it not just because it fails to give them prestige, but because they feel it actually deprives them of the prestige they have.
(3) The Galician administration has not set up a language normalisation campaign capable of effectively making the Galicians aware of the importance of keeping their language alive, of knowing it, of using it and of passing it on from one generation to the next.

(4)   The defence and the fight for the normalisation of the language, which is the only real way to ensure its survival, is a task which does not involve all sectors of society but continues to be the preserve of nationalists, and particularly of left-wing nationalists.

(5)   There are still people who believe that the Galician language is nothing more than an added extra to being Galician, whereas it is really Galicia's true *raison d'être*. Without its language, a country cannot exist.

Notes

1.   Cunqueiro, A./Camprubí, R., 1981: 5–48.
2.   For the limits between Galician and Asturian-Leonese and with Portuguese, see Fernández Rei, 1991: 18–30. For a general overview of the language, see the entry 'galego' in the *Gran Enciclopedia Gallega*, Vol. XIV.
3.   One of the first differences between the Galician and Portuguese texts, i.e. the way the palatal nasal was written (*nh* in Portugal as opposed to *nn, n* and *ñ* in Galician texts) and also the written form of the palatal lateral (*lh* in Portuguese and *ll, li* and *l* in Galician), would never have come about had the whole territory been under the same rule, because the digraphs *nh* and *lh* were imposed in a Decree issued by the Portuguese Chancellery Royal during the reign of Afonso III (1264), thus obviously failing to affect Galicia. Maia (1986: 486 and ff.).
4.   The installation of Castilian was also helped along by the cultural break between Galicia and Portugal.
5.   For an analysis of the importance of Sarmiento's work, see Santamarina (1995).
6.   The most important of these was the weekly *Tío Marcos da Portela*, created in Ourense in 1876 by the poet and journalist Valentín Lamas Carvajal. This publication survived until 1889 and ran into 4000 copies.
7.   The figures given in the *Mapa Sociolingüístico* (Fernández Rei and Rodríguez, 1995b: 1) show that Galician is the first language of 80.6% of people over 65 and of 36.7% of people between 16 and 25, thereby indicating a drop of 43.9% of potential Galician-speakers over the last 50 years. As far as usual language used is concerned, the loss amounts to 38.2% of speakers for the same period, with 84.7% of those people over 65 using Galician most of the time as compared with only 46.5% for the 16–25 age bracket.
8.   Figures for proficiency in these fields are not available for Spanish, but it would seem fair to assume that the population is generally proficient in Spanish, or at least lack of proficiency in these fields goes unrecognized.
9.   These figures come from a piece of course work carried out by Marcos Sanluís López, a student in the Faculty of Information Sciences at the University of Santiago de Compostela. The information was processed after viewing all of the advertising broadcast by the Televisión de Galicia between 4th and 5th December 1994.
10.   It is not unlikely that existing side by side in the same territory for over 500 years compounded by the unfavourable conditions for Galician has also contributed to this similarity by inhibiting the internal development of Galician and by encouraging solutions more in line with Spanish. It is perhaps this influence which could be used to explain the victory of the generally known word *pataca* for 'potato' over the alternative *castaña* or *baloca*, both of which survive as dialectal forms.
11.   Figures on the knowledge of Galician are given in Table 4.1. No figures are available for knowledge of Spanish, but knowledge of the situation means that it can be safely postulated they are no lower than those for Galician.
12.   In Portuguese 'the letters m and *n* at the end of a syllable only normally serve to indicate the nasalisation of the previous vowel' (Cunha/Cintra, 1984: 47)

13. Here this diphthong is merely a spelling convention, in as much as 'the ancient dipthong [ow] has not been maintained in Portugal or Brazil, although it does still survive in regional varieties in the North of Portugal and in Galician. In normal speech it has become reduced to [o]' (Cunha and Cintra, 1984: 49)

14. Once again, this dipthong is nothing more than a spelling convention. In standard Portuguese it is pronounced [j].

15. The digraph ch appears in all three languages despite the different ways it is pronounced.

16. Portuguese has five consonantal graphemes which can appear in final position; -m (which represents a nasal vowel), -l, -r, -s and -z, which is pronounced as an unvoiced palatal.

17. In Portuguese, final -n only exists in learned words such as *dólmen* and *líquen* which add the ending -es in the plural, e.g. *dólmenes*, *líquenes*. When a final -m is used to indicate nasalisation of the previous vowel, the plural is formed by replacing the -m with an -n before adding a final -s, e.g. *fim-fins*, *bom-bons*. Cf. Cunha and Cintra (1984: 181–5).

18. For the different usage of tu and *você*, see Cunha and Cintra (1984: 293–4).

19. In Portuguese, especially as it is spoken in Brazil, it is possible to form the possessive structure without the definite article (e.g. meu amor é só teu) in cases where this would not be acceptable Galician (e.g. *o meu amor é só teu*) Cf. Cunha and Cintra (1984: 216 and after) and Álvarez *et al.*, (1986: 152 and after).

Appendix 1

Phonetics

Feature	Galician	Portuguese	Spanish
/o/, /ɔ/	t/o/do,r/ɔ/da c/o/mo, c/ɔ/mes	t/o/do, r/ɔ/da c/o/mo, c/ɔ/mes	t/o/do, rueda c/o/mo, c/o/mes
/e/, /ɛ/	s/e/de, d/ɛ/z b/e/bo, b/ɛ/bes	s/e/de, d/ɛ/z b/e/bo, b/ɛ/bes	s/e/d, diez b/e/bo, b/e/bes
/ɐ/, /a/	c/a/ma, g/a/to Pres: am/a/mos Pret: am/a/mos	c/ɐ/ma, g/a/to Pres: am/ɐ/mos Pret: am/a/mos	c/a/ma, g/a/to Pres: am/a/mos Pret: am/a/mos
Nasal vowel phonemes	si, la, bo, sa	sim,[12] bom, la, sa	si, bueno, lana, sana
Diphthong /ie/	dera, pedra ciencia, ambiente	dera, pedra ciência, ambiente	diera, piedra ciencia, ambiente
Diphthong /ue/	podo, porto	posso, porto	puedo, puerto
Diphthong /ou/	ou, cantou	ou, cantou[13]	o, cantó
Diphthong /ei/	feira, deixar, lei	feira,[14] deixar, lei	feria, dejar, ley
/ŋ/	unha, fin	–	–
/s/, /z/	e/s/e, ca/s/a	e/s/e, ca/z/a	e/s/e, ca/s/a
/ʃ/, /ʒ/	ei/ʃ/e, /ʃ/a	ei/ʃ/e, /ʒ/á	–
/χ/	–	–	tra/χ/o
/θ/	po/θ/o	–	po/θ/o
/b/, /v/	/b/iño, /b/o	/v/inho,/b/om	/b/ino, /b/ueno
/tʃ/	/tʃ/upar, /tʃ/ispa[15]	/ʃ/upar, /ʃ/ispa	/tʃ/upar, /tʃ/ispa
/ʀ/	/r/ei, ca/r/o	/ʀ/ei, ca/ʀ/o	/ʀ/ei, ca/ʀ/o
Syll. fin. consonants	so/l/, ma/r/, me/s/, ve/θ/, no/ŋ/	so/l/, ma/r/, me/ʃ/[16]	so/l/, ma/r/,me/s/ ve/θ/, po/n/, bo/χ/ verda/d/

Morphology

Feature	Galician	Portuguese	Spanish
Compound tenses	–	Aux: *ter e haver*	Aux: *haber*
Simple Pluperfect Indicative	*amara, lera, rira*	*amara, lera, rira*	–
Conjugated Infinitive	*ver, veres, vermos, vermos, verdes, veren*	*ver, veres, ver vermos, verdes, veren*	–
Thematic vowel of Gerund	*am/a/ndo, v/e/ndo r/i/ndo*	*am/a/ndo, v/e/ndo r/i/ndo*	*am/a/ndo, v/ie/ndo, r/ie/ndo*
Thematic vowel of irregular preterites	*puid/ɛ/mos, fix/ɛ/se*	*pud/ɛ/mos, fiz/ɛ/sse*	*pud/i/mos, hic/ie/se*
Thematic vowel of regular preterites	*am/a/mos, toc/a/sedes mov/e/mos, beb/e/sedes part/i/mos, sa/i/sedes*	*am/a/mos, toc/a/sseis mov/e/mos, beb/e/sseis part/i/mos, sa/i/sseis*	*am/a/mos, toc/a/seis mov/i/mos, beb/ie/seis part/i/mos, sal/ie/seis*
Fifth person personal number marker	*amades, amabades*	*amais, amáveis*	*amáis, cantabais*
First person personal number marker for preterite of second and third declension verbs	*moví-N, partí-N*	*movi, parti*	*moví, partí.*
Second person personal number marker for preterite	*-ches: cantaches*	*-ste: cantaste*	*-ste: cantaste*
Fifth person personal number marker for preterite	*-stes: cantastes*	*-stes: cantastes*	*-steis: cantasteis*
Inf. + third person direct object pronoun	*velo*	*vê-lo*	*verlo*
Plural of nouns ending in -*n*	*sons, fins*	*sons,*[17] *fins*	*sones, fines*
Plural of nouns ending in -*l*	*animais, papeis soles, fáciles*	*animais, papeis sois, fáceis*	*animales, papeis soles, fáciles*
Gender of numeral 'two'	*dous/dúas*	*dois/duas*	*dos*
Second person subject pronoun	*ti*	*tu/você*[18]	*tu*
Polite pronoun Paradigm for poss. adjs.	*vostede meu, teu, seu miña, túa, súa*	*o senhor ... meu, teu, seu minha, tua, sua*	*usted mío, tuyo, suyo mía, tuya, suya mi, tu, su*
Comparative conjunctions CA and COMA	*menos ca el é coma nós*	–	–

Syntax

Feature	Galician	Portuguese	Spanish
Art. + poss. adjective	*o meu libro*	*o meu livro*[19]	*mi libro*
Prep. *a* + direct object	*ve-los nenos*	*ver os nenos*	*ver a los niños*
Periphrasis *ir* + infinitive	*ir + inf.*	*ir + inf.*	*ir + a + inf.*
Place of the pronoun in simple asserative sentences	postverbal: *seino*	postverbal: *sei-o*	preverbal: *lo sé*
Place of object pronoun with future and conditional	*vereino, dareicho*	*ve-lo-hei, dar-to-hei*	*te veré, te lo daré.*
Second person direct object pronoun	te: *vinte*	te: *vi-te*	te: *te vi*
Second person indirect object pronoun	che: *deiche*	te: *dei-te*	te: *te di*
Verb ending in diphthong + third person direct object pronoun	*cantouno, leveina*	*cantou-o, levei-a*	—
'Solidarity' pronoun	*fóicheme bo contóullemo*	—	—
Comparative conjunction + first person pronoun	*máis ca min, coma min*	*máis do que eu como eu*	*más que yo como yo*
Compound numbers with hundred and thousand (1532)	*mil cincocentas trinta e dúas*	*mil e quiñentas e trinta e duas*	*mil quinientas treinta y dos*

Appendix 2

Two Texts in Galician

The two texts provided below taken from the spoken language and transcribed using standard Galician are intended to give an idea of this kind of linguistic interference. The first text, recorded in 1975, comes from Roo-Noia (Fernández Rei/Hermida, 1996) and belongs to the Eastern Bloc of Galician, while the second text comes from Vences-Verín (Taboada, 1979: 204–6) and belongs to the Central Bloc. In both texts, instances of Spanish-based interference appear in bold type followed by their correct Galician form in brackets.

ROO-NOIA: Pois nas casas formábase un baile nunha casa e coa **misma** (mesma) principiábase a toca-la **pandereta** (pandeireta) e veña baile: a **ghota** (xota), a muiñeira, o **pasodoble** (pasodobre), o valse ... En fin, tódolos bailes que había: dansa, masurca ... Non había estes bailes modernos de abrasarse tanto, de apretarse tanto. Eso non: separados un do outro. E entonses si, aquelo daba ghusto. Ademais, as mulleres daquela **iban** (ían) coas saíñas **hasta** (ata) alá baixo, case a rastro do chan. Pero despois, este... a bailar, pois non nos freghábamos nada;

estábamos separados, e, en fin … Non había bicos tampouco no baile. Os bicos era cando se lle daba un bico a unha muller xa era unha cousa moi seria. **Dios** (Deus) nos libre deso. Daquela a cousa era un sagrado. Hoxe non. Hoxe xa se abrasan os mosos e as mosas, andan abrasados xa por aí adiante, á vista da xente. Nós cando nos abrasábamos naqueles nosos tempos, ai sasenta anos, sincuenta anos; daquela daba ghusto, que cando mirábamos prá nosa mosa ninghén lle podía chiscar, e coidadiño, que … estábase mirando pra ela, mirábase como pra **Dios** (Deus). Non se lle tropesaba…, **hasta** (ata) cando era no asunto de pidi-la mosa, ai, daquela si que daba ghusto; cando lla daban a un … , pero cando lle disían que non, ai, cando lle disían que non, entonses si, entonses poñíanselle os pelos de punta. Eu **tuven** (tiven) unha mosa que fun con ela sete meses e medio e non lle tropesei nin un pelo da roupa... Nadiña, nadiña. E miraba pra ela como pra María Santísima ¡alabado **sea** (sexa) ela! Pero calro, eu despois … Vai ela, e **díseme** (dime) un día … Unha noite cheghei, que eu **iba** (ía) sempre moi contento pra alí e cheghei alí … e cando cheghei vai ela e díxome: 'Mira, non volvas máis'. '¿Como dixestes?' 'Que non volvas máis'. '¿E logho por que?' 'Porque eu non quero ter moso'.

VENCES-VERÍN. Dunha vez fomos nós tocar a un **pueblo** (lugar) que se chama Feilas, e levabamos moita fame, **ibamos** (iamos) sin comer, e chegamos alá e dixemos 'mal será que non nos dean de comer'. E puxéronnos a **cena** (cea), e era moi ruín, e dixemos '¡**vamos** (imos) levar un petardo esta noite!, ¡calquera tocará na verbena!' Pero despois, ó último, sentimos fretir, ruxir a cazola, e dixemos 'agora están fretindo **costilletas** (costeletas) e bistés e **vamos** (imos) **cenar** (cear) ben. **Vamos** (imos) comer pouco desto, que era unha **cena** (cea) mal **arreglada** (amañada), **patatas** (patacas) cocidas cunhos **huevos** (ovos)'. Cando, ¿que era? Unha **fuente** (prata) de pementos fritos.

Outra vez fun tocar a Escornabois e entonces eu fun comer a unha casa e levoume o home e estaba borracho coma un coiro, e cheghei á casa e alí non había **naide** (ninguén), era á medodía. Eu dixen: '¡estouche bo!. Díxenlle ó home: '¿e aghora que? ¿e o xantar?'. Dixo: 'eu non sei onde irá a ama'.

O home **iba** (ía) borracho coma un coiro. 'Esperar un pouco a ver se ven a ama, e se nos fai algho'. 'Pois logho esperar'. Esperar esperamos, pero a muller non viña. Entonces eu díxenlle: 'eu marcho, que son hora de ir tocar á tarde, e teño que ir comer á taberna'. E foi el e díceme: 'espéra aí'. Foi, colleu un xamón, e dixen: '¡Ah!, entonces inda **vamos** (imos) estar ben'. Foi, colleu o xamón e ¡ras! meteulle o **cuchillo** (coitelo) e puxémonos a comer no xamón …

References

Alcina, J. and Blecua, J. M. (1988) *Gramática Española*. Barcelona: Ariel.

Alonso, X. (1990) Situación cultural do galego do 1900 ó 1936. In *I Congreso da Cultura*. Santiago: Consellería de Educación, Xunta de Galicia, 347–9.

Álvarez, R.; Regueira, X.L. and Monteagudo, H. (1986) *Gramática Galega*. Vigo: Galaxia.

Babarro, X. (1994) A fronteira lingüística do galego co asturiano. Delimitación e caracterización das falas de transición dos concellos de Navia, Villallón, Allande e Ibias. In F. Fernández Rei (ed.) *Lingua e Cultura Galega de Asturias*. Vigo: Xerais.

Bochmann, K. (1990) Observacións sociolingüísticas sobre a lingua galega. In *I Congreso da Cultura*. Santiago: Consellería de Educación, Xunta de Galicia, 371–4.

Castro, R. (1996) Comportamento sociolingüístico dos estudantes de xornalismo. In *O Cartafol* 12 (March 1996), 4–5.

Chacón, R. (1978) A problemática lingüística. In *Realidade Económica e Conflicto Social*, Banco de Bilbao, 359–81.

Chacón, R. (1979) Diglosia e historia, *Grial* 66, 442–52.

Cunha, C. and Cintra, L. (1984) *Nova Gramática do Português Contemporâneo*. Lisbon: Sá da Costa.

Fernández Rei, F. (1990) Nacionalismo e dignificación da lingua galega no período 1972–1980. In *A Trabe de Ouro*, 1 (1990), 43–71.

Fernández Rei, F. (1991) *Dialectoloxía da lingua Galega*. Vigo: Xerais.

Fernández Rei, F. (1994a) Delimitación xeográfica e características lingüísticas do galego de Asturias. In *Britonia. Revista de Estudios da Terra Navia-Eo*. Mesa prá defensa del galego de Asturias e da Cultura da Comarca, 1 (1994), 123–37.

Fernández Rei, F. (ed.). (1994b). *Lingua e Cultura Galega de Asturias*. Vigo: Xerais.

Fernández Rei, F. (1994c) Áreas lingüísticas. In G. Holtus; M. Metzeltin and Ch. Schmitt. *Lexikon der Romanistischen Linguitik (LRL) VI, 2* (pp. 98–110). Tübingen: Niemeyer.

Fernández Rei, F. and Hermida, C. (1996) *A nosa Fala. Bloques e Áreas Lingüísticas do Galego*. Santiago: Consello da Cultura Galega. 1 book + 3 cassettes.

Fernández Rei, M. and Rodríguez, M. (1994) *Lingua Inicial e Competencia Lingüística en Galicia*. Santiago: Seminario de Sociolingüística, Real Academia Galega.

Fernández Rei, M. and Rodríguez, M. (1995a) *Usos Lingüísticos en Galicia*. Santiago: Seminario de Sociolingüística, Real Academia Galega.

Fernández Rei, M. and Rodríguez, M. (1995b) *Addenda a Lingua Inicial e Competencia Lingüística en Galicia*. Santiago: Seminario de Sociolingüística, Real Academia Galega.

Ferro, X. (1958) Cómo e por qué os escribanos deixaron de empregar o galego. In *Homenaxe a Otero Pedrayo*. Vigo: Galaxia, 251–3.

Filgueira, X. (1990) La résurrection d'une langue: Le galicien d'hier à aujourd'hui, *Arquivos do Centro Cultural Português* 28, 111–36.

Fishman, J. (1971) *Sociolinguistique*. Labor/Natham: Brussels/París.

García, C. (1985) *Temas de Lingüística Galega*. A Coruña: La Voz de Galicia.

Goyanes, H., Núñez, C., Romero, P. and Túnez, M. (1996) *A Información en Galego*. Santiago: Lea.

Hermida, C. (1992) *Os Precursores da Normalización*. Vigo: Xerais.

Hermida, C. (1993) *A Reivindicación da Lingua Galega no Rexurdimento (1840–1891): Escolma de Textos*. Santiago: Consello da Cultura Galega.

Hermida, C. (1994) A campaña publicitaria *En galego, o que ti queiras*. In C. Rodríguez (ed.). *Comentario de Textos Populares e de Masas* (pp. 241–68). Vigo: Xerais.

Hermida, C. (1995) Contribución á historia do galego nos medios de comunicación. A prensa no século XIX. In *A Trabe de Ouro*, 20 (1995).

López, D. (1989) *O Idioma da Igrexa en Galicia*. Santiago: Consello da Cultura Galega.

Lorenzo, R. (1985) *Crónica Troiana*. A Coruña: Fundación Pedro Barrié de la Maza.

Maia, C. de Azevedo (1986) *História do Galego-Português. Estado linguístico da Galiza e do Noroeste de Portugal desde o século XIII ao século XVI (Com referência à situação do galego moderno)*. Coímbra: INIC.

Mariño R. (1990) Motivacións para o emprego da lingua galega na literatura política dos primeiros anos do século XIX. *Grial* 105, 35–67.

Mariño, R. (1990) O galego nos séculos escuros: Achegas para unha caracterización sociolingüística da Galicia dos séculos XVI, XVII e XVIII. In *I Congreso da Cultura*. Santiago: Consellería de Educación, Xunta de Galicia, 333–9.

Mariño, R. (1991) Presencia do galego na sociedade galega durante os séculos XVI, XVII e XVIII. *Grial* 110, 263–74.

Monteagudo, H. (1984) A oficialidade do galego: historia e actualidade. *Lingua e Administración* 1, 2; 2, 2–3; 3, 3–4; 4, 2–3.

Monteagudo, H. (1985) Aspectos sociolingüísticos do uso do galego, castelán e latín na Idade Media en Galicia, *Revista de Administración Galega* 1, 85–108.

Monteagudo, H. and Santamarina, A. (1993) Galician and Castilian in contact: Historical, social and linguistic aspects. In R. Posnes and J.N. Green (eds) *Trends in Romance Linguistics and Philology. Volume 5: Bilingualism and Linguistic Conflict in Romance* (pp. 117–73). Berlin/New York: Mouton de Gruyter.

Monteagudo, H. (1994) Aspectos sociolingüísticos do uso escrito do galego, o castelán e o latín na Galicia tardomedieval (ss. XII-XV). In E. Fidalgo and P. Lorenzo (coords.) *Estudios Galegos en Homenaxe ó Profesor Guiseppe Tavani* (pp. 169–85). Santiago: Centro de Estudios Ramón Piñeiro/Xunta de Galicia.

Myers-Scotton, C. (1993) *Social Motivations for Codeswitching. Evidence from Africa*. Oxford: Clarendon Press.

Ninyoles, R. Ll. (1978) *Cuatro Idiomas para un Estado*. Madrid: Cambio 16.

Noia, C. (1988) Usos e actitudes lingüísticas na 'Época Nós', *Grial* 100, 174–82.

Nussbaum, L. (1992) Manifestacions del contacte de llengües en la interlocució. *Treballs de Sociolingüística Catalana* 10, València, 99–123.

Pensado, J.L. (1974) *Opúsculos Lingüísticos Gallego del Siglo XVIII*. Vigo.

Pensado, J.L. (1989) O galego no século da Ilustración. *Grial* 102, 183–98.

Pérez, X.I. and Reboleiro, A. (1987) *História da Língua*. A Coruña: Via Láctea.

Portas, M. (1991) *Língua e Sociedade na Galiza*. A Coruña: Bahía.

Ramallo, F.F. and Rei, G. (1995) *Publicidade e Lingua Galega. Os Consumidores ante o Uso do Galego na Comunicación Publicitaria e nas Relacións Comerciais*. Santiago: Consello da Cultura Galega.

Risco, V. (1927) Da renacencia galega. A evolución do galego e os seus críticos. *A Nosa Terra* 11, 233, 9–10.

Sande, X.X. (1981) As Irmandades da Fala: Unha aproximación ás actitudes lingüísticas, *O Ensino* 3, 35–8.

Santamarina, A. (1995) Frei Martín Sarmiento, trescentos anos despois. In *A Trabe de Ouro*, 24 (1995), 89–92.

Silva-Valdivia, B. (1994) Cambios de código, alternancias e interferencias lingüísticas: unha perspectiva didáctica sociocomunicativa. In B. Silva-Valdivia (ed.) *Didáctica da Lingua en Situacións de Contacto Lingüístico* (pp. 151–76). Santiago: Instituto de Ciencias da Educación, Universidade de Santiago de Compostela.

Taboada, M. (1979) *El habla del valle de Verín*. Santiago: Servicio de Publicacións Universidade de Santiago de Compostela. Annex 15 to *Verba*.

Turell, M.T (1995) L'alternança de llengües i el préstec en una comunitat interètnica. In M.T. Turell (ed.) *La Sociolingüística de la Variació* (pp. 259–93). Barcelona: PPU.

Chapter 5

The Occitan Speech Community of the Aran Valley[1]

JORDI SUILS and ÀNGEL HUGUET

The Geographical and Historical Context

Aran is a valley situated in the central Pyrenées, through which flow the higher stretches of the river Garona. Politically, it is situated in the north of Catalonia within the Spanish State. However, as it lies on the northern side of the Pyrenees, the language spoken there is a variety of Gascon, which belongs to the Occitan linguistic area,[2] an expanse of land whose boundaries are the river Garona to the north and east, the Atlantic ocean to the west, and the western Pyrenées and Basque linguistic area to the south, as illustrated in Figure 5.1. The Aran valley is to be found at the right angle of this triangle. It is 620 km^2 in size and has a population of about 6000.

When one considers the history of the valley, one must bear in mind its geographical situation as well as the fact that it offers a 'gateway' through the mountains in the centre of the Pyrenées. At the time of the Roman Empire, its inhabitants were known to be different from the rest of the tribes of Aquitaine. Greek and Roman historians referred to the Arenosi as a group apart from the Convenae people. Throughout the Middle Ages, Aran remained loyal to the Aragonese kingdom as a means of combating the pretensions of its neighbours. First, the threat came from the counties of Pallars and Ribagorça. Then, in January 1213, Toulouse and Aragón formed an alliance in order to fight against the territorial ambitions of France. This alliance came to an end at the battle of Muret with the death of the Aragonese King Pere II in September of the same year. Nevertheless, Aran remained within the kingdom of Aragón-Catalonia. Indeed, King Jaume I confirmed the rights of Aranese people upon their own territory (rivers, forests and pastures) and, in so doing, authorised the creation of something like an autonomous state within his own kingdom.

During the 13th century, the kingdoms of France and Mallorca showed interest in gaining power over the valley, but finally the Pope established that it belonged to Aragón-Catalonia. This was a consequence of an explicit request by the Aranese people, whose representatives went to Barcelona in 1312 to pay homage to Jaume II. To show his gratitude, the

Figure 5.1 Map of the Aran Valley (own source)

king gave them a special privilege known as 'Querimonia'. This was a legal text which remained valid for four centuries and established a number of institutions for Aranese self-government. An important part of the text established new territorial divisions of Aran. The valley was divided into three parts called 'terçons' (thirds), which were, in turn, divided in 'sesterçons' (halves of thirds). As will be seen later, people are still aware of the existence of these 'terçons', which now have a symbolic value as an indigenous means of social organisation, although nowadays the term 'terçon' is used to refer to all the original 'sesterçons'. What is more, the term is also used to form a feeling of solidarity among different villages beyond the boundaries of each municipality. For example, people from Pujòlo tend to regard all the villages in their 'terçon' as having a common character, whereas a kind of traditional enmity exists with the people of Arties and Garòs in the adjoining 'terçon'.

This privilege called 'Querimonia' also established the existence of a central government for the valley called the 'Conselh Generau' (General

Council). This was composed of representatives of all the 'terçons' and was headed by a governor known as the 'Sindic' (Syndic). These institutions guaranteed the defence of the rights of Aran and enabled the valley to fend off Catalan attempts to reduce its autonomy. Moreover, the words that Aranese nationalists impute to one of the commissioners before the government of Catalonia in 1411 are brought into perspective: 'Aran has never had any owner but God'.[3]

Such a context disappeared after 1716 with the defeat of the Catalan army in Barcelona at the hands of Felipe V and the imposition of the 'Decreto de Nueva Planta' which eliminated all the autonomous institutions of Catalonia. However, the new laws were only in part applied to Aran, where a great deal of its own government activity went on as before. The 'Conselh Generau', nevertheless, was abolished by Queen Isabel II in 1834. After the creation of the Second Spanish Republic in 1931, plans were made to restore the former political institutions of Aran, but they were interrupted by the Civil War and the subsequent dictatorial period until 1977. Thereafter, a popular organisation called 'Es Terçons' represented the wishes of the Aranese people to have an explicit presence in the future text of the *Estatut d'Autonomia de Catalunya* (Catalonia's Autonomous Statute).[4]

Some Linguistic Traits of Aranese

Aranese, as it belongs to Gascon, shares the defining features of that dialect in contrast with the rest of the Occitan domain, as well as showing a particular result in some cases. In phonetical evolution, the main facts are:

- the Gascon change from the Latin F to [h] as in FILIU > hilh ([hiʎ] son). The [h] pronunciation is only conserved in some villages of the lower part of the valley (Bausén and Canejan), and in the rest of the valley only [ø] is to be found (as in [iʎ]) in such cases;
- the disappearance of N between vowels as in CADENA > cadia (chain);
- the change of the Latin LL into [t] or [tʃ] in final position and into a simple [r] between vowels as in CASTELLU > castèth (castle) or gallina > garia (hen);
- the change of L into [w] in syllable-end position as in MEL > mèu (honey).

In the vocalism one can find the general defining aspects of Occitan, for example:

- the evolution of the long Latin *u* into [y] as in French (LUCE > lutz [lyts] it shines) and the evolution of the long Latin *o* into [u] as in BONA > bona ['buna] (good);

- the diphthongisation of the open *e* and *o*, favoured by velar or palatal contexts, as in: VETULU > vielh (old); FOCU > huec ('fire'); OSSU > uas (bone).

Morphology, especially the verbal conjugation, is often one of the main features used to decide about the peculiarity of the character of a Romance language or dialect, and it is always a complex task to describe it briefly. Anyway, the presence must be mentioned in Aranese of non-consonantal plural markers (a strange case in the context of Western Romance languages). This plural morphology can be found in the masculine of some nouns, most of the masculine plural forms of the adjectives and the masculine plurals of the personal pronouns, as in:

sg. bòsc – pl. bòsqui (woods)
sg. peish – pl. peishi (fishes)
sg. carro – pl. carri (carts)
sg. poth – pl. pothi ['putSi] (chickens)
sg. bon – pl. boni (good)
sg. long – pl. longui (long)
sg. nere – pl. neri (black)
sg. bèth – pl. bèri (nice)
fem. nosates – masc. nosati (us)
fem. eres – masc. eri (they)
fem. totes – masc. toti (all)
fem. quauques – masc. quauqui (some)

The extension of this trait is not limited to the boundaries of Aran: it has a continuity through the southern area of Arièja.[5]

The morphology of the Aranese verb is too complex to be described here, but in general it follows the Gascon type with some connections with the Catalan dialects of Pallars and Ribagorça (some examples will be seen below). Syntactic aspects peculiar to Gascon, such as the presence of declarative or interrogative markers (**que mingi** I eat; **e minges?** do you eat?), have a less frequent presence in Aranese (in contrast with their systematic usage in other areas).[6]

Legislation about Language and Means for Language Planning

Aranese was recognised as an official language in Aran in the so-called *Llei de Normalització Lingüística de Catalunya* (Linguistic Normalisation Act of Catalonia, 1983). So Aran has three official languages as Catalan and Spanish are also official there. Besides this, Catalan is also the 'own' language ('llengua pròpia' in Catalan) and Aranese is recognised as having the same condition in Aran. This detail ensures that Catalan and Aranese receive special attention, at least in theory. In January 1983 the orthographic rules of Aranese were proclaimed as official for the instruction of the language at school and for the activity of language normalisation.[7] The year 1986 saw the creation of the *Centre de Normalisacion Lingüistica dera Val d'Aran* (CNLVA: Centre for Linguistic Normalisation in the Val d'Aran) which is entrusted with the protection of the language.[8]

In 1990, a new law was passed for the restoration of the traditional institutions of Aranese self-government, called *Lei de Regim Especiau dera Val d'Aran*, or simply *Lei d'Aran* (Special Regulation Act of the Government of Aran) which states that Aranese, as an official variety of Occitan in Catalonia, must be an obligatory subject at school and there should be special protection in the activities of the civil service and in the media. Aranese is now the language of common usage in the public documents of the town councils and the *Conselh Generau*. As for the media, there is only one hour a day on the radio and half an hour on Catalan television (TV3) every Friday. The written word is represented by the four-page magazine *Arenosi*, published monthly by the CNLVA for cultural information.

As a consequence of the work of the *Centre de Normalisacion*, there is a good amount of literature published in Aranese. Apart from the productions for the state schools, made by the *Centre de Recorsi Pedagogics* (Centre for Pedagogical Resources), there are a certain number of books for commercial circulation. Most of them are the result of the annual literary competition 'Jusèp Condó Sambeat' in which the participants (and consequently the texts) are from both sides of the political border.[9]

Real Use Today

Figure 5.2, from Climent (1986), shows that 79% (understand and read (54.5%); also read (15.6%); also write (8.9%)) of the population of Aran are able to speak Aranese and 13.9% are only able to understand it.

Figure 5.3, also with data from Climent (1986), illustrates that 58.5% of people in Aran use Aranese in daily life, and around 24.4% (as a second language (10.2%); sometimes (14.2%)) use it sporadically.

These statistics may have changed nowadays in favour of passive competence: according to the same data from Climent (1986), the usage of Aranese as a spoken language is about 43% in the group aged between 21 and 30 years (30% less than those people above 70). As can be seen in Figure 5.4, in people under 20 there is a clear progression in the level of oral usage of Aranese, if compared with those who are between 21 and 30. This fact is not directly explained by Climent (1986), but it could be caused by the same fact that explains the high percentage of 'Only understand' and 'No understanding': a movement of young people of Aranese origin out of the valley and the immigration of young workers of Spanish, Galician, Portuguese and Catalan origin.

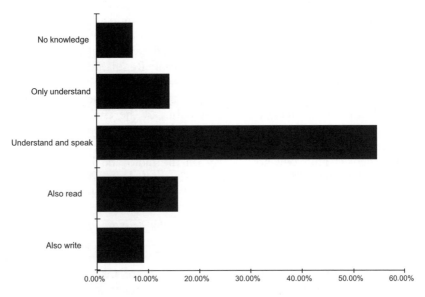

Figure 5.2 Level of knowledge of Aranese (adapted from Climent, 1986)

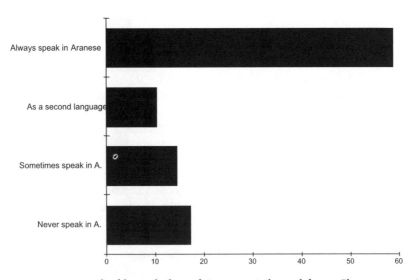

Figure 5.3 Level of knowledge of Aranese (adapted from Climent, 1986)

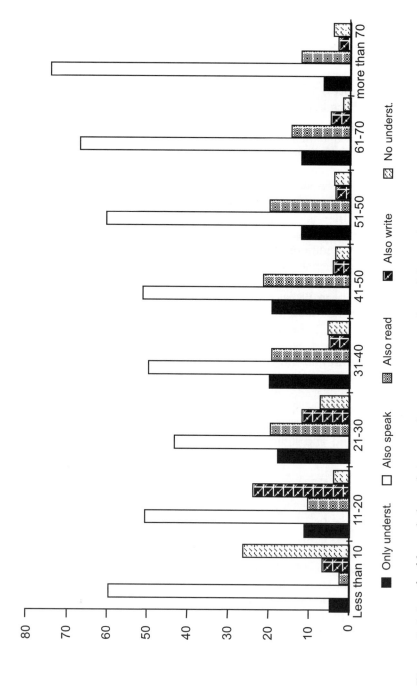

Figure 5.4 Level of knowledge of Aranese by age groups (adapted from Climent, 1986)

Aranese Occitan in Contact with other Languages

The Aranese dialect of Gascon is in historical contact with French, but not to the same extent as the rest of Gascon and Occitan. As a part of the kingdom of Aragón, Aran belonged to Catalonia since the Middle Ages, but its contact with Catalan is not comparable to the situation of Occitan in France with respect to French. Only during the last 40 years can we find in Aran a process of linguistic shift and substitution, although not in favour of Catalan but of Spanish. So, Aranese has suffered and indeed still suffers a situation of linguistic subordination that we can perceive in the case of Catalan and, in a similar way, in the case of all the languages other than Spanish to be found in Spain.

But the case of Aranese, as those of other linguistic minorities of a few thousand speakers and a very small territorial area within the Spanish State, is a special one because all the community is affected to the same extent and in the same way by changes in social organisation or by any kind of cultural innovation. As in other cases, there has been an abrupt change from a traditional society to a modern one: the transformation of an economy of shepherds and woodmen into a society based on tourism. Normally, young people work in restaurants, hotels and so on, or try to go to university in Barcelona or Lleida and then get a job in or outside Aran; maintenance of agriculture is basically the responsibility of the older people. Therefore, the changes in the economy are reflected in a kind of cultural divorce between generations. The process of linguistic substitution is a uniform one and is related to the mixing of the population and the abandonment of traditional ways of life.

The second decade of this century saw the beginning of the exploitation of hydroelectric possibilities in Aran. This in turn brought about the beginning of immigration. However, this immigration was not of a stable kind and indicated only the initial stages of the industrial advances in the valley. One area which was affected was that of the forests, whose traditional exploitation became an industrial one. During the 1940s a tunnel was cut through the mountains to ensure the connection between the valley and the road network of the rest of the state. This reduced the necessity to look for a job or go shopping on the other side of the border during the long winter months.[10] Old people still remember how different it was before the existence of the tunnel: when asked about relations to the south side of the mountains (the regions of Pallars and Ribagorça), they particularly remember the extreme weather conditions they had to suffer when walking across to the villages of Esterri or Sort when, for example, they were made to go out on military service. They also remember cases of friends who lost their lives because of the cold. So, in winter, it was naturally preferable to go to France. Men often worked on building sites whereas women got jobs in private houses as maids. They returned to their homes at the beginning of springtime. It is therefore easy to understand why elderly people normally have a good knowledge of French, even better than Catalan in some cases.

But contacts with Catalan have also been frequent for other reasons: in a society of traditional shepherds, the access of flocks to the high summer pastures is very important. Mountains have always been of common ownership in the villages of the Pyrenées (92.3% of land in the valley is of common property) and every family has the right to send its flock to the mountain belonging to the village. They can also decide whether they should accept other flocks and the price to be paid to the village. So, it has always been very important for the farmers on the south side of the mountains to maintain a good relationship with their northern neighbours, and marriages are traditionally frequent between people on both sides of the mountains, as is evident from Estrada *et al.* (1993). Language contact is then also traditional and is reflected in the fact that elderly Aranese speak the Pallarese dialect of Catalan when talking to Catalan people. People under 30 would speak central Catalan in the same situation, and this illustrates clearly the different means of language contact with Catalan: traditional activities, on the one hand, and tourism from Barcelona, on the other.

Contact with Spanish is also relatively traditional. In a border region, the presence of some kind of police force or army is an important one. Bearing in mind that Aran is an area of low demographic density, that presence is evident everywhere. The testimonies of the older people of the valley go a little further than this: the policemen ('carabinèrs', as they call the Spanish 'guardia civil') offered, for Aranese women, a real opportunity to escape from the comparatively hard prospect of work and economic difficulties. This justifies the complaint of an old man from Salardú: 'era qu'agarraue un carabinèr ja non volie saber arren de pagesi' ('if they could get off with a policeman they didn't want to know anything else about farmers'). So, contact with Spanish has been implicit in the definition of the political identity of Aran.

In this way, both the proximity of the valley to the border and the fact that it lies on the other side of the mountains ('en aute costat') have conditioned the Aranese identity. Until some years ago, the consequence of these factors had been a non-contradictory co-existence between a political identity as Spanish and a linguistic and ethnic identity as Aranese. In other words, to be Spanish there could be described as a relative concept: partially due to a generally centralised idea of Spain, Aranese people often refer to Spain and Spanish as the territory over the mountains in a geographical rather than political sense. On the other hand, speaking Aranese is a kind of function of being Aranese, but a non-explicit one. Traditionally, to be Aranese is a consequence of being born in the valley and of having Aranese parents. A special relationship exists between people in the same village or the same group of villages, a friendship based on the neighbourhood and a common character (or even enmity). This very particular and ancient relationship between truly Aranese people is reflected in a set of stereotypes and a clear sense of belonging of every person to one of a limited set of lineages. The term used for this concept is 'casa', which refers not only to the house as a building but also to its ownership, to all the members of the family who live there, and, of course, their ancestors. In this particular sense of community, it doesn't seem possible to express oneself in a language other than Aranese. In this context, Aranese is not even a language (in fact, the term 'language' is an innovation in a world like this) but a natural means of expression, the traditional way of speaking to people one has known since childhood.

Nothing threatens the normal existence of the language while this context is not disturbed, and this is the 'idyllic' state in which the dialectologist Joan Coromines found the language when he arrived in the valley at the beginning of this century. He wrote an accurate study of Aranese, a book which is still a work of necessary reference because of the state of linguistic 'purity' reflected there. Its great value is to ensure for the people the conservation, albeit only in written form, of a high amount of lexical and grammatical information.

Although the importance of Coromines (1990) is unquestionable, it has been useful basically in an erudite context and to a lesser extent for a practical work of corpus planning. As a popular dictionary, it is impractical, and illustrates to what extent there has been a rupture between the context found by Coromines and the one that exists nowadays. For a normal speaker of Aranese, there would rarely be a necessity to use Coromines' dictionary because most of its lexical entries are practically 'extinct' in modern, everyday, use. This circumstance represents a serious problem for the institutional means of language planning in their attempts to create a socially functional model of standard variety. In a conversation with a young woman on this subject, she complained about how difficult it was for the *Centre de Normalisacion Lingüistica dera Val d'Aran* (CNLVA) (Centre for Linguistic Normalisation in the Val d'Aran) to make their decisions acceptable: 'one day', she said, 'you read a strange new word and you think: oh; another invention of the Centre of Normalisation. But, the next day, you hear an old person use it and you realise how we are losing a lot of words'.

Such a circumstance is related to the idea of Aranese as a hypothetically mixed language, and these words of another young person could be an illustrative example: 'I think that Aranese people have adapted different words from the surrounding languages. They hear a new word and they say "it seems to sound O.K. it could work" and they start to use that word'. This opinion is naturally reinforced by the arrival of linguistic loans; something favoured by the cultural break-up described above. The fact that these external influences are becoming greater and greater has led to a reduction in the possibility of reaching a clear norm.

In linguistic terms a description can be formed of the features that Aranese shares with Catalan, Spanish and also with French. The similarities to the contiguous Catalan dialects illustrate the historical character of that contact, and it would be better to talk about shared facts than (mutual) influences. Some examples are:

- the presence of the prepositions *tà* and *entà* (to or for): *vau tà casa; entà qué ac vòs, aquerò?* (I am going home; what do you want it for?). These can also be found in the Ribagorçan dialect of Catalan or in Aragonese;
- the reduction of the plural article to a single form (s.m. *eth*, s.f. *era*, p. m.&f. *es*) that can also be found in Ribagorçan;
- the presence of imperfect past forms in *-eva/-iva* in both the Ribagorçan area (Alturo, 1995) and the high villages of the Aran valley (*voleva/sentiva* (I used to want/hear)); or the presence of -sc- infix (Ar.*patisqui*; Rib. *patisco* (I suffer)); or the presence of a velar insert in the subjunctive (Ar. *sènt-***ig***-a*/Rib. *sènt-***eg***-a* (that I hear));
- the sharing of some lexical forms: *gojat,-a/goiat,-a* (boy, girl); *guardar* (to look at)/*entreguardar* (to look between)/*desperguardar* (to awaken) . . .

In Aranese, there have been the same structural influences of Spanish that can be found in Catalan: lexical forms as **bueno** (in its use as a discursive connector similar to the English 'well'); **pues** (so); **pero** (but); the so-called 'neuter' pronoun **lo** (in Occitan *çò*: *tot lo de mèn qu'ei tòn*/*tot çò de mèn qu'ei tòn* (all that is mine is yours)); and, more recently, all the forms that have been introduced through cultural innovation: **coche** (car), **teléfono** (telephone), **número** (number), **pantalla** (screen), **carta** (letter), **bolígrafo** (ball-pen) with the additional loan represented by the entrance of proparoxytones.[11] These forms are one of the main problems for the definition of an Occitan-based norm for Aranese, to the extent that they are widely used and common in colloquial language. In such cases, the only realistic solution has been to adapt these lexical items to the phonological and orthographical rules and the evolution of Occitan (for example, in these specific cases the solutions would be: **coche** ['kutʃe], **telefon, numerò** [nyme'rɔ], **pantalha, carta/letra, boligraf**. Naturally, it doesn't solve the problem of the increasing linguistic distance between both sides of the political border, as for the rest of Gascon the solutions would be adapted from French (for example: *telefon, numerò* and *letra*; but *autò, ecran* and *stilò*).

Another problem, in close relation to that of Spanish influences, is the absence of genuine resources for the formal discourse in Aranese (only in recent years there has there been any written cultivation, and there is not a tradition of use in formal contexts for Occitan in general and for Aranese in particular). So, Aranese people tend to take the Spanish or even Catalan models when in a formal context, such as television or radio and for public discourse in general.

Language Attitudes and Identity

As has been mentioned above, social changes happened very fast. The most important fact was the arrival of the industrial exploitation of tourism. The excellent skiing conditions led to the opening of two stations in the valley. One of them is the most important in Spain. Consequently, agriculture and cattle raising have practically disappeared as a kind of basic economy and immigrants account for almost half of the present population. Linguistically mixed marriages are now commonplace. The majority of immigrants had Spanish as their mother tongue and, during the 1960 and 70s, this language was used exclusively in schools. Aranese became a language used only in a domestic context. Nowadays, young people use Spanish as the usual means of communication in most cases. As a consequence, although a linguistic awareness exists, the language is no longer a clear indicator of identity. On the other hand, one must remember that the valley is clearly defined in geographical terms and that Aran can be seen in a very different context when compared to the rest of the territories within the Spanish State (tourism has contributed to this awareness).

Language has its role to play in establishing an identity, but the claimed ability to speak it and its actual use has only a relative importance. Normally, those young people who claim to come from a bilingual or trilingual family (most of whom are from Aranese/Spanish families,[12] totalling about 15% of teenagers) usually state that they speak better Spanish than Aranese. However, 59% of this group also state that they regard Aranese as 'their language', whereas 13% consider that Aranese, Catalan and Spanish at the same time conform to their linguistic identity; 18% of the same group identify themselves with Spanish as their language, as can be observed in the first block of columns in Figure 5.5.

About 46% of all young people claim that Spanish is the only language they use in everyday activities at home, and practically none of these people claim any explicitly active competence in Aranese (only recently has it been taught in schools). However, a certain number of them identify themselves with Aranese (about 33%), with both Aranese and Spanish (4%) and also with all three languages – Aranese, Spanish and Catalan – at the same time (6%); 43% of them identify themselves only with Spanish, as can be observed in the third block of columns in Figure 5.5. In the case of people who claim to speak only Aranese at home, 3% of this group identify themselves only with Spanish. There is a clearly greater amount of identification with their 'own' language (81%), whereas 3% claim to have Spanish and Aranese as their languages and another 9% identify themselves with all three languages, as can be observed in the second block of columns in Figure 5.5.

So it can be stated that those who are monolingual (those who are only able to speak Spanish and whose parents use only that language) tend to

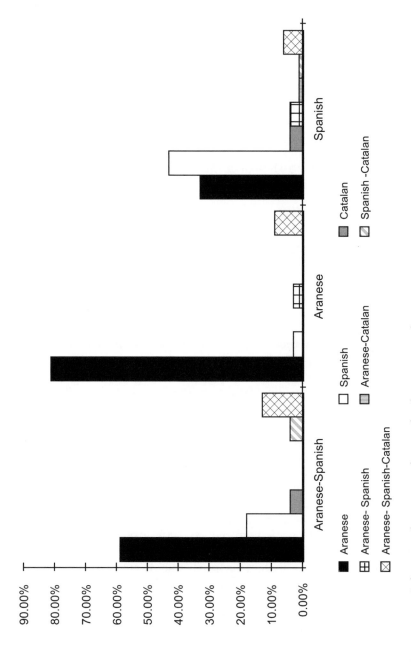

Figure 5.5 Subjective linguistic identity by language at home

assume the multilingual context of the valley as a factor of identity, and they don't always see their linguistic identity as related only to the language they speak, whereas those who are able to speak three languages (Aranese, Spanish and Catalan) and who are normally those with Aranese Occitan as language at home, tend to affirm their linguistic identity as related only to Aranese. This may indicate that, in the case of Aran, linguistic identity is partly related to the origin of one's parents and partly to the fact of being born in the valley depending on personal condition: to be of Aranese family means one is Aranese, but the same does not apply the other way round.

Patterns of Language Use and Manifestations of Language Contact

Patterns of language use

Such a kind of multilingualism causes all sorts of complex alternations in everyday conversation. In an interview with five members of *Joenessa d'Aran* (Aran Youth),[13] it was explained how it is perfectly possible to conduct a conversation in two or three languages at the same time. One said 'I talk Castilian to my father and Aranese to my mother depending on who I'm looking at while talking'. So it is possible to begin any interaction in any of the three languages and to continue in any other even within a single sentence. Another of those interviewed recounted how, as a student, he was living with two more boys from the same village, all of them with Aranese as the language of their respective homes: 'I talk in Catalan to one of them and in Castilian to the other and they talk to each other in Aranese'. But everyone has its own language: one remembers which is the language corresponding (to address oneself) to every person and acts accordingly when talking to that person. This 'personal language' is established, in the case of young people, during their childhood and it doesn't normally change thereafter: it remains as an inherent characteristic. The dynamics regarding the establishment of this 'personal language' are not clear and depend on particular contexts: a person may be of a linguistically Catalan background but his or her language may be another when talking to other people with the same background.

Nevertheless, Aranese is always in inferiority as a logical result of the fact that only those who are able to speak Aranese are also able to speak any other language of their friends.[14] In turn, Spanish is quantitatively favoured by the circumstance that, in everyday conversation, those who have Spanish as their only language at home can normally only speak Spanish and the rest of the people tend to change to Spanish when talking to them.[15] The result is that they do not attain even a passive competence in Aranese. So it is easy to understand that Spanish is the dominant language among young people in whose groups some, if not most of them, are of Spanish origin. Such a context creates a state of affairs in which Spanish finally becomes the language of conversation among people of Aranese origin. This context has changed a little in recent years, but only to a small extent. Firstly, there has been a process to restore the historical institutions and this has brought about the emergence of a certain cultural awareness. Secondly, Catalan has been introduced into state schools in all Catalonia. This has produced a need for a similar process in the case of Aranese as Aranese people regard their culture as something different in the context of an autonomous Catalonia in accordance with a long history of privileges. That has been the philosophy of 'Es Terçons'. So, at the beginning of the 1980s, a 'fashion' existed that favoured the claim for the use of Aranese and also the cultural identity of Aran. One could often see slogans like 'Jo, tostemp aranés' (me, always Aranese). So, the need to adopt a norm for literacy was seen as urgent. Once this norm became a reality, and Aranese began to be used in schools, it was felt that enough had been done. However, 10 years later it was clear that Aranese had not even started to solve the problem of quantitative recession. Indeed, the present situation still indicates that Aranese is in clear danger in the near future if everything continues as today.

Manifestations of language contact

Among the different common cases of codeswitching and code mixing, it is clear that a generic distinction must be established between those people having Aranese Occitan as their mother tongue and those who have Catalan (or Spanish in very few cases). In fact, the exceptional cases of people speaking Aranese as a second language and who speak it daily are basically people of Catalan origin. In such a situation, those who learn the language of the valley display Catalan interference in their Aranese. For these cases, the adoption of Aranese lexical elements could be observed, but with a certain fluctuation in the case of grammatical components: the verbal morphology or the definite articles, or some usages of prepositions, etc. The adoption of formal markers from central Catalan can also be found, which contrast with some forms of Aranese that, at the same time, are coincident with the corresponding forms in western Catalan. For example, a subjunctive like **passessin** shows the Catalan ending *-i-*, in contrast with the Aranese form *-e-* in *passessen*, the same form as in western Catalan. Moreover, some other formal markers from Catalan, which have tended to expand geographically as favoured forms, have begun to appear in Aranese, even in the case of native people. They are, of course, a common case for people with Catalan origin. An example is the extension of the infix *-itza-* (Catalan: **normalització** (normalisation)) when the Occitan form is *-isa- (normalisacion)*.

Other forms of interference are general, even for those with Aranese as a first language, although not from Catalan but from Spanish. Generally, such cases of interference are also common in Catalan (as a result of a situation of cultural subordination shared by Catalan and Aranese contexts). In this sense, it is possible to make a distinction between a 'traditional' type of interference and a more 'recent' one, which results from the adoption of culturally innovative contents and/or from the extension of colloquial idioms (particularly in the language of young people).

In the generic case of traditional interference, there are cases like those exposed earlier. For example, the usage of Spanish *pues* as a discourse connector. Among the cases of recent cultural contact, a simple case like **letrero** (sign) or an idiom like **pasar de todo** (not to pay much attention). All these forms are also possible to find in Catalan (*pues, lletrero, passar de tot*).

So, a difference between both cases of code mixing is that, for non-native Aranesophones, grammatical resources are more easily transferred to Aranese, and for native speakers there is a clear tendency to borrow lexical elements. The second is a more superficial kind of transfer, but it brings about structural consequences in phonological or semantic aspects.

All the different cases described above are possible to find in a couple of sentences from a conversation 'Metdia Aranés', the only daily radio programme in Aranese, on Catalunya Ràdio-Ràdio Aran. The following examples were produced by two young people of Catalan origin:

> ...jo les didaria que **passess***in* un shinhau **de tot**...
> (...I'd tell them not to pay much attention...)

> ...eth Conselh a hèt un esfòrç de normalitzacion de ... non sabi...
> **pues** de **letreros**, de libres ...
> (...the Conselh has tried to achieve normalisation by ... I don't know
> ...say with signs and notices...)

The next production is from another person of Catalan origin interviewed in the street. The cases are numbered and the corresponding text in Aranese without interferences is below, followed by a translation into English.

> **Sí, sí,**(1) **per mi**(2) òc. Ei qüestió(3) de voluntat. Ei qüestió de que (4)astimes (5)era Val d'Aran. E que ag**is**(6) de parlar, **pues**(7) normalment(8) (9)**amb la**(10) gent d'ací per que **amb** un forastèr non lo poràs parlar jamès. Jo non so(11) d'ací **pero**(12) m'agrade. E **totòm, totòm**(13) que visquen **ara**(14) Val d'Aran a de intentar parlà-lo, per qu'ei polit.

> [òc, òc, tà jo òc. Ei qüestion de volontat. Ei qüestion de qu'estimes ara Val d'Aran. E qu'ages de parlar, normauments damb era gent d'ací per que damb un forastèr non lo poràs parlar jamès. Jo non sò d'ací mès

m'agrade. E toti, toti es que visquen ena Val d'Aran an de sajar de
parlà-lo, per qu'ei polit].

('Yes, yes, I think so. It's a matter of will. A matter of whether you
love the Aran Valley. And you have to speak, sort of normally, to the
people from here because you'll never speak (Aranese) with anybody
from elsewhere. I'm not from here but I like it. And everybody,
absolutely everybody must try to speak it, because it's nice').

(1), (7), (8) and (12) are common in the use of people with Aranese as a
first language. (8) is the general case of **-al** endings (**general, principal**
(general, main)) taken from Catalan or Spanish as cultisms (the Gascon
ending for these examples is **-au**). (1), (7) and (12) are words with a discourse role, not a grammatical or deictic one, and these contexts are
normally more open to interference. But the rest are components with a
clearly syntactic calque: (2) is a double case of extension in the context of
usage of a preposition (**per** (for)) and the reduction of the contexts
corresponding to another (**tà** (for) with a final sense or (to) with directional
sense). The pronoun is not marked for case when introduced by a preposition in a context like this in Occitan, and the case marking observed in
(2) is also a Catalan influence. (5) and (14) are also relative to the general
calquing of prepositions: direct objects are introduced with preposition *a*
(to) in Aranese when they refer to human or personified beings, as in this
case (so it must be **ara -a + era-**); (14) is the case of the usage of **a** (as in
Catalan) in a context where it must be **en** (in) in Aranese. (9), (10) and (13)
are cases of the usage of Catalan lexical transfers with a grammatical
function (preposition, article and pronoun respectively). (3) is a case of
nominal morphology taken also from Catalan (**-ó** [-'o] for **-on** [-'uŋ])
and (11) a case of influence in verbal morphology (a hybrid form between
Aranese *sò* and Catalan *sóc* (I am)). (6) is also a case of the adoption of
Catalan (subjunctive) standard morphology. Finally, (4) transcribes a Catalan realisation of weak [e] in initial position.

   The main problem for a user of Aranese is to establish a clear norm: the
informant probably thinks that he is speaking Aranese, but in fact he
speaks a sort of mixed language between Catalan and Aranese. The
structural closeness between both languages is an advantage in terms of
learnability, but it also makes it difficult to keep oneself aware of the
syntactic calques, and this observation is in some measure attributable to
those who have Aranese as a first language and whose use of it has been
traditionally open to external influences. Lexical borrowing is the common
case in the language of this group. The following example was produced
by a young informant, a boy aged about 25 with Aranese as first language
and who spoke it normally with his friends:

   ... er ajuntament de Vielha mos a concedit un loca*l*, e quan ja l'*estàvem
intentant* apraià-lo tà hèr amassases de quinsevolh manèra mos a gessut

ua gotèra en loca*l*, **pero en plan salvaje** [sal'βaxe] (1), **o sea**(2) de ua **cloaca**(3) deth pis de naut, e *bueno* non se i pòt estar alavetz. Alavetz aqueth loca*l*, *pues* a quedat un shinhau … Eth darrèr còp que i anèren aueren d'anar *asta* damb **mascarilhes** [maxkariʎes] (4)… *Lo* que passe que, *claro*, **mos a talhat** molt **el ròlho**(5) *lo* dera gotèra…

('The Town Council in Vielha gave us somewhere to meet, and just when we were trying to do it up to have meetings … a leak appeared in the ceiling, a really enormous one, I mean, from some waste pipe from the flat upstairs, and, well, now we can't meet there. So, that place is now a bit … the last time they went there they had to put masks on … the thing is that, you see, the leak has really messed us up …')

(3) and (4) are cases of innovative terms borrowed from Catalan or Spanish. In (4), the ending -*ilhes* is a Spanish diminutive. The curious fact is that -*sk*- is pronounced [-xk-], as an adoption of a typical realisation of Spanish (an extension of the dialect of Madrid through the language of young people). (2) is also an innovative term, a connector whose corresponding form in Aranese is **o sigue** (that is to say). (1) and (5) are cases of codeswitching. (5) is partially adapted from Spanish **cortar el rollo** (to mess someone up), but it incorporates the foreign article **el** (Aranese *eth*). The codeswitched form shows a form with the Spanish sound [x] but, for the rest, it is really difficult to say if the whole form is adapted to Aranese or not: **pero** is an old loanword in Aranese, and **plan** is also an independent borrowing. As a consequence, although the translation to Spanish is formally identical to the form in the text, it is not easy to decide if it is really Spanish at all or an adaptation of a Spanish expression. The fact is that Spanish **salvaje** has a literal translation in Aranese *sauvatge* (savage) but, in a context like the one given here, the direct borrowing **salvaje** has a different meaning: it doesn't mean *sauvatge* but foolish (i.e. in a metaphorical sense). The primary meaning of *sauvatge* remains untouched, but the expressive possibilities of the language are unexploited in favour of foreign resources, which brings about structural consequences at least in semantics. Other traditional borrowings are transcribed in italics.

In contrast with the production of an informant of Catalan origin like the one seen above, the general aspect of this production of a native Aranesophone is the relative stability of the grammatical components. As has been stated before, the consequences of language contact are manifest at a discourse level (through connectors) and at a more specifically lexical level (those wide areas implied in different forms of cultural innovation: through colloquial idioms, for example) with clearly deeper results in structural terms.

All the examples given above are from adult people, not under 25. The case of the children following the immersion pro-gramme in Aranese in the school is still to be particularly studied.

The Role of Education

The introduction of Aranese into school took place in the 1987/88[16] school year. The need to respect the coexistence of three languages was solved by setting up three different models of scholarisation in pre-primary education (this begins when the children are three years old, in the schools known as 'escòles mairaus'). Each model used one of the three languages as the basic instrument of education. In every model, there were some classes conducted in the languages apart from the basic one. Parents chose the model that they wanted their children to follow. This system continued for the next few years, so those who began with one of the models in 1987 would continue with the same model until they were eight years old, the third year of primary education.

In fact, this plan was an experimental one, and was applied to Vielha, the main village in the centre of the valley where most of the total population (60%) and of the immigrants are concentrated. In the other villages, with low populations, there was neither the possibility of applying the strategy nor the need to do so.[17]

It must be pointed out that the need to proceed in Vielha with the experimental plan of education as described above was due to the fact that parents didn't always agree with the idea of sending their children to a school where they had to learn most of the subjects in a language other than the one they spoke at home, and Vielha is the village where live the majority of the immigrants in the valley. Those who complained for such an obligation were, for the most part, Spanish-speaking immigrants from different areas in Spain. However, this was not true in all the cases. The main dilemma was whether or not to have Aranese as the basic language of teaching. In terms of usefulness, a certain number of parents fully supported the presence of Spanish in schools. It is the language which enables a person to do anything in private or public life without having any kind of trouble, not only in the valley, but also in any other parts of Spain. This is important if one considers that, in a large number of cases, young people don't regard their future as related to the possibility of getting a job in Aran but with the need to leave the valley.

Catalan is also seen as a relatively 'useful' language; it is a fact that a good knowledge of Catalan is necessary to get a considerable number of jobs in Catalonia, especially those in the civil service. But even teenagers do not see Aranese as a useful language, at least not in economic terms. So, to choose Aranese was (is) an ideologically connoted option and to choose Spanish is a practical one. It can be easily understood that not all the opposition to Aranese as the basic means of education was expressed by parents of Spanish or Catalan origin.

After the third year of primary education, those who had followed the experimental programme went on to another system of language alternance, where the whole of teaching time was divided in three proportional parts, one for each of the three languages. In theory, there was no previous need to teach any subject in any particular language. However, in practice, it was seen as preferable to teach in Aranese the subjects related to natural sciences or society. Firstly, they were subjects with a closer connection to reality outside the school and, secondly, they were easier to adapt in linguistic terms to texts which could be used as pedagogical material in class.[18]

In 1992, the Catalan Parliament passed a series of decrees concerning linguistic usages in education (most importantly the 75/1992 and 95/1992 decrees concerning primary education). It was explicitly stated that Catalan had to be the basic language used in primary schools, while Spanish should no longer have such a role in Catalonia. It was mentioned that Aranese should be given the same attention as Catalan in the special case of Aran. This meant that the system, which offered three separate models, was to be adapted by suppressing Spanish in favour of Catalan. Of course, there have been problems. Indeed, at the beginning of every new school year there are sometimes violent arguments against the presence of Aranese in school. This is logical if one considers the contrast between the practical judgements of some parents and the procedures of language planning.

Recent Manifestations of Language Loyalty

Immersion programmes

It must be said, in this respect, that attitudes are less extreme among pupils. At least among some members of *Joenessa d'Aran*, there was a clear disagreement about the benefits of having Aranese as the only basic linguistic means of learning at school, given the fact that the so-called 'immersion programme' will probably be extended in favour of Aranese and also of Catalan. They said that this type of discussion is a typical one in the meetings of their organisation, but there seems to be a consensus of opinion that all those who live in Aran should have a similar knowledge of the three official languages. There is also a clear agreement that, in the field of technical language, knowledge only of Aranese does not present a serious problem. This is important in subjects such as Maths or Physics. 'If you go to a Catalan university', they said, 'there's not a great problem in adapting yourself to the new language. All three languages are very similar to each other.'

As mentioned earlier, those who argue against immersion in Aranese refer to the extreme lack of utility of a language spoken by only three thousand people. These people fail to consider, in such judgements, the fact that Occitan is also spoken on the other side of the border; their central argument is not the number of speakers but the practical utility of the language. In contrast, those who argue in favour of the immersion programme have resolved, in a personal decision, to speak Aranese at least when talking to people of Aranese origin. The members of *Joenessa d'Aran* also commented that the fact that they belonged to such an organisation obliged them to act in accordance with their position of representatives of a certain compromise with the Aranese traditional culture. So they decided to write all their public notices in Aranese and their leaders have to speak in Aranese when they address to those who attend their meetings. That made some people of Spanish origin adapt their linguistic habits when talking to their friends of Aranese origin. This is an important indication of how some attitudes have changed, at least in certain groups. These people are usually aged about 20, when linguistic practices are already clearly defined among friends.

Associations for the defence of Occitan

Whatever the changes may have been, it is important to point out the social impact of the existence of an organisation like *Joenessa d'Aran*. The organisation has about 150 members when the total population of Aran is no more than 6200, and they have specific objectives about the defence of the Occitan language in the valley. These efforts have contributed to the weakening of the traditional idea that Aranese is something for old people. In this sense, its situation used to be similar to that of the Catalan receding varieties spoken in the Pyrenées. An indication of how things have changed was the recent creation of a pop group composed of young people aged no more than 19 years who sing only in Aranese. There is not only the weakening of the idea that Aranese is related to traditional life and elderly people, there is also the wish to adapt the language to the normal usages of a modern one. The attitudes of the members of *Joenessa d'Aran* and others make us think that the institutional work of language planning has found its response in social activity and receptiveness.

Recently, another society has been created for the defence of Aranese, called *Lengua Viua* (Living language). At the first meeting of this organisation, which we were able to attend in the summer of 1993, people expressed the general perception that the Aranese language was in clear danger of extinction and that there was a need to awaken public awareness of this danger. Also expressed was a clear disappointment and pessimism about the first 10 years of institutional work. The basic aim should be to proclaim the right and duty to give sense of pride to the language. In the same year, *Lengua Viua* organized a popular demonstration using, as a model, an act in defence of the vernacular language, with a certain tradition in the Basque country, known as 'Korrika'. The Aranese version is called 'Corsa pera lengua' ('The language run'). A runner sets off from Plan de Beret (a high point in the valley) and the other comes from Pònt de Rei (the lowest point). They each take a key (a traditional symbol of Aran) and the key is passed on to another runner every two or three kilometres. The race passes through all the 'terçons' of the valley and, when the two keys come together at the centre of the valley, a map is formed with the smaller maps of each 'terçon'. Afterwards, music is performed throughout the afternoon and evening. The act is very well attended: about a thousand people, most of them aged between 15 and 20 years, have taken part in each edition. So far, it has taken place every year. An important thing to point out is that the guest musical band is always one from the other side of the border, so people enjoy themselves and come into contact with a variety of Gascon other than Aranese at the same time. Indeed, Nadau, a Gascon pop-folk band from Bearn are quite a social phenomenon in Aran: a good number of teenagers are able to sing their songs by heart, although they don't understand the words at all!

Some Conclusions

The next few years will perhaps be the most important in the history of Aranese. The popular opinion is that the individual attitudes of Aranese people are determinant for the definitive survival of their language. There's no doubt about this, but it also seems clear that the advances in self-government and the increasing presence of Aranese in schools have played a symbolic role of great value: positive attitudes about language are closely related to the way in which such a subject is officially considered and the extent to which it is reasonable to envisage a certain level of expectancy. The ability of Aranese people to organise themselves for the defence of their identity has always been central in this respect, and, probably, this will also be true in the near future.

The continuity of small linguistic communities like this induces those who are implied in the task of the language planning of minorities to find the essential aspect of their work: it is simply a desirable thing that these varieties continue to exist. But the continuity of Aranese will be much more than simply this. This community constitutes a point of reference for all those who work for the survival of Occitan and other linguistic varieties spoken in the Pyrenées. As long as there is the task of language planning to apply, there is also the validity of the Aranese case as a model for the other Occitan varieties in the French State, and the possibility of inviting France to recognise and protect them in a similar way within the European political context.

Acknowledgements

We must thank Jonathan Hodgson for his help in translating and correcting this article.

Notes

1. The contents of this article come from three different sources: (1) the authors' knowledge of the context described; (2) the data contained in the bibliography referred to in the text; (3) the conclusions of the answers to a questionnaire given to the students of the Collègi Garona in Vielha and Jordi Suïl's interviews with young and old people from different parts of the valley. We are very grateful to the people of Salardú who gave us their time and their help for our recordings. We must also thank Jordi and José Manuel from Salardú, Maria from Escunhau and Noelia and Maria José from Vielha, and also Mònica from Berga, for their patience and sincerity.
2. For short and clear evidence about the belonging of Aranese to the Occitan ensemble, see Lamuela (1987: 124–26). For a detailed description see also Coromines (1990).
3. These words would be repeated by J. Nart Rodès, an Aranese member of the Catalan parliament, in a speech made in the presence of President Francesc Macià in Aran in 1931.
4. More historical data could be found in Viaut (1987).
5. An article dedicated to this subject is Bec (1956). The main isoglosses that justify the attribution of a particular character to Gascon are described in Bec (1968).
6. A detailed description of Gascon and its dialects is in Rohlfs (1935).
7. Those rules were decided by a commission composed of six teachers and writers from Aran, three Occitan linguists and five Catalan linguists. They adopted the conventions of the Institut d'Estudis Occitans (Institute for Occitan Studies) as referential criteria for codification and for solving the relative chaos in the references to literacy until that moment. For details see Lamuela (1987: 117–71) and Sarpoulet (1985).
8. In spite of the importance *per se* of its existence, this institution has a very low budget and, consequently, a relatively limited scope for its activities, basically consisting of work of low cost like correction of texts and translations.
9. The main Aranese writer was Jusèp Condó Sambeat (1867–1919), a local representative of the Occitan literary movement of the 'Felibritge' in the first decades of the century. His main work was the novel *Era isla des diamants*.
10. The other traditional connection, the mountain pass of Era Bonaigua, is still normally closed in winter due to snow.
11. Proparoxytones are strange to Occitan, and this is obviously also true for Aranese with the exception of some verbal forms of the subjunctive.
12. The percentages given here are part of the data extracted from a questionnaire given to a group of 147 teenagers in Collègi Garona, the only Centre for secondary education in the valley. They represent more than 60% of the total population aged between 15 and 18 years in the valley in 1996. The questionnaire asked for some subjective data such as the perception of vitality or utility of Aranese, the need for a greater presence of Aranese in schools, and also the personal linguistic and territorial identification. We are very grateful to Miquèu Segalàs for his help.
13. *Joenessa d'Aran* is an organisation composed of young people who refute the claim that 'young people are always at the pub'. They also have an explicit wish to work for the cultural traits of Aran. They have neither religious nor political vinculations, although some have related them to *Unitat d'Aran*, the only Aranese nationalist party.
14. That is to say: trilingual people speak Aranese, Catalan and Spanish and they are normally of Aranese family, or at least one of their parents speaks Aranese; bilinguals speak normally Catalan and Spanish and have Catalan as language at home; and monolinguals speak only Spanish and have this one as the only language at home. Obviously, this can not be stated in such absolute terms: there is a certain dynamics in the fact that some monolinguals become bilinguals in Spanish and Catalan, and some bilinguals become trilinguals, but there is not a direct passage from monolingualism (in Spanish) to bilingualism in Spanish and Aranese, so Catalan has a certain role of 'first step'.
15. It must be noted that only 22% of young people between 14 and 17 years declare to have only Aranese as the language of normal use at home, and 15% to have Aranese

and Spanish for such context. In front of them, 46% state to have Spanish as the only language at home. Other combinations have little percentages: 5% for Catalan; 4% for Aranese and Catalan; 3% for Spanish and Catalan.

16. The organism entrusted with the plans for the introduction of Aranese is the SEDEC (*Servei d'Ensenyament del Català*) (Service for the Teaching of Catalan).

17. More details about Aranese in pre-primary education during the last few years can be found in Seira (1994).

18. The lack of funds has always been a serious constraint for the creation of material for didactic purposes in the teaching of or in Aranese.

References

Alturo, N. (1995) La variació d'*haver* auxiliar al català nord-occidental. In M.T. Turell (ed.) *La Sociolingüística de la Variació* (pp. 221–55). PPU: Barcelona.

Bec, P. (1956) Du pluriel en -i des adjectifs en gascon pyrenéen oriental. *Via Domitia* 3, 24–32.

Bec, P. (1968) *Les Interférences Linguistiques entre Gascon et Languedocien dans les Parlers du Comminges et du Couserans. Essai d'Aérologie Systématique.* Paris: Presses Universitaires de France.

Centre de Normalisacion Lingüistica dera Val d'Aran (CNLVA) (1991) *Prumèr Concurs Literari de Narracion 1990*. Vielha: CNLVA.

Centre de Normalisacion Lingüistica dera Val d'Aran (CNLVA) (1992a) *450 Mots que cau Saber entà Començar a Liéger, Escríuer e Parlar er Occitan dera Val d'Aran*. Vielha: Conselh Generau d'Aran.

Centre de Normalisacion Lingüistica dera Val d'Aran (CNLVA) (1992) *Racondes Bracs*. Lleida: Pagès editors.

Centre de Normalisacion Lingüistica dera Val d'Aran (CNLVA) (1993) *Dusau Concurs Literari de Narracion 1992*. Lleida: Pagès editors.

Centre de Normalisacion Lingüistica dera Val d'Aran (CNLVA) (1994a) *Tresau Concurs Literari de Narracion 1993*. Lleida: Pagès editors.

Centre de Normalisacion Lingüistica dera Val d'Aran (CNLVA) (1994b) *De quan Panèren un Peishic de País*. Lleida: Pagès editors.

Centre de Normalisacion Lingüistica dera Val d'Aran (CNLVA) (1996) *Literatura de Casa Nòsta*. Lleida: Pagès editors.

Climent, T. (1986) *Realitat Lingüística a la Val d'Aran*. Barcelona: Generalitat de Catalunya.

Comission entar estudi der normatiua lingüistica aranesa (CENA) (1982) *Nòrmes Ortografiques der Aranés*. Barcelona: Generalitat de Catalunya.

Condó, J. (1981) *Era Isla des Diamants*. St. Girons: Escòlo deras Pireneos.

Coromines, J. (1990) *El Parlar de la Vall d'Aran*. Barcelona: Curial.

Estrada, F., Roigé, X. and Beltran, O. (1993) *Entre l'Amor i l'Interès. El Procés Matrimonial a la Val d'Aran*. Tremp: Garsineu edicions

Lamuela, X. (1987) *Català, Occità, Friülà: Llengües Subordinades i Planificació Lingüística*. Barcelona: Quaderns Crema.

Rohlfs, G. (1935) *Le Gascon. Études de Philologie Pyrénéenne.* Tübingen/Pau: Max Niemeyer/ Marrimpouey Jeune, 1977.

Sarpoulet, J.M. (1985) Quatre graphies pour une langue: description diachronique succinte des différentes graphies de l'aranais. *Garona* 1, 155–63.

Seira, I. (1994) The Aranese language in pre-primary education (3 to 6 years of age) in Vall d'Aran. In A. van der Gott, W.J.T. Renkema and M.B. Stujt (eds) *Pre-primary Education* Vol. 2. Ljouwert/Leeuwarden: Mercator-Education/Fryske Akademy.

Vergés, F. (1991) *Petit Diccionari Castelhan-aranés-catalan-francés; Aranés-castelhan-catalan-francés*. Vielha: Conselh Comarcau dera Val d'Aran.

Viaut, A. (1987) *L'Occitan Gascon en Catalogne: le Val d'Aran. Du Vernaculaire au Formel*, Bordeaux: Maison des Sciences de l'Homme d'Aquitaine.

Chapter 6
The Asturian Speech Community

ROBERTO GONZÁLEZ-QUEVEDO

The Linguistic Situation in Asturias

The area in which Asturian is spoken includes the whole of the Principality of Asturias as well as adjoining areas of León. Estimates of the number of speakers vary, but if the total population of Asturias is approximately 1,100,000, various surveys have reported that around a third of these inhabitants speak Asturian, usually known as Bable. At all events it is difficult to arrive at an objective assessment since many inhabitants habitually use both Spanish and Asturian, depending on the context, and when questioned by researchers or survey-conductors tend to hide their linguistic roots. This difficulty becomes all too evident during field work, and in order to overcome it we need to avoid jumping to hasty conclusions and interpret what the informants say strictly in context, being aware of the complex and ambivalent nature of the situation. In general, Asturian is reserved for use in the family and with friends and neighbours, while the Spanish language (or if you like the Castilian spoken in Asturias) is the language of preference in more formal or official contexts. This Spanish will, however, tend to be full of features carried over from Asturian, as will be shown. Such a social division of labour running through language use is a clear instance of diglossia, as will become clear as we proceed.[1]

To be able to study the Asturian language from point of view of the society in which it is used, some brief observations about the language's present situation must be made as well as mentioning the vicissitudes that it has suffered in the past.

The Asturian language is a Romance tongue that formed in the north of the Iberian Peninsula. To begin with it diffused throughout an area that largely coincides with the old kingdom of Asturias. From there it spread southwards with the advancing Christians, into the prolongation of Asturias which became the kingdom of León. In traditional philology, the terms 'Leonese' or 'Astur-Leonese' refer to the linguistic domain which formed between Galician-Portuguese to the west and Spanish to the east. In the south of this relatively extensive area, different varieties of Leonese speech were used which have either disappeared completely or have been enormously weakened. In contrast, in the north of the domain, in an area comprising Asturias and the northern fringe of Léon, the Asturian language is still in vigorous use. These speakers call their language *Asturiano* or *Bable* (Asturian). It should be noted however, that along the western edge of Asturias, between the Rivers Navia and Eo, a transitional form known in traditional philology as Galician-Asturian is used.

Asturian, then, is a minority language which has over recent years suffered the consequences of major economic and social changes that have affected all Asturian society as a result of industrialisation and the development of the mines. These changes have affected the structure of families and communities (González-Quevedo, 1991). For the majority of Asturian speakers, living in rural areas, the use of their own language is a symptom of ignorance and social inferiority. Spanish, on the other hand, is seen as a prestigious language that opens the door to a wealth of opportunities. Some Asturian speakers actually feel there is a *stigma* attached to use of Asturian, in the sense that Barth (1976) uses the term in his analysis of what amounts to a linguistic inferiority complex.

Historical Aspects

Asturian is one of several Romance languages that developed in the Iberian peninsula, although its history is different from the other peninsular tongues. Much could be said on the internal and external history of Asturian compared to other Romance languages (Garcia Arias, 1982) but in this work we shall limit ourselves to giving some broadly general historical details, as well as commenting on the literary culture and the recent process of 'normalisation' or development of the language so that it may be used in all contexts.

Asturias was the first Christian kingdom in an Iberian Peninsula largely held by the Muslims. As the centre of gravity shifted southwards, however, Asturias began to lose political ascendancy and this loss was accentuated by the union of Castile and León. It is possible to find documents written in Asturian Romance up to the 16th century (as indicated for example by the Avilés statutes and similar documents). After that date, Spanish ousted Asturian as the written language. Spanish became the official language in all respects, while Asturian was the vernacular used by the people. It is true that religious tracts were still written in Asturian, to assist the faithful in their understanding. The church's attitude was clear: it considered Spanish to be the most suitable language for the liturgy and all religious documents. And yet we find many references to little books and pamphlets written in Asturian by the clergy to connect with the population and get the active participation of the congregation in certain religious ceremonies.

Nonetheless, from the 17th century onwards we find examples of the cultivation literature in Asturian. Thus, in 1639 there was an important literary competition in Oviedo on the occasion of the adoption of Santa Eulalia as patron saint of the diocese. The winning entry was a poem written in Asturian, one of the first such in Asturian literature. Notice, incidentally, that these classic Asturian poets did not write predominantly on rural or peasant life (as happened later on). Instead they frequently chose elaborate or sophisticated subjects, including classical mythology, and modelled their style on the great Latin and Greek authors.

From opinion expressed by authorities and writers on things literary and linguistic we deduce that until the turn of the 20th century in Asturias the local language was considered to be just another of the languages native to the peninsula. However from this point onward, the Asturian upper classes turned their back on their linguistic heritage in a way that their counterparts in Catalonia and the Basque Country did not. Thus, despite the many Asturians who have defended the Asturian language over the years, it is really only since the end of the Franco Regime that steps have been taken at political level to bring about normalisation, that is, empowerment of the language at all levels.

In 1974, the organisation known as *Conceyu Bable* (the Bable Council) was founded. This linguistic and political association was to have great social impact. Its role was to get the population to defend their linguistic rights as Asturian speakers. In this it was very active: teaching courses in Asturian, publishing magazines and pamphlets, publishing literary works, creating public opinion in the media.

In this way they succeeded in getting a large and, above all, very active sector of Asturian society to be concerned over their linguistic rights as speakers of Asturian. The swelling tide in favour of the language resulted in the setting up in 1980 of the *Academia de la Llingua Asturiana* (Academy for the Asturian Language), with the backing of all political parties. The creation of the *Academia* was an event with far-reaching consequences in many respects. In the first place, it had important symbolic repercussions, since it amounted to the official recognition – however theoretical – of the Asturian language. Secondly, the densely textured work carried out by the *Academia* at different levels (scientific studies, literary creation, language use, etc.) succeeded in getting the Asturian question increasing recognition in Asturian society and regional party politics.

The Situation of Asturian at School

Back in the days when the *Conceyu Bable* (the Bable Council) had just begun to be active, one of the most frequent complaints was that Asturian was not taught in schools in the Principality. The phrase *'Bable nes escueles!'* (Asturian in the schools) become the most popular rallying cry in the political transition period in Asturias (after Franco's death) and encapsulated the basic aspirations of all those who were defending Asturian: the survival of Asturian depended on coming generations having access to it in the educational system.

Finally, the Asturian autonomous government began to take the first steps in bringing Asturian into schools. The Asturian language became a school subject taught in certain pilot schools at elementary level. After several years of very positive experience with these centres, the scheme was extended to more schools – but progress was painfully slow, inviting criticism from Asturianist circles. Despite this, the fact that Asturian was on the curriculum in some schools was a decisive step forward for various reasons. Firstly, because it transmitted the language to the youngest in the community, which was a fundamental aim in the struggle for linguistic rights. Secondly, because it got teachers to commit themselves in a way that had very important consequences. Thirdly, because it meant raising awareness among Asturian people telling them that they possessed a language of their own that needed to be protected and cultivated.

More recent moves made by the autonomous government in power from 1991–1995 were to guarantee the teaching of Asturian in *all* centres of education (at present this is the case only in one third of them) even if only as an optional subject, in accordance with the Asturias autonomous legislation.

Linguistic Minority Status and Diglossia

To understand the Asturian linguistic situation we need to refer to the literature of the last few decades on language contact (Weinreich, 1953; Ferguson, 1959; Fishman, 1967, 1970, 1971).

There are features common to the situation of all minority languages in Europe, as well as features that are specific to each individual case. Looking at patterns of linguistic behaviour in Asturias we see certain features in common with other minority languages in Europe. Analysis of Asturian language use, for example, reveals aspects that Dorian (1981) notes for Scottish Gaelic: Dorian found the language had taken refuge in various redoubts like family and religious life and was being eliminated from the workplace. It is important to note, however, that certain industries such as mining have considerably favoured Asturian: the Asturian coalfields are the areas where there is the most favourable collective attitude to the language, despite having suffered large waves of immigration. In other sectors, however, industrialisation has had a more or less negative impact on Asturian.

There are parallels, too, with languages in other parts of the world beside Europe. Sánchez (1993) for example, notes that the Zapotec community in Mexico City rejects their own linguistic identity, convinced that their own language 'is not useful'. The fact is that minority status here, as in so many cases, is related to systems of social stratification and prestige.

As in the case of all languages that find themselves in an asymmetrical and inferior position to another, Asturian suffers from negative connotations of various sorts – although this has to be put in perspective. The attitudes and perceptions of these speakers to their mother tongue is not simple at all, but rather complex and contradictory: there is strong censure of those who try to hide the fact that they speak Asturian, in an attempt to move up the social scale. For that reason it is easy to collect anecdotes and stories in rural areas of Asturias that poke fun at those who claim to have forgotten their own language. A particularly good, and widely known example is the tale of the *engazu* (wooden rake used for hay-making). In this story, a young man goes to the New World but returns home shortly afterwards, making out that he can no longer speak or understand a word of Asturian. Until, that is, he stands on the teeth of a rake and the handle flies up and smacks him in the face. He exclaims in anger, and finds that he remembers the word *engazu*. The archetypal nature of this tale and other local stories shows very clearly the ambivalent attitude Asturian speakers commonly have to their own language; on the one hand it is seen as an inferior speech variety, but on the other there is rejection of anyone who makes exaggerated efforts to hide the fact that he/she is an Asturian speaker.

All the foregoing applies to the more traditional type of Asturian speaker. Among young people, however, what we find rather than ambivalence is a favourable and positive attitude to Asturian. As we have already observed, a significantly different attitude began to emerge several years ago in Asturias: for the first time an increasingly large section of the population were in favour of encouraging the use of Asturian, and extending its use to all levels. Twenty years ago we would not have found a single informant with a clear idea of the need to protect and foster the Asturian language to ensure its use by future generations. All that has changed: what we see now on various levels and on a whole range of issues is a clear will to transform the situation in a planned and politically viable way. While the setting up of the *Academia de la Llingua Asturiana* (Academy for the Asturian Language) was an undoubtedly important development, it is worth noting that at the same time there were far-reaching changes in society: speakers began to feel more reconciled with their own linguistic habits, and schools began to use the Asturian language. At about this time literature in Asturian ceased to be diglossic: in other words Asturian was no longer restricted to humorous, rural or local topics but began to be used in the same way as Spanish. While there is still much to do, perhaps the most difficult objective – turning the tide in favour of Asturian – has already been achieved.

But as we have already noted, much of the Asturian population lives in a diglossic situation. This calls for a constant effort to find the right expression for the right situation and constitutes one of the most interesting features of language use currently under study. In an interesting article by

González Riaño (1984) there is detailed documentation of these phenomena, including the story of the mother who tells the teacher that her
youngest son uses Asturian in the classroom because he is not *cunning*
enough to keep Asturian for use in the home, unlike her older children.

Pro-Asturian Movements

One of the aspects that best illustrates that Asturian is a minority
language that wishes to cease to be one, is the pro-Asturian pressure
groups who are at work creating public opinion and discussing the way
forward in ensuring the survival of a threatened language. This sector has
its own idiosyncratic way of looking at things, and enables the observer to
analyse the complex and at times contradictory process of linguistic
marginalisation and the redeeming of Asturian as the language of Asturias.

Just as there are similarities between the linguistic minorities in Europe,
there are corresponding similarities between the different language movements. The way political issues become institutionalised, for example, is an
important factor: it is one thing when the political majority is unanimously
nationalist and vigorously in favour of the language, and quite another
when this consensus is lacking. At all events, such situations are particularly
complex. In the case of Basque, for instance, in areas where the nationalist
parties are in power, there are pockets where the language disappeared
years ago, and as a result the process of ethnic identification takes a
different path from that in other parts of the Basque Country (Apaolaza,
1993). In the Asturian context the first thing to note is that the strictly
nationalist parties do not get many votes, although in certain contexts they
may be very active. On the other hand, there are nationalist organisations
with their own ideology that are doing important work without supporting any one political party. Another point is that among the political
forces represented in the Asturian Parliament not only are there groups
who want to see Asturian 'normalised' − that is, reintroduced at all levels
of local life − but in several cases the normalisation of Asturian is actually
the main objective.

What McDonald (1989) tells us about the pro-Breton movements in
France is very reminiscent of the Asturias situation. McDonald observes
that Breton speakers tend to fall into two groups: the country people who
often intersperse their mother tongue with French, and on the other hand
the Breton pressure groups which are fighting for the use of pure Breton
free from French influence. While the first group is not politically minded
in any way, the pressure groups are politically conscious, often university
people and usually left wing. For these politicised groups Breton holds out
the potential for bringing with it a 'different society' (McDonald,
1989: 100).

We find something similar in Asturias, where the most active groups
over recent years consist primarily of young people and students. The

vision of the future cherished by this group differs very considerably from that traditionally associated with speakers of Asturian, since traditional Asturian speakers had (and still have) no plans for the future of their language. In contrast, the young speakers who are pressing for greater use of the language do not see it as a relic from the past or as destined to live or die irrespective of the will of the Asturian people. For this new type of Asturian, the Asturian language has the right to historical continuity: they expect their politicians to pursue a policy that will guarantee the language's continuing role in the near future as the normal form of communication among Asturians. It is the young people and students with this new perspective for the future that make up a majority of the membership of organisations like *Conseyu Bable* and other *conseyos* which have opened beyond the borders of Asturias in Madrid, Barcelona, etc. They organise cultural events, festivals, parties and publish magazines, such as *Restallu* or *Secha*, in the Asturian language.

Out of this background has come the nucleus of intellectuals who supply the ideas, projects, arguments and even definite plans for linguistic and cultural revival. Certain works and studies (Garcia Arias 1975, 1976) have created the climate of revindication of linguistic rights and adopted the symbols and images that would point the way forward for the Asturian language out of diglossia as well as formulating the central ideas for combating the acculturation of Asturias.

Intellectuals of this sort normally live side by side with different views, with the common linguistic aims uniting people who are in other respects very different. Some are of rural extraction with a deep experience of the culture and language, while others are from the towns, with less experience of Asturian in the family circle. This sector, comprising students and young people (some temporarily resident outside Asturias and forming *conseyos* in non-Asturian towns and cities) have gone on to play an important role in education. It must also be mentioned that one of the notable achievements of the pro-Asturian movement is its massive influence among teachers.

Minority Languages and Literature

One of the most significant facets of the behaviour of Asturians who want their language to have a future is the fascination that the creation of written literature holds for them. And in fact a task that militants working for the Asturian cause have seriously set themselves from the beginning has been the consolidation of a new body of literature in Asturian. This would do away with the old diglossic tradition, once and for all, which dictated that Asturian was only used to write on rural or humorous topics. This was obviously nothing exceptional about Asturian — it is a pattern that can be found in other areas of Europe where there are minority languages, and the same pattern can also be seen historically, in periods far-removed from our own (González-Quevedo, 1994c). What happens next is very interesting: militants frequently go on to become writers and publish poems or stories. Literary events become important in this context, and militants become organisers of literary competitions with responsibility for obtaining attractive awards.

A collectively composed poetic work dating from 1977 is explicitly called *Del Aráu a la pluma* (from the plough to the pen). This title underscores the determination to use the language in a way that will empower it to act as a flexible modern medium, rather than relegate it to the rustic. We need to understand the literature written in Asturian in the 1970s and 80s in this light. The writers active during this period were naturally influenced by the same trends and moved by the same concerns as anywhere else in the literary world. Apart from these common characteristics, however, there were ways in which Asturian writing differed from all other literature. Most important among such characteristics were the desire to write creatively in order to keep the language and culture of Asturias alive, and the need to affirm the identity of Asturias as a people with its own personality (González-Quevedo 1986, 1994a, 1994b). One of the favourite themes in literature at this time was the supposedly Celtic origin of Asturias, an idea that become very popular among ordinary people.

One significant development was the setting up of the *El Cudoxu* theatre group run by young people. The director of the group also wrote the plays. The style and content was designed to appeal to the man in the street, but the intention was to free Asturian, once and for all, from the diglossia straitjacket that said Asturian could not be used for modern or urban subjects. This group was enormously popular with the public and went a long way to raising linguistic awareness. Their work was both literary and vernacular in approach, and carried an implicit message in favour of Asturian (González-Quevedo, 1994a).

The recent political changes[2] have had an effect on the pro-Asturian effort and on amount of literature produced in Asturian. The most committed type of literature began to disappear from the scene, and this had its effect on the way work by writers in the pro-Asturian movement was evaluated. At the same time a number of the linguistic demands have been increasingly absorbed into the political system, and this has acted to take the steam out of many of the issues. As in other areas of Europe, the struggle to defend minority languages has generally led to politicisation. One of the conclusions that can definitely be drawn after studying linguistic behaviour in Asturias is that as awareness of the language question increases, the level of general political awareness is raised at the same time. The mass of the population ranges from the highly politicised militant who speaks a very pure form of Asturian, with a clear vision of the future, to the Asturian who uses the language every day with no awareness, politically speaking, of being a minority language speaker.

Bable as an Ethnic Symbol

Observation of the linguistic behaviour of Asturian speakers reveals that in addition to being a way of communicating and of organising the world, language is a way in which we identify ourselves as a group. But to analyse this aspect we need to distinguish between language use amongst traditional speakers and that seen among young, politically minded speakers.

For the traditional type of Asturian speaker, the use of the mother tongue is more comfortable, more in harmony with their perceptions – and more efficient, since in many cases they cannot speak the official language, Spanish. But Bable is also a marker of Asturian identity, in that they will be able to classify other people according to the way they speak: speakers like themselves who are generally from a working class or peasant background; speakers who sound Asturian but who have largely or entirely shifted to speaking Spanish, speakers who exaggeratedly deepen their Asturian ('that *Llingua* lot') and, lastly, outsiders. The latter includes anyone who is plainly not Asturian.

On the other hand, for the linguistically aware speaker the language is not just a form of communication and a mark of identity, it is an active means of reaffirming and redeeming Asturian identity. Many of these are graduates or university lecturers, so they have no problem whatsoever in understanding official forms sent to them in Spanish, but they will nonetheless ask to have them in Asturian, as a way of affirming their identity.

There are a number of ritual pieces of behaviour in defence of Asturian that can be observed, both at individual and collective level. On an individual level many young couples nowadays give their children Asturian names, while adults at a particular point may change to signing their name in an Asturianised form. These can be usefully viewed as *rites du passage*, that is, symbolic acts which mark the ritual crossing of the threshold between the two languages and cultures (González-Quevedo, 1983, 1992).

Thus, study of the linguistic situation leads us to look at the question of ethnic identity (González-Quevedo, 1994b). Use of the language as an ethnic symbol does of course have its collective aspects: by observing certain public 'acts', carried out not only by Asturian activists but by community and local pressure groups in general, the Asturian language becomes a symbol of *Astur* ethnic identity. Local people may demand that certain written or spoken phrases (in different contexts, speeches, labels, posters, letter headings, etc.) be in Asturian, not to enhance communication, but simply to affirm the existence of Asturias as a linguistic and cultural entity with an identity of its own (González-Quevedo, 1992, 1994a). There are many acts throughout the year that ritually reaffirm the language as the core of Asturian identity, in acts of structure and signification similar to those studied, for example, by del Valle (1988).

Bilingualism in Asturias

A part of the population of Asturias is monolingual. Such monolinguals include those that have Spanish as their mother tongue and have no need to use Asturian. At the other extreme there are Asturian speakers who cannot speak Spanish. The latter are mostly older rural speakers. But a large proportion of the population is bilingual. Yet what exactly do we mean by this in the Asturian context? We need to analyse and characterise this bilingualism, to determine its specific features.

Firstly, this is *inorganic, disorganised* bilingualism: in other words, the great majority of Asturian bilinguals are not able to differentiate clearly between the two linguistic systems, are not aware of the dividing line or linguistic boundary between Spanish and Asturian, and as consequence tend to use a mixture of the two. Instead of a linguistic boundary therefore, what we find is a continuum[3] between the two poles – focused Spanish on the one hand and focused Asturian on the other – with the majority of the (bilingual) population situating themselves in linguistic space between the two extremes. Something which sometimes leads to a mixed variety, as it occurs in Galicia. In that region, in the north-west corner of Spain, the term *castrapo* has been coined to refer to the blend of Spanish and *Gallego* (Galician).

Asturian bilingualism is also, as we have already seen, clearly *asymmetrical*, owing to the minority status of Asturian. This means that bilingualism is not neutral and has a strong tendency to be diglossic. Also, while we are seeing increasing protection for Asturian from the politicians, this protection is clearly insufficient. In fact Asturian is not explicitly recognised as an official language of Asturias. It could be said, therefore, that bilingualism in Asturias is tolerated rather than official. This kind of bilingualism leads to a process of 'assimilation', in which Asturian is progressively replaced by Spanish, unless all necessary, essential language policy measures are taken.

Language Contact and Interference

The Asturian bilingual situation has clear linguistic repercussions, in that continued contact between the two languages, over time, produces some interesting examples of interference. In characterising this situation, the first thing to note is that there is mutual interference between Spanish and Asturian, although such interference is once again asymmetrical: there is more Spanish interference in Asturian than vice versa. Furthermore, it can be seen that Asturian interference features in local Spanish have become stabilised, while interference going in the opposite direction, from Spanish to Asturian, is on the increase owing to the dominant position of Spanish. The Asturian tongue, as the minority language, is increasingly the receiver language.

Interference from Spanish on Asturian is found at all linguistic levels. It occurs at the phonological level, for example: Spanish interferes by acting to replace the phonemes of Asturian that do not exist in Spanish. At syntactic level the impact of Spanish is less, and in fact here we see substantial carry over in the opposite direction from Asturian into Spanish. On the lexical level, too, Spanish has a powerful — and interesting — effect on Asturian. For instance, the Spanish word may replace the Asturian equivalent in all prestigious contexts, while the Asturian word survives in less prestigious contexts. Thus, for example, we frequently find Asturian speakers who use the Asturian word *fueya* (leaf) when referring to plants, but who prefer to use the Spanish *hoja* when talking about the pages (leaves) of a book.

The Asturian population is aware that their linguistic habits are often the outcome of mutual interference between their two languages — as can be seen in the study carried out by González-Quevedo and Rodríguez (1986). This research makes it clear that most speakers over a large area of the central Asturian coalfields are convinced they speak a mixture of Asturian and Spanish.

Since Asturian is a minority language with as yet limited use as a school or official language, the social use of Asturian will vary depending on the social domain we choose to look at. From fieldwork carried out on language use in different media and different milieux, we can draw the following conclusions, which incidentally recapitulate some of the points made earlier:

(1) Traditional monolingual Asturian speakers are now clearly limited to a particular area and age group: that is, rural areas and an aging population. Despite receiving all their schooling in Spanish, the Spanish language did not replace their first or mother tongue, or even add itself to the speakers' repertoire. The more recent pressures from modern communications have similarly failed to do this. However, what we do find now with such speakers is a certain amount of interference from Spanish without this actually affecting the deeper levels of the language. Thus we see Spanish vocabulary appearing as neologisms referring to *realia* that were not originally part of traditional country life. And, instead of the more correct *Estropeóse-yos la llavadora* (their washing machine broke down), — in Spanish *Se les estropeó la lavadora,* — we find *Estropeóse-yos la lavadora.* The term referring to a modern gadget appears in its Spanish variant.

(2) The majority of Asturians, even those who normally choose not to speak Asturian, generally use the syntactic structures of Asturian, rather than those of Spanish, thus making use of Asturian syntactic calques. An overwhelming majority of Asturians, for example, order pronoun clitics according to Asturian syntax even when they are speaking Spanish, and the same can be said of other structures.

Frequently, the speakers themselves are not aware of what they are doing. It is quite normal to hear utterances like *Bajáronmelu* in Asturian Spanish (they took it down for me) uttered as *Me lo bajaron*, in general Spanish, whereas in Asturian it would be: *Baxáronmelu*. The Asturian syntax is kept constant, but the diagnostic Asturian phoneme [x] is eliminated, thus adapting the phonological make-up of the word to Spanish.

(3)   At all events, the years of struggle and the efforts to recover the use of the language at all levels have certainly had their effect. For that reason we now find a section of the population, still a minority but enormously significant, who speak Asturian according to recently established criteria. Such people also speak Spanish well, but try to speak Asturian without interference from the latter language. What we have here, then, are speakers with a high degree of linguistic self-awareness who are fully aware of their linguistic usage. In many instances – although not all – these are younger people who move in university circles, in education or left wing and union politics. Speakers whose consciousness has been raised in this way, who know that their language has been, and continues to be, discriminated against, set out to right this historic wrong by speaking the purest Asturian, furthest from Spanish. To do this, such speakers may resort to terms of literary origin or Asturian words and expressions from other areas. Thus, a linguistically aware speaker in central Asturias might say: *Güei hai munchu trabayu* (Today, there's a lot of work), Spanish: *Hoy hay mucho trabajo*, but the word *güei* is typical of the west of Asturias and is not much used elsewhere. This re-Asturianisation of the language would be inconceivable outside the context of normalisation and educational change which is slowly but surely beginning to have an effect on perceptions. Among this section of the population, then, what we are seeing is the emergence of bilingualism of a genuinely ordered type.

(4)   Those who exclusively speak Spanish are found mainly in urban areas and in families of non-Asturian origin. Even in these cases, we frequently find that outsiders who have been living in the Principality of Asturias for several years begin to show Asturian features in their speech. The extent to which their children become linguistically integrated varies from area to area in Asturias. The considerable linguistic assimilation that occurs in mining areas has already been mentioned, while in towns with a more middle class ethos and large numbers of bureaucrats and government workers there is correspondingly greater resistance to linguistic Asturianisation.

(5)   It is very important to study the attitudes that Asturians entertain towards their language, especially with regard to normalisation and use in schools. In contrast to the traditional attitude which looks down on Asturian speakers as being 'uneducated' or 'village yokels',

we now find much greater tolerance and respect. The process of normalisation at first met with considerable resistance – usually accompanied by the accusation that it was 'artificial', a reference to the standardised written form, but in recent years this resistance has lessened.

(6) In all social milieux (rural/urban, social classes, etc.) the process of recovering the use of the language has had a profound effect on the sociolinguistic situation in Asturias. There is no other explanation for the findings of the most recent survey on this in Asturias (Llera, 1994: 57). When asked what the language of Asturias is: 43% of the sample said Asturian, 39% said Asturian and Spanish, and only 19% claimed that it was Spanish.

Some Real Life's Stories

The analysis of some real life stories will help us characterise the sociolinguistic and psycholinguistic aspects of the Asturian community and illustrate some of the issues that are raised.

A.'s story

As a writer, A. has made an enriching contribution to literature in the Asturian language. She had turned 50 when she began writing, at time when she felt the need to recall the world of her childhood, a world that she still remembered in intricate detail.

She spent her childhood in a valley in the north of León province. In those days the language and culture of her daily life had not been touched by Spanish; this was before Spanish began to make massive inroads in that area. A. had to do the work that traditional society expected of children: looking after the cattle and helping with the chores around the farm. Life was hard, but despite that she looks back on this as a beautiful time in her life, a time that she idealises. What helps give this stage its ideal quality is the strongly drawn, densely textured linguistic and cultural personality of daily life in her valley.

The coming of the mining industry and the railways changed all that forever. A. was witness to the way in which these changes affected the society in which she lived, although the language and native culture managed to assimilate the new conditions fairly successfully. But it was the Spanish Civil War that upset the normal unfolding of events and finally put an end to a way of life which had seemed untouched by the passage of time. She married soon after the war and went on to live in various distant parts of Spain because of her husband's work. This enabled her to see the strong linguistic and cultural identity of her home region in sharper focus, and made her more acutely aware of the rich heritage of words and customs that was being lost.

In the maturity of her years she began to record the world of her childhood and adolescence, writing about her experiences, sensations and stories. She published six books of poetry and short stories in succession, in the western dialect of the Asturian language. Her books were read with great interest particularly in the southwest of the wider Asturian cultural area, and are a real linguistic and literary landmark for scholars and specialists.

As a young girl she spoke her mother tongue thinking she did not know how to speak. Convinced of this, she experienced rites, beliefs and ways of living that, much later in life, she came to recognise as beautiful and deserving a better fate. She is naturally delighted to see the way in which the use of Asturian is being recovered, and glad to have contributed to literary creation in its western dialect. On the personal level, having written and published books based on the language and culture of her childhood has been one of the great satisfactions of her life.

A.'s conversational Asturian is interspersed with Spanish: she finds it hard not to fall back on Spanish to express abstract ideas or neologisms, because for her, Asturian is associated with everyday life, not with sophisticated thinking. And her Asturian speech is unmistakably the regional variety of her area.

B.'s story

B. is a primary schoolteacher who has been teaching for 15 years and is approximately 40 years old. He teaches in a small town in Asturias where mining is the social and economic mainstay of the community.

When he was a student B. scarcely bothered about the linguistic situation, although he always thought highly of that *Llingua lot*, and anything intended to promote Asturian. When he became a teacher, however, he became more aware of Asturian and decided to take a summer course for teachers organised by the Asturian Academy. Now he spends part of his working day teaching Asturian, something which he says he finds highly enjoyable and which takes up much of his time. In fact, his main educational concerns now focus on the teaching of the language. He attends courses and activities on the subject and eagerly reads the press and watches television whenever there is anything relating to Asturian in the schools or linguistic normalisation.

All this has meant that in addition to being a schoolteacher and teacher of Asturian, B. has also become a militant defending the use of Asturian and its complete normalisation. This has become a personal crusade in conversations with friends, in the opinions he expresses and in his vision of the culture of Asturias. B. uses as correct and 'normalised' a form of Asturian as possible, and does not hesitate to Asturianise neologisms or turn to literary Asturian for terms that are missing from his vernacular. Thus: '*La situación llinguística n'Asturies ye inxusta dafechu*' (The linguistic situation in Asturias is totally unjust) is a phrase used by B. but unlikely to be used by anyone not a part of the linguistic normalisation process in Asturias.

Not surprisingly, the pro-Asturian activity has brought about various changes in B.'s life. It is not just that he now sees the cultural and linguistic issues in a completely different way, he has also, for example, made new friends. Naturally enough he has met new people, men and women in the teaching profession with whom he feels identified. He does not just see them on the courses and socialise with them in the bar afterwards. The new links forged with those who feel the same about the Asturian language go beyond this. His 'linguistic friends' are now friends that he often sees in his leisure time for reasons that have nothing to do with the language question.

The business of teaching Asturian has become one of his important life aims. Looking back at what has happened, B. believes that these developments have enriched his life. Similarly, his union activity is now dominated by the defence of Asturian: B. is a member of an independent Asturias-based teachers' union, the most important in the area. This union is a firm defender of schooling in Asturian and Asturian normalisation – and B. is one of its most active members on this front.

C.'s story

C. is in his sixties, retired and on a pension. He is a typical Asturian peasant farmer, and has been all his life. For the first few years of his adult working life he worked for an employer, but then he took charge of the family's herds. His brothers and sisters moved away from the village to find work, and so it was left to him to carry on with the farm. Times have been very hard, and Asturian farmers have had to adapt to some very demanding new legislation imposed by the European Union.

The language that C. uses in his day to day life is Asturian, and Asturian is obviously the language his family speaks at home. When he meets other farmers, at the markets, in the celebrations, at funerals, the language they use is invariably Asturian. He may take a stab at speaking Spanish in other contexts, but he finds it an effort, and does not know how to speak it well.

Of course when he switches on his television set, listens to the radio, or glances at a newspaper, all the information reaches him in Spanish, just as the forms from the bank or tax office are in Spanish. What is more, he only learned Spanish at school. However, this diglossia is not the problem for him that one might think – it is what he is used to, it is what he has always observed around him. He finds it perfectly normal to speak Asturian and yet encounter only Spanish in the media, or in the leaflets he receives through the post on farming matters. C's speech combines the deepest Asturian with phrases that evidence interference from Spanish: '*Aninái a mercar el libru del neñu*' (Hurry up [plural imperative] and buy the child's book). Here he uses *libru* (book), a form which is half way between Asturian *llibru* and Spanish *libro*.

He cannot really see the point of things like the pro-Asturian movement, since for him Asturian occupies a natural place in the scheme of things: '*ye lo que siempre se fizo*' (it's what was always done). For him, it is perfectly reasonable to speak Asturian as he does, and for the language not to be 'normalised'. Recently he has changed his mind about the teaching of Asturian in school, which he no longer sees as a bad thing. Previously, he was against the idea, because it meant spending money on something he thought was utterly unnecessary.

Speaking to C. one becomes aware of a world that is complex and difficult to understand. The contradiction implied by a linguistically diglossic life is not surprisingly associated with attitudes and feelings that are equally contradictory. When we go more deeply into the way C. perceives and experiences his own language, we find that he harbours negative, reproachful feelings towards it. The problem with many Asturians, he says, is that they don't know how to speak well – by which he means they don't speak Spanish well. The Spanish language opens doors and confers prestige. He wants his children to speak Spanish fluently and thinks everything should be done to ensure that this happens.

But it would be wrong to conclude that C's perceptions concerning Asturian as his mother tongue are all negative. As 'diglossic' as his attitudes may be, he still thinks that the Asturian language is important for Asturias and that a good Asturian should speak it well. At bottom, and in spite of what has been said, he feels that being able to speak Asturian well is something to be proud of, a genuine mark of Asturian identity.

D.'s story

Informant D. is a young man who has left university but has not been able to get a job and is unemployed. Because of his need to find work, but also because he is interested in Asturian for its own sake, D. is watching the language situation very closely. For that reason he has been on a number of refresher courses and now has an acceptable knowledge of Asturian language teaching techniques, and this has led to him giving some adults Asturian classes paid for by local authorities. The work is unreliable and poorly paid, but at the same time it suits his tastes and interests.

D. has deeply held convictions about Asturian, the result of considerable introspection and reading. When we inquire into what Asturian means to him, we see that this is a language which has suffered great historical injustice, a language deserving a better fate. D. believes that, despite years of ill-treatment and neglect, it is not too late for the traditional language of Asturias to take its place among the European languages of the future. D.'s Asturian is textbook in its purity, he avoids interference from Spanish at all costs, and detests diglossic language use.

The fact that this is a small language (in terms of the number of speakers) is not in his view a disadvantage — for D. the important thing is that it is one's own language, the language of Asturias.

On this last point, D. is well aware that the Asturian tongue is not just one aspect of the culture and history of the Asturian people, not just another piece of Asturian folklore. For him it is the true heart of Asturias. He focuses all his concerns about Asturias on the language question. Thus the severe economic and social recession that the area is suffering at the present time is likewise linked with the future of the language. Because, as D. sees it, if Asturias does not respect the language, it certainly is not going to be able to tackle the rest of its problems. Without its linguistic personality, D. believes, his country will miss all other future opportunities.[4]

His opinions about Asturian are not primarily concerned with the instrumental value of the language: the Asturian language should be given a new impetus because this is something that should happen. On the other hand, he is completely in favour of multilingualism and multiculturalism: in his view the world of the future should be a world of tolerance and diversity, not of intolerance and homogeneity.

Notes

1. The statistics used in this work appear in the SADEI-Asturias, third regional survey 1987, and in Llera (1994).
2. A clear swing to the right in the past elections (1996).
3. This idea of a continuum in relation to bilingual speech modes was first raised by Grosjean (1990) and then applied to other bilingual contexts (i.e. Catalan-Spanish in Catalonia (Pujadas & Turell (1993), Turell (1994, 1995)).
4. This is so because in his opinion, in the Europe of the 21st century, only the regions with their own cultural identity will have the necessary edge to be able to compete in spite of the difficulties.

References

Apaolaza, Tx. (1993) *Lengua, Etnicidad y Nacionalismo.* Barcelona: Editorial Anthropos.

Barth, F. (1976) *Los Grupos Étnicos y sus Fronteras.* Mexico: Fondo de Cultura Económica.

Dorian, N. (1981) *Language Death: The Life Cycle of a Scottish Gaelic Dialect.* Philadelphia: University of Pennsylvania Press.

Ferguson, C.A. (1959) Diglossia. *Word,* 15, 325—40.

Fishman, J.A. (1967) Bilingualism with and without diglossia: Diglossia with and without bilingualism. *Journal of Social Issues* 23, 29—38.

Fishman, J.A. (1970) *Sociolinguistics: A Brief Introduction.* Rowley: Newbury House.

Fishman, J.A. (1971) *Advances in the Sociology of Language.* The Hague: Mouton.

García Arias, X. (1975) *Bable y Regionalismo.* Oviedo: Conceyu Bable.

García Arias, X. (1976) *Llingua y Sociedá Asturiana.* Oviedo: Conceyu Bable.

García Arias, X. (1982) Las lenguas minoritarias de la Península Ibérica. In *Introducción a la Lingüística.* Madrid: Alhambra Universidad.

García Arias, X. (1992) El asturiano: evolución lingüística externa. In G. Holtus, M. Metzeltin and C. Schmitt (eds) *Lexikon der Romanistischen Linguistik,* VI, 1 (pp. 681—93). Tubingen: Max Niemeyer Verlag.

González-Quevedo, R. (1983) Antropoloxía del desaniciu llingüísticu: llingua minoritaria y espacios étnicos. *Lletres Asturianes* 8, 7–15.

González-Quevedo, R. (1986) Nueva poesía asturiana. In *El Estado de las Poesías, Monografías de Los Cuadernos del Norte* (pp. 154–64). Oviedo: C.A.A.

González-Quevedo, R. (1991) *Roles Sexuales y Cambio Social en un Valle de la Cordillera Cantábrica.* Barcelona: Editorial Anthropos.

González-Quevedo, R. (1992) Langue, rite et identité. *Lletres Asturianes* 43, 7–20.

González-Quevedo, R. (1994a) Afitar la propia identidá. El Cudoxu, una experiencia de teatro popular. *Lletres Asturianes,* 51, 93–8.

González-Quevedo, R. (1994b) *Antropoloxía Llingüística. Llingua, cultura y etnicidá.* Oviedo: A.Ll.A.

González-Quevedo, R. (1994c) Respeutu al proyeutu d'una pequena lliteratura. *Lletres Asturianes* 53, 23–8.

González-Quevedo, R. and Rodríguez, V. (1986) Encuesta so la realidá llingüística: L'Entregu y L'Agüeria. *Lletres Asturianes* 22, 123–6.

González Riaño, X.A. (1994) *Interferencia Lingüística y Escuela Asturiana.* Oviedo: A.Ll.A.

Grosjean, F. (1990) The psycholinguistics of language contact and codeswitching: Concepts, methodology and data. *Papers for the Workshop on Concepts, Methodology and Data* (pp. 105–16). ESF Network on Codeswitching and Language Contact. Basel, 12–13 January 1990.

Llera, F.J. (1994) *Los Asturianos y la Lengua Asturiana.* Oviedo: Conseyería d'Educación del Principiáu d'Asturies.

McDonald, M. (1989) The exploitation of linguistic mis-match: Toward an ethnography of customs and manners. In R. Grillo (ed.) *Social Anthropology and the Politics of Language* (pp. 90–105). London: Routledge.

Pujadas, J. and Turell, M.T. (1993) Els indicadors sociolingüístics del contacte interètnic. In *Actes del Novè Colloqui Internacional de Llengua i Literatura Catalanes.* Alacant-Elx (1991). Barcelona: Publicacions de l'Abadia de Montserrat, 301–18.

Sánchez, M.J. (1993) Repensando la identidad étnica. *VI Congreso de Antroplogía.* Tenerife.

Turell, M.T. (1994) Beyond Babel: Within and across. In F. Sierra, M. Pujol and H. den Boer (eds) *Diálogos Hispánicos, n. 15. Las Lenguas en la Europa Comunitaria* (pp. 23–40). Amsterdam: Rodopi.

Turell, M.T. (1995) L'alternança de llengües i el préstec en una comunitat interètnica. In M.T. Turell (ed.) *La Sociolingüística de la Variació* (pp. 259–93). Barcelona: PPU.

Valle, T. del (1988) *Korrica. Rituales de la lengua en el espacio.* Barcelona: Editorial Anthropos.

Weinreich, U. (1953) *Languages in Contact.* The Hague: Mouton.

Chapter 7
The Sign Language Communities

ROSA VALLVERDÚ

Historical Background and Distribution

In Spain, there is written documentation of the existence of teachers of the deaf from the 16th century. Brother Pedro Ponce de León, a Benedictine monk who lived at that time, is considered to be the first teacher of the deaf, and he taught deaf children professionally. The methods he used are not documented, but it seems that he used sign language and writing to teach his disciples how to speak. Some 40 years after the death of Ponce de León, another man of the church, Juan Pablo Bonet, published his work *Reducción de las letras y arte para enseñar a hablar a los mudos* (On the arts for teaching the deaf to speak). From the 16th to the 18th centuries, all teachers of the deaf used sign language and writing to teach their students to speak and write. But throughout this period, only a privileged few (the children of the nobility) had the opportunity of being taught in this way. Furthermore, the classes were normally of only one student, or at the most two.

At the end of the 18th century, and at the beginning of the 19th century, teachers of the deaf used sign language and the classes were no longer private and restricted to the nobility, and all children were able to attend. But in 1880, after decisions taken at the *International Conference of Teachers of the Deaf and Dumb*, held in Milan, sign language was abandoned in schools in all European countries and totally oral teaching methods were adopted. So from then on, sign language became a thing of the past in Spanish schools, and in the rest of Europe, and students were not allowed to use it to communicate among themselves.

Sign language has survived this century of suppression because the deaf have taught each other. Signs have been the main form of communication in this community, and continue to be so today. When two deaf people meet, the natural tendency is to communicate via hand signals, as has been shown by studies of young children at school. It could be said, then, that sign languages have existed since two or more deaf people have had the opportunity to communicate with each other (Rodríguez González, 1992), and that signs will be used while there are still two deaf people on the face of the Earth and they meet (Schuyler Long,[1] 1910).

After the Milan Conference of 1880, as well as banning the use of sign language in teaching in schools, on many occasions the authorities even tried to stop deaf men and women from marrying each other. There are also cases of deaf women who were sterilised without being told, so that they would not have deaf children. However, despite all these attempts to eradicate sign language, it was impossible to do so. One must not forget that when the 1880 Conference was held, there was already a deaf community,[2] and there was also a certain percentage of families where the parents or the children were deaf, so sign language was passed down from parents to children. At that time, sign language was banned, but the deaf went to special schools, so the children whose first language was sign language taught it to the others. And this has continued until the present day.

Today, in the whole of Spain, there are some 100 associations of deaf people. In Catalonia, there are 26, in Madrid 6, in Andalusia 13, in Asturias 4, in Castile-León and La Rioja 9, in Galicia 8, in the Basque Country 6, in the Valencian Country 11, and in Murcia 5, as well as 13 other associations which are not federated. It is known that there are between 10,000 and 15,000 people affiliated to the *Confederación Nacional de Sordos de España* (Spanish National Confederation of Deaf People), or CNSE, but the number of deaf people who use sign language is higher than this figure since not all of them are affiliated.

There are neither official statistics nor data on the number of deaf people who make up this community, but largely because of the aid received from INSERSO it is known that in Spain there are about a million people who are deaf or who suffer from some degree of loss of hearing. Within this group, there are those who have become deaf when already adults, and people with greater or lesser degrees of impaired hearing.

The *Federació de Sords de Catalunya* (FESOCA) (Federation of Deaf People of Catalonia) distinguishes between deaf people and hypo-acoustic people. Using the criteria of the *World Federation of the Deaf*, the FESOCA considers that a deaf person is one who uses sign language as his/her main means of communication, who identifies with other deaf people and who has a hearing disability. Hypo-acoustic people are those with a reduced hearing ability, but who can improve their hearing ability with the help of technical devices, such as hearing aids. They do not necessarily communicate in sign language, and nor do they relate to, or identify with, deaf people as a group. That is, they are not part of the deaf community. So in this chapter, 'deaf people' refers to the first group, those who are part of the deaf community. Of perhaps one million people with various degrees of impaired hearing, it has been estimated that sign language is the form of communication of 120,000 deaf people.[3] It should be noted that there are non-deaf children or friends of deaf people, who should also be considered members of this community, so the real figure would be somewhat higher.

The Status of Sign Languages

The sign languages used around the world by the deaf were not studied in depth until the last quarter of this century. In 1960, William C. Stockoe, an English teacher and member of the Linguistics Research Laboratory in Washington, published the first study entitled *Sign Language Structure: An Outline of the Visual Communication System of the American Deaf*. After this, other works on sign languages and the deaf community appeared in the following years, but it was not until the 1970s that linguistic, socio-linguistic (Schaller, 1993) and psycholinguistic studies (Marchesi, 1980, 1993) of the deaf began to appear with any regularity. By the beginning of the 1980s, linguists were sure that sign language was a language in its own right, with its own grammatical structure and its own syntax, different from most oral languages (Ladd, 1991). In Spain, it was not until 1992 that the first linguistic study was made of the Spanish Sign Language (SSL), the doctoral thesis presented to the University of Valladolid by María Angeles Rodríguez González. Before this, there had been two dictionaries of the Spanish Sign Language and one of the Catalan Sign Language.[4]

However, although linguists have recognised for years that sign language is a language in its own right, in many countries governments have still not officially recognised this fact. UNESCO recognised sign language in 1985, and in 1988 the European Parliament passed a resolution recognising sign languages and the need to use them to ensure that the deaf have access to information and all areas of everyday life. But in Spain the Spanish Sign Language is still not recognised as another official language of Spain. On 23 February 1996, the qualification of Diploma in Sign Language Interpretation was approved, and if the profession of sign language interpreter has been recognised, one would think that the language itself would be recognised, but this is still not the case.

In Spain, not only is there a Spanish sign language, but as many varieties as there are Autonomous Communities. Unfortunately, no geographical-linguistic study has been made of the varieties that exist, but it is known that the essential differences are in the vocabulary. It would be interesting to carry out an in-depth study on this subject. Different sources have commented that the sign language used by the deaf in Castile, León and La Mancha is very similar to the one used in Madrid, which is SSL. Galicia, Andalusia, the Valencian Country and the Basque Country have their own variants, and in Catalonia the deaf sign with the Catalan Sign Language (CSL). SSL and CSL are probably the ones which are most different, and the deaf from outside of Catalonia recognise that there they sign a different language to the Spanish one. It is the deaf community itself that talks of the existence of different sign languages.

Paradoxically, at present the majority of those who are part of the Catalan deaf community, while signing in Catalan, speak or move their lips in Spanish, and often do not understand Catalan well. This is due to historical reasons. Under the Franco dictatorship, they were only taught in Spanish, and unlike the non-deaf, who could hear Catalan spoken, could speak it in the family, etc., the deaf could only learn it if somebody, such as a private teacher or a member of the family, taught it to them. There are people aged over 80 years who did receive their education in Catalan before Franco and thus both sign and speak in Catalan. Since the present education system was introduced, in which children are taught in Catalan, deaf children have been taught both Catalan and Spanish sign languages.

In Catalonia, the autonomous parliament has taken an important step towards the gradual equality of sign languages and oral languages by passing a motion on the *Promoció i difusió del coneixement de la llengua de signes* (Promotion and Spreading of the Knowledge of Sign Language) (No. 228/30, June 1994), which recognises the importance of knowing and making known the Catalan Sign Language, and also the need for the deaf to learn and use it.

In the 1990s, there have been articles and letters to the editor by both deaf people and by non-deaf people with an interest in the deaf, arguing that the deaf community is a linguistic community and that sign language should be taught in schools and given publicity in general. But at the same time, there are also opposing opinions from deaf people who have received a more oral-oriented education and who totally deny that such a community exists. Also, among the non-deaf, there is widespread ignorance of what it means to be deaf, to be a handicapped person who is invisible.

The Most Important Characteristics of Sign Language

A sign language is a linguistic system of non-oral communication. It is a visual, gesticulatory language, expressed through the body, hands, arms, eyes, mouth and face, which has a grammar and syntax which are different from those of oral languages. For example, there are no verb tenses, and time is expressed through a sign which refers to the past, present or future. There are no articles, the adjectives and nouns have no gender, prepositions and conjunctions either do not exist or, if a sign exists for them, they are seldom used, etc.

Mime is very important in sign languages, which means that many signs owe their origin or development to mime. For example, deaf children easily invent signs as their vocabulary increases. For the majority of signs, this imitation of reality is hard to see without knowing the meaning of the sign. That is, there is a relationship between the sign and its meaning, but this is hard to see without being aware of the meaning. For example, the sign to say that your hair stood on end is your hand on your arm with four fingers sticking straight up. If a non-deaf person knows what this gesture says, the image of your hair standing on end is quite graphic, but if not then the visual meaning is lost. There are also certain signs such as 'to eat', 'to drink', 'to see', or 'to telephone' which are practically the same as the gestures made by non-deaf people when they are talking.

Despite this relationship with mime, the invention of new signs is not a totally free process. The shape of the hand, the position and the movement are all made according to conventions. In Catalan Sign Language, there are 9 or 10 different hand shapes, some of which are more productive than others (Figure 7.1).

When a new sign is invented, it is done with one of these shapes, in conjunction with the position and movement characteristic of CSL. So signs can be analysed as a group of elements which combine to allow us to differentiate between different signs. For example, there are signs which are made with the same hand shape, the same position, but with different movements. And as Klima and Bellugi (1980) indicate, the lexical units of sign languages are formed by a restricted series of sub-lexical elements which serve as differentiators without having meaning themselves. The sign is organised as a combination of elements which occur simultaneously. A sign is really a hand or two hands in a particular shape which moves in a specific way with respect to a certain place, and all this happens simultaneously. Studies indicate that not all combinations of hand shape, movement and location are possible.

This graphic nature of signs tends to disappear as time passes, as the form is maintained but the deaf person does not always know the original meaning of the signs which he/she uses. In Catalonia, for example, the town of Sitges has the same sign as that for 'bikini', because in the 1960s it was one of the first places where women began to sunbathe in bikinis. Nowadays, many young people are unaware of this and the sign has become part of the linguistic repertoire. Other signs which have lost this visual immediacy include that for 'chemist's/pharmacy', which has its origin in the period when the chemist prepared the medicines themselves; 'diplomat', whose sign represents the two-cornered hat worn by ambassadors at the end of the 18th and beginning of the 19th centuries; 'Vitoria', the capital of one of the provinces in the Basque Country, which is represented by a gesture as if dealing cards because some well known card packs were produced there, and 'Almeria' is represented by making a pistol with each hand, because many Hollywood westerns were filmed in this province in the south of Spain. Nowadays, however, many young people are beginning to use other signs for the names of towns.

A sign language is not used for writing, and so there are no newspapers in sign language. When there is no television in sign language, not even regular programmes in sign language, the spreading of new signs will occur from one person to another. For example, when AIDS appeared, somebody invented a sign for this disease and then it spread. New signs may spread rapidly, or on the other hand, a sign may be created for a word in one place and a few kilometres away another sign may be created which means the same. There are no studies on these phenomena.

Finally, sign language is logically influenced by oral languages, since the deaf community lived within the non-deaf society. So although this is

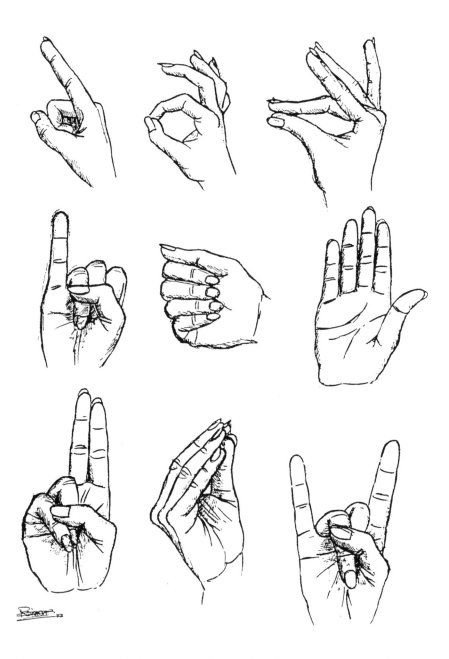

Figure 7.1 Nine of the most productive hand signs in LSC (Catalan Sign Language) (Own source)

not the most frequent case, there are signs which take into account the oral language. For example, in Catalan Sign Language the town of 'Sabadell' is represented by the same sign as for *ceba* (onion), since in oral Catalan *ceba* and *saba* are very similar phonetically, 'Europe' is often represented by the letter 'E', 'Coca-Cola' is 'CC', 'hotel' is the same as 'H', 'tongue' and 'language' are indicated by the letters 'L' (from *llengua*) and 'I' (from *idioma*) respectively, 'culture' is signed with two hands, but the shape of one of the hands is a 'C', etc. The interference between the two linguistic systems (sign/oral) suggests a consideration of bilingualism and diglossia in sign language (Rodríguez González, 1992).

Family Life

Deaf people usually marry other deaf people. Within the deaf community, there are not many marriages between deaf and non-deaf people, but when this occurs the non-deaf person is already totally integrated into the deaf community, and knows sign language, the special situation and the difficulties of the deaf. Sometimes they are non-deaf people who have an interest in the deaf world and sometimes they are non-deaf children of the deaf. Many of the members of the deaf community consider that if the non-deaf person has no interest in becoming part of the deaf community then the marriage between a deaf person and a non-deaf person will be a failure, and this has been shown to be the case on more than one occasion. So most couples are deaf and deaf people who do not have a partner say that they will marry a deaf person because no one but a deaf person can understand what it is like to be deaf.

When a couple who are both deaf have children, they may have deaf children if their deafness is hereditary, but they may also have non-deaf children. In fact, most times the latter is the case, and only 5% of deaf babies have deaf parents. These children have sign language as their first language because in the home that is how they communicate, but will learn an oral language from other relatives, at school, from TV, etc.

In Catalonia, there is a case of a deaf man married to a deaf woman, who have had six children, four of whom are deaf and two of whom have some loss of hearing but speak and hear without great difficulty. In family gatherings, they communicate in sign language, because the mother's parents are both deaf also, and her only brother, also deaf, is married to a deaf woman and has deaf children. This is one of the most numerous families with hereditary deafness in Spain, 40 people in all, and on the woman's side there are four generations of congenitally deaf people, grandparents, parents, children and grandchildren.

However, most deaf people are the children of non-deaf people, thus the situation is quite different, and at home the main language is oral. In a few cases, and especially beginning in the 1990s, there are parents who learn sign language and ensure that their children do the same (see section headed Education). If this family lives in Catalonia, they will speak Catalan, Spanish or perhaps both languages. If they live in the Basque Country, they will speak Spanish, Basque or perhaps both; similarly in Galicia with Galician and Spanish, and in the rest of Spain they will learn only Spanish. Until recently, the deaf who lived in a bilingual community faced an extra difficulty. At school, they were taught in Spanish, yet at home the language of communication might be Catalan, Basque or Galician. These people have commented that when their family spoke to them directly, they obviously spoke in Spanish, but the family conversations were in the normal language of the family. There have been cases of various deaf people born in Catalonia into a Catalan-speaking family who have ended up disconnecting from the family conversations, because of the difficulty, or the impossibility, faced by a deaf person in following a conversation with so many people, but which had been increased by the fact that the conversation was in a language which they did not know and which no one had taught them.

One informant commented: 'At home, the conversation round the family table was in Catalan. I didn't understand it and kept to myself, looking at my plate and eating. Sometimes, if I was interested in what they were saying, I would ask my sister what they had said, and she would translate for me, but many other times I would disconnect completely as I was tired of looking at the others' lips and not understanding anything.'

In the families with a deaf member, there is always some brother or sister who takes on the role of interpreter. One informant commented: 'All my family speak Basque, but I only speak Spanish, and so they always have to translate everything. I miss lots of conversations.'

Another informant from Madrid, who knows Spanish, which is the language at home, commented: 'My father doesn't open his mouth when he speaks, and I can't read his lips, but he knows a little bit of *Dactylology*,[5] and we understand each other. With my brothers and sisters, I communicate in writing.'

The vast majority of deaf children born to non-deaf parents learn the oral language first, and only as adults do they discover the organisations for the deaf and begin to learn sign language. But there are deaf children who find that any kind of spontaneous gesture they make to express themselves is suppressed. A large number of parents are afraid that their child will not learn the oral language if they let their child use signs, and they ban the use of hands for self-expression. They are scared that if they let the child use signs he/she will not make the effort needed to learn to speak an oral language. In fact, normally, when these children grow up and decide to join the organisations of the deaf, to meet other deaf people, and to learn sign language, this is very frustrating for the non-deaf parents.

One informant said: 'When I was young, my parents always scolded me when I used signs to express myself, and my mother helped me a lot to learn Catalan. So when I began to go out with a deaf boy and only communicated in sign language, that did not go down well at all at home. They were really scared that I would lose my spoken language, they said I was losing it. And they didn't want all that effort they had invested in helping me to speak well to be in vain.'

For some parents, the fact that their child joins deaf organisations and mixes with deaf people is extremely frustrating, but on the other hand, for deaf people, it can be extremely liberating. They all speak of it as discovering a new world, and in fact it is just that, a world where they do not depend on anybody to understand the conversations and to see what others are saying.

Religious Life

There are some churches where mass is said in sign language. In Madrid, in the Parish of Saint Mary of Silence, non-deaf priests who have learnt sign language say mass once a week and the church is full. In Barcelona, there is also a church where mass is held in sign language.

In Álava, in the Basque Country, when an association of the deaf was created 22 years ago, a priest began to study sign language because a fellow priest had told him that the deaf community needed a priest and that they had thought of him as the one who could do the job, so once he had learnt sign language, he began to hold masses for the deaf. He has been saying mass in sign language since then, and has also participated in the parties organised by the group, has celebrated over 20 marriages for the deaf, has baptised the children of the members and has conducted burial services for them. Mass is said on Saturdays, in the Poor Claires' Chapel ('El Correo', 20 December 1993).

Social Organisation

One can begin to speak of a deaf community from the beginning of the 20th century, when it started to be aware of being a linguistic community. The first organisations began to appear as a kind of reaction to the ban on teaching sign language that came out of the Milan Conference. In 1906, the first deaf organisation, the Deaf Mute Association of Madrid, was formed. In 1919, the first deaf organisation was formed in Catalonia, and from then on more were founded throughout Catalonia and the rest of Spain, thus facilitating relations among deaf people and the development, the practice and the spread of sign languages.

In Madrid, in 1936, the *Federación Nacional de Sociedades de Sordomudos de España* (Spanish National Federation of Deaf-mute Societies) was created, now called the *Confederación Nacional de Sordos de España* (CNSE) (Spanish National Confederation of Deaf People). Since then, it has defended the rights of the deaf, and has worked towards their enjoying the same conditions as the non-deaf. The *Federació de Sords de Catalunya* (FESOCA) (Federation of Deaf People of Catalonia) was founded in 1979 with 7 associations, and now numbers some 26 members.

The deaf do not live in geographically concentrated areas, which has meant that the associations have been essential to help deaf people to identify with the deaf community. In this way, the idea that they are a group and that they also have the ability to do many things has steadily spread, and thus the idea that they are isolated, handicapped and useless has become part of history.

Many deaf people aged between 15 and 20 years come to the deaf organisations. These people would not have had until then any relationship with other deaf people, and would have only learned to communicate orally, some with great difficulty, others more or less fluently. Different informants have explained the happiness that they have felt the first time that they participated in a deaf association, because they have been able to see another reality, to communicate with other people via a medium which is natural to them, without missing anything, for example, in a group conversation, nor needing a person who would explain what they could not hear. In this situation, they can contribute and manage for themselves.

The deaf associations (see Appendix 1 for a complete list of deaf people associations in Spain) have been very important for the consolidation, the development and the spread of sign language, and for the cultural and educational development of the deaf themselves. According to Rodríguez González (1992), the associations are perhaps the only linguistically cohesive factor among deaf people, since they often organise cultural and sporting events, such as festivals of silent cinema, poetry, theatre, etc.[6]

In Catalonia, there is an association called *Artistes Sords Units* (ASU) (United Deaf Artists), which is active in theatre and in film in sign language. They have produced over 100 films, which tend to be adaptations of well-known films such as *Cat on a Hot Tin Roof* or *Belinda*... acted in sign language by deaf actors.

The majority of the members of the deaf community participate in these activities, as well as attending the weekly gatherings in the association's meeting rooms. Many deaf people express their need to be able to communicate in sign language with other deaf people, after spending the week among only the non-deaf (at work, in shops, in the family, etc.). So these associations enable them to meet and establish friendship ties with other deaf people, when the fact of having been born into a non-deaf family normally means they would have no other way of getting together with other deaf people.

However, not all the deaf participate in these organisations. There are those who have made their circle of friends within the deaf community and prefer to arrange to meet directly with their friends to go to the cinema (needless to say, in original version with subtitles), to go on an excursion or simply for a walk.

Furthermore, the associations are also places of training and information points for their members. There, they can consult documents they do not understand, attend courses such as special classes to help pass the theory exam for a driver's licence. There are also seminars and conferences on subjects of present-day interest, so that they will not miss information which is often inaccessible to them. FESOCA also defends what they call 'the principle of affirmative action', which states that 'in equal conditions, employ a deaf person, until society totally guarantees equality of rights and opportunities'. FESOCA offers an information and advice service to companies and employers about the available incentives for employing deaf people, and about how to modify the workplace so that the deaf can do their work in conditions which allow them to be as productive as possible. They also offer a service of attention, information and advice to deaf people who are looking for employment or who wish to improve their qualifications via specialised training, and finally have a pool of jobs for those deaf who need one.[7]

These federations and associations are able to offer these services at least partly due to the subsidies they receive from the government. The Vigo association in Galicia offers courses on computing, crafts, leatherwork, and technical training, subsidised mostly by the Xunta (Regional Government), the Concello (local Council) and the ONCE (Blind Foundation). But that is not enough. Only 14 of the Galician Federation's members study at secondary level, and only three go to university. The ONCE helped them last year, but normally the Federation receives little assistance from the government. Most comes from the Council and the local government, but it is less than a million pesetas a year. In Catalonia, the president of the FESOCA, Josep Maria Segimon, comments in an interview that 'relations with the Generalitat and other Catalan government bodies are good. The FESOCA receives a subsidy although this does not cover the Federation's budget. But that does not worry me, as I'm more interested in getting my rights and changing the media, since we can't go on receiving subsidies all our lives.' (*Faro del Silencio*, 145: 10–12). On 8 July 1997, the deaf community rallied in a demonstration in front of the Social Welfare building, because the Social Welfare Department had decided to cut their subsidy by 50%, which endangered the services offered by the FESOCA.

The federations and associations of the deaf also fight for the rights of the deaf. The last Sunday in September is an important day all over the world for the deaf community, the International Day of the Deaf, when the Spanish federations of the deaf try to make their demands known to the whole of society.

In 1996, on International Day of the Deaf, the CNSE wrote a manifesto (Appendix 2) and distributed it to all its members for them to use and publicise. It placed special emphasis on the subject of communication barriers, in particular the lack of attention given to them by the news services of Spanish Television (TVE). Some of the demands of the various regional federations are: the recognition of sign language, adaptation of occupational training to the special needs of deaf people and their easier access to jobs, Civil Service entrance exams adapted to the needs of deaf people, bilingual education for the deaf, the elimination of communication barriers, the promotion and extension of interpretation services in sign language, TVE programmes with subtitles or interpretation, that the public administration take into account the opinions and suggestions of the deaf community, etc.[8]

In the demonstration held in Gerona, the president of FESOCA stated: 'We are not asking for pity, but justice. We believe that the *Generalitat de Catalunya* (autonomous government) should give priority to breaking down communication barriers. We have no voice, but we want the Government to listen to us' (*Avui*, 30 September 1996).

Education

After the International Conference of Teachers of the Deaf and Dumb held in Milan in 1880, sign language was removed from the deaf education curriculum. From then on, such education (Navarro, 1924; Granell, 1932) was entirely oriented towards training in oral skills, because the teachers, who were all non-deaf, considered that the completely deaf could learn to speak without great difficulty, and that it was precisely sign language which stopped deaf children from making progress in learning to speak. But even though sign language was banned, deaf children went to special schools for the deaf, and that meant that among themselves they spoke in the language which was most natural to them, in signs. In class, they were scolded if they signed, but in the schoolyard they were relatively free. One informant commented that he learnt sign language in the school yard, watching or speaking with his older schoolmates. All this suggests that sign language is really the most natural way of communicating for a deaf person, and that despite being prohibited, all that was needed for communication to take place in signs was for a group of deaf students to get together.

But since the *Llei d'Integració Escolar* (School Integration Act) was passed a few years ago, the tendency has been to integrate deaf children into normal schools. The special schools for the deaf began to close, and thus it was unlikely that a deaf child would find another deaf schoolmate in the same class, which meant he/she could not communicate in signs. According to this law, deaf children must be integrated into a school with non-deaf classmates to prevent them from becoming socially isolated or excluded. This policy of integration means that deaf children attend normal classes with the non-deaf, and in some subjects a special teacher comes into the class to help them, or they go to another classroom. There is normally only one deaf child in a class, and he/she can also have remedial classes with a speech therapist, whose task is to stimulate the learning of an oral language.

One informant, who has a deaf sister, commented: 'When they put me in a normal school I suffered a lot, because I knew what complete communication with my sister was like. [They communicated in sign language.] The existence of this fluent communication meant that I noticed the change much more. I knew that this fluent communication existed, and I would ask my classmates: 'What did he say?' they would answer: 'Nothing, nonsense.' And I would reply: 'What kind of nonsense? I want to know what they said.' I got used to it but I suffered a lot.' In the first two schools she went to, speaking in sign language was forbidden. She explains a story from this period: When I went to the partially integrated school, there were two other deaf children. A girl came up to me and said: 'You mustn't speak in signs, you have to speak with your mouth.' I said: 'I was speaking orally.' And she replied: 'They told me you were speaking to your friend in signs.'

Nowadays, given the results of having followed an orally oriented education policy, there are teachers and education specialists who are beginning to ask whether sign language might be useful in getting deaf children to understand certain structures and complex concepts. Three years ago, an experiment in bilingual education was begun, in which oral education was combined with the teaching of sign language (Fernández Viader, 1996). In fact, one of the points of the motion passed in the Catalan Parliament on 30 July 1994, recommends that priority be given to the use of Catalan Sign Language (CSL) in the classroom. In these schools, the deaf children are also integrated into the normal classes, but for a few hours a week the group of deaf students, of which there are various in different years, meet with a teacher who teaches them sign language.

Those who defend such a bilingual education argue that the language development process begins at an early age and therefore it is important that deaf children begin to have contact with sign language from the moment their deafness is detected. For this reason, they recommend that non-deaf parents attend courses in sign language. The supporters of bilingual education are backed by results obtained in countries such as Sweden, Denmark, France and the USA, where they have experience in bilingual education in both oral and sign languages. For example, the Kendall School, a pre- and primary school which is part of Gallaudet College, a university in Washington, has been teaching bilingually for 20 years. At the age of five, the deaf children are aware that the two codes exist, since they express themselves in sign language and also have begun to learn to speak orally. From the age of six, they have deaf teachers who use sign language, as well as non-deaf teachers. They also receive the help of a speech therapist who helps them to articulate the sounds. At the end of their primary education, these children are bilingual (Rodríguez González, 1992).

Despite these experiences, those who defend an exclusively oral education continue to believe that if the children use sign language they will lose interest in speaking or their speech will deteriorate. Both the advocates of exclusively oral education and those who defend bilingual education agree that the degree of deafness of a child must be taken into account in order to be able to decide on his/her needs. For example, a deaf child with some hearing will more easily adapt to an oral education than a totally deaf child.

A deaf education specialist, educated by oral methods and who began to learn sign language at the age of 22, commented:

> Most deaf children express themselves more easily in sign language because it adapts itself to their educational needs. Since they can't hear, they learn sign language much better as a base from which they can learn many concepts. The possibility of learning an oral language exists, but with sign language as a linguistic base. There are totally deaf children who are able to learn an oral language without sign language as a base, but they are very few.

As noted above, the parents of deaf children are mostly non-deaf (95%) and they have their own opinions about the kind of education that their children should receive. In an appearance on Channel 2 of TVE, on 11 May 1997, the parents of a totally deaf boy said: 'If we give him a signed code, he stops speaking to us. If the child already has a tendency to gesticulate, because of his deafness, in some way we are stopping the words from coming out.' But this opinion contrasts with that of other parents who have decided to take their child to a school where he also learns sign language. 'We spoke to experts and to parents of deaf children, and we reached the conclusion that the children who only use oral language do not acquire enough vocabulary to understand what is being said to them and to communicate fluently until the age of 6 or 7. And that's very sad.'

Most parents of the deaf choose the orally oriented method of education, but for a number of years there has been more and more information about the world of the deaf, and the advantage gained from learning sign language rather than an oral language, or even to facilitate the learning of the oral language, is becoming more and more recognised. Many more non-deaf parents are learning sign language themselves and helping their deaf children to learn it. For the last four years, there have been special courses for non-deaf parents of deaf children at FESOCA. These courses have more and more students enrolled, and parents recognise the progress made by their child since the parents also came into contact with sign language.

The FESOCA has a counselling service for families of the deaf, and get many requests for help from parents worried about their children. Most of these are from non-deaf parents who have a deaf child older than 15 and who has received an oral education. The results of this kind of education have not been satisfactory. They are worried because they realise that their children have great difficulties in understanding. They have worked with the oral methods for years, and with the help of specialised devices have learnt to speak more or less well, but they do not understand the meanings.

In the newspapers, various letters to the editor have appeared talking about this problem.

> Those of us who have been in the deaf community for years, and I as a mother of two deaf children, defend a better way of teaching our children, given the failure of the integration of deaf children into the final years of ordinary schools. This fact is not accepted by the public administration, but it is totally true and sad. Those who sign this letter believe that we deserve the respect and the human support and real help that those parents who defend an orally oriented education receive. (...) As a mother, I want my daughters to be truly socially integrated, as the result of the right kind of education, and not to learn an oral language and end up poorly imitating the spoken word and with a limited basic education. Nobody can demonstrate that a deaf child who signs and has access to the right kind of training will be incapable of speaking, just the contrary. (*Avui*, 17 November 1996)

But there are other parents who see it differently:

> I am the father of two totally deaf children aged 2 and 6. They were born deaf, and have been integrated into a normal school and have attended the 'Pere Barnils' Educational Resource Centre for children with auditory deficiency. The work they do there (...) is showing great results in the acquisition of oral language, concentration level and understanding of the world. The idea that for a deaf child communication and learning can only be guaranteed by learning through sign language should not be generalised. (*El País*, 11 May 1995)

And also:

> As the Parents Committee (ACAPPS), in which families which have chosen an oral education for their children coexist with others who have chosen a bilingual approach, we do not want to debate whether one system is better than another.... But we defend the need for both models to be applied, always respecting the individual characteristics of each child, such as the family and socio-economic environments, kind of development, level of hearing loss, etc. (*El País*, 24 July 1996)

Within the deaf community, they consider that children are often forced to be an artificial non-deaf person. This opinion is reflected in the words of the President of the Valladolid Association of the Deaf, in the 1985 International Conference on Sign Language in the Education of Children with Oral Communication Difficulties (Rodríguez González, 1992): 'The deaf person does not doubt the good will of his/her educators, but they are trying to create a non-deaf adult, when what is necessary is to turn the deaf child into a deaf adult who is not distanced from the non-deaf person.'

This conference took place 10 years ago, and there are still many problems in the education of the deaf in Spain. And as indicated by the Director of a Madrid special education centre for the deaf:

> They continue to show important gaps in their education, which prevent them from accessing culture and training for integration as much as they should be able to. (*El País*, 11 March 1997)

Study and Work

After 100 years of oral teaching, it has been proven that the majority of deaf people do not achieve an acceptable linguistic level in the oral and written language. Since they do not manage to express themselves or to understand well in the spoken and written language, they have great difficulty in getting through to secondary or higher education. Some have never finished primary school. For this reason, the vast majority of deaf people who work do so in jobs which do not require many qualifications.

There are not only comprehension difficulties, but also, the education system is oriented towards the non-deaf, and even if a deaf person has a high level of oral skills, he/she must have an enormous amount of willpower, because it is difficult to follow the teacher's explanations and the teacher cannot look continually at the deaf person throughout the whole of the class so the deaf student can read his/her lips. Even if he/she did, it would be impossible for one person to read another's lips for three or four hours. All informants agree on this. One of them, who has studied education and speech therapy, commented on the time spent at university: 'I had a lot of problems because people don't know what it means to be deaf. It's a handicap that you can't see, and people think nothing is happening to you. Classes get really boring. Reading lips all the time. There was a teacher who said: 'I'll try to move my lips very clearly.' But I couldn't be looking at his lips all the time. If I didn't understand him, I had to keep looking at him so he wouldn't get discouraged. If I couldn't see his lips move, I'd look away.'

This story is quite indicative of the difficulties which a deaf person may have to face, and the great effort needed to study in a society made by and for the non-deaf. Normally an interpreter who could translate what the teacher says is not available, as it would be too expensive for the administration to pay for an interpreter for every student. And it is still unimaginable that they could be taught in sign language as occurs at the Gallaudet University in the USA, where teaching is entirely in sign language and the deaf students can choose between various faculties.

Despite the difficulties that they face, there are some who reach university. There are some who study teaching or education to be able to teach deaf children. There are also some who study architecture or engineering, but these are such exceptional cases that they may have a TV programme or a newspaper article dedicated to them.

> In September, he started to study at the School of Architecture at the Polytechnical University of Catalonia, after obtaining a high mark in the entrance exam. The year before, he had studied industrial drawing. Nothing special, if it wasn't for the fact that Oscar is totally deaf, which has prevented him from speaking naturally. (*El País*, 8 May 1996)

Given Spain's present employment situation, with so many unemployed, among deaf people the situation is worsened by their low level of professional training and their limited range of job choices. We know from the CNSE that this means that the vast majority, with only a few exceptions, work as cleaners, office boys, carpenters, tailors, kitchen hands, or work in factories or companies on the production line.

Communication Barriers

In present-day society, the amount of information one receives through the sense of hearing is not only essential to have access to culture and for the intellectual development of each person, but also for everyday life. Information which reaches us via loudspeakers, television or cinema, a simple conversation with a request for information, all these and more can be problematic for a deaf person. In the home, there are more and more appliances adapted to the needs of deaf people, such as flashing lights instead of bells, fax instead of telephone, television with teletext, etc. Outside, things are quite different. It is only a few years since they began to remove the architectural barriers to handicapped people in large cities; however, the barriers to the deaf are not architectural but communicative. The deaf community complains that it is not taken into account when such changes are made. More and more architectural barriers to handicapped people are removed, in footpaths and road crossings, or in public phone boxes, but no special changes are made for the deaf. The solutions include written messages on a screen at the same time as an announcement is made over the public address system, interpreter services, more programmes on television which are subtitled or in sign language, the provision of an interpreter for those who go on to secondary or higher education, etc. One informant said that more than once he caught the wrong train because he didn't hear the announcement on the loudspeaker. Once, he was going to San Sebastián and he ended up in Bilbao. Another explained that she would have liked to see a film called *Professor Holland*, which dealt with the problem of deafness, but none of the cinemas were showing it in original version with subtitles. Foreign films in their original language provide the only opportunity for deaf people to watch films with subtitles.

The deaf community had been asking for official recognition of sign language interpreters since the 1980s, and on 22 December 1995, a Cabinet meeting approved a proposal of the Ministry of Education and Science to recognise a Diploma in *Sign Language Interpretation*. Sign language interpretation in Spain has finally attained the professional recognition that the deaf had been asking for, and this places Spain at the same level as other European Union countries in the elimination of this barrier. It is a step forward legally, but does not solve the problem. If the deaf had to pay for interpretation themselves, they would not be able to afford it, since like all such services it is very expensive. For this reason, the federations of the different Autonomous Communities in Spain have signed agreements with their regional governments to provide this service at no cost to the deaf people who request it.

In Madrid, the interpretation service was started in 1987. The first agreement was signed with the CNSE, but when the *Federación de Sordos de Madrid* (Madrid Federation of Deaf People) was founded in 1991–92, it took over the agreement. The Social Welfare Department of the Madrid Regional Government has signed an agreement with the Madrid Federation to pay for certain services. The Government pays for the interpreter, but only for a maximum of 1800 occasions per year. Also, restrictions are placed on the agreement by courts, police stations, local councils, and public or private bodies. The service does not provide interpreters for studying because he/she would have to go every day, and any such provision of services has to be through the Ministry of Education and Science or some other way. Once this limit is reached, the deaf person must pay for the interpreter, and the demand is increasing so that in October the maximum number is reached and one must wait until the following year. If it is an urgent matter, such as a court case, the deaf person will often end up paying him/herself. In this case, they do not have to pay the same rate as for services subsidised by the Madrid autonomous government but they do have to pay some 1000 or 1500 pesetas. The Interpreters' Association has a list of minimum rates for those cases where the deaf person has to pay for the service.

In Catalonia, the FESOCA offers an interpreter service in CSL for all those people or bodies which request it for different situations, such as court cases, medical and hospital consultations, consulting a lawyer or public notary, job interviews, conferences, meetings, etc. This service is free to those who request it, and in Catalonia, it is the result of the collaboration between the Social Welfare Department of the *Generalitat de Catalunya* (autonomous government), the *Diputació de Barcelona* (Barcelona's Council), the *Ajuntament de Barcelona* (Barcelona City Council), the Barcelona Red Cross, and the Ministry of Social Welfare. More and more official bodies take the deaf community into account, and are gradually becoming aware of the need for interpreters in exhibitions, museums, talks, conferences, etc. For example, in 1994 in Barcelona, the Cultural Diversity Week in the Eixample (a neighbourhood in Barcelona) was organised, and of the six talks held there four of them had simultaneous translation into sign language. Some exhibitions offer the possibility of a guided tour with a commentary in sign language. Occasionally, during the election campaign, a party will have an interpreter at a public meeting. And a few years ago, in a Barcelona theatre, there was an experiment in providing facilities for the deaf and the blind. Subtitles had been prepared for the play, but the screen with the subtitles was hung from the roof and to one side, and often the subtitles were badly synchronised with the action on stage. But it was clear that this experiment was not viable in the chosen theatre and with the available technical systems because of the need to choose between reading the text and watching the play.

Compared to the number of exhibitions, conferences and different public events, there are still few occasions on which a deaf person can enjoy a translation into sign language. Although the attempts to take into account the needs of deaf people are not frequent, it seems that these communication barriers are beginning to be taken into account.

The deaf have to deal with many communication barriers which a non-deaf person would not imagine. For example, they demand that in hospitals there be a screen where their number in the queue is shown, like in shops or supermarkets. This is easy to install but it is not done. People call them through the speaker system or out loud, and naturally they cannot hear it. In most underground carriages in Barcelona now, there is a spoken announcement of the name of the next station, but there is also a visual announcement. On the train platforms, there are screens with the destination of the next train, but if there is a last minute change of platform or destination, for example, an announcement is made on the loudspeaker. A deaf person will not hear this unless he/she asks another non-deaf person.

Television is also a communication barrier to deaf people. This is one of the most difficult barriers to overcome in a world which revolves so much around television viewing, and which thus excludes the deaf. At the moment, Spanish Television (TVE) broadcasts 40 hours a year with subtitles in videotext. Since May 1997, they have been carrying out an experiment that they first tried a few years ago, which consists of broadcasting a programme in sign language, subtitles and sound. The Basque television, *Euskal Telebista*, has subtitled its evening news programme in Spanish since October 1996 (*Faro del Silencio*, 154, September–October 1996). In Catalonia, Catalan Television (TV3) shows more than 300 hours a year of subtitled programmes, films, series, documentaries, children's cartoons, a weekly news programme and the evening news each day. Recently, the other Catalan Channel (*Canal 33*) has also begun to show some films and documentaries with subtitles. In Andalusia, *Canal Sur* has a weekly news programme called Telesigno which is shown in sign language and voice. *Canal 9*, in the Valencian Country, has been broadcasting a news programme in sign language since October 1995. This is a 10-minute programme shown from Monday to Friday.

Going to the cinema is another activity which was almost impossible for the deaf until not many years ago. These days there are more and more films shown in original version with subtitles, at least in the major cities, although it must be said that this is not because the cinema industry is thinking more of the needs of the deaf, but rather of the demands of the non-deaf who want to hear the film in the original, foreign language. But whatever the reason, deaf people can now go to the cinema and understand films without an interpreter. In the last few years, three cinema complexes have opened which show subtitled films, but this is not the norm. For example, looking at the cinema ads in the Barcelona newspapers, one finds that of the 1980s film shown, 50 are shown with subtitles (32 only in subtitled version), and 18 can be seen dubbed or with subtitles (*Avui*, 3 July 1997).

At university, there are normally no interpreters for the deaf, nor do deaf students receive special attention from the Government. *Faro del Silencio*, 154 (September–October, 1996) informs us that the University of Granada provides sign language interpreters so that deaf students can study all subjects. In the 1995–96 course, six deaf people had the help of a sign language interpreter and five other people with a hearing disability had the help of a tutor from a special programme for students with hearing disabilities. In Barcelona, an Architecture student has the help of another Architecture student who thus fulfils his obligatory social service as an alternative to military service. This deaf student's speech therapist encouraged him to sit for the university entrance exam, so he managed to gain some concessions as a result of his disability, such as not having to pass a foreign language exam and not having his spelling mistakes taken into account. But he was refused more time to do the exam and permission to use a dictionary (*El País*, 8 May 1996).

Similarly, the deaf community complains that they do not have the same opportunities to find jobs or when they sit for Government Administration entrance exams. When they try for a job, many deaf people who could do the job quite well find that they cannot understand the turns of phrases or the expressions in the questions, so they obtain much worse results than if the selection process was in sign language. So they often ask that this process be carried out in sign language, or the exam questions be explained in a language they can understand. At the Madrid deaf association, there are courses on the comprehension of oral language, but it is difficult for the students to understand the turns of phrase, the double meanings, the subtleties, etc. of this language.

The fact that non-deaf people do not understand the problems of the deaf is in itself a communication barrier. This lack of knowledge does not aid understanding or communication with this community. A clear example of this in the courts was explained in a newspaper article:

> A few months ago, in a trial of a domestic dispute, we had to put up with the rage of a judge who refused to allow us to have an interpreter because he argued that we were trying to act like simpletons in order to win him over. It was humiliating and we felt ashamed. (*El País*, 11 September 1995)

Another deaf person had problems with the government bureaucracy. Some civil servants lose patience when they have to make an effort to understand, and even more when you ask them for a piece of paper to write a message, given that they do not understand you when you speak. The deaf can normally lip-read, but a lot of people do not move their lips enough. In the non-deaf community, there are people who are sensitive to the problems of the deaf and others who are totally ignorant of the matter. This can also be seen in advertising.

In 1997, there were several ads which involved the deaf to one degree or another. In a few of these, a person communicated in sign language, for example. The *Organización Nacional de Ciegos Españoles* (ONCE) (Spanish Blind Association) had an ad about the creation of new jobs for handicapped people, and the whole ad was in sign language and subtitled. But at the same time, there are ads which hurt the feelings of the deaf community, such as one for a home language course in instalments by the publisher Planeta Agostini. Their comment was as follows:

> We, the deaf, were struck by an ad which showed a close-up of a girl while she was speaking. To us, it looked like the ad could have something to do with lip reading. But some non-deaf people explained the ad to us. While the girl's lips are moving without her voice, another voice is explaining that 'not speaking foreign languages is like being deaf'. (...) This ad doesn't tell the truth and is insulting. (*Faro del Silencio*, 155, November–December, 1996, p. 5)

With this ad, the advertising agency shows its lack of sensitivity and its total ignorance of the situation and the problems of the whole of the deaf community.

But cases like these are not the most common ones, because it is true that in recent years the interest in sign language and the removal of communication barriers has increased. For example, in 1997, the Málaga Town Council initiated a course in sign language for its employees, so that they can have the basic skills necessary to be able to attend to the deaf when they have to deal with the town council administration. There are also private companies which are aware of the problem. The Alcampo chain of large supermarkets has provided a checkout for the deaf at its Gijón (Asturias) store, where the employee knows sign language. This pilot experience could be extended to all the other stores if it is shown to be an efficient way of dealing with deaf people (*Faro del Silencio*. 157, March–April, 1997, p. 6–9).

More and more non-deaf people wish to do a course in sign language, as can be seen in the increasing number of courses offered by the different federations and associations in all Autonomous Communities of Spain.

Even the Bishop of Girona, in a September 1996, parish bulletin, defended the teaching of sign language in schools. With the headline 'An extraordinary demonstration', which referred to the demonstration in Girona on International Day of the Deaf, 29 September 1996, in support of the rights of the deaf, the Bishop drew his parishioners' attention to the limitations and the isolation imposed on the deaf. He called for their support of 'those citizens who also have the right to relationships which are as normal as possible'. And he took the side of the deaf in their demands in favour of sign language. 'It is sadly true that this language was not recognised until just a few years ago. One might ask who is deaf, them or society? When, thinking of the future, we teach our children English from an early age, is it not too much to ask that they be taught sign language, in order to foster fully human relationships?' (*Avui*, 21 November 1996). These opinions were very well received by the deaf community.

In Cantabria, reporting on the same International Day of the Deaf, the newspaper *Diario Montañés* published an article on 30 September 1996, talking about what it means to be deaf in a society where most people can hear.

> We talk about the problems faced by those who cannot see or who cannot move around, in a city designed for people who have no such problems. But we talk very little about how difficult it must be to live in the city without being able to hear, in a world of silence, when a high proportion of the communication which allows us to grow and develop in the worlds of culture, sport, education, etc, is exclusively oral.

Like the Bishop of Girona, this article also asked why sign language is ignored when we think of teaching a second or third language (*Faro del Silencio*, 155, November–December, 1996).

On the other hand, the article by the Catalan ombudsman in *Avui* (29 September 1996) was not so well received either by the deaf community or by those citizens close to it. The article defended the need to teach deaf children exclusively orally and not in sign language, which it assured us contributed to their marginalisation. More than a thousand people signed the following letter to the ombudsman:

> Dear Sir,
>   We would like to express to you some comments on your statements in the article published in the *Avui* of September 29, 1996.

Firstly, we believe that sign language is essential for many deaf people, since it has been demonstrated by the bilingual (sign language and oral language) educational experience of other countries (USA, Sweden, Denmark, Finland, France, etc) that it is this language which allows them to fully develop their thinking faculties from an early age, and thus to have access to the culture around them, without any backwardness. For this reason, the option of bilingual education for deaf people is, in our understanding, the richest, the most adequate, and the one which can create the most free citizens. The exclusively oral teaching methods, used for over a century, have led in many cases to the later appearance of basic oral language capabilities, and have caused large gaps in information and knowledge. This can be seen in the serious problems of integration suffered by the deaf to the present day. Few deaf people have managed to study secondary education and even fewer have reached university level. The majority of those who find work have unskilled jobs of low pay. As we see it, this makes them a discriminated minority.

As a final comment on the barriers to communication, the following letter to the editor is interesting. It appeared on 22 March 1997, when a group of journalists and politicians were taken around the centre of La Coruña for an hour in wheelchairs, in order to experience personally the obstacles faced by physically handicapped people. The letter summarises briefly the experience of a deaf person in Spanish society.

What would we have to do, to experience at first hand the barriers faced by the deaf and by their parents in this country? Would it be enough to use ear plugs for an hour to show that the linguistic barriers are serious obstacles which Spanish deaf people must face? No, it would not be enough. (...) To place ourselves in the same situation as the deaf, (...) we would have to renounce (for how long I do not know) the right to be taught in our own language, we would have to give up the right to receive education and training in our own language, we would have to be obliged to ignore our own culture, to live in a society which practically ignores us, and above all, we would have, in many cases, to do without our own family in exchange for an improved socialisation.

For the deaf, eliminating barriers does not only mean converting audio signals into visual ones. It means having an interpreter at the dentist, in court, in the police station, at university. It means being able to learn to speak at the right age, at the same rate as other children of your own age. It means having the right to language from the day you are born. It means being able to be taught in the language that your parents prefer, whether oral or kinesic, and thus not to have to become expert pole-vaulters in order to stroll quietly through the streets ...

Patterns of Language Behaviour and Use

It is very difficult to generalise about the linguistic behaviour of deaf people, because there is a wide range of levels of education and literacy. And it also depends on the character of the individual, and the situation. But one valid generalisation is that when a deaf person finds a breakdown in communication with a non-deaf person, whether it is because the other person does not move his/her lips or because the deaf person does not pronounce the words clearly enough, he/she will use writing to communicate.

Within the deaf community, the deaf only use sign language, although there are some who move their lips without pronouncing the words. All informants agree that they would never think of having a totally oral conversation with another deaf person. Since they were small, they have spontaneously used signs to communicate. A few informants commented that when they went to school and began to learn to speak with sounds, their parents scolded them if they used signs to make themselves understood.

Since 95% of deaf people are children of non-deaf parents, they have to use other codes to communicate within the family. This is usually spoken Spanish. In Catalonia, there are more and more deaf people who understand and even speak Catalan. Some of them speak very well, and others have great difficulties in speaking. One informant, born into a Spanish-speaking family, has learnt Catalan and now speaks it fluently. This girl commented that if a non-deaf person speaks to her in Spanish, she will reply in Spanish, but if they speak to her in Catalan, she will reply in Catalan. However, not everyone has the opportunity to choose. The majority have enough trouble learning to speak one language. A 55-year-old deaf man explained that since he only learnt Spanish at school, he only understands a few words of Catalan, and cannot follow a conversation. So when he has to talk to someone who is not part of the deaf community, he does so in Spanish, but sometimes he has had problems. 'Sometimes I'm with people who can't understand me, and they often get nervous and avoid me.' These people probably do not understand the problems of deaf people, and the difficulties they have in expressing themselves orally. This informant has deaf friends, with whom he communicates in sign language, and also non-deaf friends. He met the non-deaf friends during the period when his parents did not want him to go out with deaf people, and he speaks to them in Spanish. When he goes shopping, if he has problems with oral language, he writes messages down. He has both deaf and non-deaf children. With the deaf ones he communicates in sign language and with the non-deaf ones he speaks orally, because he says it is easier. He communicates with his wife in sign language, and when the whole family is together, most of whom are deaf, the lingua franca is sign language. During the interview, he spoke to the interviewer in sign language and at the same time pronounced many words. Sometimes, these were only conjunctions, but he also spoke words that he thought the interviewer would not know the sign for. In a conversation with deaf people, he only speaks, without sound, those words which could be confusing because there are synonyms.

Another informant from the Basque Country said that when she speaks with non-deaf people she does so in Spanish, because she does not speak Basque, even though she lives in a village whose inhabitants only speak Basque. She says that it is hard for her to speak orally, and that often when she speaks people stare at her in surprise. There are lots of people who have never had any contact with deaf people and do not understand what is going on. She has non-deaf friends because where she lives the neighbours are all non-deaf, and she has always spoken with them in Spanish. A few years ago, she found out about a deaf association and has begun to make deaf friends.

One informant explained that in her relationships with the non-deaf she no longer suffers as she did when she was young. If she does not understand, she thinks to herself: 'You don't understand. Sorry, but it's not my fault. It depends on us both; communication is between two people. It's not up to one of us. You don't move your lips and that's it. I make an effort but you don't move your lips. Don't worry, we can use writing.' She says she feels good, now that she is aware of the issues. In the interview, she spoke in Catalan, but accompanied this with sign language.

A 20-year-old architecture student from Zaragoza commented that 'to communicate amongst ourselves, sign language is the natural language to use. Oral language needs a greater effort because you have to lip-read. To communicate with non-deaf people, we need to know the oral language, although it is harder, because we have to recognise that we deaf people are a minority in a society made up mostly of non-deaf people.'

On the basis of the information obtained from interviews, it is clear that among themselves deaf people only use sign language. If they are communicating with a non-deaf person who knows sign language, they will also use sign language. If they are with a non-deaf person who does not know sign language, then they will speak orally or use writing.

Notes

1. Director of Iowa School for the Deaf. Text taken from Sachs (1991).
2. Although there is no documentation which proves that the deaf were fully aware of constituting a community, there was a group of people who communicated in sign language.
3. Some speak of 200,000 deaf people, but it is difficult to know the exact number as there are no official statistics.
4. Also see Perelló and Tortosa (1978) and Pinedo (1981).
5. *Dactylology* is a way of writing in the air. Each letter is represented by a shape of the hand. The deaf only use it for new concepts, or for place names or names of people that are not well known, and so do not have a sign yet.
6. News about deaf associations is given in *Faro del Silencio*, published by the CNSE.
7. See *Dossier Informatiu, Federació de Sords de Catalunya* (FESOCA) (Federation of Deaf People of Catalonia).

8. Also see Appendix 3 on this matter, where a manifesto of the FESORD, C.V. and the CNSE is included.

Appendix 1

List of deaf people associations in Spain (*Source*: *Confederación Nacional de Sordos de España*, CNSE):

Federación Andaluza de Asociaciones de Sordos (FAAS), in Granada.
  — Asociación de Sordos, in Motril
  — Asociación Cultural de Sordos, in Huelva
  — Asociación de Sordos de Jaén
  — Sociedad Federada de Sordos de Málaga
  — Asociación Cultural de Sordos, in Sevilla
  — Centro Cultural de Sordos 'Torre del Oro', in Sevilla
  — Asociación Cultural de Sordos, in Estepa
  — Agrupación de Sordos 'A.SO.AL' in Almeria
  — Asociación de Sordos de Cadiz
  — Asociación de Sordos, in Puerto de Santa María
  — Asociación de Sordos de Jerez, in Jerez de la Frontera
  — Asociación Provincial de Sordos, in Córdoba
  — Agrupación de Sordos de Granada
Federación de Sordos del Principado de Asturias (FESOPRAS), in Oviedo.
  — Asociación de Sordomudos, in Oviedo
  — Asociación de Sordomudos de Gijón
  — Asociación de Sordos de Avilés
  — Asociación de Sordomudos de Langreo, in La Felguera
Federación Regional de Asociaciones de Sordos de Castilla-León (FRASCL), in Valladolid.
  — Centro Cultural de Sordos, in Ávila
  — Asociación de Sordos 'Fray Ponce de León', in Burgos
  — Asociación de Sordos, in León
  — Centro de Sordos de Palencia
  — Asociación de Sordos de Salamanca
  — Sordos en Acción, in Valladolid
  — Agrupación Vallisoletana de Sordos, in Valladolid
  — Asociación de Sordos de Zamora
Federación de Sordos de la Comunidad de Madrid (FSCM), in Madrid.
  — Centro Cultural Acción Católica de Sordos, in Madrid
  — Centro Altatorre, in Madrid
  — Asociación de Sordos de Madrid
  — Asociación de Sordos, in Alcalá de Henares
  — Asociación Cultural de Sordomudos, in Móstoles
  — Asociación de Sordomudos, in Fuenlabrada, Madrid
Federació de Sords de Catalunya (FESOCA), in Barcelona.
  — CE. RE. CU. SOR, in Barcelona
  — Societat Ajuda Mútua de Sords Catalunya, in Barcelona
  — Associació de Sords Units (ASU), in Barcelona
  — Casal de Sords de Barcelona
  — Artistas Sordos Unidos (ASU), in Barcelona
  — Agrupació de Sords de Mollet
  — Associació de Sords de Sabadell
  — Unió Sociocultural de Sords, in Terrassa
  — Casal del Sord de Manresa

- Centre del Sordmut del Maresme, in Mataró
- Associació de Sords de Vic
- Llar del Sord del Vallès, in Les Franqueses
- Cercle de Sords, in Vilanova i la Geltrú
- Agrupació de Sords Com. Llobregat, in L'Hospitalet
- Llar del Sord de Badalona
- Unió de Sords de Girona
- Associació de Sordmuts de Blanes
- Agrupació de Sords de Ripoll
- Agrupació de Sords de la Garrotxa, in Olot
- Llar del Sord de Lleida
- Club de Sords de Reus

Federación de Asociaciones de Sordos de Euskalerría (FASE), in Vitoria-Gasteiz.

- Centro del Sordo de Álava, in Vitoria
- Asociación de Sordos de Navarra, in Pamplona
- Asociación de Sordos de Bilbao
- Asociación de Sordos del Duranguesado, in Durango
- Asociación de Sordos de Basauri
- Agrupación de Sordos de la Margen Izquierda, in Santurce

Federación de Asociaciones de Sordos del País Gallego (FXPG), in La Coruña.

- Agrupación de Sordos La Coruña
- Asociación Comarcal de Sordos, El Ferrol
- Agrupación de Sordos de Lugo
- Agrupación de Sordos de Ourense
- Asociación de Sordos de Vigo
- Centro Vigués de Xordos
- Sociedad Comarcal de Sordos, in Santiago de Compostela
- Agrupación de Sordos 'Río Lerez', in A Caeira-Poio

Federación de Asociaciones de Sordos de la Comunidad de Murcia (FSC Mu), in Múrcia.

- Agrupación de Sordos de Murcia
- Círculo de Sordos de Cartago, in Cartagena
- Asociación de Sordos Comarcal del Noroeste, in Caravaca de la Cruz
- Centro Murciano de Integración del Sordo
- Agrupación Recreativa de Sordos, in La Unión

Federación de Sordos de la Comunidad Valenciana (FESORD CV), in Valencia.

- Asociación de Sordos de Alicante
- Asociación de Sordos de Elche
- Asociación de Sordos de Elda
- Asociación de Sordos de Alcoi
- Asociación de Sordos, in Castelló
- Asociación Valenciana de Sordomudos, in Valencia
- Sordos 2.000 Valencia, in Valencia
- Asociación Provincial de Sordos, in Burjassot
- Agrupación de Sordos 'La Ribera', in Alzira
- Asociación de Sordos de La Safor, Gandia
- Asociación de Sordos 'La Costera', in Xàtiva

Federación de Asociaciones de Sordos de las Islas Canarias (FASICAN).

- Sociedad de Sordos 'El drago', in Tenerife
- Asociación de Sordomudos, Las Palmas de Gran Canaria

Non-confederated Associations:

- Asociación de Sordos, in Albacete
- Asociación Cultural de Sordos, in Palma de Mallorca
- Asociación Cultural de Sordos, in Cáceres
- Hermandad de Sordos de Plasencia, Cáceres

- Asociación Cultural de Sordos, in Cuenca
- Asociación de Sordos Riojanos, in Logroño
- Agrupación de Sordos, in Ciudad Real
- Asociación de Sordos 'V. de Belén', in Almansa
- Asociación de Sordos de Santander y Cantabria, in Santander
- Asociación Comarcal de Sordos de Laredo
- Asociación Provincial de Sordos, in Toledo
- Asociación de Sordos de Zaragoza

Appendix 2

The Position of the *Confederación Nacional de Sordos de España* (CNSE) on the International Day of the Deaf.

The Executive Council of the CNSE (Spanish National Confederation of Deaf People), representing the opinion of its Regional Federations (9) and Associations of Deaf People (97) throughout the country, according to the mandate given to it by its own Constitution, which charges it to inform public opinion about the needs and aspirations of Spanish deaf people, and following the custom established for some years on the occasion of the celebration of the International Day of the Deaf, announces the following:

Manifesto

Under the leadership of its National Confederation, the deaf community, with all the means at its disposal, has been carrying out a wide range of activities and advocacy, with the aim of eliminating the communication barriers which affect it. Without the elimination of these communication barriers, which presupposes the increased awareness of those who legislate and who have the means to achieve this elimination, the final goal of our integration into society will always remain only an ideal.

While in other areas of daily life, including in such an important field as education, these barriers are tending to disappear, thanks to the recognition of the profession of sign language interpreter and its integration into the Spanish education system, this is not occurring in such a vital area as that of information via television. ('A person without information is a person without opinion.')

Given that this is a right for all Spanish people, included in Article 20.1, d) of our Magna Carta, and also in Article 53.1, 'binding on all public institutions', we wish to call society's and our leaders' attentions to the unquestionable fact that Spanish deaf people suffer from complete exclusion and lack of support, because of the total lack of information and attention given to us by one kind of media, television, and especially by the Government-owned television channel, TVE, and as regards the emission of a programme specifically for deaf people.

Some time ago, from 1977 to 1982, when TVE really was *La primera* (The First), because it was the only one, it broadcast a programme ('Hablamos' (We Speak)), directed by Mr. Juan Julio Baena, at 10.00 am on Sundays, which, for all its faults, addressed the information needs of deaf people. This programme was shown in sign language, oral language and with subtitles, and could thus be watched by any person. Without any kind of explanation or alternative, it was withdrawn from the programming, and deaf people were condemned to a total silence as far as information is concerned, when this programme had given us hopes for the better.

With the coming of teletext to Spain, TVE began its teletext service, with a few pages especially for deaf people, and started to show a subtitled film once a month. At the moment, the only concessions to the deaf are some subtitled series, both locally and overseas produced, as if all our needs could be catered for with a few films and series.

As the sole achievement until now, we can only mention the King's Christmas Message in 1993, which was broadcast in sign language, achieved with the aid of different bodies such as the *Real Patronato de Prevención y de Atención a Personas con Minusvalía* (Royal Patronage for the Prevention and Assistance to the Handicapped), the Ministry of Social Affairs, and INSERSO.

The appearance of private TV and regional channels, which almost all have teletext, has not changed the panorama, although we must say that in Catalonia the regional channel TV3 has helped deaf people by subtitling with videotext the main evening news programme, 'Telenoticies Vespre', from Monday to Friday, as well as some other children's programmes, subtitled in the same way.

Two other regional channels (*Canal Sur* in Andalusia and *Euskal Televista* in the Basque Country) showed the programme 'Telesigno' for a period of time, thanks to an agreement between the *Federación Andaluza de Asociaciones de Sordos* (Andalusian Federation of Associations of Deaf People), which is a member of the CNSE, and the two television channels. 'Telesigno' was produced by the Andalusian Federation, aided by the CNSE, which helped to obtain subsidies from the Ministry of Social Affairs. It is curious that any project which comes from within the deaf community takes into account the non-deaf community, even though they ignore us, or at least those who represent it or who have the means of serving it. This programme is thus produced by deaf people for both deaf and non-deaf audiences, combining sign language, subtitles and oral language with the images, to provide the deaf with a programme they can understand, opening doors to communication which had previously been closed to them. So it is a programme for all types of audiences, and whose high quality makes it suitable for showing on any channel. The feasibility study of this same programme was repeatedly postponed by the Executive Management of RTVE and by other departments of Public Television, with the excuse of lack of funds and staff, although this was interpreted by us as a rejection of the proposal.

This same body, RTVE, is the one which, in the presentation of its Autumn programmes, this year, has made such a fuss about offering 'programmes for ALL AUDIENCES'. For ... ALL?

We are pleased to see that the regional channels are gradually becoming aware of the special needs of deaf people in television. How is it possible that some regional channels, which after all are also state channels, with less technical, human and economic resources, can respond positively to our demands, yet *La Primera* ('The First') cannot? We would be equally pleased if the private channels responded in the same way. Even though they are not obliged to do so in the same way as the government-run channels, this obligation should be part of their government-granted licences.

Could it not be, then, that behind this excuse of lack of means, and given that other channels can do it, there lies the true reason, which is lack of desire to serve the public interest? If they really wanted to, ...

There have been those, like a certain Parliamentary Party, sympathetic to our cause who have recently presented a motion in the *Congreso de los Diputados* (Parliament) urging the Government to promote access to television for deaf people, but to date there has been no response.

All of the above points to the fact that one of the most pressing needs of deaf people is to overcome the communication barriers which affect us so directly, and of these those that are directly related to information obtained through such an strong, influential and far-reaching media as is television, and specifically TVE.

So because of this, we call on those who govern us, on the communication companies and bodies, especially the Executive Management of Public Television, RTVE, and <u>demand</u>:

*that television cater for all deaf people, and not only for those who live in certain Autonomous Communities, so that EVERYBODY, both deaf and non-deaf, can have the same opportunities to have an education, information and opinions.

* an act which extends the above-mentioned Constitution to impose the obligation to respect its principles on those who occupy positions of service in the Autonomous Communities, who have in their hands the means by which the information needs of deaf people can be taken into account in television, and by which we can enjoy a truly accessible television, with programmes in sign language and subtitles, so that we have our own representatives in the planning of programmes for us, and concretely a Committee made up of representatives from interested parties, namely RTVE, film and TV companies, the Ministry of Labour and the Ministry of Social Affairs, and the representative of deaf people, which is *the Confederación Nacional de Sordos de España (CNSE).*

* an act which clearly states the principle of aid to deaf people simply because they exist, and not as a function of the availability of resources or agreements, as a right in the widest sense of the word.

Madrid, September 29, 1996
International Day of the Deaf

Appendix 3

FESORD C. V.
Federación de Sordos de la Comunidad Valenciana
(Federation of Deaf People in the Valencian Autonomous Community)

Confederación Nacional de Sordos de España
(Spanish National Confederation of Deaf People)

Manifesto

On the International Day of the Deaf, the deaf community and in its name the Federation of Deaf People in the Valencian Regional Community (FESORD, C.V) wishes to make known the following Manifesto, which sets out the most important of our demands.

1. **The elimination of the communication barriers which affect us**. To do so, the national and autonomous governments must:

1.1 Recognise sign language as a first language and heritage of the deaf community.
1.2 Recognise the profession of Sign Language Interpreter.
1.3 Continue and extend the 'Diario Actual' news programme broadcast by TVV.
1.4 Adopt the teletext subtitling technique to allow access to television programming.
1.5 Show programmes which help people to understand the deaf community.
1.6 Show programmes specifically for deaf children, which would allow their participation.
1.7 Increase the use of sign language by those professional people who deal with the public.

2. **The use of a bilingual system as another educational possibility in the education of deaf people**. To this end, we demand:

2.1 That sign language be taught at an early age and be used in school and in teaching.
2.2 That deaf adults serve as role models for schoolchildren.
2.3 That the deaf community and sign language be studied and researched.

3. **That a job creation plan for the disabled be put into practice**. To this end, we demand:

3.1 That the law in force which reserves jobs for the disabled be, in fact, enforced, and in particular that a certain number of jobs be reserved for the deaf, as in the Italian model.
3.2 The recognition of the right to have a meaningful job and to receive the same treatment as all other workers.

Finally, that the powers recognise our right to be independent and to decide for ourselves. So in the drawing up of plans or laws which affect us, the FESORD, as the highest level of representation of the deaf community in the Valencian Country, should be consulted.

Appendix 4

List of abbreviations:

ASU   Artistes Sords Units
CNSE   Confederación Nacional de Sordos de España
EGB   Educació General Bàsica
ESO   Ensenyança Secundaria Obligatòria
FESOCA   Federació de Sords de Catalunya
FP   Formació Professional
INSERSO   Instituto Nacional de Servicios Sociales
LSC   Llengua de Signes Catalana
LSE   Lengua de Signos Española
ONCE   Organización Nacional de Ciegos de España
TVE   Televisión Española
TVC   Televisió de Catalunya

References

Avui, 30 September 1996, society. Els sords reclamen la supressió de les barreres de comunicació.

Avui, 1 November 1996, opinion. El Síndic de Greuges i els sords, el claustre de professors de l'escola específica de sords CRAS.

Avui, 17 November 1996, opinion. Polèmica sobre els sords, Cecília Solanes i Traserra.

Avui, 21 November 1996, society. El bisbe de Girona vol el llenguatge dels sords a les escoles.

Avui, 21 February 1997, opinion. Rèplica al Síndic de Greuges, senyor Anton Cañellas, Carme García and 120 other signatures.

Battison, R. (1974) Phonological deleitum in American Sign Language. *Sign Language Studies* 5, 1–19.

Battison, R. (1980) *Sign Language and the Deaf Community: Essays in Honor of W.C. Stockoe.* Silver Spring: National Association of the Deaf.

Bonet, J. P. (1620) *Reducción de las Letras y Arte para Enseñar a Hablar a los Mudos,* Madrid, Francisco Abarca de Angulo, new 1930 edition.

El País, 14 December 1994, opinion. Subtitulado en TVE, Mercè Elias i Sospedra.

El País, 25 March 1995, people. El intercambio de los novios.

El País, 2 May 1995, society. Renace la lengua de los signos contra la incomunicación de los niños sordos.

El País, 11 May 1995, opinion. La comunicación del niño sordo, Raimon Jané Campos.

El País, 11 October 1995, society. Sordos, no mudos.

El País, 8 May 1996, back page, Clases en silencio, Teresa Cendrós.

El País, 24 July 1996, Catalunya. Sordera y bilingüismo. Raimon Jané Campos (representative at the parents' committee (ACAPPS).

El País, 11 March 1997, society. La clase silenciosa.

El País, 22 March 1997, opinion. Las barreras de los sordos. Inmaculada C. Báez Montero.

Faro del silencio, 145, March–April 1995, CNSE.

Faro del Silencio, 154, September–October 1996, CNSE.

Faro del silencio, 155, November–December 1996, CNSE.

Faro del Silencio, 157, March–April 1997, CNSE.

Fernández Viader, M. P. (1996) Interés de la educación bilingüe para los niños sordos. In *FIAPAS*, 49, March–April, 16–21 (published by the Federación Española de Asociaciones de Padres y Amigos de los Sordos).

FESOCA, Federació de Sords de Catalunya. *Dossier informatiu.*

FIAPAS (1994) Reflexiones sobre el bilingüismo, 36, January-February.

Frishberg, N. (1979) Arbitrariness and Iconicity: Historical Change in ASL. *Language* 51, 696–715.

Granell, M. (1932) *Historia de la Enseñanza del Colegio Nacional de Sordomudos, desde 1794 a 1932.* Madrid: Col. de Sordomudos.

Halliday, M.A.K. (1975) *Learning How to Mean.* London: Arnold.

Klima, E. and Bellugi, U. (1980) *The Signs of Language.* Cambridge, MA: Harvard University Press.

Kyle, J.G. and Woll, B. (1985) *Sign Language: The Study of Deaf People and Their Language.* Cambridge: Cambridge University Press.

Ladd, P. (1991) The British Sign Language community. In S. Alladina and V. Edwards (eds) *Multilingualism in the British Isles* (pp. 35–48). London: Longman Linguistic Library.

Lane, H. (1984) *When the Mind Hears: A History of the Deaf.* New York: Random House.

Lane, H. (1979) Histoire Chronologique de la répression de la langue des signes en France et aux États-Unis. *Langages,* 56, 92–124. Paris: Larousse.

Marchesi, A. (1980) El lenguaje de signos. *Estudios de Psicología,* 5–6, 155–84.

Marchesi, A. (1993) *El Desarrollo Cognitivo y Lingüístico de los Niños Sordos.* Madrid: Alianza Psicología.

Markowicz, H. (1972) Some sociolinguistic consideration of American Sign Language. *Sign Language Studies,* 1, 15–41.

Navarro, T. (1924) Manuel Ramírez de Carrión y el arte de enseñar a hablar a los mudos. *Revista de Filología Española,* 11, 225–66.

Perelló, J. and Tortosa, F. (1978) *Sordomudez.* Barcelona (scientific/medical).

Pinedo, F. J. (1981) *El Sordo y su Mundo.* Madrid: Federación Nacional de Sordos de España.

Pinedo, F. J. (1989) *Una Voz Para un Silencio.* Madrid: Fomento de Empleo de Minusválidos.

Rodríguez González, M.A. (1992) *Lenguaje de Signos.* Confederación Nacional de Sordos de España y Fundación ONCE. Madrid.

Rodríguez González, M.A. (1993) *Llenguatge de Signes Català.* Unitat de Qualificació Professional (UQP). Beginners level, Reports. Institut Català de Noves Professions, Generalitat de Catalunya.

Sachs, O. (1991) *Veo una Voz.* Madrid: Anaya.

Schaller, S. (1993) *Un Hombre sin Palabras.* Madrid: Anaya.

Schein, J. (1984) *Speaking the Language of Sign: The Art and Science of Signing.* New York: Doubleday.

Schein, J. (1989) *At Home Among Strangers.* Washington, DC: Gallaudet University Press.

Steward, D. A. (1983) Bilingual education: Teachers' opinions of signs, *Sign Language Studies* 39, 145–67.

Stockoe, W. (1960) *Sign Language Structure: An Outline of the Visual Communication System of the American Deaf. Studies in Linguistic Occasional Papers. 8.* Buffalo. University of Buffalo Press.

Stockoe, W. (1969) Sign Language diglossia. *Studies in Linguistics* 21, 27–41.

Stockoe, W. (1975) The use of sign language in teaching English. *American Annals of the Deaf* 120, 417–21.

Tervoort, B. (1983) The status of Sign Language in education in Europe. In J. Kyle and B. Woll (eds.) *Language in Signs: An International Perspective on Sign Language.* London: Croom Helm.

TVE2, April 25, 1996. Giravolt.

TV3, January 13, 1997. Telenotícies Vespre.

TVE2, May 11, 1997. Línea 900, Un sordo en casa.

Chapter 8

The Gitano Communities

ÁNGEL MARZO and M. TERESA TURELL

Historical and Linguistic Background

It is widely accepted that the sources which relate to the Gypsy[1] community are seldom reliable. This situation is attributed to several factors, although there is no agreement among scholars as to their real weight. First of all, the fact that the Gypsies (or the Roma, as these people like to be called) are seldom the authors of those sources; secondly, the lack of documentation, not available until the beginning of the modern era; thirdly, the Gypsy community's ethnocentrism; fourthly, the Gypsies' lack of participation in the host community's historical path, and finally, the fact that they have been prosecuted for over five centuries. A considerable effort has been made in the last 25 years to clarify their past and their present but this effort has proved to be still insufficient (San Román, 1994).

At present, there seems to be consensus as to the original location of Gypsies in India from where they would have migrated out of northern India, travelled as pilgrims to Iran around 1000 or 1100 AD, and then would have taken two different routes: one through Armenia to Byzantium, which would explain the existence of traces of Greco-Byzantine vocabulary in their language, and the other through Syria, the Middle East and the Mediterranean, which would account for the presence of Arabic vocabulary among some of the Gypsy groups.[2] However, the fact that some Germanic vocabulary is found in some European Gypsy groups, but not in those which settled in Southern Europe, would suggest that even from these first settlements there were other groups which took another alternative route towards other warmer locations. Documents and sources begin to be reliable from the 14th century onwards.[3] In 1322 the Gypsies appeared in Crete and disseminated through Europe by the second half of the 14th century. It seems that some stayed in the Balkans for a long time but that the majority of those who settled there left and migrated to other areas before the 15th century. At first, the Gypsies were welcomed in Europe, but unfortunately their settlement in Europe coincided with an intense anti-Muslim fervour and this led the European population 'to view anyone with a dark complexion and foreign language as an enemy' (Giddens, 1997: 1–2).

Very little is known about these first Gypsies to settle in Europe. Their migration pattern seems to be 'errant' even if there were periods in which they settled on a permanent basis. The Gypsies travelled in small groups of sometimes 10, 20 or even 100 men and women of all ages guided by a chief, who was often named Earl, Duke or Baron, and very often without establishing any link with the other groups. They are often described as very independent and very strange people, in their language, clothes, and customs. They travelled riding horses and with other animals, dancing and playing music. As to their religious beliefs, they were Christian but were also thought to be dealers in witchcraft.

In spite of some unfortunate experiences through which they would be chronicled stereotypically as burglars and thieves (Sánchez Ortega, 1977), the Gypsies were welcome in most places during the 15th century, partly because they were foreigners, partly because they were linked to the church. Their lucky stars deserted them with the turn of the century when they began to be prosecuted and by the middle of the 16th century they had already been deported from Spain, the Holy Roman Empire, France and England. This prosecution period extended until the 18th century with the attempt by the mainstream host communities to assimilate the Gypsies, which is still the pattern nowadays.

The language spoken by the Gypsies, generally referred to as Romani, includes varieties spoken in Europe, the Middle East, and the New World[4] and derives from a subgroup of the Indo-Aryan (Indic) languages, namely, the Central Indo-Aryan, which are spoken predominantly in western and central India, extending into Nepal and Pakistan. Hancock (1998: 10) points out that 'conservative Romani dialects remain two-thirds or more Indian in their basic lexicon and grammar'.

The Historical Background and Distribution of the Gitano Community in Spain[5]

The ancestors of those people who are nowadays known as Gitanos[6] first arrived in Spain in the 15th century, according to documents which describe how groups of Gypsies came as pilgrims. A first wave penetrated the Pyrenées at the beginning of the 15th century and by 1480 other groups which came from coastal countries appeared on the Mediterranean, their exodus being related to the Turkish invasion of Constantinople.

The Gitanos' settlement pattern followed a very similar path to that of their European counterparts, that is, they did not pay any taxes, they were given credit everywhere they went and they were associated with the popular image of a simple traveller. They travelled in groups of 10 to 100 people led by Earls, Dukes or Barons, as was said earlier, who often asked for protection of the King or the nobility against other groups with which they were confronted. The same group could duplicate or divide in two or more groups in a few years and they adopted organisational forms that still continue nowadays, travelling in search of better conditions.

These nomadic groups settled progressively in different parts of Spain, conserving their own identity and maintaining their links with their lineage, rather than links established with the local population. Although initially well received, within a few decades conflicts arose which soon became reflected in the laws that marked the beginning of a long period of rejection and legal restrictions with respect to this community. Quintana and Floyd (1972) report on the Spanish people's attitudes towards these early settlers who were described as an invading force.

Taking the legal texts as a point of reference, the picture is rather disheartening, but it is well known that the Gitanos have lived in Spain for centuries in close proximity with their neighbours without losing their own identity. During this time, they have worked principally as tinkers and in seasonal activities in agriculture. Other members of the community have worked as blacksmiths and craftsmen. Also well known is their creative participation in the artistic world, especially in music and dance. They are also well known for their participation in social activities, such as pilgrimages, gatherings and contests. The relationship between the Gitanos and the rest of the population varies between conflict and peaceful coexistence, rejection and interaction. For centuries, they have maintained a self-identity, which has been expressed, through their own social identity, based on their own lineage. Around this revolves their economic activity, internal and external social relations, and their cultural activity.

There are not many written texts about the Gitanos, because their culture and activity are expressed through an oral tradition. We can find them reflected in the legal and judicial writings of those places where they have lived or have passed through, and also in literature in Spanish and in Catalan. Well known, for example, is the work by Cervantes called *The 'Gitano' Girl*. This is based on a stereotypical vision of the Gitanos, almost certainly well established in the period, which can be seen in the first part of the work:

> Parece que los gitanos y las gitanas solamente nacieron en el mundo para ser ladrones; nacen de padres ladrones, críanse con ladrones, y, finalmente, salen con ser ladrones corrientes y molientes a todo ruedo ...

> (It seems that 'Gitanos' are born to be thieves. They are born to parents who are thieves, they grow up with thieves, they study to be thieves, and finally become common thieves all round).

But even so, Cervantes' text also reflects some of the positive aspects of the Gitanos' customs and social structure, which have been conserved till this day. Overall, it reflects the typical wavering between myth making and rejection by the non-Gitano communities.[7]

It has been estimated that nowadays, Gitanos make up 1% of the Spanish population, approximately 400,000 persons. The following groups of Spanish Gitanos exist: those from the south of Spain, which San Román (1976) calls Béticos, the Catalans, and the Castilians, those from Extremadura and the Portuguese. There are also minorities from Hungary and Central Europe. The most numerous are the Béticos, many of whom have emigrated during this century to the outskirts of the large northern cities, such as Madrid, Barcelona, Valencia, Zaragoza, Bilbao, etc. The Catalan and Portuguese Gitanos have as their own language Catalan and Portuguese respectively, although they also speak Spanish and Caló. In Catalonia, there is a minority of Gitanos from the south of France, who speak French.

The Spanish Gitano community, unlike the Central European and the British ones, is fairly settled. Nomadic Gitanos are few and in many cases they are immigrants from Eastern Europe. However, Gitanos continue to maintain family ties beyond their place of residence, and if necessary a whole family may move to another province or region. If there is some benefit to be gained, the Gitanos will readily travel. Many move for parts of the year to work as seasonal workers, and there are also groups that work in fairs or as artists, although these are not a majority nowadays.

Settlement Patterns

During the Spanish post-war period, following the Civil War, the Gitano communities settled in rural areas, some on a permanent basis. The settlement took place in small groups, which ended up with their either living on their own or living together with non-Gitano people. With the economic expansion which took place at the beginning of the 1960s, the bad economic situation in the countryside and the increasing job offer in the city, the Gitanos were attracted to the urban areas where they concentrated and created dense agglomerations in the outskirts of cities by the end of the decade. This settlement pattern also involved the settlement fixation of not only the few itinerant Gitanos that were left but also of the semi-itinerants, and this was due both to the stable occupation that some of them found and to their very profitable marginal activities, such as street vending, scrap-metal dealing and mendicity (San Román, 1994: 45–6). However, in the case of those Gitano people who had a well remunerated job this stable situation brought with it a contradictory dilemma for many of them since it cut off some of their cultural strategies and their social and work habits.

In 1978, official data from the *Centro de Investigaciones Sociológicas* (CIS) (Centre for Sociological Research) situated the distribution of Gitano people in 210,000 people in the whole of Spain,[8] representing 0.5% of the Spanish population at the time, which suggests that the Gitano community distribution has increased since the mid-1970s, if the present-day figures are considered (400,000 people, approximately). The majority were at that time concentrated in the south of Spain (Andalusia) and in big cities like Madrid and Barcelona, although there were Gitanos in other provinces of the North and much fewer in Galicia. During this period, there were four times as many Gitanos in urban than in rural areas, and the majority (90%) were sedentary, that is, temporarily settled, *vis-à-vis* a minority (10%) of nomads (San Román, 1994: 47). This situation contrasts with the settlement patterns of Gypsies in other areas of Europe since a decade later Liégeois (1988, cited by San Román, 1994: 47) estimated that there were 30% nomads, 30% sedentary and 40% settled Gypsies.

With the effects of the economic crisis, which occurred during the second half of the 1970s there was a new exodus of the Gitano communities. Street vendors left for areas of less competition from an intraethnic point of view and settled in Galicia and Asturias. In general their mobility throughout Spain was not as high as in other periods since the less fortunate tended to develop marginal activities such as scrap-metal vending and mendicity in the cities and were more or less attracted by the administration's social services and housing policy, which contributed to their sedentary pattern. However, at that period some sections of the Gitano community in Spain started to adopt a new form of mobility which had to do with a new means of transport that they used to move from one place to another. From the 1970s, the caravan, or wagon, and horses were substituted by second-hand vans and small lorries that they used to travel long-distance, sell their products and go back to their settlement to sleep.

Another factor which affected the Gitano communities' settlement patterns during this period, and which continues today, has to do with the policy of eviction from Gitano *poblados* and forced rehousing pursued by the administration, particularly in the Autonomous Communities and also by local municipalities. In many cases these city housing programmes allowed the Gitanos to settle and as a result intraethnic conflict decreased. However, in many other cases it also created some rootlessness.

Social Organisation in the Past and in the Present

One important aspect which characterises the Gitanos' settlement patterns today, and characterised them in the past, is the fact that whenever they can, the Gitanos adopt the same forms of social organisation, whether they develop their settlement spontaneously or forced by the administration. San Román (1994: 61–3) distinguishes three basic types of social structure around which the Gitano community organises its everyday life. First of all, the *household* (all those under one roof), usually a nuclear family, or several nuclear families that cook, wash and sleep in the same dwelling, although the importance of the nuclear family among the Gitanos is not very great. The majority of social activities and decisions are taken in the *domestic group*, which includes all those individual, nuclear or extended families that cooperate and help each other. Another social unit which characterises the Gitano community social structure is the *local community of relatives*, which may include a single family, a group of relatives or a big segment of a group of relatives composed of several extended or nuclear families united by a *race*, a concept which will be explained below. Social and everyday life among the Gitano people is also organised around the *neighbourhood grouping* which involves the total number of neighbours in a neighbourhood.

Although it is true that the Gitano community in Spain is undergoing big cultural changes from the point of view of social organisation, and whether or not the Gitano people have adopted more non-Gitano customs and life-style, nowadays the Gitanos reproduce the patterns that have been analysed above. On the one hand, in the city Gitanos tend to live in nuclear families which constitute a part of wider *domestic groups* and also live around a *local community of relatives* constituted by an extensive family which can also shelter other relatives. On the other, a slum village can lodge more than one *group of relatives*, which are not conflicting, because they may be neighbours of long-standing. Finally, there may be affluent Gitanos who own flats but who in general reproduce these same settlement patterns.

The Gitano Community's Cultural Strategies

The Gitano community's cultural strategies and social organisation are framed around their relationships with their relatives (parental relations). In fact, almost every aspect of their everyday life (work, leisure time, health, travel, death, and marriage) is constrained by these relations. According to San Román (1994: 48), these Gitano relationships are cut across by six fundamental trends: (1) a strong tendency to patrilocalism, (2) a strong ideology of men having the right of private property over the women's children and the women, (3) a consistent androcracy, (4) the primary role of men in the construction of social life, (5) the ultimate paternal authority, and (6) finally a truly traumatic male-chauvinist ideology. The way in which the Gitano parental relations, their groupings and their territorialisation are articulated cannot be understood unless the patrilineal filiation lines based upon these fundamental themes are taken into account. These themes vertebrate a network of parental relations and groupings of relatives which link families and local communities and create a structure of support.

An essential element in understanding the solidarity which is established between relatives is the concept of *race*[9] (*eraté, ratí* or *erraté*) and which is based upon the following criteria: the belonging of the children to the father, the Barons' primacy over the females, the paternal ultimate authority, the husband's dominance over his wife, the tendency to accept a rule of patrilocal residence after marriage, the men's absolute priority on the taking of decisions related to social life, and finally, the supreme value attributed to the solidarity and at the same time inequality between the father and the son. Two more elements could be added: one is the authority of the elderly over their descendants and the respect for their dead. Accordingly, the *race* can be understood as lineage, as the conceptual scheme of parental organisation through which it is possible to celebrate marriages and to realise spatial redistribution. But in the case of the Gitano community in Spain, the *race* behaves itself as a group. San Román states that *race* and marriage are the elements which support the network of local and dispersed groups of relatives (1994: 51), to which other cultural trends (the *quimeras* or disputes, for example) could be added.

Nowadays, the Gitanos continue to maintain the features that give them their own identity, such as marriage rites, family structures, the solidarity among the members of the extended family, the resolution of the *quimeras*, the primacy of the father and the man, etc.[10] while some of these are undergoing important changes. But in the past 20 years, a new tradition seems to be taking shape, partly forced by the imposition of the mainstream administration, partly because of the *payo* (non-Gitano) society itself, and also because new cultural and organisational forms have been emerging from inside the Gitano community itself. There is some sort of pacification, which originates among the Gitano youth, which is against revenge, and against the need to defend by all means members of the *race* or the group of relatives. Their participation in regularly paid work and the influence of the religious groups (Alleluias) have contributed to the trend to sedentary life, and with it to peace and quietness, all of which has weakened two of the most important constituents of the *race*, that is, defence and territorial control. Finally, the presence of some individuals in drug-trafficking networks is subverting the other structures and is therefore contributing to the bilateralisation of their everyday life.

On the whole, the last 20 years have been marked by a contradictory process: (1) there has been an integrative approach to economy and to the employment domain, (2) there has been judicial regulation of the family and the individual, and finally, (3) an incipient political presence in state structures which has been realised through the Gitano associations. All this has led to the Gitano community's increased social welfare, and at the same time to the emergence of a process of acculturation which includes more interest on education, a better situation for women, for people of all ages, a weakening of the role of the *races*, a tendency to reduce the groups of relatives, and the adoption of certain values related to economy and consumerism. Acculturation has allowed for permanence and innovation, on the one hand, and for emulation of the *payo* society and at the same time maintenance of their own identity, on the other, as San Román points out (1994: 108).

Flamenco as a Symbol of Emerging Gitano Consciousness

The origins of *flamenco* as it is known nowadays are to be found in Andalusia, where the majority of the Gitano population lived at the time of its emergence sometime between the end of the 18th and the beginning of the 19th centuries. The etymology of the term *flamenco* is not clear but it seems that the word was 'extended to mean Gypsies in general (...) before it came to designate their characteristic music' (Leblon, 1995: 51).[11]

That the Gitano created *flamenco* has been disputed many times, as reported in Giddens (1997: 8–10), and maybe the parties most responsible for this undermining of Gitano culture are the 'Andalusianists' who 'are primarily interested in distancing the art as much as possible from its marginalized Caló creators' (Giddens, 1997: 8), citing Leblon (1995)). And yet, the indigenous Andalusian non-Gypsy music was very different from the *flamenco* that was performed after a century of Gitano interpretation. Furthermore, the other Andalusian musics with a similar base evolved into completely different forms. And indeed there are many factors that contribute to the emergence of the unmistakable Indian, and thus Gitano, characteristics of *flamenco:* modulation, repeated use of a single note, shouts of encouragement. And particularly Gitano are the traditional themes used in *flamenco* that recall persecution: 'pride, revenge, freedom, love and jealousy, fatalism, and death' (Quintana & Floyd, 1972: 68).

Other uses of *flamenco* are related to the transmission of the Gitano community's cultural values and strategies mentioned above, in particular, a strong ideology of men having the right of private property over the women's children and the women themselves and the primary role of men in the construction of social life. *Flamenco* is usually described as a symbol of 'resistance culture' and this resistance is said to apply differently in the case of *flamenco* women who function 'outside of the bounds of normative female behaviour', stepping 'away from the norms of detached, constrained, silent feminine subjectivity', shouting, stamping, and staring you 'right in the face' (Giddens, 1997: 19). However, the position taken by the authors in this article is that this aggressive style is more directed outwards than directed inwards to the community. Directing themselves outwards, 'with their defiant bodies', Gitano women 'command both our respect and our attention, and they refuse to be marginalized' (Giddens, 1977: 21). Directed inwards it seems that in fact Gitano women use *flamenco* to seduce their men and provoke their sexual fantasy.

Flamenco music is one of the most important exponents of the Gitano's dynamic culture, as shown in the fact that it is very powerfully rooted in large sections of the community and at the same time is undergoing some shift towards purer forms. It is hoped that it will continue to be a symbol of emerging Gitano consciousness.

The Sociodemographic Profile of Present-day Spanish Gitanos

Spanish Gitanos are employed at a low professional and wage level. Their traditional trades have disappeared, as these were related to agriculture, trading and craftwork[12] and these occupational areas have gone into serious decline, forcing Gitanos to accept other, inferior jobs. Nowadays, a large proportion of Spanish Gitanos are employed as manual labourers and many others work as peddlers. This does not mean that one cannot find Gitanos working in a whole range of jobs, such as taxi drivers, bakers, painters, mechanics, drivers, guards, salespersons, or even as doctors, teachers, parliamentarians, artists, commercial salespersons, nurses, craftspersons, etc. However, the majority work in jobs with low professional status. Furthermore, the percentage of unemployed is very high, only offset to some extent by socially unrecognised activities such as buying and selling scrap or begging.

The low academic level of the Gitano population contributes to this exclusion, and the level of illiteracy is notably higher than that of the general population. Few Gitanos finish primary education, and even fewer secondary education or higher education. Although there are some attempts to provide adequate schooling for Gitano children, the education system is still a long way from offering them the programmes that they need. Another problem for the Gitano community is housing. This is often not of a habitable standard, and the problem is compounded by the large size of the Gitano families, compared to the non-Gitano families,[13] with an average of six members in the former.

In the last 20 years several changes have been taking place (San Román, 1994: 91–101). First of all, there has been a reduction of paid work in the Gitano community in Spain. Secondly, there has also been a decline of the trade of scrap dealing, particularly in Madrid and Barcelona, although it is maintained in areas of Spain (Galicia) where the Gitanos settled after the economic crisis of the 1970s. Thirdly, the Gitanos' activity in the artistic world has been reduced to the minimum, that is, to *tablaos flamencos* (flamenco shows) in summer. Fourthly, street services, such as selling Kleenex, or cleaning car windows, have proliferated, displacing other activities which were more frequent in the past (i.e. taking luggage or looking for a taxi outside stations). Fifthly, mendicity, basically practised by women of all ages, has increased slightly particularly with each economic slump, while children's mendicity has been eradicated completely. Sixthly, temporary work in the fields is no longer an option for Gitanos since it has been covered by poor *payos* and recently by foreign immigrants. Seventhly, selling of all sorts of products has been by far the most extended activity developed by Gitanos during these last 20 years. Clothes, flower and shoe stalls proliferate everywhere, both in urban and rural areas. Eighthly, there are also jobs related to the public administration which are open to members of the Gitano community who usually attend *Formación Profesional* (vocational training) and are then incorporated to the specialist fields of which they have become experts. And finally, the more delicate question of drugs which has affected many communities in the Western world and more recently the Gitano community, and which involves individual people, in general people with problems (widows or separated women with many children) and groups of relatives.

San Román (1994: 111–14) proposes a profile of certain types or groups of Spanish Gitanos which would account for the situation of the members of this community in the last 20 years, although she warns the reader not to consider them as watertight compartments that would negate the existence of other types.

(1) Very poor Gitanos who live in slums in relatively isolated towns and villages and who develop very marginal activities such as selling on the street, and cleaning car windows. Sporadically they get very low paid jobs and participate in the seasonal harvest. They may eventually end up as drug dealers. They maintain the organisational structures of the previous period although reducing the local kinship network. The Gitanos in this group resent the situation in previous periods, both intra and interethnically. Their acculturation is slight and their interest in schooling is very small. Among them there may be young people with a tendency to destructiveness and anomie.

(2) Drug dealers on a small scale who occupy slums in towns and villages and come from group 1; although they are less poor, they may be the most disruptive to the ethnic group. The degree of drug addiction is very high and this goes hand-in-hand with their individualisation. The attendance to school is almost nil and their cultural maintenance is very low because it runs counter to their interests. Interethnic relations are non-existent, and within the community they function at the level of the most immediate family, although they evince many symptoms of anomie.

(3) Poor Gitanos who live in slums, in squalid blocks of flats and suburb apartments with a low level of delinquency and who seldom sell drugs. They devote themselves to street vending and to scavenging on rubbish dumps. They are not prone to interethnic relations and keep their social structure, patterns and values, although they tend to slim down the local group of relatives. They are more persevering as to their children's schooling and exhibit a robust and stable identity, which is neither militant nor politically active.

(4) Gitanos who have non-salaried jobs, especially vendors or traders with a standard of living on a level with working-class people in Spain,

usually living in flats or small houses which they sometimes own. They do not get involved with crime and they seldom become drug dealers, although they sometimes become consumers of good quality drugs. They save money and are genuinely interested in their children's education. They are very pacific inter and intraethnically and very faithful to their parental and social organisation. The concept of *race* is less functional although it is kept as an organisational and cognitive principle, but the parental domain is more reduced, which allows the youth to establish interethnic relationships. Some of them sometimes 'pass' as *payos*, but intraethnically they keep their culture and identity, which is strong and non-militant.

(5) Old integrated Gitanos usually in a well-situated and normalised situation. They develop autonomous work activities such as small business and trade, and more recently as professional people. They value education at all levels, and save and invest. They show solidarity with their group of relatives, but insolidarity with other Gitanos in economically low positions. They combine Gitano cultural values and principles with fluid and friendly interethnic relations. The Gitanos in this group belong to Gitano associations and to the Alleluias religious Pentecostal movement.

(6) New fully integrated Gitanos who have realised their integration process via their appointment to posts of responsibility in the associations or the Alleluias cult. It seems that their level of drug consumption is higher than in the case of group 5. They tend to be more money savers than investors, to adopt individual cultural strategies and to be very interested in education. They feel very contradictory in terms of their role and obligations as Gitano leaders in non-Gitano organisations and their militant ethnic identity, which works more at the level of ethnic symbols, such as language, than in terms of the organisational patterns and values associated with it (parental solidarity, mobility, marriage age, number of children, etc.).

(7) Gitanos who are direct and stable drug dealers. They live in flats or houses that they own, although because of their activity as drug dealers they remain in slums in towns or villages, or visit them quite often. Their level of drug consumption is high and very often they save money to be able to abandon these illegal activities. They maintain certain aspects of their culture, but others, such as the distribution and hierarchic structure of loyalty within the group, are abandoned. They tend to individualisation and therefore, their acculturation is strong.

Sociolinguistic Patterns of Language Use and Language Contact

Throughout its history, the survival of the Gitano community's identity has become centred on the cohesion of the family group and the survival of its customs. So the language has not been crucial as in other communities in Spain. The Gitanos have gradually adopted the language of the place where they have settled.

While they were nomads, the use of their own language was more extended. Today, for example, the Gitanos of Central Europe, who continue to travel, conserve their own language better than those from Spain. When they have settled in an area, their use of their language has become more and more restricted to internal use, and as an instrument of self-defence against the non-Gitano population.

In Spain, the Gitano community uses Caló,[14] a Spanish-based Romani variety. Caló is sometimes called Gitano or Iberian Romani. In 1984, the numbers of speakers were variously reported as 65,000 and 170,000, mainly in Spain, with smaller numbers in France, Portugal, and Latin America. As to domains of language use, Caló is used by some older people and more usually as a language of self-defence. All this means that the use of Caló is not homogeneous but, while it does have a common base, it varies significantly as a function of the place of residence and even of the characteristics of the family where it is spoken. Its main common feature is the fact that it comes from the original Romani language, but that not all the vocabulary is shared by all speakers. Neither can one speak of dialects as such, because there is no linguistic base shared by all, which will allow variations of this to be called dialects.

From all this it seems clear that in order to account for the Gitanos' patterns of language use it will be important not only to refer to their use of Caló but also of the variety of Spanish they usually speak.

Caló. The language of the Spanish Gitanos

As mentioned, Gypsies in all countries have a common language, Romani, of which one can distinguish various dialects, according to the group of Gypsies to which we are referring. Romani has certain characteristic features as regards vocabulary, syntax, phonetics, etc., which have been recorded in various versions of its grammar. With time, Caló, the variety of Romani that the Gitano communities in Spain use, has fallen more and more into disuse, and so has weakened, as a result of the Gitanos' settling in different places and intermittent contact over centuries. Caló is commonly associated with burglars, thieves and wrongdoers, and although it tends to be more used by them, good proof that it is not exclusive nor an invention of wrong-doers is shown in the fact that it is a rich and harmonious language, which has been the object of study of many scholars, such as Borrow (1803–55), Merimée (1803–70), Valle-Inclán (1866–1936) and Cardinal Mezzofanti (1771–1848) (mentioned in Dávila and Pérez, 1991: 14–15)), who have contributed to its description.

Nowadays, Romani and Spanish have become mixed to such an extent that the grammatical base of Caló is Spanish. The syntax, phonetics, morphology and even part of the vocabulary is from Spanish, and Caló has evolved on this base.

Among the most notable features of Caló, we can mention the following:

(a) Its own vocabulary, which sets it apart, and which comes fundamentally from Romani, with local variations, at times even within Spain. For example, 'father' in Romani is *dad*, and in Caló may be *bato*, *batú* or *batico*, and even *dadá*. This vocabulary includes open-system words, such as nouns, adjectives, verbs, and also close-system words, such as articles, pronouns, prepositions, etc. Lexical and grammatical features of Caló have been studied most thoroughly, so there are various Spanish-Caló dictionaries and Caló grammars of different levels of completeness, such as Rebolledo (1909), Ropero (1978), Campuzano (1980), Torrione (1988), Dávila and Pérez (1991), Llorens (1991), Plantón García (1993) and Ramírez Heredia (1993). Many of these sources do not correspond to the present-day use of Caló, and nor have they been a reference point for the evolution of the Caló spoken by Spanish Gitanos, because their culture is an oral one, and many of them are not even aware of their existence. Furthermore, they might even disapprove of their having been published, because for large numbers of Gitanos writing down the language makes it more accessible to non-Gitanos. Nowadays, in spoken Caló, truly Romani words are mixed with Spanish words, as in these verses written down by Borrow (1874 (1979)), included in (1), (2) and (3):

(1)   Io me chale a mi quer
      En busca de mi romí
      La topisaré orobando
      Por medio de mi chaborí

(Yo me fui a mi casa/en busca de mi mujer/me la encontré llorando/ a causa de mi hija (Spanish translation))
(I went home/looking for my wife/I found her crying/because of my daughter)

(2)   La ramí que se abillela
      Debajo de los portales
      No se abillela con tun
      Que se abillela con mangue

(La Gitana que se acerca/debajo de los portales/no se va a ir contigo/ sino que se va a venir conmigo (Spanish translation))
(The 'Gitano' girl who's coming/under the arches/is not coming with you/She's coming with me)

(3)   No camelo ser aray
      que es caló mi nacimiento
      No caló ser aray
      con ser caló me contento.

(No quiero ser un señor/que es caló mi nacimiento/no quiero ser un señor/con ser caló me contento (Spanish translation))
(I don't want to be a gentleman, I was born Caló/I don't want to be a gentleman, I'm happy to be Caló)

In more colloquial language, one could say 'diquela chavoró, que viene el busnó' (Look, boy, the Payo is coming) or 'Chanela el caló este gachó' (This Payo understands Caló) and to express approval one could say 'sinela mistós' (That's OK).

(b)   Certain morphological rules peculiar to Caló, such as:

   – Masculine endings in 'ó', and feminine endings in 'í'. E.g. 'gachó'/gauche', 'chive/chive', or the formation of the diminutive with 'ill' or 'Ro'.
   – Verb conjugation following the Spanish rule-formation, even if the root verb is in Caló; the opposite pattern is also adopted since Caló affixes are added to Spanish verb roots (e.g. 'vin-el-ar') or the Spanish verb 'estar' becomes 'estu-bel-ar' (San Román, 1976: 67).
   – Caló endings such as 'imén' or 'ipén' are added to Spanish words; but endings such as 'uni' or 'una' tend to be added to the end of a word which is introduced into the Caló language.

As shown in the texts by Borrow (1874 (1979)), the above-mentioned features were already part of spoken Caló in the 19th century.

Nowadays, Gitanos do not use Caló as the normal language of communication in the family, except on specific occasions. Its use is restricted to those moments when one Gitano addresses another elderly Gitano or one with great social prestige, or when speaking in the presence of a non-Gitano to prevent that person from understanding.

The importance given to this last use, or the conservation of Caló as a language of self-defence, has meant that for a long time Gitanos were opposed to the teaching of Caló in schools, even if the teachers were of Gitano origin. Today, this situation is changing, and some members of the Gitano community have timidly begun to propose the recovery of Caló through its teaching in school.

In any case, among more highly educated Gitanos and those in contact with other European Gitanos, a kind of Caló has developed which has great affinity with Romani and which can be spoken as a language in itself. However, not all Gitanos take part in this experience. For many of them, as was mentioned, Caló is a lexical residue which has been maintained or which has evolved according to the territory and family, mixed with

Spanish vocabulary which has been made Gitano-like via word beginnings or endings, and the underlying grammar or syntax which is recognisably Spanish.

As mentioned above, there is an attempt to recover Caló, which can be seen in the publication of grammars such as the one by Plantón García(1993) and another by Ramírez Heredia (1993) published in the magazine *I tchatchipén*, and others included in dictionaries. There are various groups of Gitanos that are beginning to formulate proposals of this type, principally the Ad-Hocque group which, with the help of the European Commission, has been working on this for a number of years. Finally, some young Gitanos show a keen interest in learning Caló, but they are still a minority.

Language contact

Although the sociocultural reality of the Gitano community reflects their linguistic isolation and their exclusion, the interchange has been fluid. Spanish has adopted quite a lot of vocabulary from Caló, as shown in the study by Clavería (1951), and Caló has incorporated features of Spanish as shown above.

So the Gitanos, like other communities which have lived in Spain, have been part of the creation of the linguistic heritage of Spanish. Their contribution can be seen in words such as 'jamar', 'camelar', 'chaval', 'gachó', 'gachi', 'guipar', 'currar', and 'parné', which are included in the *Diccionario de la Real Academia Española* (Dictionary of the Royal Spanish Academy), with their origin in the Gitano language clearly indicated.

One of the communicative means in which Caló is used today is in the words of flamenco songs, and in the *rumbas*. For example, the words from songs collected by Ropero (1978), as illustrated in (4), (5) and (6):

(4) Gitana entre menda y tu
     Hay la mesma diferensia
     Que entr'er diablo y la crú.

(Gitano girl, between 'yours truly' and you/there's the same difference/as between the devil and the cross)

(5) Er dinero es un mareo
     Aquel que tiene parné
     Es bonito aunque feo.

(Money is a headache/Anyone who has some dough/Is good-looking even if he's ugly)

Another example would be the *rumba* by Peret about Anton the Gitano, who:

(6) 'sinelaba más lacho
    que un pedacito de manró'

(Era más bueno/que un pedacito de pan)
(He was as good as/a little loaf of bread)

Gitanos' use of Spanish has specific features that reflect their in-group activity. What is sometimes interpreted as an 'incorrect' use of the language is not that at all. It is not the result of an inability to speak the language, but rather an intentional, specific way of speaking. For example, they use verb forms such as 'truje' (I brought; Sp: traje), 'trujiste' (you brought; Sp: trajiste), 'trujo' (he/she brought; Sp: trajo) . . . , etc., that are Spanish archaisms which some of them have conserved, and which are uncommon in present-day Spanish. They will also use the verb 'haber' in the same way as 'ser', as in 'Habemos quince personas.' (We are fifteen people; Sp: Somos quince personas).

They also speak with a specific accent, with a characteristic intonation for both words and sentences, which they use especially in conversation in their own community and which they partially lose when they speak to people from outside.

Some words are used in different ways to the general population's use of the word, as in the use of the word 'primo' (cousin) to designate any Gitano or other person from one's own ethnic group. And particular groups use some expressions. For example, among the Gitanos of Andalusian origin in Barcelona, one can hear the turn of phrase 'Vamos a un poner' (let's say), as the beginning of a comparison. In any case, their language is the result of a particular historical background, and it is difficult to say what their own original contribution is and what they have assimilated from other communities in this historical journey.

Gitanos do not reject mixing the two languages, and include Caló words in their Spanish mode of speech, as was said. The use of language as an instrument of self-defence, so that another person will not understand what they are saying, is a well-established custom among Gitanos. Not only do they use Caló for this purpose, but some Gitanos of French or Portuguese origin use French or Portuguese as their own language so that other non-Gitano people present during the conversation will not understand. In some cases, they will even identify these languages as the language of the Gitanos, because apart from speaking them among themselves they are used for self-defence and thus are recognised as a distinguishing feature of their group.

Language and Education

The Spanish education system has ignored, and even disparaged, the contributions of the Gitano people. Of course, this includes their language also, and only marginally does the school system refer to this and in many cases the reference is a negative one. Furthermore, for a long time Gitanos have seen school as something foreign, of limited interest to them, which explains the low rate of attendance that some groups have had, and still have today.

Gitano attendance at school has been one of two kinds: in a normal school or class where they are a minority, and in a special school or class for Gitanos. In the first case, Gitano self-identity has tended to decrease and Spanish has become the dominant language, but in the second their use of their own language has continued, at least partially. But in both cases, the school's contribution is not recognised as their own. Even the language used in the classroom is sometimes inappropriate. For example, the everyday language spoken by many Gitanos makes use of analogies as a means of explanation, and the school tends to use more conceptual language. But even when the teachers try to use analogies in their teaching, they lack the means to do so because they need to know the terms used for comparison in the Gitanos' own environment.

Progress in education is perceived by the Gitano community as a loss of cultural identity. Given that Gitanos did not usually attend school because they were nomads and socially excluded, school is a recent phenomenon in their community, and many do not see any great usefulness to it. There is also reticence on their part because little consideration is normally given to minorities by the schooling system.

The high dropout rate among Gitanos may also partly be a result of the distance between the language used in school and in the community. At home, Gitanos have their own language that differs from that of the school in its meanings and, in some cases, structures. The Gitano child who begins school, or the young or adult Gitano, who enters the education system at a later age, will do so in a world whose meanings are strange to him/her.

Finally, as indicated above, some Gitanos are suspicious of the education system, but when they are offered the chance of learning a curriculum that is meaningful to them, they do not hesitate to attend school. Then their criteria for studying are normally: (1) an effort to concentrate on the subject and to obtain quick results, even if their overall comprehension may not be great, and (2) asking both their classmates and the teacher for help, to reap the greatest benefits from the classes.

Future Prospects

At present the Gitano community in Spain is undergoing a series of changes, which shows its dynamism. Some are exocentric, from Spain's mainstream culture, and have changed the Gitanos' cultural cosmos; others are endocentric, from their own dynamic process (Anta Félez, 1994: 127). These changes confirm the Gitano community's vitality that seems to ensure its development as a community, not exempt of difficulties and problems. San Román (1994: 108–9) mentions three problems that could endanger the Gitano community's cultural survival and identity. One has to do with the difficulty of finding jobs, integrated or even marginal, a situation that is more serious nowadays due to the Gitanos' rivalry with poor *payos* and foreign migrants. The second has to do with the administrative obstinacy in concentrating in the same areas Gitanos who belong to different groups of relatives. And the third problem would be drug addiction and dealing which according to San Román (1994: 109) represents the most powerful vehicle of *assimilating* the Gitanos to mainstream society.

Notwithstanding, there is evidence to suggest that the Gitanos' cultural tradition is still very powerfully rooted in large sections of the community and accordingly the Gitano community in Spain can be seen to have a very promising future, in the direction of welfare and peaceful interethnic relations, if and only if this tradition is respected and Gitano community activity and thought is taken into account. That the Gitano community has tried to take into account the Spanish mainstream society's activity and thought is reflected in the number of variations and adaptations at the historical, linguistic and space-bound levels that they have developed while they were being expelled, oppressed and marginalised. Others have described these adaptations as 'resistance culture' in face of the Spanish society's attempts to refuse their people and the pressure to annihilate and assimilate them, their culture and their social organisation. And still others redefine this culture of resistance as organisational, practical and ideological strategies that reproduce themselves to adapt to the different offers and prohibitions, which come from the mainstream society. But all this shows that the Gitano people have tried. Maybe it is time for the Spanish society to try to respect the Gitano community's alternative culture and life-style which are enriching, and hopefully will enrich, Spain's multiethnic and multilingual make-up.

Notes

1. This is the term used in this article to refer to the community as a whole even if, as Hancock (1998) points out in his paper, The Indian Origin and Westward Migration of the Romani People: 'it isn't one that is liked very much by a population whose own name for itself is Roma (singular Rom)'. According to this same author, 'this is a legacy from the English language which, since the sixteenth century, has used the word to refer to a population most often defined by its perceived behaviour rather than by its racial and cultural origins. The confusion in the minds of the Europeans about the 'gypsy' people is evident in the source of that very word, which is a shortening of *Egyptian*' (1998: 1). The Gypsies are often also called Rroma, Tsiganes, Bohemes and Gitanos, which is the term used in this article to refer to this community in Spain.

2. One hypothesis that is suggested by Hancock (1998: 20–1) is that as the Gypsy communities 'became more and more remote from their homeland, moving along the eastern periphery of the Islamic expansion, we may assume that the awareness of their shared origin in India overcame whatever newly-acquired jati or caste distinctions had divided them socially; and in time, the population became one, losing its mixed, occupational identity to acquire its emerging ethnic one. This also provides an acceptable account for

the typology of the Romani language, which demonstrates Central Indian, North-western Indian, and to a far lesser extent Dardic linguistic characteristics.'

3. Other sources (Hancock, 1998: 2) establish their arrival in Europe 'from the East at the end of the 13th century' and that is how they acquired the misnomer 'Egyptians'.

4. These Romani varieties include: **Balkan Romani**, extended in Yugoslavia, Bulgaria, Greece, Turkey, France, West Germany, Italy, Rumania, Hungary, and Iran and with 1,000,000 speakers reported in 1980; **Baltic Romani**, with 24,000 speakers reported in the Baltic region of the USRR and also in Poland; **Carpathian Romani**, with over 235,000 speakers reported (220,000 in Czechoslovakia, 12,000 in the USA, 3000 in Hungary and some in the USRR, Poland and Rumania); **Kalo Finnish Romani**, with 5000 to 8000 speakers reported in 1980 (4000 to 6000 in Finland and 1000 to 2000 in Sweden); **Sinte Romani**, with 200,000 speakers reported in 1980 (41,000 in Yugoslavia, 30,000 or more in Germany, 14,000 in Italy, 10,000 to 30,000 in France, and other countries); **Vlach Romani**, with 1,500,000 speakers reported in 1986 (in Rumania, it is the first language for 200,000 to 250,000 people and the second language for 250,000 to 300,000 people; it is also extended in Latin America (100,000 to 210,000 speakers and the US (650,000 speakers), and finally **Welsh Romani,** not to be confused with English-related Anglo-Romani, spoken in England and Wales (*International Encyclopaedia of Linguistics,* 1:244). **Anglo Romani**, also known as English Romani includes, 115,000 to 135,000 speakers reported in 1986, spread throughout the UK, the US, Australia and South Africa (*International Encyclopaedia of Linguistics,* 2: 74).

5. Teresa San Román uses several sources to document the Gitanos in Spain: Vaux de Foletier (1974) and Sampson (1926 and 1933) for the accounts before the 15th century, and Sánchez Ortega (1977 and 1986), López de Meneses (1967, 1968 and 1970), Leblon (1985), Gómez Alfaro (1980) and San Román (1976) to trace down this community from their first arrival in Spain until the 18th century.

6. The term adopted in this article to refer to this community in Spain will be Gitano, which is how these people are called in this country, although they are also known as Calé. According to Hancock (1998: 2), 'the reason that Roma are called Egyptians' not only in English but also in Greek, Albanian, Macedonian, French, Basque and Spanish (Gitanos) 'is because their arrival in Europe came on the crest of the Islamic wave which heralded the occupation of the Byzantine Empire and south-eastern Europe by the Ottoman Turks.' Special thanks are due to Yaron Matras (U. of Manchester) for suggesting our using the term Gitano in this English text.

7. The term used by Spanish Gitanos to refer to non-Gitano people is *payo.*

8. Some NGO would increase this figure up to 250,000.

9. And here *race* doesn't mean race in the racial sense.

10. For an in-depth study of the sociocultural characteristics of the Gitano community in Spain, see San Roman (1976 and 1994).

11. As Giddens (1997: 8) points out, 'these days the term functions as a noun to denote Calé and *payo* flamenco performers (and sometimes *aficionados)'.*

12. Juan de Dios Ramírez Heredia (1983) describes some of these jobs and talks about the changes they have undergone.

13. This has probably decreased since the CIS (1978) study mentioned above.

14. Following Hancock (1998: 23), the 'native ethnonym **Kalo** ('black')' is 'a self-designation among Romani populations in Spain, Wales and Finland'. In the case of the Gitanos in Spain, it is a term used to designate their own language, that is, Caló.

References

AAAV (1987) *Aprendamos Caló. Sinelamos Caló.* Zaragoza: Germinal SAL.

Acton, T. and Kenrick, D. (1984) *Romani Rokkeripen Todivvus.* London: Romanestan Publications.

Anta Félez, J.L. (1994) *Donde la Pobreza es Marginación. Un Análisis entre Gitanos.* Barcelona: Editorial Humanidades.

Borrow, G. (1874) *Romano Lavo-Lil, Word-book of the Romany, or, English Gypsy Language.* London: Sutton.

Borrow, G. (1979) *Los Gitanos en España.* Madrid: Ediciones Turner.

Borrow, G. (1983) *La Biblia en España.* Madrid: Alianza.

Campuzano, R. (1980) *Origen, Usos y Costumbres de los Gitanos y Diccionario de su Dialecto.* Madrid: Heliodoro Bibliofilia y Arte.

Cervantes, M. (1985) *La Gitanilla.* Novelas ejemplares. Madrid: Ed. Cátedra.

Clavería, C. (1951) *Estudios sobre los Gitanismos del Español.* Madrid: Anejo de la RFE, LIII, CSIC.

Dávila, B. and Pérez, B. (1991) *Apuntes del Dialecto 'Caló' o Gitano Puro.* Servicio de Publicaciones de la Universidad de Cádiz.

Giddens, A. A. (1997) *Rrom and Flamenco.* Unpublished manuscript. The University of Texas.

Gómez Alfaro, A. (1980) Los gitanos en la sociedad española, *Documentación Social,* 41.

Hancock, I. (1998) The Indian Origin and Westward Migration of the Romani people. *IRU,* Manchaca, Texas.

International Encyclopaedia of Linguistics (1992) New York and Oxford: Oxford University Press.

Leblon, B. (1985) *Los Gitanos de España. El Precio y el Valor de la Diferencia.* Barcelona: Gedisa.

Leblon, B. (1995) *Gypsies and Flamenco.* University of Hertfordshire Press.

Liégeois, J.P. (1988) *Los Gitanos.* México, D.F.: Fondo de Cultura Económica.

López de Meneses, A. (1967, 1968 and 1970) *Pomezia,* 2, 3 and 5.

López de Meneses, A. (1968) La inmigración gitana en España durante el siglo XV. In A. Martínez Ferrando (ed.), *Miscelánea de Estudios.*

Llorens, M.J. (1991) *Diccionario Gitano. Sus Costumbres.* Madrid: A.L. Mateos.

Marzo, A. (1991) Los gitanos. *Cuatro semanas,* 4.

Plantón García, J.A. (1993) *Aproximación al Caló. Chipí Cayí.* Málaga: Junta de Andalucía.

Prat, J. (1978) *Los Gitanos.* Barcelona: Dopesa.

Quintana, B. and Floyd, L. (1972) *Que Gitano!* Holt, Rinehart and Winston, Inc.

Ramírez Heredia, J.D. (1983) *Nosotros los Gitanos.* Barcelona: Ediciones 29.

Ramírez Heredia, J.D. (1985) *En Defensa de los Míos.* Barcelona: Ediciones 29.

Ramírez Heredia, J.D. (1993) A propósito de nuestra lengua. *I tchatchipen,* 2, 38–64.

Rebolledo, T. (1909) *Diccionario Gitano-Español y Español-Gitano.* Cádiz: Jiménez Mena, Artes Gráficas, editorial.

Ropero, M. (1978) *El Léxico del Caló en el Lenguaje del Cante Flamenco.* Sevilla: Secretariado de Publicaciones de la Universidad de Sevilla.

Sampson, J. (1926) *The Dialect of the Gypsies of Wales.* Oxford: Oxford University Press.

Sampson, J. (1933) *The Win of the Heath.* Gregynog Press.

San Román, T. (1976) *Vecinos Gitanos.* Madrid: Akal editor.

San Román, T. (1986) *Entre la Marginación y el Racismo.* Madrid: Alianza Editorial.

San Román, T. (1994) *La Diferència Inquietant. Velles i Noves Estratègies Culturals dels Gitanos.* Fundació Serveis de Cultura Popular. Barcelona: Editorial Alta Fulla.

Sánchez Ortega, M.H. (1977) *Los Gitanos Españoles.* Castellote.

Sánchez Ortega, M.H. (1986) Cultura e Historia de los gitanos. In T. San Román (ed.) *Entre la Marginación y el Racismo.* Madrid: Alianza Universidad.

Torrione, M. (1988) *Del Dialecto Caló y sus Usuarios: la Minoría Gitana en España.* Perpignan: Faculté de Sciences Humaines et Sociales.

Vaux de Fotelier, F. (1974) *Mil Años de Historia de los Gitanos.* Barcelona: Plaza y Janés.

Chapter 9
The Jewish Communities

BÁRBARA VIGIL

Historical and Linguistic Background

To define Judaism as a religion would not be to use this term correctly. Judaism is a humanistic term whereas the Jewish teachings (the religious dogmas) emphasise the revelation and the divinity expressed in the *Torah* (the Bible). Judaism unites the creative and dynamic elements seen in the various civilisations and cultures of which the Jews have formed a part. Thus, the Jewish community of the *Sepharad*, from before their expulsion by Ferdinand of Aragon and Isabel of Castile in 1492, has little to do with the Jewish community in Spain today. The Sephardi community does not correspond exactly to the Spanish community, and the Jewish community of the Diaspora is not the same as the Israeli Jewish community.

Sociolinguistically, the Jewish community has certain special features that differentiate it from any other linguistic group. These features are not like those of any other community, distinguished by its language and culture, but rather, a certain vocabulary, which allows us to access the Jewish world: a universal vocabulary, which serves to identify any Jew in this world, without distinguishing his/her origin. If one had to analyse the Jewish community in the context of a sociolinguistic study, something which has already been carried out in a very complete way by Berthelot (1994), one would have to talk not of a linguistic community but rather of a religious, cultural and social community, with certain features in common.

It would be wrong to call Hebrew the Jewish community's common language. It is the religious language which is common to all religious Jews, to all those who have received some kind of religious education, whether in or out of the home. In this case, it is like Latin in the era when this was the language of religious devotion for Catholics. That is, many Jews who recognise the Hebrew alphabet and pray in Hebrew do not necessarily know how to speak it.

If we looked through the *Sidur*, or prayer book, of a Jew who belonged to the Barcelona community, or to that of Madrid, or Buenos Aires, all of whom speak Spanish, we would find that each prayer is printed in Hebrew. Next to, or below, each line, is the phonetic transcription, so that it is not necessary to read Hebrew, since the words are memorised without reading them, that is, the sounds, the music of the words of the prayer, are memorised. Finally, next to, or below, each line, is the translation into Spanish. If it were a French-speaking community, the translation would be into French, etc. Given that there are Jews in such a large number of linguistic communities, it is Jewish religious works that are the most highly translated, because of the needs of so many communities, however small they may be.

Nowadays, Hebrew, as the normalised language that is spoken by some six million Hebrew-speakers, is the official language of the State of Israel. In some Spanish grammars of Hebrew, or in some histories of Hebrew, the word *ivrit* is used to distinguish between Modern Hebrew, the Hebrew in the Bible, and rabbinical Hebrew. As Hebrew is the language of the State of Israel, it has become the second language of many Jews who have migrated to Israel, but also of other non-Jewish communities that live in Israel. With the establishment of the Jewish homeland, the *Eretz Israel*, something strange has happened to Hebrew. After being the identifying language of the Jews, it became the language of the state, so that not only Jews have to speak it but also non-Jewish inhabitants, whether they be Muslims, Christians, Druse, Bedouin, etc. In fact, it would not be wrong to speak of two Hebrew-speaking communities: one which refers to those Jews who use Hebrew only as their language of worship, who are part of the Diaspora, that is, Jews outside the State of Israel, and a second community made up of Israelis, the *sabras*, or those born in Israel.

Other languages related to Judaism, and which could also be classified as languages of the Diaspora, are Yiddish and *Judeo-español*, commonly known as Ladino.[1] Both languages have a highly developed literary tradition, especially Yiddish, with its mixture of German and Hebrew vocabularies, and many of whose words have been incorporated into Modern Hebrew.

As regards Sephardi, here are the words on this question from a letter of Joseph D. Alhadeff written in Ancient Sephardi Spanish (16th century):

> *Para mi, la respuesta a Ken es Sefaradi? es muy simple y klara. Los ke son desendientes de los djudios ke bivieron en Espanya o en Portugal antes de las ekspulsiones del siglo XV, y ke estan apegados a la kultura y las tradisiones ke por mas de 500 anyos fueron transmetidas de padre a ijo y de madre a ija, eyos y solo eyos pueden ser yamados sefaradis. Seguramente la lengua es uno de los elementos de baza en la definision de ken es sefaradi, ma el fakto ke uno de los desendientes de los ekspulsados avla mas o menos el djudeo-espanyol no troka muncho. Si lo avla tanto mejor, es entonses un sefaradi kumplido.*

(For me, the answer to the question 'Who is Sephardi?' is very simple and clear. Those who are descendants of the Jews who lived in Spain or Portugal before the expulsions of the 15th century, and who are devoted to the culture and the traditions which, for more than 500 years, have been handed down from father to son and from mother to daughter, these and only these can be called Sephardim. It is true that language is one of the elements in favour in the definition of who is Sephardi, but the fact that one of the descendants of those who were expelled speaks more or less Jewish-Spanish does not change things very much. If he/she speaks Sephardi, so much the better, for he/she is then a Sephardi who does as he/she should.)

Historical Background and Distribution of the Jewish Community in Spain

The presence of Jewish communities in Spain can be characterised as long and prosperous. It seems that the origins of Spanish Judaism can be traced back to the Roman period, probably to the Phoenician times. Their organic growth started during the first century of our era and they settled along the Mediterranean coast (Beinart, 1988). The first Jewish people who settled in Spanish territory came directly from the Holy Land or through Rome. Their presence can be documented as a problematic reality already in the 4th century, as a perturbing factor for the Christians and the Roman Church. But the real difficulties began during the Visigothic period, around the 7th century when the Kingdom converted to Catholicism and the Jews were obliged to convert as well or leave the country. As in 1492, many migrated and on this occasion settled in the North of Africa.

With the invasion of Spain by the Arabs, there began a prosperous and peaceful period during which their customs and religious practices were respected and the Jewish culture in Spain developed enormously. When the Caliphate period ended because of the civil wars of the Arabs, rich and prosperous Jewish people continued to live in the Taifas Kingdoms, but it is during this time that the first prosecution and killing of Jewish people took place, and this brought with it the Jewish communities' exodus towards the Christian Kingdoms. In these territories, their kings facilitated the Jewish settlements but from the 13th century onwards hostility increased and this led to terrible killings by the end of the 14th century. This in turn caused a new exodus towards the North of Africa and other Mediterranean lands (Bel *et al.*, 1992: 15–16). In what would be the territory of the Principality of Catalonia, this period brought the end of a very enriching period for the Jewish communities of Barcelona, Girona, Besalú, Manresa, Montblanc, Tàrrega, Tarragona and others, where interchange and living together with the Christians had been possible (Berthelot & Puig, 1992: 27). As a result of this persecution in the Kingdoms of Castile and Aragón of the time, there began a period of decadence of the *aljamas* (assemblies of Jews) in the cities, leading to the appearance of small *juderías* (jewries) in rural areas so that Spanish Judaism becomes rural, although the Jews of that time continued to devote themselves to the commercial and business activities that have always characterised them.

The 1492 edict brought about the *Diaspora* of the *Sepharad*.[2] There are no reliable data as to the distribution of the Jewish communities in Spain before Expulsion or as to the number of those who were expelled, but there is an approximate estimate of the number of *aljamas* (216) that there were at the time of the Expulsion. Their destinations were varied: the majority of Jews from Castile went to Portugal; those from Andalusia chose the North of Africa and those who left from the harbours of the North and East of the Peninsula settled in the rest of Europe and in the Ottoman Empire.[3] From the 15th to the 17th century Sephardi communities settled all the provinces of the Ottoman Empire (Constantinopla, Esmirnia, Adrianopolis, Salonica and Safed). The most important Sephardi communities in Italy were Sicily, Sardinia and Naples (part of the Kingdom of Aragón), Ferrara, Venice and Liorna. And finally, as a result of the expansion of the Jewish communities beyond the Pyrenées and the Alps, it developed a western area of Hispano-Portuguese Judaism that embraced Bordeaux, Toulouse, Lyon, Nantes, Rouen, Ambers, Amsterdam, London, Hamburg, Copenhagen and Vienna.

In Spain, the Jewish population is fairly heterogeneous, due to their having come to Spain in different historical periods, when their own Jewish community was obliged to emigrate from their own country. They came from Germany and France in the second half of the 19th century, from Russia between 1881 and 1892, from Morocco and Algeria between 1860 and 1865, and later at the beginning of the 20th century. Today, little remains of this first small period of immigration. In this century, Jews arrived from Turkey and Greece between 1914 and 1930, from Germany and Poland between 1931 and 1936, and from Eastern and Central Europe (Austria, Hungary, Rumania and Bulgaria) between 1939 and 1945. This much more important second wave of immigration established Jewish communities once more in the Iberian Peninsula. Finally, there was considerable immigration from Egypt and the Middle East at the end of the 1940s, from the ex-Spanish Protectorate of Morocco from 1955 to 1975, from Argentina and Chile between 1975 and 1980, and from Israel in the 1980s.[4]

More specifically, the political events which took place in the North of Africa during the 1950s and the early 1960s made many Moroccan Jews leave their country and settle in Spain. Spain's economic growth between 1950 and 1970 attracted many other Jews to the extent that in 1969 the Jewish community in Spain amounted to 9000 people and the expansion continued until 1975. In South America, the deterioration of the political situation in countries such as Chile, Uruguay, and particularly Argentina accelerated the immigration of Jewish people to Spain, especially after Franco's death. In 1978, the total population of the Jewish community seemed to be located around 12,000 people.

The fact that different migratory movements have occurred does not mean that one can really speak of waves of immigration, since these have taken place when particular political or socioeconomic events have taken place in the country of origin: the pogroms (systematic attacks on Jewish communities) of 1881 and 1885 in Russia, the break-up of the Ottoman Empire and the rise of Turkish nationalism, the spread of Fascism and anti-Semitism before and during the Second World War, the independence of the countries of the Maghreb region, the rise of Arab nationalism and the Arab-Israeli conflict, and finally, the military dictatorships and the persecution of intellectuals in Argentina and Chile.

At present, the Jewish community in Spain is composed of some 12,000 people,[5] distributed among 12 communities, the most important of which are Madrid, with almost 4000 members, and Barcelona, with about 3500. Another of the largest and most significant Jewish communities in Spain is that of Melilla, whose special features are discussed below, since it has some linguistic aspects of its own. The community of Ceuta is similar in this respect. The other members of the Jewish communities live in different cities of varying size in Spain, attracted especially for tourist or real estate reasons, as is the case of Palma de Mallorca or Marbella, or in other places such as Málaga, Alicante, Valencia, Seville, Santa Cruz de Tenerife and Las Palmas de Gran Canaria.

It is not easy to determine the number of members in each community. The figures for those registered in the synagogues include only those who participate actively in the religious, cultural or social activities of the community, and exclude those who do not feel the need to be part of the Jewish community or who are not religious. Among the Israelis registered in the Israeli Embassy or Consulate, there are people who belong to other religious communities, and who could be Muslims, Christian Arabs or non-Arabs with Israeli nationality.

Social Organisation

As in most countries, the Jewish community in Spain has a high degree of internal organisation. This organisation is reflected in the great number of Jewish institutions and associations that there exist at the educational, cultural and political levels.

Jewish institutions in Spain

In education, it is important to speak of the different schools that exist in various Spanish regional capitals. The *Escuela Sefardita* in Barcelona began 25 years ago, and is located in the upper part of Barcelona, where over half the private schools in Barcelona are to be found. This school began teaching in 1972, and in 1980 had grown enough to need to rent a large building of three floors with $400\,m^2$ floor space for classrooms and other rooms, and a playground of $600\,m^2$. This school is a model of teaching and linguistic tolerance. Catalan, Spanish and Hebrew are the main languages, and English and French are also taught. Although the majority are local, the children are of various nationalities, including those from Israel and from the USA. What the parents wish is to give their children a good education and to pass on the Jewish traditions, knowledge of Hebrew, of the festivals, etc. The school year respects the Jewish and local festivals, such as *Rosh HaShana, Hanukah, Purim, Pésaj,* etc.

The Sephardi school in Madrid was first called *Ibn Gabirol,* then became the *Estrella Toledano.* There is also a Jewish school in Ceuta and one in Melilla, and in Melilla there is also a recently created educational centre. At least once a year, young people from the different communities in Spain meet together. The Youth Department of the Jewish Community of Barcelona is well organised and, under the supervision of the *madrijim* (religious guides), holds different activities for the various age groups.

With the coming of democracy to Spain, the Jewish community saw the need to expand their properties. In Barcelona and Madrid, they achieved large plots of land for their cemeteries; in Barcelona, they received from the City Council a section of the Collserola Cemetery with room for 2000 graves. The areas for *rejitzá* (ritual bath) and for prayer are outside the Jewish section, and have been functioning since the 1960s. There are also graveyards in the cemeteries of San Andrés and Les Corts, two Barcelona neighbourhoods. In Madrid, at the time of writing, the *Jebrá Kadishá* (Community of the Dead), headed by its president Don Fortunato Cho-crón, is purchasing a plot of land next to the Catholic cemetery in the town of Hoyos de Manzanares, 40 km from the capital. This project is architect-designed and will have about 1000 grave sites.

In 1984, the Israelite Community in Madrid renovated the Massada sports complex, also in Hoyo de Manzanares, as a sports and social centre. In the future, it will also include a home for the elderly, and the whole of this is located in the mountains near Madrid. In Barcelona, the sports complex is located in Valldoreix, a village in the Barcelona province.

When religious freedom became law in Spain, many Jews from Morocco and the Anglo-Saxon countries settled in Mediterranean coastal towns, especially on the Costa del Sol, in the city of Málaga. There has been a synagogue since around 1975, which houses a small research centre and a *Mitwéh.* In Torremolinos there is also a small synagogue, and in Marbella there is perhaps the best in Spain, in a two-storey building of its own, built 20 years ago with columns in Mozarabic style. There is also a cemetery 14 km from Málaga, with a synagogue, *rejitzá* (ritual bath) and *gueniźá* (wardrobe where deteriorated sacred documents are kept). In the Valencian Autonomous Community, there are synagogues in Valencia, Alicante and Benidorm.

In the Balearic Islands, the Jewish community is made up of retired people from Anglo-Saxon countries. In Palma, there is a small community centre that consists of a *Mikwwé* synagogue (where the ritual bath takes place) and a library. This small community holds services according to the *Ashkenazí* rite, and there is a small cemetery in Santa Eugenia. There are also very small

Jewish communities in the Canary Islands, and in Las Palmas there is a synagogue with room for 80 people. In Seville, there is a synagogue of 60 m², located in the centre of the city, and there is also a cemetery.

The great importance of the Jewish properties in Ceuta and Melilla, two cities in Africa belonging to Spain, with strong North African cultural influence, reflects the Jewish communities which have settled there, an example of tolerance and civil and religious enrichment. In Melilla, the *Yamin Benarroch* synagogue stands out. Known as *Or Zarúaj* and dating from 1925, it is in Modernist style with Mozarabic motifs, with one large rectangular room with the *hejal* (place where the Torah is kept). There are also four small synagogues, a state-subsidised Jewish school, and two cemeteries, one from last century and one from this century (Salafranca, 1995). Ceuta is another place where the Jewish community is important, with a large synagogue in the centre of the city, built at the end of the 1960s, and a cemetery.

In the 1990s, two new synagogues were created in Madrid, since for the devout it is important to have a place of worship near where they live. Also, in 1991, *El Jardín de las Tres Culturas* (The Garden of the Three Cultures) was created inspired by the gardens of the Bible and whose name refers to the *Song of Songs*. In Barcelona, a reformist synagogue was created, and the *Asociación Macabbi* commemorated the victims of the Holocaust with a monument in the Fossar de la Pedrera in Montjuic. This monument, commemorating the fiftieth anniversary of the end of the war in 1945, shows the Holocaust as it was, evoking the horror of the Nazi concentration camps.

There are also some small supermarkets, one in Barcelona opposite the synagogue, where *kosher* foods are sold, that is, foods which are approved by the rabbi, and which are appropriate for consumption according to the Jewish laws. There have been several attempts to open a *kosher* restaurant in Barcelona, but the difficulty involved, and the high cost of obtaining all the ingredients approved by the rabbi, have meant that it has not been possible.

Jewish associations and organisations in Spain

There exist a number of associations and organisations that give support to the different Jewish communities established in Spain. Worth mentioning is the existence since 1965 of the *Federación de Comunidades Judías* (Federation of Jewish Communities) which constitutes a confederated authority whose basic aim is to promote cooperation between these communities and to represent the Spanish Jewish people at the institutional level. This organisation, nowadays named the *Federación Sefardí de España* (Spanish Sephardi Federation), represented the Spanish Jewish people in the World Jewish Conference and the World Sephardi Federation (Bel *et al.*, 1992: 288).

Other Jewish associations and organisations include the following:

Macabbi. This is the international sporting organisation of the Jews. *Macabbi Barcelona* represents Spain in the Macabbi championships that are held in Israel. In Barcelona, it also plays a role in the organisation of cultural activities, especially theatre, and in public meetings to denounce anti-Semitism.

Keren Hayesod. Since the beginning of its activity 70 years ago, *Keren Hayesod*, together with the *Agencia Judía*, has organised activities in support of the Jewish people. In fact, both organisations carry out activities where there are Jewish communities to support the unity of the Jewish people, both at an international and individual level.

Keren Kayemet Leisrael. Helps with reforestation and cares for the Jewish heritage.

WIZO (*Women's International Zionist Organisation*). This is the international organisation of Zionist women, and in Spain it has its representatives in the various communities. Its task is to promote the activities carried out by the ladies of the Jewish communities.

B'nai Brith. An international organisation whose aims are cultural, social and philanthropic, in the service of Judaism and humanity. Its slogan is charity, fraternal love and harmony.

A good example of some of the other religious organisations is that of Melilla. The generosity of the Melilla Jews has allowed the creation of the following organisations:

Hozer Dalim. At the beginning of October, 1918, a group of young, single Jews founded *La Asociación Benéfica de Jóvenes Israelitas Hozer Dalim* (The 'Help the Needy' Charity Association for Youth). The objectives of this association are: medical aid to the poor, first aid, free hospital care, treatment and medical assistance for the needy, distribution of money and food help in non-Jewish disasters. And to collect funds, various activities are organised.

Jebrá Guemilut Jasadim. According to the Jewish mourning laws, when a person dies, his/her body must be wrapped in a shroud and watched over by someone of the same sex who is familiar with the Jewish laws and customs, and above all who is not a close or blood relative. The *Jebrá* has always existed for this reason. In Barcelona it is called *Jebrá Kadishá*.

Other non-Jewish bodies which have been founded in the last 15 years, and which have been active in the transition towards democracy in Spain and the freedom of organisation, as well as encouraging friendship with and knowledge of Israel and Judaism, are the following:

The *Associació de Relacions Culturals Catalunya-Israel* (Catalonia-Israel Association for Cultural Relations), founded in 1975, and called at that time the *Associació España-Israel* (Israel-Spain Association), was a pioneer in the field of relations between Spain and the State of Israel, and cultural interchange. Normal diplomatic relations between Spain and Israel were only established later, barely 10 years ago. This organisation, whose members are Jews and non-Jews, is one of the most well known for its work in the area of promoting the knowledge and acceptance of Israel. It encourages the exchange of experiences via exhibitions, conferences, travel and voluntary work on kibbutzim. Many of the students who travel to Israel first attend classes of Modern Hebrew that the Association offers regularly. All over Spain, similar organisations have been founded, friendship societies such as those in Cantabria, Valencia, León, Murcia, etc. They all promote interchange between their members and the people of Israel.

On the other hand, there are the organisations for increasing relations between the Jewish and Christian worlds. In Barcelona, the *Entesa Judeo-Cristiana* (Jewish-Christian Friends Association) has existed for some time. These organisations were initially promoted by the religious order *The Sisters of Zion*. Today, they are dedicated to the exchange of ideas, through conferences for their members. Other such organisations exist in Valencia and Madrid.

At a more scientific level, there are more intellectual organisations, such as the *Institut d'Estudis Hebraics* (Institute of Hebrew Studies), part of the *Institut d'Estudis Catalans* (Institute of Catalan Studies), whose objective is to spread and promote the study of Hebrew science, literature and language. In Girona, there is the *Institut d'Estudis Nahmànides* in the *Centre Bonastruch Ça Porta*, where they teach Hebrew, hold conferences, etc. In Toledo, there is the *Amigos del Museo Sefardí* organisation (Friends of the Sephardi Museum), which for several years now has organised an internationally known annual seminar on the subject of Sephardi culture. In Madrid, the *Asociación de Estudios Hebreos y Judíos* (Institute of Hebrew and Jewish Studies) was founded recently.

Finally, in 1991 the *Baruch Spinoza Foundation* put forward a very ambitious programme of oral history of the Jewish communities in Spain. It was initiated in Barcelona, jointly with the Barcelona Israeli Community, and is now being developed with the Jewish communities of Madrid, Seville, Ceuta and Melilla. On the one hand, this programme's main objective is to reconstruct and study the history of the Jewish people in the 12 Jewish communities in Spain, particularly during the 20th century, through the testimony of living witnesses from the existing generations and the records kept from other generations. On the other hand, a secondary objective is to find out the motivation behind the Jewish people's return and renewed settlement in Spain as a community.

Institutional Support

In spite of the fact that the establishment of diplomatic relations between Israel and Spain did not take place until 1986, the Jewish community in Spain enjoyed some privileges, particularly at the cultural level, even during Franco's times. In 1964, a Sephardi Museum was created in Toledo, in the same synagogue built by Samuel Halevi around 1357, and a library was founded. The act which institutionalised this creation involved an implicit recognition of the Jewish communities in Spain and an official link between the Spanish Government and the Jews outside Spain. After Franco's death, it was hoped that the establishment of diplomatic relations would be a reality but it soon became evident that such a resolution would have been premature. However, the association *Amistad Judeo-Cristiana* (Jewish-Spanish Friendship), which had been created in 1961, was revitalised and the *Centro de Estudios Judeo-Cristiano* (Centre for Jewish-Spanish Studies) was created (Bel, 1992: 288–89).

The Spanish Constitution (1978) establishes the configuration of Spain as a democratic and plural(istic) state. Of the state's many obligations, one of the most important is to respect all religious beliefs and, therefore, to foster cooperative relations with the different confessions or religious communities. The *Ley Orgánica de Libertad Religiosa* (LOLR) envisages the possibility of signing cooperation agreements with these religious communities in Spain. In 1990, an agreement was signed between the Spanish State and the Evangelic and the Jewish Federations, which involved very important issues for the Jewish Spanish citizens: the religious and personal situation of the rabbis, Social Security, military obligations, judicial issues, marriage according to the Jewish rite, Jewish religious teaching in school, tax relief, Jewish religious festivities, regulation of Jewish food, and the participation of the Federation of Israeli Communities in the maintenance of Jewish historical, artistic and cultural patrimony (Bel *et al.*, 1992: 290–1).

Language Use

The language use practices adopted by the Jewish community presents certain features peculiar to this community. Several studies have been made of the different groupings; the most popular of which are the *Ashkenazim* and the *Sephardim* from Morocco, different from each other in their specific varieties of language, their expressions, customs and language use.

Language use among the Ashkenazim: the use of Yiddish

The *Ashkenazim* are those members of the Jewish community who settled in Germany and Central Europe in the Middle Ages, and then later in Russia. In Germany and Poland, there was major intellectual development, despite the impediments placed upon them. Their culture and traditions developed around the Yiddish language.

After the pogroms (systematic attacks on Jewish communities) of 1881, the Jewish community resettled in the following way: part went to England, particularly London and Leeds, part went to the USA, and an important part went to Argentina, one of the communities which most preserves the study and use of Yiddish, not for its religious value, but for its intellectual and literary value. Another small part settled in Spain, responding to an invitation by King Alfonso XII, partly fleeing from the economic depression in which some of them found themselves in Poland. After the terrible disaster of the Shoa,[6] the European Yiddish-speaking community had practically disappeared. However, those Jews who were able to escape the genocide or who had emigrated beforehand, and who managed to conserve the language of their community, have kept this language alive until the present day.

Also, some of the families which settled in Spain at the beginning of this century from Poland, and brought Yiddish with them, can bear witness to the fact that at home, when the parents did not want their children to understand what they were talking about, they spoke in Yiddish. And these children, who are now parents themselves, remember expressions that they would not use with their own children. That the children did not speak Yiddish was simply due to a desire to leave behind the image of the Jewish-Polish society of the *shtetel*, of which Yiddish was the perfect symbol, that is, a society in which poverty was ever present. Nonetheless, assimilation was seen from within Judaism as a danger for the Jewish community (mixed marriages, non-celebration of the days of obligation, loss of contact with the community and its groupings, etc.). In this case, language could also play an important role, and today it is once again recognised that Yiddish has a high level of significance as a measure of Jewishness (naturally for the part of the community which has *Ashkenazi* origins), so there is now in Madrid a circle of people who meet from time to time to talk in and about Yiddish, its literature, etc.

Some of the expressions which have been passed down from Yiddish-speaking parents to their children, and which the latter no longer use but remember fondly, are the following: gunish ka sach (not important); meshiguene (crazy); shikse (maid); goi (non-Jew); shabbes goi (someone who does not respect the Sabbath); zedreit mie den kopf (you're driving me crazy). Many other refer to Jewish festivals, greetings, congratulations, typical meals, etc.

Language use among the Sephardim from Morocco: the use of Jaketía

Another linguistic modality that is barely remembered, and only studied in depth by Bendelac (1987, 1990), is the phenomenon of the

Jaketía (also called *Hakatyia*), part of the culture of the *Sephardim* from Morocco. It should be remembered that the *Sephardim* are those members of the Jewish community who, after the Expulsion of the Jews in 1492, were forced to abandon their possessions, their synagogues, and their country, which is known among the Jews as *Sepharad* (Spain). Some of the *Sephardim* settled in the Muslim countries around the Mediterranean (North Africa, the Ottoman Empire, etc.), and others emigrated to France, Holland, Italy, Germany, England, etc. Here is how Bendelac describes this language variety which is typical of the *Sephardim* from Morocco:

> Let's consider the Jaketía as one of the ways in which at some time, in some home of one of the families of the Jewish community which today make up the Jewish-Spanish community, they could use some of the utterances which come from the immigration from the north of Africa, and which expresses a rich culture. For a long time, for the Sephardim of Morocco, the Jaketía was an external sign the visible symbol by which they proclaimed their Sephardi roots and kept separate from the rest of the population. After the occupation of Morocco, as the population began to learn modern Spanish and French, whose use implied having been to school, social prestige and position, the Jaketía began to be considered as the language of the illiterate and ignorant, as a vulgar language. On the other hand, this phenomenon did not succeed in eliminating the positive value represented by the language as the symbol of a glorious past, as a link with tradition and as protection against assimilation.

Looking at the phonetics, one still often hears the peculiar intonation of the Jaketía, the oxytone accentuation, the linking of words with the [z] sound, the sounds [j] and [ch] in words, verb forms such as *dichi*, *mirí*, and *vaite*. Sometimes, Spanish and Hebrew are mixed together.

Among the most frequently heard Jaketía expressions are the following:

(1) Aquí estoy **kefseada** del **mazal**
    (A doleful, complaining expression, lamenting one's misfortune (*mazal*)).
(2) **Ba iom u ba laila**
    (From the Hebrew ('day and night'). Used to indicate that something happens continually).
(3) **Baruj ha Shem**
    (From the Hebrew ('bless the name (of God'). Used often to express faith and astonishment).
(4) **Beezrat ha Shem**
    (From the Hebrew ('God willing, with the blessing of God's name'). Used to indicate that one places one's faith in God's help that a project or situation will turn out well).

(5) **Capparah**

(An expression of resignation, fatalism, solace. It is used when some minor mishap occurs, to express the hope or belief that this mishap will have a redeeming effect, or that it will stop something worse from happening).

(6) Como **Par'ó** en la tina

(Like Pharaoh (Par'o) in the vat (tina)). A mocking metaphor to describe a difficult, unpleasant or dangerous situation, that of someone who goes through something similar to what happened to the Pharaoh in the Red Sea).

(7) Hazer **Kabod**

(To honour someone).

(8) **Shabua Tov**

(From the Hebrew ('Have a good week'), which begins when the *Shabbat* ends).

(9) Como las **makot** de noche de **pésaj**

('Like the Plagues on the night of the *pésaj*' (Passover). Used in a difficult, unfortunate or dangerous situation. *Makot* = 'plagues', referring to the Ten Plagues which God imposed upon Egypt to allow the Jews to leave, and which are commemorated on the night of Passover, by throwing wine and vinegar from a cup, alternately, at both parents, and reciting the names of the Plagues).

(10) En pasos de **mitzvot** andes siempre

(An expression of gratitude and blessing, to someone who has just done something he/she should, to compliment, to thank and to wish that they will always do and receive *mitzvot*, or 'good actions').

(11) **Jalam jajamim**

(From the Hebrew ('wise of the wise'). Said of the rabbis who are admired or venerated for their wonderful knowledge of the law, and for their great moral character).

(12) **Jatima Tová**

(From the Hebrew ('good inscription'), i.e. 'may you have a good inscription in the Book of Destiny').

Language use within the Israeli community in Spain

It is also interesting to look at the types of discourse adopted by the members of the Israeli community in Spain, who are in contact with the languages spoken in that country. The following sentences and expressions were uttered by two adult members from a young Jewish family that has quickly become part of Barcelona society. Both members of the family work in contact with the public, and both have learned Spanish through their interaction with the public. They have been in Barcelona for some nine years, and speak in Hebrew with the children, but they have already begun to codeswitch into Spanish. The following are examples of intrasentential lexical codeswitching:

(13) tiqaj et ha-**mochila**
      (Take the backpack ('mochila', in Spanish), which involves the use of an imperative verb marked for masculine gender (*tiqaj*), an accusative determiner (*et*) and the article (*ha*)).

(14) ani holejet la-**mercado**
      (I'm going to the market ('mercado', in Spanish), which involves the use of a first person, singular pronoun (*ani*), a singular verb form in present, marked for feminine gender (*holejet*), and a preposition and determinate article (*la*)).

(15) tajnisi et se la-**batidora**
      (Put this in the blender ('batidora', in Spanish), which involves the use of an imperative verb, marked for masculine gender (*tajnisi*), a particle which introduces an accusative determiner (*et*), a demonstrative article (*se*) and preposition with an article (la)).

(16) ma ba leja le-**cena**?
      (What do you feel like eating for dinner ('cena', in Spanish)?, which involves the use of an interrogative particle (*ma*), a singular verb form in present, marked for masculine gender, in impersonal form (*ba*), a preposition together with a second person, masculine pronoun, as a suffix (*lejá*), and a preposition (*le*)).

(17) tsaltsel elai la-**móvil**
      (Phone me on the mobile phone ('móvil', in Spanish), which involves the use of an imperative verb marked for masculine gender (tsaltsel), a preposition together with a first person pronoun (elai), and a preposition with an article (la)).

(18) anajnu yotsim le-**juerga**
      (Let's go out on the town ('de juerga', in Spanish) with a masculine, first person, plural pronoun (*anajnu*), a plural verb form in present, marked for masculine gender (*yotsim*), and a preposition (*le*)).

(19) naase sivuv **copas**?
      (Let's go out drinking ('de copas', in Spanish), which involves the use of a future, plural verb, in impersonal form marked for masculine gender (*naase*), and a noun (*sivuv*)).

(20) yesh li **queja** ba-inyan ha-se
      (I have a complaint ('queja', in Spanish) with a particle (*yesh*), and a preposition together with a first person, singular pronoun (*li*)).

(21) hu stam medaber ha-col **palabras**
      (He's all talk, just words ('palabras', in Spanish) with a masculine, third person, singular pronoun (*hu*). This is an expression that is almost impossible to translate, but means something like 'just because' (*stam*) and it involves the use of a singular verb form in present, marked for masculine gender (*medaber*), an article (ha), and a particle (*col*)).

(22) im ein leja **enchufe** lo tujal lehicanes le-sham

(If you haven't got connections ('enchufes', in Spanish), you can't go in there, which involves the use of a conditional (*im*), a negative particle (*ein*), a preposition together with a masculine, second person, singular suffix (*leja*), negation (*lo*), a second person singular verb form in future, marked for masculine gender (*tujal*), an infinitive verb (*lehicanes*), a preposition (*le*), and a particle (*sham*)).

(23) im tagsimi tecabli **bronca**

(If you go too far, you'll get scolded ('bronca', in Spanish), which involves the use of a conditional (*im*), a second person singular verb form in future, marked for feminine gender (*tagsimi*), and a future, second person, singular verb, marked for feminine gender (*tecabli*)).

(24) tivdeki ba-**agenda** ma ha-matsav

(Look in the diary ('agenda', in Spanish), to see how things are, which involves the use of an imperative verb form, marked for feminine gender (*tivdeki*), a preposition with an article (*ba*), an interrogative particle (*ma*), an article (*ha*), and a noun (*matsav*)).

It should be noted that most of the lexical items codeswitched in these examples are key terms denoting modern Spanish life ('juerga' (night-life), 'enchufe' (connection, i.e. for getting jobs or favours), 'queja' (complaint), 'copas' (drinks, drinking), 'bronca' (telling off, a row)) and as such are apt candidates for switching, as predicted in language contact theories and models. These are known as cultural switches.

Language Behaviour: Function and Uses of Learnt, Used and Dropped Languages

There are no global data as to the linguistic habits of and the linguistic functions attributed to the different languages learnt, used and in the process of being dropped by the 12 Jewish communities in Spain. There is a study on the patterns of linguistic behaviour of the Jewish community of Barcelona (Berthelot and Puig (1992)[7] which included those Jewish people, both of *Ashkenazim* and *Sephardi* origin, who came and settled in Barcelona from Europe but excluded those Jewish people who originated from the Maghreb, the Middle East, or South America. The results of this study, which undoubtedly shed some light on the predicted patterns of language behaviour followed by the members of all the other Jewish communities in Spain, can be summarised in terms of the following patterns:

(1) The Jewish community in Barcelona presents great original linguistic diversity reflected in the fact that there are 20 known languages[8] at stake of which the different interviewed members report several competence levels, and very often the same individual may know six languages. This linguistic richness cannot just be justified purely in

geographical terms since it is also an exponent of historical, cultural, social, economic and professional factors.

(2) Due to settlement and integration into Spain a new model of linguistic uniformity emerged, which involved the shift to the peninsula languages, first to Spanish and secondly to Catalan, any of the other historical Autonomous Communities' languages, and also to the most international European languages, mainly French but also English and German.

(3) The Jewish languages (Yiddish and Jaketía)[9] and Hebrew, as well as certain of the original languages, such as, Bulgarian, Polish, Rumanian, etc., become family or individual languages with a tendency to regress.

There is evidence to suggest that these patterns are also applicable to the other Jewish communities in Spain within which, and in spite of their original linguistic diversity and their knowledge of several languages, their members tend, (1) to use the official language, that is, Spanish, or Spanish and the other co-official language in the Autonomous Communities where two languages are spoken (Catalan, Galician and Basque, respectively); (2) then, they learn foreign languages (mainly English and French), and finally, (3) in some cases, they also learn Hebrew and maybe, Yiddish, Jaketía, also called *Hakatyia*, and the *Judeo-español* of the communities from Turkey, also called, *Djidya, Djudezma,* or *Spanioli*, depending on the family's origin.

The combination of multilingualism, language shift and complete abandonment of their original languages in favour of the languages of the communities where the Jewish people have settled is not exclusive to the Jewish communities in Spain; it has been observed in other countries: the USA, Canada, France and Israel. In Europe, and therefore in Spain, it is possible to explain this language behaviour within the context of migration, but other factors (judicial, political, economical, social, cultural, ideological, psychological) considered from a historical perspective can clarify this situation. Until the 19th century, both the *Ashkenazim* and the *Sephardim* from Central and Eastern Europe lived in communities isolated from the global society, because this isolation was either imposed from outside or from within the Jewish communities themselves to preserve their ethnic coherence and develop their traditional way of life. And they had their own language, Yiddish and *Djidya* (Judeo-español, *Djudezma* or *Spanioli*), respectively. From the 19th century and above all during the 20th century a series of internal and external factors have contributed to the transformation of the structure of these Jewish communities in such a way that they have begun participating in modern society and acquiring new patterns of life. Linguistically speaking, they have adopted habits that are seen as more universal and useful for their promotion and integration into global (mainstream) societies so that the vernacular and community languages have been steadily replaced by other languages, either as instruments and symbols of (1) assimilation in the case of German, Russian and Polish, or (2) socio-economic and cultural progress in the case of German, English and French; or finally as imposed instruments of new geopolitical realities in the case of Rumanian, Turkish, Russian and others, that they have to learn as the language of the country of adoption.

Future Prospects

The Jewish communities in Spain seem to reflect the capitalisation of two different periods and life-styles. On the one hand, there are the oldest members of the community[10] who are direct heirs of the multidirectional changes mentioned above and were exposed through their families to the original background of the community and at the same time to the non-Jewish environment. On the other hand, there are the young people or adults who have lived their own itinerary (migration, stay in different countries, immigration to Spain) and superposed different social, cultural and linguistic *substrata.*

Therefore, it seems that for the Jews of Spain a period has almost definitely come to an end, a period of spatial and temporal breakage that involved, on the one hand, their arrival to Spain, a country which in spite of the Civil War and Franco's dictatorship was and is politically speaking more stable and linguistically more homogeneous,[11] and on the other, the beginning of a much more peaceful period, at least locally. The present situation derives from this picture that has been described. Socially and culturally, the Jewish communities in Spain combine their will to integrate into the mainstream society of the community(ies) that have hosted them and their traditional and religious vocation to keep their particular traits that make them culturally rich and original. Linguistically, they will continue to be multilingual communities but they seem to be already adopting the much more reduced and homogeneous model of the Spanish global society, which involves (1) the adoption of Spanish, in Spain's monolingual areas, and Spanish and any of Spain's other languages in Catalonia, Galicia and the Basque Country, (2) the learning of foreign languages (English and French), and (3) for some, the learning of Hebrew.

Notes

1. Ladino is the term that the Jews of the Iberian Peninsula themselves used to refer to their dialect. Its origins can be traced back to the times of Ferdinand of Aragón and Isabel of Castile since it was very similar to the archaic and picturesque Castilian used as a common language in Castile and Navarra at the time, except that it was based on Spanish and Hebrew. When Spanish Jews were expelled in 1492 and settled in Esmirna, Salonica, Sarajevo or Rabat, they kept their love for Spain and its cultural values, in particular the language they had been using in Spain, that is, Ladino, which they strewed with words and idioms from the local languages with which they were in contact. Ladino has been the language of Sephardim for hundreds of years; nowadays they use it more as a second

language. Undoubtedly, what helped to keep Ladino alive was the Spanish *Romancero*, tradition which fed into Sephardic song, the most important exponent of Sephardic culture and folklore, and hence the clear similitarities between Cervantes texts and the *cancionero Sefardí*. This *cancionero* tradition is to be seen in the *Cantos Sefardíes*, published in Spain in 1979 and also popularised by the Venezuelan Soledad Bravo, one of the most significant singers of Latin America. A fragment of one of this *cantos* is reproduced below:

> Cuando veo hixa hermosa
> Una pastora yo amí
> Por la tu puerta yo pasí
> Durme, durme
> Para qué quero yo más bivir

[When I see a beautiful girl/A shepherdess I loved/I passed by your door/Sleep, Sleep/ Why should I want to live more].

2. *Sepharad* is a Hebrew toponymic with which the Spanish Jews used to name their country of origin. It is mentioned in the prophecy of Abdías in relation to old Sardia, a city in Minor Asia, where deported citizens from Jerusalem used to live. However, the Jewish tradition, particularly from the 8th century, tended to identify *Sepharad* with the most western part of the known world, that is, the Iberian Peninsula and, particularly during the Golden Age of the Hispano-Hebrew culture, the Spanish Jews would call themselves *Sephardim*, a name that they would use very proudly for their peninsular past in their Diaspora after expulsion. This term is usually used in opposition to *Ashkenazim*, another Hebrew toponym referring to a country in the High Euphrates but which the Medieval Rabbi literature identified with the first Central European Jewish settlements: Germany, France, Poland and Lithuania. It is usually used to refer to the other great common ethnic-cultural branch: the Franco-Germanic-Slav from which derived a cultural tradition, a rich folklore, religious and literary currents; linguistically, the Ashkenazi Jewish branch is characterised by its peculiar pronunciation of the Hebrew used in religious texts and by the use of Yiddish in everyday's life and in literature. The Ashkenazi Jewish, the same as the Sephardim, abandoned their ordinary central European environment and extended themselves in other areas of the world, particularly South and North America and the State of Israel.

3. Díaz Mas (1986) points out that there were two Diaspora, a primary and a secondary one, and three stages marked by two crises. The first stage, from Expulsion until the middle of the 17th century, is characterised by the migration of the expelled and converse Jews who settled in different Christian and Muslim countries (primary Diaspora). The second stage developed during the 18th century and a part of the 19th century and it involved the Sephardim community's own development and interethnic relations with other communities. The third stage started with a new political, economic and cultural crisis at the end of the 19th century and covered the two world wars which led Sephardim Jews to look for better settlements, away from their initial geographical environment and caused the secondary Diaspora towards America, Western Europe and Israel.

4. There are no reliable data, except for the place from where the migration originated, so as to be able to trace back which of these migratory settlements involved Jewish people from the Sephardim communities expelled in 1492 and which involved Jewish communities from other branches, from other secondary migrations and from Israel.

5. Which shows the Jewish community's stability.

6. The systematic extermination of the European Jews by the Nazis during the Second World War, when some six million Jews were executed.

7. The instrument used to collect the data was a sociolinguistic questionnaire which included the following parts: (a) a demographic section (interviewee's and interviewee's parents' origin; data and age of arrival), (b) languages known (mother tongue, spoken languages, and other languages known), (c) domains of language use (family, community,

work, and the place and function of Catalan), and (d) languages used everyday and the situation of the Jewish languages (Yiddish and Judeo-Español).

8. The total sample N consisted of 30 informants and the languages reportedly known were: Spanish (30), Catalan (30), French (29), English (22), German (20), Ladi (16), Hebrew (14), Italian (13), Yiddish (9), Turkish (7), Bulgarian (4), Rumanian (4), Portuguese (3), Greek (3), Polish (2), Russian (2), Hungarian (2), Serbian (1), Slavic languages (1), and Ukranian (1).

9. A language variety which is typical of the *Sephardim* from Morocco (see pp. 245–7).

10. People who were probably born around 1900.

11. Without negating Spain's multilingual make-up and the richness that the existence of Catalan, Galician and Basque involves side-by-side with Spanish.

References

Aki Yerushalayim, No. 52.

Beinart, H. (1988) La Diáspora Sefardí en Europa y especialmente en la cuenca del Mediterráneo. *Hispania Sacra* 40, 911–31.

Bel Bravo, M.A. *et al.* (1992) *Diáspora Sefardí*. Madrid: Editorial Mapfre.

Bendelac, A. Bendayan de (1987) *Los Nuestros. Sejiná, Letuarios, Jaquetía y Fraja*. New York: Peter Lang.

Bendelac, A. Bendayan de (1990) *Voces Jaquetiescas*. Caracas: Centro de estudios sefardí de Caracas, Biblioteca Popular Sefardí.

Bendelac, A. Bendayan de (1995) *Diccionario del Judeoespañol de los Sefardíes del Norte de Marruecos*. Caracas: Centro de estudios sefardí de Caracas.

Berthelot, M. (1981) Plurilinguisme au Collège Séfardi de Barcelone. B.A. Honours Dissertation. Université de Montpelier.

Berthelot, M. (1984) Les Juifs d'Espagne au XXème siècle: retour à Sefarad, identité juive et intégration à la societé catalane. Université de Montpelier.

Berthelot, M. (1994) *Cien años de Judaísmo en la España Contemporánea*. Barcelona: Eraim.

Berthelot, M. and Puig, G. (1992) Un espai lingüístic deconegut a Catalunya: la comunitat israelita de Barcelona. *Treballs de Sociolingüística Catalana* 10, 27–49.

'Del Marruecos hispanojudío'. *Raíces*, No. 18.

Díaz Mas, P. (1988) *Los Sefardíes: Cultura y Literatura*. San Sebastián: Servicio Editorial de la Universidad del País Vasco.

'El habla española de los judíos de Tánger en la actualidad'. *Raíces*, No. 27.

'Judíos argentinos en España'. *Raíces*, No. 21.

Lareda, J.A. (1993) *Retorno a Sefarad. La política de España hacia sus Judíos en el Siglo XX*. Barcelona: Riopiedras.

Salafranca, J.F. (1995) *Los Judíos de Melilla*. Málaga: Algazara.

Shalom (video). TVE S.A. El Jaketía. Jacob Hassan.

'Una Hagadá de Pésaj judeoespañola'. *Raíces*, No. 18.

Valores del judaísmo (1991) Enciclopedia Judaica. Jerusalem: Ed. Keter.

Zafir (Revista Española de la Comunidad Israelita de Barcelona), No. 48.

Zafir (Revista Española de la Comunidad Israelita de Barcelona), No. 49.

Zafir (Revista Española de la Comunidad Israelita de Barcelona), No. 51.

'1917–97. Ochenta años de sinagoga madrileña'. *Raíces*, No. 29.

Chapter 10
The Brazilian Community

M. TERESA TURELL and NEIVA LAVRATTI

Brazilian Migration throughout Recent History

Brazil can be described as a country with a history of colonisation and incoming migration, of internal influence from precolombine culture and of ongoing linguistic and cultural relations with the Spanish-speaking Latin-American countries. Brazilian migratory movements have traditionally been from overseas, from other Latin-American countries, and also internal, from inland to the coast and from rural to urban These migratory trends have contributed to Brazil patterning as a *melting-pot* of indigenous native American, African, Asian, Indian and European cultures and have converted it into a very cosmopolitan country which concentrates races and populations from practically all over the world (Lavratti, 1995).

Brazilian external migration started 10 years ago with the *Pós-Cruzado* era which led more than a million Brazilian people to look for new opportunities beyond their national frontiers. At present, in spite of the implementation five years ago of the *Plano Real*, an economic plan that brought with it a degree of economic stabilisation, Brazil continues to produce new emigrants. Their prevalent settlement pattern seems to be urban and their favourite destination seems to be Europe. In fact, Brazilian migrants prefer the most industrialised Western European countries, because job opportunities are greater and more diversified, although some Southern European and Eastern European countries also attract a considerable number of Brazilian migrants.

Nature and Distribution of the Brazilian Community in Spain[1]

Table 10.1, which includes the distribution of Brazilian migration by decreasing rate, shows that Spain occupies the middle of the distribution scale in terms of favoured destinations and that the Brazilian community in Spain can be estimated at around 12,000 people, a figure which has probably been calculated taking into account both legal residents and non-registered residents, who are attracted by cultural and linguistic affinity, apart from the economic reasons mentioned above. More conservative sources from Spanish institutions would situate the number of 1996

254

Table 10.1 Distribution of Brazilian migrants in Europe

Country	Estimated number of migrants
Germany	23,700
Portugal	22,000
Great Britain	19,500
Italy	16,800
Spain	12,000
France	8,200
Switzerland	7,500
Sweden	7,000
Belgium	2,900
Greece	2,500
Sweden	2,000
Austria	1,000
Hungary	80
Total	126,828

Source: Euro-Brazil text, 16 February 1997

Brazilian legal residents in 5694 (see the *Anuario de Migraciones*, 1997) of which only a quarter are Brazilian workers with legal work permits (see the *Anuario de Extranjería*, 1996).

According to these same official records, Brazilian migrants to Spain seem to have preferred two Autonomous Communities to settle: Madrid, with a total 1412 people, and Catalonia, with 1339 people, and within these, their capitals, Madrid and Barcelona. This preference seems to indicate that the spatial distribution of this community is moving towards the same geographical model as that of the majority of immigrant communities to Spain, that is, settlements in the large cities and on the Mediterranean coast. Table 10.2 shows the distribution of Brazilian migrants by Autonomous Community.

As to the Brazilian immigrants' geographical origin (see *Brasil, Aspectos Generales*, 1995), three areas in Brazil seem to be the source of migration into Spain: the Northeast (which includes the states of *Maranhao, Piauí, Ceará, Rio Grande do Norte, Paraíba, Pernambuco, Alagoas, Sergipe* and *Bahia*)[2], the Southeast (which includes the states of *Minas Gerais, Espírito Santo, Rio de Janeiro* and *Sao Paulo*) and the South[3] (which includes the states of *Rio Grande do Sul, Santa Catarina* and *Paraná*).

The social profile of Brazilian migrants is young, both male and female. In general, they tend to exhibit social integration, because they migrate in

Table 10.2 Distribution of Brazilian migrants by Autonomous Community (1996)

Autonomous Community	Estimated numbers
Andalusia	516
Aragón	92
Asturias	101
Balearic Islands	193
Basque Country	268
Canary Islands	232
Cantabria	64
Castile-La Mancha	51
Castile-León	216
Catalonia	1,339
Ceuta and Melilla	1
Extremadura	36
Galicia	489
La Rioja	12
Madrid	1,412
Murcia	53
Navarra	60
Valencian Country	468

Source: Anuario de Migraciones (1997) Ministerio de Trabajo y Asuntos Sociales, Madrid, 1997.

family groupings, tend to mix with the host community and adapt to Spanish life. They may even create mixed families, before or after migration to Spain, and this includes football players, who because of their social and economic status, constitute an outstanding group.

If social profile, motivation and geographical origin are correlated, the Brazilian community in Spain exhibits some differentiating features that make it uniquely idiosyncratic. In some cases, for both men and women the basic and most fundamental reason for Brazilian migration is economic and, in particular, it is linked to the need of the Brazilian middle classes to achieve a better economic level in view of the constant unstability in their Brazilian jobs; but they do not plan on staying for very long. Others, basically men, in spite of a reasonably good economic level, emigrate in search of adventure, to be able to visit new countries and learn more languages. In some cases a proportion of this group of migrants may stay

Table 10.3 1995 Brazilian immigrants to Spain by age groups

Total	−16	16−24	25−34	35−44	45−54	55−64	+65
348	39	58	164	65	16	3	3

Source: Anuario Estadístico (1996)

Table 10.4 1995 Brazilian immigrants to Spain by academic level

Total	Illiteracy	Primary education	Secondary education	Higher education	Unspecified
348	19	67	78	180	4

Source: Anuario Estadístico (1996)

up to the age of retirement. Another group, of both men and women, completed higher education and are qualified professional people (Ramírez Goicoecha, 1996: 237), who will not necessarily stay for very long. And finally, there is a group of people, which includes artists and football players, with a high degree of economic stability, who might not plan to stay for very long but tend up staying for quite a long time. All this would indicate that Brazilian immigration to Spain is integrated, generally speaking, where some migrants stay for long, but it is not very stable.

The latest available data on the influx of Brazilian citizens into Spain is for 1995 (*Anuario Estadístico 1996*) when 348 Brazilians arrived in Spain. Their distribution in Spain by Autonomous Communities is the following: 110 in Madrid, 79 in Catalonia, 36 in the Valencian Country, 34 in the Basque Country, 21 in Galicia, 19 in Andalusia, 11 in Navarra, and figures below 10 in seven more Autonomous Communities. Of those 348 Brazilian immigrants that were recorded to have migrated during 1995, one-third (121) were men and two-thirds (227), were women. As for age groups, the most represented group was aged between 25 and 34 (164), followed by those between 35 and 44 (65) and 16 and 24 (58), a pattern which seems to confirm that the motivation behind migration is economic. As to education, the 1995 Brazilian migratory wave seems to conform to the general profile described above, since the academic level of the majority of Brazilian immigrants is secondary and higher education. These patterns are illustrated in Tables 10.3 and 10.4 and they seem to suggest that the 1995 influx follows the Brazilian community's socio-demographic structure which has been described.

Settlement and Integration

The Brazilian immigrants' liking for Spain[4] can be explained in terms of the historical, cultural, religious and linguistic links between Spain and any of the Latin-American countries, from which Brazil is not excluded.

One pattern that in some cases characterises Brazilian immigrant settlement is the existence of some family and social networks waiting in the host country to welcome Brazilian citizens. These networks primarily work as a system for infrastructure, logistics, etc., locating possible jobs and financial help with travel for the incoming migrant, although they also contribute with emotional and affective support mediated through very strong family and friendship ties (Ramírez Goicoechea, 1996: 243; Romero Giménez, 1993). In the case of economic migrants, there are some isolated cases in which the women are the first to migrate, but the tendency is for the whole family to travel together, while when the reasons for migration are educational, for example pursuing further education, it is the men, usually scholars, that arrive first, but in some cases again the family travels together.

Contrastive analysis of academic level attained and their professional level in the host country, that is, Spain, shows that the Brazilian migrants' expectations have not been fulfilled, since many of them have ended up occupying posts in sectors at the bottom of the socio-economic scale, not achieving the upward mobility that they were seeking via migration. Their work is structured on an age and sex basis. In the case of the economic migrants, some young women, married and unmarried, work as maids, and the latter tend to live in their employer's house, while young men are employed in unskilled jobs, and a surprisingly high proportion, both men and women, end up working as artists (i.e. in dance academies, etc.). However, in the case of migrants who arrive in Spain in search of adventure or to pursue their higher education, there is no such distribution since both men and women end up finding jobs similar to what they were doing in Brazil, or at least close to their professional and educational background: teachers, nurses, musicians, etc.

The majority of Brazilian migrants are not very motivated to study Spanish in a formal instruction context. They feel that they can use colloquial Portuguese and converge on a sort of broken Spanish (*Españogués*[5] or falso *castellano*, as they call it) to ensure communication. This factor and the above mentioned language proximity between Spanish and Portuguese favour a high degree of interference from Portuguese when Brazilian speakers try to speak Spanish. This is illustrated in (1) an excerpt from L.R., a 36-year old (at the time of the interview) *capoeirista*[6] in Spain, who migrated to Europe in the mid 1960s and has been living in Spain, more specifically Catalonia, since 1991:

(1)   Olha, aqui na Espanha, ou seja, na Catalunha, Barcelona ... eu uso o meu espanhol, ou seja, castelhano, não? E de uma outra forma, assim na Europa, o que me segura a onda mesmo é o meu francês, falso francês. Eu falo francês ... um pouco de francês ... eu não falo nada na realidade, não? Mas me comunico melhor em francês do que em

espanhol; parece incrível mas acho que é porque eu passei um maior tempo falando ... e aqui eu falo o castelhano com sotaque, jeitinho brasileiro, aí meus alunos não entendem ... dali a pouco eles tão falando português também!

Well, here in Spain, or rather in Catalonia, Barcelona ... I use my Spanish, or rather Castilian, don't I? And otherwise, here in Europe, what enables me to keep up with things is my French, false French. I speak French ... a little French ... I don't speak it all, really, do I? But I communicate better in French than in Spanish; it seems incredible but I think that it's because I spent more time talking ... and here I speak Spanish with a Brazilian accent and my students can't understand me ... in a little while from now they'll be speaking Portuguese, too!

Social Organisation and Institutional Support

The Brazilian community in Spain presents a quite rich level of social organisation with a number of associations and societies in different cities in Spain giving social, professional and personal support. In Barcelona, there is the *Associação para investigadores e estudantes brasileiros de Catalunha* (APEC) (Association for Brazilian Researchers and Students in Catalonia) founded by university teachers and researchers in humanistic and scientific fields of study. Its headquarters are located in the *Centro de Estudos Brasileiros* (Centre for Brazilian Studies) of the Brazilian Consulate. As regards its members, it is interesting to note that in spite of their quite high economic status and educational linguistic level, their attitudes towards Spanish and Catalan, and the host community people and culture, are not very positive and they prefer to learn a third language, English, with more clout internationally.

Another association at national level, again located in Barcelona, is the *Associação do Amigos do Brasil* (AAB) (Association for Friends of Brazil), with sociocultural goals. For several years since its foundation in the late 1980s, this association brought together Brazilian couples or mixed Brazilian-Spanish families with residence permit, with primary or secondary education, and low linguistic awareness *vis-à-vis* the host community language, although evidencing positive attitudes towards the host community people and their culture. For the past five years, the AAB has also attracted other Brazilian people, and even Spaniards, of all ages and educational level, including some APEC members.

There is a third section of the Brazilian community in Spain that does not belong to any society and which includes professional people, artists, and football players – that is, people with an impressive degree of economic and professional stability. These people show, in general, a positive attitude towards the host community people, with their culture and language(s), probably because of their decision to stay in Spain for a lengthy period of time, although the exception would be the football players who show a positive attitude for integration but less interest in learning the host community(ies) language(s).

Finally, the Brazilian community in Barcelona has at its disposal the *Centro de Estudos Brasileiros* (Centre for Brazilian Studies) which comes under the Cultural Department of the Brazilian Consulate. This centre offers courses of Portuguese as a foreign language, has a library, a video and audio club, and promotes joint sociocultural activities between the Brazilian Consulate and some Spanish institutions. It has a current membership of 805 people, more than half of them Spaniards. It is frequented by Brazilian students and professional people, resident in Barcelona, who are in search of documentation and references on historical and contemporary Brazil, and as well as Brazilian visitors to Barcelona looking for artistic and cultural activities, news and events to attend while they are in the city. In Madrid, where the Brazilian Embassy is located, there is only a *Casa do Brasil*, which is a hall of residence, similar in its present-day functions to the *Residencia de Estudiantes*.[7] Originally, the *Casa do Brasil* was founded by the Brazilian Ministry of Foreign Affairs and is now affiliated to the Universidad Complutense de Madrid. Finally, there is also the *Escuela Oficial de Idiomas*, which is a state language school that teaches Brazilian Portuguese, as well as other languages, and which also exists in other Spanish big cities, such as Barcelona, Valencia and Bilbao.

Another section of the Brazilian community in Spain which is worth mentioning is composed of those Brazilians who came to Spain ostensibly as tourists and then looked for any means of survival, as they in fact planned to stay in Spain after their arrival. Generally, at a preliminary stage, these people show little motivation for learning the host community language(s) and even think that colloquial Portuguese is sufficient to ensure communication with Spanish speakers, mixing their mother tongue with Spanish.[8]

At an even more official level, it must be mentioned that in their procedure to become legal residents or be granted Spanish nationality, apart from having to follow all the ordinary steps, Brazilian migrants to Spain enjoy certain advantages, as a result of Brazil and Spain's signature of several international agreements on Social Security: an agreement dating from 1971 published in the *Boletín Oficial del Estado* (BOE) on 12 August 1971, as well as an additional protocol published in the BOE on 12 February 1982, and an administrative resolution also published in the BOE on 26 February 1982. There exists a cultural agreement between Brazil and Spain that was signed in 1960, approved by law in 1964 and ratified in 1965. More recently (7 October 1997), the Republic of Brazil and the Kingdom of Spain signed a collaboration agreement on cultural issues (printed books, audio-visual aids, archives and libraries, cultural and educational centres) and artistic matters (painting, theatre).

Domains of Language Use

As mentioned, Brazil is a very cosmopolitan and diverse country, where a *melting-pot* of European, African, Asian, Indian and American indigenous races live together, and a country which not only concentrates races and cultures from all over the world but which possesses a startling number of indigenous languages.[9] Nowadays, and with a population of approximately 160 million inhabitants, Brazil nonetheless presents a solid linguistic unity from North to South. Furthermore, Brazilian Portuguese enjoys standardisation and unification and its use has been extended to all the domains: home, street, school, the media (press, radio and TV).

Within this scenario, it is interesting to note that in spite of positive integration into Spain, reflected in the Brazilian migrants'extended use of the host community's language(s), the overall in-group communication pattern among adults and between parents and children, involves a high use of their own language, that is, Brazilian-Portuguese. However, language choice in the family adopts different forms. The use of Brazilian-Portuguese predominates in Brazilian families, with second-generation members introducing Spanish or Catalan, or using bilingual modes of discourse. This bilingual usage, which occurs particularly in mixed families, may take two specific forms: (1) codeswitching where Spanish (or Catalan, or any of the other Autonomous Communities' languages (Basque or Galician)) and Portuguese are kept separate but are used in the course of the same interaction, and (2) mixed modes which reflect other language contact phenomena, such as borrowing, interference at the level of phonology and morphology, and semantic and syntactic calques. The terms that are proposed in this article to refer to these mixed modes are *Portunhol* and *Españogués*, which will be described below.

On the whole, language proximity between Portuguese and Spanish is a decisive factor in the form taken by patterns of language behaviour and use adopted by members of the Brazilian community in Spain. Brazilians themselves are aware of this, as is illustrated in (2) an excerpt from a 35-year old architect who migrated to Barcelona in 1989:

(2) Não, me cuida não, ela (her mother) fica desesperada, porque claro, quatro anos aqui falando castelhano, aí tem coisas do português que eu já eu me embarralho todo e palavras que já estão introspectadas na cabeça que a gente mesmo falando, mesmo na rodinha de brasileiros aqui falando, tem palavras que cê já põe no meio, né, não sei o que sei lá vamo, com o que a gente vai? Vai a pé ou vai de **coche** (Portuguese: *carro*), não fala mais vai de carro, de **coche** e ... às vezes os verbos, os provérbios os pronomes eu me embarralho todo já ... eu creio que a ... é o ponto de conflito de falar duas línguas que são muito parecidas com a mesma raiz não, com a mesma se eu falasse um alemão, seguramente eu falaria ... voltaria a escrever português talvez com não, não tanta dificultade. Mas isso, **mi madre** é professora

primária, meus irmãos, bom cada, um com sua profissão tem dentistas, engenheiros agrônomo, econmomistas, advogado, minha irmã minha irmã se ... é matemática, apesar que não segue a profissão, basicamente isso.

No, she doesn't look after me; she (the speaker's mother) despairs of me, because of course, four years here speaking Spanish, so that I've got things from Portuguese that are all mixed up, and words that I have fixed in my head, that with people speaking, the little circle of Brazilians over here speaking, I have words that I know are a little better. I don't know how people, how we are getting there ... How are people travelling? They're going on foot or they're going by **car**, they don't ever say going by car, by **car** ... and at times the verbs, the proverbs, the pronouns, I just mix it all up ... I think it's a source of conflict to speak two languages that are very similar, with the same root, no? with the same ... if I were to speak German, I'd surely speak ... I'd start writing Portuguese perhaps with less difficulty. But you know, **my mother** is a primary school teacher, my brothers and sisters, well, they each have their own profession, dentists, agronomic engineers, economists, a lawyer, my sister ... my sister knows ... is a mathematician, although that isn't a profession, that's it, basically.

Codeswitching Practices

In a situation of language contact with Spanish, Brazilian speakers make use of both lexical and grammatical intrasentential codeswitching (Fontana & Vallduví, 1990; Pujadas & Turell, 1993), as illustrated in (3) and (4):

(3) ... eu colocaria o **catalán** ...
     (I would say Catalan)
(4) Isto é muito, desculpa, posse ver algo **muy interesante**.
     (This is very, sorry, I can see something very interesting)

Brazilian speakers also make use of codeswitches which are pragmatically motivated (Turell, 1994), as in (5), where the speaker uses an extra-sentential codeswitch, in the form of a Spanish confirmation check:

(5) Você contou tudo, **no?**
     Você contou tudo, né? (Portuguese: não é > né)
     (You narrated everything, didn't you?)

Bilingual Speech Modes

In the context of language contact between Brazilian Portuguese and Spanish, it has been suggested that there are two varieties of language or bilingual modalities of discourse referred to in this article as *Portunhol* and

Españogués. In general, in acquisition/learning contexts, *Portunhol* is viewed as an interlanguage stage with marked levels of fossilisation. According to Ferreira (1994), it is the term used in practice and in specialised literature to refer to Spanish speakers' intermediate production when they attempt to speak Portuguese. Others, such as Colin Rodea (1990, cited by Ferreira (1994)) prefer to define *Portunhol* 'as the most immediate expression of the contact between Brazilian Portuguese and Spanish' and use it to describe the variety of language used both by Portuguese speakers in contact with Spanish when they use Portuguese and by Spanish speakers in contact with Brazilian Portuguese when they use Spanish. Additionally, the term *Españogués* has been proposed to refer to an interlanguage variety in the context of language acquisition and learning as well as the actual modality of discourse used by Portuguese speakers when they try to speak Spanish in natural situations.

The use of *Portunhol* and *Españogués* becomes relevant in the context of the Brazilian community in Spain in the sense that these two varieties of language could be described as two extreme poles within a *continuum* (Pujadas & Turell, 1993; Turell, 1994). According to this framework of analysis, *Portunhol* would be the term used to refer to the variety of language used by Brazilian migrants in Spain when they speak Portuguese as a result of contact in natural situations and with a considerable degree of language interference both at the phonological, morphological and lexical levels (*overt* contact), and also at the syntactic and semantic ones (*covert* contact). On the other hand, *Españogués* would be the term used to refer to an interlanguage variety used by Brazilian learners of Spanish in an acquisition/learning situation, that is, when they learn and try to use Spanish, which reflects different stages of interference at the levels mentioned above, depending on their progress as learners. For our purposes in this article, we shall take these as our working definitions of these terms.

The use of *Portunhol*

Portunhol, as the variety of Portuguese influenced by Spanish that Brazilian speakers use in a situation of language contact, can be characterised on different linguistic areas: interference at phonological and morphological levels, lexical borrowing, and semantic and syntactic calquing.

Phonology

At the phonological level, the use of *Portunhol* in this contact situation involves the following patterns, among others:

(1) Monothongisation of Portuguese dipthongs: *um pouco > um poco* (Spanish: *poco;* a little).
(2) Dipthongisation of monothongs: *tempo > tiempo* (Spanish: *tiempo;* time).

(3) Lack of nasalisation of /a/ preceded by /n/: *não > nao;* (Spanish: *no*).
(4) Confusion between fricatives since Spanish has only three (/f/, /s/ and /x/) whereas Brazilian Portuguese has three voiced (/v/, /z/ and /ʒ/ and three voiceless (/f/, /s/ and /ʃ/).

Morphology

At the morphological level, three interference processes define the *Portunhol* used by Brazilian migrants living in Spain:

(1) substitution of Brazilian Portuguese articles (*o/a*) by Spanish articles (*el/la*): *a minha casa > la minha casa;* (my house); *o meu livro > el meu livro,* (my book).
(2) Substitution of the Brazilian Portuguese preposition-article contraction (*na*) by the Spanish counterpart (en *la*): *na escola > en la escola;* (at school).
(3) Substitution of Brazilian Portuguese personal pronouns by their Spanish counterparts: *ele < él,* or in the case of the preposition-article contraction: *nele > en él.*

Lexical borrowing

Interference occurs as borrowing, through the use of Spanish words which may either have a very similar cognate in Brazilian Portuguese, or be very distant words, such as, **busquei** (a Spanish verb (to look for) and Brazilian Portuguese morphology) instead of *procurei;* **flotador**, instead of *bóia* (*lifebelt*); **permissao** (Spanish noun, Portuguese morphology) instead of *licença* (*licence*), that they adapt phonologically and morphologically to Brazilian Portuguese.

Syntax

Portunhol presents a number of interesting patterns at the level of syntax, particularly in the area of calquing.[10]

(1) In terms of tenses, calquing the Spanish present subjunctive form in substitution for the Brazilian Portuguese future subjunctive, as in (6):

> (6) Quando meu irmão **estudie** será aprovado (*Portunhol*)
> Quando meu irmão *estudar* será aprovado (*Brazilian Portuguese*)
> (When my brother gets down to studying, he will pass)

(2) At the morphosyntactic level, calquing the use of Spanish auxiliary *haber*, in substitution for Brazilian Portuguese auxiliary *tener*, as in (7):

> (7) O Brazil **ha** feito muitos acordos com países vizinhos (*Portunhol*)
> O Brazil *tem* feito muitos acordos com países vizinhos (*Brazilian Portuguese*)
> (Brazil signed many agreements with neighbouring countries)

(3) Calquing of the Spanish clitic order. In *Portunhol*, speakers make use of the Spanish clitic order, that is, instead of placing the clitic, either between the main verb and the infinitive (*quero te dizer*) or between an auxiliary and the main verb (*estava me procurando*), they calque the Spanish word order, as in (8):

> (8) **Te** quero dizer (I want to tell you...)
> **Me** estava procurando (I was trying to get...)

Semantic calques

Although in the context of lexically-based grammatical models it has been argued that the dividing line between syntax and semantics is fused (Corcoll, 1999), it seems interesting to consider some examples of semantic calques, as in (9), (10) and (11):

> (9) **E já tá** (*y ya está*) instead of *E mais nada*
> (and that's all)
> (10) **Seguro que não** (*seguro que no*) instead of *Com certeza que não*
> (I'm sure it isn't or wasn't)
> (11) Não **me sai** (*no me sale*) instead of *não consigo*
> (I can't do it)

The use of *Españogués*

In the context of the acquisition and learning of Spanish by Brazilian learners some relevant developments at the phonological and intonation levels occur. Phonologically, Brazilian Portuguese phonemes which are inexistent in Spanish are commonly used precisely when the word is identical in Spanish and Portuguese, graphically and semantically, but not phonologically. At the intonation level, the most striking aspect to note is that Brazilian speakers of Spanish use Brazilina Portuguese intonation contours very often, which gives a certain impression of artificiality to the Spanish they use and may cause them insecurity, depending on the extent to which they are motivated to speak the host community language correctly.

The patterns of language contact in *Españogués* (that is, the interlanguage variety produced by Brazilian learners of Spanish in their different stages of language acquisition) also affect different linguistic levels.

Phonology

At the phonological level, interference occurs in the following areas:

(1) Dipthongisation of Spanish simple vowels: *poco* > *pouco* (*a little*)
(2) Monothongisation of Spanish dipthongs: *huevo* > *ovo* (egg)
(3) Unvoicing of Spanish consonants: *gato* > *cato*; (cat)
(4) Confusion between Spanish and Brazilian Portuguese fricatives

Morphology

At the morphological level, *Españogués* presents the same interference patterns as *Portunhol* in the opposite direction, that is, for example, Brazilian Portuguese speakers of Spanish sometimes use Brazilian Portuguese articles, pronouns and prepositions (i.e. *en la escuela* > **na** *escuela*.

Syntax

Similarly, at the syntactic level, the tendency for Brazilian users of *Españogués* will be to substitute:

(1) The form of the Spanish present used in a real condition context for the Brazilian Portuguese future subjunctive, as in (12):

(12) Si nosotros **jugarmos** (*Españogués*)
Si nosotros *jugamos* (*Spanish*)
(If we play)

(2) Spanish auxiliary *haber* for Brazilian Portuguese *tener*, as in (13):

(13) En mi casa **tiene** árboles (*Españogués*)
En mi casa *hay* árboles (*Spanish*)
(There are trees in my property...)

(3) Spanish clitic order for Portuguese clitic order, as in (14):

(14) Va **me** dando (*Españogués*)
Me va dando (*Spanish*)
(He/she is giving me...)

Learning Strategies

The learning strategies (Oxford *et al.*, 1989) used by Brazilian migrants who are attending Spanish classes and those used by Brazilian migrants who are mere users of Spanish without having received any formal instruction in it are very similar. On the one hand, Brazilian migrants show learning strategies based on the migrant's mother tongue (L1). As with *Españogués*, these strategies include the use of Brazilian-Portuguese syntactic and semantic variables (Bialystok, 1990; Dijk & Kintsch, 1983). Sometimes, these learners of Spanish resort to anglicisms as an interlanguage between Spanish and Portuguese. On the other hand, they adopt acquisition and communication strategies which draw upon the resources of the interlocutor's language, in this case Spanish.[11] These include generalisations, periphrasis, coinage of new words, and reformulation. More specifically, (1) they use Brazilian Portuguese words phonetically adapted to Spanish (i.e. *beijitos* from *beijinhos* (Brazilian Portuguese) instead of *besitos* (kisses) in Spanish); (2) they adopt expression literally translated from Brazilian Portuguese (i.e. *En hipótesis alguna haré el trabajo* from *Em hipótese alguna farei o trabalho* (Brazilian Portuguese) instead of *No pienso hacer el trabajo bajo ningún concepto* (I'm not going to do this job by any means); (3) they borrow verbs from Brazilian Portuguese and adapt them to Spanish morphology (i.e. *El coche se estragó* (from the verb 'estragar') instead of *El coche se estropeó* (the car broke down)). Finally, both Brazilian migrants in general and Brazilian formal learners of Spanish make use of non-linguistic strategies, such as facial and body gesture, tone of voice, vocalisation, not only as universal strategies but also as a trademark of the Brazilian speaker's personality and linguistic behaviour.

Nonetheless it is important to note that Brazilian formal learners of Spanish (or Catalan, Basque and Galician) make less use of language contact phenomena than Brazilians who are mere users of Spanish without having had formal instruction, and so they keep Portuguese and Spanish separate to a greater extent, since they are conscious of the linguistic system and structure of the host community's language that they are learning.

Conclusion

The prospects for and nature of Brazilian migration into Spain have to be considered within the general Brazilian migratory trend, which seems to be of continuous external migration and of a geographical model of settlement similar to other migrant communities which settle in large cities. The basic and most fundamental reason for Brazilian migration is economic and, in particular, it is linked to the Brazilian middle classes' need to seek better economic prospects in view of their constant unstability in their Brazilian jobs. Brazilian immigrants to Spain tend to integrate, if they stay for long, but in general there is constant instability. The social profile of Brazilian migrants is young and single, in general, but they also come with their Brazilian family, or establish a mixed family in Spain.

As to the Brazilian migrants' geographical origin, there are three areas in Brazil in which migration has traditionally been favoured: the Northeast, the Southeast and the South. Their settlement pattern, family grouping and their work is structured on an age and sex basis. Moreover, the migrants' social and educational level varies according to the family's economical situation and the parents' educational level that would have affected their educational and professional future. Finally, the Brazilian community in Spain presents a relatively rich level of social organisation as is shown by the existence of a number of associations and societies, particularly in big cities,[12] which give the Brazilian migrants into Spain social, professional and personal support.

As to language use, the overall communication pattern among adults and between parents and children is a high use of their own language, that is, Brazilian-Portuguese. However, language choice in the family adopts different forms. Furthermore, even if Brazilian migrants are not very motivated to study Spanish in a formal instruction context, their use of the host community's language(s) is extended. As a result of social and, therefore, linguistic contact, Brazilian migrants make use of two mixed varieties of language: *Portunhol*, that is, Brazilian-Portuguese influenced by Spanish, and *Españogués*, that is, Spanish influenced by Brazilian-Portuguese. However, these specific language use practices seem to be more attributable to language proximity between Brazilian-Portuguese and Spanish than to incomplete competence and knowledge of Spanish.

Notes

1. In order to draw a general profile of the Brazilian immigrant in Spain, a pilot study was conducted by interviewing 20 Brazilian people living in Catalonia and particularly Barcelona (see Appendix 1: Catalogue of Informants). Barcelona was chosen since it can be taken as a prototypical city of the sort that Brazilian migrants seem to prefer. The method that was used to interview them was the life story, very similar to the socio-linguistic interview, which lasted between 45 and 60 minutes and dealt with various topics: demographic information, linguistic competence, family, social networks, work, friendship, hobbies and interests, and finally neighbourhood life. All interviews follow the same pattern and were all conducted in Brazilian-Portuguese. This information was then used to compare the data collected in the pilot study and official data, with the purpose, as has been said, of drawing a more general profile type of the Spanish-based Brazilian immigrant. We would like to thank Catia Tavares for her excellent work in transcribing the informants' life stories and doing some preliminary interview analysis.
2. In this state, African roots are very striking at the level of culture, customs, folklore, etc. because of their inhabitants' African extraction.
3. Whose inhabitants are mostly of European origin, particularly Italian and German.
4. Which does not exclude their liking for Northern European countries, as Table 10.1 illustrates, or even the US, probably the most natural destination for reasons of work and relative geographical proximity.
5. Whose exact nature will be considered in the section headed 'Domains of Language Use'.
6. A *capoeirista* is a dancer who simulates an Afro-Brazilian fight, the capoeiria, which was performed as a dance by 17th and 18th century slaves in Brazil so that slave-owners would not notice that the slaves were getting ready to fight them.
7. But very different in nature and history, since the Residencia de Estudiantes was created during the Second Republic (1931–36) and with time turned into a kind of stronghold and avant-garde resort for art, literature, history, science, etc., during the Civil War and during Franco's Dictatorship.
8. It should be mentioned that Brazilian-Portuguese is not 'naturally' intelligible to Spanish, Catalan and Basque speakers.
9. In Amazonia, for example, 718 indigenous languages became extinct before they could even be studied. In the whole of the Brazilian territory, languages from 40 different branches divided into 94 linguistic families have been identified. With the discovery of the New World by Columbus and other Spanish 'descubridores' (discoverers), a slow process of erosion and homogenisation of indigenous cultures and languages was initiated. Between 1616 and 1757, the religious missions favoured the grouping of different tribes into bigger communities. Nheengatu, the simplified version of Tupi, spoken in Amazonia, was being taught in those times. In 1757, the expansion of Portuguese began and nowadays a considerable part of the great Precolombian linguistic diversity has been lost for ever (See *Escola, A revista do ensino fundamental*, 1999).
10. Following Corcoll (1999), 'a syntactic calque is the syntactic manifestation of the extension, reduction, addition or suppression of one or several (semantic) features included within a particular lexical entry' which occurs in a sociolinguistically marked situation and

is always motivated by a lexical entry. Another given condition for the calque to occur is that its result may not violate the grammar of the host language, in this case, Brazilian-Portuguese.

11. And of any of the other languages spoken in other Autonomous Communities (Catatonia, Galicia and the Basque Country), in the case of those few migrants who settle there.

12. The fact that the Brazilian migrants' most usual settlement pattern is urban (Western big cities) means that the choice of Barcelona, as the site to undertake the pilot study, is consistent with the authors' preliminary observation.

Appendix 1: Catalogue of Informants

Name	Age	Place of birth	Profession
Ionara Dalcol	27	Rio Grande do Sul	Chemist
Aluisio	30	Rio de Janeiro	Portuguese teacher
Júlio Cézar	34	Rio de Janeiro	Hotel/catering manager
Patrícia Schweler	25	Rio de Janeiro	Actress
Valdemar	32	São Paulo	Machinist
Laércio Raimundo	36	São Paulo	Capoeirista
Dirceu Tavares	36	Recife, Pernambuco	University teacher
Beda	35	Recife, Pernambuco	Engineer
Maria Lúcia	36	Santa Catarina	Nurse
Maria Helena	30	Paraná	Language teacher
Manuel Castro	33	Rio de Janeiro	Chemist
Leda María	29	Rio de Janeiro	Maid
Lu	35	São Paulo	Architect
Rosângela Franco	35	São Paulo	Psychologist
Deise Carrero	51	São Paulo	Catalan teacher
Silvia Mello	42	Rio Grande do Sul	Portuguese teacher
Maria da Glória	50	Mato Grosso	Cleaning lady
Armelinda	(50)	Rio de Janeiro	English teacher
Hilda	40	Pernambuco	Maid
Cintia Tavares	22	São Paulo	Administrative

References

Anuario de Extranjería (1996) Ministerio de Trabajo y Asuntos Sociales. Madrid.
Bialystok, E. (1990) *Communication Strategies. A Psychological Analysis of Second Language Use.* Oxford: Blackwell.
Brasil. Aspectos Generales (1995) Consulado Geral do Brasil em Barcelona.
Colin Rodea, M. (1990) *Você não é brasileiro? Um estudo dos planos pragmáticos na relação Português/Espanhol.* Dissertation. Unicamp.

Corcoll, C. (1999) A reassessment of the notion of syntactic calque: Grammatical and socio-linguistic evidence. Research work presented within the PhD Programme on Applied Linguistics, Institut Universitari de Lingüística Aplicada. Universitat Pompeu Fabra. Barcelona.

Dijk, V. and Kintsch, W. (1983) The notion of strategy in language and discourse understanding. In *Strategies of Discourse Comprehension* (pp. 61–98). London: Academic Press.

Escola. A revista do ensino fundamental, XIV, No. 121. O índio redescoberto. April 1999.

Ferreira, I.A. (1994) A interlíngua do falante de Espanhol e o papel do professor: aceitação tácita ou ajuda para superá-la? 39–47.

Fontana, J.M. and Vallduví, E. (1990) Mecanismos léxicos y gramaticales en la alternancia de códigos. In M.T. Turell, Nuevas Corrientes Lingüísticas. Aplicación a la descripción del Inglés. *Revista Española de Lingüística Aplicada, Anejo I*, 171–92.

Instituto Nacional de Estadística (1996) *Anuario Estadístico 1996*. Madrid.

Ministerio de Trabajo y Asuntos Sociales. *Anuario de Migraciones 1996 and 1997*. Madrid.

Lavratti, N.T. (1995) *Proyecto de Tesis Doctoral. El Contacto de Lenguas: La Comunidad Brasileña en Barcelona*. Barcelona: Universitat de Barcelona.

Ministerios de Asuntos Sociales (1995) *Boletín Estadístico de Datos Básicos*. Madrid:, 2nd term, No. 20.

Oxford, R.L., Lavine, R.Z. and Crookall, D. (1989) Language learning strategies, the communicative approach, and their classroom implications. *Annals Foreign Language*, Vol. 22, No. 1.

Pujadas, J.J. and Turell, M.T. (1993) Els indicadors sociolingüísticas del contacte inter-ètnic. *Actes del IXè Col.loqui Internacional de Llengua i Literatura Catalanes*, Alacant (1991), 301–18.

Ramírez Goicoechea, E. (1996) *Inmigrantes en España: Vidas y Experiencias*. Madrid: Centro de Investigaciones Sociológicas, 147.

Romero Gimenez, C. (coord) (1993) *Inmigrantes Extranjeros en Madrid*. Madrid: Serie Informes Técnicos, Tomo I.

Turell, M.T. (1994) Code-switching as communicative design. *Actas del XVI Congreso de AEDEAN*, Valladolid (1992), 59–78.

Chapter 11

The Cape Verdean Community

LORENZO LÓPEZ TRIGAL

Nature and Distribution of the Cape Verdean Community in Spain

For the last 20 years there have been a significant number of Portuguese speakers in Spain other than the Portuguese themselves. These include the Portuguese speakers from the Americas, in the case of the Brazilians, or from various ex-colonies in Africa, especially Angola and Cabo Verde. People from very different areas geographically are grouped together linguistically as a result of Portugal's maritime expansion, and the emigration that took people from that country to such far-flung areas – a result, too, of the forced moving of populations to islands that until then had been unpopulated, such as the Cabo Verde or São Tomé and Príncipe. Portuguese has thus become the official language of Brazil and of five African states even though some of these co-exist with indigenous African (Niger Congo) languages or with mixed languages (Portuguese Creole) in a more or less bilingual situation, depending on the country and on their recent situation, after gaining independence.

The African Portuguese speakers who in varying numbers, depending on the nationality, have migrated to Spain over recent years fall within this cultural, ethnic and geographical context. Estimates of the numbers from various sources indicate that there are hundreds of people from Mozambique, Guinea Bissau and São Tomé, some three thousand Angolans; some of these are political refugees as are some of those from the other countries mentioned, as well as some 7000 from the Cabo Verde islands. Official data (Ministerio de Trabajo y Asuntos Sociales) estimate that in 1996 there were 2166 Cape Verdean residents (See *Anuario de Migraciones 1997*). Altogether, then, there could be around 11,000 Africans from Portuguese-speaking countries now living in Spain. This is not a large number compared with the total number of around a half million immigrants currently settled in the country. But they are distinctive in that they typically came to Spain quite recently, after their countries gained independence, and have generally followed a migratory pattern that took them first to Portugal, above all Lisbon and its metropolitan area. The latter is the distribution point from which they moved to various Spanish localities. This dispersal brought the Cape Verdeans to a variety of

271

different areas in mainland Spain, including Madrid, Barcelona, mining areas of León, fishing ports in Galicia, while the other Portuguese-speaking Africans have gone very largely to Madrid.

All of Spain to a lesser or greater degree, depending on the region, has become an extension of the Portuguese-speaking Brazilian and African migration to Portugal and its bridgehead to Europe. It would seem that in the future much of this migration will necessarily settle permanently in Spain – despite the current situation that makes it easier for refugees who wish to return home to actually do so. These people will then swell the numbers of economic immigrants from Africa, Latin American and Portuguese extraction of the type most usual in Spain. Cape Verdeans in particular represent some of the longest-established immigrants with a greater proportion who have reunited their families in the new country. They are more settled, and their knowledge of Portuguese brings them closer to their Spanish neighbours.

Note that these immigrant communities are both 'African and Portuguese-speaking', that is, they have the Portuguese language to some extent as an intercultural factor, as a means of communicating nationally. There are also cultural ties with metropolitan Portugal as the colonising country and form part of the international family of 'falantes de portugês' (Portuguese speakers). And there are other factors, too, in common, such as the migratory chain we have already described that passes through Lisbon, as well as the discrimination encountered in Spain as in other parts of Europe because of the colour of their skin, as well as the experience of maintaining links with the family back home particularly through the regular sending of their savings. Lastly, there is the common experience of setting up cultural associations, and the defence of their interests (if not the lingering hope in the background of returning home one day) and not losing their cultural and national identity.

The various African countries where Portuguese is spoken as an official language are known in Portugal as PALOP countries, although in the opinion of the Mozambican writer Mia Couto, rather than being 'Lusophone' (Portuguese speaking), Mozambique is actually 'Luso-aphonic' (Portuguese nonspeaking) – a false unity in other words that is Portuguese speaking by decree. Yet Cape Verdeans are a particular case that deserves special study for several reasons, above all because they constitute the largest group of African Portuguese speakers in Spain, and are the third-largest community of African origin after the Moroccans and Senegalese.

A Brief History of Cape Verdean Emigration

Emigration is a fundamental issue for Cabo Verde: over the course of the 20th century emigration has formed a vital part of the economy of the country, to the extent that in recent years the money sent home by Cape Verdeans abroad makes up 15% of the national income. In fact there are more Cape Verdeans abroad than remaining in their country of origin (420,000 as opposed to 375,000 according to the 1990 census). Emigration, 'which the Cape Verdeans were the first to make an effective weapon against the colonisers (Margarido, 1994), is the result both of the economic crisis that every Cape Verdean family has to confront as a result of years of relentless drought and the effect on agriculture, and the demand for unskilled labour in most of the countries that Cape Verdean immigration has gone to: the United States (with 250,000, representing slightly more than half the emigration total to date), Portugal (with 70,000, mostly living in the greater Lisbon area), the Netherlands, Italy, France, Luxembourg, Spain and Switzerland, as well as to developing countries such as Angola, Senegal (Dakar), Sâo Tomé and Brazil. On this point it is worth looking at what Lesourd (1994) has to say about the strong sense of insularity in this state. He writes that 'distributed around the Atlantic, the migrants carry their insularity with them, an insularity that distance can activate. In their new islands of Cape Verdeanness surrounded by foreign country, they generate new features of insularity, fed by economic or cultural influences from the outside world.' It does indeed seem from a geographical point of view that they have settled within the ambit of the Atlantic and that they have made the Atlantic their home. It is from this ocean that they obtain their best raw material, fish – just as the movement of people and goods increasingly uses the islands as a bridge between Europe and Africa, on the one hand, and Brazil and the rest of Latin America, on the other. This they have in common with the Spanish Canary Islands and the Portuguese Azores and Madeira, which together form a great complementary chain of archipelagos with the network of Atlantic relations. The way in which the Cape Verdean region works, according to Lesourd (1994) with its central islands, outer islands, foreign 'islands' in the Atlantic Diaspora, itself highlights the strong and problematic insularity of this state.

Origin, Culture and Language Use Patterns

The population itself is diversified, in that 71% are mulattos (part Black African), 28% are Black African, and Europeans make up the other 1%. This is due to the fact that Cabo Verde has essentially been a convergence point for West Africans and Europeans (Portuguese), each side bringing with it its language and culture. Thus, two languages co-exist here, as a result of the country's history in which peoples mingled: these are Portuguese and *Kriolu* (Creole, *crioulo* in Portuguese). The latter is a mixed language (or, in the view of some Portuguese, a dialect of Portuguese, or Portuguese 'mal falado') transmitted by unlettered natives from West

Africa, and is defined as a Portuguese Creole both in Cabo Verde and São Tomé.

This *Kriolu* can be described taking into consideration different aspects which are relevant in Pidgin and Creole studies, such as, the Creole's substrate, the settlement patterns, the Creole's linguistic characterisation and the sociolinguistic context, in terms of speakers' distribution and future perspectives.[1]

As to its substrate, it is important to mention that 'the Cape Verdean Islands were populated by slaves from Guinea-Bissau speaking West Atlantic and Mande languages, whereas the Gulf of Guinea Islands were populated with slaves' speaking Kwa and Bantu languages. Since both groups of languages belong to the Niger-Congo family, the two groups of Portuguese Creoles (the Cape Verdean *Kriolu* and the Gulf of Guinea Creoles) exhibit 'certain basic structural similarities' but also 'significant structural differences' (Holm, 1989: 272).

The specific linguistic characterisation of this Portuguese 'kriolu', which is viewed by some authors as 'a continuum of varieties (Meintel, 1975: 236, cited by Holm, 1989: 274) with a general movement towards decreolisation', is also variably constrained by the specific nature of the settlement, the time when and the specific island on which the settlement took place. The Cape Verdean Islands are usually classified into two groups: the *Barlavento* (Santo Antão, São Vicente, Santa Luiza, São Nicolau, Boa Vista, and Sal) and the *Sotavento* (São Tiago, Fogo, Maio, and Brava). 'Brava and the Barlavento islands remained uninhabited until the late 17th and 18th centuries' (Holm, 1989: 273), then 'the settlement from Portugal led to a more mixed population' and subsequently the varieties of *kriolu* spoken in those islands exhibit more European features. However, in São Tiago and the other Sotavento islands the settlements occurred before and involved a higher proportion of Africans and therefore the *kriolu* shows more African features similar to the Creole of Guinea-Bissau. (Holm, 1989: 273–4).

Sociolinguistically speaking, this *kriolu* is now a fully developed means of communication, and a universally understood mother tongue, even though educated speakers will use Portuguese as much as Creole, despite the fact that the former is their second language. According to Lane (1986, cited by Holm, 1989: 274), though, 'the rate of literacy in Portuguese is 37%'. It is also important to mention that 'a sociolinguistic survey in 1972 indicated that most Cape Verdeans thought that Portuguese had gained ground over Creole during their lifetime' (Valkhoff, 1975: 53, cited by Holm, 1989: 274), but that 'after independence in 1975 (...) the domains of spoken Portuguese receded in favour of the *Kriolu*, a symbol of nationalism' (Cuhna, 1981: 77).

At all events, the first generation of Cape Verdean immigrants who arrived in Spain with no education or elementary education only, use Creole almost exclusively when at home or talking among themselves. Here, too, the insularity mentioned above can be seen in the varieties of

Creole used, since each island's Creole shows certain differences from the others, 'a lingua de cada um' ('...'). The more windward and northerly islands show greater European influence and mulattos are clearly in the majority. The leeward and southerly islands, on the other hand, show greater Black African influence. This, then, is a sociolinguistically complex, multicultural situation, as a result of these factors and of the factors of education and family or work setting.

Related to this language situation is the well-known Cape Verdean music, formerly associated with the Guinean slaves and known as 'Morna', which singers such as Cesaria Évora have popularised. An example of this Creole, then, would be the poem sung by her: 'Sodade'.[2] In this poem-song the singer tells of the way she sees the return-trip distance for an emigrant who may never return:

> Quem mostra' bo/Ess caminho longe?/
> Ess caminho /Pa Sâo Tomé/Sodade sodade/
> Sodade/Dess nha terra Sâo Nicolau/
> Si bô 'screvê'me/'M ta 'screvê'me/
> Si bô 'screvê'me/M ta 'screvê'me
> Ate' dia/Qui bô voltá

(Who was indicating you this long way/this way to Sâo Tomé/you're longing, longing, longing from the land of Sâo Nicolau/if you write to me, I'll write back/if you write to me, I'll write back, until the day you come back).[3]

What we have here is a microcosm within a micro-state of some $4000\,\text{km}^2$ set in the Atlantic ocean opposite the coastlines of Senegal and Mauritania, and just as arid. Hence, rather than agriculture and fishing, the islands' income is based more on foreign aid from United Nations and a small number of countries, on money sent home by emigrants, and tourism. The latter, incidentally, is in its infancy but increasing — it suffers from a lack of infrastructure, but its future is promising. This is a state which

> bases its legitimacy on its inhabitants' awareness that they belong to a part of the Portuguese African world, an awareness of a cultural identity based on linguistic unity (Portuguese creole) as well as a dramatic past (slavery, hunger, economic neglect, emigration under duress or economic pressure, struggle for freedom) which has contributed to this awareness, and which in turn has its cultural base (poetry, music, traditional crafts, religion, and *mestizaje*, or creole blending of cultures). All this is in sharp contrast to what we find in neighbouring African countries on the mainland. (Lesourd, 1994)

Within this national consciousness there is considerable local inter-island rivalry in terms of economics and culture, and the migrants take this with them when they form communities abroad.

Cape Verdean Migration Patterns

The migration from the Cabo Verde islands began as much as a century ago, 'after [Cape Verdeans] realised they would get nothing out of the Portuguese colonists' (Margarido, 1994). At first, migration was from the smaller uncultivated islands and the ultimate destination was the North Eastern United States. Today there are more Cape Verdeans in that region than anywhere else in the Diaspora. As a consequence, a new language variety arose known as New Bedford creole, as the Cape Verdean creole took on English vocabulary. This early period served as an apprenticeship for later migration, from the 1970s onwards going to Dakar or Lisbon, and then after independence at an increased rate going into Europe via Lisbon. Over this period the three values that characterised the Cape Verdeans who settled in the United States were to be reaffirmed: readiness to work for an employer, earning money – they were not much interested in other activities – and saving. Savings were then sent as 'tokens of love' to those who remained in the islands, mainly women, children and old people.

On the other hand, affirmation of the national and cultural identity was done through the retention of a number of typical features that included speaking Cape Verdean creole and cooking traditional dishes, reminiscing about the islands in one's conversations at home (where other customs might be retained such as the pounding of meal on certain occasions). And in their clubs and cultural associations, from the 1980s onwards in Burela (on the Galician coast) or Bembibre and Villaseca de Laciana (León Province, northern Spain), Cape Verdeans would be listening to their own distinctive music, holding dances, forming football teams, and getting news from home, if not actually travelling back to Cabo Verde at intervals of around five years in many instances. These gregarious activities are typical of immigrant Cape Verdean communities, since the associations and their premises represent a small, cherished piece of home.

As regards the particular ties formed during the process of this immigration, what we find is that island loyalties are constantly present, each Cape Verdean community tends to be from a particular island in the archipelago, and the money sent back goes there. Thus, Cape Verdean ex-patriots in the United States send their savings to the southerly or leeward islands (Fogo, Sâo Tiago and Brava); those in Portugal send them to Sâo Tiago, Sal, Sâo Nicolau and Sâo Vicente, and so on (Lesourd, 1994). Cape Verdeans in Spain generally come from Sâo Nicolau and Santo Antâo and send money to those islands.

The process of settlement in Spain has been under way since 1975. At first, during the early years of the process, Cape Verdeans came via Lisbon. Later they came directly to Spain, encouraged by those relatives already settled there, or to a lesser extent in other European countries including the Netherlands and Italy, and areas that had been reached by an earlier wave of migration. Reasons for not coming directly from Cabo

Verde include the visa requirement. Since Cape Verdeans do not have diplomatic representation in Spain they need to come via another country, such as Portugal. Cape Verdeans receive hardly any institutional help either from their own country or from the Spanish State, but they do receive assistance from the relevant Spanish local authorities.

There is a clear tendency for these migrants to cluster settlement in particular cities. This is especially clear in the case of women opting for Madrid to be employed in domestic service, and men choosing to go to ports like Vigo or Burela (Galician coast) or to the Western León coalfield (municipal areas of Bembibre, Villablino and Torre del Bierzo). Over the ensuing 20 years since the immigrants began to arrive, a double pattern has emerged: on the one hand, there are new immigrants entering the country (as well as families reuniting often despite the economic difficulties involved) via informal or spontaneously arising networks of friends and relatives who came before them. On the other, there are the community-internal networks formed by marriages of couples who met in the immigrant communities. As a result, we find miners of Cape Verdean origin in León living with Cape Verdean maids or domestic helps who were pre-viously working in Madrid. Marriage with a Spanish or Portuguese person is not usual. Consequently, the Cape Verdean community often moves from the original settlement area, where they were young and separated according to sex, depending on employment. Typically, as we have already suggested, men would be employed in fishing-mining-building and women in domestic service and catering.

The number of Cape Verdean workers officially registered in Spain in 1991 was 1174, with rather more women than men (58.6%) and dis-tributed in the primary sector (6.2%) secondary sector (30.7%) and above all in the tertiary sector (62.4%) according to figures from the Ministerio de Trabajo (Ministry of Employment (1993)).

Turning to the demographic structure, this was analysed in detail for the León coalfield in López Trigal (1991) and López Trigal and Prieto Sarro (1993a, 1993b) and this data can be extrapolated, to some extent, to the rest of the community. The ratio of males to females was found to be slightly skewed, with rather more women (55%) except in certain mining areas in León and fishing localities in Galicia previously mentioned. This is also a very youthful population. Basing estimates on the 1991 census and consular registers (Portugal assumes responsibility for Cape Verdean representation in Spain, through the embassy in Madrid and a number of consulates) it can be observed that the great majority of the population was born after 1950, more exactly in the decade from 1951 to 1960 in the case of the adults (all born in Cabo Verde) and even more markedly in the period from 1977 to 1990 in the case of the second generation, born mainly in Spain but with also a notable proportion from Portugal. Families consist on average of 5.2 members, somewhat larger than the mean among Portuguese immigrants (4.8) and the Spanish families in the mining areas (4.4). It is important to note that the falling birth-rate phenomenon has also affected the number of births in the last five-year period analysed, from 1986 to 1991, so that Cape Verdean families appear to be increasingly similar to the Spanish host community families around them in this respect.

It can be seen from the study of the Cape Verdeans in León, and from other studies of the community in Madrid, that levels of education are extremely low. Part of the population, especially the women, are illiterate or have had no formal education, while a proportion of the adults and young people have primary education, and in some cases secondary education when they have been born in Spain. In fact, there has recently been a reinforcement of Portuguese culture in this community thanks to the widespread application of the *Programa Hispano-Luso para la Acción Educativa y Cultural* (Hispano-Portuguese programme of Action for Education and Culture). This was set up jointly by the Spanish and Portuguese governments in 1988 and is aimed in the first place at Portuguese people resident in Spain. This is available in principle in state primary schools in areas of Portuguese settlement, and often also involves Cape Verdean and Spanish pupils.

The Difficult Process of Integration

The degree of integration (in social, economic and cultural terms) achieved by Cape Verdean immigrants into the host community will, judging from surveys carried out, depend on the locality where they live (urban or coal-mining area) the number of years they have been in the country, the occupation or job situation. It can be seen firstly that there is greater integration in mining areas as opposed to cities like Madrid, and secondly that integration is enhanced where both spouses are employed or have been in Spain for a relatively long time. At all events, the fact that they will know Portuguese to a greater or lesser extent, and that this makes it easier for them to understand Spanish and communicate with the host community, is undoubtedly a factor in favour of Cape Verdeans and Portuguese-speaking Africans as compared to other immigrants. This helps integration at school as well as in the street or in the workplace.

The community does show a degree of stability in immigration, based on the children and their progress in school, in employment after becoming skilled or experienced workers in the mining industry and other occupation – leading in turn to monthly earnings that range from the stipulated minimum wage in domestic work or building (60,000 to 80,000 pts) to the wages of skilled workers in the fisheries and mining (200,000 to 300,000 pts).This provides a stable living to a lesser or greater extent, and enabling money to be put by and then sent to the family in the Cabo Verde, and perhaps to fulfil the 'émigrés' dream of returning one day to live decently in their own country.

Until that time comes, integration will involve a series of variables such as access to work and a stable and consolidated occupation, the school success (or failure) of the children, the quality of housing and whether this is owned or rented property, and the amenities. Also relevant is the degree of unionisation of the occupation and relationships at work and in the wider community. On these measures Cape Verdeans have a number of aspects in their favour in the Spanish society: they have some access to the language via Portuguese, as well as their work ethic and their wish to integrate. On the other hand, they are dark-skinned mulattos and for that reason they run up against difficulties in a society that was not multiracial until now, with all the attendant negative reactions from the indigenous Spanish: 'at work they're all equal and the "blackies" [Cape Verdeans] are generally the best coal-face workers, but I don't want to live next to Blacks and Portuguese, and I wouldn't want my daughter to marry a blackman,' comments a mining engineer to a journalist (Fuentes, 1989). In fact, the opinion of the miners themselves would not coincide and could even be diametrically opposed to the views expressed by this manager.

Some Biographic Data

Some *life stories* recounted by Cape Verdeans better describe this situation: António, born in Nossa Senhora do Rosário in 1945, primary school education, lives in the village of El Escobio in León, a truly multiethnic immigrant community, where a third of the population are Cape Verdeans, a third are immigrants from elsewhere in Spain and a third are Portuguese). He is employed at the pit face and there are 11 in the family, with four older children born between 1969 and 1975 in Cabo Verde and five more born in the hospital in Ponferrada in León. 'Yes, I've felt rejected because of my colour. There is racism, that's here to stay, even though we're only off sick when we need to be, not like the Spaniards, even though when we're down the pit we're all exploited the same, even though we belong to *Comisiones Obreras*.[4] I can assure you that a black immigrant's life is very hard ... But, in spite of everything, I'd like my children to choose Spanish nationality.' Fuentes (1989). This is an example of full integration, and the speaker will, finally, choose to remain in Spain.

Another case study is provided by someone who also lives in El Escobio, and who is also called António. Born in Sâo Nicolau in 1955, he is married to a Spanish woman who was born in the same mining village (who already had a child born in Barcelona). Both had elementary education. They have four children from their union who were born in Ponferrada between 1981 and 1989. He says: 'down the pit, we're almost a cut above the Spaniards. The only thing keeping me here is the money. I'm dying to go back and eat lobsters and enjoy the beaches where you can swim in warm water' (Fuentes, 1989). But Cabo Verde seems like a distant paradise, and it will be the Spanish-born family that finally decide to stay for good like the above-mentioned family — since he, António, is the only member of the family to be born in Africa.

João Teófilo, resident in Caboalles, a town in Villablino, is 44 years old and was one of the first to come to the district in 1975 on the advice of a friend; he lives with his wife and several children, and works for a regular wage in the building industry, earning around 100,000 pesetas a month. In his rented flat he has some facilities including an automatic washing machine, but he does not have a car or a telephone, because of his limited earnings. His economic situation, as he describes it, is not satisfactory. On the other hand he is quite satisfied with his social situation in terms of integration, and relations at work, home and school. He is not thinking of staying indefinitely and he dreams a lot about going back to his country and his home village when he retires.

Miguel, aged 44, suffers from *saudade* (longing) for São Nicolau. He left the island in 1975 where he was a teacher and has gone back on two occasions. He emigrated first to Portugal and then left for Italy and Holland after a few days. However he did not succeed in getting a job. Then, he received a letter from a cousin who was working in the mines in Villablino, urging him to move there and settle down in the little Leonese town. That was 20 years ago. Now he is not sure whether to go back to Lisbon where two of his brothers live, or to stay in Villablino where he has his own house and is well integrated.

At the same time the story of two women could be indicative as regards concern for one's children and the mining industry: Idalina was born in Cabo Verde in 1955, never went to school, married to Aristide and they have three children, who were born in Ponferrada between 1979 and 1986. In her little flat in El Escobio she cares that her children do not go hungry, especially when there are strikes as there were quite frequently in the past. Constantly hanging over their head is the threat of pit-closures. Lastly, there is the story of Filamena, resident in Villaseca (León) since 1981 and born in Cabo Verde in 1956. 'I still don't feel I belong here' she admits, 'but I don't feel I belong there either, so in the end we don't fit in [anywhere]'. This is the fate of the 'the children who stayed in Cabo Verde, and then came later with their parents, with the language only half there, to fit in with a different world.' 'Now our future is in the balance because of the problems with the big mining company', the *Minero Siderúrgica de Ponferrada*, generally known as the MSP, where around 100 Cape Verdeans are employed.

These comments and personal assessments are a reflection of the different types of family and people in the Cape Verdean community settled in Spain, specifically those living in the mining villages of León. In the end, a large number of these immigrants will return to their Atlantic islands, but others are putting down roots for good among their Spanish neighbours (in some instances, as in León, among Portuguese neighbours also). In this way the fabric of Spanish society will take on new multiracial, ethnic and cultural features, as to a greater or lesser extent has done our European society.

Notes

1. For a more detailed analysis of this Cape Verdean 'Kriolu', see Holm, 1989.
2. *Saudade*, the Portuguese word so widely known and so difficult to translate, meaning approximately *longing*.
3. Many thanks are due to Neiva Lavratti and Glaucemira Maxinino, teachers of Brazilian-Portuguese at the *Centro de Estudos Brasileiros* in Barcelona, who provided the Spanish translation of this song so that it could then be translated into English.
4. One of the two largest Spanish trade unions.

References

Aranda-Vasserot, C. (1994) Inmigrantes caboverdianos en El Bierzo. *Polígonos* 4, 99–105.

Cunha, C. (1981) *Lingua, Nação, Alimentação*. Rio de Janeiro: Editora Nova Fronteira.

Diehl, J-P., Dessalieu, C. and Lesourd, M. (1989) *Emigration et Transferts des Capverdiens Emigrés*. Paris: SEDES.

Fuentes, J. (1989) El oscuro destino de ser minero y negro en León. *Cambio 16*, 10 Julio, 67–9.

Holm, J. (1989) *Pidgins and Creoles*. Cambridge: Cambridge University Press.

Lane, H.U. (1986) *The World Almanack and Book of Facts*. New York: Doubleday.

Lesourd, M. (1994) Le problème du contrôle territorial dans les petits espaces: L'exemple de la République du Cap Vert, Micro-État insulaire. En H. Thery (dir.) *L'Etat et les Stratégies du Territoire*. Paris: CNRS.

Lesourd, M. (1994) Insularismes et développement en République du Cap-Vert. *Lusotopie*, 1, 113–33.

Lopes da Silva, B. (1984) *O Dialecto Crioulo de Cabo Verde*. Lisboa: Imprensa Nacional.

López Trigal, L. (1991) *La Inmigración Extranjera en León*. León: Universidad de León.

López Trigal, L. and Prieto Sarro, I. (1993a) Portugueses y caboverdianos en España. *Estudios Geográficos* 210, 75–96.

López Trigal, L. and Prieto Sarro, I. (1993b) Caracterización de la inmigración portuguesa y caboverdiana en la provincia de León. *IV Jornadas de la Población Española*. La Laguna: Universidad de La Laguna, 611–17.

Mallart, L. (1986) *Cap Verd*. Barcelona: Oikos-Tau.

Margarido, A. (1994) Pour une histoire des géopolitiques culturelles des îles du Cap-Vert. *Lusotopie* 1, 103–12.

Medeiros, C. (1994) *Difusão Geográfica da Lingua Portuguesa*. Lisboa: Instituto Camões.

Meintel, D. (1975) The criole dialect of the island of Brava. In M.F. Valkhoff (ed.) *Miscelânea Luso-Africana: Colectânea de Estudos Coligidos*. Lisboa: Junta de Investigações Científicas de Ultramar.

Ministerio de Trabajo y Asuntos Sociales. *Anuario de Migraciones 1997*. Madrid.

Rodrigues, W. (1989) Comunidade caboverdiana: marginalização e identidade. *Sociedades e Território* 8, 96–103.

Valkhoff, M.F. (1975) *Miscelânea Luso-Africana: Colectânea de Estudos Coligidos*. Lisboa: Junta de Investigações Científicas de Ultramar.

Chapter 12

The Chinese Community

JOAQUÍN BELTRÁN and CRESCEN GARCÍA

Diversity of Origins

The Chinese ethnic community in Spain is not homogeneous. It is made up of numerous sections or sub-communities, each one of which has its own history, dynamics and structure. If they have anything in common, it is the feeling of being 'Chinese' in a foreign country. The Chinese have a long history of presence in Spanish territories. They were there in the Philippines when it was colonised by Spain, and during the 19th century they were taken to Perú and Cuba to work in the mines and plantations. In the Spanish Peninsula, some Chinese sailors and traders appeared at the beginning of this century but did not settle. The earliest news of resident Chinese dates from the 1920s and 1930s, when Chinese peddlers roamed the length and breadth of Europe, selling small articles, such as ties, stockings, cheap jewellery, soap, etc. Reports from this period describe them in the following way, highlighting certain pronunciation difficulties which became a stereotype:

> ... they will sell you 'collales a peseta' (cheap 'collares' (necklaces)) in any street in any town of our country. (Tato, 1939: 22)

> ... muttering out loud: 'Colbatas, collales' ('corbatas' (ties), 'collares' (necklaces)). So the image of the Chinese became fixed in my memory, as itinerant peddlers with a poverty-stricken look about them, who could also not pronounce the letter *r*. (Llorca, 1980: 10)

In Madrid in the 1950s, two Chinese circuses were set up (Wang, 1991). Most of the peddlers and acrobats were peasants from the south of the Zhejiang Province, and were the origin of the largest Chinese sub-community in Spain, which makes up 70% of the total. During the Civil War, a Chinese battalion made up of students who were in Europe and the USA participated in the International Brigades. Shortly afterwards, a large number of Chinese fled to Spain from the Second World War, of which a group in Hortaleza Street in Madrid in the 1940s is worthy of mention. The Franco regime's diplomatic relations with the Republic of Taiwan (1953–73) encouraged the arrival of Chinese from this island. Many came with the help of Spanish missionaries to continue their studies and ended up settling in Spain as professionals.

During the 1970s, an interesting phenomenon increased the number of members and diversity of the Chinese community. Chinese who lived in other European countries saw how the local population travelled to Spain for holidays, and they followed in their footsteps, opening restaurants along the coast and in the islands. The origin of these Chinese-European investors is not clear, but those from Hong Kong and the neighbouring province of Guandong stand out. Another group which Spain accepted in 1979–80 were the ethnically-Chinese Vietnamese refugees. About 1000 of these arrived to be distributed in settlements in quite different parts of Spain.

In 1979, the restrictive Chinese migratory policy changed. The Popular Republic 'opened its doors to the outside', and allowed the exit of a greater number of citizens by the application of more flexible criteria for the granting of passports. This new flow of emigrants fundamentally consisted of those from Zhejiang, but other groups began to arrive from provinces such as Shanghai, Tianjin, Beijing, Shandong, Guangxi, Yunnan and Fujian. Recently, also, the number of Chinese from Hong Kong has grown, and for the first time Chinese from Singapore and Malaysia have arrived.

China is a subcontinent with nine and a half million km^2. As well as this, in many Southeast Asian countries, the Chinese are a considerable ethnic minority with a long history of residence. The complex question of the geographical limits of the Chinese community is complicated by the presence of two colonies on Chinese soil, Hong Kong and Macao, and by

Table 12.1 Origins of Chinese immigrants

People's Republic	Other Chinese countries	Other countries
Zhejiang	Taiwan	Vietnam
– Wenzhou	Hong Kong	Singapore
– Qingtian	Macao	Malaysia
– Hangzhou		USA
Guangdong		Great Britain
Shanghai		Holland
Tianjin		France
Beijing		Rest of Western Europe
Shangdong		
Anhui		
Guangxi		
Yunnan		
Fujian		

the existence of the Republic of China in Taiwan, which, from the point of view of the Popular Republic, is one more Chinese province and sooner or later will have to be united with mainland China. Table 12.1 shows the origins of Chinese immigrants in Spain, according to three categories: the People's Republic, other Chinese countries and other countries.

Each one of these origins potentially forms the basis for a sub-community, more or less structured around different types of voluntary groupings. Often, the fundamental criterion for the grouping is the sharing of a common language or dialect which can bring together or, alternatively, divide the criterion of the place of origin. Two examples: some from areas outside the People's Republic have their roots in that country, and part of their family, with whom they still have links, still live there; or the clear division which exists between those from the municipality of Wenzhou and its neighbouring district of Qingtian, both from the same province of Zhejiang.

Work and Geographical Distribution

The evolution of the spatial dispersion of Chinese residents has followed patterns which are directly related to their main jobs. From the end of the Second World War, in certain European countries, the Chinese restaurant sector has undergone rapid development, and over time the Chinese immigrants have abandoned their previous jobs. They have created and moved into economic and ethnic niches which have ended up being practically self-sufficient. Around this activity in their restaurants, as before when they were peddlers, have arisen a number of complementary and dependent services: companies which import products from China, shops which sell Chinese products, travel agents, farmers who produce soy beans, construction workers and tradesmen who renovate and decorate the restaurants, transport companies, distributors of products for their kitchens, gambling establishments, credit societies, etc.

Once the supply of restaurants has reached saturation point, there are various alternatives, among these occupational diversification and investment. In Spain, this is directed especially towards clothing workshops, following in the footsteps of Italy (Campani & Maddii, 1992). Table 12.2 shows an approximate indication of the distribution of the Chinese community by provinces and years.

The provinces listed for each year in Table 12.2 concentrate more than 70% of the officially registered Chinese population. The official data is only an approximation. The collective of Chinese immigrants is characterised by a large number of illegal immigrants (Beltrán, 1991; Conde, 1994; García, 1994). At present, it is estimated that there are about 60,000 Chinese living in Spain. One fact which corroborates the importance of illegal immigrants is that in the two processes of legalisation of immigrants carried out in

Table 12.2 Chinese residents by province and years of residence

1971		1981		1986		1993	
Madrid	176	Madrid	282	Madrid	719	Madrid	2700
Barcelona	77	Barcelona	111	Valencia	335	Barcelona	1455
Las Palmas	59	Las Palmas	99	Las Palmas	203	Valencia	577
Malaga	24	Santa Cruz	54	Barcelona	168	Alicante	508
		Baleares	44	Alicante	111	Malaga	365
		Valencia	31	Malaga	88	Las Palmas	252
		Malaga	25	Baleares	85	Vizcaya	221
				Santa Cruz	82	Seville	190
						Zaragoza	190
Total	336		646		1791		6458

Source: Dirección General de Migraciones

Spain, the Chinese have occupied important positions in the number of immigrants legalised. In the 1985–86 campaign, they were ninth with 1192 applications out of a total of 43,815, and in the 1991–93 one, they moved up to third place with 7531 applications, making up 5775 of the total (Izquierdo, 1991; Aragón and Chozas, 1993). More recent official sources (Ministerio de Trabajo y Asuntos Sociales) estimate that in 1996 there were 10,816 Chinese residents (See *Anuario de Migraciones 1997*).

In the 1952 census of foreigners, there were 116 resident Chinese. The increase in the size of the Chinese community was continual, and accelerated during the 1980s and 1990s to increase by a factor of 11 from 1981 to 1993. Madrid has always been by far the province with the largest Chinese community, followed by Barcelona. Noteworthy is the important early presence in the Canary Islands, Majorca and Minorca, Málaga, Valencia and Alicante, provinces with important tourist industries. In 1993, their presence in industrial centres such as Bilbao and Zaragoza was already important. At the moment, they are in almost all towns and cities which have a population of at least 10,000.

The change in their distribution corresponds closely to the predominant work that they do. The largest clientele for the Chinese restaurants is found in the big cities and in the tourist areas. In Spain, the Chinese community is one of the immigrant minorities most highly concentrated in a single productive sector, with 98% working in the service industries. Using information on work permits granted in 1993, Table 12.3 shows the distribution of the Chinese community by productive sectors.

Table 12.3 shows the dominance of the service and hotel sectors. Commerce and selling are another of their traditional ethnic occupations.

Table 12.3 Work permits granted, by occupation (1993)

Sector	Taiwan	China
Professionals and skilled workers	10	106
Civil servants and company directors	5	21
Administrative workers and similar occupations	3	53
Traders and sellers	11	172
Services and hotel industries	48	4590
Agricultural workers	0	2
Industry, construction and transport	1	58
Others	0	2
Total	78	5004

Source: Ministerio de Trabajo y Seguridad Social. Dirección General de Informática y Estadística

Of the total permits granted in 1993, 2030 (40%) are for 'self-employment', a high proportion in the foreign community. The number of these 'autonomous' workers is similar to the number of Chinese restaurants in Spain. Immigrant Chinese tend to be self-employed, to be the owners of their own businesses. Until they can be so, they work in businesses owned by other Chinese. Apart from the above-mentioned jobs, there are others such as professionals, civil servants and administrative workers which increase the social hierarchy within the Chinese community. This last group corresponds to those with a high educational level, and who are more or less integrated into Spanish society, outside the ethnic enclave.

The Emigration Chain

The present structure of the Chinese population in Spain shows quite a large presence of children, pensioners, housewives and students. This situation is the result of a long process which began with the emigration of single men before the 1950s, most of whom returned to China. Until the end of the 1970s, the standard of living in Spain was rather low compared to the rest of Europe, and for this reason Spain was not especially attractive to emigrants until the 1980s. A combination of various factors, such as Spain's entry into the EEC, China's open door policy, and the oversupply of Chinese restaurants in some European countries, made Spain a more attractive target for the Chinese, because of the enormous possibilities for the development of their businesses in an area which was practically unexplored.

The new immigrants who began to arrive from the end of the 1970s had higher educational levels than previous generations. Now, their intention is not so much to spend a few years working and saving money in Spain, as to settle in this country on a long-term basis. Deep down, they all wish to return to China some day, but the reality is that they do so only to visit, especially those who have been economically successful. However, some pensioners return to their villages to spend the last few years of their lives there.

Despite the changes in attitudes towards returning to China, they continue to maintain close contact with the villages and towns they came from. They keep in touch by telephone and/or letter, send money to their families, and return for a visit, to get medical treatment, to get married, to study, for business reasons, to donate money to the community and, finally, to be buried.

The development of small businesses stimulates the reunification of families. The members of the family group are also the employees of the business. The emigration chain is exploited to the utmost. Relatives, friends and neighbours are helped to leave China as much as is allowed by the possibilities of their contacts in Spain, and the restrictive migratory policies both in Spain and in China. The present desire to emigrate has created a demand which is much greater than the legal opportunities, giving rise to a large increase in the number of illegal immigrants.

The logic of this chain is self-perpetuating. The first exclusively male immigrants, as time passes and after saving some capital, open a business either alone but more often in partnership, where they themselves are both the owners and the workers. As the profits increase, some set up their own individual businesses and then they call the members of their family group to come and help them. Thus arrive their wives, children, brothers and sisters, cousins, etc. If the business expands or if they open other ones, then they call upon more distant relatives, neighbours, friends, etc, whom they help to leave China. Thus, dependent networks are created around powerful bosses who 'sponsor' new and dependant immigrants. Each new arrival aspires to become the head of a new chain.

In the new generation, the whole domestic group settles overseas, and new members are born outside of China. The families established in Spain are interrelated among each other by multiple connections of kinship, economics, place of origin, etc, creating and recreating extended 'families' or 'lineages', which hold power and exercise authority within the community (García, 1994).

The Chinese Language: Official Language, Dialects and Variants

Both the Chinese language and the culture and society are complex and varied. They can only be described on the basis of their differences, rather than in general. Chinese, and its many variants, belong to the Sino-Tibetan group of languages, and are spoken by more than 1500 million people, a fifth of the world's population. The Chinese language and ethnic groups are called Han, a name taken from the Han dynasty (202 BC to 220 AD). The unification of the different Chinese kingdoms and territories under an empire in the third century BC led to the adoption of a common system of writing which has been part of the basis for Chinese identity until the present day (Gernet, 1969).

Chinese languages form part of the isolating group. The words normally consist of a single syllable, which does not change, and takes neither inflections nor suffixes. Word order gives meaning to the sentence. Each character or ideograph has its own semantic and grammatical content, which may vary according to its position in the sentence structure, the pronunciation or the intonation. Sometimes, several characters are combined to create new structures or concepts with a different meaning. There is no univocal relation between sound and written phoneme, so a character may be pronounced in different ways, with a large tonal variety (the official language has four tones and Cantonese has eight). The vowels have various phonemes which vary from one dialect to another (Alladina & Edwards, 1991).

Chinese has eight linguistic variants officially considered in China as dialects, although these are as different phonetically and lexically as are French and Spanish. Some linguists dispute this classification and consider, for example, that Cantonese is a distinct language. Over more than two thousand years, the system of writing has undergone various changes. At the beginning of this century, a revolutionary change was to abandon Wenhua or 'written language of culture' for Baihua or 'written vernacular'. This was an attempt to bring together the written and spoken languages, since these had become completely separate. Baihua became the language used in literature, newspapers and modern education. The most recent change has been the simplification of the number of strokes in some characters under the People's Republic. Outside of the 'continent', in Taiwan, Hong Kong, Singapore, etc, the traditional style is still used.

The Chinese dialects are the following: (1) the Northern Dialect, with the Northern, Lower Yangzi, North Eastern and North Western variants; (2) the Wu dialect, spoken in Shanghai, south Jiangsu and in Zhejiang; (3) the Yue dialect (Cantonese); (4) the northern and southern Min dialects, from Fujian; (5) the Hakka dialect, spoken among the peoples of the southern mountains; (6) the Gan dialect, spoken in Jiangxi; and (7) the Xiang dialect, from Hunan. Apart from its many variants, each dialect has developed different kinds of local slang. Both local variants and dialects can be mutually quite unintelligible. It is their writing that provides their unity. However, some written characters can be read and pronounced in more than one way, and their semantic and even grammatical content can vary according to the pronunciation and intonation used.

In 1952, the 'standardised' or 'widely understandable' Putonghua, based on the northern dialect popularly called 'Beijing Mandarin', became the official language of the People's Republic, taught in all schools and used in national mass media. Speakers of the different local variants communicate with each other in Putonghua, and when spoken communication fails, people resort to the written language, which is thus the basis for Chinese linguistic self-identity. Variants mostly have the same syntax, although some linguists suggest relevant differences between some of them. Syntactic and semantic comprehension depend greatly on the level of cultural and linguistic education of each person, and this in turn varies greatly from urban to rural areas, between different generations and among individuals. In the 1960s, a phonetic transcription into the Latin alphabet, called Pinyin, was created, based on a standardised pronunciation of Putonghua. In Taiwan and Hong Kong, this is called Guoyu ('national language'), and in Singapore it is one of the official national languages, taking the name of Huayu ('language of the Chinese').

Chinese Culture and Education

Education in China plays a fundamental role and is highly valued as a means of upward social mobility. For over a thousand years, civil servants have been selected via an examination system, and to know how to read and write has been the privilege of a few and the aspiration of all. In Chinese society, education is a means of wielding power and plays an essential role in the social hierarchy, together with money. Throughout history, the most powerful families had schools so that their children could learn to read and write. The most outstanding of these were given every opportunity to sit for and to pass the official state examinations, in order to gain a high government post, which not only was a source of pride to the family of the successful candidate, but also benefited those who had helped him to reach this position.

Language is the basic pillar of Chinese education and culture. Years of study and great effort must be dedicated to learning the thousands of characters which must be known in order to read and write in Chinese. Learning them is based on copying, repeating and memorising the ideograms. In primary education, most of the time is spent in teaching the language. Calligraphy is highly esteemed by the different social classes, becoming something with intrinsic aesthetic value. Houses are decorated with words and written sayings hung on the walls. The level of language skill is a function of the number of years at school; that is, the more years spent learning, the more characters known and used.

Despite the importance given to learning the language in Chinese culture, not everyone knows how to read and write to the same extent as each other, or even at all. In Catalonia, illiterate immigrants represent

Table 12.4 Reading and writing capacities of Chinese immigrants who applied for legalisation of their residence situation, 1991

Can read and write	No.	(%)
Own mother tongue	172	65.15
Spanish	7	2.65
Own mother tongue and Spanish	47	17.8
Other languages	5	1.89
Own mother tongue and other languages	15	5.68
Spanish and others	2	0,76
Own mother tongue, Spanish and other languages	16	6.06
Total	264	87.5

Source: Aragón and Chozas (1993)

about 3.5% of the total immigrants. Newly illiterate persons, who used to be literate but have lost this skill, are more common and are usually older men and women. People who read and write with difficulty are most frequently found, according to their age and origins. In the process of learning Spanish, when attempting to write a Spanish word in their own language, these immigrants often know the word in Chinese but not how to write it. Furthermore, about 20% do not know the Latin alphabet, and many are unable to transcribe their own name. This fact makes cultural differences relevant in Chinese society. In immigration, these differences are fundamental, as the hardest and most marginal jobs are done by those with least education.

A survey of 264 Chinese immigrants during the amnesty for illegal immigrants in 1991 (Aragón and Chozas, 1993: 265–433) indicates several characteristics of this particular population, although it is unclear how valid this data is, for it is not representative of the whole Chinese immigrant community. Many only speak their native tongue, and a large number do not even attempt to legalise their situation. Also, the Chinese tend to state their position as better than it really is; it is a question of face or prestige. With these limitations, the data suggests that 90% of those surveyed have been to school for more than 6 years, and in particular 77 of them (29% of the total) have studied for more than 11 years; 72% are men, 76% are married, 86% have arrived since 1986 and 16% came via another European country.

As Table 12.4 illustrates, 27% claim to be able to read and write Spanish and 30% claim the same for their own language and another language; 10% read and write at least one language but not Chinese; 30% read and write more than one language. This data shows a relatively privileged group, and the only generalisation that could be made about the whole Chinese community is that among the younger members of this community illiteracy is quite low compared to the levels found in other immigrant minorities.

Since the decade of the 1920s, many emigrant Chinese who have become economically successful donate money to their villages to found schools. In Communist China, the traditional 'family school' has become a new kind of school which is an important centre of lineage in times when other focal points of identity, such as once were the owning of land or temples dedicated to the ancestors, have been lost.

Language and Culture as Grouping Factors in the Host Country

The great majority of immigrant Chinese are from the Han ethnic group, and share common social and cultural features. They all continue to speak Chinese as their first language, which allows them to communicate with each other and to conserve their Chinese identity in the country of immigration, in spite of the large differences between them, and the boundaries of their areas of movement are well defined. From the outside, the tendency is to treat them as a homogeneous whole, but the differences can in fact be more pronounced than in European society as a whole, even though the many variations are lost in a complex 'Chinese identity' and in the so-called 'Chinese' language.

The languages used in the various Chinese communities in Europe depend mainly on the numbers of people from the different places of origin. In Holland, most Chinese speak Cantonese, which is the language of greatest prestige, because it is the language of the majority of the Dutch Chinese (Pieke & Van der Berg, 1993). In contrast, the Chinese in Spain largely speak the Wu dialect, in its variants from the south of the Zhejiang province. Although at a communicative level many varieties of Chinese can be found, Putonghua is the lingua franca and the language of culture.

Among immigrant Chinese, one's language is very important since they often regroup according to families, friendships or places of origin. Getting together on the basis of one's place of origin guarantees easy verbal communication. Wherever the Chinese immigrate, they build their own communities in isolation from mainstream society, with their own culture, values and language. This self-exclusion is very important for them because they believe that if they live isolated from the rest of society they will keep their own culture intact, a culture they consider to be 'superior' to Western culture, and their language richer and more complex. To all this one must add the lack of curiosity displayed towards them by the host society, such as Spanish society.

This 'Sino-centric' behaviour does not allow the Chinese to value other cultures in a positive way, and they in turn must face the local 'Euro-centrist' attitudes and behaviour. Some societies do not receive immigrants in such a sufficiently motivating way as to awaken their interest. This is the case of Spain and particularly Chinese immigration to Spain. Often, the Chinese do not seem to exist even in the organisations which help immigrants. They are a silent and invisible minority which contrasts with the characteristic features of Spanish society. They are not a competing labour supply, nor do they make any visible demands, so it is as if they did not exist. On the other hand, the differentiation established by their own culture prevents the two from getting to know each other or understanding the many and varied values expressed by each group. Preserving their language is very important and in the family and other groupings the language used is their own local dialect. Such attitudes as 'If (s)he doesn't speak Chinese, (s)he is not a good Chinese', or 'You can't be Chinese if you don't speak the language' are not uncommon.

One of the strategies used to preserve their culture is to send the children to study in China when they reach the age of eight or nine. That is, when the language of the host society has been assimilated enough for it not to be forgotten. When they are 16 or 17, they return to Europe, and in this way the parents guarantee the continuation of their own self-identity, and of the language as the main expression of this identity. On other occasions, they are sent shortly after birth and return as adolescents. Sometimes, they come to Spain to continue studying, or are born here, and just stay, although it is likely that they will return to China one day to know their roots.

Language Attitudes

The language of everyday use is Chinese, and some Chinese immigrants neither speak nor understand Spanish even at a basic level after living in Spain for 10 or 12 years. Some families even prevent recently arrived adolescents from learning Spanish. This attitude is a way of preserving their identity and preventing young Chinese from relating to and mixing with the local culture, and losing their own culture or, worse still, undergoing any process of assimilation. Also, in their everyday life, they do not need to speak Spanish because they work for, and with, other Chinese. They shop in Chinese shops, and spend their spare time speaking Chinese in places such as Chinese karaoke bars or gambling establishments. Many young people, and especially women, have no emotional attachments at all with the mainstream society. In other situations, the attitudes are very different, and the young people learn the local language in order to help their parents, family or other adults. The avoidance/mixing strategies vary from one group to another; immigrants from Hong Kong and Taiwan are more accepting of, and relate better to, the host population.

At a linguistic level, relationships established with the local population tend to be purely functional, such as the acquisition of a simple level of language skill so as to be able to communicate in everyday activities. Some families consider that to live in Spain, and to get on, it is essential to speak Spanish, although this does not imply a process of integration, much less assimilation. Some families even spend a large part of their economic resources on paying for their children to go to a good school or to have a private teacher. In these cases, the idea of returning to China gets less and less likely, although it does not disappear, and in theory the children should learn both languages without losing their own identity based on the Chinese language and culture. Those who encourage their children to learn Spanish, or even other officially recognised languages, such as Catalan, value progress and upward social mobility highly, since the greater the educational and cultural level, the greater the prestige within the community.

The Chinese look for the practical advantages to be found in knowing the local language. Speaking Spanish opens doors and makes life easier in Spain. What they are most interested in from Spain is earning money ('the pesetas'), and secondly in getting an education. In itself, Spain is of little interest to them. Many would prefer to live in other European countries such as Holland or Germany, and the majority would like to emigrate to the United States. The 'American Dream' is more common among young Chinese than in other immigrant minorities.

It is understandable that a collective which emigrates for mainly economic or political motives be afraid of integration, since it has come not to get to know another society or to live with different people, but to satisfy certain needs. It is obvious that in other circumstances they would not have emigrated. Belonging as they do to a society where the superiority of their own values is accepted, they do not establish work or emotional relationships with the host society and build a community on the edge of it. Integration is neither an immediate need nor a desire. In the integration process, in some countries, such as the USA or France, the Administration tends to equate equality with assimilation and not with respect for cultural differences and diversity; and the same happens in the different Spanish autonomous communities which have a high immigration rate. This would also explain why certain collectives such as the Chinese, who have their own unique characteristics, are so resistant to so-called integration and even more to assimilation. Since language is the fundamental vehicle of integration, the result is a large amount of fossilisation in the language learning process, and a lack of motivation and curiosity towards the host society.

Learning the Chinese Language and Maintaining one's Own Culture

In Spain there are second generation Chinese, some of whom were born in Spain and others who arrived when very young with their parents or other relatives. These children go to school in the Spanish educational system. Their families ensure that the fact of learning at school in another language and in the culture transmitted by it does not exclude learning the Chinese language and culture. Different strategies are used to preserve these: paying for private teachers of Chinese, studying Chinese as a second language at language schools, where children of both mixed and purely Chinese marriages attend, and returning to China to become reacquainted with one's roots. Returning to learn to read, write and speak Chinese is quite frequent, whether from one's own decision or because of one's parents' decision. The age of return depends on each particular case.

Older Chinese who have been in Spain longer are very worried about the risk of the new generations losing their identity. For this reason, they have begun to found schools to teach Chinese language. The first was opened in 1977 in Madrid, by the 'Association of Chinese Restaurants in Spain', a grouping of Chinese from Taiwan. In 1987, the 'Spanish Formosa Association' set up the 'Chinese College of Spain', in Madrid also. In 1996, the 'Friends of China Association' opened a school in Valencia. The children go to school after normal school hours, especially on Saturdays and Sundays. There is very little collaboration on the part of the governments of the People's Republic and Taiwan, largely restricted to providing text books and materials. The organisation, buildings and teachers' salaries are paid for by the immigrants themselves. The business associations, the Chinese embassy or individual people try to find the resources needed to be able to perpetuate the Chinese identity and the values that this represents.

Learning the Official Languages of Spain

Some Chinese immigrant associations in Madrid offer basic services to the recently arrived, such as teaching them basic functional and survival skills in Spanish. The classes are taught by Chinese teachers or other immigrants, and usually last a short time. Most go to the Official Language Schools or to adult education centres, both of which are free, or at least cheap, and government funded. In particular, the largest grouping of Chinese in Catalonia is in an adult literacy school in the centre of Barcelona. In this centre, the Chinese learn Spanish, some learn Catalan and even English, travelling from the outskirts of Barcelona and from nearby towns. The school is not only somewhere to learn Spanish, but a meeting place and point of contact for them with each other, with other immigrant groups and with the local society.

Only a minority of immigrants are so immersed in their community that they are motivated enough to learn the local languages. The frame of reference is not Spanish society but their own immigrant community and their homelands. Most work exclusively in ethnically based businesses.

Those with a higher cultural level tend to have a high communicative level in the target language. Among the groups which best speak Spanish is the limited subgroup of the mixed marriages. The recent arrivals have a higher cultural level than the first generation immigrants, although their interest in learning Spanish is not very different. The long working day increases their isolation and de-motivates them to learn the language. On the other hand, some employers help their employees to learn Spanish, since a waiter needs to know how to speak and understand a little of the language of the host society. But in family circles, at work and in spare time, their daily activities are carried out in Chinese.

The Chinese use direct and metacognitive learning strategies, such as memorising techniques. They especially use visual memory, analogies, contrasts and opposites, as well as social strategies and learner autonomy and self-direction. The strategies developed in the language learning process are directly related to their culture, language and values. Their life experience, languages learnt previously and the degree of expertise in their own language all play an important part. Other aspects which are relevant to the language learning process are age, gender and relationships which have been established with the target language (García, 1993).

Turning now to the language itself, the disparity implied by beginning from an isolating language and learning an inflected language like Spanish means that they do not use Chinese to any great extent as a help in creating an interlanguage. Not more than 6% speak another language, such as English, come mostly from Hong Kong and Taiwan, and use this third language for an interlanguage. The main objective when beginning to learn is to become familiar with the phonetics and the structures of the target language. That is, to understand how the language they are learning works. Women develop more strategies than men. Many work as waitresses or shop assistants, and are in more direct contact with the host society and thus with the target language (Chuang, 1994).

During the adult learning process there is a strong interference from the cultural background, particularly the scale of values. Chinese behaviour and attitudes are very much determined by the need to avoid conflict, and thus any risk of losing face in front of other people. This interference prevents the use of the target language out of insecurity or fear of speaking or pronouncing incorrectly, or of doing things which are not considered acceptable in their own culture. Women and young people have less prejudices and fear of making a fool of themselves or of contact with others.

In class, with non-Chinese classmates, there are activities which only the Chinese students refuse to do. For a Chinese person, it is difficult to say a word without being completely sure of what it means or how to use it correctly. Normally, they show a great reluctance to speak about anything which implies giving an opinion about something, or explaining their ideas in front of others. They are thus different from other immigrants such as Arabs, Africans, Brazilians, Europeans, etc., who show no fear of expressing their own point of view. Yet the most important part of language learning is precisely the skill of communicating, of speaking, expressing ideas and talking about experiences. The very concept of Chinese teaching and schooling is in opposition to the communicative methods of teaching which emphasise communication and carrying out activities which are directly related to everyday language use in their daily lives. Thus, pragmatic errors are frequent, given the cultural differences with the target language and the values that this carries.

Adults show all kinds of errors: phonological, lexical, syntactic, morphosyntactic, spelling, semantic and especially pragmatic (Fang, 1993). There is strong fossilisation as well as a tendency to stop learning once they have gained the essential communicative resources needed in their lives. Fossilisation of errors has become the characteristic feature of Chinese speakers who speak a second language, especially if the target language has been learned in adulthood. Important here is the self-isolation and self-exclusion of cultural and emotional life from the target language, although this does not exclude the possibility that some adults show great interest and motivation towards learning Spanish. In the same conditions, Chinese women learn more quickly and more successfully than the men. Women immigrants are generally more motivated, and more curious about the local society.

The second generation of immigrants is composed of those born in Spain, who have gone or who go to school in the Spanish educational system and who are spread over the country as a result of the main Chinese economic activity, their restaurants. This distribution prevents their concentration in particular schools, which may help their assimilation. As well, there are the Chinese children born in China who come to Spain at different ages and who go to school in Spain.

Small Chinese children are slower to learn the Spanish language than other communities, but their great determination helps them to overcome their special learning problems. This difficulty is not due only to the particular characteristics of their language, culture and family self-isolation, but also to a lack of resources and information on the part of the school. Even so, and taking into account the difficulties and needs of their schooling, Chinese children obtain good results at school. This can also be seen in other countries such as Holland or Italy.

Adolescent Chinese who go to school in Spain have many difficulties. Firstly, there are deficiencies in the school system. There are few special teachers who can cover the pressing needs in the language learning of Chinese children, and neither are there many qualified teachers in this respect. In one case, a girl with excellent handwriting copied anything she could, without understanding even 30% of what she was writing. Then there is the shock of joining a strange system. They need months to emotionally adapt to and understand their school environment. The fact that they live in the Chinese community stops them from establishing personal relationships with other children and their parents are concerned to find them Chinese friends.

They also begin to work at a very early age. When they finish their studies, many adolescents begin working in restaurants or doing other tasks required by their parents. Some girls aged 13 who have not been to school are already doing all the housework. Some adolescents know very little about Spain after living here for five or six years. Usually, however, through their schooling and knowledge of the language, they become the medium through which general information and events reach the family. Those who go to school tend to have good results in comparison with the high failure rate of the Spanish education system, and with the results obtained by other immigrants such as children from the Maghreb region of North Africa. Chinese school children in Spain normally speak good Spanish, and in Catalonia, good Catalan. Deficiencies can be seen at the vocabulary level, when those who read Chinese have to divide their time between the language of school and Chinese. There are more and more adolescents who neither read nor write Chinese, which is a continual worry for their parents. These adolescents highlight the importance of being Chinese, and express their strong desire to return to China when they have learnt many things in Spain. They are more interested in technical and science subjects than arts or humanities.

Patterns of language use

Adult Chinese do not exhibit interference or linguistic borrowing from the local language. In private, conversations are always in Chinese. In the restaurants, even the waiters and waitresses who speak good Spanish translate the clients' orders, even if it is only the number of the dish. Only those who wait on tables need to understand some Spanish. The rest of the workers neither need it nor do they understand it. In their personal life, they relate mainly to other Chinese, and only a minority of young men go out to discotheques or other leisure centres, and relate to Spaniards. Although the women are more communicative than the men, their personal relationships tend to be only with other Chinese. Only infrequently do some more independent people establish relationships with Spaniards, but these are not approved of by the rest of the community.

Children who have been to school in Catalonia show some borrowing from Spanish or Catalan in family circles and at work, such as numbers, exclamations and swearwords. When the parents do not speak Spanish the child will interpret for them to solve those problems related to bureaucratic practices and Spanish society. Children very seldom speak Spanish or Catalan among themselves in the presence of adults, since these do not always understand them and this would show a lack of respect. For those who have been to school, the language used in contact with the host society is generally Spanish or, in some cases, Catalan, but for expressing feelings it is Chinese and it is in a Chinese environment where most of their life is lived. Away from school, they barely relate to young non-Chinese, nor to the local culture. Most begin working at an early age and spend their non-school hours working.

To improve their Chinese, they use such means as watching videotapes of Chinese films, copying letters in Chinese and reading Chinese books, magazines and newspapers. The members of the family who remain in China often send them Chinese books and there are also special importers of books, magazines and videos from Hong Kong. They also have a large number of private and cultural activities in their personal lives, and rituals play a large and varied part in their lives.

Generally, it can be said that when Chinese use the target language, they do not borrow from their native language, and if they do not know a word they do not fall back on their own or another language to express themselves. They are very aware that nobody understands their language, so they do not borrow words which no one will understand. If they do not know a word, they remain silent or ask another Chinese person to help them.

Chinese Students in Spain

Sending students abroad to finish their schooling has been done since the beginning of the 19th century in China. First preference is Japan, then the USA, and some European countries. For example, the present education system in Taiwan is totally oriented towards the USA, and there the Chinese are the largest foreign minority in higher education. The phenomenon has created a special class within the Chinese community, of scientists, technicians and professionals who rapidly undergo a process of integration in the USA. To a lesser extent, this can be seen in Spain. Within the Chinese community, there is a highly qualified minority which has become integrated into Spanish life.

For Chinese from Taiwan, this tradition of coming to Spain to study began in the 1950s. Many of these students have settled in Spain after finishing their studies. Some have married Spaniards, and their children are quite well integrated into Spanish society. At the moment, there are as many post-graduate students from Taiwan as there are from the People's Republic.

Although still in small numbers, children of Chinese immigrants are beginning to go to Spanish universities, something which is not always approved of by their compatriots, who think they should study in China, and if they study in Spain it should be a practical, prestigious, scientific degree in order to return to China and help the family, or to get a well-paid job. Chinese culture is very pragmatic, and tends to use intellectual resources in a very utilitarian way. That is, one's studies should serve to earn money and gain prestige. Those who go to the university are normally male, since the family favours their getting an education over the daughters. On the other hand, it is expected that the daughters should marry a 'good match' from within the Chinese community, because of their privileged situation as an immigrant. Money and education are the most highly valued signs of prestige in the Chinese community. The children's education is an investment to which the available family resources are dedicated, with preference given to the male child.

The Chinese ethnic minority has been considered by researchers as a good example of educational success in an immigrant community, for their results are better than the local population in the countries to which they have immigrated (Jong, 1988; Hirshman & Wong, 1986). For example, in Australia, the second generation of Chinese immigrants has taken its place among the most outstanding intellectuals of the country. The high school success rate of this 'model' minority is attributed to the strong striving for success and the high value placed on education by Chinese culture. Pieke (1991) disputes this interpretation, which simplifies a much more complex reality. Those who go to school do so because they are good at their studies, but there are many other children who do not go to school and a large number who drop out after primary school.

Success at school is also related to a rejection of failure, instilled at an early age. Adolescent Chinese show a striving to do better and a fear of failure which are much higher than in other immigrant minorities. Another factor is that the Chinese community is a very hierarchical and family-oriented society. Respect for elders and their decisions is unquestionable, and every individual success or failure is interpreted as that of the family. Finally, success at school is a means of upward social mobility, and gives great prestige and the possibility of gaining some kind of well-paid job.

References

Alladina, S. and Edwards, V. (1991) *Multilingualism in the British Isles.* London: Longman.

Aragón Bombín, R. and Chozas Pedrero, J. (1993) *La Regularización de Inmigrantes durante 1991–1992.* Madrid: Ministerio de Trabajo y Seguridad Social.

Beltrán Antolín, J. (1991) Los chinos en Madrid: Aproximación a partir de datos oficiales. Hipótesis para una investigación. In *Malestar Cultural y Conflicto en la Sociedad Madrileña* (pp. 295–304). II Jornadas de antropología de Madrid. Madrid: Comunidad de Madrid.

Campani, G. and Maddii, L. (1992) Un monde à part: les Chinois en Toscane. *Revue Européenne des Migrations Internationales* 8 (3), 51–71.

Chuang, Yuan-Ling (1994) El uso de estrategias de aprendizaje en la comunidad china de Barcelona. M.A. thesis in Teacher Education in Spanish as a Foreign Language. Universidad de Barcelona.

Conde, P. (1994) La mafia china mata en España, *INTERVIU* 924, January 10–16, 11–15.

Fang, Shu-Ru (1993) Estudio comparativo de las gramáticas china y española. MA thesis in Teaching Spanish as as Foreign Language. Universidad de Barcelona.

Gernet, J. (1969) China. Aspectos y funciones psicológicos de la escritura. In M. Cohen and J.S. Fare (eds) *La Escritura y Psicología de los Pueblos.* Madrid: Siglo XXI.

García Mateos, C. (1993) La adquisición del español como segunda lengua por personas analfabetas y con dificultades de aprendizaje: una propuesta didáctica. MA thesis in Teacher Education in Spanish as a Foreign Language. Universidad de Barcelona.

García Mateos, C. (1994) L'immigrazione cinese in Spagna. In G. Campani, F. Carchedi and A. Tassinari (eds) *L'immigrazione silenziosa. Le comunità cinesi in Italia* (pp. 183–92). Milano: Edizioni della Fondazione Giovanni Agnelli.

Hirshman, C. and Wong, M.C. (1986) The extraordinary educational attainment of Asian-Americans. *Social Forces* 65 (1), 1–27.

Izquierdo Escribano, A. (1991) La inmigración ilegal en España. Análisis de la operación extraordinaria de regularización 1985–86. *Economía y Sociología del Trabajo* 11, 8–38.

Jong, M. (1988) Ethnic origin and educational careers in Holland. *The Netherlands Journal of Sociology* 24 (1): 65–75.

Llorca, C. (1980) *Diario de un Viaje a la China de Mao.* Madrid: Erisa.

Ministerio de Trabajo y Asuntos Sociales. *Anuario de Migraciones 1997.* Madrid.

Pieke, F.N. (1991) Chinese educational achievement and 'Folk Theories of Success'. *Anthropology and Education Quarterly* 22 (2), 162–80.

Pieke, F.N. and Van Der Berg, M. (1993) Chinese. In G. Extra and L. Verhoeven, L. (eds) *Community Languages in the Netherlands.* University of Tilburg: Swets and Zeitlinger Publishers.

Tato Cumming, G. (1939) *China, Japón y el Conflicto Chino-japonés.* San Sebastián: Editorial Española.

Wang, Dingxi (1991) *Xibanya, Putaoya huaqiao gaikuang* (The Situation of Chinese International Immigrants in Spain and Portugal). Taibei: Zhengzhong shuju.

Woon, Yuan-Fong (1989) Social change and continuity in South China: Overseas Chinese and the Guan Lineage of Kaiping County, 1949–1987. *China Quarterly* 118, 324–44.

Chapter 13

The Italian Community

ROSA M. TORRENS

Nature and Distribution of the Italian community in Spain[1]

Interest in the community of Italians abroad has existed for a long time,[2] and extends over a wide range of viewpoints: sociological, sociolinguistic, anthropological, cultural (distribution of the community, features of the settlement in different areas, linguistic variation, spread of the Italian language and culture abroad, etc.). This can be seen in the large number of conferences[3] that have taken place and of studies[4] that have been done in recent times.

In Spain, especially in the last few years, the Italian community has become more and more noticeable, with a 1996 population of 21,362 residents according to official state figures (see *Anuario de Migraciones 1997*) and 24,164 people according to official consular data (given in April–July 1996), although in this last case it is estimated that the numbers are as high as 34,000 (Table 13.1), concentrated mainly in Catalonia[5] and the Autonomous Region of Madrid,[6] followed by Andalusia and the Balearic Islands. In the Regions of Aragón, Balearic Islands, Catalonia, Valencia, Murcia, and the Principality of Andorra, the data for age groups show 43.5% aged between 18 and 45 years, and for gender 57% are men and 43% are women.

Not only is the number of Italians high, but their presence dates back many centuries, due to the flourishing trading and financial relations which already existed in the 13th century. So by the decade 1860–70, the Italian

Table 13.1 The Italian community in Spain

	1995		1996	
	Official	*Estimated*	*Official*	*Estimated*
Catalonia, Aragón, Valencia, Balearic Islands, Murcia, Andorra	8997	15,000	10,194	16,000
Rest of Spain	–	–	13,970	18,000
Total			24,164	34,000

Sources: Italian Consulate General in Barcelona; Italian Consulate General in Madrid

community had grown to as many as 2000 members in Catalonia, which promoted the organised establishment of this community in Barcelona from the end of the 19th century to the beginning of this century, with the foundation of the Italian School and the 'Casa degli Italiani'.

Characteristics of the Italian Community: Motivation, Settlement and Relations with Social Institutions

It is well known that a country's place in the international economy[7] is one of the contributing factors to the formation of the image abroad of an immigrant community, and the economic factors are very often the reason for internal and external migratory flows, as is the case of Italy. Leaving aside the economic and cultural differences between the north and south of Italy, which deepened during the first half of this century[8] as Italy became more economically developed, the international integration of the country became more and more consolidated. Even though its industrial economy depends on the foreign supply of raw materials and energy sources, Italy's productive capacity has expanded, especially since the 1950s and 1960s, thanks to the almost continually positive balance of trade with European markets (even when this has been the frequent result of the devaluation of the Italian currency), mainly with Germany, France and the United Kingdom, and to a lesser extent with countries like Spain, whose trading relations have increased and improved in recent years.[9] More specifically, the Italian economic expansion of the last few decades is mainly due to the decisive push of small and medium-sized companies and in fact to the individual success of businessmen and women with a high capacity for adaptation and innovation, and to whom is largely due the international consolidation of the prestige of the label 'Made in Italy'. And Italians abroad have taken with them this singular business spirit, as we shall see.

In relation to the economic oscillations and the process of consolidation of Italy in the international context, the following fundamental immigration flows must be considered (Valussi, 1993: 85–90):

(1) from 1875 to 1886, to European and Mediterranean countries;
(2) until 1916, when the maximum number of emigrants was reached, mainly to the USA, Argentina, Brazil, and to a lesser extent, Tunisia and Algeria;
(3) after the First World War, to France and Belgium, and to a lesser extent to the above-mentioned American countries. There was an important decrease from around 1925, when the dictatorship began in Italy;
(4) and as from 1945, when restrictions on emigration were abolished, to Europe (Switzerland and West Germany), Canada, Venezuela and Australia, with a peak in 1961.

On the basis of these migratory flows, some Italian communities became well established, and continue so, as in Argentina, which in 1987 was 60% Italian in origin (Betolaja, 1987: 479), and the USA, where in 1980 there were six million Italian-Americans (Haller, 1986: 37). However, during the last few decades and especially since 1972,[10] the emigration flow has been decreasing until the present (Dittmar & Sobrero, 1990: 194): the trend was reversed in 1989, and 66,000 left (45% aged between 20 and 39 years), while 81,000 returned (mostly elderly), and 75% of this migration was within Europe.

From the above data, we can see that until the end of the 1960s, Italian settlement abroad occurred in a context of a negative socioeconomic situation which created large emigrations in search of jobs, and so the Italian immigrant arrived with the stigma of sociocultural (and linguistic) inferiority which the host society confirmed (Sabatini *et al.*, 1974: 125). However, according to some authors (Collicelli & Di Cori, 1986: 431; Dittmar & Sobrero, 1990: 195), the migratory flows of the 1980s and 1990s, having decreased considerably since the 1970s, have become during the 1980s and the 1990s a kind of 'elitist' emigration, a voluntary and more individual change of residence, related to experiences of sociocultural growth of the individual, in a context of population interchange between countries of equal prestige. The typical Italian emigrant has changed, both in the reasons for the move and in the duration and kind of job. According to these studies, it is: (1) a 'technological' emigration, for a limited period and in international companies; or (2) a change of country of less than two years' duration for reasons of tourism or employment; or (3) emigration related to the 'Made in Italy' phenomenon, with the image of Italy consolidated thanks to its foreign trade and the strength of its small and medium-sized companies.

This characterisation of the Italian community is confirmed, in general terms, by the pilot study carried out in Catalonia, and more specifically in Barcelona (capital and province) (see Appendix 1). The survey done for the pilot study, with a total number of 11 informants, indicates important variations with regard to sex, age and town or region of origin. Most came from small or medium rural or slightly industrialised towns, while others came from large cities where there were large service industries. Although, regardless of their origin, almost all had visited different European countries before coming to Spain, whether for tourism or employment, some of them had lived for up to 10 years in an English-speaking country.

With few exceptions, their parents were Italian.[11] Their fathers were businessmen and skilled or specialist workers, self-employed or employees, and their mothers, when they were employed, worked in different sectors. The data on their housing in their country of origin, together with their parents' profession, confirms that they came from middle and upper middle class backgrounds. Furthermore, all the respondents – with the exception of two, who for their own reasons were studying full time – had jobs that were the same or better than their present employment in Spain.

From the above, it can be deduced that in no case did they emigrate for economic reasons,[12] but that their reasons were one of the following, in this order: sentimental reasons, which sometimes arose after arriving in Spain; because they did not like the area where they used to live (cities or villages, or climatic aspects); to finish their studies of the Spanish language, or to do specialist courses; because there were aspects of Italy that they did not like (privileged social groups, fiscal pressure, deficient health system); because they felt good in Spain or had always wanted to live in this country; because they liked Spanish culture; or because they had established strong links of friendship. These observations thus confirm the previous ones, with respect to a kind of elitist emigration.

Furthermore, those respondents who came voluntarily without a pre-arranged job had great possibilities of finding one. Sometimes they had the help of their partner's family or friends, but the majority relied on their own efforts, and found a job by sending letters, self-employment in a liberal profession, founding a family company, or by establishing contacts with the Italian or Spanish communities, so that even in the few cases were there had been difficulties, their conclusion was that 'there are other communities which must have it worse', whereas they were well received and cannot be considered as foreigners, or 'although being a foreigner is a hard road, when you prove that your work is good they respect you more than the locals'.

In fact, leaving aside those who came to study or to retire, only in less than half of the interviewees does finding work come to mind when thinking of the initial period of adaptation. Those slightly conflictive elements of their settling in Spain have to do with emotional aspects, and are the main features of any initial inability to adapt and/or of the few problems which have continued since then. Among these, are missing close friends or their relationship with the family they have left behind. More than half have emigrated alone, and thus some of them indicate, using the highly descriptive term 'black sheep', that they are seen as, or feel they have become, different from the rest of the family. This is compensated for by strong family ties which are conserved during the initial adaptation period, and which mean that they can return to Italy if things do not work out in Spain, given that in some cases their home town and their family are relatively close.[13] Also, the perceived level of acceptance on the part of the host community is a determining factor in the ability to adapt to the new society, as expressed, for example, in their socio-psychological position in the host society with respect to socio-cultural clichés.

It is well known that Italians and Spaniards identify with each other in many ways. As early as the end of last century, the actor Ernesto Rossi, travelling through the Iberian Peninsula, apart from documenting an important Italian presence in the city of Barcelona, compared the Catalans with the Piedmontese (for their tough character of few words, but tenacious and intelligent), and the qualities of the Spaniards in general with those of the Italians (Rossi, 1887: 321–5).

The pilot study highlights some of these features and adds to them. The first positive memories of their stay are generally related to the host population's sociable, friendly nature, warmth and helpfulness, openness, freedom, simplicity, straightforwardness and sincerity, civic pride and hardworking qualities. Also mentioned are some characteristics of the city: the pleasant temperature, the sun, the sea, or the wide boulevards, Modernist art, nightlife, not feeling observed, and the feeling of being at home.

On the other hand, apart from the family ties or close friendships in Italy mentioned above, less positive memories are related to socially differentiating aspects, such as a small versus a large town, Italy versus Spain, which make the immigrants feel different from their host community because of their work patterns or the timetables. They mention that in Italy friends stay more in contact with each other, but in Barcelona the family is more important than friendships, and that Spaniards are less concerned about the quality of their work and are not very competitive, and the discontent with the timetables refer mainly to the long lunch hour. As regards the economic side, the inferior standard of living and/or technological level compared to Italy now belong to the past, the turning points being seen as the World Cup (1982), and above all the Olympics and the Expo World Fair (1992), although these stereotypes about Spain are still believed by some of those who have never been in this country. Finally, among the less positive aspects of their adaptation, they also mention the difficulty in distinguishing between Catalan and Spanish.

These aspects mentioned above contribute to the construction of the images of the Spanish and/or Catalan communities and of those of their own community before and after arriving. So three important factors need to be considered: (1) how the informant sees the other members of the community as integrated; (2) whether he/she sees the host community as homogeneous; (3) his/her opinions about the stereotypical ways in which one community sees the other.

These aspects are of great importance in this context, since these considerations[14] are decisive in determining the level of integration, in the same way as employment would be for other communities. Also, given that we are talking here of an 'elitist' kind of immigration and thus voluntary (with the exception of those who come because of an obligatory job position within their company), the level of integration will depend on much more subtle and less quantifiable factors. Finally, because of their complexity and inter-relatedness, these aspects must be studied separately, but for obvious reasons of space, only a few examples will be presented in this article. One of the interviewees indicates that he has a very affectionate relationship with Italians in his job, that they like him, but that he considers them to be 'snobbish', because they have a 'superior way of being', like a 'marchio' (distinguishing mark). He sees this as precisely the reason why they have certain difficulties in integrating, which increases in proportion to lesser cultural background, lower social class and greater wealth. According to the interviewee, it is these characteristics that describe those Italians who emigrate for a temporary change of occupation, who only relate to Italians, who do not adapt to certain Spanish eating habits, and consider Spain to be less economically developed. It should be noted that the person to whom we refer had always wanted to live in Spain and feels at home in this country, so that given these characteristics we should say that, as regards identification with one or another community (Deprez, 1993: 102ff),[15] he identifies more with the host community than with the Italian one.

However, there are many other aspects which affect those mentioned above. According to the same interviewee, a low cultural level is characteristic of those Spaniards who see Italians as 'Mafia types', which he does not like, since he considers the Mafia to be a phenomenon related only to the south of Italy, and also because Spain has its own problem of violence (terrorism). As regards the general image of Spaniards, he considers them to be similar in character and culture, and values highly the fact that they know how to have a good time, compared to the Italians' work habits. Although from another point of view, this aspect is also negative, as he sees the work habits in Spain as slow and low quality, and Spanish workers as informal and thus not very competitive.

Looking at Spaniards' stereotypes of Italians, some disapproved of these, while others thought that these were natural, since this works both ways, and in the end when you get to know them they change their opinion of you. The Italians associate the Spaniards with sociocultural and gastronomic stereotypes (bullfights, flamenco, paellas) and stereotypes of character (friendly, unassuming, open) and of human relations (not especially competitive). They see themselves as different in sociocultural and gastronomic terms (Mafia, opera, pizza, pasta), commercially (Italian fashion industry), and describe their own character as friendly, arrogant, elegant, and themselves as good talkers (this last characteristic in both the good and the bad senses).

Another of the indicators of the level of integration is the relation to the Italian institutions and associations. According to Consulate sources, Italians do not associate themselves with these institutions, as each Italian's self-identity is highly individualised and barely related to the wider community. The pilot study confirms these features. The interviewees rarely visit the Italian Consulate in Barcelona, and only for specific goals, and only visit the *Instituto Italiano di Cultura* to use the library or a videotape, and none of them regularly visits the *Casa degli Italiani*. Furthermore, on few occasions do they recommend these places to an Italian who is looking for work, whereas they would recommend official offices of a Spanish/Catalan institution (INEM, *Centre Català d'Ocupació*) or newspapers or magazines (*La Vanguardia*, Barcelona daily newspaper). This absence of identification of the individual with institutions is compensated for, however, by a high sense of group belonging, expressed privately in relationships of friendship. The interviewees keep in contact with between 3 and 40 other Italians, and have an average of 5 Italian friends.

Patterns of Behaviour and Language Use

After describing the Italian community and its relationship with the host community, this article analyses the relationship between this community and the various linguistic codes in its environment, plus the way these are used. This study is, of course, inseparable from the previous analysis.

The Italian's community speech varieties

The Italian community is characterised by a large geographical linguistic variety. Apart from those speech communities different from Italian,[16] it is necessary to indicate that in Italy there are five basic, different, dialectal varieties (Pellegrini, 1972): Tuscan, Friulian, Sardinian, the northern dialects (north of a line between Spezia and Rimini), and the central and southern dialects (South of this line).[17] The prestige and connotation in terms of social use associated with each variety can be established on the basis of their pronunciation (De Mauro, 1972: 172ff; Marazzini, 1994: 431–33). Although known outside Italy, the southern variety is the least prestigious, and the northern one is the most prestigious. The Roman dialect, coming from the political and cultural capital, has given rise to new linguistic features, influencing the others through the media, whereas the Tuscan dialect is the closest to the literary language, for historical reasons, and enjoys a special prestige of its own.

On the basis of this brief classification, we can sketch the social patterns of use of the dialects in comparison to the standard variety. Italy is different from other countries in that, although standard Italian has a higher prestige than the dialects, either one can be used in informal situations, whereas in other countries the use of the higher variety would be highly amusing (Bruni, 1990: 103–4).

So on the basis of this map of linguistic varieties, geographically distributed but interchangeable with standard Italian in many situations, the sociolinguistic characteristics of the Italian immigrant are formed. According to Bettoni (1993: 415), in his study of post-war (1950–60) Italian immigration, the typical Italian immigrant has an Italian dialect as his/her mother tongue, although in many cases (like the southern immigrants in Turin), the opening up to the new and foreign may have encouraged a bilingual condition between dialect and spoken Italian ('anticipatory socialisation' (Sobrero, 1973)) which in those years was already more common than was thought.

The immigrants studied by Bettoni (1993) had moved in search of work, in a situation of socioeconomic inferiority on the part of Italy with respect to the host countries, and hardly any of them spoke the language of the target country. On the other hand, as indicated above, the migratory flows of the 1980s and 1990s corresponded to a kind of 'elitist' emigration. Furthermore, in Spain, and in particular in Barcelona, there are no numerous groups of Italian immigrants, nor whole families,[18] concentrated in particular neighbourhoods, and neither are there large migratory flows such as, for example, the Friulians to Rumania (Iliescu, 1972), or to the communities in other European countries (like Switzerland or Germany) or outside of Europe (such as USA, Argentina or Australia).

So we must conclude, as do other studies, that the distinguishing features of the typical, contemporary, Italian emigrant arise from the balanced images that Spaniards and Italians have of Italy and Spain respectively, from the present-day motivation of the 'elitist' kind of emigration, from the size and level of homogeneity of this movement, and one would suppose from the individual immigrant's relationship to the dialect in his/her place of origin.

With respect to this last point, we might suppose that, as far as our informants are concerned, in the host country the regional variety of Italian,[19] or original dialect, would be used very little or not at all, except for the immediate family environment,[20] whereas standard Italian would be used in most cases, in interactions with the Italians or with the Spanish husband/spouse who would be more or less bilingual.

This fact, which the pilot study has confirmed, in some cases means the more or less total abandonment of the dialect or of a regional or colloquial variety of Italian partially mixed with the dialect to some extent, which before they had alternated with standard Italian.[21] For example, this is the case with the Milanese interviewee (G.) and the one from Naples (K.), as it had also been for the emigrants in previous decades, for whom the move meant a definite strengthening of their use of standard Italian to the detriment of the dialect (Berruto, 1987: 180; De Mauro, 1972: 53–63).

At present, the importance of this fact lies, in the first place, in the distancing of the linguistic variety emotionally closest to the subject, according to the situation; and, in second place, in the following hypothesis: some aspects of the sociolinguistic situation experienced by the interviewee in Italy determine that once in Catalonia they consider and use Catalan and Spanish in different ways, due to both their use and to the past perception of the relationship between the dialect (or regional variety) and the standard variety, and also their previous experience in partially similar situations of bilingualism. Also, their knowledge of other communities and foreign languages in their country of origin will be a determining factor. During the period of their primary socialisation, some northern Italian interviewees came into contact with southern Italian children of the same age, and received some dialectical or regional input from their parents. When adults, a considerable number of interviewees continued to use the regional Italian, and a minority the dialect itself, in the family and with friends, whereas at work they used standard Italian, which confirms the sociolinguistic description mentioned above (Bruni, 1990: 103–4).

Language choice

On the basis of the sociolinguistic situation in the place of origin, it seems that the pilot study informants mainly prefer to speak Italian, rather than a dialect (only one person preferred a dialect (Milanese) to standard Italian), together with Spanish, although they seem to identify with their native tongue. Their especially flexible patterns of use confirm this. In the mixed family, when the husband/spouse is sufficiently competent, they continue to speak Italian, slightly mixed with Spanish to express some things, or as involuntary interferences which indicate a high level of integration. With friends and acquaintances, they all speak in Italian with Italians, and in Spanish with Spaniards, and at least half of them use Catalan with some friends, although with more difficulty. At work, leaving aside those who teach Italian or do not work, most people use almost exclusively Spanish although Catalan is required, which suggests that it is either a personal decision or that they subjectively think that their knowledge of Catalan is insufficient.

Considering the relationship established by the interviewees between the dialect and standard Italian in the place of origin and their patterns of usage, a closer look at the Catalan language is now taken. In many cases, there is no identification with Catalan, because it reminds the speakers of their own dialects, because it is not considered to be a language in its own right, because it is not considered necessary for socioeconomic success, or because it is a political problem. On other occasions, the reasons are more subjective, such as harshness or lack of musicality; others partially identify with Catalan, pointing to its history for an explanation of its present situation.[22] In interactions with Catalan speakers, those who do not identify with it are annoyed when the other person does not change to Spanish, and fail to understand why they do not since the most important thing is to communicate, although at the same time they consider that learning Catalan is a way of respecting the place they are in and 'demonstrating' that they are integrated. In any case, both groups usually successfully negotiate the choice of language used in the interaction. If they do not manage to communicate, they will ask the other person to change language, asking if he/she minds if they speak in Spanish, or doing so directly themselves.

On the basis of these considerations, the hypothesis proposed above seems to be confirmed. The interviewees who used their own dialect more extensively, even as an adult, and who preferred it to standard Italian, and in whose socialization area there is no stigma attached to such use, are the ones who use Catalan most and who do not understand why this should be a problem. Those who have lived in a bilingual environment, find it similar to the Italian situation, and try to be as flexible as possible in situations of possible conflict. On the other hand, other interviewees, particularly those who had experienced a greater degree of dissociation between the dialects and the standard variety, explicitly said that they did not like Catalan because it reminded them of the dialects, or they compared its function with the dialects. They also do not like the way it sounds, comparing it with German, although they repeatedly declare that this does not influence their opinion of the Catalan people, with whom they get on well.

So for some informants there are definite connections, which should be explored more deeply, between their opinion of, their use of and the interrelation between the linguistic varieties in their country of origin and their individual perception of the linguistic varieties in a bilingual part of the host country. For some, Catalan is inferior to Italian and Spanish, while their own dialect is, to a greater or lesser extent, even more lowly valued. But for others, Catalan is valued as highly as, or only slightly less than, Spanish and Italian, and the dialect is considered to be inferior to these three. In only one case, mentioned above, did the interviewee value all four varieties at the same level, in spite of not speaking the dialect as well as before. This data is important, since it partially modifies the classification made by Bettoni (1993: 416–17) when discussing Italian immigration, who placed the host country's language as most highly valued, below this its dialects, then spoken Italian and lowest of all the Italian dialect. In fact, as we have seen above, the reasons for emigrating, the Italian political and economic situation, and the knowledge of foreign languages before emigrating are different for the present Italian immigration in Spain from previous migration flows.

Turning now to other aspects of the learning of languages, the similarity between Spanish and Italian is well known. The learning of similar languages has been studied objectively on the basis of a comparison of the two (contrastive analysis, from the 1950s onwards) and subjectively, looking at the perceived distance between speakers (Kellerman & Shaarwood Smith, 1983). The common features of similar languages allow the speaker to take advantage of his/her knowledge of foreign languages, whichever ones they may be. The term 'transparent languages' is used by teachers of especially similar foreign languages in the education system in Catalonia, although in fact this term had been used previously in a more specific sense, *'la ricerca di transparenza'* (search of transparency) (Calvi, 1995: 89). This term suggests a perceptive analogy: when the speaker makes hypotheses (whether or not these are correct) about a fragment of a 'transparent' foreign language, he/she has to look round less obstacles in order to understand, since the target language is less 'opaque' than to native speakers of other languages.

Various studies of the similarity between Spanish and Italian have highlighted: (1) contrastive studies of convergence and divergence (Arce *et al.*, 1984; Carrera Díaz, 1985), (2) features of the learning of Spanish by Italians, especially the extremely similar vocabulary (Calvi, 1995: 89),[23] (3) strategies for learning Italian by Spaniards (Schmid, 1994: 109ff), and (4) the use of particular communicative strategies and of teaching/learning strategies (Torrens, 1994, 1997, 1998), sometimes partially related to codeswitching (Alber & Py, 1986: 85–9; Nussbaum, 1992: 116–19; Calvi, 1995: 71), such as the fact that the non-native speaker can overcome a communicative problem by using particular language items which involve a mixed code between his/her own language and the foreign language, and which the speaker identifies as such via the intonation, but which he/she uses without hesitation nor clarification, based on his/her confirmed knowledge of the similarity between the two languages.

Some of this has been confirmed by the pilot study. Some of the interviewees had studied Spanish at university level in Italy (from one to three years' study) and/or in Spain in summer courses, while the others came without knowing any Spanish at all, although they may have visited Spain before. Most of the first group had had some contact with Spanish speakers in Italy, and most of the second attended classes in Spain. They all indicated the ease, or at least the lack of difficulty, of their learning process. Some suggested that the difficulty was the same as for learning other languages, such as English, which they partly attributed to their being 'good at learning languages', to their knowledge of other languages, to their open-mindedness, or to being able to use Spanish every day. In short, they put it down to their motivation, although others are conscious of the dangers of a superficial knowledge of the language or the fossilisation of lexical or syntactic errors. Some also point out that the strong similarity between the two languages allowed them to understand texts from the very beginning, without having studied the language previously (although without appreciating stylistic differences), to make themselves understood and to understand without studying, and to use Spanish from the beginning by using Italian but making double consonants single and putting on the s's. In no case was the similarity between the two languages suggested to them, but rather they spontaneously referred to it themselves.

Language use and language contact patterns

The above discussion has looked at the patterns of language behaviour on the basis of the interviews in the pilot study, and now the relationship between these and the language behaviour demonstrated by the interviewees during the interviews will be analysed, with the aim of indicating as a conclusion how these features allow us to establish the level of contact and kind of integration.

To illustrate the language contact phenomena in the pilot study, the approach was qualitative (Auer, 1984; Bettoni, 1993; and others),[24] considering the parameters internal to the micro-situation and the establishment of the relation between the language contact phenomena and the replies obtained via the modules. Thus, in a superficial way, some correlations can be made, while a more detailed analysis is left to later research, which will have to be an individual analysis of each interviewee. In the transcriptions, the capital letter at the beginning of each quote indicates the interviewee, according to the catalogue of informants presented in Appendix 1, and 'In.' indicates the interviewer.[25]

Lexical borrowing[26]

In this section, only lexical borrowing, both adapted and non-adapted, and both from Italian and Spanish, will be analysed. However, it should be noted that many other phenomena of language contact have been observed at all other levels (phonetic, morphological, morphosyntactic and syntactic).

Examples (1) to (3) of lexical borrowing from Italian have been observed in other interviewees, apart from those in this study. Some are also very frequent in non-natural situations, such as 'teaching Italian or Spanish as a foreign language' classrooms, as indicated by the author's teaching experience and the analysis of specific typescripts (Torrens, 1994).

(1) **G:** hablas en el **idioma madre** ¿no? (you speak in the **idioma madre** (mother tongue), don't you?) (S)[27]

(2) **F:** o sea que es mi **lengua madre** ¿no? ¿se dice? (I mean, it's my **lengua madre** (mother tongue) isn't it? Do you say that?) (S)

(3) **J:** es bastante [...] **madrelengua**, digamos es bastante (it's quite ... **madrelengua** (mother tongue), well it's quite...) (S)[28]

On many occasions, speakers are not aware of borrowing words (4), whereas on other occasions they realise immediately after speaking, and then switch exolingually to the other language (5), in this case Spanish, or simply request agreement or clarification (6). In contrast, at other times although they realise what they are doing, they repeat the borrowing form or give two synonyms (which are not being regarded as a 'repair' because of their order of appearance), probably because the borrowed word occurs frequently in their interlanguage (7), (8).

(4) **H:** es un poco, el **espejarse** un poco [...] la gente se encontra parecida (it's a little **espejarse** a little) (S)[29]

(5) **E:** alle officine della Inem **oficinas de la Inem** (I); (in the officine **INEM offices**)

(6) son las **tanas**, las, los sitios donde van a dormir ¿no? ¿**tanas** se llama? (S); (they are **tanas**, the, the places where they sleep, right? Are they called **tanas**? where tanas refers to an animal's burrow).

(7) **G:** ho trovato un signore qua a Arco de Triunfo che c'aveva una negozio che vendeva, una **ferretteria** (I found a man here at Arco de Triunfo who had a shop which sold, a **ferretteria** (hardware store))

   In: mm

   G: beh, ferramenta in italiano una **ferretteria** (I) (err, 'ferramenta' in Italian a **ferretteria** (hardware store))

(8) **H:** molti eh tedeschi, **alemani**, cioè, parlano l'inglese (I). (lots of, err, Germans, **alemani** (Germans), I mean, they speak English)

There were also phraseological interferences:

(9) **H:** yo le pido un'opinión, nadie tiene de ser el **padre eterno**, señora (INF) (I'm asking for your opinion, nobody has to be the **padre eterno** (Holy Father))[30]

There are innumerable examples of hesitators and gap fillers, but it is difficult to decide whether they are borrowing or codeswitching phenomena.[31] One would suppose that in an interview in Spanish (S) or in the parts in Spanish in the informal context (INF) the hesitators and gap fillers in Italian would be mostly borrowed. However, on some occasions some interviewees saw these[32] as borrowing and on others as codeswitching.[33] Consider the following examples:

(10a) **In:** i tuoi genitori sono di Potenza? o sono di diverse (Are your parents from Potenza, or are they from different)

   B: i miei sí **bueno** mia madre **bueno** mia madre è di un paesino là vicino (I) (My parents, Yes, **bueno** (well), my mother **bueno** (well) is from a village nearby)

(10b) **In:** e italiani che abitassero in Spagna? (the Italians who lived in Spain)

   A: **tampoco** nemmeno (I); (**tampoco** (neither) not even)

(10c) **In:** li vedi come una comunità unica o sottodivisa in comunità, cioè gruppo di gente (Do you look at the community as a whole or divided into sub-communities, I mean, into groups of people?)

   A: **a ver** diciamo che se, normalmente sono ognuno per conto suo (I) (**a ver** (let's see) let's say that if normally each one separately)

(10d) **In:** cioè gli italiani a volte considerano gli spagnoli come sottosviluppati (I mean, the Italians sometimes see the Spaniards as from an underdeveloped country)

>   **A:** a volte sí, sottosviluppati nel senso di **a ver como se puede decir**, di strutture (I). (sometimes, yes, underdeveloped in the sense of **a ver como se puede decir** (let's see how we can say it), of structures)

In (10a), B. sees something strange in her Italian (she pauses and laughs), but uses it again. At least in the second case she switches. (10b) is clearly an example of borrowing, with a later correction. In (10c) it is not possible to decide whether it is borrowing or codeswitching. In (10d), the same person as in (10c), places the same expression (**a ver**) next to a similar one (**como se puede decir**), and in this case one can probably speak of codeswitching.

Codeswitching

It distinguishes between: (a) *bilingual* codeswitching (Nussbaum, 1990, 1992; Torrens, 1997) which can take different forms; (b) *exolingual* codeswitching (Nussbaum, 1992; Torrens, 1997, which are resources to cover a gap in linguistic competence; and (c) *situational* codeswitching,[34] which, unlike the previous two types, indicates a modification of one of the parameters of the situation.

(a) *Bilingual* codeswitching can involve an expressive resource, a quotation, or a geographical or cultural reference.

Expressive resource. (11), (12) and (13) are examples of bilingual codeswitching used as an expressive resource and they have a clear intensifying effect:

(11)   **G:** è una cosa è un **chanchullo** (I) (it's a thing it's a **chanchullo** (fiddle))

(12)   **C:** ci son parole tedesche quindi c'è **una barreja de tot** (I) (There are German words so it's **una barreja de tot** (mixture of everything))

(13)   **C:** poi ho detto aspetta un momentino che qua se non parlo lo spagnolo **malament** (I) (so I said: wait a minute, if I don't speak Spanish here **malament** (not good))

There are other language contact phenomena (i.e. borrowings) whose function is similar according to some authors, because of their expressive or witty nature, but only from a formal point of view (code-mixing in the same element) would they be borrowing. In any case, they are a particularly expressive playing with words whose use shows a certain control of the interconnection between the two language codes (a high level of bilingual ability), as well as a special sensitivity for the language contact phenomena of which the interviewee is aware, as illustrated in (14), (15) and (16):

(14) **B:**   [ad **alquilare**] come diciamo io ed Antonio ([ad **alquilare** (to
               rent)] as Antonio and I say

      In: hm B. vado un momento ad **alquilare** il video (I) (I'm going
               out for a moment to **alquilare** (to rent)[35]

(15) **G:**   Gli italiani **ligoni** e i brasiliani **samboni** (I) (the Italians, **ligoni**
               (womanisers),[36] and the Brazilians, **samboni** (samba dancers))

(16) **B:**   los **polentones** (S)[37]

Quoting

Quoting is a type of codeswitching which, in this case, refers to the
Catalans or the Spaniards, to their ways of behaving or seeing the other
community, as in (17). They are also related to customs or cultural
characteristics (18), or make comparisons between linguistic codes (19),
not excluding references to the speaker's position *vis-à-vis* the Catalan
language.

(17) **A:**   e quindi ah italiani! **chicos italianos no por favor ¡qué
               chicos!** (I) (and so ahh, the Italians! **chicos italianos no por
               favor** (Italian boys, no thanks) **¡qué chicos!** (what boys!),
               where the Spanish girls' commentary on the Italian boys are
               reproduced).

(18) **G:**   alla frontiera la policía **¡documentación!** (I) (at the border
               ¡documentación! (papers!))

(19) **H:**[38] come dicono qua: **son idiomas diferentes** (I) (as they say
               here: **son idiomas diferentes** (they are two different lan-
               guages))

Some codeswitching corresponds to what is known as 'self-polyphony', or
the repetition of one's own words in a different situation, in relation to key
facts such as the patterns of trilingual use of Italian/Spanish/Catalan, as in
(20), where the matrix language is Spanish, or the length of time they have
been here, as in (21) and (22). In this last case, the utterance corresponds to
the reply probably given by the interviewee when the matrix language
is Italian to members of the host community when she meets them.[39]
She thus responds to the interviewer 'as a member of the host community'
(a Spanish speaker), forgetting for a moment the formal interview situation
and placing herself temporarily in a spontaneous informal situation.

(20) **C:**   al saludar dice **adéu** cuando les saludo digo **adéu** y luego digo
               madonna! (S) (when he/she says goodbye he/she says **adéu**
               (goodbye) when I say goodbye I say **adéu** (goodbye) and then
               I say **madonna!** (My God!))

(21) **C:**   dall'89 vado verso il sett settimo **año** (I) (since '89 it's getting
               on for seven **año** (years))

(22) **B:**   quattro **cuatro años** (I) four **cuatro años** (four years))

Social, cultural o geographic characteristics

On some occasions, the change of language indicates a distancing from the Spanish language or culture.

(23) **H:** c'è un termine, qua, che in Italia non c'è, **chapuza, una chapuza** (I) (there's a word which doesn't exist in Italian, **chapuza, una chapuza** (shoddy job))[40]

A large number of codeswitches related to the stereotypes about each of the cultures have been observed. For example, in (24), B. shows how she has incorporated the word 'fantasma' into the Italian repertoire, a sign of a high level of exchange between the two codes.

(24) **B:** l'idea che gli spagnoli italiani uomini l'idea che gli spagnoli si fanno degli italiani uomini, oh definizione letterale **fantasma**. (the idea that the Spanish Italian men the idea that the Spanish get of the Italian men, the exact definition is **fantasma** (someone who is all talk))

 In: ah ahhaa

 B: li definiscono **fantasma**,[41] beh in italiano non si dice però insomma (I) (they describe them as a **fantasma**, well, in Italian you don't say it, but anyway)

Other times, they attribute stereotypes about the Spaniards to other Italians, or distance themselves from the Spaniards' opinions of the Italians, among whom they include the bilingual interviewer. This is close to Gumperz (1982)'s notion of quotation or Bakhtine (1977)'s idea of polyphony, with the stereotypes in the mouth of the 'others'.

(25) **E:** c'abbiamo molto più **la sangre caliente** (I) (we are much more **la sangre caliente** (hot-blooded))

(26) **J:** con esa aire de superioridad que se la lleva encima como un **marchio** un poco (S) (with that air of superiority they have about them like a **marchio**)[42]

(27) **C:** a nosotros nos ven **spaghetti pizza mafia** y **mafia spaghetti pizza** y (S) (they see us as spaghetti pizza Mafia and Mafia spaghetti pizza)

(28) **G:**[43] tipico spanish tipico spanish **paella, tortilla y corridas y mucho sol y las chica olé** (I) (tipico spanish (typically Spanish) tipico spanish **paella, tortilla y corridas y mucho sol** (bullfights and lots of sun) **y las chica olé** (and the girls, wow!))

Some codeswitching occurs because the items do not exist in the other language, whereas others indicate a preference for one or the other code because of the cultural reference implied. The following examples illustrate this type of codeswitching related to Spanish culture (29) and to the Government administration, bodies or offices of the two countries, or to television or educational institutions (30–32).

(29) **C:** molto toro toro toro e **sangría** e **paella** come dicono gli italiani no? (I) lots of bulls, bulls and **sangria** and **paella**, as the Italians say it, right?, where C. even indicates the Italians' incorrect pronunciation and where the matrix language is Italian.

(30) **A:** o come è il caso qua di Cataluña alla **Generalitat, Departament de Treball** (I) (or as is the case here in Catalonia in the **Generalitat, Department de Treball** (Department of Labour)

(31) **J:** a livello di **COU**, ecco che si esce da un ottavo d'**EGB** in Italia molto più preparati (I) (at **COU** (final year secondary school) level, you finish eighth year **EGB** (primary school) in Italia much better prepared)

(32) **B:** y el **Consolato italiano** (S) (and the Italian Consulate), where the matrix language is Spanish

In other cases, as in (33), some items with the same semantic content and function show a heterogeneous switching, because it is easier for the speaker, who can focus on the content:

(33) **C:** gli italiani in **Cataluña**, Baleari e **Aragón** iscritti al Consolato (I) (the Italians in **Cataluña** (Catalonia), the Balearic Islands and **Aragón** (Aragón) who are registered at the Consulate), where Cataluña is the only form used by C. in all three sections of the typescript. Catalongna (it.) never occurs and Aragón appears to focus on the content.

(b) *Exolingual* codeswitching is a result of gaps in linguistic competence, and is used as a resource to make communication easier. Sometimes, the speaker is more interested in communicating than in avoiding codeswitching, as in (34), (35) and (36):

(34) **H:** anzi, un italiano è favore adesso come si dice? favorezzato, **favorecido**, va beh, insomma, perchè (I) (so an Italian is favour, how do you say? Favorezzato (Favoured), **Favorecido** (Favoured), yeah, well, anyway, because)

(35) **H:** non solo in pensione, **jubilad** cioè **jubilados** (I) (not only retired, **jubilad** (pens …) I mean, **jubilados** (pensioners)

(36) **E:** en italiano se dice **terziaria** porque vive del tercer sector (S). (in Italian you call it **terziaria** (tertiary) because it lives from the tertiary sector

On other occasions, the speaker asks for the interviewer's agreement, or that he/she tell him/her the vocabulary needed, as in example (37):

(37) **C:** stanno aprendo varie eh come si dice **tintorería** in italiano? (I) (they are learning various err how do you say **tintorería** (dry cleaners) in Italian?)

Other times (38–41), the immediate cause of the switch is not a gap in linguistic competence (there is no pause) but constitutes a habitual interlanguage mixture, keeping the two codes separate, which indicates a certain flexibility in the use of the two languages and is really a momentary slip.

(38)   **A:**   se tu mi parli in castigliano evidentemente risponderò nella **misma** forma medesima forma no?[44] (I) (If you speak to me in Castilian I'll reply in the **misma** (same) way medesima (same) way, won't I?)

(39)   **B:**   sí sí no non si può definire un lucano anche se **ahora** ora diciamo[45] (I) (yes, yes, no. You can't define a person from Basilicata although if we say **ahora** (now) now I mean)

Excerpt (40) is an interesting example of codeswitching in which phraseological elements in both languages are rearranged. In Italian it is 'essere il prezzemolo di ogni minestra' and the literal translation into Spanish would be 'ser el perejil de todas las salsas' (to be the parsley in every sauce). C. applies it to the Italians, since they are a 'very numerous' community.

(40)   **C:**   siamo come **el perejil**, qua si dice, no? (I); (we are like **perejil** (parsley), you say that here, don't you?)

This example involves codeswitching not so much because of the form *el perejil*, as because of the content ('qua si dice no?') and there are other interesting examples.[46]

(c) *Situational* codeswitching is different from the previous types in that it modifies one of the situational parameters. It was produced in all the interviews ((I) and (E)) and in the semi-spontaneous recordings (INF) with multiple functions, a fact which indicates a great flexibility in moving from one language to another, and as a result a high level of bilingualism. So in some cases, the codeswitch functions to articulate the movement from one argument to the next. In (41), A. replies to the question as to whether she knew any Spaniards before emigrating, and gets partially side-tracked on to talking about the procedures for contact or exchange between Italy and Spain for students or young workers, as well as her personal experience in the Petra Programme. (She had worked in the Italian Tourist Office before moving to Spain.)Then she switches into Spanish momentarily ('y tal ¿no? y bien'), and continues talking ('quindi conoscenti...' (being aware of)) about the Spaniards she knew before moving to Spain.

(41)   **A:**   comunque sono andata nell'ufficio **oficina de turismo** di Gran Vía (However, I went to the office **oficina de turismo** (Tourist Office) in Gran Via)

       In: hm

>   A: chiaro ti metti un po' lo que es la vita quotidiana ¿no? il lavoro **y**
>   **tal ¿no? y bien** quindi conoscenti di anche lí, chiaro sempre che
>   ho bisogno di qualcosa e so che loro mi possono aiutare
>   insomma c'è sempre un punto d'appoggio voglio dire (I)
>   (Of course, they give you an idea of what everyday life is like,
>   right? work **y tal ¿no? y bien** (and so on, right? so) so acquaint-
>   ances also at work, of course, whenever I need something, and
>   I know they can help me, well, it's always a help, I mean)

In other cases, the switch into the other language indicates the end of the
interview, as in (42), where the importance of the codeswitch is increased,
given that In. does not speak Italian and that B. knows this. Obviously, the
factor of linguistic transparency has an influence.

(42)   **In:** bueno, pues nada, ya está (well, that's it)
       B: ya está, bueno, **che velocità eh?** (that's it, good, **che velocità**
               eh? (that was quick, wasn't it)) (S)

A switch can also indicate an attempt to change the matrix or base
language of the interaction (since In. is bilingual), because of the speaker's
linguistic preference (even if it is momentary).

(43)   **In:** parli anche il catalano? (Do you also speak Catalan?)
       B: sí **una mica** (I) (yes **una mica** (a little))
(44)   **In:** lo parli? (Do you speak it?)
       C: **una miqueta, molt poquet** (...) ho intento però no hi ha
               manera (a little bit, very little (...) I try, but there's no way I can)
       In: **a poc a poc no?** (little by little, right?)
       C: **a poc a poc** (little by little)
       In: e pensi che sia utile? (I) (and do you think it's useful?)
(45)   **P:**   te gusta? (Do you like it?)
       E: sí que haremos esta noche, ¿salimos? (...) (yes, What shall we
               do tonight? Shall we go out? (...))
       P: máximo de tarde, eso quiere decir siete y media probablemente
               estoy en casa (At the most, which means I'll be home by seven
               thirty)
       E: **molt bé**[47] (...) e **poi ritorniamo a casa?** (very well (...) and
               then we'll go home?)
       P: a mí me hace ilusión ver a R. y a S. pero ir y volver no hacerles
               una visita rápida (I'd quite like to see R and S., but go and come
               back, no just a quick visit)
       E: **va beh,** (...) **non lo so** (...) (well, (...) I don't know (...))
       P: che devo dire? (What should I say?)
       E: **Boh.** Este es una canción de The Cure (INF). **Boh** (Dunno).
               This is a song by The Cure.)

Other situational codeswitching changes the subject. The following example is the continuation of the previous conversation (46).

(46)   **P:**   che devo dire? (What should I say?)
       E: boh. **Este es una canción de The Cure** (Dunno. **Este es una canción de The Cure** (This is a song by The Cure.))
       P: **la conozco. Está en el LP kiss kiss me que te dejé** (INF). (I know it. It's in the *Kiss Kiss* album that I lent you.)

In any case, in the semi-spontaneous recording (INF) of E. it can be seen that P. prefers Catalan, even though his usual language of use with E. is Spanish. For his part, E. also shows his preference for Italian, but uses Catalan (a language which she does not normally speak with P.) to make jokes or give an indulgent tone to the conversation, moving closer to P. by using Catalan.

In the next extract, each one of the speakers uses the language of their choice, and E. uses Catalan again with the above mentioned functions.

(47)   **P:**   se va a oír todo el ruido de la comida (You'll hear the sound of the food.)
       E: è l'unico momento che abbiamo per registrare (It's the only moment we've got to record.)
       E: Sono pazzi! (They're crazy!)
       P: a mí no me gusta este programa para nada (I don't like this programme at all.)
       E: **ah, es bonic!** (Catalan) (Ahh, it's nice.)
       P: **bonic** (Catalan), es estúpido (**bonic** (Wonderful), it's stupid)
       E: ma per questo! (INF) (Just because of that!)

Here is an example of P.'s preference for Catalan.

(48)   **P:**   ¿sabes qué estaba pensando? En aquello que me comentaste de las casas de italiano (You know what I was thinking? About what you said about the Italian houses)
       E: qua? (Where?)
       P: sí: **no te'n recordes? ha trucat la teva companya** (Catalan) (Don't you remember? Your friend called.) (INF)

Conclusions

This study has shown that the methodology used for the collection of data, via interviews in Spanish (S) and in Italian (I) and in semi-spontaneous situations (INF), allows us to determine with more certainty the interviewees' beliefs and information they have about the characteristics of the community, their reasons for emigrating, the settlement patterns, and language use, and to establish correlations between all this and language contact phenomena. The characteristics of the Italian community in

Spain have been established by looking at previous studies and socio-linguistic and socio-economic features in the place of origin, focusing on the general characteristics and only occasionally looking at individuals. Up until the end of the 1960s, Italian emigration was the result of a socio-economic situation which was inferior to that of the host country, and was motivated fundamentally by the search for employment, which meant that the host community viewed the Italian immigrant as socially inferior. However, this aspect was probably lessened in Spain, because until the 1980s this country's foreign image was not so very high itself. In other countries or states, such as the USA, the Italian immigrant community settled and became semi-integrated, a phenomenon seen also in their preference for the available linguistic codes, with the language of the host country first, then the local dialects, then standard Italian and finally the Italian dialect.

However, the pilot study allowed us to describe a different kind of Italian immigration, confirming and expanding some previous studies (Dittmar & Sobrero, 1990) with respect to the type of settlement and the motivation for it in the last few decades, as well as allowing us to distinguish with particular precision the determining factors in the integration and to carry out a detailed study of the patterns of language use.

These transfers have decreased progressively since 1970, and now occur in the context of socio-economic equality in the host country, and so in Spain occur for sentimental or personal reasons (need for a change), and within multinational companies. The immigrants interviewed in this study left jobs which were as good or better than those they have in Spain, and those who came without a job or without contacts were able to find work largely through their own efforts. In this way, the movement is generally considered a phenomenon of 'cultural growth', on the basis of a 'solid psychological predisposition', mostly positive, towards the new community and host country with which and where they had chosen to live. However, in such a particularly favourable context, some counter-acting features can be found, such as the geographical proximity of the country of origin, which accentuates the feelings of nostalgia for loved ones or for one's own linguistic code, especially for those who were used to using their own dialect or dialectal forms, and also their perception of a strong, uninterrupted link with their own country, and a few differentiating sociocultural aspects, among which the interviewees emphasised the kind of relationship with friends and family, and above all the level of quality at work, lesser in the host country. One could thus suppose that the level of identification with the home community is high, a hypothesis which is confirmed at the personal level (friends), but which is denied at the institutional level, where it is almost non-existent, suggesting a strong sense of individual identity.

With regard to patterns of behaviour and language use, the Italian immigrant normally knows perfectly the standard variety of his/her language, being able to switch between this and other low-status or dialectal varieties, and often Spanish too, as well as any host community's language. This normally allows a faster linguistic integration, helped by a certain psychological closeness between the two codes, felt even by those who did not speak Spanish before emigrating, and by the objective closeness of the two languages. The immigrants found Spanish easy, and its linguistic clarity immediately allowed them to use communicative strategies which are typical of situations of language contact between similar languages, such as lexical simplification. From this, together with interference and codeswitching typified as 'resource' (Turell, 1994) and used as bilingual patterns of communication, one can conclude that their level of bilingual ability is quite high. Exolingual codeswitching corresponds sometimes to momentary slips, and in other cases it is minimised because it is not seen as interrupting communication but rather helping it.[48]

So to establish the linguistic features of the speaker's level of identification with the host community and the community of origin, the replies which refer to the stereotypes about the Italian and Spanish/Catalan communities and to the perception of the host community during and after the initial period of adaptation, are determinant, as are the patterns of use of Italian, Spanish and Catalan, and the formal aspects of languages contact. In fact, integration in Catalonia in this case shows specific features because of the value placed on languages and the differing patterns of use of the native language compared to the language of the host community, and because of the relation, real or perceived, of each of the individual interviewees with other language codes in his/her place of origin.[49] According to these parameters, Italian and Spanish would always seem to have a high status, independently of their actual use, while the various Italian dialects and the regional varieties of Italian are valued more lowly. Catalan varies between a mainly low status, slightly above the Italian dialects, and an occasional high status, which on some occasions is of the same level as Italian and Spanish. The speakers switch between Italian and Spanish in all contexts, whereas few Italians speak Catalan as well as they speak Spanish and its use is subject to negotiation in the conversation. The relationship which the Italian immigrants establish with the Catalan language is thus directly linked to their integration and they describe it as a symbol of the desire to integrate, rather than just the amount or quality of their integration. This can be seen both in the study of the content of the interviews and in that of the language contact patterns observed in the bilingual speech modes of the members of the Italian community in Spain.

Notes

1. I am grateful to I. Gelabert, without whose colaboration in the majority of the interviews the collection of the data would not have been possible, and to those who replaced her on a few occasions. I would also like to thank all those workmates and students who

helped to partially transcribe the interviews, as well as the advice given by F. Amella, M.N. Muñiz, R. Pinto and H. Puigdoménech, lecturer at the *Universitat de Barcelona*, and L. Nussbaum, lecturer at the *Universitat Autònoma de Barcelona*.

2. As the large immigration flows developed. These flows are hard to quantify, since, as Dittmar and Sobrero (1990: 196–7) indicate, the data from the Italian National Institute of Statistics (ISTAT) does not distinguish between temporary and permanent migration. Furthermore, this data does not contemplate changes related to legislation on population movement. For example, the statistical data seems to indicate a decrease in the number of Italian emigrants, which is related to a new law which repealed the obligation of the emigrant to register in the local municipal council.

3. For example, the Montecatini Congress (26–28 March 1996) *'sulle iniziative per l'insegnamento e la diffusione della lingua e cultura italiana all'estero, nel quadro promozione culturale e della cooperazione internazionale'*, promoted by the *Direzione Generale dell'Emigrazione e degli Affari Sociali* of the Italian Ministry of Foreign Affairs and by the General Council of Italians Abroad. For this Congress, an extensive, up-to-date bibliography was published on Italian immigration (Tassello & Vedovelli, 1996).

4. Among others, Giacolone Ramat (1988; 1993), Bettoni (1993) and a study on Spanish immigrants in Switzerland (Schmid, 1994).

5. Italian Consulate General in Barcelona (Electoral area of Barcelona): Catalonia, Aragón, Valencia and the Balearic Islands: 8779 enrolled. Estimated: 15,000 (on 23/8/95). Catalonia, Aragón, Valencia, Balearic Islands, Murcia (193) and Andorra (103): 10,194 enrolled. Estimated: 16,000 (on 10/7/96). As can be seen, increasing.

6. Italian Consulate General in Madrid (Electoral area of Madrid): The rest of Spain: 13,970. Estimated: 18,000 (on 25/4/96). These figures do not include Andalucia, Murcia and Extremadura (estimated: 4000), for which data is not available. In both cases, the data was obtained via a personal communication from the Italian Ambassador in Madrid and Consul General in Barcelona, E. Kelescian and D. Vecchioni, respectively, to whom I am extremely grateful for their collaboration.

7. Also politically. Italy was one of the first European countries to enter NATO and the EU.

8. The industrial triangle of Milan-Turin-Genova and the growing separation of Rome as the political capital and Milan as the heart of the industrialised north have contributed to the present stratified, socio-economic situation, where three areas of Italy can be distinguished according to their level of industrialisation, a situation which has changed slightly in recent decades.

9. For example, Spain is the main agricultural-food supplier to Italy, together with Morocco, and Italy is the third-largest foreign market for Spain, after France and Germany (data for 1996).

10. Probably because of the economic crisis caused by the increase in the cost of energy (Valussi, 1993: 88).

11. For each of the persons interviewed, their parents came from the same place of origin as those indicated in Appendix 1 or from close by.

12. E. *'io mi sono spostato stando bene (. . .) io non personalmente però la mia famiglia (. . .) non è un'emigrazione'* (When I moved I was fine (. . .) not me personally, but my family (. . .) it's not emigration).

13. Talking of the migratory flows that took place until the 1970s, Sabatini *et al.* (1974) have indicated the positive importance of this last point.

14. H. *'non esiste più la emigrazione (. . .) la gente si sposta solo perchè ha piacere di andare, di cambiare'* (There isn't emigration any longer (. . .) people move because they want to go, to change).

15. J. *'non [sono venuto] per poter mangiare (. . .) io no me siento affatto **un emigrante con necesidad de trabajo (. . .) sino por elección de vida (. . .) me iban muy bien las cosas allá (. . .) no me sitúo en este globo no me englobo digamos en este grupo'*** (I didn't come because I was starving (. . .) I don't feel **an emigrant at all who needs to work (. . .) but because of my life style (. . .) things were going well back there (. . .) I don't put myself in, I don't fit into this group**).

16. French-speaking (mainly in the Aosta Valley, and the Friuli, Carnic and Dolomites) Sardinian-speaking in Sardinia, German-speaking (mainly in Bolzano Province and the Tirol), and to a lesser extent, Greek and Catalan (in l'Alguer). See M.A. Pradilla (Chapter 2 in this volume.)

17. The classification is only tentative. Each one of the five varieties obviously includes other sub-categories: the complexity of the present classification of the Italian linguistic varieties is due to the equally complex political situation in Italy before the unification which took place in the second half of the 19th century. Until then, Italy was politically and thus culturally and linguistically divided into a large number of small states. This fragmentation caused the linguistic divergence that still characterises some dialects such as the Sicilian which differ from standard Italian, very distant from the Tuscan variety, to the extent of their being considered as linguistically independent.

18. 'Whole families' includes the different nuclear families of the various children, brothers and sisters, etc. That is, different generations and their horizontal and vertical branches.

19. By 'regional variety' is meant that neo-standard Italian which is most influenced by regional differences, that is, by the different intonation, vocabulary, etc., partly due to the coexistence with the local dialect.

20. When the husband/spouse, partner or other member of the family moved with the interviewee.

21. The greater or lesser use of the dialect or of varieties of standard Italian influenced by the dialects depends on various factors, such as educational level, social class, age, opinion of the teachers and parents of the dialect, geographical situation, apart from the situation in which the language is used (degree of informality, participants in the inter-action, etc.).

22. Mainly those interviewees who were acquainted with bilingual situations (such as C., whose parents were Slovenian, who learnt a Slavic dialect and who as an adult described herself as bilingual in the Slavic language and in Italian, switching between both languages with friends and at work), or those who considered their dialect and standard Italian as equal and used them both (such as G. from Milan).

23. Which is extremely useful in the early stages of learning, and helps with communicative interaction via the use of various kinds of simplification, although this may create some misunderstandings and the large number of real or supposed homonyms and synonyms may be an obstacle.

24. Bettoni (1993: 429) states that there is a tendency to move away from the quantitative analysis of data collected in large surveys, towards 'a subtler, qualitative and inter-pretative analysis, even of one person', and also to carry out micro-interpretations of the codeswitching *in loco*, by looking at the speaker's motivation or the effects produced on other speakers, rather than macro-correlations between the patterns of linguistic use and the situational factors which can be defined beforehand or the persons involved in the interaction.

25. The letters in brackets at the end of each example indicate the section of the transcript in which it occurs. ((I) = Interview in Italian, (S) = Interview in Spanish, (INF) = Informal inter-view in semi-spontaneous context). Bold type indicates the language contact phenomena.

26. See Turell (1993, 1995) for a more exhaustive description.

27. Capital letters + stop (A.) indicate specific informants (See Appendix 1); In. = interviewer.

28. From *lingua madre* and *madrelingua* (in Italian), respectively.

29. From *(ris)pecchiarsi*, used in a slightly different way to the Italian (regard someone as a role model), meaning to see oneself reflected in another person, to look similar.

30. From *fare il padreterno* (behave like someone who is infallible).

31. Also, completely separating one language from the other as an indication of switching (the expressions in question appear in Spanish or Italian without language contact) is not a rigorous practice, because of the particular functions that the hesitators and gap fillers fulfill, because they are more or less isolated from the constructions in which they occur, and because they are mostly invariable.

32. Especially *bueno*, and to a lesser extent, others such as *pues* (well), *es que* (the thing is), *o sea* (that is), *a ver* (let's see), *¿sabes?* (you know?). A. often uses *¿sabes?*, but which he alternates with *¿sai?*. Among the Italian hesitators and gap-fillers, the most common in these interviews are *però* (but), *cioè* (I mean), *insomma* (any way) and then others such as *ma* (but), *beh* (well), *perchè* (because), *anzi* (so).

33. This aspect deserves greater attention. It would be necessary to verify the number, and where they appear, the Italian and Spanish forms of the same hesitator or gap-filler, as well as its function *in loco*, for each one of the individual interviewees.

34. Or commutations, as in Nussbaum (1992: 106).

35. Here, the Spanish verb *alquilar* has been Italianised using the Italian 1st conjugation ending (-are).

36. From *ligones* (sp.) 'womanisers' whose ending has been transformed by the Italian morphology.

37. Which is the Spanish transformation of the Italian 'polentoni', polenta eaters, from the north of Italy.

38. Talking of Spanish vs. Catalan applied to Italian vs. dialects.

39. Such as '*¿Cuánto tiempo llevas aquí?*; *Pues hablas muy bien el español*' (How long have you been living here for?; Well, you speak very good Spanish), etc. A dialogue with members of the host community which is focused on these subjects constitutes a reinforcement of her condition of 'foreigner', as there is a date when she came, and a period of adaptation to the language. and an important transformation of her linguistic and cultural identity from those of the host community.

40. Where *chapuza* refers to the inferior quality of Spanish workmanship compared to the Italian one.

41. In this case, given that *fantasma* (Spanish) (person who is all talk) coincides syntactically with *fantasma* (Italian) in the singular but not in the plural, B.'s clarification could refer to: (a) voluntary switching; or (b) borrowing which she realised was such afterwards. In any case, the following borrowing was observed in this interviewee: '*Anche se sono fantasmi*' (Also if they are all talk).

42. Where *marchio* means a mark of distinction, possessed by the Italians.

43. Spanish stereotypes that he saw as a tourist in Malaga, but which he no longer believes, unlike many other Italians.

44. The typescript of A.'s conversations shows examples of this kind of switching, with the immediate juxtaposition of an equivalent item in the base language.

45. The juxtaposition of *ahora* and *ora* (now), with this function, is also sometimes present in A.'s and G.'s speech.

46. (40b) '*ti ho detto, siamo come il prezzemolo, come il **perejil**, da tutte le parti (I)*" (I told you, we're like parsley [...] like *perejil* (parsley), everywhere). (40c) '*somos como el perejil del Carlos Arguiñano en todas las salsas. Dime dónde no haya un italiano porque yo voy allí (E)*' (we're like Carlos Arguiñano's (a Basque cook) parsley in every sauce. Tell me where there are no Italians because that's where I'm going). (40d) 'C. *se sono qui come il prezzemolo vuol dire che li vedono bene (I)*' (a play on words: if they're like parsley, this means they have a high regard for them). Note that two examples of switching appear in Spanish (I) in (40a) -*el perejil*- and in (40b) -*il prezzemolo/il **perejil***- and no other example in the other two extracts, with Spanish base or matrix language (E) (40c) and Italian (I) in (40d).

47. For E's use of Catalan, see examples (47)–(48).

48. The specific characteristics of their interlanguage were not determined in this study.

49. As is the case of dialects and other languages in a bilingual situation in relation to standard Italian.

Appendix 1

Interviewee	Gender	Partner/spouse	Childhood residence	Age	Year of arrival	Session	Profession	
							country of origin	host country
A	F	–	Montegalda/Vicenza	28	1994	(III)	secretarial work	secretarial work
B	F	SC	Potenza	28	1991	(III)	student	teacher of Italian
C	F	–	Gorizia	30	1989	(III)	manager	secretary
D	F	I	R. Emilia	63	1963	(I)	manager	business manager
E	M	SC	Potenza	22	1992	(III)	student	teacher of Italian
F	M	–	Agliana (Pistoia)	34	1984	(III)	employee/worker	teacher of Italian
G	M	SC	Milan	39	1983	(III)	designer	designer
H	M	SC	Milan/Verona/Rome	52	1987	(III)	designer	designer
I	M	SC	Ferrara	46	1993	(I)	shop owner	restaurant owner
J	M	–	Florence	29	1991	(II)	electrician	electrician
K	M	SC	Naples	71	1997	(III)	sales person	retired

Total number of informants: 11

Key:

Sex: M = male, F = female

Spouse/partner: SC = Spanish or Catalan, I = Italian

Childhood residence: place of birth and residence or town lived in for most of childhood

Year of arrival in Spain: emigration, not visit

Sessions recorded:
I = sociolinguistic interview in Italian
II = sociolinguistic interviews in Italian and Spanish
III = sociolinguistic interviews in Italian and Spanish and recording without interviewer in the host country and in the country of origin

Profession:

References

Alber, J.L and Py, B. (1986) Vers un modèle exolingue de la comunication interculturelle. *Études de Linguistique Appliquée* 61, 78–90.

Arce, J., Carrera, M., Fernández de Murga, F. and Muñiz, M.N. (1984) *Italiano y Español-Estudios Lingüísticos*. Universidad de Sevilla, Sevilla.

Auer, J.C.P. (1984) *Bilingual Conversation*. Amsterdam/Philadelphia: John Benjamins.

Backtine, M. (1977) *Le Marxisme et la Philosophie du Langage*) (1st edition 1929). Paris: Les Éditions du Minuit.

Berruto, G. (1987) *Sociolinguistica dell'Italiano Contemporaneo*. Roma: La Nuova Italia Scientifica.

Betolaja, E. (1987) L'Unione Latina. In V. Lo Cascio (ed.). *L'Italiano in America Latina*. Firenze: Le Monnier.

Bettoni, C. (1993) Italiano fuori d'Italia. In A.A. Sobrero (ed.). *L'Italiano. La Variazione e gli Usi* (pp. 41–60). Roma: Laterza.

Bruni, F. (1990) *L'italiano. Elementi di Storia della Lingua e della Cultura* (1st edition 1984). Torino: Utet.

Calvi, M. (1995) *Didattica di Lingue Affini: Spagnolo e Italiano*. Milano: Guerini Scientifica.

Carrera Díaz, M. (1985) *Manual de Gramática Italiana*. Barcelona: Ariel.

Collicelli, C. and Di Cori, S. (1986) L'immigrazione straniera in Italia nel contesto delle problematiche migratorie internazionali. *Studi Emigrazione* 82–83, 429–41.

De Mauro, T. (1972). *Storia Linguistica dell'Italia Unita* (1st edition 1963). Bari: Laterza.

Deprez, C. (1993) L'entretien autobiographique ou la (re)presentation de soi: un exemple de dialogue à trois. *Cahiers d'Acquisition et de Pathologie du Language (CALaP)* 10, 101–15.

Dittmar, N. and Sobrero, A.A. (1990) L'italiano in europa: dalla parte di chi emigra. In V. Lo Cascio (ed.). *Lingua e Cultura Italiana in Europa*. Firenze: Le Monnier.

Giacalone Ramat, A. (1988) *L'Italiano tra le altre Lingue: Strategie di Acquisizione*. Bologna: Il Mulino.

Giacalone Ramat, A. (1993) Italiano di stranieri. In A.A. Sobrero (ed.). *L'Italiano. La Variazione e gli Usi* (pp. 341–409). Bari: Laterza.

Gumperz, J.J. (1982) *Discourse Strategies*. Cambridge: Cambridge University Press.

Haller, H. (1986) Come si parla l'italiano negli Stati Uniti. *Italiano e Oltre* 1. Firenze.

Iliescu, M. (1972) *Le Frioulan à partir des Dialectes Parlés en Roumanie*. The Hague: Mouton.

Kellerman, E. and Sharwood Smith, M. (1983) Now you see it, now you don't. In S.M. Gass and L. Selinker (eds) (1986) *Crosslinguistic Influence in Second Language Acquisition* (pp. 112–13). Cambridge: Cambridge University Press.

Marazzini, C. (1994) *La Lingua Italiana*. Bologna: Il Mulino.

Ministerio de Trabajo y Asuntos Sociales. *Anuario de Migraciones 1997*. Madrid.

Nussbaum, L. (1990) *El Contacte de Llengües a Classe de Francès. Una Aproximació Pragmàtica*. PhD Dissertation. Universitat Autònoma de Barcelona.

Nussbaum, L. (1992) Manifestacions del contacte de llengües en la interlocució. *Treballs de Sociolingüística Catalana* 10, València, 99–123.

Pellegrini, G.B. (1972) I cinque sistemi linguistici dell'italo-romanzo. In G.B. Pellegrini (1975) *Saggi di Linguistica Italiana* (pp. 55–87). Torino: Boringhieri.

Rossi, E. (1887) *Quarant'anni di Vita Artistica* Vol. 2 (pp. 317–420). Firenze: L.Niccolai.

Sabatini, F., Lombardi Satriani, L.M. and Simone, R. (1974) Emigrazione italiana, lingua e processi di acculturazione in Europa. In Centro per lo studio dell'insegnamento dell'italiano all'estero (Università degli studi di Trieste) (ed.) *Italiano d'Oggi. Lingua non Letteraria e Lingue Speciali* (pp. 113–32). Trieste: Lint.

Schmid, S. (1994) *L'italiano degli Spagnoli. Interlingue di Immigrati nella Svizzera Tedesca*. Milano: Franco Angeli.

Sobrero, A.A. (1973) L'integrazione linguistica in giovani immigrati a Torino. In *Parole e Metodi* 6, 165–212.

Tassello, G. and Vedovelli, M. (eds) (1996) *Scuola, Lingua e Cultura nell'Emigrazione Italiana all'Estero* (bibliografia generale (1970–1995). Roma: Centro Studi Emigrazioni di Roma (CSER).

Torrens, R. (1994) *Las Estrategias de Intercomprensión y de Enseñanza/Aprendizaje en el Aula de Italiano y Español Lengua Extranjera: un Estudio de los Cambios de Lengua*. Research Paper for PhD Courses, Universitat de Barcelona.

Torrens, R. (1997) La función del análisis del discurso en la comprensión de las estrategias de enseñanza/aprendizaje de una lengua extranjera: la perspectiva interaccionista de los cambios de lengua. *Ies Jornades de Llengües Estrangeres*, Departament d'Ensenyament, Tarragona. Anuari de Filologia, Vol XX, secció G, no. 8, 87–100. Universitat de Barcelona.

Torrens, R. (1998) L'analisi del codeswitching: uno strumento pedagogico nell'insegnamento dell'italiano Lingua Straniera. *Quaderns d'italià*, 3, Universitat Autònoma de Barcelona, 47–56.

Turell, M. (1993) Els indicadors sociolingüístics del contacte interètnic. *Actes del IXè Col.loqui Internacional de Llengua i Literatura Catalanes*, Alacant (1991), 301–18.

Turell, M. (1994) Codeswitching as communicative device. *Actes del XIV Congreso de AEDEAN*. Valladolid: Universidad de Valladolid (1992), 59–78.

Turell, M. (1995) L'alternança de llengües i el préstec en una comunitat interètnica. In M. Turell (ed.) *La Sociolingüística de la Variació* (pp. 259–93). Barcelona: PPU.

Valussi, G. (1993) *L'italia Geoeconomica* (1st edition 1987). Torino: Utet.

Chapter 14

The Maghrebi Communities

BELÉN GARÍ

Nature and Distribution of the Maghrebi Communities

Immigration to Spain has increased enormously over the last two decades, especially from the Third World. One of the biggest immigration groups are the Maghrebi communities. The majority are Moroccans, but some Algerians and Tunisians can also be found. The number of Libyans and Mauretanians is statistically insignificant. According to the *Instituto Nacional de Estadística* (Spanish Institute of Statistics) the Moroccan community of 1992 legal residents contains 29,265 members, but the estimates of the non-governmental organisations consider the real number to be between 60,000 and 100,000. In terms of Algerians and Tunisians there are 1411 legal residents and about 8000 clandestine ones, the general status of whom is that of 'economic immigrants', with only a few being considered 'political refugees'. The possibility of legalising this situation is low, because the residence permit can only be obtained with a legal job or studies in the country. More recent official figures (see the *Anuario de Migraciones 1997*) situate the number of 1996 Moroccan migrants in 77,189 and Algerian migrants in 3706.

As Table 14.1 indicates the majority of the Maghrebi immigrants are very young. Those younger than 15 constitute 17% of the population and the active young population (between 15 and 45 years) represent 55%.

Table 14.1 Maghrebians with residence permit by age groups

Age	Moroccans	(%)	Other Africans	(%)
<15	5,105	17	1,366	14
15–30	9,351	32	2,775	28
30–45	6,839	23	3,735	38
45–65	2,102	7	526	5
>65	305	1	142	1
Unknown age	5,563	19	831	8
Total	29,265		9,853	

Source: Anuario de Migraciones 1993; Ministerio de Asuntos Sociales (1994)

These figures indicate a very high birth rate considering that 40% of the men are unmarried or have their family still in the country of origin. Therefore, in terms of immigration, we can consider the Maghrebi community as being in an initial phase, with a second generation still under 15 years.

There are more men than women in the group (about 65%). There is no information on the number of men in the clandestine category, but the proportion of men is probably even greater (about 70%). In general, adult male immigration precedes that of the wife and children, who normally travel to Spain when the father's situation is relatively stable.

The community's distribution in Spain is very heterogeneous, as can be observed in Table 14.2, where figures by Autonomous Community are

Table 14.2 Maghrebians in Spain by Autonomous Community and country of origin

	Moroccans	*Algerians*	*Other Maghrebians*	*Total*
Catalonia	20,461	499	160	21,120
Madrid	11,061	303	206	11,570
Andalusia	7,963	235	80	8,278
Valencian Country	3,665	967	44	4,676
Murcia	3,705	217	4	3,926
Canary Islands	2,373	36	120	2,529
Balearic	1,448	125	11	1,584
Extremadura	1,410	13	1	1,424
Castille-La Mancha	1,271	69	8	1,348
Basque Country	1,260	38	35	1,333
Aragón	834	320	17	1,171
Castille-León	637	31	5	673
Galicia	482	16	2	500
Rioja	314	78	1	393
Ceuta and Melilla	684	2	–	686
Navarra	233	51	2	286
Asturias	133	9	7	149
Cantabria	55	6	5	66
Unknown	3,314	244	116	3,674
Total Spain	61,303	3,259	824	65,386

Source: Anuario de Migraciones 1993; Ministerio de Asuntos Sociales

included by decreasing number. Nearly all the Maghrebi communities live in just seven of Spain's Autonomous Communities, above all Catalonia (21,120), Madrid (11,570) and Andalusia (8,278). There are also a fair number to be found along the remaining areas of the Mediterranean coast (the Valencian Country, Murcia), and on the islands (the Balearic Islands and the Canary Islands). There are also some members of these communities in the two African colonies (Ceuta (345) and Melilla (341)). The rest of the country has very few Maghrebi settlers.

Table 14.3 shows the distribution of Maghrebi migrants in Spain by provinces with more than 1000 immigrants and country of origin. With regard to the provinces in these above-mentioned Autonomous Communities, Barcelona is the one with the largest population (14,863), followed by Madrid (11,570) and the provincial capitals on the Mediterranean coast (Murcia, Girona, Málaga, Tarragona, Almería, Valencia, Majorca, Alicante, Castelló, etc.). The Atlantic coast and the centre of Spain (except Madrid) do not have Maghrebians in significant numbers.

Even if newspapers and mass media are constantly publishing stories about illegal networks 'smuggling people', this is not the commonest way of coming into the country and staying on illegally. There is no doubt that

Table 14.3 Maghrebians in Spain by provinces with more than 1000 immigrants and country of origin.

	Moroccans	*Algerians*	*Other Maghrebians*	*Total*
Barcelona	14,492	272	99	14,863
Madrid	11,061	303	206	11,570
Murcia	3,705	217	4	3,926
Girona	3,035	21	43	3,099
Malaga	2,627	37	25	2,689
Tarragona	2,158	82	9	2,249
Las Palmas	1,974	28	109	2,111
Almeria	1,726	106	20	1,852
Valencia	1,237	565	20	1,822
Balearic Islands	1,448	125	11	1,602
Alicante	1,259	205	14	1,478
Cadiz	1,883	19	6	1,408
Castelló	1,169	197	10	1,376
Cáceres	1,089	9	–	1,098

Source: Anuario Estadístico 1992; Instituto Nacional de Estadística

the largest number of illegal immigrants come in legally either as 'tourists' or with a three months' visa, and lose legality when this initial time period is finished. Another illegal situation which is very common arises when a legal job is lost because the contractual period is over and not renewed. Such immigrants are much sought after because they constitute a pool of little-valued workers who will adapt to almost any kind of situation and need because of their marginal position and lack of labour union help (López García & Montabes Pereira, 1994).

The most pathetic situation, very frequent in the last 10 years can be seen in the *pateras* (small boats) which attempt to disembark on the Spanish coasts. These *pateras*, 'into which a large number of North African migrants from Morocco and Argelia are crammed, are frequently stopped by the Spanish police before their passengers can even disembark. Besides, these passengers, who spend all their money on the journey and suffer abuse from intermediaries, are in the majority of cases repatriated' (See M.T. Turell, Ch. 1 in this volume).

In Spain, as in the rest of Europe, the Maghrebi communities settle in urban areas and work in the services sector. The tendency is to group together in the same neighbourhood and villages. This phenomenon of concentration is typical of new immigrant groups such as the Maghrebi community. At all events, the number of Maghrebi immigrants is expected to increase, despite political restrictions on the Spanish side.

Language and Culture

Maghrebi culture is basically oral. There is a rich popular unwritten culture, transmitted by people who cannot read or write. The most important manifestations of this culture are poetry, popular songs, *malhuns* (a sort of sung poetry) and stories. All these date from ancestral times and are now under threat. The first crisis came with colonisation of the countries by the Europeans (mainly French); the second, with the abandoning of the villages to go to the big cities. But the experience of immigration is what has done the greatest harm to oral culture. Being separated from the members of the family, all these poems, songs and stories have lost their medium of transmission. Nowadays, in situations such as these, oral tradition has no channel of diffusion and is sentenced to neglect and indifference. Many of these poems and songs are in Berber and decreasing use of this language makes the survival of the tradition even more problematic. In Spain the oral traditional Maghrebi culture is not known at all by the host community mainly due to the difficulty of understanding or translating it.

Another aspect of the Maghrebi culture is the role that women play in society. When women come to the new society they find it difficult to get to know people, make friends and go out. In Maghrebi countries women are accustomed to interact in groups of women, with no male present. But in Spain it is nearly impossible for them to be in an atmosphere, except at home, with only women. It is hard to accept that in the cultural centre, in the market, in the park, or wherever they go there are men and women. They are not used to Spanish cultural patterns, but at the same time, they have lost much of their own because of migration. Many women are illiterate and it is only in this kind of oral, traditional group (where they make clothes or tapestry while they tell stories and sing songs), that they can express and develop their sense of culture.

As a last point it must be mentioned that, in Maghrebi countries, culture is very much related to religion. They celebrate Islamic rituals of the year. The most important is *Ramadan* when they do not eat during daylight hours, and they pray many times during the day. Once again, these traditions are difficult to keep up in the new community, because there are no concessions made in the school timetable or the working day, and they are not helped by the general ethos.

Education

The area of education involves a range of aspects. On the one hand, there is the first generation immigrant who needs to be incorporated into the Spanish education system; but this is not easy given the level of language and general knowledge required. When the family is finally reunited in the new country, children between 0 and 16 years travel to Spain. Getting these children to enter school with children of the same age is likely to be problematic, because they lack the prior knowledge assumed by the curriculum and are not fluent in Spanish. In addition, those over 14 have no right to free education. On the other hand, the children of immigrants who are born in Spain need special attention; but the teachers are not, in many cases, prepared to understand and support the immigrant properly. There are, of course, the so-called 'support teachers', whose job it is to follow the children with adaptation problems. Unfortunately, in some cases these teachers' efforts have done more harm than good, as a result of overtly sympathetic or patronising attitudes.

The high incidence of failure in education in the new community is also partly due to the parents. The latter do not have a coherent long-term view of education, and are trying to adapt themselves. The school offers models and values which are completely different from those of their community, and the family's tendency is to turn inwards on their community values in order to survive as a group. This leads to reaction on the part of the school radicalising the new values, creating confusion in the child who becomes a stranger in both communities (Cummins, 1981). There are some non-governmental institutions who are active in trying to make up for this lack of institutional help by providing supportive supplementary education: evening schools, literacy classes, Arabic lessons for children, etc.

At present, in Spain there are only 30 schools, distributed in Madrid, Andalusia, the Valencian Country, Asturias, Ceuta and Melilla, where Islam is taught as an extracurricular activity. During the academic year 1999–2000 a new experience will be developed in Catalonia whereby Islamic language, culture, customs and traditions will be taught to Maghrebi children in those centres where a sufficient number of pupils apply, without detriment to their integrating into the Spanish educational system and in the direction of summing cultures as part of humankind's cultural and linguistic heritage (*La Vanguardia*, 9 September 1999).

Girls, unfortunately, usually leave school at the onset of puberty (that is, between 11 and 14), because their presence in a coeducative institution after this age is not acceptable to the family; furthermore, a woman's education needs are supposed to be covered elsewhere. At this age some of them have not finished the basic education, so they miss the chance of obtaining an official diploma. A high percentage of the boys drop out of school as well, because they are expected to work to bring some money into the family when they are only 15–16: the poor results they usually have at school often leads to a family decision to take them out of school.

This lack of support to the immigrant Maghrebi communities by the institutions is based upon the so-called *Ley de Extranjería* (Immigration Act). Under this law it is not legal to work in Spain without a work permit. To obtain the permit one needs a residence permit and a request from an employer who is willing to employ the person. This is nearly impossible to obtain and very easy to lose when the contract is over. Because of this situation, many immigrants have no rights or benefits and they are considered 'undesirable aliens' by the police. This term means, according to a spokesman of the *Dirección General de la Policía* (Police General Headquarters), 'an immigrant who has not yet committed any crime, but who is involved in questionable or shady activities'.

The official status most often used by immigrants in Spain is 'tourist' status so they can be in the country with a visa for three months, during which time they cannot work, and have no social, cultural or healthcare rights. They usually live and work in a total lack of support from social services. Unions, laws and social assistance are reserved for the legal minority.

Language Status in the Country of Origin and in the Host Country

Maghrebians live in a complex, trilingual situation in their own country. French, Arabic and Berber are present in a diglossic system. Berber is the language with lowest status, Arabic has two status levels (Low and High) and French is the High status language. Morocco is the country with most Berbers, nearly the whole population is Berber in origin, but at present the language is spoken only in certain places like the

Rif, the Atlas and Sús in Morocco, and Kabilia, Chauía and Mzab in Algeria. The use of the language is restricted to the family domain, and especially used by women and children. Interaction among men is usually in Arabic. The public use of Berber is considered a transgression of the national union and a break of the ideal of an entire Arabic nation.

Arabic is spoken with several registers from the very highest sacred Classic Arabic of the Al-Koran to the lowest variants of familiar and casual Arabic in national variants. In the middle we have school Arabic, institutional Arabic, political Arabic (used for speeches and meetings), religious Arabic, etc. Even if the leaders in the Maghrebi countries pretend that there is a totally uniform Arabic language, the sociolinguistic situation is quite different. This language policy produces in the Maghrebi speaker a heightened sense of linguistic unity and a feeling of linguistic affinity to any other language of the Arabian world – which is totally artificial. Far from this ideal, the real situation is one of complex heterogeneity.

Lastly, a third language completes the sociolinguistic map of the Maghreb. People with higher education, in general men, speak French. It is the language used to maintain relations with the Western world and for transmitting science and research at university level. Women have a survival level of French but in many cases this is forgotten because of lack of practice. To know and speak French means to side with progressive ideas, against the integrism proposed by many political leaders of these countries. The hope of immigrating to Europe and the history of immigration to France have increased the willingness and ability to communicate in French.

In the new community, in this case Spain, Arabic has less status than in Maghrebi countries. Theoretically, it is considered an important language, redolent with culture, literature and thought. But in an everyday context it is not very accepted by the population as it has come to be related to crime, drugs and terrorism. Berber is unknown in the new community. French is well considered and accepted in an initial phase, but not completely accepted after a while. Spanish and other European national languages have a high status in Spain.

In Catalonia, the situation of Moroccan and Algerian migrants of *Amazigh* origin deserves a separate mention. These people call their own language *Amazigh*, which is an Afro-Asiatic language, more specifically, Northern Berber. The most important *Amazigh* varieties are: *Tarifit* (with almost 2,000,000 speakers, mainly in Morocco), *Kabyle* (with 2,500,000 speakers, mainly in Algeria), *Tamazight* (with 3,000,000 speakers, mainly in Morocco), *Tachelhit* (with 3,000,000 speakers, distributed in both Morocco and Algeria), and finally, *Tamaceq*, spoken by the Tuareg in the Sahara (with 260,000 speakers) (*International Encyclopaedia of Linguistics*, 1: 175). In spite of the fact that most African countries in this area are independent, *Amazigh* is not a fully recognised language; it is only official in Nigeria and Mali, whereas in Morocco, Algeria, Tunisia, Libya, Mauritania and Txad it has not been granted any political status. If anything, these migrants are still more isolated than the rest of the Maghrebi people, who usually speak Arabic or French, since the fact of not mastering any of these two more international languages may have negative effects on their psychological development, in the case of *Amazigh* children and, in general, on the development of cultural identity and the process of socialisation. Moreover, according to Timaltine *et al.* (1995) this situation reinforces the isolation of the *Amazigh* community in its patterns of settlement in the host community.

Patterns of Language Use

The languages used by Maghrebians in Spain are the following: Berber, national variants of Arabic, Spanish, French and Classic Arabic. These languages are used in different situations and interactions. These include: family, cultural centre, work, relations with officialdom, mosque, friends and education.

Domain 1: the family

Interactions in the family vary according to two factors: whether or not the members live in the household and whether or not the members come from a Berber-speaking family. With regard to the first factor, the Maghrebians who live in the family household with wife and children speak national variants of Arabic at home, and there is little or no use of Berber, even if they spoke it in their country of origin. But those who live in all male groups or in residences or boarding houses, carry on speaking Berber when they go back to their country of origin for holidays. The reason seems to be that the Berber families by preference choose to speak a variety of Arabic of their country of origin, as a question of sociolinguistic identity, since they feel more Arabic than Berber. The normal interaction between men is traditionally in Arabic, and Berber has a restricted domain in the family and mainly for women and children.

The other factor, of course, is whether the member is Berber or Arabic. In the latter case he will only speak Arabic in the family. So the loss of Berber is very considerable in the community. Second generation immigrants have practically no access to the Berber language or opportunity to acquire it, and one underlying reason for this is the lack of prestige suffered by this language.

Domain 2: the cultural centre

There are 46 Maghrebi associations in Spain with a variety of cultural and educational goals. The majority have fewer than 100 fixed members, although they all have a large number of sporadic members who, in some cases, may number up to 500 per year. The languages spoken in the cultural centres are national variants of Arabic, Spanish and French. In these centres there are two types of interaction: either between Maghrebians, in which case Arabic is always spoken, or between Spaniards and Maghrebians, and in this case Spanish is the most spoken language because the volunteers, people visiting the centre, the teachers, etc. do not speak Arabic. But sometimes the Maghrebians' Spanish level is too low to make communication in Spanish feasible, in which case they may use French as a lingua franca.

Domain 3: work

At work Maghrebians tend to use Spanish or French. Those who work with the public (waiters, house cleaning, etc.) must speak Spanish. The use of French is only accepted by the employers in the initial phase. Reaching a survival level of Spanish in order to get a job is the main reason for attending the cultural centres' courses.

Domain 4: institutions

Institutional interaction, for example with public administration, police, the officials at the Department of Employment, Immigration Department, etc. takes place only in Spanish, because the government employees will typically not speak other languages. Such interaction tends to be frustrating especially if the Maghrebi speaker does not yet have a good level of Spanish.

Domain 5: the mosque

The common language used by Muslims in their prayers and rituals in the mosque is Classic Arabic. It is the sacred language of the Al-Koran. All Muslims, both Arabic and non-Arabic, can speak the sacred language of Islam, since they have to learn by heart extracts from the Al-Koran in the original. In their countries of origin they would have kept the religious observances and visited the mosques quite frequently. But when they come to the new country, especially in the case of Spain, the frequency of attendance decreases considerably. Second generation immigrants in most cases do not visit the mosque, nor do they learn Classic Arabic. Their knowledge of Classic Arabic is confined to some prayers and sentences learned from their parents (or grandparents if they go to the old country on holidays) but only a small number of them continue as practising Muslims.

Domain 6: friendship

In interactions with friends, Spanish and Arabic are the main languages. Spanish (or occasionally French) is used in interethnic (Spanish–Arabic) friendship, while Arabic is used for monocultural interaction. Within their group of friends there are normally no other Muslims from other speech communities such as Pakistanis or Senegalese, with whom they might have spoken Arabic.

Domain 7: education

Those who are studying in Spain use Spanish for interaction both with teachers and other students. In some Autonomous Communities there is another language in the education system, for example, Basque in the Basque Country and Catalan in Catalonia. They can understand Basque or Catalan, but seldom or never use these languages themselves.

Figure 14.1 shows the language used by Maghrebians across domains. As can be seen, Arabic and Spanish are the two languages used the most by the Maghrebi community. Spanish is predominant, and is present in nearly all situations (except in family and mosque). Arabic, however, is present in many situations and interactions, increasing in the family domain, and monolingually in in-group Maghrebi interaction. Second generation immigrants continue speaking Arabic within the group, but only Spanish if a member of the host community is present.

Other languages, on the contrary, tend to decrease, especially in the second generation: French is used as a bridge language and not used any longer when they reach a sufficient level of Spanish, and then not transmitted to the second generation. Classic Arabic and Berber tend to be reduced to a few formulas and usages, mainly set phrases and expressions.

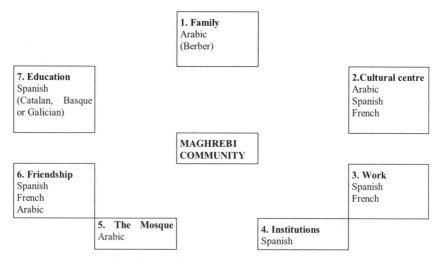

Figure 14.1 Maghrebi speech communities across domains

Acquisition and Use of the Host Communities' Language(s)

In order to analyse the whole area of acquisition and use of the host community language(s) by the Maghrebi communities in Spain, that is, Spanish in the monolingual areas of Spain, or Spanish and any other of the officially recognised languages in bilingual areas, it is necessary to consider the structural linguistic differences between Spanish and the host community language(s) and the other languages and Arabic, contrastively, first to understand their learning strategies better, and their patterns of language use in the host community's language(s).

Contrastive analysis between Spanish and Arabic

Arabic belongs to the Hamito-Semitic family of languages. The Berber languages also belong to the Hamito group. Arabic is a very widely spoken language, in different national variants over a vast area from Saudi Arabia, Syria and Iraq to the Maghrebi countries.[1] It is the official language of all five of the latter countries: Mauritania, Libya, Tunisia, Algeria and Morocco. Arabic is a very highly inflected and fusional language, with very complex declensions, conjugations and derivational system, and a rich lexicon. It has 28 consonants and three vowels. It is morphologically based on a combination of roots and affixes (prefixes, infixes and suffixes), on the one hand, and modification of the root, on the other. Its syntax is the most developed and complex of all Semitic languages.

Arabic's main typologically distinctive features are:

(1) In the vowel system, there are only three vowels (a, u, i), not present in writing except as apostrophe in didactic texts; there is no diphthongisation or tripthongisation. It distinguishes between long and short vowels.
(2) As regards the consonant system, it has 28 consonants which are not combined in closed syllables. It does not have the bilabial, plosive, voiceless sound /p/.
(3) In accentuation, even if Arabic gives stress to some syllables and not others, this phenomenon is not distinctive. In writing, accentuation and intonation phenomena are not reflected, so that each morpheme is written in isolation from the root.
(4) Nouns, adjectives and pronouns have three cases: nominative, genitive and accusative.
(5) The Possessive adjective system is constructed by a suffix added to the name's root.
(6) In the verbal system, since there is no tense morpheme, information on time is given in the aspect morpheme (perfective-past/imperfective-present or future). There are three moods (indicative, subjunctive and conditional). Also, due to its richness in derivation and inflexion there is comparatively little use of phrasal and auxiliary verbs.

(7) In agreement, substantives and adjectives agree in gender and number making a copular sentence. It is not necessary to add imperfective *be*. The verb, on the contrary, agrees in gender and case with the subject, but not in number. When *be* is perfective, it functions as a transitive and, therefore, there is no agreement.

(8) The written language is full of polyvalence (homophones and homonyms).

Finally it must be added that in the modern Arabic spoken in Morocco the language shows two new tendencies: the enrichment of the vocalic system and the reduction of desinential syntax, tending towards structures based more on word order.

Language use in the host community's language(s)

Taking into account Arabic's structural make-up, the following features have been observed in the Maghrebians' use of the host community's language(s) in their process of acquisition and learning. Because of this the following features commonly occur in speech:

(a) As to the vowel system, the Maghrebi students have problems in understanding and pronouncing the differences between *i/e* and *o/u*, thus producing *grandi* for *grande* (big) or *peru* for *pero* (but); they generally assimilate diphthongs and tripthongs to one of the vowels (normally a, i, u) as in *Marrucos* for *Marruecos* (Morocco), *bin* for *bien* (good), *limpas* for *limpiáis* (you (plural) clean).

(b) As to the consonant system, they frequently add an epithetic vowel when two consonants occur together in a syllable as in *boligarafo* for *bolígrafo* (ball pen), *comparar* for *comprar* (to buy). And they substitute the consonant b for p, as in *beso* (kiss) for *peso* (weight) and *roba* (he/she steals) for *ropa* (clothes). In conversation they have accentuation and intonation problems both with production and reception. Problems increase when reading aloud.

(c) In the area of syntax and concerning words marked for case, there is no use of a rich preposition system as in English or Spanish. As a result, their Spanish may lack prepositions like *a, para* (to, for), *de* (of, from), *con, en, por, sin, tras* (with, in/on, for/through, without, after), as in *la casa Alí* for *la casa de Alí* (Ali's house). *Todas amigas trabajan las casas* for *Todas mis amigas trabajan en las casas* (All my friends work as domestic helps). This example also shows lack of possessive pronoun due to the morphological system in Arabic. The use of *ser* (to be) as equative copula is also problematic for them. They tend to omit the verb in present tense like *la vida larga* for *la vida es larga* (life [is] long). And they may fail to make the subject agree with the nominal predicate in the past tense, as in *las vidas era bello* for *las vidas eran bellas* (the lives were beautiful; used as masculine singular). Finally they tend to add a plural marker to the first person verb form so that they agree with the verb in number and person: as in *quieros a mis padres* for *quiero a mis padres* (I love-PLURAL my parents) and apply this to other person forms, as in *quieres a tí* for *te quiero* (I love-2 PERS you).

Learning strategies

The analysis of the data[2] on learning strategies (LS) used by Maghrebi learners of Spanish as a foreign language in a situation of migration reveals that their use of LS is constrained by three factors: the learners' personality,[3] their degree of integration in the host community and the specific skill that they may be applying. For example, in the learning of vocabulary and grammar, these learners prefer academic strategies such as rules, textbooks, controlled practice of exercises, and show little interest in the study of grammar in general, thus preferring communicative skills. They make use of 'compensatory' LS (Oxford, 1990) in speaking and reading and in many cases of self-stimulus, particularly in reading. As to LS use in general, Maghrebi learners of Spanish make use of LS whatever their level of Spanish is, their educational level and their frequency in attending Spanish courses. It is true that some of these patterns are also valid for other groups of learners, as the analysis of the control group shows, and that therefore these LS are not specific to this group of migrants. However, in Maghrebi learning processes two traits seem to characterise the use and individualisation of LS: self-stimulus and the urgency of learning to be able to find a job.

Unfortunately, this initial interest disappears as they attain an acceptable degree of understanding Spanish, their self-stimulus decreases and so does their use of resources and in general the use of indirect LS. On the other hand, their use of compensatory LS increases as they are more trained to create authentic speech acts in real situations. Nevertheless, these new strategies may produce a slowing down of the learning process. And very frequently what happens is that the time they spent trying to learn a new language is then replaced by time and effort devoted to the search for a new or better job, so that learners quit the courses when they attain this minimal competence level and this does not involve a parallel autonomous process in the use of metacognitive LS.

Future Prospects

In the future, the Maghrebi community is expected to increase in numbers and importance. The reuniting of families, the demographic tendency of the Maghrebi countries to higher birth rates[4] as well as the lack of employment in these countries, make it more than likely that immigration will increase considerably in the next few years. If Europe simply closes its eyes to this situation, making it difficult to achieve legal status in the new country, the number of illegal immigrants will increase, benefiting only the backdoor economy and the climate of injustice.

In principle, three solutions can be envisaged as to positive future prospects for the Maghrebi communities in Spain:

(1) There must be legalisation that will make easier to be legally resident in Spain and other communities in the First World. The Maghrebi communities have to obtain a new level of consideration and respect and not be classified as criminals or 'undesirables' (as the police tend to) but rather as citizens with the right to vote, work, be attended in health centres, education, etc., like any Spaniard.

(2) There is a need to help the Maghrebi governments to set up job creation schemes. Many immigrants come to Spain because they are trapped in a dead-end situation in their own country, but are not happy in Spain. If they could choose freely whether to come or to stay at home it would be a less frustrating experience. The idea of being able to work in their own country would induce them to stay there. First World governments should devote more money to job creation.

(3) It is also important to educate and support the immigrants in their new community to help them integrate and establish intercultural conditions of exchange with the host community. Once in the new community the most positive thing that can be done is to try to integrate the immigrants by giving them education and institutional support. The administration and the institutions give the communities little support, and it is only thanks to voluntary non-governmental organisations that these immigrants get some help. There is a need to train teachers who will be able to understand and encourage the Maghrebi students. A related problem is the great lack of suitable educational materials. And, finally, there needs to be more research on the needs, goals and hopes of Maghrebi immigrants, as well as ongoing monitoring of the results. The biggest problem existing between Spanish and Maghrebi communities is that, although they are neighbours, neither communities on either side of the Mediterranean know anything about the other, and those who have migrated are seen as strangers. Spain has ignored them as a culture and has imposed its own values, languages and thoughts.

Notes

1. In fact, Maghreb means West in Arabic.
2. These data were collected in Catalonia, more specifically in the centre *Bait Al-Thaqafa* in Barcelona. The instruments used were: (a) a questionnaire on LS, divided into different

sections according to field (vocabulary and grammar) and skills (reading, speaking, writing and listening), and (b) class observation through the use of an observational check list. In the case of the questionnaire on LS, the sample consisted of 37 Arab learners of Spanish and 8 European learners used as control group, whereas for class observation, the sample consisted of 50 learner subjects (out of the 170 Maghrebians who usually visit the centre) and 30 Maghrebians who visit the centre very frequently.

3. Which is true of other situations of learning, such as first language learning.
4. Because of better health conditions at birth and during the first few years.

References

Ajuntament de Barcelona (1991) *Actitud dels Barcelonins envers els Immigrants provinents d'Altres Cultures.* Opuscule.

A.P.I.P. (Associació per a la Promoció i Inserció Professional) (1992) III. *Annexos al Document de Treball sobre Refugiats i Estrangers.* Opuscle.

Centro di Studi Mediterranei. Agrigento (1990) *Unione del Magreb Arabo: Realtà e Prospettive, Ricerche e Proposte.* Opuscule.

Churchill, S. (1986) *The Education of Linguistic and Cultural Minorities in the OECD.* Clevedon: Multilingual Matters.

Colectivo I.O.E. Intervención Sociológica (1992) *Balance Análisis de los Trabajos Realizados sobre la Inmigración.* Opuscule.

Consell Municipal de Benestar Social (1991) *Refugiats i Estrangers.* Ajuntament de Barcelona.

Cummins, J. (1981) *Bilingualism and Minority Language Children.* OIES.

Cummins, J. and Swain, M. (1986) *Bilingualism in Education.* London: Longman.

Instituto Nacional de Estadística. *Anuario Estadístico 1992.* Madrid.

International Encyclopaedia of Linguistics (1992) New York and Oxford: Oxford University Press.

La Vanguardia, 9 September 1999.

López García, B. and Montabes Pereira, J. (eds) (1994) *El Magreb tras la Crisis del Golfo: Transformaciones Políticas y de Orden Internacional.* Biblioteca de Ciencias Políticas y Sociología. Universidad de Granada.

Ministerio de Asuntos Sociales. *Anuario de Extranjería 1992.* Madrid.

Ministerio de Trabajo y Asuntos Sociales. *Anuario de Migraciones 1997.* Madrid.

Ministerio de Asuntos Sociales. *Anuario de Migraciones 1993.* Madrid.

Oxford, R.L. (1990) *Language Learning Strategies.* New York: Newbury House Publishers.

Pinilla de las Heras, E. (1992) *Immigració i Mobilitat Social a Catalunya, 1–4.* Opuscles.

Roque, M.A. (ed) (1994) *Les Cultures del Magreb.* Enciclopedia Catalana.

Servier, J. (1990) *Les Berebères.* Presses Universitaries de France.

Timaltine, M. *et al.* (1995). *La llengua rifenya. Tutlayt tarifit.* Bellaterra: Servei de Publicacions. Universitat Autònoma de Barcelona.

Chapter 15

The Portuguese Community

LORENZO LÓPEZ TRIGAL

Portuguese Migration to Spain Throughout Recent History

Throughout the 20th century, Portuguese migratory movements have traditionally been towards other countries, rather than from overseas to Portugal. Until 1960, emigration was predominantly to Brazil and other Latin American countries, and since then has been mainly, and in greater numbers, to other European countries. At the present moment, the *Instituto de Apoio à Emigração* (Institute for Emigrant Support) estimates that some 4.47 million Portuguese are resident outside of Portugal, a very high figure when one compares it to the population resident in Portugal, less than 10 million. The same source puts the number of Portuguese resident in Spain as 70,000, which makes it the ninth ranked country in the world, in numbers of Portuguese immigrants, and the fourth in Europe, after France, Switzerland and Germany. Table 15.1 includes the estimated number of emigrants by source and year.

Table 15.1 Estimates of Portuguese emigration

Source	*Year*	*Estimated no. emigrants*	*Observations*
Colectivo I.O.E. – Caritas Española (1987)	1987	76,524	45,000 illegal
I.N.E. (1987)	1986	32,901	Born in Portugal, resident in Spain
Instituto Español de Emigración (1992)	1990	57,047	23,779 in irregular situation
Ministerio de Trabajo y Seguridad Social (1993)	1991	11,608	Workers with work permits
Ministerio Negócios Estrangeiros (1993)	1992	70,000	
Portuguese Embassy (Galaz, J. (1993))	1992	57,000	19,384 in irregular situation
I.N.E. (1993)	1992	28,631	
Eurostat (1994)	1993	25,400	

Source: López Trigal, L. (1996: 113)

Foreign emigration from Portugal has been such a permanent phenomenon throughout the 20th century that Serrão (1977: 27) has called it a
present and past national drama, which has repercussions in the contemporary Portuguese socio-economic and cultural process. However,
Spain has always been a secondary target for Portuguese migration. In the
1970s, this migratory flow reached several tens of thousands of workers
and their families, who spread out over Spain, although previously
emigrants had settled in the areas near Portugal, as is normal on the border
areas of two countries. There were three main centres: the provinces on the
border with Portugal, Madrid and Barcelona, and the León-Asturias area.
Their numbers have tripled over the last 50 years, although as a proportion
of the total Portugese rate of immigration to Spain has decreased from 25%
to 7% (I.N.E. various years). Updated official figures (see *Anuario de
Migraciones 1997*) situate the 1996 Portuguese population in 38,316. This

Table 15.2 Portuguese residents in Spain

Autonomous Community	Regular (1990)	Irregular (1989–90)	Regular + irregular	% increase	% irregular
Andalusia	3,783	524	4,307	13.9	12.2
Aragón	294	233	527	79.3	44.2
Asturias	1,739	6,500	8,239	373.8	78.9
Balearic Islands	212	303	515	142.9	58.8
Basque Country	3,635	132	3,767	3.6	3.5
Canary Islands	672	0	672	0.0	0.0
Cantabria	159	178	337	111.9	52.8
Castile-La Mancha	193	34	227	17.6	15.0
Castile-León	4,095	6,705	10,800	163.7	62.1
Catalonia	2,428	0	2,428	0.0	0.0
Ceuta and Melilla	98	0	98	0.0	0.0
Extremadura	1,364	35	1,399	2.6	2.5
Galicia	8,174	8,557	16,731	104.7	51.1
La Rioja	58	29	87	50.0	33.3
Madrid	4,860	261	5,121	5.4	5.1
Murcia	88	0	88	0.0	0.0
Navarra	432	288	720	66.7	40.0
Valencian Country	984	0	984	0.0	0.0
Total	33,268	23,779	57,047	71.5	41.7

Source: Anuario de Migraciones 1993. Ministerio de Trabajo y Seguridad Social

immigration has been more like migration from Third World countries than from other European countries. Table 15.2 shows the distribution of Portuguese migrants to Spain by Autonomous Community.

According to Pinto dos Santos (1995), the size of this emigration has created, on the one hand, a negative demographic balance, resulting in the ageing of the population and a decrease in available labour. But on the other hand, it has been basic to the socio-economic improvement of the whole country in terms of house ownership, bank savings, and also to the change in the way of life and behaviour, reflecting the increase in the standard of living and a higher consumption. The money sent home and the return of the emigrants to their lands, and especially to the Portuguese cities, play an important, even decisive, part in the present-day changes in Portugal, which is becoming more and more urban and less rural. In this way, the Portuguese are moving closer to the average European way of life, and the difference in earnings with respect to the rest of the European countries is becoming lesser. This difference, however, still exists, so it is still possible that there will be new immigration flows from Portugal in the future.

Characteristics of the Community

Nowadays the Portuguese community in Spain exhibits some differentiating features which make it uniquely different. Unlike the other communities of European origin, the Portuguese emigrate for economic reasons, are mainly unskilled workers, and look for jobs in the service sector, construction, mining, fishing or agriculture (in this last case, of a seasonal nature). But neither is this community the same as immigrant communities from the developing world in Spain, because of its greater social integration, emigration in family groupings and marriage to Spanish nationals, creating mixed families, as well as the cultural and linguistic similarities to the Spanish population. They also stay longer, in many cases up to the age of retirement. All this would indicate, according to Izquierdo (1992: 87), that the Portuguese immigration is generally for a longer period, is more stable and is more integrated.

Among all the European migrants in Spain, the Portuguese make up a social group composed mainly of unqualified workers, coming from rural, and in particular, agricultural, sectors, half of whom do not register as emigrants as such. That is, some 30,000 have come to Spain without the necessary legal documentation, if we take into account the difference between the immigrants registered by Spanish authorities and the estimates made by the Portuguese Embassy and Consulates in Spain (Tables 15.1 and 15.2). Furthermore, there is also a specific minority group of Portuguese, that of the Gitano[1] communities (*gitanos trasmontanos*), whose members exhibit the worst of these social and economic characteristics, working in unofficial or illegal jobs and without permanent residence, moving from one place to another, living in urban shacks, and often becoming the stereotype of the Portuguese immigrant, when in fact they are seasonal workers who have settled on the outskirts of the cities.

While the Portuguese areas which have seen most emigration are the Azores, Madeira, Porto, Lisbon and Aveiro, the emigration towards Spain has come from northern districts such as the villages of Braga and Braganca, or Petisqueira, where work in the fields of rye and potatoes 'non da nada e todo o que habia foi para fora' ('doesn't produce anything and all those who were here have left'), and only the old folk are left there. So the process of rural decomposition has given rise to real communities in Spain with the same regional origins. These communities have spread throughout Spain, further and further from Portugal because, as Izquierdo has pointed out (1992: 222), the area near the Portuguese border is more a temporary place of passage than a permanent destination. Thus, according to the *Instituto Nacional de Estadística* (Spanish Institute for Statistics) (various years), whereas in 1950 the seven Spanish provinces on the Portuguese border (especially Pontevedra, Orense and Huelva) received 74% of Portuguese immigration, in 1990 this had become 34%. In recent years, important destinations have been the mining areas of León and Asturias, with 13.3%, and the large cities of Madrid and Barcelona (20%), and other distant destinations made up a third of the total. In this sense, the spatial distribution of this community in recent years is moving towards the same geographical model as that of the rest of the immigrant communities, characterised above all by settlements in the large cities and the Mediterranean coastal region. Table 15.3 shows the increase in Portuguese immigration from 1950 to 1990.

The adult members of this community who arrived in previous decades were characterised by their lack of professional qualifications, with little previous specialisation, and by little educational training, not finishing primary education or even without any schooling at all. But in the second

Table 15.3 Portuguese legally resident in Spain (1950–90)

Year	Portugal	Total	1950 = 100	% total
1950	14,570	56,517	100.0	25.8
1955	16,871	66,043	116.9	25.5
1960	14,798	64,660	114.4	22.9
1965	19,427	99,582	176.2	19.5
1970	25,483	148,400	262.6	17.2
1981	24,713	198,042	350.4	12.5
1990	33,268	407,647	721.3	8.2

Source: I.N.E. (various years). *Anuario*

generation this changes, as the young people are integrated into the Spanish system of compulsory schooling. On the other hand, those who are employed in productive activities are spread out over a variety of professions, without any particular one dominating, a characteristic which distinguishes them from other immigrant communities. This has a positive aspect, since in times of crisis they do not depend on only one main activity, as is the case with other communities. There are miners in the mining areas of western León and central Asturias, construction workers, female servants in the metropolitan area of Madrid, hotel workers in the Balearic Islands, the Mediterranean coast and Andorra, fishermen in the Galician ports, and seasonal pickers who travel to Spain at harvest times without any legal coverage of their temporary jobs and in precarious conditions, mainly in the Spanish provinces of Huelva, Badajoz and Orense.

According to the latest censuses, their work is structured on an age and sex basis. Young, unmarried women live in their employer's house as live-in servants (maids in cities such as Madrid), whereas young men are employed in fishing, construction and mining. Other jobs, such as seasonal agricultural work, employ both men and women. The activities of the Portuguese workers in all these examples is in jobs that are either very tough work or simply not wanted by the native Spanish workers, creating a pool of jobs that attracts large numbers of immigrants.

López Trigal (1994) and Lora-Tamayo (1995) studied the socio demographic structure of the Portuguese community in Spain and concluded that, although there are different characteristics according to the settlement areas, the following general features are present: (1) the age structure in the last censuses of 1986 and 1991 reflect the predominance of the 20–39 age group, with the demographic pyramid showing much reduced numbers in the older and younger extremes, since most of the immigration was of young people in the period from 1975 to 1985, (2) although until 1990 the general decrease in the fertility rate in this community is barely perceptible, it is to be expected that in the 1996 census this decrease will be more noticeable, following the rapid fall of this index in both Spain and Portugal, (3) one can observe a balance in the gender proportion or sex ratio, although there are more females in the most common age groups, such as young adults, and (4) the active population represents some 50%, but decreases to 40% among the women. Similarly, the unemployment figure is higher for men, being 20% in 1990 (similar to the Spanish average), and the rate of temporary employment is as high as 35%.

Mainly Positive Integration

This research and other studies show that in general the social integration of the Portuguese community is quite satisfactory, with the exception of the Portuguese Gitano minority, because of its own characteristics.

However, it does vary from greater (in mining or rural areas) to lesser (in metropolitan areas), which is related to the geographical distribution and the kinds of occupations. Being a population that comes from mainly rural areas, sometimes of Gitano origin, the Portuguese population resident in Spain is somewhat heterogeneous, so that one can only appreciate the extent of their integration into Spanish society by looking at specific groups and their particular economic and cultural features.

This different evaluation of their integration can be seen if we compare two such different areas as the León mining zone and the outer, urban suburbs of Madrid. In the first case, according to the pioneering study by the Colectivo IOE (1987: 253), the essential characteristic of this mining group is its relative stability, based on the children and their progress at school, and on having achieved a reasonable level of skill in the mining profession and a salary which allows a relatively comfortable life. At the same time, specific features of this area are the high number of Portuguese–Spanish mixed marriages, and to a lesser extent Spanish–Portuguese ones, the owning of their own home by a good number of families, and the Portuguese Language and Culture Programme for Portuguese students (López Trigal, 1991, 1994).

In a very different situation, at times bordering on social exclusion, we find the very varied kinds of integration of the metropolitan area of Madrid, as studied by Giménez Romero and Perales Díaz (1993). In this big city, the Portuguese community shows large contrasts, caused by employment in very different professions, a range of income and educational levels, and kinds of settlements, etc. These features define a variety of social groupings, ranging from the businessmen and professionals, who have settled in Madrid and become well integrated, to the domestic servants who are integrated to varying degrees, and to the slum-dwelling Portuguese Gitanos on the outskirts of the city, in unplanned settlements such as the Pitis[2] in Fuencarral (Madrid), where unemployment and begging have been prevalent for some time.

Integration and Language Use

In any case, the degree of integration will depend, of course, on the number of years' residence in the country, on the area of residence, on the work situation, on age, on the type of dwelling and neighbourhood. So normally children and young people will be more integrated than their parents and their grandparents, because of their knowledge of one of the languages of Spain, and their schooling, since school is always one of the most favourable means of integration. The sociocultural differences resulting from the professional and economic levels of this population, translated into the differing standards of living, go together with cultural differences to make social integration difficult.

In contrast, there is a certain continuity in the different Portuguese communities with regard to the high use of their own language in communication among adults and between parents and children. Outside the home, however, this use decreases considerably in both cases, for this kind of communication is influenced by the mass media, and sometimes the adults try to use Spanish. They often speak in *Portunhol*,[3] a mixture of Portuguese and Spanish (español), as a means of increasing social status, and devaluing their own origins in many cases, as indicated by the last *Seminar on the Portuguese Language and Culture*, held in León in January 1996. The level of proficiency in their own language of the children of Portuguese who have settled in Spain is quite high, since from age 3 to 5, before going to school, they all learn to speak it and understand it orally, but they read it less well and write it quite poorly, depending on the socio-economic conditions of the family, among other variables. The adults' proficiency in spoken Spanish is intermediate, but that of the written word is low. In this context, certain problems can be observed among the Portuguese community, such as problems of parent–child interaction, of personal identity and of self-esteem, depending on the family conditions or the level of acceptance or rejection by the wider community in which they live.

Biographical Data

A few brief biographies of some Portuguese who live in the León area will tell us more about the characteristics of this Portuguese community (see Nuno Ferreira, 1994). Manuel is 41, comes from the village of Trás-os-Montes (Bragança), and at present works as a miner down a mineshaft, after having worked in the mines in France and in Pamplona. He has got used to living in the León town of Villablino, where he is married to a Spanish woman with three children. He has no aspirations to return to his country of origin, for he earns a good salary and lives better, fighting alongside his workmates from the mine against the economic crisis and the threatened closure of the mines.

Antonio is also from the Trás-os-Montes region, where he began work as a waiter and at a similar age to Manuel he moved to Torre del Bierzo, in León, to work on the roads and then soon went down the mines. He is now on a disability pension because of a work-related illness, and spends his time doing community work. He is married to a Portuguese woman and, with his family well settled in Spain, does not expect to return to Portugal in the near future.

Somewhat younger is Arnaldo, at the age of 30, who works in the construction industry and arrived in the neighbourhood eight years ago. He speaks in *Portunhol* and hopes to return to his family in Portugal if they can find a job for him, since 'It's our country.' He came to Spain as an illegal immigrant, contracted by a Portuguese businessman, and spent a year and a half in this situation and six months in Portugal before he was able to become a legal immigrant, with the help of the Consulate.

Diamantino, at 43, travelled more until he also came to Villablino 20 years ago. Spending his youth in Angola as a soldier and a mechanic, he returned to Portugal when Angola gained its independence, lived for a while in Bragança and now has his own automotive workshop with an Argentinean partner. A relative helped him to come to León, where he prefers to stay because of the higher standard of living and because it is a nice place to live. Curiously, his Portuguese wife lives in Bragança with the children, because 'she didn't want them to study Spanish', and he visits them on the weekend whenever he can.

Anabela is 20, also speaks *Portunhol* like the others, and is a waitress in a small hotel in the mining town of Bembibre. She was born in a village near Mirandela, in Trás-os-Montes, which she left with her family when her father, a miner in this area, took them to their new home. Her mother works as a house help, and hopes to return with the family savings to live in Portugal, but Anabela wishes to be a professional hairdresser and she likes the atmosphere of youth and fun in Spain more than Portugal, so it is likely she will not return with her family.

Institutional and Educational Support

Given that there are some difficulties in integration, and a certain loss of their own language and culture by many Portuguese immigrants, the Spanish and Portuguese Governments have carried out various programmes to change this situation. In the issue of the magazine *Polígonos* dedicated to international migration in the European Union, authors such as Galaz (1993) outline the measures taken to combat the social exclusion of this community, to resolve problems such as slum dwelling, begging and delinquency, as well as encouraging community involvement and educational and cultural programmes. These last two initiatives will be considered in more detail, because of their integrating nature.

The Portuguese are involved in the wider community through the *Asociaciones de Padres de Alumnos* (APAS) (Parents Associations) at the schools where their children go, and the workers are affiliated to the national trade unions, especially those in the fishing, mining and construction sectors. But here mention must be made of the Portuguese Cultural Associations, under the wing of the Portuguese State, through its 19 Consulates and its Spanish Embassy. This community movement, through its network of organisations in the world of the immigrants, tries to defend their rights as citizens, helps those Portuguese in need, organises adult education courses and occupational training, and organises 'fiestas'.[4] There are not many Associations, two being found in Madrid (in the centre and on the outskirts), and the others in Mieres, La Coruña, Vigo, Pamplona, Barcelona, Las Palmas, Miranda de Ebro, and in four mining towns in León province.

Secondly, an agreement between Spain and Portugal has given rise to a programme called *Programa Hispano-Luso para la Acción Educativa y Cultural* (Hispano-Portuguese Programme for Educational and Cultural Action). This promotes the Portuguese language and culture in the schools where there are significant groups of Portuguese students. The programme has expanded continually since its beginnings in 1987–88 in the mining area of León. In the 1990–91 school year, there were 1039 students enrolled in 23 schools, and in 1995–96 these numbers had increased to some 4000 students taught by Portuguese teachers in the relevant subjects in 60 primary schools, in 10 provinces in the north of Spain and Madrid, and in two secondary schools in León. It is most developed in León Province, with 2000 students, and, surprisingly, the majority (56.6%) are Spanish students, which could be because these are children of Portuguese immigrants who want to study Portuguese language and literature and the history and geography of Portugal. Similarly, there is a large minority of children from the Cabo Verde Islands (12.0%), although until now there have been no classes in Cabo Verde culture.[5] Only 31.2% of the students are of Portuguese nationality. Given its special extension and focus, this could be considered an excellent way of integrating students via the implicit recognition of cultural diversity, with its strategy of teaching in a multicultural context. At present, Portuguese television is beginning to become available via satellite, and this will produce positive changes, especially as regards the children's use of and competence in their parents' native language.

Future Prospects

It is not expected that there will be significant increases in the number of Portuguese immigrants in Spain in the near future, but there could be some movement of the Portuguese now settled in Andorra, which is undergoing a severe economic crisis, to Barcelona or the Mediterranean coast, as well as seasonal agricultural workers or in tourism and hotels, and construction, since these jobs are normally available in Spain. Some professionals and skilled workers will arrive. Those Portuguese who have been settled for a long time in Spain will probably stay since they are well integrated. On the other hand, the present economic crises in the mining and fishing areas in the north-west of Spain directly affect the Portuguese, and will produce a certain readjustment of the territorial distribution of the Portuguese in Spain, rather than provoke their return to their home country. At least between 50,000 and 70,000 Portuguese immigrants will remain in Spain, and those who return to Portugal will be replaced by new immigrants, who sometimes settle in Spain on their way to France, in areas where they are welcomed.

Notes

1. The term 'Gitano' is used here to refer to the Gypsy communities in Spain and Portugal, as proposed by Yaron Matras (U. of Manchester). See Chapter 8 and also Chapter 1 (Note 1) in this book for more details on this term.
2. See Aguirre, B. En Pitis se habla portugués (1993). *El País* (18-VI-1993, p. 4).
3. In practice and in the specialised literature (Ferreira, 1993; Lombello and Ferreira, 1993, cited by Ferreira, 1993) the term *Portunhol* (Portuñol in Spanish) is used to describe the linguistic production of a Spanish-speaking person when trying to speak Portuguese, particularly in relation to South America. This variety of language is viewed as an index of Latin American integration (to occur, according to him, within a century) in the context of which linguistic integration will involve the convergence of Spanish and Portuguese into a unique language, which is indistinctively referred to as either *Portunhol* or *Espanhoguês*. The term *Portunhol/ Portuñol* is also used (in the context of the Portuguese and Brazilian communities which migrated to Spain) to refer to the speech modalities of the members of these two migrated communities when they try to speak Spanish. Unfortunately there are no recorded samples of the Portuguese community's use of such modalities. See Chapter 10 on the Brazilian community for a more linguistic characterisation of *Portunhol.*
4. The "festas de emigrantes" are genuine reaffirmations of their own cultural heritage as expressed in their new places of residence.
5. See Chapter 11 for more details on this community.

References

Aguirre, B. (1993) En Pitis se habla portugués. *El País*, 18 June, p. 4.

Colectivo I.O.E.-Caritas Española (1987) Los Inmigrantes en España. *Documentación Social 66.*

Ferreria, N. (1994) Portugueses no Reino de Leáo. *O Publico Magazine*, 11-XII, 57—67.

Ferreria, I.A. (1993) A interlíngua do falante de Espanhol e o papel do professor: aceitaçao tácita ou ajuda para superá-la. *Anais do Seminário Educação sem Fronteiras* (pp. 39—48). Secretaria de Estado da Educação do Paraná.

Galaz, J.A. (1993) La inmigración portuguesa en España. *Polígonos 3*, 159—62.

Giménez Romero, C. and Perales Díaz, J.A. (eds) (1993) *Inmigrantes Extranjeros en Madrid.* Madrid: Comunidad de Madrid.

Instituto Nacional de Estadística (I.N.E.) (various years). *Anuario.* Madrid.

Instituto Español de Emigración (1992) *Anuario.* Madrid.

Izquierdo Escribano, A. (1992) *La Inmigración en España, 1980—1990.* Madrid: Ministerio de Trabajo y Seguridad Social.

Lombello, L.C. and Ferreira, I.A. (1993) O ensino de Português para falantes de Espanhol: Português o Portunhol. *Anais do Seminário Educação sem Fronteiras.* Secretaria de Estado da Educação do Paraná.

López Trigal, L. (1991) *La Inmigración Extranjera en León.* León: Universidad de León.

López Trigal, L. (dir.) (1994) *La Inmigración de Portugueses en España.* León: Universidad de León.

López Trigal, L. (1995) Revisión de los estudios sobre la migración portuguesa en España. *População e Sociedade 1*, 109—18.

López Trigal, L. (1996) La migration portugaise en Espagne. *Revue Européenne des Migrations Internationales 12*, 1, 109—19.

López Trigal, L. and Prieto Sarro, I. (1993a) Inmigración portuguesa en ciudades del Norte de España. In Various Authors. *Nuevos Procesos territoriales* (pp. 507—11).

López Trigal, L. and Prieto Sarro, I. (1993b) Portugueses y cavoverdianos en España. *Estudios Geográficos 210*, 75—96.

Lora-Tamayo, G. (1995) Características de la población extranjera en España – Censo de 1991 –, *Cuadernos de Formación, 6.*

Ministerio de Trabajo y Seguridad Social. *Anuario de Migraciones* (various years). Madrid.

Pinto dos Santos, N. (1995) As dimençōes da emigração na sociedade portuguesa contemporânea. *Cadernos de Geografia* 14, 35–76.

Serrão, J. (1977) *A Emigração Portuguesa.* Lisboa, Horizonte.

Various Authors (1993) *Nuevos Procesos Territoriales.* XIII Congreso Nacional de Geografía. Universidad de Sevilla. Sevilla.

Chapter 16

The UK Community

M. TERESA TURELL and CRISTINA CORCOLL

Nature and Distribution of the British-English Speech Community in Spain

The British community's visiting or moving to Spain is not a recent trend. In fact, Spain has historically been one of the favoured sites for British to come and live after retiring, in search of new horizons, peace and sun. This is so much so that one can now find in some villages along the Mediterranean coast institutions like the *Sociedad Cívica Internacional* (International Civic Society) that have been created in order to serve the needs of retired Britons who have moved to Spain. Data given by this society allows one to draw a profile of one of the largest groups of British immigrants in Spain: over 50, middle-class, retired and with little competence in Spanish (Enguix, 1994).

It is also interesting to note that Spain is one of the favourite holidaying places for the British, and this may explain their coming here to live later in their lives. When they come on holiday, British prefer the Canary and the Balearic Islands, the Andalusian and Valencian coasts, and Catalonia (Vallejo, 1994). When looking at the data, a correlation can be made between these holiday destinations and the sites of residence of British immigrants. This correlation is further shown through the socio-linguistic interviews carried out in Lanzarote (Canary Islands), where most British residents explain that they first came and knew the island as a holiday place and, on the basis of that experience, they decided to stay and settle there for good.

Recent official figures situate the 1996 British population in Spain in 68,359 residents (see the *Anuario de Migraciones 1997*). According to the *Instituto Nacional de Estadística* (INE) statistics (1999), there was a total of 255,379 foreign residents in Spain in 1999. Of these, the highest number were from Great Britain, followed by Germany, Portugal and France. Figure 16.1 (*Anuario Estadístico 1995* (INE (1996)) shows how the immigration rate has evolved during the las two decades: 39,052 UK immigrants lived in Spain in 1985; 46,914 (1986); 55,318 (1987); 64,081 (1988); 73,535 (1989); 78,210 (1990); 50,071 (1991); 53,441 (1992); 58,168 (1993); 62,317 (1994). These statistics show that, although subject to change, British immigration to Spain has followed a relatively steady pattern: there

BRITISH RATE OF IMMIGRATION

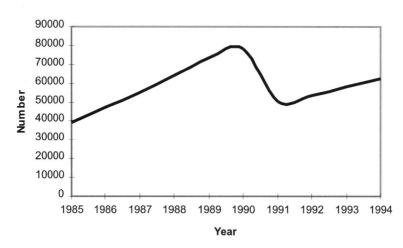

Figure 16.1 Rate of immigration of UK citizens to Spain (1985–94)
Source: Anuario estadístico 1995; INE (1996)

was an important peak between 1989–90, a decrease between 1990–91 and a steady increase since 1992.[1]

The British Consulate General of Barcelona has provided the following estimates of British residents in Spain by consular areas[2] (1994): 75,000 British in Málaga, 70,000 British in Alicante, 60,000 in Tenerife, 41,000 in Palma, 15,500 in Barcelona, 11,500 in Las Palmas, 10,000 in Madrid, 7,000 in Bilbao, 4,000 in Ibiza, 4,000 in Seville, and 3,000 in Vigo. The total figure is then 291,000, although this figure is purely an estimate, since there is no obligation on the immigrants' part to register with Consulates. It will be noticed that there is a considerable difference in overall numbers between the figures offered by the INE and those supplied by the British Consulate General for 1994 (62,317 versus 291,000). This is due to the fact that the Consulate considers not only British residents, but also all those British who come to spend a limited period of time in Spain. The latter group could be formed by students, who may spend a year out while at university, or retired people, who come to Spain to spend the winter.

In order to draw the profile type of the UK immigrant to Spain, a pilot study was conducted by interviewing British people living in Barcelona, Lanzarote and Tarragona, and surrounding areas (see Appendix 1 and 2: Catalogue of Informants). For study purposes, these sites were chosen since they represent what are apparently the favourite destinations for the British who immigrate to Spain. Each site seems to be chosen by the immigrants for different reasons. Thus, first, Barcelona was chosen since it can be taken as a prototypical city for those who come to Spain to further their career or their studies, and want to enjoy a rich social and cultural life; secondly, Lanzarote seems to be the favourite site for the British who move to Spain to retire and to enjoy a sunny, peaceful life; finally, Tarragona could be placed somewhere in the middle because it offers both a pleasant environment and the possibility to develop a professional career. A second argument that favours the election of these sites for our analysis is the data offered by the British Consulate General, according to which these sites receive some of the largest numbers of British immigrants: 71,700 in the Canary Islands, which are covered by two consular areas (60,000 immigrants are registered in the consular area of Tenerife, which covers the islands of Tenerife, La Palma, Gomera and Hierro; and 11,500 in the consular area of Las Palmas, which covers the islands of Gran Canaria, Lanzarote and Fuerteventura); and 15,500 in Catalonia, which is covered by the consular area of Barcelona, which consists of Catalonia, Andorra and part of Aragón.

Motivation

There seem to be three main motivations for British immigration to Spain: firstly, the wish to learn a language and have the experience of living abroad; secondly, to develop professionally; and thirdly, to retire. The first group consists of younger Britons, who come because they have studied some Spanish in the UK and want to improve it, or simply because they fancy living in a new place. The second group includes migrants who come for professional reasons, bring the family with them, and integrate, if they stay for long. The third group involves those British migrants who settle on the Mediterranean coast, mainly the Valencian Country (Alicante) and Andalusia (Málaga), and the Canary Islands. They accept that they have created a kind of ecosystem with others of the same nationality and that they do not integrate within the host community, or try to speak its language. The majority of residents in these coastal sites are retired people (75%), although this tendency has changed during the last decade since there are already second generation residents who were born in Spain. These include children of first generation migrants who migrated for professional reasons and also live in these coastal sites. Also of those older couples who come to Spain to retire, some are known as 'snowbirds', that is, people who spend the summer in England and the winter in Spain.

By correlating motivation and place of settlement, it is possible to notice that the UK community in Spain exhibits some internal differentiation. Different groups, then, have rather different reasons for coming to Spain and this is why they choose to settle down in one place or another. As an illustration, many more retired Britons move to Lanzarote or any of the other islands than to Barcelona, while many Britons in their thirties will prefer moving to Barcelona for professional reasons. In the

Tarragona sample, while some of the migrants initially lived in Barcelona, they moved and nowadays they live in Tarragona, Reus, Salou and smaller towns.

All this would indicate that UK immigration to Spain tends to be stable within certain limits,[3] that is, except for those young people who come for adventure to live a different life, British migrants stay for long in general, and are integrated, if they come for professional reasons.

Arrival and Settlement

In general, it seems that settling into the new community does not present great problems for the British, although it could be argued that at least one group of immigrants (the retired) never seem to really settle down in Spain. Rather, it is characteristic that some of this group only spend half the year in Spain (the winter) and tend to live in areas with many other British people, where they can buy and eat British products, attend clubs for foreigners and speak English at all times. The picture is rather different, however, for the group of migrants who migrate to Spain for professional reasons, bring their family with them and enjoy meeting Spaniards and live a way of life different from the one in their home country.

When asked how easy or difficult it was to settle into the new community, almost all migrants who came to Spain for professional reasons say that it was quite easy to meet people and integrate. Most met people through work, sports clubs, and so on. In any case, many admit that there are things that are difficult to get used to, such as the length of time it takes to get through any administrative paperwork. For the retired migrants settling on coastal sites the situation was obviously quite different, since most immigrants speak little or no Spanish and, as mentioned, live in British areas and meet people through foreigners' clubs. In these situations it will evidently be more difficult for Britons to engage in social relationships with Spaniards.

The pilot study informants[4] seem to fall into these patterns and corroborate these general tendencies. For example, the group interviewed in Lanzarote consists mainly of retired couples or middle-aged Britons (40–55) who do not need to work and move to have a better life. The group interviewed in Barcelona comprises younger migrants and professional middle-aged couples who come to Spain for sentimental reasons or simply in search of a new experience or a better job, and most of them work as English teachers; the third group, in Tarragona, includes migrants with both patterns of settlement, that is, retired and professional people.

The UK Migrants' Social Profile

The latest detailed data available on the arrival of British citizens to Spain is for 1994 (*Migraciones 1995*, INE), when 1129 British arrived in

Table 16.1 1994 incoming UK immigrants by areas of residence

Total	Provincial capital	−10,000	10,001– 20,000	20,001– 50,000	50,001– 100,000	+100,000
1129	163	319	159	388	88	12

Source: Migraciones 1995; INE (1996)

Table 16.2 1994 incoming UK immigrants by age-groups

Total	−16	16–24	25–34	35–44	45–54	55–64	+65
1129	103	69	302	170	157	194	134

Source: Migraciones 1995; INE (1996)

Table 16.3 1994 incoming UK immigrants by academic level

Total	Illiterates	Elementary education	Secondary education	Higher education	Unknown
1129	59	375	276	391	28

Source: Migraciones 1995; INE (1996)

Spain. Their distribution by areas is relatively even within the geographical patterns of settlement mentioned when referring to motivation: 245 in Andalusia, 226 in the Valencian Country, 183 in the Canary Islands, 162 in the Balearic Islands, 136 in Catalonia, 91 in Madrid, 42 in the Basque Country and the rest (44) in other cities and villages. As for the size of the cities or towns of residence, Table 16.1 shows that a majority settled in provincial towns of between 20,001 and 50,000 inhabitants (388), followed by towns of less than 10,000 inhabitants (319), which proves that the British migrants' pattern of settlement is fundamentally urban.

The distribution by sex is equally even: 604 men and 525 women. As for age-groups, Table 16.2 shows the figures: the largest age-group is aged between 25 and 34 (302), followed by those between 55 and 64 (194) and 35 and 44 (170). The fact that the two largest groups are those between 25 and 34, and 55 and 64 tends to reflect the motivations that bring these British immigrants to Spain: middle-aged migrants who come to further their career and the older ones who come to retire.

The correlation between age data and the geographical site where UK migrants settle shows how the informants follow the community's general pattern described above: many young middle-aged Britons tend to move to big urban areas because their main motivation is to develop professionally, while the older generation retires to holiday resort areas like Lanzarote.

As Table 16.3 illustrates, the majority of UK immigrants that arrived in Spain in 1994 were quite qualified since of the total of 1129, 391 had a university degree and a further 276 completed sixth form. The data available from the pilot studies undertaken in Barcelona, Tarragona and Lanzarote confirm the UK migrants' high qualifications[5] since most British immigrants in these samples in these three cities went to university. This fact seems to corroborate the tendency that has been observed that British people do not migrate for economic or social reasons, but rather because they are seeking to develop professionally, to learn a foreign language, or to begin a new life in Spain.

Attitudes Towards the Spanish Language and Culture

The migrants' attitudes towards the Spanish language and culture (or any language and culture in the different Autonomous Communities in Spain) seems to be quite different depending on the group of immigrants considered. As mentioned, the settlement area is chosen in accordance with the interests and the motivation that the immigrants have: younger and middle-aged professionals tend to move to areas such as Barcelona in Catalonia, while the older, retirement-age migrants tend to move to tourist areas such as the Valencian Country (Alicante), Andalusia (Málaga) and the Canary Islands (Lanzarote and Tenerife). Obviously, these different interests and motivations make it either more or less necessary for Britons to mix with Spaniards.

With respect to the first group, the younger or middle-aged professionals, it should be noted that some do marry Spaniards, come on their own and thus they will have met the people with whom they relate (family, friends, etc.) in Spain; and many work with Spaniards. The picture is substantially different for the second group, that of the retired. Most confess that they would like to learn Spanish but since they do not really need to speak it, they do not make much of an effort. Some also say that they feel that the host community people do not really want to mix or share any activities with them. This and the fact that it is very easy for them to stay within the British community, since most of these retirement-age migrants come with their families, live in areas of British settlement and do not work, make them less willing to socialise with local people and to adapt to a new culture. In the words of one of the consultants, the British people who move to Lanzarote 'bring England to the island, they want little England here' (an/93/UK). It must be noticed, however, that some of the informants in Lanzarote actually complained about this situation. What was the point, they implied, in leaving their country to go to a new place where they lead a life similar to the one they were leading in their home country. For that reason, some immigrants have actually moved out of the British areas and are, after all, learning Spanish. One of the scenarios where this willingness to mix emerges is in the case of the younger or middle-aged immigrants who have little children and have to make decisions on their language education.

Social Life

Socially, it is relatively more difficult for a non-British to enter the community, insofar as it exists. British people pride themselves on keeping their roots and, in a way, many pride themselves on not adapting to wherever they may be.[6] In this sense, there are places where they get together with other Britons, but having access to them has proved a hard task and, in general, entering the British community as a group may tend to be quite difficult. However, this attitude has been changing during this last decade, particularly in relation to second generation migrants, younger people who want to have the same rights as Spaniards and take part in Spanish social life. Some predict that this change in attitude will also involve a social change and the beginning of a more intercultural stage.

The UK community in Spain presents a rich level of social organisation. UK residents in coastal sites, such as Alicante in the Valencian Country, have their own papers (*The Weekly Post* and *The Costa Blanca News*) which give regular and detailed information not only on social and political news but also on cultural and leisure activities. Britons in this area also have their own theatre group and supervise their British school which is located in Alfaz del Pi (a village in the Alicante province). On the other hand, retired migrants are taken care of by the municipal authorities that offer them cultural activities, travelling, games, dancing and health care.

There are other British institutions, such as British schools in the majority of big cities in Spain and, above all, the British Council, that make it possible for British and non-British to meet in a cultural and educational environment. The British Council is probably the largest British institution overseas. It was set up by the British government in 1934 and 'promotes educational, cultural and technical co-operation between Britain and other countries (...) designed to establish long-term and world-wide partnerships and to improve international understanding' (British Council, 1996). The British Council was established in Madrid in 1940 and in Barcelona three years later. British Council branches may now be found in many other cities: Bilbao, Las Palmas, Málaga, Palma de Mallorca, Salamanca, Seville and Valencia, although they do not all offer as many services as the big cities. The main activity offered in the three largest ones (Barcelona, Bilbao and Madrid) is the teaching of English, but other activities are carried out, including seminars on English Language Teaching and Literature, business sponsorships, research links, exchange programmes, self-access learning, etc. Smaller branches (such as the ones in Palma de Mallorca and Salamanca) are linked to the university and only offer English courses and examinations.

The existence of a high number of English, Irish and Scottish pubs and taverns in itself confirms that the British like to keep their traditions and way of life. Obviously, these pubs are open to everybody, but there is little contact between different communities in them, unless for example a

Spaniard is taken there by a Briton. British may also meet at associations such as the British Council, the American and International Women's Club (A&IWC) at a national level, and the Catalan Irish Association or the British Society of Catalonia, in this Autonomous Community.

Particularly in Lanzarote, an association that seems to bring together all foreigners and especially the British is the Residents' Club, which was created in 1990 to become the place where newly arrived immigrants would get all the information and help they needed and where immigrants would mix with the Canary Islanders. The truth is that it never succeeded as a meeting place between the communities and, so, it is practically only frequented by immigrants. Other informants also mention the Anglican Church or other associations such as *Amigos de Lanzarote* (Friends of Lanzarote) and the Association for the Defence of Animals as sites where they may get together and also mix with the locals.

Patterns of Language Behaviour

As will be recalled, Table 16.2 shows the age distribution of the UK migrants who settled in Spain: the largest age-group being aged between 25 and 34 (302 people), followed by those between 55 and 64 (194), and 35 to 44 (170). The first and the second group highlight the potential presence of two generations of immigrants: first and second generations. Clearly, this has important consequences in terms of the role of education in both determining and maintaining specific language use and choice patterns.

As a general rule, British people in Spain – those who mix with Spaniards – may use up to three languages (English, Spanish and any of the other three community languages (Catalan, Galician and Basque). The distribution of these three languages by domain of language use is very varied. The fact is that whichever language is chosen in every domain depends on the immigrant's professional activity and on their family type.[7] Regarding linguistic behaviour towards children, since many parents would like their children to be competent in as many languages as possible and try to develop their linguistic competence in all directions, they may leave Spanish or the other host community languages for the school in the case of monolingual families; or use two languages at home in the case of mixed families where the mother uses Spanish and the father uses English, for instance. Many English-speaking parents persist in talking in English to their children even where (as they point out) children are young and do not understand why they use different languages in and out of the home. This can also be observed in the Catalonia and Canary Islands pilot studies: many of the informants interviewed are concerned that their children should learn Spanish or Canarian Spanish in the case of Lanzarote, and Spanish and Catalan in the case of Catalonia, without forgetting their mother tongue. They want their children to mix and, therefore, to learn the language(s) used in the new community, while staying in touch (through the language) with their home country. This viewpoint is illustrated in (1) and (2):

(1) But the aspect of the satellite was also a consideration in that in our home it was ... we needed to improve our children's English because you can well imagine, they go to school, they're taught in **castellano** and in **catalán**, and their time in the home we have to make sure their English is kept to a good level and it's easier if we can get them watching English programmes on television because obviously if the only English they're learning is from myself and my wife it does become limited and with the, with the aid of television, they're gonna get accustomed to hearing different accents, different expres-sions and learn the difference between, for example, English spoken by English people and, say, by American, there's a vast difference, it's the same language, but it's the words they usually raise, they're totally different, so that's the two reasons for having, for having the facility of the satellite television. (jo/93/UK)

(2) **I:** And, at home, which language do you speak?
  N: Spanish, Castilian. My husband is not **catalán**. Both my children are **catalán** or Catalonian, they were born in **Tarragona**, but my husband is not from Catalonia and so Castilian is the middle, the middle language. Until my eldest daughter was 2, I used to speak to her in English but as soon as she started kindergarten, she said, no, no, Mummy, no Spanish, no English, only Spanish, no, but she does speak English. (ni/92/UK)

In our sample, the most important patterns of language behaviour and use can be summarised as follows:

(a) When retired migrants and those migrants who settle in coastal sites (the Canary Islands, the Valencian Country, Andalusia) are asked, they state that their most usual language is English and that most of their friends are British. It is precisely their low level of Spanish that many British people use to justify their enclosure within the British community. Another argument that seems to explain this isolation to the extent that it exists is the fact that most informants live in Spain with their most immediate family (partner and children), so this makes it more difficult not to follow a British way of life. The only group that does not seem to follow this pattern is that comprising mixed professional families. In their case, the UK migrants will have met many Spanish people through their partners and this has made it easier for them to lead their lives outside the British community and to improve their language skills in any of the host community languages, but particularly in Spanish.

(b)   The members of the UK community in Spain are frequently asked by Spanish people to speak English because they want to practice and improve their language skills, and, on the other, they may relate to other foreigners, which usually makes English their most usual language.

(c)   There are also some demographic or social facts that account for this maintenance of English among English-speaking immigrants, such as family, professional activity or language instruction. There is a comparatively large number of British immigrants who move to Spain with their families and, thus, keep English as their home language. Professionally, a great percentage of migrants work as English teachers or own pubs or restaurants, which become meeting points for the foreigners of the area.

(d)   It does not seem to be the general rule for British to learn Spanish and/or any of the other official languages in Spain (Basque, Catalan or Galician) in a formal setting. Rather, they learn these languages through living in Spain, which may make it more difficult for them to gain linguistic confidence in certain aspects.

(e)   The members of the UK community living in Spain may switch from one language to another depending on whom they are talking to, on what they are talking about and also on what the style of the conversation is. This variation in code choice and code change takes different forms and is viewed differently depending on migrant profile. This is shown in (3) and (4) below, where UK immigrants talk about the real need they have to use any language other than English, and about how they can manage to make themselves understood although their knowledge of Spanish and/or Catalan may not be so good:

(3)   (...) I have lots of Spanish friends as well but because I can't say what I want to say in Spanish, it's difficult, you know (...) I can communicate but to a degree, but it's not really enough, you know, it's not really enough and the counter thing is it's too easy because there are too many English-speaking people, if there weren't so many English-speaking people I would have needed far more of an effort and learnt, book learningwise from, to learn Spanish but I haven't, it's wrong. (fa/93/UK)

(4)   (...) Catalan, I can understand, more or less, I can understand it, reading, to a certain extent, and listening I have a comprehensive comprehension ability in Catalan, I can watch the news in Catalan and know more or less what's going on and some of my students speak to me in **catalán** (uttered in Catalan), after a class, for example, or if they don't understand something or if they can't express themselves because their first language is **catalán**, so they just come out with "how do you say...?" and they say it in **catalán** (uttered in Catalan) and usually I seem to be able to understand. (ru/92/UK)

Domains of Language Use

According to Fishman, 'in many studies of multilingual behaviour the family domain has proved to be a very crucial one. Multilingualism often begins in the family and depends upon it for encouragement if not for protection' (1965: 76). In accordance with Fishman's view, the family domain has proved to be significant in the case of the UK community in Spain. At all events, great importance is given to the children's use of English in a British-English speaking household, as illustrated in (1), a fragment of which is reproduced in (5):

(5) But the aspect of the satellite was also a consideration in that in our home it was ... we needed to improve our children's English because you can well imagine, they go to school, they're taught in **castellano** and **catalán**, and their time in the home we have to make sure their English is kept to a good level and it's easier if we can get them watching English programmes on television (...). (jo/93/UK)

However, a difference must be made between monolingual families and mixed families, keeping in mind that the proportion of mixed families in the UK community is not very high, at least according to our findings. Beginning with the group of English *monolingual* families, the general rule would be: English spoken at home between partners and between the parents and children, who may speak English, Spanish or any of the other host community languages among themselves, mainly depending on the school they attend. The second group, that of *mixed* families, may combine any of the three languages at home: Spanish, English and any of the other three host community languages; most of them say that their most usual language (which is considered to be the language spoken at home) is English, while only a minority say that it is either Spanish or Catalan.

As to the employment domain, the UK migrants' professional activity will generally involve the use of some, or even mostly, Spanish or any other host community language, apart from English (in the case of English teachers or pub owners, especially). In fact, most Britons from this professional group will have learnt either Spanish, Catalan, Galician or Basque once settled in Spain. The process of learning is in general not formal, but achieved through the interaction with people from the host communities in their settlement area.[8]

Language Contact Patterns

In line with the hypotheses presented in the introduction of this book (Chapter 1), immigrants in contact with speakers of the host community's language(s), in this case UK migrants in contact with Spanish, Catalan, Basque and Galician speakers, may present different discourse patterns in terms of the types of language contact phenomena that they produce – overt, non-overt, or both – which are constrained by a number of internal and external factors. Overt phenomena include codeswitching, where the two languages in contact are kept separate, and borrowing, which, while it may involve some phonological and morphological adaptation, does not require much cognitive effort. Non-overt phenomena include syntactic and semantic calque, which often involve a mixing of the grammars of the languages in contact.

Codeswitching

In order to account for the UK community patterns of codeswitching, we follow Fontana and Vallduví's framework of analysis (1990) and take the distinction between lexical (usually one-word codeswitches)[9] and grammatical codeswitching. Lexical codeswitching occurs when a LEX2 element is inserted in the L1 grammar, or the other way round, as illustrated in (6) and (7):

(6)   because of the presence of the **Guardia Civil,** yeah? (jb/92/UK)
       (because of the presence of the **Civil Guard**)

(7)   The first job I had after school, I was a plumber, an apprentice, **fontanería**. (jb/93/UK)
       (The first job I had after school, I was a plumber, an apprentice, **plumbing**)

Grammatical codeswitching, on the other hand, involves the use of two grammars in the same syntactic unit, that is, the alternation between two grammatical systems, as in (8) and (9):

(8)   making an extractor, extract popper **más fuerte** and making the patio. (fa/93/UK)
       (making an extractor, extract popper **more powerful** and making the patio)

(9)   and, of course, they spelled **averiado con b en vez de v**, I knew that right off. (jb/92/US)
       (and, of course, they spelled **out of order with a b instead of a v**, I knew that right off)

A further distinction can be made according to their place of occurrence, that is, depending on whether they occur intersententially (between sentences), intrasententially (between sentence constituents) and extrasententially (outside the boundary of a sentence). Some instances of these types are illustrated in examples (10), (11) and (12):

(10) Well, I'm sure, I'm sure that something good will come out of it, well, to start with **Barcelona, posa't guapa**. (ni/92/UK)
(Well, I'm sure, I'm sure that something good will come out of it, well, to start with '**Barcelona, make yourself pretty**')

(11) I've done because we are **an ático**, but we had, when we first came. (ar/93/UK)
(I've done because we are **a loft**, but we had, when we first came)

(12) − Do you speak it properly?
− **Bastante**, yes. (di/92/UK)
(Do you speak it properly? **Quite a lot**, yes)

As to the specific codeswitching patterns used by the UK migrant community (Turell & Corcoll, 1998) find that lexical codeswitching is preferred to grammatical codeswitching, because it is less costly cognitively speaking, and that intrasentential sites are preferred to extrasentential and intersentential, because the latter require much more cognitive effort and more L2 competence.

Borrowing

Following Pujadas and Turell (1993: 307), a borrowing may be characterised by being phonologically and (sometimes) morphologically integrated into the matrix or base language so, in this case, an example would be a Spanish or Catalan word adapted to English phonology and/or morphology. Also, in accordance with Myers-Scotton's Matrix Language Frame Model (1993), words which designate a reality only known to a certain culture, whether phonologically and morphologically adapted or not, can be classified as borrowings because they can be seen as an insertion in the English lexicon of items that have no equivalent in English and, therefore, that have become part of the English lexicon. Some examples ((13), (14) and (15)) taken from the UK migrants' modality of discourse illustrate this type of borrowing:

(13) (. . .) every three or four shops there is a **cafetería** or a bar, isn't there. (fa/93/UK)   (café, coffee bar)

(14) I got involved in translation by the typical Spanish habit of **enchufe**,[10], yeah?. (jb/92/UK)   (pulling strings)

(15) I think in Spain it's geared for outdoor life, whether we go to the beach or to the mountains, to ski or even to have a **calçotada**[11] or something like this. (ri/93/UK)   (open air picnic with braised shallots)

Syntactic calque

In recent research on syntactic calque, a new conception of this manifestation of language contact (Corcoll, 1999) has been developed which characterises it as a phenomenon occurring within the realm of semantic features included within lexical entries, rather than at structural level (where structure is understood basically as word order).[12] This calque of structures may involve different parts of speech, such as the over-generalization of the use of definite articles and prepositions, a change in word order, or a different construction of noun and verb phrases. (16), (17), (18) exemplify this type of calque:

(16) so I think buses should still go **all the day**, they still go, but the ser-vices reduce (...). (jb/93/UK)   (all day)

(17) we can't give you any work because you're only here for **one week more or two weeks more**. (ar/92/UK)
      (one more week or two more weeks)

(18) Now obviously they **have a lot more years**, and I don't even think I've had a coarse word with them in many years. (ri/93/UK)
      (are a lot older)

Semantic calque

Following Pujadas and Turell (1993: 397), this type of calque may be defined as the literal translation from one language to another of the con-cept represented by a linguistic unit, with no external indication showing its linguistic provenance. Examples (19) and (20) illustrate this linguistic phenomenon:

(19) I've never been robbed in the street, but once when we went on holiday to America, they **entered in** our house and stole some, some vases and things. (di/92/UK)   (broke in)

(20) – And what do you get out of working besides money?
      Pains in the head. (mf/93/UK)
      (headaches)

As a final remark, it is interesting to note how language contact, even if unconsciously caused, is viewed by consultants when they comment on the effects that the coexistence of two or more languages, whatever these may be, has had on their mother tongue, as in (21):

(21) sometimes I can't find the words in English to translate what I'm doing, do you understand, but then in Spanish it's a **técnico de mantenimiento y de control de calidad de la automoción,** you can just imagine now again trying to put it all back together in English. (mf/93/UK)
          (maintenance and automotion quality control technician)

Conclusion

The analysis of the UK community in Spain seems to suggest that Spain has historically been and still is one of the favoured sites for the British to come and live after retiring, in search of new horizons, peace and sun, but also that it is an attractive destination for professional British people to come, work and settle. In fact, there seem to be three main motivations for British immigration to Spain: firstly, the wish to learn a language and have the experience of living abroad; secondly, to develop professionally; and thirdly, to retire. Different groups, then, have rather different reasons for coming to Spain and this may be why they choose to settle down in one place or another. British migrants stay for long in general, and this would indicate that UK immigration to Spain tends to be stable within certain limits and is integrated, if they come for professional reasons, but not for those who come to retire.

The attitudes towards the Spanish language and culture (or any language and culture in the different Autonomous Communities in Spain) seem to be quite different depending on the group of immigrants considered. Also, the distribution of these languages by domain of language use is very varied. The fact is that whichever language is chosen in every domain depends on the immigrant's professional activity and on their family type. This variation in code choice and code change takes different forms and is viewed differently depending on migrant profile.

Clearly, prospects are bright for the English-speaking communities from the UK in Spain and for their language. The fact that quite a precise 'identikit' picture can be described for the UK immigrants and that the immigration rate is relatively steady and persistent over time suggests that UK citizens will continue to come to Spain at more or less the same rate and for more or less the same reasons as they do now. Moreover, the ever growing importance of English seems to point to the same direction: English has become the international language *par excellence* and native speakers of English will be necessary in Spain, for a long time and in a variety of professions. Finally, it must be said that, in the case of the UK community, the sense of community is built not only by the migrants themselves by developing associations and schools, establishing relationships with other foreigners and so on, but also by the host society that surrounds them.

Notes

1. The fact that there was a decrease not simply in numbers 'arriving' but in overall total shows considerable instability compared to the most typical pattern of migration.
2. A consular area is that area that falls within the jurisdiction of a particular Consulate. The consular areas in Spain are Alicante, Barcelona, Bilbao, Ibiza, Las Palmas, Madrid, Málaga, Palma, Seville, Tenerife and Vigo.

3. This is confirmed by data extracted from our case study in the two settlement sites: Catalonia (Barcelona and Tarragona) and the Canary Islands (Lanzarote). Half the informants who migrated to Catalonia have lived there for more than five years; as to the informants who reside in Lanzarote, a vast majority migrated more than five years before the interview was conducted in 1993.

4. Following the methodological design used with all new migrant communities, the members of the UK community were interviewed and the conversations were tape-recorded. The interviews lasted between 30 and 45 minutes and dealt with topics that ranged from demographic facts, including age, place of birth, studies and so on, to linguistic competence, family, neighbourhood, hobbies and interests. All interviews follow the same pattern and they were all carried out in English. At certain points, the interviewees also used some Spanish in the case of Lanzarote and some Spanish and/or Catalan in the case of Tarragona and Barcelona. Language interference and language contact will be the object of study of a later section: Language contact patterns.

5. As to the pilot study informants, in both samples the difference in numbers between those that have a university degree and those that only completed secondary education is not very significant. In Catalonia, a majority are English teachers and pub owners, and an overwhelming majority are English, although there are also Irish and Welsh. In Lanzarote, well over half have a university degree and most of them do not work there either because they have retired (those over 50) or because they do not need a job. The majority of those who work there are English teachers or have a job related to tourism. All the informants were English.

6. Obviously, this is an overgeneralization and it does not rule out the possibility of keeping both attitudes at once: to keep one's roots and to integrate into the host community.

7. As far as the sample informants' pattern of integration, there seems to be a difference between the first and the second generation. The first generation to arrive keep English as their most usual language in most cases, with the exception of some mixed families. In the case of the informants in Catalonia, the younger ones generally use Catalan or Spanish at work, with friends, etc. and so English becomes limited to the family circle.

8. As to the friendship domain, more often in *mixed* rather then in *monolingual* families, Spanish or the other host community languages are spoken with friends, although there may be cases within the British community where the number of Spanish friends is small.

9. The definition of lexical codeswitching is extended to multiword switches (toponyms, titles in general) or even idioms which by their nature involve the same cognitive markedness as one-word switches.

10. When one gets something by *enchufe*, one gets it thanks to the influence of a friend or an acquaintance, not through one's own merits. This use may be compared with English expressions such as 'string-pulling' or 'old-boys' network'.

11. A *calçotada* is an outdoor activity typical of some parts of Catalonia which consists in a celebration where people get together and eat roasted *calçots*, a variety of onion (braised shallots).

12. This analysis of syntactic calque was carried out within a lexically-based model of grammar, which would consider as *syntax* the sum of pure structure and the semantic features included within lexical entries. For further details, see Corcoll (1999).

13. The number of years is counted as of the year when the interview was carried out, which is indicated by the two figures in the code for every informant.

Appendix 1: Catalogue of Informants

Catalonia (Barcelona and Tarragona)

Name	Age	Profession	Academic level	Years in Spain[13]	Other languages	Code
Arthur	56	Plumber	Secondary	5	Sp	ar/93/UK
Digsby	25	English teacher	Secondary	4.5	Sp, Cat, Fr	di/92/UK
Edi	43	Restaurant owner	University	6	Sp, Cat, Fr, Ge	ed/92/UK
Emma	28	English teacher	University	6	Sp, some Cat	em/97/UK
Fay M. Davies	50	Bartender	University	9	Sp, Cat	fa/93/UK
Helen Jones	25	English teacher	Secondary	?	Sp	he/93/UK
John Bates	31	English teacher	University	7	Sp, Cat, Fr	jb/92/UK
Johnny	47	Businessman	University	22	Sp, Rus	jo/93/UK
Michael	29	Painter	Secondary	10	Sp.	mf/93/UK
Mike	27	English teacher	University	5	Sp, Cat, Fr	mi/92/UK
Nissy	40	English teacher	University	10	Sp, Cat	ni/92/UK
Richard	38	Engineer	University	?	Sp, Cat	ri/93/UK
Ruth Maguire	22	English teacher	University	2	Sp, Cat, It, Fr	ru/92/UK

Appendix 2: Catalogue of Informants

Lanzarote (Canary Islands)

Name	Age	Profession	Academic level	Years in Spain	Other languages	Code
Anni	?	Retired secretary	College	11	some Sp	an/93/UK
Bonny	52	Retired secretary	College	8	Fr, some Sp	bo/93/UK
Inna	46	Retired beauty therapist	Secondary	5	some Sp	in/93/UK
Jonathan	65	Retired barrister	University	9	some Sp	jon/93/UK
Lay	46	Musician	College	11	some Sp	la/93/UK
Lidia	12	Student	Primary	10	Sp	li/93/UK
Moira	65	Retired secretary	Secondary	9	Fr, some Sp	mo/93/UK
Ray	43	Builder	College	7	Fr, some Sp	ra/93/UK
Robert	52	?	College	5	some Sp	ro/93/UK
Robin	50	Retired civil servant	College	12	some Sp	rob/93/UK
Rosy	37	Fashion designer	College	10	some Sp	ros/93/UK
Sandra	32	Waitress (in Spain)	?	11	Sp	sa/93/UK
Shasha	51	Retired secretary	College	3	some Sp	sh/93/UK

References

British Council of Barcelona (1996) *Some Facts and Figures 1995/96.*

Corcoll, C. (1999) *A Reassessment of the Notion of Syntactic Calque: Grammatical and Sociolinguistic Evidence.* Research work presented within the PhD Programme on Applied Linguistics. Institut Universitari de Lingüística Aplicada. Universitat Pompeu Fabra. Barcelona.

Enguix, S. (1994) Ni ¡help! ni ¡auxilio! *La Vanguardia*, 31 (May 23).

Enguix, S. (1999) Elecciones en el paraíso. *La Vanguardia, 12* (June 13).

Fishman, J. (1965) Who speaks what language to whom and when? *Linguistique, 2,* 67–88.

Fontana, J.M. and Vallduví, E. (1990) Mecanismos léxicos y gramaticales en la alternancia de códigos. In M.T. Turell (ed.) *Nuevas Corrientes Lingüísticas. Aplicación a la Descripción del Inglés* (pp. 171–92). *Revista Española de Lingüística Aplicada, AESLA,* año VI. Anejo I. Granada.

Instituto Nacional de Estadística (INE) (1996) *Anuario Estadístico 1995. España.* Madrid.

Instituto Nacional de Estadística (INE) (1996) *Migraciones Año 1995.* Madrid.

Instituto Nacional de Estadística (INE) *Anuario Estadistico 1999.* Madrid.

Ministerio de Trabajo y Asuntos Sociales. *Anuario de Migraciones 1997.* Madrid.

Myers-Scotton, C. (1993) *Social Motivations for Codeswitching.* Oxford: Clarendon Press.

Pujadas, J. and Turell, M.T. (1993) Els indicadors sociolingüístics del contacte interètnic. In *Actes del IXè Col.loqui Internacional de Llengua i Literatura Catalanes.* Alacant-Elx (1991). Barcelona: Publicacions de l'Abadia de Montserrat, 301–18.

Turell, M.T. and Corcoll, C. (1998) The effect of socio-collective factors on the bilingual speech modes of British and American English-speaking communities in Spain. Paper presented at the *Sociolinguistics Symposium 12.* Institute of Education. University of London. London.

Vallejo, E. (1994) Vuelven los ingleses. *La Vanguardia.*

Chapter 17

The US American Speech Community

M. TERESA TURELL and CRISTINA CORCOLL

Nature and Distribution of the US American-English Speech Community in Spain

The people of the United States are not a very migratory community. Many young people may move to and live in Europe for a short period of time either before or after university, to then go back and settle down in the US. The latter country, however, has one of the highest rates of immigration in the world. According to a prediction made by the US Census Office, towards the year 2050 white people will only account for 53% of the population in the US. The remaining 47% will be divided between Hispanic (25%), black (14%) and Asian people (8%). Moreover, by 2050 the population will, it is predicted, to have grown by 124 million people, 80 million of whom will be immigrants. All this will shape a new American nation (Mas, 1997).[1]

Even though a minority, some US citizens do migrate to Europe and, according to the 1994 *American Citizens Abroad* (ACA),[2] while the total number of US citizens living abroad is not known exactly, the current estimate is between 2,500,000 and 5,000,000. Of these, more than

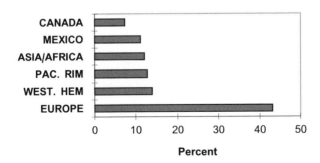

REGIONS OF RESIDENCE

Figure 17.1 US immigrants by areas of residence
Source: ACA, 1994

US CITIZENS IN SPAIN

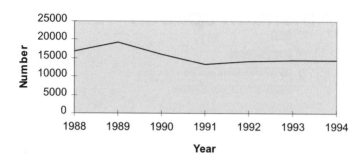

Figure 17.2 Rate of immigration of US citizens to Spain (1985–1994)
Source: *Anuario Estadístico* (1995)

900,000 are US Government employees and military people. Figure 17.1 shows how they are distributed by regions of residence: the largest proportion (43.1%) lives in Europe, the Western Hemisphere accounts for 13.8%, the Pacific Rim represents 12.8%, Asia/Africa 12.1%, Mexico 11% and Canada trails with 7.2% (ACA, 1994: 5).[3]

Spain is not one of the most favoured destination for US citizens in Europe, which accounts for 43.1% of Americans abroad, as was mentioned earlier. According to the ACA Survey (1994), 45% of Americans who come to Europe live in Austria, Germany, Italy and Switzerland. The 1994 *Instituto Nacional de Estadística* (INE) (Spanish National Institute of Statistics) statistics (*Anuanrio de Migraciones* (1995)) indicate that there were at that time a total of 14,528 US citizens living in Spain. They were mainly concentrated in Madrid (4880), Andalusia (2420) and Catalonia (1648). In these areas, they also tended to live in major cities, such as Seville (667) and Barcelona (1470).[4] Figure 17.2 shows how the immigration rate has evolved over the past decade and also US immigration to Spain as increasing steadily between 1985 and 1989, falling a little between 1990 and 1991 and increasing again as of that year.[5]

Motivation

In terms of their motivation for leaving the US and coming to Spain, migrants can be classified into the following groups: firstly, those, a great majority, who come for professional reasons (teachers and businessmen), whether it in search of an economic advancement or in search of a challenge, but who in spite of this cannot be considered as economic migrants; secondly, there are those who come for sentimental reasons and either marry somebody from the host community they migrate to or finally decide to stay because they like being in Spain; thirdly, there are

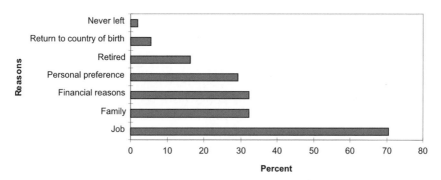

REASONS FOR LIVING ABROAD

Figure 17.3 US immigrants' reasons for living abroad
Source: ACA, 1994

those who come to study or simply to get to know a different place and enjoy a different kind of life. Finally, another group that has to be mentioned are the American Army and Air Force personnel, who came to Spain to work on the American bases when these were set up and, in some cases, decided to stay in Spain after these bases were dismantled in recent years.

Figure 17.3, which has been extracted from the ACA Survey (1994), shows the main reasons why US citizens live abroad according to that source: 70.5% said they were living abroad for professional reasons, almost half that number (32.3%) cited family reasons and an approximately equal number mentioned financial reasons, 29.2% said they lived abroad because of personal preference, 16.4% retired abroad, 5.5% returned to their country of birth, and 1.9% never left their country.

Arrival and Settlement

The general rule seems to be that US migrants move to Spain almost by chance: some informants arrive first in other European countries, they visit some Spanish big cities, such as Barcelona, Madrid or Seville, and then decide either to stay or to come back after a while. When asked, they also report that, in the beginning, they found it difficult to meet people in Spain, but that once they began to make friends, they made many.

A difference can be made here between two age-groups that, at the time of their arrival and settlement, are made up of younger people, on the one hand, and slightly older to middle-aged, on the other. The tendency among the first group is to spend a time in Spain either before or after university, and then go back to the US to settle down. The second group is much more likely to end up settling down in Spain, since on many occasions they form a family in this country and then it becomes more difficult to leave. In fact, many of those who have children would rather have them all living in Spain, although they visit the US as often as they can.

As to place of settlement, the majority of US immigrants to Spain typically move to big urban areas[6] where they can develop professionally and mix with Spaniards. It must be noted, however, that most US citizens that decide to stay in Spain after having lived in such urban areas move to smaller towns. The tendency among professional groups of US citizens is for them to stay longer than those younger citizens who come to look for adventure or a new way of life.

The correlation between motivation and settlement area would indicate that US migration is related to professional rather than economic or political factors and that it is quite stable,[7] particularly in the case of professional migrants, and this means that, once they migrate and settle, they tend to stay.

The US Migrants' Social Profile

The most recent official data available on the arrival of US citizens to Spain is for 1994 (see *Anuario de Migraciones 1995*) and these data corroborate the general pattern described above in terms of settlement area. In that year, 316 US citizens arrived in Spain and they concentrated in the following areas: Madrid (100), Catalonia (63) and Andalusia (42). Turning to the size of the destinations of the immigrants, Table 17.1 shows how half these US immigrants (152) chose to live in provincial capitals, that is, big urban areas, while the rest chose towns of between 20,001 and 50,000 inhabitants (51) or between 50,001 and 100,000 (43), which confirms that the US migrants' pattern of settlement is essentially urban.

Distribution according to sex is quite even: 161 women and 155 men. As to age, Table 17.2 illustrates that the largest group of US immigrants (94) is aged from 25 and 34 years of age, followed by the 35 to 44 age group. These are first generation migrants, although the US community in Spain also includes families with relatively young children, who thus have to decide what kind of education they want for them.

Table 17.1 1994 US immigrants by areas of residence

Total	Provincial capitals	−10,000	10,001– 20,000	20,001– 50,000	50,001– 100,000	+100,000
316	152	41	18	51	43	11

Source: Migraciones 1995; INE (1996)

Table 17.2 1994 US immigrants by age-groups

Total	−16	16/24	25/34	35/44	45/54	55/64	+65
316	50	20	94	56	38	35	23

Source: Migraciones 1995; INE (1996)

Table 17.3 1994 US immigrants by academic level

Total	Illiterates	elementary school	Completed through 8th grade	High School diploma/Higher Education	Unknown
316	18	46	29	214	9

Source: Migraciones 1995; INE (1996)

As regards their academic level, the majority of 1994 US immigrants (214) have a university degree and most of them work in the public service sector, as Table 17.3 illustrates. At the other end of the scale, 46 did not study beyond elementary school.[8]

These figures relating to the 1994 flux of US of migrants into Spain suggest that the socio-demographic structure described above is correct. The social profile of US migration that emerges is of young people in search of adventure and young middle-aged professionals, who settle with their families or constitute mixed families with a highly positive integration pattern. The exception to this picture would be the US citizens who worked on the US military bases, before they were dismantled in the early 1990s, and who tended to live in the bases or in areas with many other English-speaking people, where they could buy and eat US products, attend clubs for foreigners and speak English at all times, creating real ghettos.

Attitudes towards the Spanish Language and Culture

US immigrants' attitudes towards the Spanish language and culture, and the languages and cultures of the other autonomous communities in Spain, are generally very positive. That the US community on the whole[9] integrates into the local community can be ascertained through different facts; the most important is the fact that on our evidence most US immigrants are able to, at least understand and, in many cases, speak, read and write both Spanish, and Catalan, Galician or Basque, depending on the settlement area. Also, in line with their motivation for migrating and their age (young or middle-aged), it seems that they typically end up marrying a Spaniard and having children in Spain. In general, these children attend local schools instead of attending American or British schools. Moreover, although US migrants meet other foreigners, they tend not to stay enclosed within their community, but rather they mix with the local community.[10] There is evidence to suggest, therefore, that, in comparison with other migrant communities which have settled in Spain, the US community is a relatively open community, which is also shown on the US immigrants' greater wish to mix and integrate into the new community than to create strong ties with other foreign people who live in the area, whether they are from the US or other countries.

The Role of Education

There is no official information available as to the US migrants' children who are growing up in Spain and attending secondary school and university. The information relating to some opinions that parents or future parents have about education in Spain and in the US was extracted from the pilot study that was conducted within the US migrant community in Spain. As a general rule, the children of Americans living in Spain know either two or three languages. They learn English from their American parents and Spanish and perhaps another language at school. They are able to use English and at least one other language, and they will use one or the other depending on their interlocutor. The usual situation seems to be using English at home (either with the American parent or with both of them), and Spanish and/or any of the other official languages in Spain[11] with friends. When there is more than one child, they tend to use Spanish and/or any of the other official languages in Spain among themselves.

It is not a very difficult task for US migrants' children to keep in touch with English. Apart from whatever language they speak at home, if these children attend a local school, they are exposed to the same amount of English as any other child in Spain: they study English at school, listen to music in English, watch movies in English, and so on.[12] However, many parents state that they use English at home to make sure that their children will learn it. In many cases, children may not want to use English during the early period of their lives, particularly after they have been attending a local school for a year or two, because they may not want to speak differently from their schoolmates or simply because they cannot understand the need to know more than one language. In general, this situation seems to change in time, and children eventually become proficient in the two or three languages they have around. This is reflected upon by some of the sample informants, as in (1) and (2):

(1)   (...) Yeah, my daughter is ... six and a half and my son is eight and they've been here for four years, so they're completely trilingual, in fact, I think their favourite language to speak is Spanish, it's really interesting, their language at school is **catalán**, their family language is English, but their language to have fun and play is Spanish (j/95/US)

(2)   (...) My son speaks in **catalán**, but he understands absolutely everything in English 'cause I knew that he was understanding me all these months, but now that my parents have come, he understands everything that they're saying ... he responds in **catalán**, he speaks in **catalán**, but if I say 'No, Julian' or we play this game 'Julian, momma says **casa** and poppa says "house"' and he goes 'house', and then, you know, we try to get him to repeat things. He'd come into the kitchen from outside and he'd wanna like water the plants and he says '**Més aigua, papa**' and I say 'No, Julian, more water, please' and he goes 'more water, please' (m/95/US)

In the case of the informants who participated in the pilot study, all their children are attending Catalan schools, in spite of the fact that there are several American and British schools, basically in Barcelona. In a few cases, parents mention that their children are attending or will attend university in the United States. Scholarships and specialisation are mentioned as factors that may make these families send their children to study in the US. Accordingly, the ACA survey mentions education as one of the topics of major concern for Americans living abroad. On the one hand, 21.2% respondents believed that since it was their choice to live overseas, education was the parents' responsibility and that the US Government should not get involved in educating children abroad. On the other hand, 56.8% felt that the Government *should* get involved and that their children should get the same educational benefits as they would in the US.

As to the parents' attitude towards their children's language competence and use, both English monolingual families and mixed families have similar opinions, since parents tend to want their children to be competent in as many languages as possible and, therefore, try to develop their linguistic competence in all directions, usually leaving Spanish or Catalan for the school in the case of the first group (monolingual families); or using two languages at home in the case of the second group, making use of the *one parent-one language* pattern. Many English-speaking parents try to keep talking to their children in English, in spite of the difficulties encountered when the children are young and do not understand why they use different languages in and out of the home.

Social Life

In general, the US community abroad seems to be open and receptive to the host community's life-style and culture with which they are in contact when they settle. Members of this migrant group get involved and integrate into the host community. At the same time, however, they like keeping in touch with their roots: 65.2% of respondents to the ACA Survey are members of some organisation representing Americans living abroad. These organisations are normally non-profit social and cultural associations where Americans can get together for pleasure and can also obtain information on any legal, health care, social security or any other need they may have.[13]

Some examples of this type of association are the American Citizens Abroad (ACA) itself, the American Benevolent Society (ABS), the American Womeńs Club (AWC), the American Society, the Association of American Residents Overseas (AARO), etc. The American Consulate in any Spanish big city will have information on which of these associations can be found and on how to contact them. Taking Barcelona as an example, the following ones are represented: the American and International Women's Club (A&IWC), the American Society of Barcelona and the Institute of American Studies (IAS). The three of them organise events of many kinds both for Americans and non-Americans. In the particular case of the A&IWC, these events include celebrating American celebrations and holidays, such as Halloween or Thanksgiving; holding meetings for American citizens and their families; organising talks on issues that may affect Americans as immigrants (citizenship, health care, social security, etc.); or holding sports competitions. The IAS, for its part, organises conferences, courses, exhibitions, etc. to spread American culture. In general, the main goal of these associations seems to be keeping in touch with American culture and encouraging relations between US Americans abroad.

At the same time, American immigrants keep in touch with their relatives and friends, and visit each other quite frequently. The family is probably the strongest tie that the informants have with the US. Still, they would rather stay in Spain than go back. In particular, those informants who have children would prefer them to grow up in Spain. One informant who lives in a town outside Barcelona describes life in Spain in the following way, as (3) illustrates:

(3)   it's really nice for the kids, they can, you know, go outside by themselves, everything is just really calm and peaceful compared to New York (j/95/US)

Patterns of Language Behaviour

US migrants living in Spain exhibit variation in code choice and code change into Spanish, or the other host community's languages (Catalan, Galician and Basque). They may change from one language to another depending on whom their interlocutors are, on the conversation topic and on the style of the conversation. This variation is viewed differently by the speakers themselves, who are often quite competent in these languages. The members of the US community in Spain tend to talk about their linguistic use according to level of formality (friends, work, family, etc.), to whether training has been received in one language or another, or to the existence or lack of certain terminology, as illustrated in (4), (5) and (6):

(4)   (...) I prefer English, but when I'm with, when I'm working I have to speak Spanish and when I am with friends, if they are not English friends or American friends (...) who speak English, but if they are Spanish friends, of course, I speak Eng ... Spanish. It's kind of 50–50 right now. I always speak English with my children, yes, always, because with my wife it's very difficult for me to speak in Eng ... in Spanish (jb/92/US)

(5)   – [Is there any specific topic that you feel you can express yourself better in English than in Spanish?]
        – Feelings (...) but I think English is better at that ... not because, let me think, not because ... I don't think it's any lack of competence on my part ... (...) but I really think English has better words ... (am/95/US)

(6)   Is there any one topic that I would prefer to speak in English about? Yeah, I'll give you an example ... music, there's a very specific language that, that goes along with, you know, describing all the music terminology (...) since I started playing music when I was 8 or 9 years old, that's so ingrained (...) it's hard to express nuances of like musical concepts in Catalan (m/95/US)

The most important language communication patterns can be summarised as follows:

(a)   There are some demographic or social facts that account for the maintenance of English among US immigrants, such as family, professional activity or language instruction.
(b)   The use of other languages by the US community in Spain depends very much on a number of individual and community factors that will contribute to our picture of differentiating integration patterns.
(c)   These language communication patterns, which suggest that US Americans in Spain should be characterised as an *open-type* community, are related to these migrants' specific demographic profile and to settlement patterns. This community is distinctive for the high number of immigrants who come alone and, from the very outset, begin mixing with the members of the host community. This situation favours greater integration that can be discerned in the high number of mixed families, the development of professions related to the host community, and the fact that a majority of them attend formal classes in Spanish and, in the communities where they are spoken, also in Catalan, Galician or Basque.
(d)   The members of the US community in Spain are frequently asked by Spanish people to speak English because they want to practice and

improve their language skills, and they may also relate to other foreigners, which frequently makes English their most usual language.

Domains of Language Behaviour

In accordance with Fishman's view (1965: 76), the family domain has proved to be significant in the analysis of the US community in Spain. In general, in the households of US Americans living in this country a minimum of two languages are spoken and it is very likely that the language used between the parents and between the parents and the children is different from that used between the children when they play in the household. These patterns of language behaviour are illustrated in (7):

(7)   (...) they (the children) have been here for four years, so they're completely trilingual, in fact, I think their favorite language to speak is Spanish, it's really interesting. Their language at school is Catalan, their family language is English, but their language to have fun and play is Spanish (j/95/US)

First of all, a difference must be made between *monolingual* families and *mixed* families, keeping in mind that in the US American community the incidence of the latter is quite high. This difference is of great importance since it will account for different linguistic uses at home and with the children. Beginning with the *monolingual* families, the general rule would be that English is spoken at home between the couple and between the parents and children, who may speak English, Spanish or Catalan among themselves mainly depending on the school they attend; in *mixed* families sometimes any of the three languages which are available to the migrant community are combined at home.

The migrants' professional activity will generally also involve the use of some Spanish or Catalan in Catalonia, apart from English (in the case of English teachers especially), or mostly Spanish or Catalan; and, Spanish or Catalan is spoken in the friendship domain with friends from the host communities.

As for their linguistic background, that is, the language(s) they have spoken and/or studied throughout their lives, the norm for the US American community is not to have spoken any other language apart from English in their childhood. However, the situation differs when considering the questions of what the migrants' most usual language is at present and of the way they learnt Spanish and/or Catalan. In the case of the US immigrants, a substantial section has adopted Spanish as their most usual language. As mentioned above, those who have a Spanish partner and have children may use up to three languages at home (English, Spanish, and either Catalan, Galician or Basque) and a great majority have taken or are currently taking Spanish and/or Catalan, Galician or Basque courses.

Language Contact Patterns

The view which is taken in this article is that immigrants may present different patterns concerning the types of language contact phenomena which are constrained by a number of internal and external factors. These manifestations of language contact phenomena include: codeswitching, where the two languages in contact are kept separate; borrowing, which, even if it may often involve some phonological and morphological adaptation, does not require much cognitive effort; and syntactic and semantic calque, which often involve a mixing of the grammars of the languages in contact.

Codeswitching

In order to account for the UK community patterns of codeswitching, we follow Fontana and Vallduví's framework of analysis (1990) and take the distinction between lexical (usually one-word codeswitches)[14] and grammatical codeswitching. Lexical codeswitching occurs when a LEX2 element is inserted in the L1 grammar, or the other way round, as illustrated in (8):

(8)   it was like in a **tiovivo**, you know? (mi/92/US)
      (It was like in a **merry-go-round**, you know?)

Grammatical codeswitching, on the other hand, involves the use of two grammars in the same syntactic unit, that is, the alternation between two grammatical systems, as in (9):

(9)   what do you call it? **un cepillo** (jb/92/US)
      (what do you call it? **a plane**)

Apart from considering the instances of codeswitching from this viewpoint, a further distinction is made according to site of occurrence, that is, depending on whether switches occur intersententially (between sentences, as in (9)), intrasententially (between sentence constituents) and extrasententially (outside the boundary of a sentence). Some examples of intra and extrasentential codeswitches are presented under (10) and (11), respectively:

(10) the parties in the summer and the **verbenas** are excellent here
      (k/93/US)   (celebration, festival)

(11) **Uy**, if I can remember, that's not very easy (am/95/US)
      (**Gosh**, if I can remember, that's not very easy)

In line with general findings on codeswitching, Turell and Corcoll (1998) show that in their codeswitching practices US community people prefer lexical codeswitching rather than grammatical codeswitching, because it is less costly cognitively speaking. As to the correlation between internal and external factors, it seems that type of community,[15] and in particular, degree of contact,[16] have a significant effect on codeswitching frequency and type. For example, in terms of the switch's grammatical form, High contact US migrants use more complex and more cognitively costly codeswitches, such as, bare NPs, than Average or Low contact members of the US community, while the latter prefer less complex and less cognitively costly codeswitches, such as, bare nouns. As far as syntactic and pragmatic functions, High contact has a favouring effect on the use of complex arguments.

Borrowing

Following Pujadas and Turell (1993: 307), a borrowing is usually characterised by being phonologically and sometimes morphologically integrated into the mother tongue so, in this case, an example would be a Spanish or Catalan word adapted to English phonology and/or morphology. Examples (12) and (13) illustrate this type of language interaction phenomenon:

(12) it's a very **touristic** city (k/93/US)
       (it's a city **for tourists**)

(13) He is in the United States now, he is getting his doctorate in microbiology, **biochemic**, biochemistry and genetical engineering (mi/92/US)
       (He is in the United States now, he is getting his doctorate in microbiology, **biochemistry**, biochemistry and genetical engineering)

Also, in accordance with Myers-Scotton's Matrix Language Frame Model (1993), words which designate a reality only known to a certain culture, whether phonologically and morphologically adapted or not, can be classified as borrowings because they can be seen as an insertion in the English lexicon of items that have no equivalent in English and, therefore, become part of the English lexicon. Examples (14) and (15) illustrate this type of phenomenon:

(14) (...) we get together, if it's not for a **calçotada**,[17] it's for a **paella**[18] party (k/93/US)

(15) (...) the parties in the summer and the **verbenas**[19] here are excellent (k/93/US)

Syntactic calque

Following recent research on this language contact phenomenon (Corcoll, 1999), a new conception of syntactic calque has been developed which characterises it as a calque occurring within the realm of semantic features that are included within lexical entries, rather than at the level of their structure (when structure is understood basically as word order).[20] This calque of structures may involve different parts of speech, such as the overgeneralisation of the use of definite articles and prepositions, a change in word order, or a different construction of noun and verb phrases. The instances (16), (17), (18) and (19) exemplify this type of calque:

(16) I **like** painting with acrylic **more**, this one here is acrylic (mi/92/US) (like (...) better)

(17) (...) to learn other languages and it must be **one of the more**, most difficult accents (b/92/US)   (one of the most)

(18) I worked for two years with **paralysis cerebral** for a state hospital in New York (mi/92/US)   (cerebral paralysis)

(19) they don't feel the need to learn English as much as the **olders** do (mi/92/US)   (older ones)

Semantic calque

Following Pujadas and Turell (1993: 397), this type of calque may be defined as the literal translation from one language to another of the concept represented by a linguistic unit, with no external indication showing its linguistic provenance, as is illustrated in (20) and (21):

(20) (...) but I have no time now **to do it with tranquillity**, to draw, to paint (mi/92/US)   (to do it in no rush, at my leisure)

(21) (...) the woman, she's cleaning or Jet is **making food** or whatever (...) (ji/95/US)   (cooking)

As a final remark, it is interesting to note how language contact, even if it is unconscious, is viewed by informants when they comment on the effects that the coexistence of two or more languages, whatever these may be, has had on their mother tongue, as in (22), (23) and (24):

(22) (...) because English is not difficult for me, not as difficult as Spanish but, **with the time,**[21] every, now I'm starting to forget how to speak English, not that I'm forgetting but it's not as easy, that I have to think now to speak in English and before I didn't need to think, it's harder for me to express myself (b/92/US)

(23) (...) and my Spanish is right now my strongest language. It's probably better than my English, I would say (am/95/US)

(24) I read almost exclusively in English on purpose, to make sure that I still speak English (ja/95/US)

Conclusion

Even if US Americans do not constitute a very migratory community, the US continues to produce new emigrants whose most favourite destination seems to be Europe. In Spain, the basic and most fundamental reason for US migration seems to be professional and the migrants' pattern of settlement seems to be urban. In general, US migrants in Spain tend to integrate, if they stay for long. The social profile of the US citizens who migrate and settle in Spain is young and middle-aged. Some are single and migrate on their own, but others come with their family, or establish a mixed family in Spain. At the social and organisational level, their sense of community is built not only by the migrants themselves, who develop associations and schools, establish relationships with other foreigners and so on, but also by the host society that surrounds them. They exhibit a very positive approach to integration, as the considerable number of mixed marriages shows, and very positive attitudes towards the host community(ies)' culture and language(s). As to language use, the overall communication pattern among adults and between parents and children is a high use of English. However, in mixed families language choice adopts different forms which seem to be constrained by sociolinguistic factors (domains of language use) and psycholinguistic factors (competence in the host community's language(s)).

The fact that the US immigration rate is relatively steady suggests that the US citizens will continue to come to Spain for more or less the same reasons as they do at present and adopt similar patterns of settlement. Also, the ever growing importance of English seems to point to the same direction, since English has become the international language *par excellence* and, the same as in the case of UK migrants, native speakers of English will be necessary for a long time in a variety of professions.

Notes

1. The information on present percentages and predictions was extracted from an article published in *La Vanguardia* on 12 September 1997. It is worth noting how the Amerindians, the native population of the US, do not appear within any of the groups considered.
2. This association is concerned with protecting and promoting the welfare, rights and benefits of American citizens living outside the United States. Its European headquarters is in Geneva, Switzerland.
3. Regarding these data, it should be mentioned that, in taxonomic terms, some of these areas are overlapping (i.e. Canada, Western Hemisphere and the Pacific Rim). However, these are categories used in the ACA Survey and are presented in this article as such.
4. No percentages related to these data are available.
5. In order to arrive at a cross-section profile of the US immigrants in Spain, a pilot study was conducted in which 12 American people who live in Barcelona and its surrounding area took part (see *Appendix 1: Catalogue of Informants*). Following the methodological design used with all communities, the members of the US community were interviewed and the conversations were tape-recorded. The interviews lasted between 45 and 60 minutes and dealt with topics that ranged from demographic facts (age, place of birth, studies, etc.) to languages, family, neighbourhood hobbies and interests. The interviews

were carried out in English, although many words and expressions were used in both Spanish and Catalan.

6. This is one of the reasons behind the choice of Barcelona as a prototypical city to conduct the pilot study.

7. This point is illustrated by figures related to length of migration. According to the number of years they have lived in Spain, the sample informants can be divided into the following groups (the number of years is counted as of 1995, when the majority of the interviews were carried out): 2 to 5 years, 4 informants; 6 to 10, 6 informants; 11 to 15, 1 informant, and, more than 20, 1 informant. Most informants arrived in Spain in the 1980s, which also corroborates the data from the INE. Most of them came alone, although in almost every case they already knew somebody in the country. Only a small group came with their families. Although the informants now live in small towns located in the province of Barcelona, such as Sitges, Argentona or Sant Pere de Ribes, almost all of them lived first in Barcelona city and then moved.

8. Most of the sample informants have a university degree (10) and they all work in the services sector. Finally, they all have kept their American nationality and it is also worth noting that a great majority comes from the Eastern states of the US, while only 3 informants come from Western (1) and Southern States (2) of America.

9. Except in the case of the US Army and Air Forces personnel.

10. This may be connected with the fact that most informants in our pilot style end up moving out of Barcelona and into smaller towns, where meeting local people might be easier.

11. Any other official language that is spoken in the area where the immigrants live. In the case of the majority of informants, this language is Catalan. Other official languages are Basque and Galician, in the Basque Country and Galicia, respectively.

12. Also, since English seems to be considered by the sample informants and their families as a *prestige language*, they enjoy using it.

13. As to the pilot study's informants, although they claim that they know other informants, only a small minority belongs to one of these associations. Many seem to be more involved with the local people from the area where they live, the place where they work or where they study than with the US Americans living in Spain. However, a few of them hold periodical meetings and mix with members of the US community and their families.

14. The definition of lexical code-switching is extended to multiword switches (toponyms, titles in general) or even idioms which by their nature involve the same cognitive markedness as one-word switches.

15. Drawing from information related to the informants' social networks, it was possible to characterise the American US community in Spain as a relatively open type of community.

16. The instrument used to measure the degree of contact that the informants have with the members of the host community(ies) is the *index of contact*, which is defined according to sociolinguistic parameters. This instrument consisted of a questionnaire which included questions relating to their process of arrival and settlement, to their social networks and to any factors that would bring them in closer contact with host community members. Values were attributed to each of the answers to reach a scale between 1 and 8 in such a way that values between 1 and 2 would characterise **low** contact, values between 3 and 6, an **average** contact, and values between 7 and 8, a **high** contact.

17. A *calçotada* is an outdoor activity typical of some parts of Catalonia which consists in a celebration where people get together and eat *calçots*, a variety of onion.

18. A *paella* is a typical Spanish dish whose main ingredients are rice and seafood.

19. A *verbena* is a celebration usually hold on Saint John's or Saint Peter's day, where fires are lit and fireworks displayed. It usually takes place in Catalonia, the Valencian Country and the Balearic Islands, but there are *verbenas* in other areas of Spain.

20. This analysis of syntactic calque was carried out within a lexically-based model of grammar, which would consider as *syntax* the sum of pure structure and the semantic features included within lexical entries. For further details, see Corcoll (1999).

21. Which is a remarkable example of calque.

Appendix 1: Catalogue of Informants

Name	Age	Ethnicity	Profession	Education	Yrs in Spain	Other languages	Code
Anne	29	Michigan	Student	University	5	Sp, Cat, De, Fr	am/95/US
Brian	20	Washington	Student	Secondary	5	Sp, Cat	b/92/US
Derrall	38	Philadelphia	Translator/musician	Secondary	14	Sp, Cat	d/95/US
JB	37	Missouri	Lorry driver	Associate degree in Arts	4	Sp, Cat	jb/92/US
Jackie	43	Alabama	English teacher	University	4	Sp	j/95/US
Janet	40	Maryland	University teacher	Doctorate	8	Sp, Cat	ja/95/US
Jim	39	New York	English teacher	Master	2	Sp, Cat, Fr	ji/95/US
Jon	33	Caracas	Interpreter/teacher	University	4	Sp, Cat, Fr, It	jo/95/US
Kelly	27	Michigan	English teacher	University	5	Sp, Cat	k/93/US
Michael	41	New York	Musician	University	5	Sp, Cat	m/95/US
Mimi	52	New York	Housewife	Graduate in occupational therapy	19	Sp, Cat	mi/92/US

References

American Citizens Abroad (ACA) (1994) *A Survey of the Worldwide Overseas American Community*. Geneva: ACA.

Corcoll, C. (1999) *A Reassessment of the Notion of Syntactic Calque: Grammatical and Sociolinguistic Evidence*. Dissertation presented within the Programme of the Doctorate on Applied Linguistics, Institut Universitari de Lingüística Aplicada, Universitat Pompeu Fabra, Barcelona.

Fishman, J. (1965) Who speaks what language to whom and when? *Linguistique, 2,* 67–88.

Fontana, J.M. and Vallduví, E. (1990) Mecanismos léxicos y gramaticales en la alternancia de códigos. In M.T. Turell (ed.) *Nuevas Corrientes Lingüísticas. Aplicación a la Descripción del Inglés* (pp. 171–92). *Revista Española de Lingüística Aplicada, AESLA,* año VI, Anejo I. Granada.

Instituto Nacional de Estadística. *Anuario de Migraciones 1995.* Madrid.

Instituto Nacional de Estadística. *Anuario Estadístico 1995.* Madrid.

Mas, J. (1997) A new American nation. *La Vauguardia* (September 12).

Myers-Scotton, C. (1993) *Social Motivations for Codeswitching.* Oxford: Clarendon Press.

Pujadas, J. and Turell, M.T. (1993) Els indicadors sociolingüístics del contacte interètnic. In *Actes del IXè Col.loqui Internacional de Llengua i Literatura Catalanes. Alacant-Elx (1991).* Barcelona: Publicacions de l'Abadia de Montserrat, 301–18.

Turell, M.T. and Corcoll, C. (1998) The effect of socio-collective factors on the bilingual speech modes of British and American English-speaking communities in Spain. Paper presented at the *Sociolinguistics Symposium 12,* Institute of Education, University of London, London, 26–28 March.